About This Boo

This book is designed to help you teach yourself the new and necessa with Turbo C++ 4.5. In 21 days, you'll learn about such fundamen environment, managing I/O, loops and arrays, object-oriented programming, game programming OLE2, VBX creation, and creating basic OWL applications—all in well-structured and easy-to-follow lessons. Each lesson provides a sample listing—complete with sample output and an analysis of the code—to illustrate the topics of the day. Syntax examples are clearly marked for handy reference.

To help you become more proficient, each lesson ends with a set of common questions and answers, exercises, and a quiz. You can check your progress by examining the quiz answers provided in the book's appendix.

Who Should Read This Book

You don't need any previous experience in programming to learn Turbo C++ with this book. You'll find the numerous examples of syntax and detailed analysis of code an excellent guide as you begin your journey into this rewarding environment. If you have programmed before or have some familiarity with C++, you will see that this book treats many important new features of the Turbo product. Whether you are just beginning or need only to learn the latest about Turbo C++ 4.5, this book's clear organization makes doing so fast and easy.

Conventions

Note: These boxes highlight information that can make your Turbo C++ 4.5 programming more efficient and effective.

Warning: These boxes focus your attention on problems or side effects that can occur in specific situations.

These boxes provide clear definitions of essential terms.

DO use the "Do/Don't" boxes to find a quick summary of a fundamental principle in a lesson.

DON'T overlook the useful information offered in these boxes.

This book uses various typefaces to help you distinguish C++ code from regular English. Actual C++ code is typeset is a special `monospace` font. Placeholders—words or characters used to represent the real words or characters you would type in code—are typeset in *`italic monospace`*. New or important terms are typeset in *italic*.

In the listings in this book, each real code line is numbered. If you see an unnumbered line in a listing, you'll know that the unnumbered line is really a continuation of the preceding numbered code line (some code lines are too long for the width of the book).

Teach Yourself Turbo C++ 4.5 for Windows in 21 Days

Teach Yourself Turbo C++ 4.5 for Windows in 21 Days

Craig Arnush

SAMS PUBLISHING

201 West 103rd Street
Indianapolis, Indiana 46290

This book is dedicated to René for her patience and support.

FIRST EDITION

International Standard Book Number: 0-672-30727-8

Library of Congress Catalog Card Number: 95-67646

98 97 4

Interpretation of the printing code: the rightmost double-digit number is the year of the book's printing; the rightmost single-digit, the number of the book's printing. For example, a printing code of 95-1 shows that the first printing of the book occurred in 1995.

Composed in AGaramond and MCPdigital by Macmillan Computer Publishing

Printed in the United States of America

Publisher
Richard K. Swadley

Acquisitions Manager
Greg Wiegand

Managing Editor
Cindy Morrow

Acquisitions Editor
Grace Buechlein

Development Editor
Dean Miller

Production Editor
Jill D. Bond

Editorial Coordinator
Bill Whitmer

Editorial Assistants
Carol Ackerman
Sharon Cox
Lynette Quinn

Technical Reviewer
Bruneau Babet

Marketing Manager
Gregg Bushyeager

Assistant Marketing Manager
Michelle Milner

Cover Designer
Tim Amrhein

Book Designer
Alyssa Yesh

Director of Production and Manufacturing
Jeff Valler

Production Manager
Kelly Dobbs

Team Supervisor
Katy Bodenmiller

Manufacturing Coordinator
Paul Gilchrist

Production Analysts
Angela Bannan
Dennis Clay Hager
Bobbi Satterfield
Mary Beth Wakefield

Graphics Image Specialists
Teresa Forrester
Clint Lahnen
Dennis Sheehan
Greg Simsic
C. Small
Jeff Yesh

Page Layout
Charlotte Clapp
Mary Ann Cosby
Louisa Klucznik
Ayanna Lacey
Jill Tompkins
Tina Trettin
Dennis Wesner

Proofreading
Don Brown
Mona Brown
Donna Harbin
Kevin Laseau
Donna Martin
Cheryl Moore
Brian-Kent Proffitt
Linda Quigley
Erich J. Richter
SA Springer

Indexer
Chris Cleveland

Overview

		Introduction	xxiii
Week 1 at a Glance			**1**
Day	1	Getting Started	3
	2	C++ The Preprocessor, Variables, and Operators	41
	3	The Decision-Making Constructs and Loops	79
	4	User-Defined Types and Pointers	117
	5	Functions	149
	6	Arrays	173
	7	Strings and Managing I/O	205
Week 1 in Review			**243**
Week 2 at a Glance			**247**
Day	8	Object-Oriented Programming and C++ Classes	249
	9	Basic Stream File I/O	283
	10	The C++ *string* Class, Templates, and the Class Library	305
	11	Programming Windows with OWL 2.5	341
	12	Basic Windows	359
	13	OWL Controls	377
	14	Dialog Boxes	405
Week 2 in Review			**423**
Week 3 at a Glance			**427**
Day	15	Grouped Controls	429
	16	List Box Controls	443
	17	Scroll Bars, Combo Boxes, and VBX Controls	471
	18	MDI Windows	501
	19	The Application and Class Experts	527
	20	OLE 2	579
	21	Debugging	649
Week 3 in Review			**663**

Appendix

A	Answers	677
	Index	703

Contents

Introduction xxiii

Week 1 at a Glance 1

Day 1 Getting Started 3

The Basics of C++ Programs 4
Reading the Documentation 5
The Acrobat Reader 5
Reference Information and Help Files 7
Loading the Turbo C++ IDE 8
An Overview of the Turbo C++ IDE 8
The File Menu 9
The Edit Menu 13
The Search Menu 15
The View Menu 18
The Project Menu 22
The Debug Menu 25
The Tool Menu 26
The Options Menu 26
The Window Menu 31
The Help Menu 32
The EasyWin Applications 33
Introduction to Projects and Nodes 34
Your First C++ Program 35
Exiting the IDE 38
Summary 38
Q&A 39
Workshop 40
Quiz 40
Exercise 40

Day 2 C++ The Preprocessor, Variables, and Operators 41

Predefined Data Types in Turbo C++ 4.5 42
Naming Items in Turbo C++ 4.5 44
The Preprocessor 44
The *#include* Directive 45
The *#define* Directive 46
Declaring Variables 46
Declaring Constants 48
Using Macro-Based Constants 49
Using Formal Constants 51
Operators and Expressions 52
Arithmetic Operators 52
Arithmetic Expressions 55

Increment Operators 55
Assignment Operators 57
The *sizeof* Operator 60
Typecasting 62
Relational and Logical Operators 65
Boolean Expressions 67
Bit-Manipulation Operators 70
The Comma Operator 72
Operator Precedence and Evaluation Direction 72
Summary 74
Q&A 76
Workshop 76
Quiz 76
Exercises 78

Day 3 The Decision-Making Constructs and Loops 79

Decision-Making Constructs 80
The Single-Alternative *if* Statement 80
The Dual-Alternative *if-else* Statement 82
The Multiple-Alternative *if-else* Statement 85
The *switch* Statement 87
Nested Decision-Making Constructs 91
Exception Handling 92
Loops 94
The *for* Loop 94
The *do-while* Loop 99
The *while* Loop 102
Skipping Loop Iterations 104
Exiting Loops 106
Nested Loops 106
Summary 108
Q&A 110
Workshop 113
Quiz 113
Exercises 116

Day 4 User-Defined Types and Pointers 117

Type Definition in C++ 118
Enumerated Data Types 119
Structures 122
Unions 126
Reference Variables 127
Overview of Pointers 129

Pointers to Existing Variables 130
A Short Introduction to Arrays 133
Pointers to Arrays 134
The Pointer Increment/Decrement Method 136
Pointers to Structures 138
Pointers and Dynamic Memory 141
Far Pointers 145
Summary 145
Q&A 147
Workshop 148
  Quiz 148
  Exercises 148

Day 5 Functions **149**

Declaring and Prototyping Functions 150
Local Variables in Functions 153
Static Variables in Functions 155
The *#define* Statement Revisited 156
Inline Functions 157
Exiting Functions Prematurely 160
Default Arguments 160
Passing Arguments by Reference 162
  Using *const* in Arguments 163
Recursive Functions 164
Function Overloading 166
Summary 169
Q&A 170
Workshop 171
  Quiz 171
  Exercise 172

Day 6 Arrays **173**

Using Single-Dimensional Arrays 174
Initializing Single-Dimensional Arrays 176
Array Parameters in Functions 179
Sorting Arrays 183
Searching Arrays 187
Multidimensional Arrays 192
Initializing Multidimensional Arrays 196
Multidimensional Array Parameters 197
Summary 200
  Q&A 202
Workshop 203
  Quiz 203
  Exercise 204

Day 7 Strings and Managing I/O **205**

Formatted Stream Output 206
Stream Input 208
The *printf* Function 210
C++ Strings An Overview 215
String Input 216
Using the STRING.H Library 216
Assigning Strings 217
The Length of a String 219
Concatenating Strings 219
String Comparison 223
Converting Strings 228
Reversing Strings 229
Locating Characters 231
Locating Strings 234
Summary 238
Q&A 239
Workshop 240
  Quiz 241
  Exercises 242

Week 1 in Review **243**

Week 2 at a Glance **247**

Day 8 Object-Oriented Programming and C++ Classes **249**

Basics of Object-Oriented Programming 250
  Classes and Objects 250
  Messages and Methods 251
  Inheritance 251
  Polymorphism 251
Declaring Base Classes 252
  The Sections of a Class 252
Constructors 256
Destructors 258
  Examples of Constructors and Destructors 259
Declaring a Class Hierarchy 262
Virtual Functions 266
  Rule for Virtual Functions 270
Friend Functions 272
Operators and Friend Operators 275
Summary 278
Q&A 279
Workshop 280
  Quiz 280
  Exercise 281

Day 9 **Basic Stream File I/O** **283**

The C++ Stream Library 284
Common Stream I/O Functions 284
Sequential Text Stream I/O 286
Sequential Binary File Stream I/O 290
Random Access File Stream I/O 297
Summary 302
Q&A 302
Workshop 303
  Quiz 303
  Exercise 303

Day 10 **The C++ *string* Class, Templates, and the Class Library** **305**

Benefits of the C++ *string* Class 306
The *string* Class Header File CSTRING.H 308
Bug Busters 315
Reading and Comparing Strings 315
String Search, Substitution, and File I/O 319
Other C++ *string* Class Functions 325
Templates 327
The Class Libraries 331
Summary 336
Q&A 337
Workshop 338
  Quiz 339
  Exercises 339

Day 11 **Programming Windows with OWL 2.5** **341**

OWL and Windows Issues 342
Hungarian Notation 343
The Basic Structure of OWL 344
  Event Handling, *TEventHandler* 344
  Streamable or Persistent Objects, *TStreamableBase* 345
Module Management, *TModule* and *TApplication* 345
  Window Management, *TWindow* 345
A Sample OWL Program 345
Windows Messages and OWL 347
A Real OWL Program Resources, Menus, Screen Writing 349
Summary 357
Q&A 357
Workshop 358
  Quiz 358
  Exercise 358

Day 12 Basic Windows 359

Creating a Read-Only Text Window ... 360
Scrolling Through Text ... 365
A Scrolling Window ... 367
The *SetupWindow* Member Function ... 373
Summary ... 375
Q&A ... 375
Workshop ... 375
  Quiz ... 375
  Exercise ... 375

Day 13 OWL Controls 377

The *TControl* Object ... 378
The Static Text Control ... 379
The Edit Control ... 382
  The *TEdit* Class ... 382
  Clipboard-Related Editing Functions ... 384
  Query of Edit Controls ... 385
  Altering the Edit Controls ... 388
The Pushbutton Control ... 389
  The *TButton* Class ... 389
  Handling Button Messages ... 390
  Manipulating Buttons ... 390
Mr. Calculator ... 391
Summary ... 402
Q&A ... 402
Workshop ... 403
  Quiz ... 403
  Exercises ... 403

Day 14 Dialog Boxes 405

Constructing Dialog Boxes ... 406
Creating Dialog Boxes ... 407
Connecting OWL Objects with Windows Controls ... 413
Transferring Control Data ... 414
Data Transfer for Modal Dialog Boxes ... 415
Transferring Data for Modeless Dialog Boxes ... 420
Summary ... 420
Q&A ... 421
Workshop ... 421
  Quiz ... 421
  Exercises ... 421

Week 2 in Review 423

Week 3 at a Glance 427

Day 15 **Grouped Controls** 429

The Check Box Control 430
The *TCheckBox* Class 430
Responding to Check Box Messages 432
The Radio Button Control 432
The *TRadioButton* Class 432
The Group Control 433
The *TGroupBox* Class 433
The Widget Selection Application 433
Summary 441
Q&A 442
Workshop 442
Quiz 442
Exercise 442

Day 16 **List Box Controls** 443

The List Box Control 444
The *TListBox* Class 444
Responding to List Box Notification Messages 453
The List Manipulation Tester 454
Handling Multiple-Selection Lists 462
The Multiple-Selection List Tester 463
Summary 467
Q&A 468
Workshop 468
Quiz 468
Exercise 469

Day 17 **Scroll Bars, Combo Boxes, and VBX Controls** 471

The Scroll Bar Control 472
The *TScrollBar* Class 472
Responding to Scroll Bar Notification Messages 475
The Count Down Timer 477
The Combo Box Control 482
Responding to Combo Box Notification Messages 485
Combo Boxes as History List Boxes 486
The Son of Mr. Calculator Application 486
VBX Controls 494
Initializing the VBX Subsystem 494
Using the VBX Mixin Class 494
Defining a VBX Response Table 495
The *TVbxControl* OWL Interface Class 497

Summary 499
Q&A 500
Workshop 500
Quiz 500
Exercise 500

Day 18 **MDI Windows** **501**

The MDI Application Features and Components 502
Basics of Building an MDI Application 503
The *TMDIFrame* Class 503
Building MDI Frame Windows 504
The *TMDIClient* Class 505
The MDI Child Window Class 507
Building MDI Child Windows 508
Managing MDI Messages 508
Simple Text Viewer 509
Revised Text Viewer 516
Summary 525
Q&A 525
Workshop 526
Quiz 526
Exercises 526

Day 19 **The Application and Class Experts** **527**

Using the AppExpert Utility 528
The Application Topic 529
The Main Window Topic 533
The MDI Child/View Topic 538
Studying the AppExpert Output 539
The *Expert* Project 540
Altering AppExpert's Options 563
Invoking ClassExpert 564
Adding New Member Functions 565
Summary 577
Q&A 577
Exercises 577

Day 20 **OLE 2** **579**

What Is OLE 2? 580
How Does Borland Implement OLE 2? 583
OLE *Doc/View* 584
Defining a *TOleDocument* Class 585
Step 1: Define the Document Storage 585
Step 2: Define Notifications to Tell Views to Update Themselves 585

Defining a *TOleView* Class 586
Step 1: Define the Presentation 586
Step 2: Add Data Editing Methods 587
Step 3: Add Notification Responses 587
Step 4: Support Embedded Objects, if Required 587
The OLE Registry 588
Creating an OLE Application 591
Step 1: Declare a *Doc/View* Template and Register its Details 591
Step 2: Add the Application Registration Details 592
Step 3: Implement the Application Class 593
Step 4: Implement an OLE *OwlMain* 595
Creating OLE Applications with AppExpert 596
OLE Automation 631
Step 1: Design the Server Class 632
Step 2: Declare the Class to Be Automatic 632
Step 3: Define the Automatic Methods and Properties 633
Step 4: Build the Application Engine 634
Step 5: Build a Type Library and C++ Class 635
Step 6: Use the C++ Class 635
Whither Automation? 645
Summary 646
Q&A 646
Workshop 647
Quiz 647
Exercise 647

Day 21 Debugging 649

The Integrated Debugger 650
The Debug Menu 650
The View Menu 653
Debugging a Program 654
Other Debugging Tools 660
Summary 661
Q&A 661

Week 3 in Review 663

How To Play 664
Scoring 664
The Deal 665
The Discard 665
The Turn 665
The Play 665
Counting Player Hands 666
Counting the Crib 666
The Cribbage Example 666
Variations and Expanding the Game 675

Appendix

A **Answers** **677**

Answers to Day 1, "Getting Started" ... 678
Answers to Day 2, "C++ The Preprocessor, Variables, and Operators" ... 678
Answers to Day 3, "The Decision-Making Constructs and Loops" ... 680
Answers to Day 4, "User-Defined Types and Pointers" ... 684
Answers to Day 5, "Functions" ... 686
Answers to Day 6, "Arrays" ... 688
Answers to Day 7, "Strings and Managing I/O" ... 690
Answers to Day 8, "Object-Oriented Programming and C++ Classes" ... 694
Answers to Day 9, "Basic Stream File I/O" ... 695
Answers to Day 10, "The C++ *string* Class, Templates, and the Class Library" ... 697
Answers to Day 11, "Programming Windows with OWL 2.5" ... 699
Answers to Day 12, "Basic Windows" ... 700
Answers to Day 13, "OWL Controls" ... 700
Answers to Day 14, "Dialog Boxes" ... 700
Answers to Day 15, "Grouped Controls" ... 700
Answers to Day 16, "List Box Controls" ... 701
Answers to Day 17, "Scroll Bars, Combo Boxes, and VBX Controls" ... 701
Answers to Day 18, "MDI Windows" ... 701
Answers to Day 20, "OLE 2" ... 702

Index **703**

Acknowledgments

I would like to thank Grace Buechlein at Sams Publishing for having the patience to deal with the likes of me. Also, thanks to Dean Miller, who listened to my suggestions and even liked my bugs; and Jill Bond, who had some insightful comments on my prose. My thanks go out to all those at Sams who participated in putting this book together.

Another hearty thank you goes out to Bruneau Babet's diligence in picking up on all the twiddly bits I had missed. He must surely have been more awake than I.

A very special dedication to Ian Spencer who appeared in a crisis, waved his wand, and made the problems disappear. Thanks, Ian. I needed that.

Last but by *absolutely no means* least, super-special thanks with sugar on top go out to all the people who took the time to contact me and let me know where I had screwed up in earlier incarnations of this book: Greg Bowerbank, Matt Clayton, Manuel Derieux, John Fischer, Huy Viet Le, Aaron Moy, Brian Poff, and Jim Willeke.

About the Author

Craig Arnush is an independent software consultant in San Diego and is an expert on Windows. He volunteers his time answering technical questions on the Borland CompuServe forums as a member of Team Borland. Craig can be reached via his CompuServe account at `71333,3052` or via the Internet at `craiga@netcom.com`.

Introduction

This book has three major goals: to teach you to program in C++, teach you to create Windows applications using Turbo C++, and teach you the new features of Turbo C++ 4.5. No prior programming experience is required. However, knowing how to program in other languages, such as BASIC or Pascal, certainly helps. This book is not for the faint-hearted, because becoming familiar with the new features of a new compiler is hard enough, but also learning to program in C++ and learning to write Windows applications in C++ are two nontrivial tasks!

The book contains 21 chapters, one for each study day. The material is somewhat fast-paced in order to meet the goals of the book. Each chapter contains a Q&A section, a Quiz section, and an Exercise section. Appendix A provides the answers to the quizzes and to many of the exercises.

Day 1 gives you a brief tour of the Turbo C++ IDE, the Windows environment that you use to develop C++ programs. This chapter also presents your first C++ program to demonstrate the basic components of a non-Windows C++ program.

Day 2 looks at C++ program components in more detail. This chapter discusses the preprocessor as well as naming and declaring variables, constants, and functions. This book also provides an early focus on C++ functions because they are important program building blocks.

Day 3 covers C++ decision-making constructs and loops. The constructs include the various types of `if` statements as well as the `switch` statement, while loops include the `for`, `while`, and `do-while` loops. The chapter demonstrates how to use the `for` loop as an open loop. In addition, the chapter discusses skipping loop iterations, exiting loops, and nesting loops.

Day 4 covers user-defined types and pointers. This chapter discusses enumerated data types, structures, unions, reference variables, and pointers. The text demonstrates how to declare and use pointers with simple variables, arrays, structures, and dynamic memory.

Day 5 examines functions and how they are constructed. This chapter discusses the differences between preprocessor macros, regular functions, and inline functions.

Day 6 presents arrays in C++. This chapter covers both single-dimensional and multidimensional arrays and discusses how to declare them and initialize them. In addition, this chapter discusses sorting and searching single-dimensional arrays.

Day 7 focuses on strings and the STRING.H library, which is inherited from C. The chapter covers topics such as assigning, concatenating, comparing, converting, and reversing strings. In addition, this chapter discusses searching for characters and substrings in strings before moving on to formatted stream input and output, as well the famous `printf` function. The latter function supports versatile formatted output.

Day 8 introduces you to the world of object-oriented programming (OOP). This chapter covers the basics of OOP and presents C++ classes. The text discusses the basic components of a C++ class and the rules related to using these components.

Day 9 discusses the basic stream file I/O, which is supported by the C++ stream library. This chapter covers common stream functions, sequential text stream I/O, sequential binary stream I/O, and random-access stream I/O.

Day 10 covers the string class, an alternative to strings, and the functions in STRING.H that work with them. This class conforms to the preliminary strings class from the ANSI C++ committee and is prototyped in the header file CSTRING.H. This chapter then goes on to discuss templates and the Borland Class Library.

Day 11 presents very simple OWL-based Windows applications. Object Windows Library version 2.5, or OWL 2.5, is included with Turbo C++ 4.5. It is a C++ library for use in Windows programming, and using it shortens the time and effort in developing a Windows program.

Day 12 focuses on drawing text in a window. This chapter presents both nonscrolling and scrolling windows and illustrates how to draw text (as graphics) in these windows.

Day 13 presents the OWL library classes, which model static text controls, edit controls, and pushbutton controls. This chapter also presents a nontrivial command-oriented line calculator as an example that uses these controls.

Day 14 focuses on creating and using dialog boxes. This chapter shows you how to use resource files to define modal and modeless dialog boxes. In addition, this chapter discusses data transfer between a dialog box and its parent window.

Day 15 presents the OWL library classes that model the check box control, the radio button control, and the group control.

Day 16 covers the OWL library class that models list box controls. This chapter discusses both single-selection and multiple-selection list boxes. The programs in the chapter illustrate both types of list boxes.

Day 17 presents the OWL library classes, which model the scroll bar control and the combo box control. This chapter also discusses how to create history boxes using combo boxes. In addition, the chapter presents a version of the calculator program that uses the combo boxes. Finally, VBXs are introduced and explained.

Day 18 looks at Multiple Document Interface (MDI) windows. The chapter presents the classes that support MDI-compliant applications and illustrates how to manage MDI-child windows.

Day 19 shows how to use the Application and Class Experts to automatically generate the skeleton of your Windows applications, then modify them in a browser-like atmosphere.

Day 20 describes OLE2 and how it's implemented by Borland's ObjectComponents Framework (OCF). This chapter concentrates on how OCF is integrated into OWL.

Day 21 gives a quick tutorial on some simple debugging techniques. No program is perfect, but this chapter will help you get as close to perfect as possible.

The book contains Windows programs that illustrate aspects of programming that go beyond the trivial aspects of using various visual controls. Study these programs, as they contain techniques and tricks that can enrich your Windows programming. We all learn to program by looking at examples (including nontrivial ones) and by asking friends questions.

Note: You can obtain the source code and the project files presented in this book by downloading the files from CompuServe; type `GO SAMS`. The files can be found in the Sams Programming Library 9.

The files are also available via anonymous FTP to `ftp.netcom.com` in the `pub/cr/craiga` directory.

Happy programming!

About This Book

This book is designed to help you teach yourself the new and necessary aspects of programming with Turbo C++ 4.5. In 21 days, you'll learn about such fundamentals as the Turbo C++ 4.5 environment, managing I/O, loops and arrays, object-oriented programming, creating basic OWL applications, and using OLE2—all in well-structured and easy-to-follow lessons. Each lesson provides a sample listing—complete with sample output and an analysis of the code—to illustrate the topics of the day. Syntax examples are clearly marked for handy reference.

To help you become more proficient, each lesson ends with a set of common questions and answers, exercises, and a quiz. You can check your progress by examining the quiz answers provided in the book's appendix.

Who Should Read This Book

You don't need any previous experience in programming to learn Turbo C++ with this book. You'll find the numerous examples of syntax and detailed analysis of code an excellent guide as you begin your journey into this rewarding environment. If you have programmed before or have some familiarity with C++, you will see that this book treats many important new features of the Borland product. Whether you are just beginning or need only to learn the latest about Turbo C++ 4.5, this book's clear organization makes doing so fast and easy.

Conventions Used in This Book

Note: These boxes highlight information that can make your Turbo C++ 4.5 programming more efficient and effective.

Warning: These boxes focus your attention on problems or side effects that can occur in specific situations.

This icon indicates clear definitions of essential terms.

DO	DON'T

DO use the "Do/Don't" boxes to find a quick summary of a fundamental principle in a lesson.

DON'T overlook the useful information offered in these boxes.

The type icon denotes a new program for you to enter into your editor.

The output icon highlights the results of compiling and executing the program.

Analysis of the program reveals insights and information about key lines of the listing.

This book uses various typefaces to help you distinguish C++ code from regular English. Actual C++ code is typeset is a special `monospace` font. Placeholders—words or characters used to represent the real words or characters you would type in code—are typeset in *`italic monospace`*. New or important terms are typeset in *italic*.

In the listings in this book, each real code line is numbered. If you see an unnumbered line in a listing, you'll know that the unnumbered line is really a continuation of the preceding numbered code line (some code lines are too long for the width of the book).

WEEK 1 AT A GLANCE

1
2
3
4
5
6
7

The first week of your journey into learning to write Windows applications starts with an introduction to the Turbo C++ 4.5 environment—the IDE (integrated development environment). The remaining days in this week present the basics of the C++ language itself. You learn about the following:

- Predefined data types
- Naming constants, variables, and functions
- C++ operators and expressions
- Managing basic input and output
- Making decisions
- Writing loops
- Declaring and using arrays

You also will learn about simple user-defined types and pointers along with basic string operations. Thus, this week covers the basic components of the C++ language.

Week 1 at a Glance

You might be interested to note that the topics covered this week are all the components included in the C language. Starting with the second week, you will be introduced to the portions of the language that are new with C++ along with the basics of Windows programming.

WEEK 1

Getting Started

Welcome to the world of C++ and Windows programming. Your journey into this exciting world begins today. Most of the information in today's lesson familiarizes you with the Turbo C++ Integrated Development Environment (IDE). You will learn about the following topics:

- The basics and history of C++ programs
- Reading the Turbo C++ documentation
- Loading and using the Turbo C++ IDE
- EasyWin applications
- Projects and nodes
- Typing and running your first C++ program

The Basics of C++ Programs

You don't need any previous experience in programming to learn Turbo C++ with this book; but if you have programmed before, things will be easier. As with other languages, C++ is made up of declarations and statements that specify exact instructions to be executed when the program runs.

C++ was developed by Bjarne Stroustrup at Bell Labs. The language is meant to supersede and build on the popular C language, mainly by adding object-oriented language extensions.

NEW TERM An *object-oriented language* represents the attributes and operations of objects.

In addition, C++ offers a number of enhancements to C that are not object-oriented. Thus, learning C++ gives you the bonus of becoming very familiar with C. However, unlike C, which has been standardized, C++ is still undergoing the standardization process by the ANSI/ISO committee. As of this writing, it looks like a standard for C++ will be finalized and ratified by the end of 1996.

Programming in C++ requires that you become aware of the supporting libraries, which perform various tasks such as input/output, text manipulation, math operations, file I/O (input/output), and so on. In languages such as BASIC, support for such operations is transparent to programs, meaning that it is automatically available to these programs. As a result, many programs come across as single components that are independent of any other programming components. By contrast, programming in C++ makes you more aware of a program's dependency on various libraries. The advantage of this language feature is that you are able to select between similar libraries, including ones that you develop. Thus, C++ programs are modular. C++ compilers, including Turbo C++, use project files and program files. The Turbo C++ IDE uses project files to manage the creation and updating of a program.

NEW TERM *Project files* specify the library. *Program files* create an application.

Reading the Documentation

While this book makes a good learning tool, it always will be necessary to refer back to the original Borland-supplied documentation from time to time. There you will find reference manuals containing all the functions and all the classes provided by Turbo C++, as well as tutorials for subjects that are beyond the scope of this book.

Starting with version 4.5, Turbo C++ no longer comes automatically with printed manuals. Instead, the CD-ROM version has all the manuals available on the CD itself, and they can be read or printed directly from Windows. You can, however, order printed documentation from Borland for an additional fee.

The Acrobat Reader

All the documentation on the CD-ROM is in the Acrobat format and can be read with the Acrobat Reader v2.0, included with the Turbo C++ package. Table 1.1 lists the books available with Turbo C++ and what is in them.

Table 1.1. List of Turbo C++ Books

Book Title	Contents
Turbo C++ Programmer's Guide	A guide to the Turbo C++ compiler
Turbo C++ User's Guide	A guide to the Turbo C++ IDE and its various supporting tools
ObjectWindows Programmer's Guide	A guide to the OWL classes
ObjectWindows Tutorial	A step-by-step guide to using OWL

The Acrobat Reader is a simple application to use. Access it by double-clicking on the Turbo C++ 4.5 Online Books icon in the Turbo C++ 4.5 Program Manager group. You should see the screen as shown in Figure 1.1 which shows the various books you can select to read. There also is a button here that will lead you to some easy instructions on using the Acrobat Reader, mostly just a list of what the buttons on the toolbar do. You should probably take some time to study this help screen and experiment with the toolbar buttons.

Upon selecting one of the books by double-clicking on the appropriate button, a new window will open up to display the beginning of that book, such as in Figure 1.2.

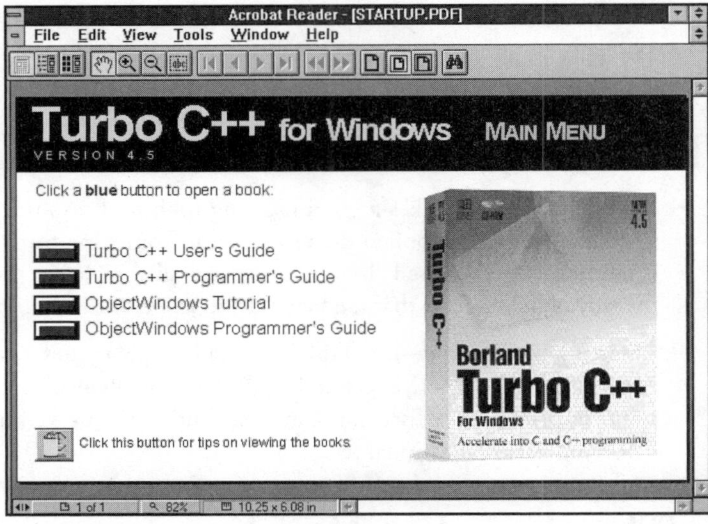

Figure 1.1.
The Acrobat Reader Book List.

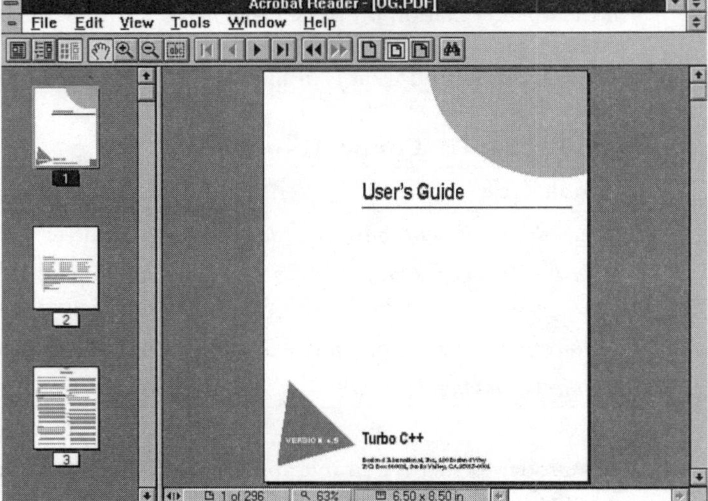

Figure 1.2.
The Turbo C++ User's Guide.

Here, you see a window containing two separate sections. The left side of the window shows all the sections in the chapter, while the right side shows the actual text of the book. At the bottom of the window is a status bar in which the separate sections can be used as buttons to provide extra functionality to the reader. Following is a description of the various buttons:

- The first button looks like a pair of arrows separated by a vertical line. By clicking on this and then moving the mouse, you can adjust the various sizes of the two main sections of the view window.
- The next button shows the current page number and the total page count of the document you are viewing. When you click on this button you will be presented with a dialog asking you to select a page number. This enables you to instantly jump to any page in the document.
- Next is a button that shows the current magnification level. You can manipulate this to better view the document in the main window. Clicking the button pops up a menu that enables you to select from various magnification levels.
- The last button before the horizontal scroll bar is one that displays the size of the page you are viewing. You can't click on this button for any sort of functionality, but you can consult it to determine the size of the page if you decide to print it.

I advise you to take some time now and explore the Acrobat Reader to find out what it can do. The Find function can be extremely useful in locating various topics in the supplied books.

Reference Information and Help Files

It is important to note that not all information can be obtained via the online manuals. There is a large amount of reference information covering details of the C++ language itself that are contained in various help files. The files are integrated into the Turbo C++ IDE in several ways. You can either select one of the Help menu items that will be described later this chapter, or you can click the right mouse button while in the IDE's editor window. Also, pressing the F1 key will access the help system.

From the Turbo C++ help window, you can click any one of a number of buttons that will enable you to change to specific reference help files. These buttons are shown in Table 1.2.

Table 1.2. List of Turbo C++ References in Help

Button Label	Reference Manual
Class Ref	The Class Library is a group of classes and functions you can use to hold collections of other objects. This is described later in Day 10.
OWL	The ObjectWindows Library (OWL) is a system whereby the large complexity of writing to the Windows operating system can be concealed behind easy-to-use classes. OWL is described starting on Day 11 and its description will continue through the rest of the book.

continues

Table 1.2. continued

Button Label	Reference Manual
OCF	The ObjectComponents Framework (OCF) is Borland's solution to building complex OLE2 applications with relatively little work. OCF, while it doesn't depend upon OWL, can be combined seamlessly with it. OCF is described on Day 20.
Win16	The Windows 16-bit Reference describes the Application Program Interface (API) for the direct Windows system calls available in the 16-bit version of Windows (Windows 3.1 and Windows for Workgroups 3.11). While OWL makes it easy for you to ignore the actual Windows functions, you will find yourself needing to bypass OWL occasionally, and this reference will be invaluable.

One of the most important methods of reaching the reference manual help you will use is when you're editing a file. By placing the editing cursor over a keyword in the file and pressing F1, you can tell Turbo C++ to search the manuals for the entry that describes the particular keyword. It's immensely useful for getting quick help on keywords, including all the information describing their precise usage and limitations.

Loading the Turbo C++ IDE

The Turbo C++ IDE is the visual interface for the C++ compiler, linker, debugger, and other tools that are used to create, manage, and maintain C++ programs. You can load the IDE by simply clicking the Turbo C++ icon or by double-clicking the TCW.EXE program from the File Manager. (The file TCW.EXE is located in the directory \TCWIN45\BIN.)

An Overview of the Turbo C++ IDE

The Turbo C++ IDE is an MDI-compliant application with the following main components:

- The frame window with the menu system, minimize, and maximize icons. You can resize, move, maximize, and minimize the main Turbo C++ IDE window.
- The system menu, which offers numerous options
- The speed bar, which contains special bitmapped buttons that offer shortcuts to specific commands. The IDE enables you to customize the bitmapped buttons on the speed bar. In addition, these buttons are context sensitive. Their number and type can change, depending on the current task or active window. The IDE supports a nice feature that displays what a bitmapped button does (the text appears in the status line) when you move the mouse over that button.

- The client area, which contains various windows, such as the source-code editing window, the message window, the variable watch window, and so on
- The status line located at the bottom of the IDE window. This line displays brief online help as you move the mouse over the buttons in the speed bar, offers a brief explanation for the various menu items, displays the cursor location, and shows the status of the insert/overwrite mode.

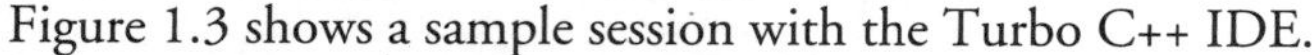

Figure 1.3 shows a sample session with the Turbo C++ IDE.

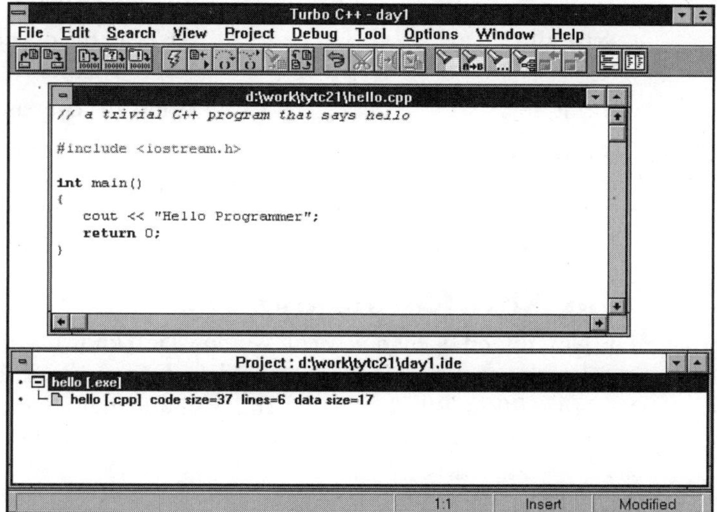

Figure 1.3.
The Turbo C++ IDE.

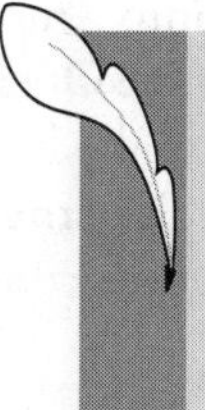

Note: Because the IDE is meant to accommodate software developers, many of the options will seem advanced to you if you are a novice programmer. However, you only need to be familiar with the options and their related terms. As you become more experienced, these options and terms will become part of your knowledge as a Turbo C++ programmer.

The File Menu

The File menu provides options that enable you to manage files, print text, and exit the IDE. Table 1.3 summarizes the options on the File menu. The File menu also includes a dynamic list of the most recently opened source-code files.

Table 1.3. Summary of the options in the File menu.

Command	Shortcut Keys	Function
New		Opens a new edit window
Open...		Loads an existing source-code file into a new edit window
Save	Ctrl+K S	Saves the contents of the active edit window
Save as...		Saves the contents of the active edit window using a new filename
Save all		Saves all the opened source-code windows in their respective files
Print...		Prints the contents of a source code window
Print setup...		Sets up the printer
Exit		Exits the IDE

The New Command

The **New** option opens a new edit window (also known as a source-code window) and assigns it a default associated filename. The default filename of the first new window you open is NONAME00.CPP. Likewise, the default filename of the second new window is NONAME01.CPP, and so on. The newly opened window initially is empty.

The Open... Option

The **Open...** option enables you to load the contents of an existing source code file into a new edit window. In fact, the IDE is capable of loading multiple files. The option invokes the Open a File dialog box, shown in Figure 1.4. The dialog box contains several list box and combo box controls that enable you to locate the source-code file and then select it. These controls permit you to choose the drive, directory, and filename wildcards that help you locate the source-code file you seek.

The Save Option

The **Save** option assists you in saving the contents of the active edit window to its associated file. If you invoke this option with a new edit window, the **Save** option invokes the Save File As dialog box, shown in Figure 1.5. This dialog box enables you to optionally specify the nondefault filename, as well as the destination drive and directory. The shortcut keys for the **Save** option are normally Ctrl+K, S; note, however, that they can change if you modify the key mappings (in the Options|Environment menu).

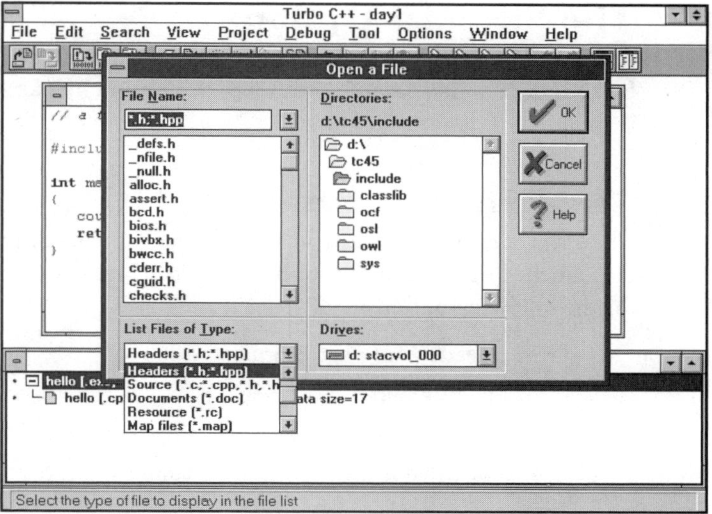

Figure 1.4.
The Open a File dialog box.

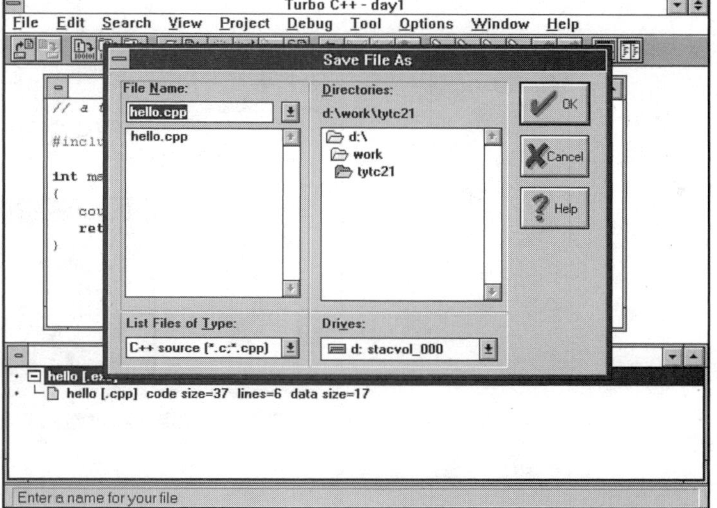

Figure 1.5.
The Save File As dialog box.

The Save As... Option

The Save **A**s... option enables you to save the contents of the active edit window in a file that is different from the currently associated file. In fact, the new filename becomes the new associated file for the active edit window. The Save **A**s... option invokes the Save File As dialog box, shown in Figure 1.5. If you select an existing file, the option displays a message dialog box that asks you whether you want to overwrite the contents of the existing file with those of the active edit window.

The Save All Option

The Save All option writes the contents of all the modified edit windows to their associated files. If the IDE contains new edit windows, this option invokes the Save File As dialog box to save these new windows.

The Print... Option

The **Print**... option enables you to print the contents of the active edit window. The option displays the Print Options dialog box, shown in Figure 1.6. This dialog box contains check boxes for the following options:

- Print a header and page numbers
- Print line numbers
- Highlight syntax keywords by printing them in bold characters
- Use color (if your printer supports colors)
- Wrap lines
- Left margin edit box option

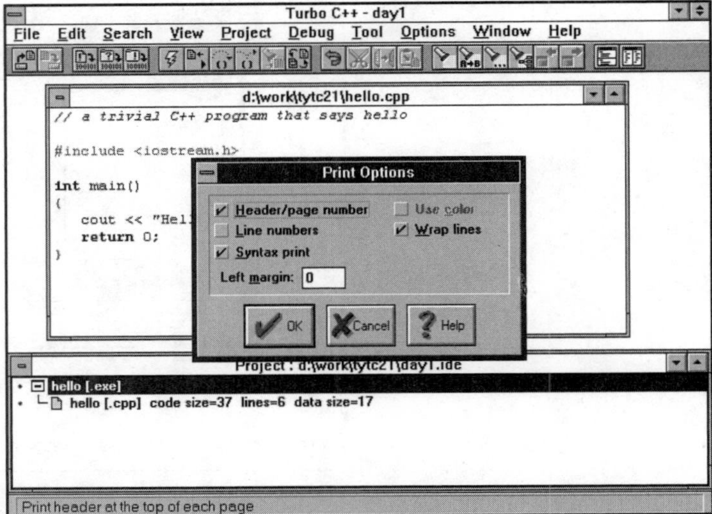

Figure 1.6.
The Print Options dialog box.

The Print Setup... Option

The Print Setup... option enables you to set up your printer using the **Print**... option before you print. The printer setup option displays the Setup dialog. This is the same dialog box that will appear whenever you select Print Setup... from any program.

The Exit Option

The Exit option enables you to exit altogether the Turbo C++ IDE. The IDE prompts you for any modified edit window that has not been saved.

The Edit Menu

The Edit menu contains options that enable you to edit the text in the edit windows. Table 1.4 summarizes the options in the Edit menu.

Table 1.4. Summary of the options in the Edit menu.

Command	Shortcut Keys	Function
Undo	Ctrl+Z	Undoes the last editing action
Redo	Shift+Ctrl+Z	Reverses the action of the last Undo option
Cut	Ctrl+X	Deletes the selected text and copies it to the Clipboard. The previous contents of the Clipboard are lost.
Copy	Ctrl+C	Copies the selected text to the Clipboard. The previous contents of the Clipboard are lost.
Paste	Ctrl+V	Inserts the contents of the Clipboard at the current cursor location
Clear	Ctrl+Delete	Deletes selected text but does not write it to the Clipboard
Select all		Selects all the text in the active edit window
Buffer list...		Displays the Buffer List dialog box

The Undo Option

The **U**ndo option enables you to reverse the effect of the last editing task and restore the contents of the active edit window. The shortcut keys for this option are Ctrl+Z. This option enables you to quickly and efficiently deal with editing errors—especially after working long hours.

The Redo Option

The **R**edo option enables you to reverse the action of the **U**ndo option. The shortcut keys for the **R**edo option are Shift+Ctrl+Z. The **R**edo option enables you to switch between two versions of edited source code. This option is beneficial to the truly exhausted programmer who cannot make up his mind about how the source code should look!

The Cut Option

The Cut option deletes selected text and places it in the Clipboard. The previous contents of the Clipboard are lost. The shortcut keys for the Cut option are Ctrl+X.

The Copy Option

The Copy option copies the selected text into the Clipboard. The previous contents of the Clipboard are lost. The shortcut keys for the Copy option are Ctrl+C.

The Paste Option

The Paste option inserts the contents of the Clipboard at the current insertion point. The contents of the Clipboard remain unaffected. Thus, you can use the Cut and Paste options to move text in the same edit window or across different edit windows. You also can use the Copy and Paste options to duplicate blocks of text in the same edit window or across different edit windows. The shortcut keys for the Paste option are Ctrl+V.

The Clear Option

The Clear option clears the selected text without copying it to the Clipboard. This does not mean that the deleted text is irreversibly lost, because you can use the Undo option to undelete that text. The shortcut keys for the Clear option are Ctrl+Delete.

The Select All Option

The Select All option selects all the text in the active edit window. You can copy this text to the Clipboard by using the Copy option. You then can write the contents of the Clipboard to another edit window using the Paste option.

The Buffer List... Option

The Buffer List... option enables you to examine the list of buffers used with the various edit windows. This option displays the Buffer List dialog box. This dialog box enables you to load a buffer into an edit window. The dialog box contains the list of buffers; those that have changed since they were last loaded have the word `MODIFIED` (placed in parentheses) after them.

The dialog box is a feature borrowed from the BRIEF editor. In that, you have a list of buffers and a single window; you switch between the different files, changing the currently viewed buffer in the edit window. The IDE's buffer list dialog box enables you to replace the contents of the current edit window without closing the associated file. If the replaced file is not loaded into another edit window, it is hidden. You may use the buffer list later in order to load the hidden buffer into an edit window.

You can use the Save pushbutton of the Buffer List dialog box to update the file associated with the selected buffer. This action causes the word `MODIFIED` to disappear from the selected buffer entry. You also can use the Delete pushbutton to remove the selected buffer from memory, if that buffer is not in an Edit window.

The Search Menu

The Search menu contains options that enable you to locate various types of information, such as text, symbol definitions, function declarations, and program-building errors. Table 1.5 summarizes the options in the Search menu.

Table 1.5. Summary of the options in the Search menu.

Command	Shortcut Keys	Function
Find...	Ctrl+Q F	Searches for text in the active edit window
Replace...	Ctrl+Q A	Replaces text in the active source-code window
Search again	F3	Repeats the last Find or Replace operation
Browse symbol...		Locates a symbol in any source code that is part of the current project
Locate function...		Locates a function
Previous message	Alt+F7	Selects the previous program-building message and places the cursor at the offending line in an edit window
Next message	Alt+F8	Selects the next program-building message and places the cursor at the offending line in an edit window

The Find... Option

The **F**ind... option supports searches for text in the active edit window. This option, which has the shortcut keys Ctrl+Q F, displays the Find Text dialog box, shown in Figure 1.7. This dialog box has the following controls:

- The **T**ext to find combo box control, which enables you to type in the search text or to recall recently searched text.
- The Options check boxes, which include
  - The Case sensitive check box, which enables you to select case-sensitive or case-insensitive text search.

- The Whole words only check box, which enables you to choose between matching entire words or matching any text.
- The Regular expression check box, which turns on or off the use of the BRIEF editor's regular expressions feature. Such expressions result in using the text in the Text to find control as the text pattern.
- The Direction diamond-shaped radio button controls. These controls enable you to choose between Forward and Backward search.
- The Scope diamond-shaped radio button controls. These controls enable you to choose between searching the entire text and limiting the search to the Selected text.
- The Origin diamond-shaped radio button controls. These controls enable you to choose between searching the Entire edit window and searching From the cursor position.

- The OK, Cancel, and Help buttons.

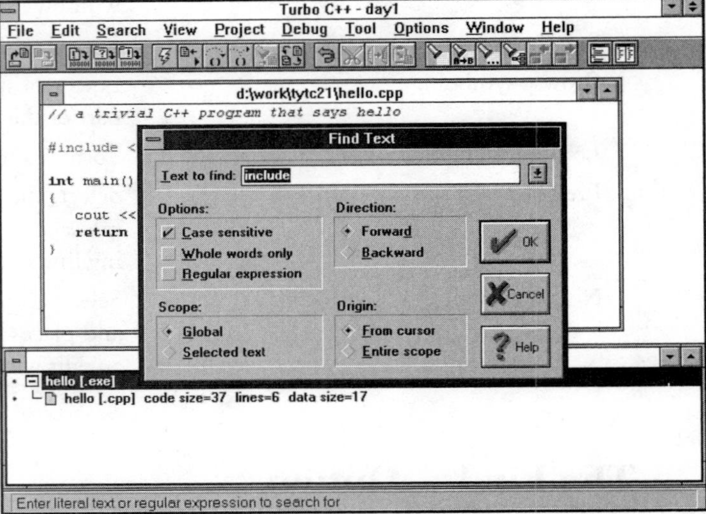

Figure 1.7.
The Find Text dialog box.

The Replace... Option

The **R**eplace... option supports replacing text in the active edit window and has the shortcut keys Ctrl+Q A. This option displays the Replace Text dialog box, which looks exactly like the Find... dialog box, except for a few additions. There's a single edit field into which you can enter the text that will be used to replace the found text, and there's a Change All button that will make changes to all occurrences instead of simply the next one.

The Search Again Option

The **S**earch Again option enables you to repeat the last **F**ind... or **R**eplace... option. The shortcut key for this option is the F3 function key.

The Browse Symbol... Option

The **B**rowse Symbol... option enables you to browse the makeup of a symbol, including classes, functions, and variables. These symbols need not be defined in the active edit window, as long as they are defined in one of the current project's source-code files (your files or the library's included files); the symbols depend upon the symbolic information produced by a compile with debugging on. Figure 1.8 shows a sample symbol-browsing dialog box.

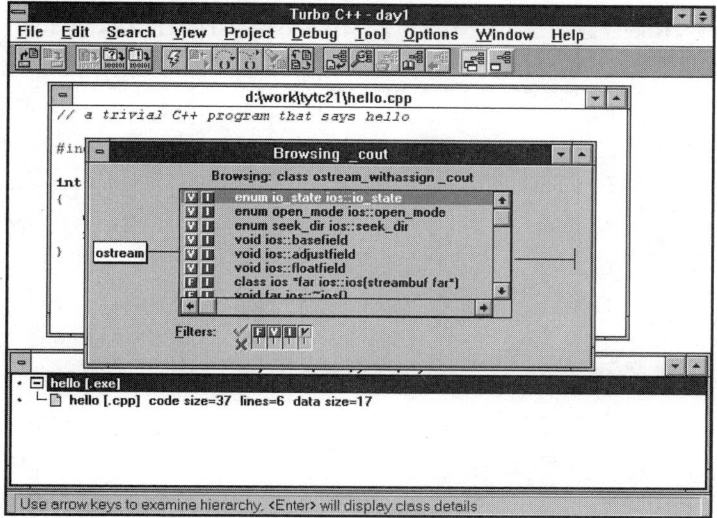

Figure 1.8.
A sample symbol-browsing dialog box.

The Locate Function... Option

The **L**ocate Function... option enables you to find the definition of a function. This option displays the Locate Function dialog box which prompts you to enter the name of the function you want to find. The IDE responds by moving to it in an existing edit window or by displaying the function definition in a new edit window, if necessary.

The Previous Message Option

The **P**revious Message option enables you to zoom in on the offending source-code line that is associated with the previous message in the Message window. The IDE responds to this option by displaying the edit window that contains the offending source-code line. The shortcut keys for this option are Alt+F7.

The Next Message Option

The **N**ext Message option enables you to zoom in on the offending source-code line that is associated with the next message in the Message window. The IDE responds to this option by displaying the edit window which contains the offending source-code line. The shortcut keys for this option are Alt+F8.

The View Menu

The View menu contains options that enable you to view and browse through a wide variety of information. This information goes beyond the declarations in the source-code files of your own project. Table 1.6 summarizes the options in the View menu.

Table 1.6. Summary of the options in the View menu.

Command	Shortcut Keys	Function
C**l**assExpert		Invokes the ClassExpert utility, which works with project files generated by AppExpert
Project		Displays the Project window
Message		Displays the Message window
Classes		Browses through the classes
Globals		Browses through global data types, constants, and variables
Watch		Selects or opens the Watch window
Breakpoint		Selects or opens the Breakpoints window
Call **s**tack		Selects or opens the Call Stack window
Register		Selects or opens the Registers window
Event log		Selects or opens the Event Log window
Information...		Displays system or status information

The ClassExpert Option

The C**l**assExpert option invokes the ClassExpert utility, which works only with project files created by the AppExpert (both of these topics are discussed on Day 19). This option invokes the ClassExpert window, which has three panes, as follows:

- The Classes pane lists the classes involved in the project created using AppExpert. The information in the other two panes is related to the currently selected class in this pane.

- The Events pane lists the command notification, control notifications, virtual functions, Windows messages, and other events related to the class selected in the Classes pane.
- The source-code window, in which the selected class is defined.

The Project Option

The **P**roject option selects or opens the Project window, which lists the targets in the nodes in the current .IDE file. The Project window displays the files of a target in the form of a tree-like outline. The outline is made up of nodes that you can expand and collapse (if they have child nodes). Each node has a bitmap to its left. If the bitmap graphic has a + sign, then the node has child nodes that are currently hidden. If you click the + sign, you expand that node, and the IDE replaces the + sign with a – sign. The child nodes without + or – signs have no child nodes of their own.

If you click the right mouse button on a node in the Project window, the IDE displays a floating menu that enables you to view various components of the project, manage nodes, and edit project-related components.

The project window is discussed in more detail later on today.

The Message Option

The **M**essage option displays, selects, or opens the Message window, which contains the source-code compiler, resource compiler, and linker messages. These messages inform you of the progress of building the .EXE program file. In addition, the Message window contains any warning or error messages generated by the compilers or by the linker.

The Classes Option

The **C**lasses option displays the Browsing Objects window, showing a graph of the various classes in the current project and how they are interlinked. Typically, the Browsing Objects window has a vertical and horizontal scroll bar to enable you to scroll through the various classes involved in the current project. This topic is covered a little later, when there are some classes to browse.

The Globals Option

The **G**lobals option displays the Browsing Globals window, which shows the global data types, constants, variables, and functions. Figure 1.9 shows a sample Browsing Globals window. The window identifies each item by using the following special bitmaps:

- The bitmap T indicates that the symbol is a data type.

- The bitmap `C` signals that the symbol is a constant.
- The bitmap `F` signifies that the symbol is a function.
- The bitmap `V` indicates that the symbol is a variable.

The Browsing Globals window contains switches that enable you to filter the viewing of certain global symbols. The window also contains an edit box control that enables you to type in the name of the symbol you want to find. The edit box control filters the symbols with every keystroke you enter.

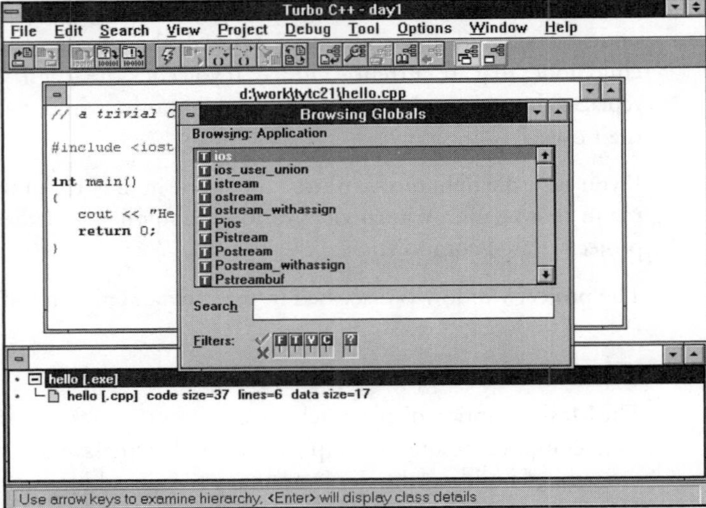

Figure 1.9.
A sample Browsing Globals window.

The Watch Option

The **W**atch option selects or opens the Watch window. This window lists the currently watched variables in your program during debugging. The window displays a check box to the left of each variable. The check box is checked by default to display and update the value in the associated variable. You can uncheck the control to temporarily disable displaying the value of a variable. This task especially is meaningful when the watched variable is not defined in the currently traced function. The Watch window is discussed on Day 21.

The Breakpoint Option

The **B**reakpoint option displays the Breakpoints window, which lists the location and type of breakpoints. A *breakpoint* is a program statement at which the program stops to enable you to inspect its variables. The Breakpoints window displays the following information:

- The filename that contains the breakpoint

- The line number where the breakpoint is located
- The state of the breakpoint
- The number of passes (that is, the number of times the statement is executed before the program stops at the breakpoint)

If you double-click any entry in the Breakpoints window, the IDE displays the Breakpoints Properties dialog box. This dialog box enables you to edit the breakpoint's data. This dialog box is discussed on Day 21.

The Call Stack Option

The Call **S**tack option displays the Call Stack window, which lists the pending program and the DLL functions that were called (and not yet returned) when the program reached the current breakpoint or the current single-stepped line. The DLL functions are referenced by the name of the DLL library, followed by the address of the function. Again, this is a debugging-related function and will be covered on Day 21.

The Register Option

The **R**egister option displays the Registers window, which reveals the current values in CPU registers. The information in this window helps you perform a low-level debug and trace of a program, and it requires some knowledge of assembly language and how C++ is translated into it.

The Event Log Option

The **E**vent Log option displays the Event Log window, which lists the sequence of breakpoint events that have occurred. Each log entry includes the breakpoint address, followed by text that identifies the related Windows messages, output messages, or exceptions.

The Information... Option

The **I**nformation... option displays the Information dialog box. This dialog box contains the following information:

- The current directory
- The Windows version and mode
- The MS-DOS version
- The total free memory space
- The largest free memory block
- The percent of USER, GDI, and total free heap space

This information can be useful when mysterious problems start showing up in Windows. It lets you know just how much memory is available and how much is free, and informs you of just how many resources are available. If any of these numbers get too low, things can start to get rather weird in Windows.

The Project Menu

The Project menu offers options that manage a project to build an executable program or a library. Table 1.7 summarizes the options in the Project menu.

Table 1.7. Summary of the options in the Project menu.

Command	Shortcut Keys	Function
AppExpert...		Invokes the AppExpert utility to generate the files of a project
New project...		Creates a new project
Open project...		Opens an existing project and closes the current project
Close project		Closes the current project
New target...		Creates a new target in the current project
Compile	Alt+F9	Compiles the file in the active edit window
Make all		Updates the project files by compiling and linking the necessary source-code files
Build all		Unconditionally compiles and links all of the project source-code files

The AppExpert... Option

The AppExpert... option invokes the AppExpert utility, which is a valuable and sophisticated tool for rapid program development. Day 19 discusses using the AppExpert.

The New Project... Option

The New project... option triggers the process that enables you to create a new project without involving the AppExpert utility. This option displays the New Project dialog box, shown in Figure 1.10. The dialog box enables you to specify the following information:

- The path and name of the new project
- The target name (that is, the name of the .EXE file)

- The target type, which can be one of the following:
  - A Windows .EXE application
  - A Windows .DLL dynamic library
  - An EasyWin .EXE program.
  - A .LIB static library
  - A .LIB import library
  - A Windows .HLP help file
- The application's platform, which must be 16-bit Windows 3.*x*. In order to develop for other platforms, such as Win32 or MS-DOS, you will need to upgrade to the full Borland C++ product.
- The target's memory model, which can be small, compact, medium, or large
- A variety of choices related to the libraries included; these are sensitive to the target type and change correspondingly.
- The options to specify child node files with .C or .CPP extension along with an optional .RC resource file and a .DEF definition file. The Advanced pushbutton control in the dialog box offers these options through a special dialog box.
- The option to select the path for the project. The Browse pushbutton control in the dialog box offers this option.

This is discussed a little bit later in this chapter when projects are introduced.

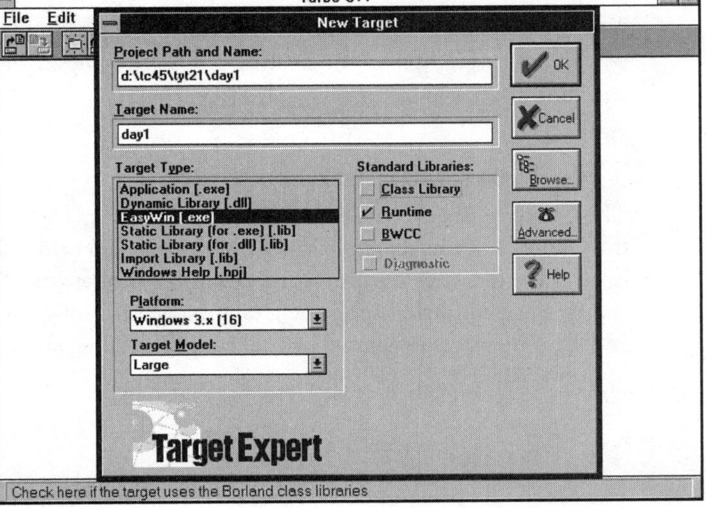

Figure 1.10.
A sample New Project dialog box.

The Open Project... Option

The **O**pen Project... option enables you to open a new project and automatically close the current one. This option displays the Open Project File dialog box, which resembles the File Open dialog box. The Project File dialog box enables you to specify the drive, directory, and filename wildcards involved in selecting the .IDE or .PRJ project files. The .PRJ project files from previous versions of Turbo C++ can still be loaded for backward compatibility; they are converted automatically to .IDE files. Project files from the full Borland C++ product also can be loaded, but if they contain any options that aren't supported in Turbo C++, the options will be ignored unless they conflict. If you load a project that targets Win32, for example, then the option will be changed to Win16 as that is the only platform supported.

The Close Project Option

The C**l**ose Project option closes the current project and its edit windows.

The New Target... Option

The New **T**arget... option enables you to add another target to the project. The option first displays the New Target dialog box, which enables you to enter the name and type of the target. The target type may be AppExpert, Standard, and SourcePool. If you choose the AppExpert target type, the IDE invokes the AppExpert once you close the New Target dialog box. If you select the Standard target type, the IDE invokes the Add Project dialog box. If you choose the SourcePool target type, the IDE quietly adds a SourcePool target node. The Project window reflects the addition of the new target and indicates its type.

A source pool target contains a set of nodes that are not built in the project. Instead, source pools play the role of templates for creating reference copies, which allow different targets to employ common source code.

The Compile Option

The **C**ompile option compiles the source code in the active edit window. The option displays the Compile Status dialog box, which informs you of the files being compiled, the number of lines, the number of warnings, and the number of errors. When the compilation process ends, the Message window displays general messages for the compilation steps and includes warning and error messages generated by the compiler, linker, and other tools. The shortcut key for this option is Alt+F9.

The Make All Option

The **M**ake All option updates the project's target by compiling and linking only those files that have been changed since the previous program make or build operations. The option also uses the Compile Status dialog box to display the progress of the compilation and linking

steps. Once this process is terminated, the Message window displays messages that reflect the progress of compiling and linking, along with any warning and error messages.

The Build All Option

The **B**uild All option is similar to the **M**ake All option, except that it systematically recompiles and links all of the project's files.

The Debug Menu

The Debug menu provides you with options that enable you to manage debugging and executing your C or C++ source code. Table 1.8 summarizes the options in the Debug menu. Day 21 offers a short tutorial on some simple debugging techniques.

Table 1.8. Summary of the options in the Debug menu.

Command	Shortcut Keys	Function
Run	Ctrl+F9	Runs the program of the current target. If necessary, this option also compiles and links the project source-code files.
Step over	F8	Runs the next statement without tracing into the parts that make it up. Contrast this with tracing into a function, the next command.
Trace into	F7	Single-steps through the next statement and also traces the statements of functions that are called in the next statement. This is a way of following the contents of a function.
Toggle brea**k**point	F5	Toggles making the line at the current cursor location an unconditional breakpoint
Find execution point		Shows the source code at the point of execution
Pause program		Pauses the program and switches to the debugger
Terminate pro**g**ram	Ctrl+F2	Stops the program. If you start or step into the program again, it will restart at the beginning as if you never had run it before.

continues

Table 1.8. continued

Command	Shortcut Keys	Function
Add **w**atch...	Ctrl+F5	Opens the Watch Properties dialog box to add a variable to watch
Add **b**reakpoint...		Opens the Breakpoint Properties dialog box to add a breakpoint
Evaluate/Modify...		Evaluates an expression and modifies the value in a variable
Inspect...	Alt+F5	Inspects the contents of a variable.
Load symbol table...		Loads DLL symbol table

The Tool Menu

The Tool menu provides you with access to several programming utilities. The IDE **T**ools... option in the Options menu enables you to customize the list of programming tools that appear in the Tool menu. Table 1.9 summarizes the default options in the Tool menu.

Table 1.9. Summary of the default options in the Tool menu.

Command	Shortcut Keys	Function
Resource Workshop		Invokes the Resource Workshop utility
Grep		Runs the Grep utility on the currently selected nodes
WinSight		Invokes the WinSight utility to monitor Windows messages
W**i**nSpector		Runs the WinSpector utility to perform postmortem analysis
Key map compiler		Compiles the IDE key map file

The Options Menu

The Options menu enables you to fine-tune the operations of the compiler, linker, editor, and all the other components of the IDE. Table 1.10 summarizes the options in the Options menu.

Table 1.10. Summary of the options in the Options menu.

Command	Shortcut Keys	Function
Project...		Inspects and edits the setting of the current project
Target...		Allows you to use the TargetExpert to modify the build options of the current project's targets
Environment...		Views and edits the setting of the environment.
Tools...		Adds or deletes (or both) tools in the Tool commands
Style Sheets...		Edits the options style sheets
Save...		Configures to save the project, desktop, and environment

The Project... Option

The **P**roject... option displays the dialog box with the title Project Options, as shown in Figure 1.11. The Project Option dialog box contains a list of topics on the left side and a set of controls on the right. Those controls are changed according to the topic selected in the left list. Following are the Project Options topics:

- The Directories topic enables you to specify the directories for the include, library, and source code files, as well as to specify the paths for intermediate and final files.
- The Compiler topic enables you to fine-tune the compiling of C and C++ source code, specify the preprocessor definitions, manage the inclusion of debug information, and manage precompiled header files.
- The Advanced Compiler topic enables you to manage compiling for 16-bit Windows 3.*x* applications, select the processor type, and choose the memory model for the compiled files.
- The C++ Options topic assists you in determining how the C++ compiler interprets your source code to manage new and old C++ language features.
- The Messages topic enables you to determine the type of messages emitted during the creation of the program. The options in the Message topic enables you to choose anything from a very strict to a very relaxed level of warnings and errors.
- The Linker topic enables you to control the creation of .OBJ, and .LIB files, which are united into the executable .EXE files.
- The Librarian section enables you to combine a set of .OBJ files into a .LIB file and control this process.

- The Resources section enables you to specify the target Windows version in order to create the right type of .RES compiled resource file and how it is bound to the .EXE.
- The Make section offers options that control the integrated make process.

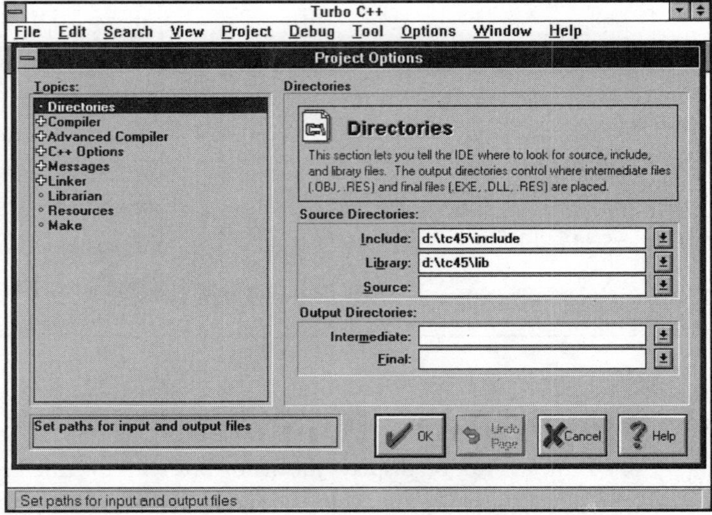

Figure 1.11.
A sample session with the Project Options dialog box.

The Target... Option

The Target... option displays a small dialog box that contains a list of the top-level targets in the current project. These targets then can be selected and edited in order to change such things as their target type, platform, memory model, and standard libraries.

The Environment... Option

The Environment... option displays the Environment Options dialog box, shown in Figure 1.12, which enables you to customize various aspects of the IDE. These aspects are organized and controlled by the following sections that appear in the dialog box:

- The Editor topic controls the operations of the IDE's text editor. The Editor's subtopics enable you to select the default text editor (which is similar to WordStar), select the IDE classical text editor, emulate the BRIEF editor, emulate the Epsilon editor, or customize various aspects of the current text editor.
- The Syntax Highlighting topic enables you to determine both the color and style used by the editor to display the source code. The syntax topic offers a few predefined sets of colors and styles.

- The Browser topic enables you to determine the default filters for the Browser. In addition, the topic enables you to request the creation of new windows as you traverse through the hierarchy of classes.
- The Debugger topic enables you to select between hard mode and soft mode debugging and to select smart mode debugging. (The hard and soft debugging modes determine how the Windows messages are intercepted by the debugger.) In addition, this topic enables you to select the capture of Windows messages, output messages, and breakpoints.
- The Speedbar section enables you to customize the location and contents of the speed bar.
- The Preferences section provides options related to saving various IDE components, such as the editor files, the environment, the desktop, and the project. The section also provides options to specify which parts of the desktop to save.
- The Project View section provides options that determine the type of information to include in the Project window—code size, data size, location, name, number of lines, node type, and so on.

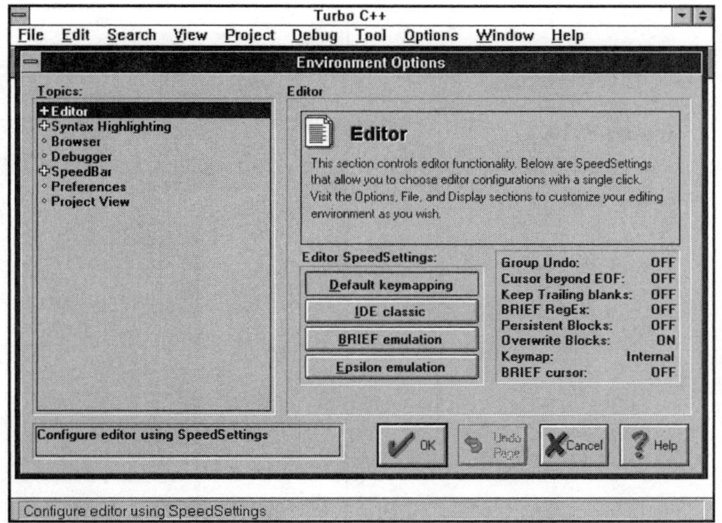

Figure 1.12.
A sample session with the Environment Options dialog box.

The Tools... Option

The **T**ools... option enables you to add new menu items to the Tool menu and to delete items from that menu. Figure 1.13 shows the Tools dialog box, which contains a Tools list box that shows you the available tools. If you click the Edit pushbutton, the dialog box displays the Tools Options dialog box, as shown in Figure 1.14. The latter dialog box enables you to specify the name of the tool, along with its path, command line, menu text, and help hint (which appears in the status line).

Note that most of the tools displayed in the list actually are internal tools and don't appear in the Tool menu. Some of the listed tools can be added to the menu if desired; however, many wouldn't make sense there.

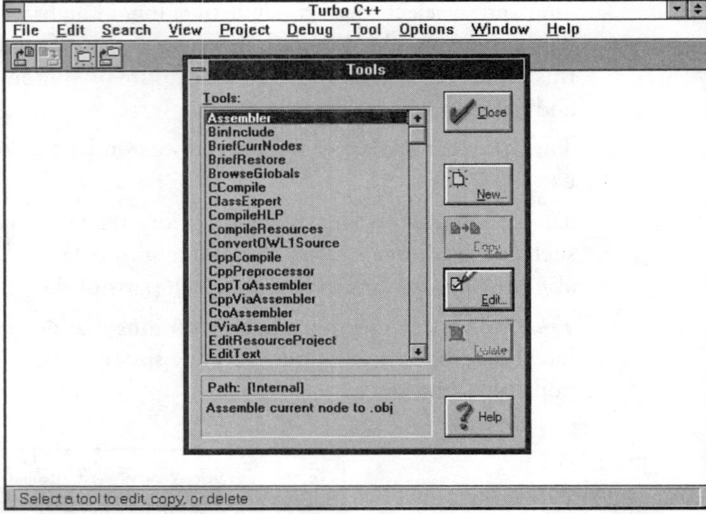

Figure 1.13.
The Tools dialog box.

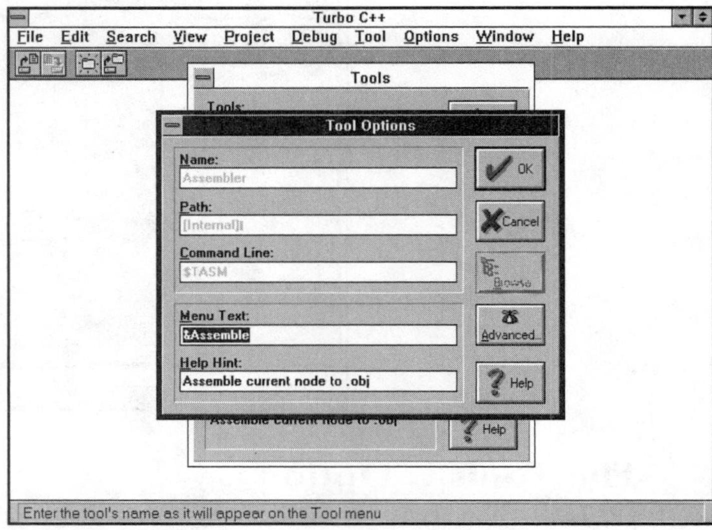

Figure 1.14.
The Tools Options dialog box.

The Style Sheets... Option

The Style Sheets... option displays the Style Sheet dialog box, shown in Figure 1.15, which enables you to select a configuration for the compile and runtime settings for a project. Each style sheet is a predefined collection of settings that can be affiliated with a node.

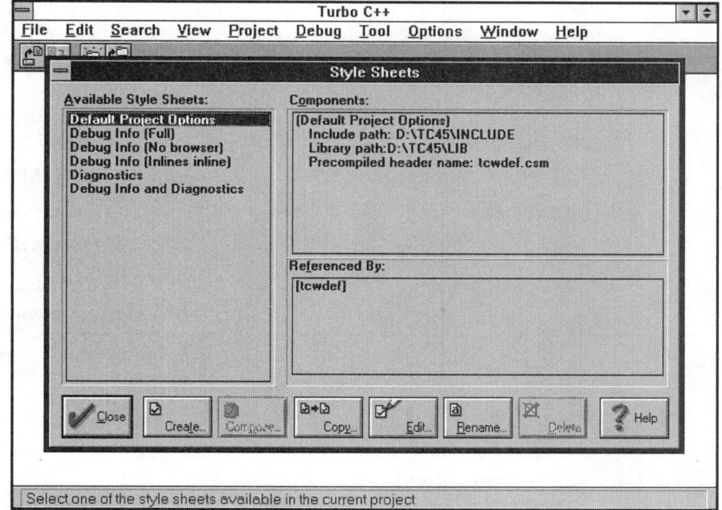

Figure 1.15.
The Style Sheet dialog box.

The Save... Option

The **S**ave... option enables you to specify to automatically save the desktop, environment, and project file. This option invokes the Save Options dialog box, which offers check boxes for saving these three IDE components.

The Window Menu

The Window menu offers options to manage windows in the IDE client area. These options, which are summarized in Table 1.11, enable you to arrange, close, minimize, and restore some or all the windows. In addition to the standard options, the Window menu also lists the current windows.

Table 1.11. Summary of the options in the Window menu.

Command	Shortcut Keys	Function
Cascade	Shift+F5	Cascades the windows in the client area of the IDE.

continues

Table 1.11. continued

Command	Shortcut Keys	Function
Tile **h**orizontal	Shift+F4	Tiles the windows horizontally on the client area of the IDE
Tile vertical		Tiles the windows vertically on the client area of the IDE
Arrange **i**cons		Arranges the icons in the client area of the IDE
Close **a**ll		Closes all windows—debugger windows, browser windows, or editor windows
Mi**n**imize all		Minimizes all windows, debugger windows, browser windows, or editor windows
Restore all		Restores all windows, debugger windows, browser windows, or editor windows

The Help Menu

The Help menu provides you with the kind of online help you may have gotten from other software. Table 1.12 summarizes the options in the Help menu.

Table 1.12. Summary of the options in the Help menu.

Command	Shortcut Keys	Function
Contents		Displays the table of contents for the online help system
Keyword **s**earch	F1	Displays help regarding the keyword on which the cursor is situated
Keyboard		Displays information about the mapping of the keyboard.
Using **h**elp		Displays information to assist you in using the online help system
Quick Tour		This offers a tutorial-like tour through Turbo C++.
Tips		Displays a list of special tips for using Turbo C++. Clicking on these tips displays a help screen with the appropriate information.
Windows API		Takes you to the Win16 API reference mentioned earlier

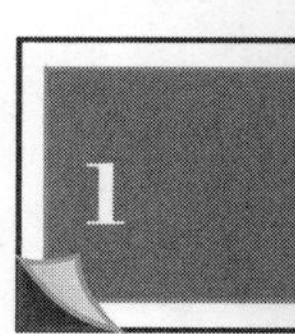

Command	Shortcut Keys	Function
OWL API		Opens up the OWL reference mentioned earlier
About...		Displays information regarding the software version and copyright

The EasyWin Applications

Microsoft Windows is a complicated environment. Applications are responsible for creating windows, providing support for mouse events, and all sorts of other things. Before windowing environments came about, programs ran in simple console environments like that found in standard MS-DOS. When a program is run, it has simple input from the keyboard and simple output directly to the screen on a character-by-character basis. Although the interface isn't very pretty, it's good for writing simple programs without having to worry about all the many features required for a full windowed program.

The Turbo C++ IDE enables you to build a special kind of program called an EasyWin application that provides a simple window that acts like an old-style console program. The programs in Days 1 through 10 of this book are EasyWin applications that enable you to focus on learning C++ using a console interface and input/output procedure. The EasyWin window is the standard input and output for C++ programs (compiled as EasyWin applications). The EasyWin window has a simple menu with few options and a few selections.

To create an EasyWin application, perform the following steps:

1. Load the Turbo C++ IDE.
2. Choose the Project menu from the menu bar.
3. Select the **N**ew Project command to invoke the New Project dialog box.
4. Enter the path and name of the .IDE project file in the topmost edit box. The dialog box echoes the pathname (as you type it) in the Target name edit box (that is, it makes the program name match the name of the project). You need to edit the target name if the name of the program does not match the name of the .IDE project file. You can use the Browse pushbutton to select the directory that will contain the project files.
5. Click the Advanced pushbutton to invoke the Advanced Options dialog box. Select the check box labeled .cpp node. This selection causes the IDE to insert the .CPP node for the EasyWin source-code file. This dialog also enables you to add or remove an .RC or .DEF module. Because these are useful only for real Windows applications and not for EasyWin, make sure these two options are unchecked. Close the Advanced Options dialog box by clicking on the OK button.

6. Select the EasyWin [.exe] item in the Target type list box.
7. Click the OK pushbutton to create the new project file.
8. The IDE displays the Project window, which lists the nodes for the various programs. When you first create a project file, the Project window will have only one node.
9. Click the main node to view the files contained in that node. The nodes of EasyWin programs contain only one file, a .CPP file, which has the source code. Double-click the .CPP file to request editing the file. Initially, the source window for the .CPP file is empty.
10. Enter the source code for the EasyWin program.
11. Press the Ctrl+F9 keys to compile, link, and run the EasyWin program. The compiler flags any errors and lists them in the Message window. If the EasyWin program is correct, the IDE will launch it.

Introduction to Projects and Nodes

When you create a new project or load an old one from disk, the Turbo C++ IDE creates a Projects window at the bottom of the IDE. This window contains all the nodes and sub-nodes needed for the application.

NEW TERM A *node* is the term used to describe the various items found in the project window. These nodes each have specific rules associated with them that the IDE uses to decide how to build applications. Furthermore, each node may, in turn, depend on one or more nodes for compilation. This means that before any particular node can be dealt with, the nodes on which it depends must already have been dealt with successfully.

You can add more than one program to an .IDE file. I suggest that you group the separate programs of each of the first twelve days in .IDE files named for their respective days, such as DAY1.IDE, DAY2.IDE, and so on. Grouping related program files in a single IDE saves space because the .IDE files are not small.

To add another target to an existing .IDE file, follow these steps:

1. Load the Turbo C++ IDE.
2. Choose the Project menu from the menu bar.
3. Select the New Target command to invoke the New Target dialog box.
4. Enter the name of the new program and click the OK pushbutton.
5. The IDE displays the New Project dialog box. Simply click the OK pushbutton to add a new program node in the Project window. All the changes you made earlier, including those made in the Advanced dialog, are remembered from last time.
6. The IDE displays the Project window, which lists the new nodes for the new program.

This last step just adds a new top-level target to the project with a single .CPP file for its main source code. You can add more nodes as dependencies to any target by selecting that node, clicking the right mouse button, and selecting the Add Node option from the resulting pop-up menu. A dialog box entitled Add to Project List appears and enables you to set the filename of the new node.

You also should note that some nodes have either a plus or a minus sign in their bitmaps. This operates in much the same way as the File Manager's folder bitmaps. A plus sign means there are node dependencies that have been hidden in order to help clean up the display. By clicking on the bitmap, the plus sign will change to a minus sign, and the node will expand to show its dependencies. Clicking on the node's bitmap again will collapse the display and change the minus back into a plus.

It can be extremely useful to have multiple files in conjunction with a single application. Eventually, when you start writing full-fledged Windows applications in Day 11, you're going to start seeing some rather large programs. Putting all the source code for the program in a single file can get extremely unwieldy, so splitting up that source code into multiple files can make life for the programmer much easier. You can find more about this on Day 11, which also discusses the AppExpert and its output.

Your First C++ Program

The first C++ program presented in this book displays a one-line greeting message. This simple program enables you to see the very basic components of a C++ program.

Listing 1.1 contains the source code for the program HELLO.CPP with numbered lines. *Do not* enter the line numbers when you type the program. These line numbers serve as reference only. This simple program displays the string `Hello Programmer!` Carry out the following steps to create and run this first C++ program. (Note that, with minor modifications, the line numbers can be used for all the program examples in the book that you type in yourself; the IDEs all are provided for you if you obtain the source disk):

1. Load the Turbo C++ IDE if it is not already loaded.
2. Choose the Project menu from the menu bar.
3. Select the **N**ew Project command to invoke the New Project dialog box.
4. Type **`\tcwin45\tc21day\day1\hello.ide`** in the edit box requesting the Project path and name. The dialog box also shows the name `"hello"` in the Target name edit box.
5. Click the Advanced pushbutton to invoke the Advanced Options dialog box. Select the check box labeled .cpp Node and turn off the RC and DEF options. Close the Advanced Options dialog box.
6. Select the EasyWin [.exe] item in the Target type list box.
7. Click the OK pushbutton to create the new project file.

The IDE displays the Project window, which lists the node for the hello program.

8. Click the hello.exe node to view the hello.cpp node. Double-click the hello.cpp node to invoke the IDE editor.
9. Enter in the new window the program shown in Listing 1.1.
10. Choose the **S**ave command in the File menu.
11. Press the Ctrl+F9 keys to compile, link, and run the HELLO.EXE program.

When an EasyWin program ends, the runtime system alters the title of the program's window to include the word `Inactive`. To close the program's window, select the **C**lose command from the system menu, or simply press Alt+F4.

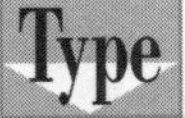

Listing 1.1. Source code for the program HELLO.CPP.

```
// a trivial C++ program that says hello

#include <iostream.h>

int main()
{
  cout << "Hello Programmer!";
  return 0;
}
```

The output of the program appears in Figure 1.16. Notice that the caption of the output window starts with the word `Inactive` to indicate that the program has terminated.

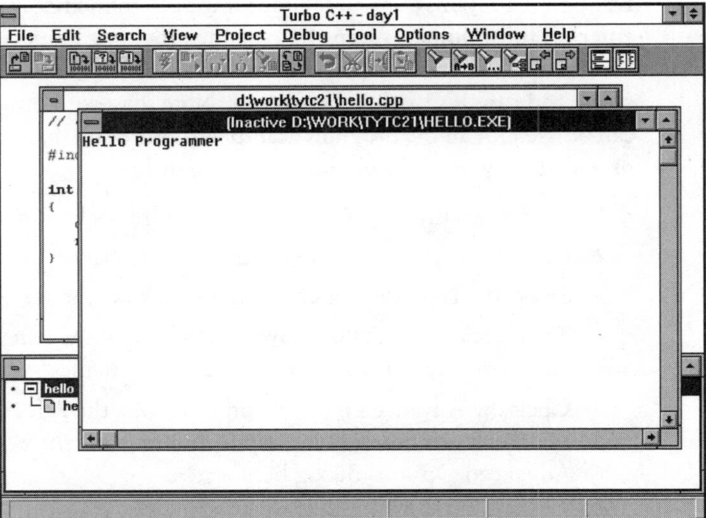

Figure 1.16.
The output of the HELLO.EXE program.

1

Analysis Examine the short code of the C++ program and notice the following characteristics:

- C++ uses the `//` characters for comments that go to the end of the line. C++ also supports the C-style comments that begin with the `/*` characters and end with the `*/` characters. Line 1 contains a comment that briefly describes the program.

NEW TERM *Comments* are remarks that you put in the program to explain or clarify certain parts of the program. The compiler ignores comments but the programmer relies on them to figure out what is meant in a program, especially if the code hasn't been looked at in a long time.

- The C++ program has no reserved keywords that declare the end of a program. In fact, C++ uses a rather simple scheme for organizing a program. This scheme supports two levels of code: global and single-level functions. In addition, the function `main`, which starts on line 5, plays a very special role because runtime execution begins with this function. Therefore, there can be only a single function `main` in a C++ program. You can place the function `main` anywhere in the code.
- The C++ strings and characters are enclosed in double and single quotes, respectively. Thus, `'A'` is a single character, whereas, `"A"` is a single-character string. Mixing C++ single-character strings and characters is not allowed.

NEW TERM Strings can have any number of characters, including no characters. A string without any characters is called the *empty string*.

- C++ defines blocks using the `{` and `}` characters. See examples in lines 6 and 9, respectively.
- Every statement in a C++ program must end with a semicolon (`;`). When looking at other code, it might appear that there are exceptions to this rule, but there really isn't, and this will be discussed later on.
- C++ contains the `#include` compiler preprocessor directive. An example of this is in line 3, instructing the Turbo C++ compiler to include the IOSTREAM.H header file. C++ extends the notion of streams, which already exists in C. IOSTREAM.H provides the operations that support basic stream input and output. The C++ language does not include built-in I/O routines. Instead, the language relies on libraries specializing in various types of I/O.

NEW TERM A *compiler directive* is a special instruction for the compiler and will be described under the Preprocessor heading in Day 2.

A *header file* contains the declarations of constants, data types, variables, and function prototypes.

A *stream* is a sequence of data flowing from one part of a computer to another.

- The C++ program outputs the string `Hello Programmer!` to the standard output stream `cout`, which is the EasyWin window. In addition, the program uses the output operator, `<<`, to send the emitted string to the output stream.

- ☐ The function `main` must return a value that reflects the error status of the C++ program. Returning the value `0` signals to the operating system that the program terminated normally.

Exiting the IDE

To exit the IDE, choose the Exit command from the File menu.

Summary

Today's lesson introduced you to a tremendous amount of material about the Turbo C++ IDE and presented you with the first C++ program. You learned these basics:

- ☐ C++ programs are modular and rely on standard and custom libraries.
- ☐ The DynaText documentation reader can be used to access the manuals that come with Turbo C++ on the CD-ROM.
- ☐ Reference information is available via the help system, which is available via the top menu; pop-up menus when the right mouse button is clicked; and by pressing either F1 or Ctrl+F1.
- ☐ The two ways to load the Turbo C++ IDE are by clicking the Turbo C++ icon or double-clicking the TCW.EXE file when using the File Manager (or any similar utility).
- ☐ The Turbo C++ IDE is a versatile environment for developing, maintaining, and debugging C and C++ programs and libraries for Windows applications.
- ☐ The File menu manages the creation of new files, the opening of files, the saving of files, printing, and exiting the IDE.
- ☐ The Edit menu offers options to perform popular editing operations (such as undo, cut, copy, paste, and delete).
- ☐ The Search menu enables you to find and replace text, as well as to browse through symbols, locate functions, and visit the offending source-code lines.
- ☐ The View menu enables you to view a wide variety of information. Among the viewable information are the project nodes, compiler and linker messages, the hierarchy of the project classes, global symbols, watched variables, the stack of called functions, and the CPU registers.
- ☐ The Project menu provides options to create, open, close and manage a project. The project options enable you to compile and link related source code files.
- ☐ The Debug menu offers options that enable you to debug and single-step in the source code from within the IDE and watch the values of variables in the Watch window.

- The Tool menu enables quick access to a variety of Windows programming tools, such as the Turbo Debugger for Windows, the message-tracing WinSight utility, the postmortem WinSpector utility, and your own tools.
- The Options menu enables you to fine-tune various aspects of your project—environment, tools, and project style sheets.
- The Window menu is for managing, arranging, closing, and restoring the windows in the IDE desktop.
- The Help menu provides you with the online help.
- EasyWin applications are Windows applications providing special windows that act as standard input and output devices. EasyWin applications enable you to write DOS-like programs.
- New projects are easy to create by setting certain options on a simple dialog box.
- Turbo C++ Project files enable you to create multiple targets and to have these targets contain multiple files.
- The first C++ program in this book is a simple greeting program that illustrates the basic components of a C++ program. These components include comments, the `#include` directive, and the `main` function.
- You exit the IDE through the Exit selection on the File menu.

Q&A

Q Does C++ use line numbers?

A No. We are using line numbers in the listings in this book only for the sake of reference.

Q Does the IDE's editor monitor what I type?

A Yes, it does. In fact, when you type a C++ keyword, the IDE quickly colors that keyword.

Q What happens if I forget to type the second double quote in the first program?

A The compiler tells you that there is an error in the program. You need to add the second double quote and build the project.

Q How do I delete all occurrences of some text in the currently edited window?

A Use the Replace selection in the Edit option and specify nothing for the replacement string, or use the Edit menu's Cut and Clear commands.

Workshop

The Workshop provides quiz questions to help you solidify your understanding of the material covered and exercises to provide you with experience in using what you've learned. Try to understand the quiz and exercise answers before continuing on to the next day's lesson. (Answers are provided in Appendix A.)

Quiz

1. What is the output of the following program?

```
// quiz program #1

#include <iostream.h>

main()
{
  cout << "C++ in 21 Days?";
  return 0;
}
```

2. What is the output of the following program?

```
// quiz program #2

#include <iostream.h>

main()
{
  // cout << "C++ in 21 Days?";
  return 0;
}
```

3. What is wrong with the following program?

```
// quiz program #3

#include <iostream.h>

main()
{
  cout << "C++ in 21 Days?"
  return 0;
}
```

Exercise

Write a program that displays the message `I am a C++ Programmer`.

WEEK 1

C++ The Preprocessor, Variables, and Operators

Day 1 presented the Borland IDE and a simple C++ program. Today you will focus on the basic components of C++ programs, including data types, variables, constants, and functions. You will learn about the following topics:

- The predefined data types in Turbo C++ 4.5
- Naming items in Turbo C++ 4.5
- The `#include` directive
- Declaring variables
- Declaring constants
- Arithmetic operators and expressions
- Increment operators
- Arithmetic assignment operators
- Typecasting and data conversion
- Relational operators and conditional expressions
- Bit-manipulating operators
- The comma operator

Predefined Data Types in Turbo C++ 4.5

Turbo C++ 4.5 offers the `bool`, `int`, `char`, `float`, `double`, and `void` data types to represent booleans, integers, characters, single-precision floating-point numbers, double-precision floating-point numbers, and valueless data, respectively. C++ uses the `void` type with a function's returned values to indicate that the function does not yield a significant result—that is, the function acts as a procedure. Functions are described in more detail on Day 5.

C++ adds more flexibility to data types by supporting data type modifiers. The type modifiers are as follows: `signed`, `unsigned`, `short`, and `long`. Table 2.1 shows the predefined data types in C++ (and includes the type modifiers), along with their sizes and ranges. Notice that `int` and `unsigned int` are system-dependent.

NEW TERM *Data type modifiers* alter the precision and the range of values.

Table 2.1. Predefined data types in C++.

Data Type	Byte Size	Range	Examples
`bool`	1	`false to true`	`true, false`
`char`	1	–128 to 127	`'A','!'`
`wchar_t`	2	–32768 to 32767	L'A', L'!'

Data Type	Byte Size	Range	Examples
`signed char`	1	–128 to 127	`23`
`unsigned char`	1	0 to 255	`200,0x1a`
`int`	2	Depends on system –32768 to 32767 for 16-bit	`3000`
`unsigned int`	2	Depends on system 0 to 65535 for 16-bit	`0xffff,` `65535`
`short int`	2	–32768 to 32767	`100`
`unsigned short int`	2	0 to 65535	`0xff, 40000`
`long int`	4	–2147483648L to 2147483647L	`0xfffffL,` `-123456L`
`unsigned long int`	4	0L to 4294967295L	`123456L`
`float`	4	3.4E–38 to 3.4E+38 and –3.4E–38 to –3.4E+38	`2.35,` `-52.354` `1.3e+10`
`double`	8	1.7E–308 to 1.7E+308 and –1.7E–308 to –1.7E+308	`12.354` `-2.5e+100` `-78.32544`
`long double`	10	3.4E–4932 to 1.1E+4932 and –1.1E–4932 to –3.4E+4932	`8.5e-3000`

NEW TERM C++ supports *hexadecimal numbers.* Such numbers begin with the characters `0x`, followed by the hexadecimal value. For example, the number `0xff` is the hexadecimal equivalent of the decimal number 255.

Note: Although I've listed `bool` here, and although some of the libraries supplied with Turbo C++ make use of it (particularly OWL), it hasn't quite made it into the language proper as of yet. When the appropriate header file (classlib\defs.h) is included, a special version of the `bool` type is set up to "fake it" until the compiler is outfitted with the proper equipment. This header file is included automatically whenever you make use of the Class Libraries or OWL, or you can add `#include <classlib\defs.h>` to your program manually.

Also note that C++ regards `0` as false and any nonzero value as true. The "faked" `bool` type in classlib\defs.h sets up `false` to be `0` and `true` to be `1`. In previous versions of the Turbo C++ compiler, (and in the standard Windows header files) `TRUE` and `FALSE` (in all capitals) were used.

Naming Items in Turbo C++ 4.5

Turbo C++ 4.5 requires you to observe the following rules with identifiers:

- The first character must be a letter or an underscore (_).
- Subsequent characters can be letters, digits, or underscores.
- The maximum length of an identifier is 32 characters by default (that can be changed in the compiler options).
- Identifiers are case-sensitive in C++. Thus, the names `rate`, `RATE`, and `Rate` refer to three different identifiers.
- Identifiers cannot be reserved words, such as `int`, `double`, or `static` to name just a few.

The following are examples of valid identifiers:

```
X
x
aString
DAYS_IN_WEEK
BinNumber0
bin_number_0
bin0Number2
_length
```

And here are some invalid ones.

```
123aNumber
const
NoSpaces Allowed
NorAre*Most+Symbols
```

DO	DON'T

DO use descriptive names that have a reasonable length.

DON'T use identifier names that are too short or too long. Short names yield poor readability, and long names are prone to typographical errors. Some notable exceptions would be with iterators used in loops (to be explained on Day 3). In those cases, a simple `i` or `ix` often is used.

The Preprocessor

A long time ago, on a computer far, far away, compilers were a lot simpler than they are today. Back then, compilers required multiple passes through the source code in order to successfully create the machine code that could run on the computer. In those days, the preprocessor was an integral part of the compiling process. The preprocessor would do a quick run through the code in order to bring extra files together and to process macros.

2

The instructions that were meant for the preprocessor alone were called *directives*, and while the preprocessor as a separate entity doesn't really exist in the same way today, the terminology has. In C and C++, all directives must begin with a number sign (sometimes called sharp or pound—`#`) on the far left of a line followed by the directive name. There are a number of directives, most of them meant to control how the compiler operates, but the most important ones are `#include` and `#define`.

The *#include* Directive

The C++ program in Day 1 contains an `#include` directive. This directive tells the compiler to include the text of a file as if you have typed that text yourself. Thus, the `#include` directive is a better alternative than cutting text from one file and pasting in another file. Instead, one can create a header file that includes the common code and then simply include it in all the relevant programs.

It is vitally important, however, to recognize the difference between including a header file and separating code out into separate source files that all combine later into the target. Once a variable is created in memory, another creation is illegal. Therefore, if you actually create a variable in a header file, then include it in two different source files that combine into a single target, you will get compiler errors informing you of duplicate symbols. Typically, the only things that get placed in a header file are macro definitions, structure definitions, type definitions, and function prototypes. All of these will be described in time.

Syntax

The *#include* Directive

The general syntax for the `#include` directive is

```
#include <filename>
#include "filename"
```

The filename represents the name of the included file. The two forms differ in how the `#include` directive searches for the included file. The first form searches for the file in the special directory for included files. The second form extends the search to involve the current directory before searching the include directory.

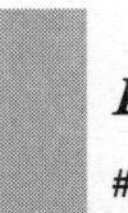

Examples

```
#include <iostream.h>
#include "string.h"
```

The *#define* Directive

The `#define` directive is what creates macro definitions. The most common of these is a simple substitution-type of macro: you tell the preprocessor to substitute every occurrence of a particular text pattern with another. In these cases, the compiler proper never really sees what you originally typed into the source code, but rather its substitution.

The other, slightly less common usage for the `#define` directive is to create macros that involve some sort of substitution via parameters. This is similar to functions that will be described on Day 5, except, again, the compiler proper never even sees the original source code, but rather is shown only the substitution. Because of that similarity, they will be described then.

Syntax

The *#define* Directive

The general syntax for the `#define` directive is

```
#define constantName constantValue
```

The `#define` directive causes the preprocessor to perform text substitution to replace the macro-based constants with their values. This text replacement step occurs before the compiler processes the statements in the source file. Consequently, the compiler never sees the macro-based constants themselves, only what they expand to.

Examples

```
#define ASCII_A 65
#define DAYS_IN_WEEK 7
```

Note the tendency for macros to be in all uppercase. This merely is a convention that has survived from the original C macros, but it helps to keep the macros separate from other parts of the program, and makes them easier to pick out from all the other code.

Declaring Variables

Declaring variables requires you to state the data type of the variable and the name of the variable. The word *variable* indicates that you can alter the data of these data containers.

NEW TERM *Variables* are identifiers used to store and recall information.

In order to help in understanding variables, imagine that there are a number of cardboard boxes, and they are each made to hold only a certain type of object. These objects are called `ints` and `chars`, and so on. You can have any number of any type of box, but you need to have one for each object you want to store; you cannot store an object without a box. So, for example, if you wanted to hold on to an int, you would need to have the appropriate type of variable into which you could store the number. Then, when you want to use that number later on, you can just refer to the box to find out what's in it.

2

Syntax

Declaring Variables

The general syntax for declaring variables is

```
type variableName;
type variableName = initialValue;
type var1 [= initVal1], var2 [= initVal2], ...;
```

Examples

```
int j;
double z = 32.314;
long fileSize, diskSize, totalFileSize = 0;
```

C++ enables you to declare a list of variables (that have the same types) in a declarative statement, such as the following:

```
int j, i = 2, k = 3;
double x = 3.12;
double y = 2 * x, z = 4.5, a = 45.7;
```

The initializing values may contain other variables defined earlier.

DO	DON'T

DO resist using global variables. It's considered to be very bad form, especially in object-oriented languages like C++.

DON'T declare variables within the same program unit with names that are different in character case (such as `rate` and `Rate`).

Look at a simple example that uses variables. Listing 2.1 shows the source code for the program VAR1.CPP. The program declares four variables, two of which are initialized during their declarations. The program then assigns values to the uninitialized variables and displays the contents of all four variables. Create the project DAY2.IDE (in the directory \TCWIN45\TC21DAY) and include the VAR1.CPP file as a node. Compile and run the VAR1.EXE program.

Type

Listing 2.1. Source code for the program VAR1.CPP.

```
1:  // C++ program that illustrates simple variables
2:
3:  #include <iostream.h>
4:
5:  main()
6:  {
7:    int i, j = 2;
8:    double x, y = 355.0 / 113;
9:
10:   i = 3 * j;
11:   cout << "i = " << i << "\n"
12:        << "j = " << j << "\n";
13:
14:   x = 2 * y;
15:   x = x * x;
16:   cout << "y = " << y << "\n"
17:        << "x = " << x << "\n";
18:   return 0;
19:
20: }
```

Here is a sample session with the program in Listing 2.1.

```
i = 6
j = 2
y = 3.14159
x = 39.4784
```

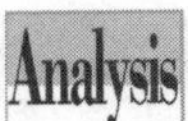

The program uses the `#include` directive in line 3 to include the stream I/O header file IOSTREAM.H; it is this header file that defines the code necessary for output. The function main appears in line 5. The function contains the declarations of the int-typed variables `i`, `j` in line 7, and the double-typed variables `x` and `y` in line 8. The declarations initialize the variable `j` and `y`. The statement in line 10 multiplies the value in variable `j` (which is `2`) by `3` and stores the result in variable `x`. The stream output statement in lines 11 and 12 displays the values of variables `i` and `j`. The statement includes strings that label the output.

The statement in line 14 doubles the value in variable `y` and stores it in variable `x`. The statement in line 15 squares the value in variable `x` and assigns the result back to variable `x`. This statement uses the variable `x` on both sides of the equal sign. The stream output statement in lines 16 and 17 displays the values in variable `x` and `y`. The statement in line 18 returns `0` as the result of function `main`.

Declaring Constants

Many languages, such as BASIC (the more recent implementations), Modula-2, Ada, C, Pascal, and C++, support constants. No one can deny that constants enhance the readability of a program by replacing numeric constants with identifiers that are more descriptive. Moreover, using constants enables you to change the value of a program parameter by merely changing the

value of that parameter in one location. This capability is more convenient and less prone to generate the errors that may occur when you employ your text editor to replace certain numbers with other numbers.

NEW TERM *Constants* are identifiers that are associated with fixed values. C++ offers constants in two varieties: *macro-based* and *formal*. The macro-based constants are inherited from C and use the `#define` compiler directive.

Syntax

The Formal Constant

The general syntax for the formal constant is

```
const dataType constantName = constantValue;
```

The `dataType` item is an optional item that specifies the data type of the constant values. If you omit the data type, the C++ compiler assumes the `int` type.

Examples

```
const unsigned char ASCII_A = 65;
const DAYS_IN_WEEK = 7;
const char FIRST_DISK_DRIVE = 'A';
```

DO	DON'T

DO use uppercase names for constants. This naming style enables you to determine quickly if an identifier is a constant.

DON'T assume that other people who read your code will know what embedded numbers mean. Use declared constants to enhance the readability of your programs.

Using Macro-Based Constants

Now consider an example that uses macro-based constants. Listing 2.2 shows the source code for the program CONST1.CPP. The program prompts you to enter the number of hours, minutes, and seconds since midnight. The program then calculates and displays the total number of seconds since midnight. Add the CONST1.CPP file as a node in the project file DAY2.IDE, and then compile and run the CONST1.EXE program.

Listing 2.2. Source code for the program CONST1.CPP.

```
// C++ program that illustrates constants

#include <iostream.h>

```

continues

Listing 2.2. continued

```
5:  #define SEC_IN_MIN 60
6:  #define MIN_IN_HOUR 60
7:
8:  main()
9:  {
10:   long hours, minutes, seconds;
11:   long totalSec;
12:
13:   cout << "Enter hours: ";
14:   cin >> hours;
15:   cout << "Enter minutes: ";
16:   cin >> minutes;
17:   cout << "Enter seconds: ";
18:   cin >> seconds;
19:
20:   totalSec = ((hours * MIN_IN_HOUR + minutes) *
21:               SEC_IN_MIN) + seconds;
22:
23:   cout <<"\n\n" << totalSec << " seconds since midnight";
24:   return 0;
25: }
```

Here is a sample session with the program in Listing 2.2.

```
Enter hours: 10
Enter minutes: 0
Enter seconds: 0

36000 seconds since midnight
```

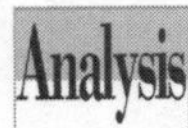

The program uses the `#include` directive in line 3 to include the header file IOSTREAM.H; in addition to providing the definitions necessary for output, IOSTREAM.H also is required for input. Lines 5 and 6 contain the `#define` directive that declares the macro-based constants `SEC_IN_MIN` and `MIN_IN_HOUR`. Both constants have the value `60`, but each value has a different meaning. The function `main`, which starts at line 8, declares 4 `long`-typed variables: `hours`, `minutes`, `seconds`, and `totalSec`.

The function uses pairs of statements to output the prompting messages and receive input. Line 13 contains the stream output statement that prompts you for the number of hours. Line 14 contains the stream input statement. The identifier `cin` is the name of the standard input stream and uses the input operator >> to read data from the keyboard and to store it in the variable `hours`. The input and output statements in lines 15 through 18 perform a similar task of prompting for input and obtaining keyboard input.

Line 20 contains a statement that calculates the total number of seconds since midnight and stores the result in the variable `totalSec`. The statement uses the macro-based constants `MIN_IN_HOUR` and `SEC_IN_MIN`. As you can see, using these constants enhances the readability of the statement, compared to using the number 60 in place of both constants. Line 23 contains a stream output statement that displays the total number of seconds since midnight (stored in the variable `totalSec`), followed by qualifying text to clarify the output.

Using Formal Constants

Now look at a new version of the program—one that uses the formal C++ constants. Listing 2.3 shows the source code for the program CONST2.CPP. This program works like the CONST1.CPP program. Add the CONST2.CPP file as a node in the project file DAY2.IDE. Compile and run the CONST2.EXE program.

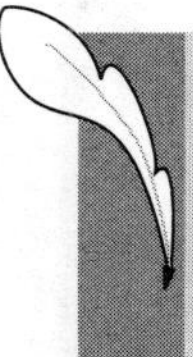

Note: At this point, we assume that you are familiar with the process of creating the .CPP source file, creating the .IDE project file, and adding .CPP files as nodes in the project file. From now on we will not mention creating these files, unless there is a special set of source files in a project.

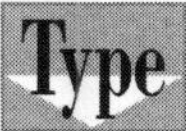

Listing 2.3. Source code for the program CONST2.CPP.

```
// C++ program that illustrates constants

#include <iostream.h>

const SEC_IN_MIN = 60; // global constant

main()
{
  const MIN_IN_HOUR = 60; // local constant

  long hours, minutes, seconds;
  long totalSec;

  cout << "Enter hours: ";
  cin >> hours;
  cout << "Enter minutes: ";
  cin >> minutes;
  cout << "Enter seconds: ";
  cin >> seconds;

  totalSec = ((hours * MIN_IN_HOUR + minutes) *
                SEC_IN_MIN) + seconds;

  cout <<"\n\n" << totalSec << " seconds since midnight";
  return 0;
}
```

Here is a sample session with the program in Listing 2.3.

```
Enter hours: 1
Enter minutes: 10
Enter seconds: 20

4220 seconds since midnight
```

The programs in Listings 2.2 and 2.3 are similar. The difference between them is how they declare their constants. In Listing 2.3, the formal C++ constant syntax is used to declare the constants. In addition, the constant `SEC_IN_MIN` in line 5 is declared, outside the function `main`. This type of declaration makes the constant global. That is, if there were another function in the program, it would be able to use the constant `SEC_IN_MIN`. By contrast, the constant `MIN_IN_SEC` is declared inside the function `main`. Thus, the constant `MIN_IN_SEC` is local to the function `main`.

Operators and Expressions

The manipulation of data involves expressions made up of operands and operators. C++ supports several kinds of operators and expressions.

NEW TERM Operators are special symbols that take the values of operands and produce a new value.

If you've taken any simple algebra in school, you will recognize the types of things that are described in this section. They're mostly extensions of the familiar equations you were taught.

Arithmetic Operators

Table 2.2 shows the C++ arithmetic operators. The compiler carries out floating-point or integer division, depending on the operands. If both operands are integer expressions, the compiler yields the code for an integer division. If either or both operands are floating-point expressions, the compiler generates code for floating-point division.

Table 2.2. C++ arithmetic operators.

C++ Operator	Purpose	Data Type	Example
`+`	Unary plus	Numeric	`x = +y + 3;`
`-`	Unary minus	Numeric	`x = -y;`
`+`	Add	Numeric	`z = y + x;`
`-`	Subtract	Numeric	`z = y - x;`
`*`	Multiply	Numeric	`z = y * x;`
`/`	Divide	Numeric	`z = y / x;`
`%`	Modulus	Integers	`z = y % x;`

Look at an example that uses the mathematical operators with integers and floating-point numbers. Listing 2.4 shows the source code for program OPER1.CPP. The program performs the following tasks:

- ☐ Prompts you to enter two integers (one integer per prompt).
- ☐ Applies the +, -, *, /, and % operators to the two integers, storing the results in separate variables.
- ☐ Displays the results of the integer operations.
- ☐ Prompts you to enter two floating-point numbers (one number per prompt).
- ☐ Applies the +, -, *, and / operators to the two numbers, storing the results in separate variables.
- ☐ Displays the result of the floating-point operations.

Listing 2.4. Source code for the program OPER1.CPP.

```
// simple C++ program to illustrate simple math operations

#include <iostream.h>

main()
{

    int int1, int2;
    long long1, long2, long3, long4, long5;
    float x, y, real1, real2, real3, real4;

    cout << "\nType first  integer : ";
    cin >> int1;
    cout << "Type second integer : ";
    cin >> int2;
    cout << "\n";
    long1 = int1 + int2;
    long2 = int1 - int2;
    long3 = int1 * int2;
    long4 = int1 / int2;
    long5 = int1 % int2;
    cout << int1 << " + " << int2 << " = " << long1 << '\n';
    cout << int1 << " - " << int2 << " = " << long2 << '\n';
    cout << int1 << " * " << int2 << " = " << long3 << '\n';
    cout << int1 << " / " << int2 << " = " << long4 << '\n';
    cout << int1 << " mod " << int2 << " = " << long5 << '\n';
    cout << "\n\n";
    cout << "Type first  real number : ";
    cin >> x;
    cout << "Type second real number : ";
    cin >> y;
    cout << "\n";
    real1 = x + y;
    real2 = x - y;
    real3 = x * y;
    real4 = x / y;
```

continues

Listing 2.4. continued

```
37:     cout << x << " + " << y << " = " << real1 << '\n';
38:     cout << x << " - " << y << " = " << real2 << '\n';
39:     cout << x << " * " << y << " = " << real3 << '\n';
40:     cout << x << " / " << y << " = " << real4 << '\n';
41:     cout << "\n\n";
42:     return 0;
43: }
```

Here is a sample session with the program in Listing 2.4.

```
Type first  integer : 10
Type second integer : 5

10 + 5 = 15
10 - 5 = 5
10 * 5 = 50
10 / 5 = 2
10 mod 5 = 0


Type first  real number : 1.25
Type second real number : 2.58

1.25 + 2.58 = 3.83
1.25 - 2.58 = -1.33
1.25 * 2.58 = 3.225
1.25 / 2.58 = 0.484496
```

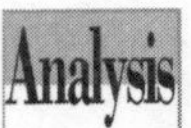

The program in Listing 2.4 declares a set of `int`-typed, `long`-typed, and `float`-typed variables in the function `main`. Some of these variables store your input, and others store the results of the mathematical operations. The output statement in line 12 prompts you to enter the first integer. The input statement in line 13 obtains your input and stores it in the variable `int1`. Lines 14 and 15 perform a similar operation to prompt you for the second integer and store it in variable `int2`.

The program performs the integer math operation in lines 17 through 21 and stores the results of these operations in variables `long1` through `long5`. These variables were declared as `long`-typed to guard against possible numeric overflow. The output statements in lines 22 through 26 display the integer operands, the operators used, and the results.

The output statement in line 28 prompts you to enter the first floating-point number. The input statement in line 29 obtains your input and stores it in the variable `x`. Lines 30 and 31 perform a similar operation to prompt you for the second floating-point number and to store it in variable `y`.

NEW TERM A floating-point number also is known as a *real number*.

The program performs the floating-point math operation in lines 33 through 36 and stores the results of these operations in variables `real1` through `real4`. The output statements in lines 37 through 40 display the operands, the operators used, and the results.

Arithmetic Expressions

The simplest types of expressions are the ones that contain literals, such as

```
-12
34.45
'A'
"Hello"
```

NEW TERM In general terms, an *arithmetic expression* is part of a program statement that contains a value.

The literal constants `-12` and `35.45` are the simplest arithmetic expressions. The next level of arithmetic expressions includes single variables or constants, such as

```
DAYS_IN_WEEK // a constant
i
x
```

Yet another level of arithmetic expressions contains a single operator with numbers, constants, and variables as operands. Following are a few examples:

```
355 / 113
4 * i
45.67 + x
```

More advanced arithmetic expressions contain multiple operators, parentheses, and even functions, such as

```
(355 / 113) * square(radius)
PIE * square(radius)
((2 * x - 3) * x + 2) * x - 5
(1 + x) / (3 - x)
```

The order of executing the operators are discussed at the end of today's lesson, after other types of operators are introduced.

Increment Operators

C++ supports the special increment and decrement operators.

NEW TERM *Increment* (++) and *decrement* (–) *operators* enable you to increment and decrement, respectively, the value stored in a variable by 1.

Syntax

Increment Operators

The general syntax for the increment operators is

```
variable++  // post-increment
++variable  // pre-increment
```

Examples

```
lineNumber++;
++index;
```

Decrement Operators

Syntax

The general syntax for the decrement operators is

```
variable  // post-decrement
variable  // pre-decrement
```

Examples

```
lineNumber;
index
```

This general syntax demonstrates that there are two ways to apply the ++ and – operators. Placing these operators to the left of their operand changes the value of the operand *before* the operand contributes its value in an expression. Likewise, placing these operators to the right of their operands alters the value of the operand *after* the operand contributes its value in an expression. If the ++ or – operators are the only operators in a statement, there is no practical distinction between using the pre- or post-forms.

Following are a few simple examples:

```
int n, m, t = 5;

t++; // t is now 6, same effect as ++t
-t; // t is now 5, same effect as t-
t = 5;
n = 4 * t++; // t is now 6 and[]is 20
t = 5;
m = 4 * ++m; // m is now 6 and[]is 24
```

The first statement uses the post-increment ++ operator to increment the value of variable t. If you write ++t instead, you get the same result when the statement finishes executing. The second statement uses the pre-decrement operator. Again, if you write t instead, you get the same result. The next two statements assign 5 to variable t and then use the post-increment ++ operator in a simple math expression. This statement multiplies 4 by the current value of t (that is, 5), assigns the result of 20 to the variable n, and then increments the values in variable t to 6. The last two statements show a different outcome. The statement first increments the value in variable t (the value in variable t becomes 6), and then performs the multiplication, and finally assigns the result of 24 to the variable n.

Look at a simple program that illustrates the feature of the increment operator. Listing 2.5 shows the source code for the program OPER2.CPP. The program requires no input from you. It simply displays two integers whose values were obtained using the increment operator.

Type

Listing 2.5. Source code for the program OPER2.CPP.

```
/*
   C++ program to illustrate the feature of the increment operator.
   The ++ or  may be included in an expression.  The value
   of the associated variable is altered after the expression
   is evaluated if the var++ (or var) is used, or before
   when ++var (or var) is used.
```

```
 7: */
 8:
 9: #include <iostream.h>
10:
11: main()
12: {
13:    int i, k = 5;
14:
15:    // use post-incrementing
16:    i = 10 * (k++); // k contributes 5 to the expression
17:    cout << "i = " << i << "\n\n"; // displays 50 (= 10 * 5)
18:
19:    k; // restores the value of k to 5
20:
21:    // use pre-incrementing
22:    i = 10 * (++k); // k contributes 6 to the expression
23:    cout << "i = " << i << "\n\n"; // displays 60 (= 10 * 6)
24:    return 0;
25: }
```

Here is a sample session with the program in Listing 2.5.

```
i = 50

i = 60
```

The program in Listing 2.5 has the function `main`, which declares 2 `int`-typed variables, `i` and `k`. The function initializes the variable `k` by assigning it the value `5`. Line 16 contains a statement that applies the post-increment operator to the variable `k`. Consequently, the statement multiplies `10` by the initial value in `k`, `5`, and assigns the product, `50`, to variable `i`. After assigning the result to variable `i`, the program increments the value in variable `k`. The output statement in line 17 displays the value in variable `i`. The statement in line 19 decrements the value in variable `k` back to `5`. The statement in line 22 applies the pre-increment operator to the variable `k`. Therefore, the program first increments the value in variable `k` (from `5` to `6`) and then multiplies `10` by the updated value in `k`. The program assigns the result of the multiplication, `60`, to the variable `i`. The output statement in line 23 displays the current value of variable `i`.

Assignment Operators

As a programmer, you often may come across statements that look similar to the following:

```
IndexOfFirstElement = IndexOfFirstElement + 4;
GraphicsScaleRatio = GraphicsScaleRatio * 3;
CurrentRateOfReturn = CurrentRateOfReturn / 4;
DOSfileListSize = DOSfileListSize - 10;
```

The variable that receives the result of an expression also is the first operand. (Of course, the addition and multiplication are commutative operations. Therefore, the assigned variable can be either operand with these operations.) Notice that we chose relatively long names to remind you of your need to shorten the expression without making the names of the variables shorter.

NEW TERM C++ offers *assignment operators* that merge with simple math operators.

You can write the following statements:

```
IndexOfFirstElement += 4;
GraphicsScaleRatio *= 3;
CurrentRateOfReturn /= 4;
DOSfileListSize -= 10;
```

Notice that the name of the variable appears only once. In addition, notice that the statements use the operators +=, *=, /=, and -=. Table 2.3 shows the arithmetic assignment operators. C++ supports other types of assignment operators.

Table 2.3. Arithmetic assignment operators.

Assignment Operator	Long Form	Example
`x += y`	`x = x + y`	`x += 12;`
`x -= y`	`x = x - y`	`x -= 34 + y;`
`x *= y`	`x = x * y`	`scale *= 10;`
`x /= y`	`x = x / y`	`z /= 34 * y;`
`x %= y`	`x = x % y`	`z %= 2;`

Look at a program that applies the assignment operators to integers and floating-point numbers. Listing 2.6 shows the source code for the program OPER3.CPP. The program performs the following tasks:

- Prompts you to enter two integers (one integer per prompt).
- Applies a set of assignment and increment operators to the two integers.
- Displays the new values of the integers.
- Prompts you to enter two floating-point numbers (one number per prompt).
- Applies a set of assignment and increment operators to the two numbers.
- Displays the new values of the floating-point numbers.

Listing 2.6. Source code for the program OPER3.CPP.

```
// C++ program to illustrate math assignment operators

#include <iostream.h>

main()
{
    int i, j;
    double x, y;

```

```
10:     cout << "Type first  integer : ";
11:     cin >> i;
12:     cout << "Type second integer : ";
13:     cin >> j;
14:     i += j;
15:     j -= 6;
16:     i *= 4;
17:     j /= 3;
18:     i++;
19:     j;
20:     cout << "i = " << i << "\n";
21:     cout << "j = " << j << "\n";
22:
23:     cout << "Type first  real number : ";
24:     cin >> x;
25:     cout << "Type second real number : ";
26:     cin >> y;
27:     // abbreviated assignments also work with doubles in C++
28:     x += y;
29:     y -= 4.0;
30:     x *= 4.0;
31:     y /=  3.0;
32:     x++;
33:     y;
34:     cout << "x = " << x << "\n";
35:     cout << "y = " << y << "\n";
36:     return 0;
37: }
```

Here is a sample session with the program in Listing 2.6.

```
Type first  integer : 55
Type second integer : 66
i = 485
j = 19
Type first  real number : 2.5
Type second real number : 4.58
x = 29.32
y = -0.806667
```

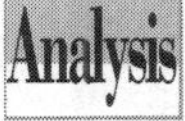

The program in Listing 2.6 contains the function `main`, which declares two `int`-typed variables (`i` and `j`) and two `double`-typed variables (`x` and `y`) in lines 7 and 8, respectively. The output statement in line 10 prompts you to enter the first integer. The input statement in line 11 receives your input and stores it in the variable `i`. Lines 12 and 13 are similar to lines 10 and 11—they prompt you for the second integer and store it in variable `j`.

The program manipulates the values in variables `i` and `j` using the statements in lines 14 through 19. In line 14, the program uses the `+=` operator to increment the value in variable `i` by the value in variable `j`. Line 15 uses the `-=` operator to decrement the value in variable `j` by `6`. Line 16 applies the `*=` operator to multiply the value in variable `i` by `4` and to assign the result back to variable `i`. Line 17 utilizes the `/=` operator to divide the value in variable `j` by `3` and to store the result in `j`. Lines 18 and 19 apply the increment and decrement operators to variables `i` and `j`, respectively. The output statements in lines 20 and 21 display the contents of variables `i` and `j`, respectively.

The output statement in line 23 prompts you to enter the first floating-point number. The input statement in line 24 receives your input and saves it in the variable x. Lines 25 and 26 are similar to lines 23 and 24; they prompt you for the second floating-point number and store it in variable y.

The program manipulates the values in variable x and y using the statements in lines 28 through 33. In line 28, the program uses the += operator to increment the value in variable x by the value in variable y. Line 29 uses the -= operator to decrement the value in variable y by 4. Line 30 applies the *= operator to multiply the value in variable x by 4 and to save the result back to x. Line 31 utilizes the /= operator to divide the value in variable y by 3 and to store the result in y. Lines 32 and 33 apply the increment and decrement operators to variable x and y, respectively. The output statements in lines 34 and 35 display the contents of variables x and y, respectively.

The *sizeof* Operator

Frequently, your programs need to know the byte size of a data type or of a variable. C++ provides the sizeof operator, which takes an argument of either a data type or the name of a variable (scalar, array, structure, and so on).

Syntax

The *size*of Operator

The general syntax for the sizeof operator is

```
sizeof({variable_name ¦ data_type})
sizeof {variable_name ¦ data_type}
```

Examples

```
int sizeDifference = sizeof(double) - sizeof(float);
int intSize = sizeof int;
```

DO	DON'T

DO use sizeof with the name of the variable rather than its data type. This approach is safer because if you alter the data type of the variable, the sizeof operator still returns the correct answer. By contrast, if you use the sizeof operator with the data type of the variable and later alter the variable's type, you create a bug if you do not update the argument of the sizeof operator.

DON'T use numbers to represent the size of a variable. This approach often causes errors.

Look at an example that uses the sizeof operator with variables and data types. Listing 2.7 contains the source code for the program SIZEOF1.CPP. The program displays two similar tables that indicate the sizes of the short int, int, long int, char, and float data types. The

program displays the first table by applying the `sizeof` operators to variables of these types. The program displays the second table by directly applying the `sizeof` operator to the data types.

Listing 2.7. Source code for the program SIZEOF1.CPP.

```
/*
  simple program that returns the data sizes using the sizeof()
  operator with variables and data types.
*/

#include <iostream.h>

main()

{
    short int aShort;
    int anInt;
    long aLong;
    char aChar;
    float aReal;

    cout << "Table 1. Data sizes using sizeof(variable)\n\n";
    cout << "    Data type         Memory used\n";
    cout << "                        (bytes)\n";
    cout << "    ";
    cout << "\n     short int             " << sizeof(aShort);
    cout << "\n      integer              " << sizeof(anInt);
    cout << "\n   long integer            " << sizeof(aLong);
    cout << "\n     character             " << sizeof(aChar);
    cout << "\n      float                " << sizeof(aReal);
    cout << "\n\n\n\n";

    cout << "Table 2. Data sizes using sizeof(dataType)\n\n";
    cout << "    Data type         Memory used\n";
    cout << "                        (bytes)\n";
    cout << "    ";
    cout << "\n     short int             " <<  sizeof(short int);
    cout << "\n      integer              " <<  sizeof(int);
    cout << "\n    long integer           " <<  sizeof(long);
    cout << "\n     character             " <<  sizeof(char);
    cout << "\n       float               " <<  sizeof(float);
    cout << "\n\n\n\n";

    return 0;
}
```

Here is a sample session with the program in Listing 2.7.

```
Table 1. Data sizes using sizeof(variable)

Data type          Memory used
(bytes)
--------           -----------
short int            2
integer             2
```

```
long integer          4
character           1
float             4


Table 2. Data sizes using sizeof(dataType)

Data type          Memory used
(bytes)
----------         ------------
short int            2
integer            2
long integer          4
character           1
float            4
```

The program in Listing 2.7 declares five variables in the function `main`. Each variable has a different data type and derives its name from its data type. For example, the variable `anInt` is an `int`-typed variable, the variable `aLong` is a `long`-typed variable, and so on.

The statements in lines 17 through 25 display the table of data sizes. The output statements in lines 21 through 25 use the `sizeof` operator with the variables.

The statements in lines 28 through 36 also display the table of data sizes. The output statements in lines 32 through 36 use the `sizeof` operator with the data-type identifiers.

Typecasting

Automatic data conversion of a value from one data type to another compatible data type is one of the duties of a compiler. This data conversion simplifies expressions and eases the frustration of both novice and veteran programmers. With behind-the-scenes data conversion, you do not need to examine every expression that mixes compatible data types in your program. For example, the compiler handles most expressions that mix various types of integers or mix integers and floating-point types. You get a compile-time error if you attempt to do something illegal.

NEW TERM *Typecasting* is a language feature that enables you to specify explicitly how to convert a value from its original data type into a compatible data type. Thus, typecasting instructs the compiler to perform the conversion you want and not the one the compiler thinks is needed.

Syntax

Typecasting

C++ supports the following forms of typecasting:

```
type_cast(expression)
```

and

```
(type_cast) expression
```

Examples

```
int i = 2;
float a, b;
a = float(i);
b = (float) i;
```

Look at an example that illustrates implicit data conversion and typecasting. Listing 2.8 shows the source code for the program TYPCAST1.CPP. The program declares variables that have the character, integer, and floating-point data types. Then the program performs two sets of similar mathematical operations. The first set relies on the automatic conversions of data types, performed by the compiler. The second set of operations uses typecasting to explicitly instruct the compiler on how to convert the data types. The program requires no input—it provides its own data—and it displays the output values for both sets of operations. The program illustrates that the compiler succeeds in generating the same output for both sets of operations.

Type

Listing 2.8. Source code for the program TYPCAST1.CPP.

```
// simple C++ program that demonstrates typecasting

#include <iostream.h>

main()
{
    short shortInt1, shortInt2;
    unsigned short uShort;
    int anInt;
    long aLong;
    char aChar;
    float aReal;

    // assign values
    shortInt1 = 10;
    shortInt2 = 6;
    // perform operations without typecasting
    uShort = shortInt1 + shortInt2;
    anInt = shortInt1 - shortInt2;
    aLong = shortInt1 * shortInt2;
    aChar = aLong + 5; // conversion is automatic to character
    aReal = shortInt1 * shortInt2 + 0.5;

    cout << "shortInt1 = " << shortInt1 << '\n'
         << "shortInt2 = " << shortInt2 << '\n'
         << "uShort = " << uShort << '\n'
         << "anInt = " << anInt << '\n'
         << "aLong = " << aLong << '\n'
         << "aChar is " << aChar << '\n'
         << "aReal = " << aReal << "\n\n\n";

    // perform operations with typecasting
    uShort = (unsigned short) (shortInt1 + shortInt2);
    anInt = (int) (shortInt1 - shortInt2);
```

continues

Listing 2.8. continued

```
35:     aLong = (long) (shortInt1 * shortInt2);
36:     aChar = (unsigned char) (aLong + 5);
37:     aReal = (float) (shortInt1 * shortInt2 + 0.5);
38:
39:     cout << "shortInt1 = " << shortInt1 << '\n'
40:          << "shortInt2 = " << shortInt2 << '\n'
41:          << "uShort = " << uShort << '\n'
42:          << "anInt = " << anInt << '\n'
43:          << "aLong = " << aLong << '\n'
44:          << "aChar is " << aChar << '\n'
45:          << "aReal = " << aReal << "\n\n\n";
46:     return 0;
47: }
```

Here is a sample session with the program in Listing 2.8.

```
shortInt1 = 10
shortInt2 = 6
aByte = 16
anInt = 4
aLong = 60
aChar is A
aReal = 60.5


shortInt1 = 10
shortInt2 = 6
aByte = 16
anInt = 4
aLong = 60
aChar is A
aReal = 60.5
```

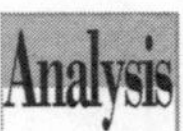

The program in Listing 2.8 declares the following variables in the function `main`:

- The `short`-typed variables `shortInt1` and `shortInt2`
- The `unsigned short`-typed variable `uShort`
- The `int`-typed variable `anInt`
- The `long`-typed variable `aLong`
- The `char`-typed variable `aChar`
- The `float`-typed variable `aReal`

Lines 15 and 16 assign the integers `10` and `6` to variable `shortInt1` and `shortIn2`, respectively. Lines 18 through 22 perform various mathematical operations and assign the results to variables `uShort`, `anInt`, `aLong`, `aChar`, and `aReal`.

Note: C and C++ treat the `char` type as a special integer. Each `char`-type literal (such as `'A'`), constant, or variable has an integer value that is equal to its ASCII representation. This language feature enables you to store an integer in a `char`-type variable and treat a `char`-type data item as an integer. The statement in line 21 adds the integer `5` to the value of the variable `aLong` and assigns the result, an integer, to the variable `aChar`. The value of the assigned integer, `65`, represents the ASCII code for the letter A.

2

The output statement in lines 24 through 30 displays the values stored in the variables. Notice that the output for variable `aChar` is the letter `A`. If you write the output term for variable `aChar` as `<< (int) aChar`, you get `65`, the ASCII code of the character stored in `aChar`.

The statements in lines 32 through 37 perform similar operations to the statements in lines 18 through 22. The main difference is that the statements in lines 32 through 37 use typecasting to explicitly instruct the compiler on how to convert the result. The output statement in lines 39 through 45 displays the contents of the variables.

Relational and Logical Operators

Table 2.4 shows the C++ relational and logical operators. Notice that C++ does not spell out the operators `AND`, `OR`, and `NOT`. Rather, it uses single- and dual-character symbols. Also notice that C++ does not support the relational `XOR` operator.

NEW TERM The *relational operators* (less than, greater than, and equal to) and the *logical operators* (`AND`, `OR`, and `NOT`) are the basic building blocks of decision-making constructs in any programming language.

Table 2.4. C++ relational and logical operators.

C++ Operator	Meaning	Example
`&&`	Logical `AND`	`if (i > 1 && i < 10)`
`||`	Logical `OR`	`if (c==0 || c==9)`
`!`	Logical `NOT`	`if (!(c>1 && c<9))`
`<`	Less than	`if (i < 0)`
`<=`	Less than or equal to	`if (i <= 0)`
`>`	Greater than	`if (j > 10)`
`>=`	Greater than or equal to	`if (x >= 8.2)`

continues

Table 2.4. continued

C++ Operator	Meaning	Example
`==`	Equal to	`if (c == '\0')`
`!=`	Not equal to	`if (c != '\n')`
`? :`	Conditional assignment	`k = (i<1) ? 1 : i;`

Although these macros are permissible in C++, you might get a negative reaction from veteran C++ programmers who read your code. Who says that programming is always objective?

Warning: Do *not* use the = operator as the equality relational operator. This common error is a source of logical bugs in a C++ program. You may be accustomed to using the = operator in other languages to test the equality of two data items. In C++, you *must* use the == operator. What happens if you employ the = operator in C++? Do you get a compiler error? The answer is that you may get a compiler warning. Other than that, your C++ program should run. When the program reaches the expression that it is supposed to test for equality, it actually attempts to assign the operand on the right of the = sign to the operand on the left of the = sign. Of course, a session with such a program most likely leads to weird program behavior or even a system hang.

Notice that the last operator in Table 3.3 is the `?:` operator. This special operator supports what is known as the conditional expression.

NEW TERM The *conditional expression* is a shorthand for a dual-alternative simple `if-else` statement. (See Day 3 for more information about the if statement.)

For example, the following is an `if-else` statement that can be compressed into a conditional expression:

```
if (condition)
variable = expression1;
else
variable = expression2;
```

The equivalent conditional expression is as follows:

```
variable = (condition) ? expression1 : expression2;
```

The conditional expression tests the condition. If that condition is `true`, it assigns `expression1` to the target variable. Otherwise, it assigns `expression2` to the target variable.

Boolean Expressions

Often, you need to use a collection of relational and logical operators to formulate a nontrivial condition. Here are examples of such conditions.

```
x < 0 || x > 11
(i != 0 || i > 100) && (j != i || j > 0)
x != 0 && x != 10 && x != 100
```

NEW TERM *Boolean* (also called *logical*) *expressions* are expressions that involve logical operators and/or relational operators.

DO | **DON'T**

DO double-check to avoid Boolean expressions that are either always true or always false. For example, the expression `(x < 0 && x > 10)` is always false, because no value of `x` can be negative and greater than 10 at the same time.

DON'T use the = operator to test for equality.

Consider now an example that uses relational and logical operators and expressions. Listing 2.9 shows the source code for the program RELOP1.CPP. The program prompts you to enter three integers and then proceeds to perform a battery of tests. The program displays the relational and logical operations, their operands, and their results.

Type

Listing 2.9. Source code for the program RELOP1.CPP.

```
/*
   simple C++ program that uses logical expressions
   this program uses the conditional expression to display
   TRUE or FALSE messages, since C++ does not support the
   BOOLEAN data type.
*/

#include <iostream.h>

const MIN_NUM = 30;
const MAX_NUM = 199;
const int TRUE = 1;
const int FALSE = 0;

main()
{
    int i, j, k;
    int flag1, flag2, in_range,
        same_int, xor_flag;

    cout << "Type first  integer : "; cin >> i;
```

continues

Listing 2.9. continued

```
    cout << "Type second integer : "; cin >> j;
    cout << "Type third  integer : "; cin >> k;

    // test for range [MIN_NUM...MAX_NUM]
    flag1 = i >= MIN_NUM;
    flag2 = i <= MAX_NUM;
    in_range = flag1 && flag2;
    cout << "\n" << i << " is in the range "
         << MIN_NUM << " to " << MAX_NUM << " : "
         << ((in_range) ? "TRUE" : "FALSE");

    // test if two or more entered numbers are equal
    same_int = i == j || i == k || j == k;
    cout << "\nat least two integers you typed are equal : "
         << ((same_int) ? "TRUE" : "FALSE");

    // miscellaneous tests
    cout << "\n" << i << " != " << j << " : "
         << ((i != j) ? "TRUE" : "FALSE");
    cout << "\nNOT (" << i << " < " << j << ") : "
         << ((!(i < j)) ? "TRUE" : "FALSE");
    cout << "\n" << i << " <= " << j << " : "
         << ((i <= j) ? "TRUE" : "FALSE");
    cout << "\n" << k << " > " << j << " : "
         << ((k > j) ? "TRUE" : "FALSE");
    cout << "\n(" << k << " = " << i << ") AND ("
         << j << " != " << k << ") : "
         << ((k == i && j != k) ? "TRUE" : "FALSE");

    // NOTE: C++ does NOT support the logical XOR operator for
    // boolean expressions.
    // add numeric results of logical tests.  Value is in 0...2
    xor_flag = (k <= i) + (j >= k);
    // if xor_flag is either 0 or 2 (i.e. not = 1), it is
    // FALSE therefore interpret 0 or 2 as false.
    xor_flag = (xor_flag == 1) ? TRUE : FALSE;
    cout << "\n(" << k << " <= " << i << ") XOR ("
         << j << " >= " << k << ") : "
         << ((xor_flag) ? "TRUE" : "FALSE");
    cout << "\n(" << k << " > " << i << ") AND("
         << j << " <= " << k << ") : "
         << ((k > i && j <= k) ? "TRUE" : "FALSE");
    cout << "\n\n";
    return 0;
}
```

Here is a sample session with the program in Listing 2.9.

```
Type first  integer : 55
Type second integer : 64
Type third  integer : 87

55 is in the range 30 to 199 : TRUE
at least two integers you typed are equal : FALSE
55 != 64 : TRUE
```

```
NOT (55 < 64) : FALSE
55 <= 64 : TRUE
87 > 64 : TRUE
(87 = 55) AND (64 != 87) : FALSE
(87 <= 55) XOR (64 >= 87) : FALSE
(87 > 55) AND(64 <= 87) : TRUE
```

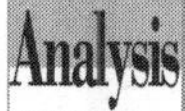

The program in Listing 2.9 declares 4 global constants. The constants MIN_NUM and MAX_NUM define a range of numbers used in the logical tests. The constants TRUE and FALSE represent the Boolean values. The function main declares a number of int variables that are used for input and various testing. The statements in lines 21 through 23 prompt you for 3 integers and store them in the variables i, j, and k, respectively.

2

The statements in lines 26 through 31 involve testing whether the value in variable i lies in the range of MIN_NUM and MAX_NUM. The statement in line 26 tests if the value in i is greater than or equal to the constant MIN_NUM. The program assigns the Boolean result to the variable flag1. The statement in line 27 tests whether the value in i is less than or equal to the constant MAX_NUM. The program assigns the Boolean result to the variable flag2. The statement in line 28 applies the && operator to the variable flag1 and flag2, and it assigns the Boolean result to the variable in_range. The output statement in lines 29 through 31 states what the test is and displays TRUE or FALSE depending on the value in the variable in_range. The statement uses the conditional operator ?: to display the string TRUE if in_range has a nonzero value and to display the string FALSE if otherwise.

The statements in lines 34 through 36 determine whether at least two of the three integers you entered are equal. The statement in line 34 uses a Boolean expression that applies the == relational operators and the || logical operators. The statement assigns the Boolean result to the variable same_int. The output statement in lines 35 and 36 states the test and displays the TRUE/FALSE outcome. The output statement uses the conditional operator to display the strings TRUE or FALSE depending on the value in variable same_int.

The statements in lines 39 through 49 perform miscellaneous tests that involve the input values, and they display both the test and the results. Please feel free to alter these statements to conduct different tests.

Note: The statements in lines 54 through 60 perform an XOR test and display the outcome. The program uses a simple programming trick to implement the XOR operator. The statement in line 54 adds the Boolean value of the subexpressions (k <= i) and (j >= k). The result is 0 if both subexpressions are false, 1 if only one of the subexpressions is true, and 2 if both subexpressions are true. Because the XOR operator is true only if either subexpression is true, the statement in line 57 assigns TRUE to the variable xor_flag if the previous value is 1. Otherwise, the statement assigns FALSE to xor_flag. The statements in lines 61 through 63 perform another miscellaneous test.

Bit-Manipulation Operators

C++ is a programming language that is suitable for system development. System development requires bit-manipulating operators.

NEW TERM *Bit-manipulating operators* toggle, set, query, and shift the bits of a byte or a word.

Table 2.5 shows the bit-manipulating operators. Notice that C++ uses the symbols `&` and `¦` to represent the bitwise AND and OR, respectively. Recall that the `&&` and `¦¦` characters represent the logical AND and OR operators, respectively. In addition to the bit-manipulating operators, C++ supports the bit-manipulating assignment operators, shown in Table 2.6. (Using bit-manipulating operators is a part of advanced programming that involves fiddling with single bits. As a novice C++ programmer, you most likely will not use these operators in the near future.)

Table 2.5. C++ bit-manipulating operators.

C++ Operator	Meaning	Example
`&`	Bitwise AND	`i & 128`
`¦`	Bitwise OR	`j ¦ 64`
`^`	Bitwise XOR	`j ^ 12`
`~`	Bitwise NOT	`~j`
`<<`	Bitwise shift left	`i << 2`
`>>`	Bitwise shift right	`j >> 3`

Table 2.6. C++ bit-manipulating assignment operators.

C++ Operator	Long Form	Example
`x &= y`	`x = x & y`	`i &= 128`
`x ¦= y`	`x = x ¦ y`	`j ¦= 64`
`x ^= y`	`x = x ^ y`	`k ^= 15`
`x <<= y`	`x = x << y`	`j <<= 2`
`x >>= y`	`x = x >> y`	`k >>= 3`

Let us present a C++ program that performs simple bit manipulation. Listing 2.10 contains the source code for the program BITS1.CPP. The program requires no input, because it uses internal data. The program applies the `¦`, `&`, `^`, `>>`, and `<<` bitwise operators and displays the results of the bitwise manipulation.

Listing 2.10. Source code for the program BITS1.CPP.

```
1:  // C++ program to perform bit manipulations
2:
3:  #include <iostream.h>
4:
5:  main()
6:  {
7:
8:       int i, j, k;
9:
10:      // assign values to i and j
11:      i = 0xF0;
12:      j = 0x1A;
13:
14:      k = j & i;
15:      cout << j << " AND " << i << " = " << k << "\n";
16:
17:      k = j ¦ i;
18:      cout << j << " OR " << i << " = " << k << "\n";
19:
20:      k = j ^ 0x1C;
21:      cout << j << " XOR " << 0x1C << " = " << k << "\n";
22:
23:      k = i << 2;
24:      cout << i << " shifted left by 2 bits = " << k << "\n";
25:
26:      k = i >> 2;
27:      cout << i << " shifted right by 2 bits = " << k << "\n";
28:      return 0;
29: }
```

Here is a sample session with the program in Listing 2.10.

```
26 AND 240 = 16
26 OR 240 = 250
26 XOR 28 = 6
240 shifted left by 2 bits = 960
240 shifted right by 2 bits = 60
```

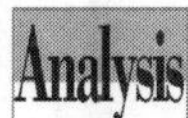

The program in Listing 2.10 declares three `int`-typed variables, `i`, `j`, and `k`. The statements in lines 11 and 12 assign hexadecimal numbers to the variables `i` and `j`, respectively. The statement in line 14 applies the bitwise `AND` operator to the variables `i` and `j`, and it stores the result in variable `k`. The output statement in line 15 displays the operands, the bitwise operator, and the results. The statement in line 17 applies the bitwise `OR` operator to the variable `i` and `j`, and it saves the result to variable `k`. The output statement in line 18 displays the operands, the bitwise operator, and the results. The statement in line 20 applies the bitwise `XOR` operator using the variable `j` and the hexadecimal integer `0x1C`. The output statement in line 21 displays the operands, the bitwise operator, and the results.

The statements in lines 23 through 27 apply the shift-left and shift-right operators to variable `i`. These operators shift the bits of the variable `i` by two bits and assign the result to variable `k`. The effect of the left-shift operator is the same as multiplying the value in the variable `i` by `4`. Similarly, the effect of the right-shift operator is the same as dividing the value in the variable `i` by `4`.

The Comma Operator

The comma operator requires that the program completely evaluate the first expression before evaluating the second expression. Both expressions are located in the same C++ statement. What does located in the same C++ statement mean exactly? Why use this rather unusual operator in the first place? Because the comma operator with its peculiar role does serve a specific and very important purpose in the `for` loop.

NEW TERM *Loops* are powerful language constructs that enable computers to excel in achieving repetitive tasks. The *comma operator* enables you to create multiple expressions that initialize multiple loop-related variables.

Syntax

The Comma Operator

The general syntax for the comma operator is

```
expression1, expression2
```

Example

```
for (i = 0, j = 0; i < 10; i++, j++)
```

You will learn more about the `for` loop in Day 3. For now, this example shows you how to apply the comma operator.

Operator Precedence and Evaluation Direction

Now that you are familiar with most of the C++ operators (there are a few more operators that deal with pointers and addresses), you need to know two related aspects: first, the precedence of the C++ operators; and second, the direction (or sequence) of evaluation. Table 2.7 shows the C++ precedence of the C++ operators covered so far and also indicates the evaluation direction.

Table 2.7. C++ operators and their precedence.

Category	Name	Symbol	Evaluation Direction	Precedence
Monadic				
	Post-increment	`++`	Left to right	2
	Post-decrement	–	Left to right	2
	Address	`&`	Right to left	2
	Bitwise `NOT`	`~`	Right to left	2
	Typecast	`(type)`	Right to left	2
	Logical `NOT`	`!`	Right to left	2
	Negation	`-`	Right to left	2
	Plus sign	`+`	Right to left	2
	Pre-increment	`++`	Right to left	2
	Pre-decrement	–	Right to left	2
	Size of data	`sizeof`	Right to left	2
Multiplicative				
	Modulus	`%`	Left to right	3
	Multiply	`*`	Left to right	3
	Divide	`/`	Left to right	3
Additive				
	Add	`+`	Left to right	4
	Subtract	`-`	Left to right	4
Bitwise Shift				
	Shift left	`<<`	Left to right	5
	Shift right	`>>`	Left to right	5
Relational				
	Less than	`<`	Left to right	6
	Less or equal	`<=`	Left to right	6
	Greater than	`>`	Left to right	6
	Greater or equal	`>=`	Left to right	6
	Equal	`==`	Left to right	7
	Not equal	`!=`	Left to right	7

continued

Table 2.7. continued

Category	Name	Symbol	Evaluation Direction	Precedence
Bitwise				
	AND	&	Left to right	8
	XOR	^	Left to right	9
	OR	¦	Left to right	10
Logical				
	AND	&&	Left to right	11
	OR	¦¦	Left to right	12
Ternary				
	Cond. express.	?:	Right to left	13
Assignment				
	Arithmetic	=	Right to left	14
		+=	Right to left	14
		-=	Right to left	14
		*=	Right to left	14
		/=	Right to left	14
		%=	Right to left	14
	Shift	>>=	Right to left	14
		<<=	Right to left	14
	Bitwise	&=	Right to left	14
		¦=	Right to left	14
		^=	Right to left	14
	Comma	,	Left to right	15

Summary

Today's lesson presented the basic components of C++ programs. These components include data types, variables, constants, and expressions. You learned the following basics:

- The predefined data types in Turbo C++ 4.5 include the `bool`, `int`, `char`, `float`, `double`, and `void` data types. C++ adds more flexibility to data types by supporting data-type modifiers. These modifiers alter the precision and the range of values. The type modifiers are `signed`, `unsigned`, `short`, and `long`.

- Turbo C++ 4.5 identifiers can be up to 32 characters long and must begin with a letter or an underscore. The subsequent characters of an identifier may be a letter, digit, or underscore. C++ identifiers are case-sensitive.
- The `#include` directive is a special instruction to the compiler. The directive tells the compiler to include the contents of the specified file as though you typed it in the currently scanned source file.
- Declaring constants involves using the `#define` directive to declare macro-based constants or using the `const` keyword to declare formal constants. The formal constants require that you specify the constant's type (the default is `int`, when omitted), the name of the constants, and the associated value.
- Declaring variables requires you to state the data type of the variable and the name of the variable. C++ enables you to initialize a variable when you declare it. You can declare multiple variables in a single declarative statement.
- The arithmetic operators include `+`, `-`, `*`, `/`, and `%` (modulus).
- The arithmetic expressions vary in complexity. The simplest expression contains a single data item (literal, constant, or variable). Complex expressions include multiple operators, functions, literals, constants, and variables.
- The increment and decrement operators come in the pre- and post-forms. C++ enables you to apply these operators to variables that store characters, integers, and even floating-point numbers.
- The arithmetic assignment operators enable you to write shorter arithmetic expressions in which the primary operand also is the variable receiving the result of the expression.
- The `sizeof` operator returns the byte size of either a data type or a variable.
- Typecasting enables you to force the type conversion of an expression.
- Relational and logical operators enable you to build logical expressions. C++ does not support a predefined Boolean type and instead considers `0` as false and any nonzero value as true.
- Boolean expressions combine relational and logical operators to formulate nontrivial conditions. These expressions allow a program to make sophisticated decisions.
- The conditional expression offers you a short form for the simple dual-alternative `if-else` statement.
- The bit-manipulation operators perform bitwise `AND`, `OR`, `XOR`, and `NOT` operations. In addition, C++ supports the `<<` and `>>` bitwise shift operators.
- The bit-manipulation assignment operators offer short forms for simple bit-manipulation statements.

Q&A

Q Is there a specific style for naming identifiers?

A There are a few styles that have become popular in recent years. The one we use has the identifier begin with a lowercase character. If the identifier contains multiple words, such as `numberOfElements`, make the first character of each subsequent word an uppercase letter.

Q How does the compiler react when you declare a variable in a function but never assign a value to it?

A The compiler issues a warning that the variable is unreferenced.

Q What is the Boolean expression for checking that the value of a variable, `i`, is in the range of values (for example, defined by variables `lowVal` and `hiVal`)?

A The expression that determines whether the value in variable `i` is located in a range is

```
(i >= lowVal && i <= hiVal)
```

Workshop

The Workshop provides quiz questions to help you solidify your understanding of the material covered and exercises to provide you with experience in using what you've learned. Try to understand the quiz and exercise answers before continuing on to the next day's lesson. Answers are provided in Appendix A.

Quiz

1. Which of the following variables are valid, and which are not? Why?

```
numFiles
n0Distance_02_Line
0Weight
Bin Number
static
Static
```

2. What is the output of the following program?

```
#include <iostream.h>

main()
{
  int i = 3;
  int j = 5;
  double x = 33.5;
  double y = 10.0;
```

```
  cout << 10 + j % i << "\n";
  cout << i * i - 2 * i + 5 << "\n";
  cout << (19 + i + j) / (2 * j + 2) << "\n";
   cout << x / y + y / x << "\n";
  cout << i * x + j * y << "\n";
  return 0;
}
```

3. What is the output of the following program?

```
#include <iostream.h>

main()
{
  int i = 3;
  int j = 5;

  cout << 10 + j % i++ << "\n";
  cout << -i * i - 2 * i + 5 << "\n";
  cout << (19 + ++i + ++j) / (2 * j + 2) << "\n";
  return 0;
}
```

4. What is the output of the following program?

```
#include <iostream.h>

main()
{
  int i = 3;
  int j = 5;

  i += j;
  j *= 2;
  cout << 10 + j % i << "\n";
  i -= 2;
  j /= 3;
  cout << i * i - 2 * i + j << "\n";
  return 0;
}
```

5. What is the output of the following program?

```
#include <iostream.h>

main()
{
  int i = 5;
  int j = 10;

  cout << ((i < j) ? "TRUE" : "FALSE") << "\n";
  cout << ((i > 0 && j < 100) ?  "TRUE" : "FALSE") << "\n";
  cout << ((i > 0 && i < 10) ? "TRUE" : "FALSE") << "\n";
  cout << ((i == 5 && i == j) ? "TRUE" : "FALSE") << "\n";
  return 0;
}
```

2

Exercises

1. Use the conditional operator to write the function `max`, which returns the greater of two integers.
2. Use the conditional operator to write the function `min`, which returns the smaller of two integers.
3. Use the conditional operator to write the function `abs`, which returns the absolute value of an integer.
4. Use the conditional operator to write the function `isOdd`, which returns `0` if its integer argument is an odd number and yields `1` if otherwise.

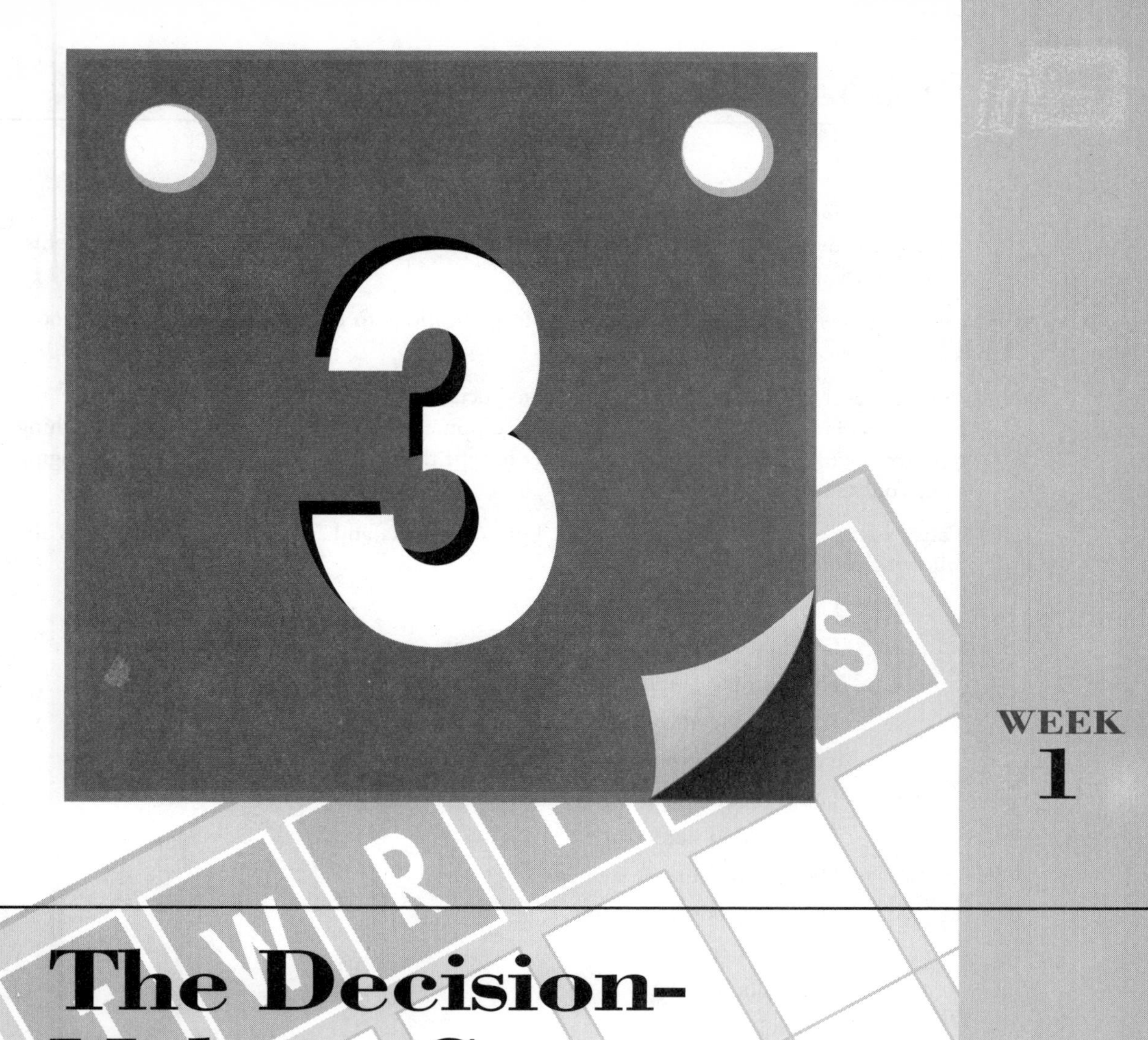

WEEK 1

The Decision-Making Constructs and Loops

Different programming languages offer varying support for decision-making constructs. Some languages provide only simple decision-making constructs, whereas others offer more sophisticated constructs.

NEW TERM *Decision-making constructs* allow your applications to examine conditions and choose courses of action.

Another facet of the decision-making constructs in C++ are the loops that improve the processing of repetitive tasks. They allow the computer to take over the job of doing something repeatedly without forcing the programmer to type the same stuff in over and over, changing things only slightly for each version.

Today's lesson looks at the decision-making constructs and loops in C++ and covers the following topics:

- The single-alternative `if` statement
- The dual-alternative `if-else` statement
- The multiple-alternative `if-else` statement
- The multiple-alternative `switch` statement
- Nested decision-making constructs
- The `try`, `catch`, and `throw` statements
- The `for` loop statement
- The `do-while` loop statement
- The `while` loop statement
- Skipping iterations
- Exiting loops
- Nested loops

Decision-Making Constructs

Today's lesson starts with decision-making constructs. These are methods by which an application can perform different tasks based on differing conditions. For example, if a program asks the user whether to continue an action, the program needs to be able to actually continue (or not continue) based on the user's input. These are the first of the decision-making constructs.

The Single-Alternative *if* Statement

Unlike many programming languages, C++ does not have the keyword `then` in any form of the `if` statement. This language feature may lead you to ask how the `if` statement separates the tested condition from the executable statements. The answer is that C++ dictates that you enclose the tested condition in parentheses.

NEW TERM An `if` statement is a *single-alternative* statement.

Syntax

The Single-Alternative *if* Statement

The general syntax for the single-alternative `if` statement is

```
if (condition)
   statement;
```

for a single executable statement, and

```
if (condition) {
   <sequence of statements>
}
```

for a sequence of executable statements.

Examples

```
if (numberOfLines < 0)
   numberOfLines = 0;

if ((height - 54) < 3) {
   area = length * width;
   volume = area * height;
}
```

C++ uses the open and close braces `{}` to define a block of statements. Figure 3.1 shows the flow in a single-alternative `if` statement.

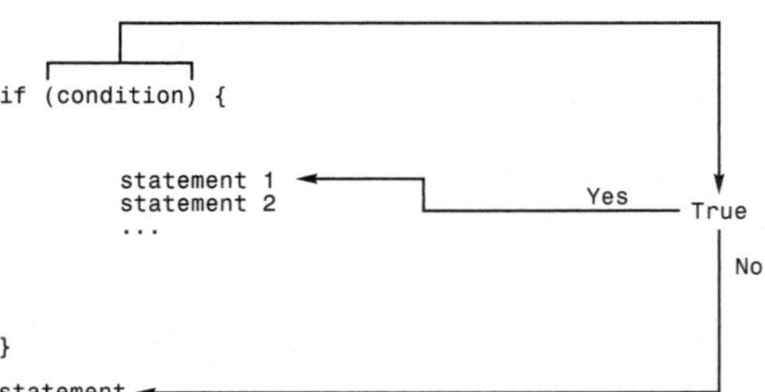

Figure 3.1.
The program flow in the single-alternative `if` *statement.*

Look at an example. Listing 3.1 shows a program with a single-alternative `if` statement. The program prompts you to enter a nonzero number and stores the input in the variable `x`. If the value in `x` is not zero, the program displays the reciprocal of `x`.

Type

Listing 3.1. Source code for the program IF1.CPP.

```
// Program that demonstrates the single-alternative if statement

#include <iostream.h>

main()
```

continues

Listing 3.1. continued

```
6: {
7:   double x;
8:   cout << "Enter a non-zero number : ";
9:    cin >> x;
10:   if (x != 0)
11:     cout << "The reciprocal of " << x
12:          << " is " << (1/x) << endl;
13:   return 0;
14: }
```

Here is a sample session with the program in Listing 3.1.

```
Enter a non-zero number : 25
The reciprocal of 25 is 0.04
```

The program in Listing 3.1 declares the `double`-typed variable `x` in the function `main`. The output statement in line 8 prompts you to enter a nonzero number. The input statement in line 9 stores your input in variable `x`. The `if` statement in line 10 determines whether `x` does not equal zero. If this condition is true, the program executes the output statement in lines 11 and 12. This statement displays the value of `x` and its reciprocal, `1/x`. If the tested condition is false, the program skips the statements in lines 11 and 12 and resumes at the statement in line 13.

The Dual-Alternative *if-else* Statement

In the *dual-alternative* form of the `if` statement, the `else` keyword separates the statements that are used to execute each alternative.

NEW TERM The *dual-alternative* `if-else` statement provides two alternate courses of action based on the Boolean value of the tested condition.

Syntax

The Dual-Alternative *if-else* Statement

The general syntax for the dual-alternative `if-else` statement is

```
if (condition)
   statement1;
else
   statement2;
```

for a single executable statement in each clause, and

```
if (condition) {
   <sequence #1 of statements>
}
else {
   <sequence #2 of statements>
}
```

for a sequence of executable statements in both clauses.

Example

```
if (moneyInAccount > withdraw) {
   moneyInAccount -= withdraw;
   cout << "You withdrew $" << withdraw << endl;
   cout << "Balance is $" << moneyInAccount << endl;
}
else {
   cout << "Cannot withdraw $" << withdraw << endl;
   cout << "Account has $" << moneyInAccount << endl;
}
```

Figure 3.2. shows the program flow in the dual-alternative `if-else` statement.

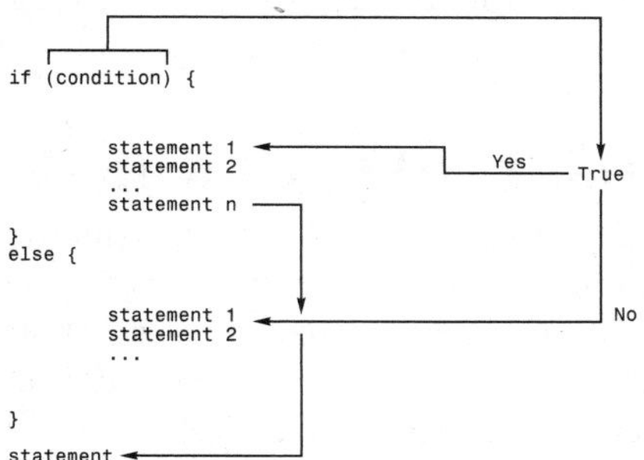

Figure 3.2.
The program flow in the dual-alternative `if-else` *statement.*

Look at an example that uses the dual-alternative `if-else` statement. Listing 3.2 contains the source code for the program IF2.CPP. The program prompts you to enter a character and then determines whether you entered a letter. The program output classifies your input as either a letter or a nonletter character.

Type

Listing 3.2. Source code for the program IF2.CPP.

```
// Program that demonstrates the dual-alternative if statement

#include <iostream.h>
#include <ctype.h>

main()
{
  char c;
  cout << "Enter a letter : ";
  cin >> c;
  // convert to uppercase
  c = toupper;
  if (c >= 'A' && c <= 'Z')
    cout << "You entered a letter\n";
  else
    cout << "Your input was not a letter\n";
  return 0;
}
```

Here is a sample session with the program in Listing 3.2.

```
Enter a character : g
You entered a letter
```

The program in Listing 3.2 declares the `char`-typed variable `c` in line 8. The output statement in line 9 prompts you to enter a letter. The input statement in line 10 obtains your input and stores it in variable `c`. The statement in line 12 converts the value in the variable to uppercase by calling the function `toupper` (prototyped in the CTYPE.H header file). This character case conversion simplifies the tested condition in the `if-else` statement at line 13. The `if-else` statement determines if the variable `c` contains a character in the range of A to Z. If this condition is true, the program executes the output statement in line 14. This statement displays a message stating that you have entered a letter. Alternatively, if the tested condition is false, the program executes the `else` clause statement in line 16. This statement displays a message stating that your input was not a letter.

Potential Problems with the *if* Statement

There is a potential problem with the dual-alternative `if` statement. This problem occurs when the `if` clause includes another single-alternative `if` statement. In this case, the compiler considers that the `else` clause pertains to the nested `if` statement. (A nested `if` statement is one that contains another `if` statement in the `if` and/or `else` clauses. You learn more about nesting in the next section.) Here is an example.

```
if (i > 0)
   if (i = 10)
      cout << "You guessed the magic number";
else
   cout << "Number is out of range";
```

In this code fragment, when the variable `i` is a positive number other than 10, the code displays the message `Number is out of range`. The compiler treats these statements as though the code fragment meant

```
if (i > 0)
   if (i = 10)
      cout << "You guessed the magic number";
   else
      cout << "Number is out of range";
```

To correct this problem, enclose the nested `if` statement in a statement block.

```
if (i > 0) {
   if (i = 10)
      cout << "You guessed the magic number";
}
else
   cout << "Number is out of range";
```

The Multiple-Alternative *if-else* Statement

C++ enables you to nest `if-else` statements to create a multiple-alternative form. This alternative gives a lot of power and flexibility to your applications.

NEW TERM The *multiple-alternative* `if-else` statement contains nested `if-else` statements.

Syntax

The Multiple-Alternative *if-else* Statement

The general syntax for the multiple-alternative `if-else` statement is

```
if (tested_condition1)
   statement1; ¦ { <sequence #1 of statement> }
else if (tested_condition2)
   statement2; ¦ { <sequence #2 of statement> }
...
else if (tested_conditionN)
   statementN; ¦ { <sequence #N of statement> }
[else
   statementN+1; ¦ { <sequence #N+1 of statement> }]
```

Example

```
char op;

int opOk = 1;
double x, y, z;
cout << "Enter operand1 operator operand2: ";
cin >> x >> op >> y;
if (op == '+')
   z = x + y;
else if (op == '-')
   z = x - y;
else if (op == '*')
   z = x * y;
else if (op == '/' && y != 0)
   z = x / y;
else
   opOk = 0;
```

The multiple-alternative `if-else` statement performs a series of cascaded tests until one of the following occurs:

- One of the conditions in the `if` clause or in the `else if` clauses is true. In this case, the accompanying statements are executed.
- None of the tested conditions are true. The program executes the statements in the catch-all `else` clause (if there is an `else` clause).

Figure 3.3 shows the program flow in the multiple-alternative `if-else` statement.

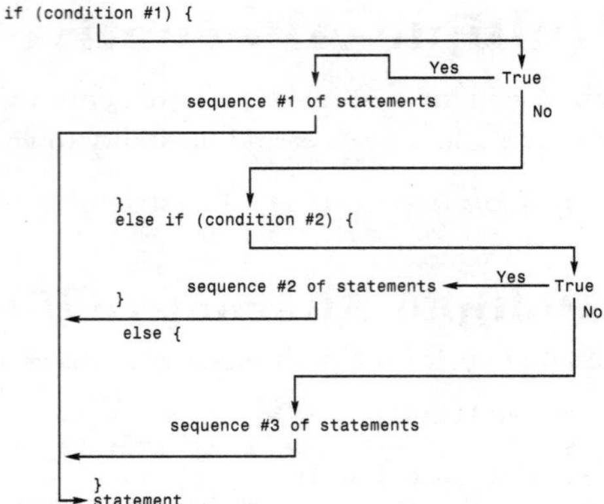

Figure 3.3.
The program flow in the multiple-alternative `if-else` statement.

Consider the following example. Listing 3.3 shows the source code for the program IF3.CPP. The program prompts you to enter a character and uses the multiple—alternative `if-else` statement to determine whether your input is one of the following:

- An uppercase letter
- A lowercase letter
- A digit
- A non-alphanumeric character

Type

Listing 3.3. Source code for the IF3.CPP program.

```
// Program that demonstrates the multiple-alternative if statement

#include <iostream.h>

main()
{
  char c;
  cout << "Enter a character : ";
   cin >> c;
   if (c >= 'A' && c <= 'Z')
     cout << "You entered an uppercase letter\n";
   else if (c >= 'a' && c <= 'z')
     cout << "You entered a lowercase letter\n";
   else if (c >= '0' && c <= '9')
     cout << "You entered a digit\n";
   else
     cout << "You entered a non-alphanumeric character\n";
   return 0;
}
```

Here is a sample session with the program in Listing 3.3.

```
Enter a character : !
You entered a non—alphanumeric character
```

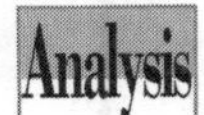

The program in Listing 3.3 declares the `char`-typed variable `c` in line 7. The output statement in line 8 prompts you to enter a letter. The input statement in line 9 obtains your input and stores it in variable `c`. The multi-alternative `if`-`else` statement tests the following conditions:

- In line 10, the `if` statement determines whether the variable `c` contains a letter in the range of A to Z. If this condition is true, the program executes the output statement in line 11. This statement confirms that you entered an uppercase letter. The program then resumes at line 18.
- If the condition in line 10 is false, the program jumps to the first `else if` clause, in line 12. There the program determines whether the variable `c` contains a letter in the range of a to z. If this condition is true, the program executes the output statement in line 13. This statement confirms that you entered a lowercase letter. The program then resumes at line 18.
- If the condition in line 12 is false, the program jumps to the second `else if` clause, in line 14. There the program determines whether the variable `c` contains a digit. If this condition is true, the program executes the output statement in line 15. This statement confirms that you entered a digit. The program then resumes at line 18.
- If the condition in line 14 is false, the program jumps to the catch-all `else` clause in line 16 and executes the output statement in line 17. This statement displays a message telling you that your input was neither a letter nor a digit.

The *switch* Statement

The `switch` statement offers a special form of multiple-alternative decision-making. It enables you to examine the various values of an integer-compatible expression and choose the appropriate course of action.

Syntax

The *switch* Statement

The general syntax for the `switch` statement is

```
switch (expression) {
   case constant1_1:
   [     case constant1_2: ...]
      <one or more statements>
      break;
   case constant2_1:
   [     case constant2_2: ...]
      <one or more statements>
      break;
...
   case constantN_1:
   [     case constantN_2: ...]
      <one or more statements>
```

```
        break;
    default:
        <one or more statements>
}
```

Example

```
OK = 1;
switch (op) {
    case '+':
        z = x + y;
        break;
    case '-':
        z = x - y;
        break;
    case '*':
        z = x * y;
        break;
    case '/':
        if (y != 0)
            z = x / y;
        else
            OK = 0;
        break;
    default:
        Ok = 0;
}
```

Following are the rules for using a `switch` statement:

1. The `switch` requires an integer-compatible value. This value may be a constant, variable, function call, or expression. The `switch` statement does not work with floating-point data types.
2. The value after each `case` label *must* be a constant.
3. C++ does not support `case` labels with ranges of values. Instead, `each` value must appear in a separate case label.
4. You need to use a `break` statement after each set of executable statements. The `break` statement causes program execution to resume after the end of the current `switch` statement. If you do not use the `break` statement, the program execution resumes at the subsequent `case` labels.
5. The `default` clause is a catch-all clause.
6. The set of statements in each `case` label or grouped `case` labels need not be enclosed in open and close braces.

Note: The lack of single `case` labels with ranges of values makes it more appealing to use a multiple-alternative `if-else` statement if you have a large contiguous range of values.

Figure 3.4 shows the program flow in the multiple-alternative `switch` statement.

Look at an example that uses the `switch` statement. Listing 3.4 contains the source code for the program SWITCH1.CPP that you obtained by editing Listing 3.3. The new program performs the same task of classifying your character input, this time using a `switch` statement.

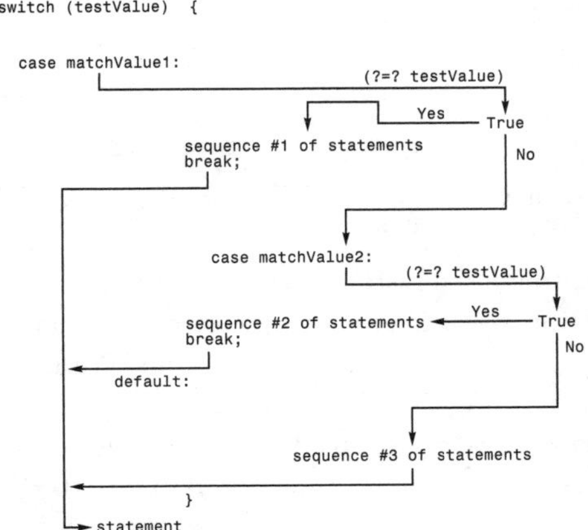

Figure 3.4.
The program flow in the multiple-alternative `switch` *statement.*

3

Type

Listing 3.4. Source code for the SWITCH1.CPP program.

```
// Program that demonstrates the multiple-alternative switch statement

#include <iostream.h>

main()
{
  char c;
  cout << "Enter a character : ";
  cin >> c;
  switch  {
    case 'A':
    case 'B':
    case 'C':
    case 'D':
    // other case labels
      cout << "You entered an uppercase letter\n";
      break;
    case 'a':
    case 'b':
    case 'c':
    case 'd':
    // other case labels
      cout << "You entered a lowercase letter\n";
      break;
    case '0':
    case '1':
    case '2':
    case '3':
```

continues

Listing 3.4. continued

```
29:     // other case labels
30:       cout << "You entered a digit\n";
31:       break;
32:     default:
33:       cout << "You entered a non-alphanumeric character\n";
34:   }
35:   return 0;
36: }
```

Here is a sample session with the program in Listing 3.4.

```
Enter a character : 2
You entered a digit
```

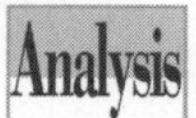

The program in Listing 3.4 declares the `char`-typed variable `c`. The output statement in line 8 prompts you to enter a character. The statement in line 9 stores your input in variable `c`. The `switch` statement starts at line 10. Lines 11 through 14 contain the `case` labels for the letters A through D. You omitted the case labels for the rest of the uppercase letters to keep the program short. If the character in variable `c` matches any value in lines 11 through 14, the program executes the output statement in line 16. This statement confirms that you entered an uppercase letter. (Because you reduced the number of `case` labels, the program executes the statement in line 16 only if you enter one of the letters A through D.) The `break` statement in line 17 causes the program flow to jump to line 35, past the end of the `switch` statement.

If the character in variable `c` does not match any of the `case` labels in lines 11 through 14, the program resumes at line 18 where it encounters another set of `case` labels. These labels are supposed to represent lowercase characters. As you can see, you reduced the number of labels to shorten the program. If the character in variable `c` matches any value in lines 18 through 21, the program executes the output statement in line 23. This statement confirms that you entered a lowercase letter. (Because you reduced the number of `case` labels, the program executes the statement in line 23 only if you enter one of the letters a through d.) The `break` statement in line 24 causes the program flow to jump to line 35, past the end of the `switch` statement.

If the character in variable `c` does not match any of the case labels in lines 18 through 21, the program resumes at line 25, where it encounters another set of `case` labels. These labels are supposed to represent digits. Again, you can see that you reduced the number of labels to shorten the program. If the character in variable `c` matches any value in lines 25 through 28, the program executes the output statement in line 30. This statement confirms that you entered a digit. (Because you reduced the number of case labels, the program executes the statement in line 30 only if you enter one of the digits 0 to 3.) The `break` statement in line 31 causes the program flow to jump to line 35, past the end of the `switch` statement.

If the character in variable `c` does not match any `case` label in lines 25 through 28, the program jumps to the catch-all clause in line 32. The program executes the output statement in line 33. This statement tells you that you entered a non-alphanumeric character.

Nested Decision-Making Constructs

Often you need to use nested decision-making constructs to manage nontrivial conditions. Nesting decision-making constructs enables you to deal with complicated conditions using a divide-and-conquer approach. The outer-level constructs help you to test preliminary or more general conditions. The inner-level constructs help you deal with more specific conditions.

Look at an example. Listing 3.5 shows the source code for the program IF4.CPP. The program prompts you to enter a character. Then the program determines if your input is an uppercase letter, a lowercase letter, or a character that is not a letter. The program displays a message that classifies your input.

Listing 3.5. Source code for the program IF4.CPP.

```
1:  // Program that demonstrates the nested if statements
2:
3:  #include <iostream.h>
4:
5:  main()
6:  {
7:    char c;
8:    cout << "Enter a character : ";
9:    cin >> c;
10:   if ((c >= 'A' && c <= 'Z') || (c >= 'a' && c <= 'z'))
11:     if (c >= 'A' && c <= 'Z')
12:       cout << "You entered an uppercase letter\n";
13:     else
14:       cout << "You entered a lowercase letter\n";
15:   else
16:     cout << "You entered a non-letter character\n";
17:   return 0;
18: }
```

Here is a sample session with the program in Listing 3.5.

```
Enter a character : a
You entered a lowercase letter
```

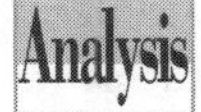

The program in Listing 3.5 declares the `char`-typed variable `c`. The output statement in line 8 prompts you to enter a character. The statement in line 9 stores your input in variable `c`. The program uses nested `if-else` statements that begin at lines 10 and 11. The outer `if-else` statement determines whether the variable `c` contains a letter. If the tested condition is true, the program executes the inner `if-else` statement in line 11. Otherwise, the program resumes at the `else` clause of the outer `if-else` statement and executes the output statement in line 16. This statement tells you that your input was not a letter.

The program uses the inner `if-else` statement to further examine the condition of the outer `if-else` statement. The `if-else` statement in line 11 determines whether the variable `c` contains an uppercase letter. If this condition is true, the program executes the output statement in line 12. Otherwise, the program executes the `else` clause statement in line 14. These output statements tell you whether you entered an uppercase or a lowercase letter. After executing the inner `if-else` statement, the program jumps to line 17, past the end of the outer `if-else` statement.

Exception Handling

Exception handling was introduced into the ANSI/ISO C++ standard as a way of letting a program deal with unexpected problems that might occur, and also as a means of presenting a universal method of specifying errors. Before exceptions, it sometimes was difficult to tell when something was supposed to be an error and when something was supposed to be a valid number. This especially was true with the return values from functions, which is discussed on Day 6, and with class constructors, which is discussed on Day 9.

The exception mechanism revolves around placing the statements that might generate a runtime error in a special block—the `try` block. This block is followed by one or more `catch` blocks that identify and handle the errors generated in the `try` block.

Syntax

The *try* and *catch* Blocks

The syntax for the `try` and `catch` blocks is

```
try {
   // place code that may generate an exception
}
catch(T1 [X1]) {
   // handle exception type T1
}
[catch(T2 [X2]) {
   // handle exception type T2
}]
[other catch blocks]
[catch(...) {
   // handle remaining types of exceptions
}]
```

The types `T1` and `T2` are structures or classes that support user-defined exceptions. The parameter `X1` can have the type `T1`, `T1&`, `const T1`, and `const T1&`. The parameter `X2` can have the same variations for type `T2`. The last `catch` block uses the ellipsis (three dots) to indicate that it is a catch-all block.

```
try {
   // Do something to a file
   DoSomething("filename.ext");
}
catch(char* str) {
   cout << "Couldn't " << str << endl;
}
```

```
catch(...) {
   cout << "Unknown exception\n"
}
```

The preceding example has a `try` block that attempts to call a function to manipulate a file called FILENAME.TXT (functions are discussed on Day 6). This function *throws* (that is, generates) an exception. The `catch` block handles the `xmsg` exception type by displaying an error message that contains the message generated by the exception. The last `catch` block uses an ellipsis (...) rather than actually specifying a type to handle. This enables you to handle exceptions you didn't expect; any exception for which you don't actually specify the type gets handled in this all-encompassing block.

NEW TERM An *exception* is runtime error. To *throw* an exception means to generate a runtime error.

3

C++ enables you to define your own exception types, using structures or classes (discussed on Day 4). An exception type can be an empty structure or object if you only need the name of the structure or object type. If you want to provide more information related to the nature of the exception, the exception type can include data members and member functions that support manipulating the exception state.

The last component of handling exceptions deals with throwing them. C++ supplies the keyword `throw`, which throws an exception.

The *throw* Keyword

Syntax

The syntax for the `throw` keyword is

```
throw(exceptionInstance);
```

The `exceptionInstance` is an instance of an exception structure or class.

Example

```
try {
   int rslt;
   if (!(rslt = DoSomething(filename)))
      throw "do something";
   if (!UseRslt(rslt))
      throw "use rslt";
   if (rslt >= 100)
      throw rslt;
}
catch(char* str) {
   cout << "Couldn't " << str << endl;
}
catch(int i) {
```

```
    cout << "Result was too high: " << i << endl;
}
```

The preceding function throws the exception instances whenever it encounters an error. Note the use of the `char*` type. This is a pointer to a character which is one of the ways that C++ can handle strings. Pointers are discussed in more detail on Day 4, and strings are discussed in depth on Day 8.

Loops

Loops are employed in order to get C++ to do things repeatedly. Rather than have the programmer type in the same code over and over again, each time modifying it slightly so that it will perform actions in sequence, you can use a loop to perform the repetition automatically.

The *for* Loop

The `for` loop in C++ is a versatile loop because it offers both fixed and conditional iterations. The latter feature of the `for` loop deviates from the typical use of the `for` loop in other programming languages, such as Pascal and BASIC.

The *for* Loop

Syntax

The general syntax for the `for` loop statement is

```
for (<initialization of loop control variables>;
     <loop continuation test>;
     <modification of loop control variables, often an increment or decrement>)
```

Example

```
for (i = 0; i < 10; i++)
   cout << "The cube of " << i << " = " << i * i * i << endl;
```

The `for` loop statement has three components, each of which is optional. The first component initializes the loop control variables. (C++ enables you to use more than one loop control variable.) The second part of the loop is the condition that determines whether the loop makes another iteration (sort of like an `if` statement without the actual `if` keyword). The last part of the `for` loop is the clause that modifies the loop control variables; often this simply is an increment and/or decrement operation.

Note: The C++ `for` loop enables you to declare the loop control variables. Such variables exist in the scope of the loop and also immediately outside in the containing scope. This scope is defined by the block of statements that contains the loop.

So, for example, the following is possible:

```
for (int i = 0; i < 10; ++i)
   cout << "Hello" << endl;
cout << "i is still accessible: " << i << endl;
```

Look at an example. Listing 3.6 contains the source code for the program FOR1.CPP. The program prompts you to define a range of integers by specifying the lower- and upper-bounds. The program then calculates the sum of the integers, as well as the average value, in the range you specify.

Type

Listing 3.6. Source code for the program FOR1.CPP.

```
// Program that calculates a sum and average of a range of
// integers using a for loop

#include <iostream.h>

main()
{
    double sum = 0;
    double sumx = 0.0;
    int first, last, temp;

    cout << "Enter the first integer : ";
    cin >> first;
    cout << "Enter the last integer : ";
    cin >> last;
    if (first > last) {
      temp = first;
      first = last;
      last = temp;
    }
    for (int i = first; i <= last; i++) {
      sum++;
      sumx += (double)i;
    }
    cout << "Sum of integers from "
         << first << " to " << last << " = "
         << sumx << endl;
    cout << "Average value = " << sumx / sum;
    return 0;
}
```

Here is a sample session with the program in Listing 3.6.

```
Enter the first integer : 1
Enter the last integer : 100
Sum of integers from 1 to 100 = 5050
Average value = 50.5
```

The program in Listing 3.6 declares a collection of `int`-typed and `double`-typed variables in function `main`. The function initializes the summation variables, `sum` and `sumx`, to `0`. The input and output statements in lines 12 through 15 prompt you to enter the integers that define a range of values. The program stores these integers in the variables `first` and `last`. The `if` statement in line 16 determines whether the value in variable `first` is greater than the value in variable `last`. If this condition is true, the program executes the block of statements in lines 17 through 19. These statements swap the values in variables `first` and `last`, using the variable `temp` as a swap buffer. Thus, the `if` statement ensures that the integer in variable `first` is less than or equal to the integer in variable `last`.

The program carries out the summation using the `for` loop in line 21. The loop declares its own control variable, `i`, and initializes it with the value in the variable `first`. The loop continuation condition is `i <= last`. This condition indicates that the loop iterates as long as `i` is less than or equal to the value in the variable `last`. The loop increment component is `i++`, which increments the loop control variable by 1 for every iteration. The loop contains two statements. The first statement increments the value in the variable `sum`. The second statement adds the value of `i` (after typecasting it to `double`) to the variable `sumx`.

Note: You can rewrite the `for` loop to move the first loop statement to the loop increment component.

```
for (int i = first; i <= last; i++, sum++)
   sumx += (double)i;
```

The output statement in lines 25 through 27 displays the sum and average of integers in the range you specified.

To illustrate the flexibility of the `for` loop, we created the program FOR2.CPP, shown in Listing 3.7, by editing the program FOR1.CPP.

Listing 3.7. Source code for the program FOR2.CPP.

```
// Program that calculates a sum and average of a range of
// integers using a for loop

#include <iostream.h>

main()
{
    double sum = 0;
    double sumx = 0.0;
    int first, last, temp, i;

    cout << "Enter the first integer : ";
```

```
13:     cin >> first;
14:     cout << "Enter the last integer : ";
15:     cin >> last;
16:     if (first > last) {
17:       temp= first;
18:       first = last;
19:       last = temp;
20:     }
21:     i = first;
22:     for (; i <= last; ) {
23:       sum++;
24:       sumx += (double)i++;
25:     }
26:     cout << "Sum of integers from "
27:          << first << " to " << last << " = "
28:          << sumx << endl;
29:     cout << "Average value = " << sumx / sum;
30:     return 0;
31: }
```

Here is a sample session with the program in Listing 3.7.

```
Enter the first integer : 10
Enter the last integer : 100
Sum of integers from 10 to 100 = 5005
Average value = 55
```

The FOR1.CPP and FOR2.CPP programs perform the same tasks and interact identically with the user. The changes we made are in line 10 and lines 21 through 25. Line 10 declares the loop control variable. In line 21, we initialize the variable `i` using the value in the variable `first`. The `for` loop is located at line 22. The loop has no initialization part, because we took care of that in line 21. In addition, we removed the loop increment component and compensated for it by applying the post-increment operator to the variable `i` in line 24.

Open Loops Using the *for* Loops

When we introduced you to the C++ `for` loop, we stated that the three components of the `for` loop are optional. In fact, C++ permits you to leave these three components empty.

NEW TERM When you leave the three components of a loop empty, the result is an *open loop*.

It is worthwhile to point out that other languages, such as ADA and Modula-2, do support formal open loops and provide mechanisms to exit these loops. C++ permits you to exit from a loop in the following two ways:

- The `break` statement causes the program execution to resume after the end of the current loop. Use the `break` statement when you want to exit a `for` loop and resume with the remaining parts of the program.

- The `return` statement will return from the current function (including `main`). You'll learn more about `return` and functions on Day 5.
- The `throw` statement causes an exception to be thrown. This is used when an error has occurred and you can't continue with the rest of the program without some sort of error handler. You'll learn more about exceptions later today.
- In very extreme cases, the `exit` function (declared in the STDLIB.H header file) enables you to exit the program. Use the `exit` function in dire emergencies when there isn't even any hope of recovering from an error. This will stop iteration and exit the program.

Consider the following example. Listing 3.8 contains the source code for the program FOR3.CPP. The program uses an open loop to prompt you repeatedly for a number. The program takes your input and displays it along with its reciprocal value. Then the program asks you whether you want to calculate the reciprocal of another number. If you type in the letter `Y` or `y`, the program performs another iteration. Otherwise, the program ends. If you continue to type `Y` or `y` for the latter prompt, the program keeps running—at least until the computer breaks down!

Type

Listing 3.8. Source code for the program FOR3.CPP.

```
// Program that demonstrates using the
// for loop to emulate an infinite loop.

#include <iostream.h>
#include <ctype.h>

main()
{
   char ch;
   double x, y;

   // for loop with empty parts
   for (;;) {
      cout << "\nEnter a number : ";
      cin >> x;
      // process number if non-zero
      if (x != 0) {
        y = 1/ x;
        cout << "1/(" << x << ") = " << y << endl;
        cout << "More calculations? (Y/N) ";
        cin >> ch;
        ch = toupper(ch);
        if (ch != 'Y')
           break;
      }
      else
        // display error message
        cout << "Error: cannot accept 0\n";
   }
```

```
30:    return 0;
31: }
```

Here is a sample session with the program in Listing 3.8.

```
Enter a number : 5
1/(5) = 0.2
More calculations? (Y/N) y

Enter a number : 12
1/(12) = 0.0833333
More calculations? (Y/N) y

Enter a number : 16
1/(16) = 0.0625
More calculations? (Y/N) n
```

The program in Listing 3.8 declares the `char`-typed variable `ch` and two `double`-typed variables, `x` and `y`. The function `main` uses the `for` loop, in line 13, as an open loop by eliminating all three loop components. The output statement in line 14 prompts you to enter a number. The input statement in line 15 obtains your input and stores it in variable `x`. The `if-else` statement in line 17 determines if the value in variable `x` is not zero. If this condition is true, then the program executes the block of statements in lines 18 through 24. Otherwise, the program executes the `else` clause statement in line 28. This statement displays an error message.

The statement in line 18 assigns the reciprocal of the value in variable `x` to variable `y`. The output statement in line 19 displays the values in variables `x` and `y`. The output statement in line 20 prompts you for more calculations, and requires a Y/N (in either uppercase or lowercase) type of answer. The input statement in line 21 stores your single-character input in variable `c`. The statement in line 22 converts your input into uppercase, using the function `toupper`. (This function is prototyped in the CTYPE.H header file.) The `if` statement in line 23 determines whether the character in variable `c` is not the letter `Y`. If this condition is true, the program executes the `break` statement in line 24. This statement causes the program execution to exit the open loop and to resume at line 30.

The *do-while* Loop

The `do-while` loop in C++ is a conditional loop that tests the iteration condition at the end of the loop. Therefore, the `do-while` loop iterates at least once.

NEW TERM A *conditional loop* iterates as long as a condition is true. This condition is tested at the end of the loop.

Syntax

The *do-while* Loop

The general syntax for the `do-while` loop is

```
do {
   <sequence of statements>
} while (condition);
```

Example

The following loop displays the squares of 2 to 10:

```
int i = 2;
do {
   cout << i << "^2 = " << i * i << endl;
} while (++i < 11);
```

Look at an example. Listing 3.9 shows the source code for the program DOWHILE1.CPP, which essentially calculates square root values. The program performs the following tasks:

- ☐ Prompts you to enter a number. (If you enter a negative number, the program reprompts you for a number.)
- ☐ Calculates and displays the square root of the number you entered.
- ☐ Prompts you to enter another number. (If you enter the letter Y or y, the program resumes at step number 1; otherwise, the program ends.)

Listing 3.9. Source code for the program DOWHILE1.CPP.

```
// Program that demonstrates the do-while loop

#include <iostream.h>

const double TOLERANCE = 1.0e-7;

double abs(double x)
{
  return (x >= 0) ? x : -x;
}

double sqroot(double x)
{
  double guess = x / 2;
  do {
    guess = (guess + x / guess) / 2;
  } while (abs(guess * guess - x) > TOLERANCE);
  return guess;
}

double getNumber()
{
  double x;
  do {
    cout << "Enter a number: ";
    cin >> x;
```

```
27:    } while (x < 0);
28:    return x;
29: }
30:
31: main()
32: {
33:    char c;
34:    double x, y;
35:
36:    do {
37:       x = getNumber();
38:       y = sqroot(x);
39:       cout << "Sqrt(" << x << ") = " << y << endl
40:            << "Enter another number? (Y/N) ";
41:       cin >> c;
42:       cout << endl;
43:    } while (c == 'Y' || c == 'y');
44:    return 0;
45: }
```


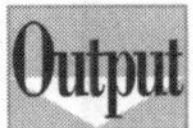

Here is a sample session with the program in Listing 3.9.

```
Enter a number: 25
Sqrt(25) = 5
Enter another number? (Y/N) y

Enter a number: 144
Sqrt(144) = 12
Enter another number? (Y/N) n
```

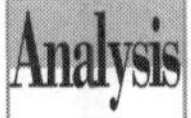

The program in Listing 3.9 declares the global constant `TOLERANCE` and the functions `abs`, `sqroot`, `getNumber`, and `main`. The function `abs`, located in line 7, returns the absolute value of `double`-typed arguments. Note that, even though functions have not yet been introduced, you should have relatively little trouble understanding their use in the preceding listing. Functions are discussed formally on Day 6.

The function `sqroot`, located in line 12, returns the square root of the parameter `x`. The function sets the initial guess for the square root to `x / 2` in line 14. Then the function uses a `do-while` loop to refine iteratively the guess for the square root. The condition in the `while` clause determines whether the absolute difference between the square of the current guess and the parameter `x` is greater than the allowable error (represented by the constant `TOLERANCE`). The loop iterates as long as this condition is true. The function returns the guess for the square root in line 18. The function `sqroot` implements Newton's method for iteratively obtaining the square root of a number.

The function `getNumber`, located in line 21, prompts you for a number and stores your input in the local variable `x`. The function uses a `do-while` loop to ensure that you enter a non-negative number. The `while` clause in line 27 determines if the value in variable `x` is negative. As long as this condition is true, the `do-while` loop iterates. In line 28, the `return` statement yields the value of `x`.

The function `main`, located in line 31, uses a `do-while` loop to perform the following tasks:

- ☐ Prompts you for a number by calling function `getNumber`. (The statement in line 37 contains the function call and assigns the result to the local variable `x`.)
- ☐ Calculates the square root of `x` by calling function `sqroot`, and assigns the result to the variable `y`. (The statement that contains this function call is in line 38.)
- ☐ Displays the values in variables `x` and `y`.
- ☐ Prompts you to enter another number. (The input statement in line 41 takes your single-character Y/N input and stores it in variable `c`.)

The `while` clause, located in line 43, determines whether the variable `c` contains either the letter `Y` or `y`. The `do-while` loop iterates as long as this condition is true.

The program in Listing 3.9 illustrates the following uses for the `do-while` loop:

1. *Iterative calculations.* The loop in function `sqroot` demonstrates this aspect.
2. *Data validation.* The loop in function `getNumber` demonstrates this aspect.
3. *Program continuation.* The loop in function `main` demonstrates this aspect.

The *while* Loop

The `while` loop in C++ is another conditional loop that iterates as long as a condition is true. Thus, the `while` loop may not iterate if the tested condition is initially false.

Syntax

The *while* Loop

The general syntax of the `while` loop is

```
while (condition)
   statement; ¦ { sequence of statements }
```

Example

```
double power(double x, int n)
{
   double pwr = 1;
   while (n-- > 0)
      pwr *= x;
   return pwr;
}
```

Look at the next example. Listing 3.10 shows the source code for the program WHILE1.CPP. This program performs the same operations as the program FOR1.CPP, in Listing 3.6. The two programs interact with the user in the same way and yield the same results.

Listing 3.10. Source code for the program WHILE1.CPP.

```
1: // Program that demonstrates the while loop
2:
3: #include <iostream.h>
4:
5: main()
6: {
7:     double sum = 0;
8:     double sumx = 0.0;
9:     int first, last, temp, i;
10:
11:     cout << "Enter the first integer : ";
12:     cin >> first;
13:     cout << "Enter the last integer : ";
14:     cin >> last;
15:     if (first > last) {
16:       temp= first;
17:       first = last;
18:       last = temp;
19:     }
20:     i = first;
21:     while (i <= last) {
22:       sum++;
23:       sumx += (double)i++;
24:     }
25:     cout << "Sum of integers from "
26:          << first << " to " << last << " = "
27:          << sumx << endl;
28:     cout << "Average value = " << sumx / sum;
29:     return 0;
30: }
```

Here is a sample session with the program in Listing 3.10.

```
Enter the first integer : 1
Enter the last integer : 100
Sum of integers from 1 to 100 = 5050
Average value = 50.5
```

Because the programs in Listings 3.10 and 3.6 are similar, we focus here on lines 20 through 24, where lies the main difference between the two programs. The statement in line 20 assigns the value of the variable `first` to the variable `i`. The `while` loop starts at line 21. The loop iterates as long as the value in the variable `i` is less than or equal to the value in the variable `last`. The variable `i` plays the role of the loop control variable. The statement in line 22 increments the value in the variable `sum`. The statement in line 23 adds the value in variable `i` to the variable `sumx` and also increments the variable `i`. The statement performs the latter task by applying the post-increment operator to the variable `i`.

Skipping Loop Iterations

C++ enables you to jump to the end of a loop and resume the next iteration using the `continue` statement. This programming feature permits your loop to skip iteration for special values that may cause runtime errors.

Syntax

The *continue* Statement

The general form for using the `continue` statement is

```
<loop-start clause> {
   // sequence #1 of statements
   if (skipCondition)
      continue;
   // sequence #2 of statements
} <loop-end clause>
```

Example

```
double x, y;
for (int i = -10; i < 11; i++) {
   x = i;
   if (i == 1)
      continue;
   y = 1/sqrt(x * x - 1);
   cout << "1/sqrt(" << (x*x-1) << ") = " << y << endl;
}
```

This form shows that the evaluation of the first sequence of statements in the `for` loop gives rise to a condition tested in the `if` statement. If that condition is true, then the `if` statement invokes the `continue` statement to skip the second sequence of statements in the `for` loop.

Look at an example. Listing 3.11 shows the source code for the program FOR4.CPP. The program displays the table of values for the function `f(X) = =(`X^2`-9)` at integer values between `-10` and `10`. Because the integers between `-2` and `2` yield complex results, which the program avoids, the table does not display the complex values for `f(X)` between `-2` and `2`.

Type

Listing 3.11. Source code for the program FOR4.CPP.

```
// Program that demonstrates using the continue statement
// to skip iterations.

#include <iostream.h>
#include <math.h>


double f(double x)
{
  return sqrt(x * x - 9);
}

main()
```

```
14: {
15:    double x, y;
16:
17:    cout << "          X";
18:    cout << "             f(X)\n";
19:    cout << "___________________________________\n\n";
20:    // for loop with empty parts
21:    for (int i = =10; i <= 10; i++) {
22:      if (i > =3 && i < 3)
23:        continue;
24:      x = (double)i;
25:      y = f(x);
26:      cout << "      ";
27:      cout.width(3);
28:      cout << x << "          ";
29:      cout.width(7);
30:      cout << y << endl;
31:    }
32:    return 0;
33: }
```

Here is a sample session with the program in Listing 3.11.

```
X           f(X)
___________________________________

-10          9.53939
-9          8.48528
-8           7.4162
-7          6.32456
-6          5.19615
-5                4
-4          2.64575
-3                0
3                 0
4          2.64575
5                4
6          5.19615
7          6.32456
8           7.4162
9          8.48528
10          9.53939
```

The program in Listing 3.11 declares the function `f` to represent the mathematical function `f(X)`. The function `main` declares the `double`-typed variables `x` and `y` in line 15. The output statements in lines 17 through 19 display the table's heading. The `for` loop in line 21 declares its own control variable and iterates between `-10` and `10`, in increments of 1. The first statement inside the loop is the `if` statement located at line 22. This statement determines if the value in variable `i` is greater than `-3` and less than `3`. If this condition is true, then the program executes the `continue` statement in line 23. Thus, the `if` statement enables the `for` loop to skip error-generating iterations and resume with the next iteration. The statement in line 24 assigns the value in variable `i` to variable `x`. The statement in line 25 calls the function `f` and supplies it with the argument x. The statement then assigns the result to variable y. The output statements in lines 25 through 30 display the values of the variables x and y. The statements use the function width for simple formatting.

Exiting Loops

C++ supports the break statement to exit a loop. The break statement makes the program resume after the end of the current loop.

Syntax

The *break* Statement

The general form for using the break statement in a loop is

```
<start-loop clause> {
   // sequence #1 of statements
   if (exitLoopCondition)
      break;
   // sequence #2 of statements
} <end-loop clause>
// sequence #3 of statements
```

Example

```
// calculate the factorial of n
factorial = 1;
for (int i = 1; ; i++) {
   if (i > n)
      break;
   factorial *= (double)i;
}
```

This form shows that the evaluation of the first sequence of statements in the for loop gives rise to a condition tested in the if statement. If that condition is true, then the if statement invokes the break statement to exit the loop altogether. The program execution resumes at the third sequence of statements.

For a good example that uses the break statement, we recommend that you reexamine the FOR3.CPP program in Listing 3.8.

Nested Loops

Nested loops enable you to contain repetitive tasks as part of other repetitive tasks. C++ enables you to nest any type of loop to just about any level needed. Nested loops frequently are used to process arrays (which are covered in Day 5).

Following is an example that uses nested loops. Listing 3.12 shows the source code for the program NESTFOR1.CPP. The program displays a table for square roots for whole numbers

in the range of 1 to 10. The program uses an outer loop to iterate over this range of numbers and employs an inner loop to iteratively calculate the square root.

Listing 3.12. Source code for the program NESTFOR1.CPP.

```
// Program that demonstrates nested loops

#include <stdio.h>

const double TOLERANCE = 1.0e-7;
const int MIN_NUM = 1;
const int MAX_NUM = 10;

double abs(double x)
{
  return (x >= 0) ? x : -x;
}

main()
{
   double x, sqrt;

   printf("  X       Sqrt(X)\n");
   printf("_____________________\n\n");
   // outer loop
   for (int i = MIN_NUM; i <= MAX_NUM; i++) {
     x = (double)i;
     sqrt = x /2;
     // inner loop
     do {
       sqrt = (sqrt + x / sqrt) / 2;
     } while (abs(sqrt * sqrt - x) > TOLERANCE);
     printf("%4.1f     %8.6lf\n", x, sqrt);
   }
   return 0;
}
```

Here is a sample session with the program in Listing 3.12.

```
X       Sqrt(X)
_____________________

1.0     1.000000
2.0     1.414214
3.0     1.732051
4.0     2.000000
5.0     2.236068
6.0     2.449490
7.0     2.645751
8.0     2.828427
9.0     3.000000
10.0     3.162278
```

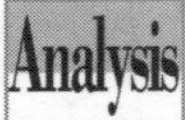

The program in Listing 3.12 includes the header file STDIO.H in order to use the `printf` output function with its powerful formatting capabilities. Lines 5 through 7 define the constants `TOLERANCE`, `MIN_NUM`, and `MAX_NUM` to represent, respectively, the tolerance in square root values, the first number in the output table, and the last number in the output table. The program defines the function `abs` to return the absolute number of a `double`-typed number.

The function `main` declares the `double`-typed variables `x` and `sqrt`. The output statements in lines 18 and 19 display the table's heading. Line 21 contains the outer loop—a `for` loop. This loop declares its control variable, `i`, and iterates from `MIN_NUM` to `MAX_NUM` in increments of 1. Line 22 stores the typecast value of `i` in variable `x`. The statement in line 23 obtains the initial guess for the square root and stores it in variable `sqrt`. Line 25 contains the inner loop, a `do-while` loop that iterates to refine the guess for the square root. The statement in line 26 refines the guess for the square root. The `while` clause in line 27 determines whether the refined guess is adequate. The output statement in line 28 displays the formatted values for the variables `x` and `sqrt`.

Summary

Today's lesson presented the various decision-making constructs and loops in C++, including the following:

- The single-alternative `if` statement, such as

```
if (tested_condition)
     statement; ¦ {     <sequence of statements> }
```

- The dual-alternative `if-else` statement, such as

```
if (tested_condition)
    statement1; { <sequence #1 of statements> }
else
    statement1; { <sequence #1 of statements> }
```

- The multiple-alternative `if-else` statement, such as

```
if (tested_condition1)
     statement1; ¦ { <sequence #1 of statement> }
else if (tested_condition2)
     statement2; ¦ { <sequence #2 of statement> }
...
else if (tested_conditionN)
     statementN; ¦ { <sequence #N of statement> }
[else
     statementN+1; ¦ { <sequence #N+1 of statement> }]
```

- The multiple-alternative `switch` statement, such as

```
switch (caseVar) {
    case constant1_1:
    case constant1_2:
    <other case labels>
         <one or more statements>
         break;
    case constant2_1:
    case constant2_2:
    <other case labels>
         <one or more statements>
         break;
    ...
    case constantN_1:
    case constantN_2:
    <other case labels>
         <one or more statements>
         break;

    default:
         <one or more statements>
         break;
}
```

You also learned about the following topics:

- The `if` statements require you to observe the following two rules:
  - The tested condition must be enclosed in parentheses.
  - Blocks of statements are enclosed in pairs of open and close braces.
- Nested decision-making constructs enable you to deal with complex conditions using a divide-and-conquer approach. The outer-level constructs help you in testing preliminary or more general conditions. The inner-level constructs assist in handling more specific conditions.
- The `try`, `catch`, and `throw` statements enable you to use exception handling for error control.
- The `for` loop in C++ has the following general syntax:

```
for (<initialization of loop control variables>;
     <loop continuation test>;
     <increment/decrement of loop control variables>)
```

The `for` loop contains three components: the loop initialization, loop continuation condition, and the increment/decrement of the loop variables.

- The conditional loop `do-while` has the following general syntax:

```
do {
     sequence of statements
} while (condition);
```

The `do-while` loop iterates at least once.

- The conditional `while` loop has the following general syntax:

```
while (condition)
     statement; ¦ { sequence of statements }
```

The `while` loop might not iterate if its tested condition is initially false.

- The `continue` statement enables you to jump to the end of the loop and resume with the next iteration. The advantage of the `continue` statement is that it uses no labels to direct the jump.
- Open loops are `for` loops with empty components. The `break` statement enables you to exit the current loop and resume program execution at the first statement that comes after the loop. The `exit` function (declared in STDLIB.H) enables you to make a critical loop exit by halting the C++ program altogether.
- Nested loops enable you to contain repetitive tasks as part of other repetitive tasks. C++ enables you to nest any kind of loops to just about any level needed.

Q&A

Q Does C++ impose any rules for indenting statements in the clauses of an `if` statement?

A No. The indentation purely is up to you. Typical indentations range from two to four spaces. Using indentations makes your listings much more readable. Following is the case of an `if` statement with unindented clause statements:

```
if (i > 0)
     j = i * i;
     else
     j = 10 - i;
```

Compare the readability of that listing with this indented version.

```
if (i > 0)
  j = i * i;
else
  j = 10 - i;
```

The indented version is much easier to read.

Q What are the rules for writing the condition of an `if-else` statement?

A There are two schools of thought. The first recommends that you write the condition so that it is more often true than not. The second school recommends avoiding negative expressions (those that use the relational operator `!=` and the Boolean operator `!`). Programmers in this camp translate this `if` statement,

```
if (i != 0)
    j = 100 / i;
else
    j = 1;
```

into the following equivalent form,

```
if (i == 0)
    j = 1;
else
    j = 100 \ i;
```

even though the likelihood of variable `i` storing 0 might be very low.

Q How do I handle a condition such as the following, which divides by a variable that can possibly be zero?

```
if (i != 0 && 1/i > 1)
    j = i * i;
```

A C++ does not always evaluate the entire tested condition. This partial evaluation occurs when a term in the Boolean expression renders the entire expression false or true, regardless of the values of the other terms. In this case, if variable `i` is `0`—the runtime system does not evaluate the term `1/i > 1`. This is because the term `i != 0` is false and would render the entire expression false, regardless of what the second term yields.

Q Is it really necessary to include an else or default clause in multi-alternative `if-else` and `switch` statements?

A Programmers highly recommend the inclusion of these catch-all clauses to ensure that the multiple-alternative statements handle all conditions. However, they are not technically required for a program to compile.

Q How can a `while` loop simulate a `for` loop?

A Here is a simple example.

```
int i;
for (i = 1; i <= 10; i +=2){
   cout << i << endl;
}
```

```
int i = 1;
while (i <= 10) {
   cout << i << endl;
   i += 2;
   }
```

The `while` loop needs a leading statement that initializes the loop control variable. Also notice that the `while` loop uses a statement inside it to alter the value of the loop control variable.

Q How can a `while` loop simulate a `do-while` loop?

A Here is a simple example.

```
i = 1;                      i = 1;
do {                        while (i <= 10) {
   cout << i << endl;          cout << i << endl;
   i += 2;                     i += 2;
} while (i <= 10);             }
```

The two loops have the same condition in their `while` clauses. Note, however, that if the loop is designed in such a way that it doesn't necessarily know the initial value of `i`, it could have different effects if, for example, `i` starts out as `10`. The loop on the left would run through once while the loop on the right would never make it through a single iteration.

Q How can the open `for` loop emulate the `while` and `do-while` loops?

A The open `for` loop emulates the other C++ loops by placing the loop-escape `if` statement near the beginning or end of the loop. Here is how the open `for` loop emulates a sample `while` loop.

```
i = 1;                      i = 1;
while (i <= 10) {           for (;;) {
                               if(i > 10) break;
   cout << i << endl;          cout << i << endl;
   i += 2;                     i += 2;
}                           }
```

Notice that the open `for` loop uses a loop-escape `if` statement as the first statement inside the loop. The condition tested by the `if` statement is the logical reverse of the `while` loop condition. Here is a simple example showing the emulation of the `do-while` loop.

```
i = 1;                      i = 1;
do {                        for (;;) {
   cout << i << endl;          cout << i << endl;
   i += 2;                     i += 2;
                               if (i > 10) break;
} while (i <= 10);             }
```

The open `for` loop uses a loop-escape `if` statement right before the end of the loop. The `if` statement tests the reverse condition as the `do-while` loop.

Please take note, however, that these examples are rather crude and inelegant. One would never use an open `for` loop in this manner. Rather, one might skip one of the three clauses inside the `for` loop's parentheses (like the initialization clause if the control variable already has been initialized). Open `for` loops are more often used in cases where exiting the loop would be a rare occurrence, such as if one were accepting and processing a user's keystrokes, but exiting when the Esc key is encountered.

Q In nested `for` loops, can I use the loop control variable of the outer loops as part of the range of values for the inner loops?

A Yes. Not only does C++ not prohibit such use, it actually is rather quite common. Here is a simple example.

```
for (int i = 1; i <= 100; i += 5)
    for (int j = i; j <= 100; j++)
         cout << i * j << endl;
```

Q Does C++ restrict nesting of the various types of loops?

A No. You can nest any combination of loops in a C++ program.

Workshop

The Workshop provides quiz questions to help you solidify your understanding of the material covered and exercises to provide you with experience in using what you've learned. Try to understand the quiz and exercise answers before continuing on to the next day's lesson. (Answers are provided in Appendix A.)

Quiz

1. Simplify the following nested `if` statements by replacing them with a single `if` statement:

```
if (i > 0)
  if (i < 10)
     cout << "i = " << i << endl;
```

2. Simplify the following `if` statements by replacing them with a single `if` statement:

```
if (i > 0) {
    j = i * i;
    cout << "j = " << j << endl;
}
if (i < 0) {
    j = 4 * i;
    cout << "j = " << j << endl;
```

```
}
if (i == 0) {
    j = 10 + i
    cout << "j = " << j << endl;
}
```

3. True or false? The following `if` statements perform the same tasks as the subsequent `if-else` statement:

```
if (i < 0) {
     i = 10 + i;
     j = i * i;
     cout << "i = " << i << endl;
     cout << "j = " << j << endl;
}
if (i >= 0) {
     k = 4 * i + 1;
     cout << "k = " << k << endl;
}

if (i < 0) {
     i = 10 - i;
     j = i * i;
     cout << "i = " << i << endl;
     cout << "j = " << j << endl;
}
else {
     k = 4 * i + 1;
     cout << "k = " << k << endl;
}
```

4. Simplify the following `if-else` statement:

```
if (i > 0 && i < 100)
  j = i * i;
else if (i > 10 && i < 50)
  j = 10 + i;
else if (i >= 100)
  j = i;
else
  j = 1;
```

5. What is wrong with the following `if` statement?

```
if (i > (1 + i * i)) {
```

```
    j = i * i
    cout << "i = " << i << " and j = " << j << endl;
}
```

6. What is wrong with the following loop?

```
i = 1;
while (i < 10) {
  j = i * i - 1;
  k = 2 * j - i;
  cout << "i = " << i << endl;
  cout << "j = " <<  j << endl;
  cout << "k = " << k << endl;
}
```

7. What is the output of the following `for` loop?

```
for (int i = 5; i < 10; i + 2)
     cout << i - 2 << endl;
```

8. What is the output of the following `for` loop?

```
for (int i = 5; i < 10; )
     cout << i - 2 << endl;
```

9. What is wrong with the following code?

```
for (int i = 1; i <= 10; i++)
     for (i = 8; i <= 12; i++)
          cout << i << endl;
```

10. Where is the error in the following nested loops?

```
for (int i = 1; i <= 10; i++)
  cout << i * i << endl;
for (int i = 1; i <= 10; i++)
  cout << i * i * i << endl;
```

11. Where is the error in the following loop?

```
i = 1;
while (i > 0) {
  cout << i << endl;
  i++;
}
```

12. The factorial of a number is the product of the sequence of integers from 1 to that number. The following general equation defines the factorial (which uses the symbol `!`):

```
n! = 1 * 2 * 3 * ... * n
```

Following is a C++ program that calculates the factorial of a number. The problem is that for whatever positive value you enter, the program displays a `0` value for the factorial. Where is the error in the program?

```
int n;
double factorial;
cout << "Enter positive integer : ";
cin >> n;
for (int i = 1; i <= n; i++)
   factorial *= i;
cout << i << "! = " << factorial;
```

Exercises

1. Write the program IF5.CPP to solve for the roots of a quadratic equation. The quadratic equation is

   $Ax^2 + Bx + C = 0$

   The roots of the quadratic equation are

   $root1 = (-B + \sqrt{B^2 - 4AC}) / (2A)$
   $root1 = (-B - \sqrt{B^2 - 4AC}) / (2A)$

   If the term in the square root is negative, then the roots are complex. If the term in the square root term is zero, then the two roots are the same and are equal to `-B/(2A)`.
2. Write the program SWITCH2.CPP, which implements a simple four-function calculator. The program should prompt you for the operand and the operator, and display both the input and the result. Include error checking for bad operators and for the attempt to divide by zero.
3. Write the program FOR5.CPP, which uses a `for` loop to obtain and display the sum of odd integers in the range of 11 to 121.
4. Write the program WHILE2.CPP, which uses a `while` loop to obtain and display the sum of the squared odd integers in the range of 11 to 121.
5. Write the program DOWHILE2.CPP, which uses a `do-while` loop to obtain and display the sum of the squared odd integers in the range of 11 to 121.

WEEK 1

User-Defined Types and Pointers

Creating user-defined data types is one of the necessary features of a modern programming language. Today's lesson looks at the enumerated data types and structures that enable you to better organize your data. In addition, this lesson discusses using pointers with simple variables, arrays, structures, and dynamic data. Today, you will learn about the following topics:

- The type definition using `typedef`
- Enumerated data types
- Structures
- Unions
- Reference variables
- Pointers to existing variables
- Simple arrays
- Pointers to arrays
- Pointers to structures
- Using pointers to access and manage dynamic data
- Far pointers

Type Definition in C++

C++ offers the `typedef` keyword, which enables you to define new data type names as aliases of existing types.

Syntax

The *typedef* Keyword

The general syntax for using `typedef` is

```
typedef knownType newType;
```

Examples

```
typedef unsigned word;
typedef unsigned char byte;
typedef unsigned char boolean;
```

The `typedef` keyword defines a new type from a known one. You can use `typedef` to create aliases that shorten the names of existing data types or to define names of data types that are more familiar to you. (See the second of the preceding examples, which `typedef`s a byte type). In addition, the `typedef` statement can define a new type name that better describes how the data type is used. The third of the preceding examples illustrates this use of `typedef`. You also can use `typedef` to define the name of an array type.

Syntax

An Array Type Name

The general syntax for defining the name of an array type is

```
typedef baseType arrayTypeName[arraySize];
```

The `typedef` statement defines the `arrayTypeName`, whose basic type and size are `baseType` and `arraySize`, respectively.

Examples

```
typedef double vector[10];
typedef double matrix[10][30];
```

Thus, the identifiers `vector` and `matrix` are names of data types.

Enumerated Data Types

The rule to follow with enumerated data types is that although the enumerated identifiers must be unique, the values assigned to them need not be unique.

NEW TERM An *enumerated type* defines a list of unique identifiers and associates values with these identifiers.

Syntax

An Enumerated Type

The general syntax for declaring an enumerated type is

```
enum enumType { <list of enumerated identifiers> };
```

Examples

```
enum Boolean { false, true };
enum YesNo { no, yes, dontCare, maybe };
enum weekday { Sunday, Monday, Tuesday,
               Wednesday, Thursday, Friday, Saturday };
```

Following is an example of declaring an enumerated type:

```
enum CPUtype { i8088, i80286, i80386DX, i80386SX,
               i80486DX, i80486SX };
```

C++ associates integer values with the enumerated identifiers. For example, in this type, the compiler assigns 0 to i8088, 1 to i80286, and so on.

C++ is very flexible in declaring an enumerated type. First, the language enables you to explicitly assign a value to an enumerated identifier. Following is an example:

```
enum weekday { Sunday = 1, Monday, Tuesday, Wednesday,
               Thursday, Friday, Saturday };
```

This declaration explicitly assigns `1` to the enumerated identifier `Sunday`. The compiler then assigns the next integer, `2`, to the next identifier, `Monday`, and so on. C++ enables you to explicitly assign a value to each member of the enumerated list. Moreover, these values need not be unique. Following are some examples of the flexibility in declaring enumerated types in C++:

```
// explicit value assignment for every list member
enum colors { black = 1, red = 2, blue = 3, green = 5,
              yellow = 7, white = 11 };

// intermittent value assignment
enum colors { black = 1, red, blue, green = 5,
              yellow = 7, white = 11 };

// duplicate values
enum CPUtype { i8088 = 1, i80286 = 2,
               i80386DX = 3, i80386SX = 3,
               i80486DX = 4, i80486SX = 4 };

enum choiceType { false, true, dontCare = 0 };
```

In the last example, the compiler associates the identifier `false` with `0` by default. However, the compiler also associates the value `0` with `dontCare` because of the explicit assignment.

C++ enables you to declare variables that have enumerated types in the following ways:

- The declaration of the enumerated type may include the declaration of the variables of that type. The general syntax is

  ```
  enum enumType { <list of enumerated identifiers> }
                <list of variables>;
  ```

  Following is an example.

  ```
  enum weekDay { Sun = 1, Mon, Tue, Wed, Thu, Fri, Sat }
       recycleDay, payDay, movieDay;
  ```

- The separate declaration of the enumerated type and its variables includes multiple statements to declare the type and the associated variables separately. The general syntax is

  ```
  enum enumType { <list of enumerated identifiers> };
  enumType var1, var2, ..., varN;
  ```

Look at an example. Listing 4.1 shows the source code for the program ENUM1.CPP. The program implements a simple one-line, four-function calculator that performs the following tasks:

- Prompts you to enter a number, an operator (+, –, *, or /), and a number.
- Performs the requested operation, if valid.
- Displays the operands, the operator, and the result, if the operation was valid; otherwise, displays an error message that indicates the type of error. (You either entered a bad operator or attempted to divide by 0.)

Type

Listing 4.1. Source code for the program ENUM1.CPP.

```
/*
C++ program that demonstrates enumerated types
*/

#include <iostream.h>

enum mathError { noError, badOperator, divideByZero };

void sayError(mathError err)
{
  switch (err) {
    case noError:
      cout << "No error";
      break;
    case badOperator:
      cout << "Error: invalid operator";
      break;
    case divideByZero:
      cout << "Error: attempt to divide by zero";
  }
}

main()
{
  double x, y, z;
  char op;
  mathError error = noError;

  cout << "Enter a number, an operator, and a number : ";
  cin >> x >> op >> y;

  switch (op) {
    case '+':
      z = x + y;
      break;
    case '--':
      z = x -- y;
      break;
    case '*':
      z = x * y;
      break;
    case '/':
      if (y != 0)
        z = x / y;
      else
        error = divideByZero;
      break;
    default:
      error = badOperator;
  }

  if (error == noError)
```

continues

Listing 4.1. continued

```
53:     cout << x << " " << op << " " << y << " = " << z;
54:   else
55:     sayError(error);
56:   return 0;
57: }
```

Here is a sample session with the program in Listing 4.1.

```
Enter a number, an operator, and a number : 355 / 113
355 / 113 = 3.14159
```

The program in Listing 4.1 declares the enumerated type mathError in line 7. This data type has three enumerated values: noError, badOperator, and divideByZero.

The program also defines the function `sayError` in lines 9 through 21 to display a message based on the value of the enumerated parameter `err`. The function uses the `switch` statement in line 11 to display messages that correspond to the various enumerated values.

The function `main` declares the `double`-typed variables `x`, `y`, and `z` to represent the operands and the result, respectively. In addition, the function declares the `char`-typed variable `op` to store the requested operation, and the enumerated variable `error` to store the error status. The function initializes the variable `error` with the enumerated value `noError`.

The output statement in line 29 prompts you to enter the operands and the operator. The statement in line 30 stores your input in variables `x`, `op`, and `y`, in that order. The function uses the `switch` statement in line 32 to examine the value in variable `op` and perform the requested operation. The `case` labels in lines 33, 36, 39, and 42 provide the values for the four supported math operations. The last `case` label contains an `if` statement that detects the attempt to divide by zero. If this is true, then the `else` clause statement assigns the enumerated value `divideByZero` to the variable `error`.

The catch-all `default` clause in line 48 handles invalid operators. The statement in line 49 assigns the enumerated value `badOperator` to the variable `error`.

The `if` statement in line 52 determines whether the variable `error` contains the enumerated value `noError`. If this condition is true, then the program executes the output statement in line 53. This statement displays the operands, the operator, and the result. Otherwise, the program executes the `else` clause statement that calls the function `sayError` and passes it the argument `error`. This function call displays a message that identifies the error.

Structures

C++ supports structures, and these members can be predefined types or other structures.

NEW TERM *Structures* enable you to define a new type that logically groups several fields or members.

Syntax

A Structure

The general syntax for declaring a structure is

```
struct structTag {
 <list of members>
};
```

Examples

```
struct point {
   double x;
   double y;
};

struct rectangle {
   point upperLeftCorner;
   point lowerRightCorner;
   double area;
};

struct circle {
   point center;
   double radius;
   double area;
};
```

Once you define a `struct` type, you can use that type to declare variables. Following are examples of declarations that use structures that we declared in the syntax box:

```
point p1, p2, p3;
```

You also can declare structured variables when you define the structure itself.

```
struct point {
double x;
double y;
} p1, p2, p3;
```

Untagged structures enable you to declare structure variables without defining a name for their structures.

Note: Interestingly, C++ permits you to declare untagged structures. For example, the following structure definition declares the variables `p1`, `p2`, and `p3` but omits the name of the structure:

```
struct {
     double x;
     double y;
} p1, p2, p3;
```

C++ enables you to declare and initialize a structured variable. Here is an example:

```
point pt = { 1.0, -8.3 };
```

Accessing the members of a structure uses the dot operator. Following are a few examples:

```
p1.x = 12.45;
p1.y = 34.56;
p2.x = 23.4 / p1.x;
p2.y = 0.98 * p1.y;
```

Note: This method of initializing a `struct` is the old C way of doing things. C++ has a better way: by using a constructor. This can work because `struct`s are actually just special forms of classes. The `class` is covered on Day 8.

Consider an example. Listing 4.2 shows the source code for the program STRUCT1.CPP. The program prompts you for four sets of coordinates that define four rectangles. Each rectangle is defined by the `x` and `y` coordinates of the upper-left and lower-right corners. The program calculates the areas of each rectangle, sorts the rectangles by area, and displays the rectangles in the order of their areas.

Type Listing 4.2. Source code for the program STRUCT1.CPP.

```
/*
  C++ program that demonstrates structured types
*/

#include <iostream.h>
#include <stdio.h>
#include <math.h>

const MAX_RECT = 4;

struct point {
  double x;
  double y;
};

struct rect {
  point ulc; // upper left corner
  point lrc; // lower right corner
  double area;
  int id;
};

typedef rect rectArr[MAX_RECT];

main()
{
```

```
27:   rectArr r;
28:   rect temp;
29:   double length, width;
30:
31:   for (int i = 0; i < MAX_RECT; i++) {
32:     cout << "Enter (X,Y) coord. for ULC of rect. # "
33:          << i << " : ";
34:     cin >> r[i].ulc.x >> r[i].ulc.y;
35:     cout << "Enter (X,Y) coord. for LRC of rect. # "
36:          << i << " : ";
37:     cin >> r[i].lrc.x >> r[i].lrc.y;
38:     r[i].id = i;
39:     length = fabs(r[i].ulc.x -- r[i].lrc.x);
40:     width = fabs(r[i].ulc.y -- r[i].lrc.y);
41:     r[i].area = length * width;
42:   }
43:
44:   // sort the rectangles by areas
45:   for (i = 0; i < (MAX_RECT -- 1); i++)
46:     for (int j = i + 1; j < MAX_RECT; j++)
47:       if (r[i].area > r[j].area) {
48:         temp = r[i];
49:         r[i] = r[j];
50:         r[j] = temp;
51:       }
52:
53:   // display rectangles sorted by area
54:   for (i = 0; i < MAX_RECT; i++)
55:     printf("Rect # %d has area %5.4lf\n", r[i].id, r[i].area);
56:   return 0;
57: }
```

Here is a sample session with the program in Listing 4.2.

```
Enter (X,Y) coord. for ULC of rect. # 0 : 1 1
Enter (X,Y) coord. for LRC of rect. # 0 : 2 2
Enter (X,Y) coord. for ULC of rect. # 1 : 1.5 1.5
Enter (X,Y) coord. for LRC of rect. # 1 : 3 4
Enter (X,Y) coord. for ULC of rect. # 2 : 1 2
Enter (X,Y) coord. for LRC of rect. # 2 : 5 8
Enter (X,Y) coord. for ULC of rect. # 3 : 4 6
Enter (X,Y) coord. for LRC of rect. # 3 : 8 4
Rect # 0 has area 1.0000
Rect # 1 has area 3.7500
Rect # 3 has area 8.0000
Rect # 2 has area 24.0000
```

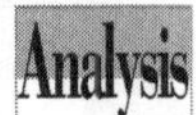

The program in Listing 4.2 includes the header files IOSTREAM. MATH.H, and STDIO.H. The program declares the global constant `MAX_RECT` to specify the maximum number of rectangles. Line 11 contains the declaration of structure point, which is made up of two double-typed members: `x` and `y`. This structure models a two-dimensional point. Line 16 contains the declaration of structure rect, which models a rectangle. The structure contains two point-typed members, `ulc` and `lrc`, the double-typed member area, and the int-typed member id. The members ulc and lrc represent the coordinates for the upper-left and lower-right corners that define a rectangle. The member area stores the area of the rectangle. The member id stores a numeric identification number.

The typedef statement in line 23 defines the type recArr as an array of MAX_RECT elements of structure rect.

The function main declares the rectArr-typed array r, the rect-typed structure temp, and the double-typed variables length and width.

The function main uses the for loop in lines 31 through 42 to prompt you for the coordinates of the rectangles, calculate their areas, and assign their id numbers. The output statements in lines 32 and 33, and in lines 35 and 36, prompt you for the x and y coordinates of the upper-left and lower-right corners, respectively. The input statements in lines 34 and 37 store the coordinates you enter in members r[i].ulc.x, r[i].ulc.y, r[i].lrc.x, and r[i].lrc.y, respectively. The statement in line 38 stores the value of the loop control variable i in member r[i].id. The statement in line 39 calculates the length of a rectangle using the x members of the ulc and lrc members in the element r[i]. The statement in line 40 calculates the width of a rectangle using the y members of the ulc and lrc members in the element r[i]. The statement in line 41 calculates the area of the rectangle and stores it in member r[i].area.

The nested loops in lines 44 through 51 sort the elements of array r using the member area. The loops implement the simple bubble sort method (which is useful for very small arrays). The if statement in line 47 compares the areas of elements r[i] and r[j]. If the area of rectangle r[i] is larger than that of rectangle r[j], the statements in lines 48 through 50 swap all the members of r[i] and r[j]. The swap uses the structure temp. This task illustrates that you can assign all the members of a structure to another structure in one statement.

The for loop in lines 54 and 55 displays the rectangles sorted according to their areas. The output statement in line 55 uses the printf function to display the rectangle id numbers and areas.

Unions

The size of a union is equal to the size of its largest member.

NEW TERM *Unions* are special structures that store members with shared address spaces.

Syntax

Unions

The general syntax for unions is

```
union unionTag {
   type1 member1;
   type2 member2;
   ...
   typeN memberN;
};
```

Example

```
union Long {
   unsigned mWord[2];
   long mLong;
};
```

The union `Long` stores either two unsigned integers (each requiring two bytes) or a four-byte long integer. In addition, the union `Long` enables you to access the lower or higher words (two-byte integers) of a long integer.

Unions offer an easy alternative for quick data conversion. Unions were more significant in the recent past, when the price of computer memory was much higher and it was feasible to use unions to consolidate memory. Accessing union members involves the dot access operators, just as in structures.

Reference Variables

In Day 2, you learned that you declare reference parameters by placing the `&` symbol after the parameter's type. Recall that a reference parameter becomes an alias to its arguments. In addition, any changes made to the reference parameter affect its argument. In addition to reference parameters, C++ supports *reference variables.* You can manipulate the referenced variable by using its alias. As a novice C++ programmer, your initial use of reference variables will most likely be limited. On the other hand, you probably are using reference parameters more frequently. As you advance in using C++, you will discover how reference variables can implement programming tricks that deal with advanced class design. This book discusses only the basics of reference variables.

NEW TERM Like reference parameters, *reference variables* become aliases to the variables they access.

Syntax

A Reference Variable

The general syntax for declaring a reference variable is

```
type& refVar = Var;
type& refVar = aVar;
```

The `refVar` is the reference variable that can be initialized when declared. You must ensure that a reference variable is initialized or assigned a referenced variable before using the reference variable.

Examples

```
int x = 10, y = 3;
int& rx = x;
int& ry = y; // take the reference
```

Here is a simple example that shows a reference variable at work. Listing 4.3 shows the source code for the program REFVAR1.CPP. The program displays and alters the values of a variable using either the variable itself or its reference. The program requires no input.

Listing 4.3. Source code for the program REFVAR1.CPP.

```
1: /*
2:   C++ program that demonstrates reference variables
3: */
4:
5: #include <iostream.h>
6:
7: main()
8: {
9:     int x = 10;
10:    int& rx = x;
11:    // display x using x and rx
12:    cout << "x contains " << x << "\n";
13:    cout << "x contains (using the reference rx) "
14:         << rx << "\n";
15:    // alter x and display its value using rx
16:    x *= 2;
17:    cout << "x contains (using the reference rx) "
18:         << rx << "\n";
19:    // alter rx and display value using x
20:    rx *= 2;
21:    cout << "x contains " << x << "\n";
22:    return 0;
23: }
```

Here is a sample session with the program in Listing 4.3.

```
x contains 10
x contains (using the reference rx) 10
x contains (using the reference rx) 20
x contains 40
```

The program in Listing 4.3 declares the `int`-typed variable `x` and the `int`-typed reference variable `rx`. The program initializes the variable `x` with 10 and the reference variable `rx` with the variable `x`.

The output statement in line 12 displays the value in variable `x` using the variable `x` itself. By contrast, the output statement in lines 13 and 14 displays the value in variable `x` using the reference variable `rx`.

The statement in line 16 doubles the integer in variable `x`. The output statement in lines 17 and 18 displays the new value in variable `x` using the reference variable `rx`. As the output shows, the reference variable accurately displays the updated value in variable `x`.

The statement in line 20 doubles the value in variable `x` by using the reference variable `rx`. The output statement in line 21 displays the updated value in variable `x` using variable `x`. Again, the output shows that the variable `x` and the reference variable `rx` are synchronized.

Overview of Pointers

Each piece of information, both code and data, in the computer's memory resides at a specific address and occupies a specific number of bytes. When you run a program, your variables reside at specific *addresses*. With a high-level language such as C++, you are not concerned about the actual address of every variable. That task is handled transparently by the compiler and the runtime system. Conceptually, each variable in your program is a *tag* for a memory address. Manipulating the data using the tag is much easier than dealing with actual numerical addresses, such as `0F64:01AF4`.

NEW TERM An *address* is a memory location. A *tag* is the variable's name.

Going back to the box analogy (in Day 3), imagine that your computer's memory is just a large number of tiny boxes. Now, imagine that when you declare a variable, you're really just setting aside a box to hold the value of that variable. But what if you weren't so much interested in what that box contained, but rather you wanted to know just where that box was in memory? You would create a pointer to that box. Creating a pointer is just declaring another variable, but the value that can be found in the pointer's box really is just the address of another variable's box. Regard Figure 4.1 as it relates to the following code snippet:

```
int myInt = 42;
int *pInt = &myInt;
```

Figure 4.1.
Memory depicted by boxes.

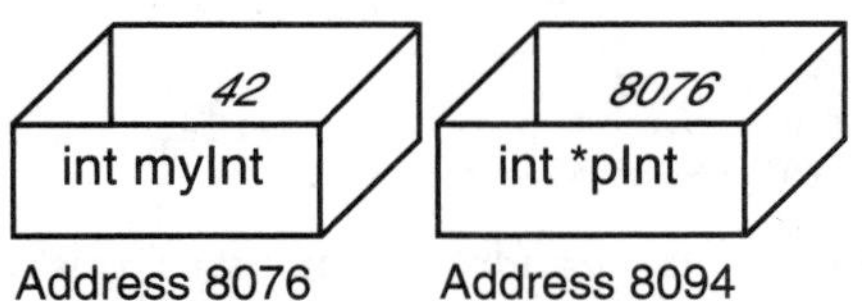

The variable `myInt` has been declared, which created a box for it, and the value 42 has been placed into it. That box happens to be at memory address `8076`. When the pointer `pInt` was declared, another box was created at another memory address. In this particular case, that memory happens to be `8094`. It's important to note that the memory addresses will not necessarily be next to each other, as in this case. When `pInt` was declared, it was initialized with the address (that's what the `&` means) of `myInt`. So, the memory address at which `myInt` resides was placed inside of `pInt`'s box. `pInt` is a variable of its own, but its value just happens to be the address of another variable. Note that it is entirely possible, at this point, to declare yet another box, and have that be a pointer to `pInt`; this would be called a *pointer to a pointer*.

C++ and its parent C are programming languages that also are used for low-level systems programming. In fact, many programmers regard C as a high-level assembler. Low-level system programming requires that you work frequently with the address of data. This is where pointers, in general, come into play. Knowing the address of a piece of data enables you to set and query its value.

4

NEW TERM A *pointer* is a special variable that stores the address of another variable or information.

Warning: Pointers are very powerful language components. They also can be dangerous if used carelessly, because they may hang your system. This malfunction occurs when the pointer hasn't been set up yet. Don't forget that simply declaring something doesn't automatically give it any value. Until you've set the value of a pointer (with the address of another variable), that pointer is just referring to something random in memory, and if you use that pointer, you could get some really weird results.

Pointers to Existing Variables

In this section, you learn how to use pointers to access the values in existing variables. C++ requires that you associate a data type (including `void`) with a declared pointer. The associated data type may be a predefined type or a user-defined structure.

Syntax

A Pointer

The general syntax for declaring a pointer is

```
type* pointerName;
type* pointerName = pointerVariable;
type* pointerName = &variable;
```

The `&` operator is the address-of operator (this is not the reference operator, which also uses the `&` symbol) and is used to take the address of a variable. The address-of operator returns the address of a variable, structure, function, and so on. By contrast, the reference operator creates an alias to a variable using another variable.

Example

```
int *intPtr; // pointer to an int
double *realPtr; // pointer to a double
char *aString; // pointer to a character
long lv;
long* lp = &lv;
```

You also can declare nonpointers in the same lines that declare pointers.

```
int *intPtr, anInt;
double *realPtr, x;
char *aString, aKey;
```

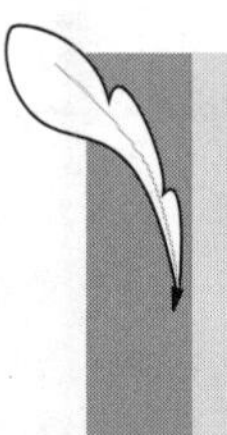

Note: C++ allows you to place the asterisk character right after the associated data type. You should not interpret this type of syntax to mean that every other identifier appearing in the same declaration is automatically a pointer.

```
int* intPtr; // pointer to an int
double* realPtr; // pointer to a double
char* aString; // pointer to a character
int *intP, j; // intP is a pointer to int, j is an int
double *realPtr, *doublePtr;  // both identifiers
                              // are pointers to a double
```

DO **DON'T**

DO initialize a pointer before you use it, just as you do with ordinary variables. In fact, the need to initialize pointers is even more pressing—using uninitialized pointers invites trouble that can lead to unpredictable program behavior or a system hang. Whenever you see a General Protection Fault (a GPF) in a program, it usually is caused by using a pointer that has not been initialized properly.

DON'T assume that uninitialized pointers are harmless.

Once a pointer contains the address of a variable, you can access the value in that variable using the `*` operator followed by the name of the pointer. For example, if `px` is a pointer to the variable `x`, then you can use `*px` to access the value in variable `x`.

DO **DON'T**

DO include the `*` operator to the left of a pointer to access the variable whose address is stored in the pointer.

DON'T forget to use the `*` operator. Without it, a statement ends up manipulating the address in the pointer instead of the data at that address.

Following is a simple example that shows a pointer at work. Listing 4.4 shows the source code for the program PTR1.CPP. The program displays and alters the values of a variable using either the variable itself or its pointer. The program requires no input.

Listing 4.4. Source code for the program PTR1.CPP.

```
1:  /*
2:    C++ program that demonstrates pointers to existing variables
3:  */
4:
5:  #include <iostream.h>
6:
7:  main()
8:  {
9:    int x = 10;
10:   int* px = &x;
11:   // display x using x and rx
12:   cout << "x contains " << x << "\n";
13:   cout << "x contains (using the pointer px) "
14:        << *px << "\n";
15:   // alter x and display its value using *px
16:   x *= 2;
17:   cout << "x contains (using the pointer px) "
18:        << *px << "\n";
19:   // alter *px and display value using x
20:   *px *= 2;
21:   cout << "x contains " << x << "\n";
22:   return 0;
23: }
```

Here is a sample session with the program in Listing 4.4.

```
x contains 10
x contains (using the pointer px) 10
x contains (using the pointer px) 20
x contains 40
```

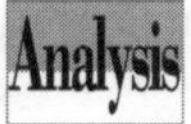

The program in Listing 4.4 declares the `int`-typed variable `x` and the `int`-typed pointer `px`. The program initializes the variable `x` with 10 and the pointer `px` with the address of variable `x`.

The output statement in line 12 displays the value in variable `x` using the variable `x`. By contrast, the output statement in lines 13 and 14 displays the value in variable `x` using the pointer `px`. Notice that the statement uses `*px` to access the value in variable `x`.

The statement in line 16 doubles the integer in variable `x`. The output statement in lines 17 and 18 displays the new value in variable `x` using the pointer `px`. As the output shows, the pointer accurately displays the updated value in variable `x`.

The statement in line 20 doubles the value in variable `x` by using the pointer `px`. Notice that the assignment statement uses `*px` on the left side of the `=` operator to access the variable `x`. The output statement in line 21 displays the updated value in variable `x` using variable `x`. Again, the output shows that the variable `x` and the pointer `px` are synchronized.

A Short Introduction to Arrays

An *array* is one of the most useful components in a programming language. It enables the programmer to store a number of data items in a single location. The single-dimensional array is the simplest kind of array. In a single-dimensional array, each variable is individually accessed using a single index.

NEW TERM An *array* is a group of variables that share the same name (the name of the array).

A Single-Dimensional Array

Syntax

The general syntax for declaring a single-dimensional array is

```
type arrayName[numberOfElements];
```

C++ requires you to observe the following rules in declaring single-dimensional arrays:

- The lower bound of a C++ array is set at 0. C++ does not allow you to override or alter this lower bound.
- Declaring a C++ array entails specifying the number of members. Keep in mind that the number of members is equal to the upper bound plus one.

The valid range of indices for this form extends between `0` and `numberOfElements - 1`.

Examples

```
int intArray[10];
char name[31];
double x[100];
```

Using a single-dimensional array involves stating both its name and the valid index in order to access one of its members. Depending on where the reference to an array element occurs, it can either store or recall a value. Following are the simple rules to remember:

- Assign a value to an array element before accessing that element to recall data. Otherwise, you get garbage data.
- Use a valid index. This is of paramount importance, because trying to access an array with an invalid index is like using an uninitialized pointer; it can lead to strange behavior in your program and GPFs in Windows.

DO	DON'T

DO make reasonable checks for the indices that access the arrays.

DON'T assume that indices are always valid.

The following is a simple example of accessing arrays:

```
double nums[5];
for (int i = 0; i < 5; ++i)
   {
   cout << "Enter number " << i << ": ";
   cin >> nums[i];
   }
cout << "You entered the following numbers: ";
for (i = 0; i < 5; ++i)
   cout << "nums[" << i << "] is " << nums[i];
cout << endl;
```

Pointers to Arrays

C++ and its parent language, C, support a special use for the names of arrays. The compiler interprets the name of an array as the address of its first element. Thus, if `x` is an array, the expressions `&x[0]` and `x` are equivalent. In the case of a matrix—call it `mat`—the expressions `&mat[0][0]` and `mat` also are equivalent. This aspect of C++ and C makes them work as high-level assembly languages. Once you have the address of a data item, you've got its number, so to speak. Your knowledge of the memory address of a variable or an array enables you to manipulate its contents using pointers.

NEW TERM A *program variable* is a label that tags a memory address. Using a variable in a program means accessing the associated memory location by specifying its name (or tag, if you prefer). In this sense, a variable becomes a name that points to a memory location—a pointer.

C++ enables you to use a pointer to access the various elements of an array. When you access the element `x[i]` of array `x`, the compiled code performs two tasks. First, it obtains the base address of the array `x` (that is, where the first array element is located). Second, it uses the index `i` to calculate the offset from the base address of the array. This offset equals `i` multiplied by the size of the basic array type.

```
address of element x[i] = address of x + i * sizeof(basicType)
```

Looking at the preceding equation, assume that you have a pointer `ptr` that takes the base address of array `x`.

```
ptr = x; // pointer ptr points to address of x[0]
```

You now can substitute `x` with `ptr` in the equation and come up with the following:

```
address of element x[i] = ptr + i * sizeof(basicType)
```

In order for C++ and C to be high-level assemblers, they simplify the use of this equation by absolving it from having to explicitly state the size of the basic array type. Thus, you can write the following:

```
address of element x[i] = p + i
```

This equation states that the address of element `x[i]` is the expression `(p + i)`.

The PTR2.CPP program in Listing 4.5 illustrates the use of pointers to access one-dimensional arrays. This program is a modified version of the program ARRAY1.CPP that calculates the average value for data in an array. The program begins by prompting you to enter the number of data points and the data itself. The program then calculates the average of the data in the array and displays the average value.

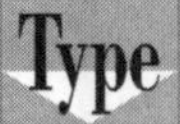

Listing 4.5. Source code for the program PTR2.CPP.

```
/*
   C++ program that demonstrates the use of pointers with
   one-dimension arrays.  Program calculates the average
   value of the data found in the array.
*/

#include <iostream.h>

const int MAX = 30;

main()
{

    double x[MAX];
    // declare pointer and initialize with base
    // address of array x
    double *realPtr = x; // same as = &x[0]
    double sum, sumx = 0.0, mean;
    int n;
    // obtain the number of data points
    do {
        cout << "Enter number of data points [2 to "
             << MAX << "] : ";
        cin >> n;
        cout << "\n";
    } while (n < 2 ¦¦[]> MAX);

    // prompt for the data
    for (int i = 0; i < n; i++) {
        cout << "X[" << i << "] : ";
        // use the form *(x+i) to store data in x[i]
        cin >> *(x + i);
    }

    sum = n;
    for (i = 0; i < n; i++)
    // use the form *(realPtr + i) to access x[i]
        sumx += *(realPtr + i);
    mean = sumx / sum;
    cout << "\nMean = " << mean << "\n\n";
    return 0;
}
```

Here is a sample session with the program in Listing 4.5.

```
Enter number of data points [2 to 30] : 5

X[0] : 1
X[1] : 2
X[2] : 3
X[3] : 4
X[4] : 5

Mean = 3
```

The program in Listing 4.5 declares the double-typed array x to have MAX elements. In addition, the program declares the pointer realPtr and initializes it using the array x. Thus, the pointer realPtr stores the address of x[0], which is the first element in array x.

The program uses the pointer for `*(x + i)` in the input statement at line 32. Thus, the identifier `x` works as a pointer to the array `x`. Using the expression `*(x + i)` accesses the element number `i` of array `x`, just as does using the expression `x[i]`.

The program uses the pointer `realPtr` in the `for` loop at lines 37 and 38. The expression `*(realPtr + i)` is the equivalent of `*(x + i)`, which in turn is equivalent to `x[i]`. Thus, the `for` loop uses the pointer `realPtr` with an offset value, `i`, to access the elements of array `x`.

The Pointer Increment/Decrement Method

The preceding C++ program maintains the same address in the pointer `realPtr`. Employing pointer arithmetic with the `for` loop index `i`, you can write a new program version that increments the offset to access the elements of array `x`. C++ provides you with another choice that enables you to access sequentially the elements of an array without the help of an explicit offset value. The method merely involves using the increment or decrement operator with a pointer. You still need to initialize the pointer to the base address of an array and then use the ++ operator to access the next array element. Following is a modified version of the preceding program, a version that uses the pointer increment method. Listing 4.6 shows the source code for the PTR3.CPP program.

Listing 4.6. Source code for the program PTR3.CPP.

```
/*
  C++ program that demonstrates the use of pointers with
  one-dimension arrays.  The average value of the array
  is calculated.  This program modifies the previous version
  in the following way:  the realPtr is used to access the
  array without any help from any loop control variable.
  This is accomplished by 'incrementing' the pointer, and
  consequently incrementing its address.  This program
```

```
   illustrates pointer arithmetic that alters the pointer's
   address.

*/

#include <iostream.h>

const int MAX = 30;

main()
{

    double x[MAX];
    double *realPtr = x;
    double sum, sumx = 0.0, mean;
    int i, n;

    do {
        cout << "Enter number of data points [2 to "
             << MAX << "] : ";
        cin >> n;
        cout << "\n";
    } while (n < 2 || n > MAX);

    // loop variable i is not directly involved in accessing
    //  the elements of array x
    for (i = 0; i < n; i++) {
        cout << "X[" << i << "] : ";
        // increment pointer realPtr after taking its reference
        cin >> *realPtr++;
    }

    // restore original address by using pointer arithmetic
    realPtr -= n;
    sum = n;
    // loop variable i serves as a simple counter
    for (i = 0; i < n; i++)
       // increment pointer realPtr after taking a reference
        sumx += *(realPtr++);
    mean = sumx / sum;
    cout << "\nMean = " << mean << "\n\n";
    return 0;

}
```

Output

Here is a sample session with the program in Listing 4.6.

```
Enter number of data points [2 to 30] : 5

X[0] : 10
X[1] : 20
X[2] : 30
X[3] : 40
X[4] : 50

Mean = 30
```

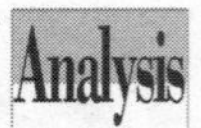

The program in Listing 4.6 initializes the `realPtr` pointer to the base address of array `x`, in line 22. The program uses the `realPtr` pointer in the keyboard input statement in line 38. This statement uses `*realPtr++` to store your input in the currently accessed element of array `x` and then to increment the pointer to the next element of array `x`. When the input loop terminates, the pointer `realPtr` points past the tail of array `x`. To reset the pointer to the base address of array `x`, the program uses the assignment statement in line 42. This statement uses pointer arithmetic to decrease the current address in pointer `realPtr` by *n* times `sizeof(real)`. The statement resets the address in the pointer `realPtr` to access the array element `x[0]`. The program uses the same incrementing method to calculate the sum of data in the second for loop in line 47.

Pointers to Structures

C++ supports declaring and using pointers to structures. Assigning the address of a structured variable to a pointer of the same type uses the same syntax as with simple variables. Once the pointer has the address of the structured variable, it needs to use the `->` operator to access the members of the structure.

Syntax

Accessing Structure Members

The general syntax for a pointer to access the members of a structure is

```
structPtr->aMember
```

Example

```
struct point {
   double x;
   double y;
};

point p;
point* ptr = &p;

ptr->x = 23.3;
ptr->y = ptr->x + 12.3;
```

Here is a sample program that uses pointers to structures. Listing 4.7 shows the source code for the program PTR4.CPP. This program is the version of program STRUCT1.CPP that uses pointers. The program prompts you for four sets of coordinates that define four rectangles. Each rectangle is defined by the x and y coordinates of the upper-left and lower-right corners. The program calculates the area of each rectangle, sorts the rectangles by area, and displays the rectangles in the order of their areas.

Listing 4.7. Source code for the program PTR4.CPP.

```
/*
  C++ program that demonstrates pointers to structured types
*/

#include <iostream.h>
#include <stdio.h>
#include <math.h>

const MAX_RECT = 4;

struct point {
  double x;
  double y;
};

struct rect {
  point ulc; // upper left corner
  point lrc; // lower right corner
  double area;
  int id;
};

typedef rect rectArr[MAX_RECT];

main()
{
  rectArr r;
  rect temp;
  rect* pr = r;
  rect* pr2;
  double length, width;

  for (int i = 0; i < MAX_RECT; i++, pr++) {
    cout << "Enter (X,Y) coord. for ULC of rect. # "
         << i << " : ";
    cin >> pr-->ulc.x >> pr-->ulc.y;
    cout << "Enter (X,Y) coord. for LRC of rect. # "
         << i << " : ";
    cin >> pr-->lrc.x >> pr-->lrc.y;
    pr-->id = i;
    length = fabs(pr-->ulc.x -- pr-->lrc.x);
    width = fabs(pr-->ulc.y -- pr-->lrc.y);
    pr-->area = length * width;
  }

  pr --= MAX_RECT; // reset pointer
  // sort the rectangles by areas
  for (i = 0; i < (MAX_RECT -- 1); i++, pr++) {
    pr2 = pr + 1; // reset pointer pr2
    for (int j = i + 1; j < MAX_RECT; j++, pr2++)
      if (pr—>area > pr2—>area) {
        temp = *pr;
```

continued

Listing 4.7. continued

```
53:         *pr = *pr2;
54:         *pr2 = temp;
55:       }
56:   }
57:
58:   pr --= MAX_RECT -- 1; // reset pointer
59:   // display rectangles sorted by area
60:   for (i = 0; i < MAX_RECT; i++, pr++)
61:     printf("Rect # %d has area %5.4lf\n", pr-->id, pr-->area);
62:   return 0;
63: }
```

Here is a sample session with the program in Listing 4.7.

```
Enter (X,Y) coord. for ULC of rect. # 0 : 1 1
Enter (X,Y) coord. for LRC of rect. # 0 : 2 2
Enter (X,Y) coord. for ULC of rect. # 1 : 1.5 1.5
Enter (X,Y) coord. for LRC of rect. # 1 : 3 4
Enter (X,Y) coord. for ULC of rect. # 2 : 1 2
Enter (X,Y) coord. for LRC of rect. # 2 : 5 8
Enter (X,Y) coord. for ULC of rect. # 3 : 4 6
Enter (X,Y) coord. for LRC of rect. # 3 : 8 4
Rect # 0 has area 1.0000
Rect # 1 has area 3.7500
Rect # 3 has area 8.0000
Rect # 2 has area 24.0000
```

The program in Listing 4.7 declares the pointers `pr` and `pr2` in lines 29 and 30, respectively. These pointers access the structure of type `rect`. The program initializes the pointer `pr` with the base address of array `r`.

The first `for` loop, which begins at line 33, uses the pointer `pr` to access the elements of array `r`. The loop increment part contains the expression `pr++`, which uses pointer arithmetic to make the pointer `pr` access the next element in array `r`. The input statements in lines 36 and 39 use the pointer `pr` to access the members `ulc` and `lrc`. Notice that the statements use the pointer access operator `->` to allow pointer `pr` to access the members `ulc` and `lrc`. The statements in lines 40 through 43 also use the pointer `pr` to access the members `id`, `ulc`, `lrc`, and `area`, using the `->` operator.

The statement in line 46 resets the address stored in pointer `pr` by `MAX_RECT` units (that is `MAX_RECT * sizeof(double)` bytes). The nested loops in lines 48 through 56 use the pointers `pr` and `pr2`. The outer `for` loop increments the address in pointer `pr` by one before the next iteration. The statement in line 49 assigns `pr + 1` to the pointer `pr2`. This statement gives the pointer `pr2` the initial access to the element `i + 1` in array `r`. The inner `for` loop increments the pointer `pr2` by 1 before the next iteration. Thus, the nested `for` loops use the pointers `pr` and `pr2` to access the elements of array `r`. The `if` statement in line 51 uses the pointers `pr` and `pr2` to access the `area` member in comparing the areas of various rectangles. The statements in line 52 through 54 swap the elements of array `r`, which are accessed by pointers `pr` and `pr2`. Notice that the statements use `*pr` and `*pr2` to access an entire element of array `r`.

The statement in line 58 resets the address in the pointer `pr` by subtracting `MAX_RECT - 1`. The last `for` loop also uses the pointer `pr` to access and display the members `id` and `area` of the various elements in array `r`.

This program illustrates that you can completely manipulate an array using pointers only. They are powerful and versatile.

Pointers and Dynamic Memory

The programs presented thus far create the space for their variables at compile-time. When the programs start running, the variables have their memory spaces preassigned. There are many applications in which you need to create new variables during the program execution. You need to allocate the memory space dynamically for these new variables at runtime. The designers of C++ have chosen to introduce new operators, which are not found in C, to handle the dynamic allocation and de-allocation of memory. These new C++ operators are `new` and `delete`. While the C-style dynamic memory functions `malloc`, `calloc`, and `free` are still available, you should use the operators `new` and `delete`. These operators are more aware of the type of dynamic data that is created than are functions `malloc`, `calloc`, and `free`. Also, the standard C functions for creating and deleting dynamic memory won't handle class constructors and destructors (which are discussed on Day 8).

Syntax

The *new* and *delete* Operators

The general syntax for using the `new` and `delete` operators in creating dynamic scalar variables is

```
pointer = new type;
delete pointer;
```

The operator `new` returns the address of the dynamically allocated variable. The operator `delete` removes the dynamically allocated memory accessed by a pointer. If the dynamic allocation of operator `new` fails, it throws an exception of type `xalloc` (declared in the EXCEPT.H header file). Therefore, you should make sure that you enclose your dynamic memory allocations in `try` blocks if you suspect trouble.

Example

```
try {
   int *pint;
   pint = new int;
   *pint = 33;
   cout << "Pointer pint stores " << *pint;
   delete pint;
}
catch(xalloc)
{
   cout <<< "Couldn't allocate memory." << endl;
}
```

Syntax

A Dynamic Array

To allocate and de-allocate a dynamic array, use the following general syntax:

```
arrayPointer = new type[arraySize];
delete[] arrayPointer;
```

The operator `new` returns the address of the dynamically allocated array. If the allocation fails, the operator throws an `xalloc` exception. The operator `delete` removes the dynamically allocated array that is accessed by a pointer.

Example

```
try {
   const int MAX = 10;
   int* pint;
   pint = new int[MAX];
   for (int i = 0; i < MAX; i++)
      pint[i] = i * i;
   for (i = 0; i < MAX; i++)
      cout << *(pint + i) << endl;
   delete [] pint;
}
catch(xalloc)
{
   cout << "Couldn't allocate memory." << endl;
}
```

DO | **DON'T**

DO maintain access to dynamic variables and arrays at all times. Such access does not need the original pointers that were used to create these dynamic variables and arrays. Here is an example.

```
int* p = new int;
int* q;
*p = 123;
q = p; // q now also points to 123
p = new int; // create another dynamic variable
*p = 345; // p points to 345 whereas q points to 123
cout << *p << " " << *q << " " << (*p + *q) << "\n";
delete p;
delete q;
```

DON'T forget to delete dynamic variables and arrays at the end of their scope. If you do, there is the potential of a "memory leak." This is the condition when memory seems to keep getting lower in your system for no apparent reason. It means that something has allocated memory without freeing it.

Using pointers to create and access dynamic data can be illustrated with the next program, PTR5.CPP (Listing 4.8). This program is a modified version of program ARRAY1.CPP that calculates the average value for data in an array. The program begins by prompting you to enter the actual number of data and validates your input. Then the program prompts you for the data and calculates the average of the data in the array. Next, the program displays the average value.

Type

Listing 4.8. Source code for the program PTR5.CPP.

```
/*
  C++ program that demonstrates the pointers to manage
  dynamic data
*/
#include <iostream.h>
#include <except.h>

const int MAX = 30;

main()
{

    double* x;
    double sum, sumx = 0, mean;
    int *n;

    try { n = new int; }
    catch {xalloc&) { return 1; }

    do { // obtain number of data points
        cout << "Enter number of data points [2 to "
             << MAX << "] : ";
        cin >> *n;
        cout << "\n";
    } while (*n < 2 || *n > MAX);
    // create tailor-fit dynamic array
    try { x = new double[*n]; }
    catch (xalloc&) {
      delete n;
      return 1;
    }
    // prompt user for data
    for (int i = 0; i < *n; i++) {
        cout << "X[" << i << "] : ";
        cin >> x[i];
    }

    // initialize summations
    sum = *n;
    // calculate sum of observations
    for (i = 0; i < *n; i++)
        sumx += *(x + i);

    mean = sumx / sum; // calculate the mean value
    cout << "\nMean = " << mean << "\n\n";
```

continued

Listing 4.8. continued

```
46:     // deallocate dynamic memory
47:     delete n;
48:     delete [] x;
49:     return 0;
50: }
```

Here is a sample session with the program in Listing 4.8.

```
Enter number of data points [2 to 30] : 5

X[0] : 1
X[1] : 2
X[2] : 3
X[3] : 4
X[4] : 5

Mean = 3
```

The program in Listing 4.8 uses two pointers for dynamic allocations. Line 13 declares the first pointer, which is used to allocate and access the dynamic array. Line 15 declares the pointer to create a dynamic variable.

The statement in line 17 uses the operator `new` to allocate the space for a dynamic `int` variable. The statement returns the address of the dynamic data to the pointer `n`. The `catch` statement in line 18 determines whether the dynamic allocation failed. If so, the function `main` exits and returns an exit code of `1` (to flag an error).

The `do-while` loop in lines 20 through 25 prompts you to enter the number of data points. The statement in line 23 stores your input in the dynamic variable accessed by pointer `n`. The statement uses the pointer reference `*n` for this access. The `while` clause also uses `*n` to access the value in the dynamic variable. In fact, all the statements in the program access the number of data points using the pointer reference `*n`.

The statement in line 27 creates a dynamic array using the operator `new`. The statement creates a dynamic `double`-typed array with the number of elements that you specify. This feature demonstrates the advantage of using dynamic allocation to create custom-fit arrays. The `catch` statement in line 28 determines whether the allocation of the dynamic array was successful. If not, the statements in lines 29 and 30 de-allocate the dynamic variable accessed by pointer[ ] and exit the function with a return value of `1`.

The `for` loop in lines 33 through 36 prompts you to enter values for the dynamic array. The statement in line 35 stores your input to the element `i` of the dynamic array. Notice that the statement uses the expression `x[i]` to access the targeted element. This form resembles that of static arrays. C++ treats the expression `x[i]` as equivalent to `*(x + i)`. In fact , the program uses the latter form in the second `for` loop in lines 41 and 42. The statement in line 42 accesses the elements in the dynamic array using the form `*(x + i)`.

The last statements in function `main` delete the dynamic variable and array. The statement in line 47 de-allocates the space for the dynamic variable accessed by pointer `n`. The statement in line 48 deletes the dynamic array accessed by pointer `x`.

Far Pointers

The architecture of processors, such as the family of Intel 80×86, features segmented memory. Each segment is 64 kilobytes (KB) in size. Using segments has advantages and disadvantages. This storage scheme supports two types of pointers: *near pointers* and *far pointers.*

NEW TERM Within a segment you can use near pointers to access data in the same segment. The pointers only store the offset address in the segment and, thus, require fewer bytes to store their address. By contrast, far pointers store the segment and offset addresses and, thus, they require more space. Windows applications use far pointers.

To declare far pointers, insert the keyword `__far` (or sometimes `_far`) between the type and the name of the pointer.

It's important to note that far pointers are extremely non-portable. That is, they only apply to applications written for the IBM PC and compatible computers, and only then when in a 16-bit mode, such as MS-DOS or Windows 3.1. If you upgrade to the full Borland C++ compiler and write for Windows NT or any other 32-bit version of Windows, you will be able to ignore far pointers completely.

You also should note that far pointers really only make sense when compiling in something other than the large memory model (changeable in the Project dialog box accessible from the Options menu in the IDE). I strongly recommend that you always compile in large model and never leave it. The memory savings you get from using other memory models is minimal compared to the potential for bugs and consternation in mixing and matching far and near pointers.

Summary

Today's lesson introduced you to user-defined data types and covered the following topics:

- You can use the `typedef` statements to create alias types of existing types and define array types. The general syntax for using `typedef` is

  ```
  typedef knownType newType;
  ```

- Enumerated data types enable you to declare unique identifiers that represent a collection of logically related constants. The general syntax for declaring an enumerated type is

  ```
  enum enumType { <list of enumerated identifiers> };
  ```

- Structures enable you to define a new type that logically groups several fields or members. These members can be predefined types or other structures. The general syntax for declaring a structure is

```
struct structTag {
< list of members >
};
```

- Unions are a form of variant structures. The general syntax for unions is

```
union unionTag {
type1 member1;
type2 member2;
 ...
typeN memberN;
};
```

- Reference variables are aliases of the variables that they reference. To declare a reference variable, place the `&` after the data type of the reference variable or to the left of the variable's name.
- Pointers are variables that store the addresses of other variables or data. C++ uses pointers to offer flexible and efficient manipulation of data and system resources.
- Pointers to existing variables use the `&` operator to obtain the addresses of these variables. Armed with these addresses, pointers offer access to the data in their associated variables. To access the value by using a pointer, use the `*` operator followed by the name of the pointer.
- Arrays are groups of variables stored in a list with the same name, and they're useful for holding on to collections of the same type of data.
- Pointers access the elements of arrays by being assigned the base address of a class. C++ considers the name of an array as equivalent to the pointer of the base address. For example, the name of the array `X` is treated as `&X[0]`. Pointers can be used to sequentially traverse the elements of an array to store and/or recall values from these elements.
- Pointers to structures manipulate structures and access their members. C++ provides the `->` operator in order to allow a pointer access to the members of a structure.
- Pointers can create and access dynamic data by using the operators `new` and `delete`. These operators enable you to create dynamic variables and arrays. The `new` operator assigns the address of the dynamic data to the pointer used in creating and accessing the data. The operator `delete` assists in recuperating the space of dynamic data when that information is no longer needed.
- Far pointers are pointers that store both the segment and the offset addresses of an item. Near pointers only store the offset address of an item. Far pointers require more storage than near pointers.

Q&A

Q Does C++ support pointers to the predefined type `void`?

A Yes, `void*` pointers are considered typeless pointers and can be used to copy arbitrary data.

Q Because C++ pointers (including `void*` pointers) have types, can I use typecasting to translate the data accessed by the general-purpose `void*` pointers to non-`void*` pointers?

A Yes. C++ enables you to typecast pointer references, such as

```
void* p = data;
long *lp = (long*) p;
```

The pointer `lp` uses the typecast to translate the data it accesses.

Q What happens if I delete a dynamic array by using the `delete` operator without following it with the empty brackets?

A The effect of deleting an array with a plain `delete` operator is undefined. Expect the plain `delete` operator to leave orphaned dynamic memory and cause memory leaks.

4

Q Can a structure contain a pointer to itself?

A Yes. Many structures that model dynamic data structures use this type of declaration. For example, the following structure models the nodes of a dynamic list with pointer-based links:

```
struct listNode {
dataType data;
listNode *next;
};
```

Q Does C++ allow the declaration of a pointer-to-structure type before declaring the structure?

A Yes. This feature makes declaring nodes of dynamic data structures possible.

Q Does C++ allow pointers that access the addresses of other pointers?

A Yes. C++ supports pointers-to-pointers (also called *double pointers*). To declare such pointers, use two `*` characters, as shown in the following example, which declares the double pointer `p`:

```
int x;
int *px = &x;
int **p = &px;
```

The expression `*p` accesses the pointer `px`, and the expression `**p` accesses the variable `x`.

Workshop

The Workshop provides quiz questions to help you solidify your understanding of the material covered and exercises to provide you with experience in using what you've learned. Try to understand the quiz and exercise answers before continuing on to the next day's lesson. Answers are provided in Appendix A.

Quiz

1. What is the error in the following statements?

```
enum Boolean { false, true };
enum State { on, off };
enum YesNo { yes, no };
enum DiskDriveStatus { on , off };
```

2. True or false? The declaration of the following enumerated type is incorrect.

```
enum YesNo ( no = 0, No = 0, yes = 1, Yes = 1 };
```

3. What is the problem with the following program?

```
#include <iostream.h>
int main()
{
  int *p = new int;
  cout << "Enter a number : ";
  cin >> *p;
  cout << "The square of " << *p << " = " << (*p * *p);
  return 0;
}
```

Exercises

1. Modify the program PTR4.CPP to create the program PTR6.CPP, which uses the `Comb` sort method to sort the array of rectangles.
2. Define a structure that can be used to model a dynamic array of integers. The structure should have a member to access the dynamic data and a member to store the size of the dynamic array. Call the structure `intArrStruct`.
3. Define a structure that can be used to model a dynamic matrix. The structure should have a member to access the dynamic data and two members to store the number of rows and columns. Call the structure `matStruct`.

WEEK
1

Functions

Today you will be introduced to a vital aspect of C++: functions. Functions provide a way of compartmentalizing parts of a program into more easily accessible pieces.

- Declaring and prototyping functions
- Local variables in functions
- Static variables in functions
- Macro expansion
- Inline functions
- Exiting functions
- Default arguments
- Passing arguments by reference
- Recursive functions
- Function overloading

Declaring and Prototyping Functions

Most programming languages use functions and procedures. C++ does not support formal procedures. Instead, all C++ routines are functions.

NEW TERM *Functions* are the primary building blocks that conceptually extend the C++ language to fit your custom programs. One could think of each function as a small routine that gets a small, very specific piece of a job done.

Syntax

Declaring Functions

The general form for the ANSI C style of declaring functions (which is maintained by C++) is

```
returnType functionName(typedParameterList)
```

Examples

```
double sqr(double y)
{ return y * y; }

char prevChar(char c)
{ return c - 1; }
```

Remember the following rules when declaring C++ functions:

- The return type of the C++ function appears before the function's name.
- If the parameter list is empty, you still use empty parentheses. C++ also allows you the option of using the `void` keyword to explicitly state that there are no parameters, but this is a throwback to the C language. I only mention the `void` keyword here so that you can recognize old code you might encounter that has been updated from C.

- The typed parameter list consists of a list of typed parameters that use the following general format:

  ```
  [const] type1 parameter1, [const] type2 parameter2, ...
  ```

  This format shows that the individual parameter is declared like a variable—you state the type first and then the parameter's identifier. The list of parameters in C++ is comma-delimited. In addition, you cannot group a sequence of parameters that have exactly the same data type. You must declare each parameter explicitly. If a parameter has the `const` clause, the compiler makes sure that the function does *not* alter the arguments of that parameter.

- The body of a C++ function is enclosed in braces ({}). There is no semicolon after the closing brace.

- C++ supports passing arguments either by value or by reference. By default, parameters pass their arguments by value. Consequently, the functions work with a copy of the data, preserving the original data. To declare a reference parameter, insert the `&` character after the data type of the parameter. A reference parameter becomes an alias to its arguments. Any changes made to the reference parameter also affect the original variable used as the argument. The general form for reference parameters is

  ```
  [const] type1& parameter1, [const] type2& parameter2, ...
  ```

  If a parameter has the `const` clause, the compiler makes sure that the function does not alter the arguments of that parameter. (Yes, there are good reasons for passing arguments by `const` reference, and they are discussed later in this chapter.)

- C++ supports local constants, data types, and variables. Although these data items can appear in nested block statements, C++ does not support nested functions.

- The `return` keyword returns the function's value.

- If the function's return type is `void`, you do not have to use the `return` keyword, unless you need to provide an exit route in the middle of the function.

5

NEW TERM C++ dictates that you either declare or define a function before you use it. Declaring a function, commonly called *prototyping*, lists the function name, return type, and the number and type of its parameters. Including the name of the parameter is optional. You also need to place a semicolon after the close parenthesis. C++ requires that you declare a function if you call it before you define it.

The following is a simple example of prototyping:

```
// prototype the function square
double sqr(double);

main()
{
   cout << "5^2 = " << sqr(5) << "\n";
   return 0;
}
```

```
double sqr(double z)
{ return z * z; }
```

Notice that the declaration of function sqr only contains the type of its single parameter. This is a common practice; however, I discourage it. By placing the name of parameters in prototypes, it makes figuring out the purpose of a function easier, especially if it's been a while since you wrote the function and can't remember exactly what it's supposed to do.

Typically, the declaration of a function is global. You still may prototype a function within its client function. This technique conceals the prototype from other functions.

Calling a function requires you to supply its parameter with arguments. The arguments are mapped onto the parameter by the sequence in which the parameters are declared. The arguments must be data types that match or are compatible with those of the parameters. For example, you may have a function volume, defined as follows:

```
double volume(double length, double width, double height)
{
   return length * width * height;
}
```

To call the function volume, you need to supply double-typed arguments or arguments with compatible types (which, in this case, are all of numeric data types). Here are a number of sample calls to the function volume.

```
double len = 34, width = 55, ht = 100;
int i = 3;
long j = 44;
unsigned k = 33;

cout << volume(len, width, ht) << endl;
cout << volume(1, 2, 3) << endl;
cout << volume(i, j, k) << endl;
cout << volume(len, j, 22.3) << endl;
```

Note: C++ enables you to discard the result of a function. This type of function call is used when the focus is on what the function does rather than its return value.

Syntax

The Declaration of Exceptions Thrown by a Function

The syntax for declaring functions that can or cannot throw exceptions is

```
[returnType] functionName([parameterList]);
```

The preceding syntax declares that the function functionName can throw any type of exception.

```
[returnType] functionName([parameterList]) throw();
```

The preceding syntax declares that the function `functionName` should *not* throw an exception.

```
 [returnType] functionName([parameterList])
throw(exceptionTypeList)
```

The preceding syntax declares that the function `functionName` can only throw an exception in the comma-delimited exception type list, `exceptionTypeList`.

Examples

```
void parse();
void calc() throw();
void input() throw(TFileErr, TMemoryErr);
```

The declaration of function `parse` states that the function can throw any type of exception. By contrast, the declaration of function `calc` states that the function cannot throw any type of exception. The declaration of function `input` states that the function can only throw the exceptions of type `TFileErr`, `TMemoryErr`, or their descendant classes. This function `throws` an exception of type `TFileError` (a user-defined exception type). The catch block handles the `TFileError` exception type by displaying an error message.

Turbo C++ requires that you declare the `throw` clause in both the declaration and the definition of a function.

Local Variables in Functions

5

Good structured-programming techniques foster the notion that functions should be as independent and as reusable as possible. Consequently, functions can have their own data types, constants, and variables to give them this independence.

NEW TERM The *local variable* in a function exists only when that function is called. Once the function terminates, the runtime system removes the local variables. Consequently, local variables lose their data between function calls. In addition, the runtime system applies any initialization to local variables every time the host function is called.

DO	DON'T

DO use local variables to store and alter the values of parameters that are declared with the `const` clause.

DON'T declare a local variable to have the same name as a global variable that you need to access in the function.

Look at an example. Listing 5.1 displays the value of the mathematical function

```
f(X) = X2 - 5 X + 10
```

and its slope at the argument 3.5. The program calculates the slope using the approximation

```
f'(X) = (f(X + h) - f(X - h)) / 2h
```

where `h` is a small increment.

Listing 5.1. Source code for the program VAR2.CPP.

```
1:  // C++ program that illustrates local variables in a function
2:
3:  #include <iostream.h>
4:
5:  double f(double x)
6:  {
7:    return x * x — 5 * x + 10;
8:  }
9:
10: double slope(double x)
11: {
12:   double f1, f2, incrim = 0.01 * x;
13:   f1 = f(x + incrim);
14:   f2 = f(x — incrim);
15:   return (f1 — f2) / 2 / incrim;
16: }
17:
18: main()
19: {
20:  double x = 3.5;
21:
22:   cout << "f("  << x << ") = " << f(x) << "\n"
23:        << "f'(" << x << ") = " << slope(x) << "\n";
24:
25:   return 0;
26: }
```

Here is a sample session with the program in Listing 5.1.

```
f(3.5) = 4.75
f'(3.5) = 2
```

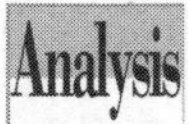

The program in Listing 5.1 declares three functions, namely `f` (in line 5), `slope` (in line 10), and `main` (in line 18). The function `f` is simple and returns the value of the mathematical function. The function `f` is void of local variables. By contrast, the function `slope` declares the local variables `f1`, `f2`, and `incrim`. This function also initializes the latter variable. Line 13 assigns the value of `f(x + incrim)` to the local variable `f1`. Line 14 assigns the value of `f(x - incrim)` to the local variable `f2`. Line 15 returns the value for function `slope` using the local variables `f1`, `f2`, and `incrim`. The function `main` simply displays the values of the mathematical function and its slope when `x = 3.5`.

Static Variables in Functions

In Listing 5.1, the local variables in the function `slope` lose their values once the function terminates. C++ enables you to declare a local variable as static simply by placing the `static` keyword to the left of its data type. Static variables usually are initialized. This initialization is performed once, when the host function is called for the first time.

NEW TERM There are a number of programming techniques that require maintaining the values of local variables between function calls. These special local variables are called *static variables*. They're sort of like global variables, in that they are always around, but they can only be accessed from within the function in which they're declared—they are local to that function.

When the host function terminates, the static variables maintain their values. The compiler supports this language feature by storing static variables in a separate memory location that is maintained while the program is running. You can use the same names for static variables in different functions. This duplication does not confuse the compiler because it keeps track of which function owns which static variables.

Look at a simple program. Listing 5.2 uses a function with static variables to maintain a moving average. The program supplies its own data and calls that function several times in order to obtain and display the current value of the moving average.

Type

Listing 5.2. Source code for the program STATIC1.CPP.

```
// C++ program that illustrates static local variables

#include <iostream.h>

double mean(double x)
{
  static double sum = 0;
  static double sumx = 0;

  sum = sum + 1;
  sumx = sumx + x;
  return sumx / sum;
}

main()
{
  cout << "mean = " << mean(1) << "\n";
  cout << "mean = " << mean(2) << "\n";
  cout << "mean = " << mean(4) << "\n";
  cout << "mean = " << mean(10) << "\n";
  cout << "mean = " << mean(11) << "\n";
  return 0;
}
```

Here is a sample session with the program in Listing 5.2.

```
mean = 1
mean = 1.5
mean = 2.33333
mean = 4.25
mean = 5.6
```

The program in Listing 5.2 declares the function `mean`, which contains static local variables. Lines 7 and 8 declare the static variables `sum` and `sumx`, respectively. The function initializes both static variables with `0`. The statement in line 10 increments the variable `sum` by 1. The statement in line 11 increments the variable `sumx` by the value of parameter `x`. Line 12 returns the updated moving average, obtained by dividing `sumx` by `sum`.

The function `main` issues a series of calls to function `mean`. The stream output statements in lines 17 through 21 display the updated moving average. These results are possible thanks to the static local variables `sum` and `sumx` in function `mean`. If static variables were not supported by C++, you would need to resort to using global variables—a highly questionable programming choice.

The *#define* Statement Revisited

It now is time to come back to the `#define` statement. It was mentioned on Day 2 that the `#define` statement really was creating macros, and then I went over the simple macro substitution in which a single identifier was replaced with another. Actually, macros also can take parameters in much the same way as regular functions, but you first must take a little care.

Syntax

Parameters in the *#define* Macro

The parameterized syntax for the `#define` function is

```
#define macroName(arg1, arg2, ..., argN) substitution
```

The `substitution` expression can be anything, and doesn't even need to make use of the parameters given to the macro name (it's common to turn off a macro simply by defining it as blank, with no `substitution` expression). It also is important to note that there are no types involved here; the parameters are just names that are to be used in the `substitution` expression. Furthermore, be very careful to not put a semicolon on the end of the `substitution` expression. The following is an example of how to use a macro to figure out the smallest (`min`) and greatest (`max`) of two variables:

```
#define min(n1, n2) (((n1) < (n2)) ? (n1) : (n2))
#define max(n1, n2) (((n1) > (n2)) ? (n1) : (n2))
```

Note all the parentheses used in that last example. In order to help explain that, I'm going to digress slightly from the topic and discuss how arguments are passed to functions.

When a parameter is sent to a function, a brand new variable is declared (the one inside the function definition's parentheses) and the passed argument is copied into this new declaration. When you use the variable inside the function, you really are using the copy of the original value. This actually explains why actions taken on the parameter inside the function don't affect the originally passed value: you're not even using it. References are a slightly different case, and I'll explain why when I describe passing pointers to functions later on today.

Getting back to the macro's parameters, you might begin to understand a little more about just how different they are from functions. Their arguments really are just substitutions; no new declarations are made and no variables are copied. To expand on the previous example, regard the following which shows a before and after picture, comparing the original source code to what the preprocessor produces for the compiler to use:

```
#define min(n1, n2) (((n1) < (n2)) ? (n1) : (n2))
double num1 = 50, num2 = 5, rslt;
rslt = min(num1 / 2, num2 * 2);
```

Now take a look at that last line when the preprocessor is done with it.

```
rslt = (((50 / 2) < (5 * 2)) ? (50 / 2) : (5 * 2));
```

First note that if there had been a semicolon at the end of the first line, there would have been two at the end of the final result, because the last line of the original source line that calls `min` has a semicolon at its end.

Finally, to explain about all the parentheses, look at what that expression would have looked like without all the parentheses in the original macro definition.

```
rslt = 50 / 2 < 5 * 2 ? 50 / 2 : 5 * 2;
```

What operator is doing what to what else? By placing the parentheses, you ensure that if an expression is used as an argument (rather than just a simple variable or constant), it won't confuse the compiler when the preprocessor is done with the substitutions.

Inline Functions

Using functions requires the overhead of calling them, passing their arguments, and returning their results. While macros get around this problem, they have the added problem of being only macros, and they lose all the advantages of local variables, and so on, that are available in full-fledged functions. C++ enables you to use *inline functions* that expand into their statements. Thus, inline functions offer faster execution time—especially helpful where speed is critical—at the cost of expanding the code.

Syntax

The *inline* Function

The general syntax for the `inline` function is

```
inline returnType functionName(typedParameterList)
```

Examples

```
inline double cube(double x)
{ return x * x * x; }

inline char nextChar(char c)
{ return c + 1; }
```

The alternative to using inline functions is the use of the `#define` directive to create macro-based pseudo-functions. Many C++ programmers strongly recommend foregoing this method in favor of inline functions. The justification for this is that inline functions provide type checking. Macros created with the `#define` directive do not. However, this lack of type checking is exactly what makes macros so appealing: one can write a single macro that will act on many different types of data by expanding the same code in place for each instance.

Also, because the parameters to an inline function are used as if they were sent into a real function, rather than expanded in a macro, there is less risk of side effects. Regard the `min` macro, again, and a dangerous use of it.

```
#define min(n1, n2) (((n1) < (n2)) ? (n1) : (n2))
int num1 = 5, num2 = 10;
rslt = min(++num1, num2);
```

The last line expands to the following:

```
rslt = (((++num1) < (num2)) ? (++num1) : (num2);
```

Note that both `rslt` and `num1` will end up with the value of 7. This is because `num1` is incremented twice: once in the comparison and once in the result portion of the `?:` operator. An inline function would only increment `num1` once before executing the contents of the function.

There is a middle ground that allows for macro-like expansion of full-fledged functions. These are called templates and are explained on Day 10.

DO | **DON'T**

DO start by declaring inline functions as ordinary functions when you develop your programs. Non-inline functions are easier to debug. Once your program is working, insert the inline keyword where needed.

DON'T use inline functions on anything really large. Again, it's important to stress that inline functions are expanded as if they were typed directly at the location from where they are called. There also are some restrictions on what the compiler will let you do within an inline function; but, if you put the `inline` keyword on something the compiler doesn't like, it will just give you a warning and ignore the `inline` keyword. Your program still will compile and run just fine.

DON'T declare inline functions with many statements. The increase in .EXE program size may not be acceptable.

Here is a simple example of a program that uses inline functions. Listing 5.3 contains the source code for the program INLINE1.CPP. This program prompts you for a number, and then calculates and displays the square and cube values for your input.

Listing 5.3. Source code for the program INLINE1.CPP.

```
1:  // C++ program that illustrates inline functions
2:
3:  #include <iostream.h>
4:
5:  inline double sqr(double x)
6:  {
7:    return x * x;
8:  }
9:
10: inline double cube(double x)
11: {
12:   return x * x * x;
13: }
14:
15: main()
16: {
17:   double x;
18:
19:   cout << "Enter a number: ";
20:   cin >> x;
21:
22:   cout << "square of "  << x << " = " << sqr(x) << "\n"
23:        << "cube of " << x << " = " << cube(x) << "\n";
24:
25:   return 0;
26: }
```

Here is a sample session with the program in Listing 5.3.

```
Enter a number: 2.5
square of 2.5 = 6.25
cube of 2.5 = 15.625
```

The program in Listing 5.3 declares the inline functions `sqr` and `cube` on lines 5 and 10, respectively. Each function heading starts with the keyword `inline`. The other aspects of the inline functions resemble short normal functions. The function `main` calls the functions `sqr` and `cube` on lines 22 and 23 to display the square and cube values, respectively.

Exiting Functions Prematurely

Usually you make an early exit from a function because particular conditions do not allow you to proceed with executing the statements in that function. C++ provides the `return` statement to exit from a function. If the function has the `void` type, you then employ the statement `return` and include no expression after the return. By contrast, if you exit a non-`void` function, the return statement should produce a value that indicates the purpose for exiting the function.

Default Arguments

Default arguments are a language feature that is quite simple and yet very powerful. When you omit the argument of a parameter that has a default argument, that argument is used automatically.

Note: C++ permits you to assign default arguments to the parameters of a function.

Using default arguments requires that you follow these rules:

- Once you assign a default argument to a parameter, you must do so for all subsequent parameters in the same parameter list. You cannot randomly assign default arguments to parameters. This rule means that the parameter list can be divided into two sublists: the leading parameters, which do not have default arguments, and the trailing parameters, which do.
- The caller of the function must provide an argument for every parameter that has no default argument.
- The caller may omit the argument for a parameter that has a default argument.
- Once you omit the argument for a parameter with a default argument, the arguments for all subsequent parameters also must be omitted.

Note: The best way to list the parameters with default arguments is to locate them according to the likelihood of using their default arguments. Place the least-likely-to-be-used arguments first and the most-likely-to-be-used arguments last.

Look at a simple example that uses a function with default arguments. Listing 5.4 shows the source code for the program DEFARGS1.CPP. The program prompts you to enter the x and y coordinates of two points. The program then calculates and displays the distance between the two points and between each point and the origin (0, 0).

Listing 5.4. Source code for the program DEFARGS1.CPP.

```
1:  // C++ program that illustrates default arguments
2:
3:  #include <iostream.h>
4:  #include <math.h>
5:
6:  inline double sqr(double x)
7:  { return x * x; }
8:
9:  double distance(double x2, double y2,
10:                  double x1 = 0, double y1 = 0)
11: {
12:   return sqrt(sqr(x2 — x1) + sqr(y2 — y1));
13: }
14:
15: main()
16: {
17:   double x1, y1, x2, y2;
18:
19:   cout << "Enter x coordinate for point 1: ";
20:   cin >> x1;
21:   cout << "Enter y coordinate for point 1: ";
22:   cin >> y1;
23:   cout << "Enter x coordinate for point 2: ";
24:   cin >> x2;
25:   cout << "Enter y coordinate for point 2: ";
26:   cin >> y2;
27:
28:   cout << "distance between points = "
29:        << distance(x1, y1, x2, y2) << "\n";
30:   cout << "distance between point 1 and (0,0) = "
31:        << distance(x1, y1, 0) << "\n";
32:   cout << "distance between point 2 and (0,0) = "
33:        << distance(x2, y2) << "\n";
34:
35:   return 0;
36: }
```

Here is a sample session with the program in Listing 5.4.

```
Enter x coordinate for point 1: 1
Enter y coordinate for point 1: 1
Enter x coordinate for point 2: --1
Enter y coordinate for point 2: 1
distance between points = 2
distance between point 1 and (0,0) = 1.41421
distance between point 2 and (0,0) = 1.41421
```

The program in Listing 5.4 includes not one but two header files. Line 4 uses the `#include` directive to include the MATH.H header file, which declares the square-root math function, `sqrt`. The program declares the inline `sqr` function in line 6. This function returns the square value of the arguments for parameter `x`. The program also declares the function `distance` with four `double`-typed parameters. The parameters `x2` and `y2` represent the x and y coordinates, respectively, for the second point, whereas the parameters `x1` and `y1` represent the x and y coordinates, respectively, for the first point. Both parameters `x1` and `y1` have the default argument of `0`. The function returns the distance between the two points. If you omit the arguments for `x1` and `y1`, the function returns the distance between the point (x2, y2) and the origin (0, 0). If you omit only the argument for the last parameter, the function yields the distance between the points (x2, y2) and (x1, 0).

The function `main` prompts you to enter the x and y coordinates for two points, using the statements in lines 19 through 26. The output statement in lines 28 and 29 calls the function `distance`, providing it with 4 arguments, namely, `x1`, `y1`, `x2`, and `y2`. Therefore, this call to the function `distance` uses no default arguments. By contrast, the statement in lines 30 and 31 calls the function `distance`, supplying it with only three arguments. This call to the function `distance` uses the default argument for the last parameter. The statement in lines 32 and 33 calls the function `distance`, providing it with only two arguments. This call to the function `distance` uses the two default arguments for the third and fourth parameters. You can omit the third argument in the second call to the function `distance` and still compile and run the program.

Passing Arguments by Reference

It's time to talk a little more about how arguments are passed by reference. You already have learned about pointers in general and how they hold the addresses of other variables. References are very similar, except that all the pointer stuff is hidden from you. When you make a reference to another variable, somewhere deep in the compiler is a pointer that is pointing at the original variable, and the reference just hides that fact by allowing you to use the reference as if it were a regular variable, only it continues to modify the original.

Remember that, when it comes to passing arguments to a function, the contents of the original variable is copied into the function's newly declared version of the variable, and it then can be used throughout the life of the function. If you want to modify the original version, you can pass it by reference. At this point, you really are only copying a pointer to the original variable rather than the entire contents of the original. While inside the function, you can use the variable as normal— it's just that you're really modifying the original.

Now, when you're copying the contents of something such as an `int` or a pointer, which are only going to be a few bytes, there's no problem with copying their contents. When it comes to passing something such as a structure, however, you could start copying a tremendous amount of data. Some structures can be in the kilobyte range or larger. If you were to copy its contents every time you passed it to a function, it is conceivably possible that you could slow down your system enough that you would even notice it in realtime.

The solution, of course, is to pass the structure by reference. Now, rather than copying the entire contents of the structure, you are only copying a few bytes to create the reference to the original structure, which is much more manageable.

The problem, of course, is that the function now is capable of modifying the original structure, and that's not always a good thing.

Using *const* in Arguments

The `const` type modifier comes to the rescue here. So far, we've only really discussed it with respect to creating constant variables. It's best to use it as a modifier of such types as pointers and references. By specifying a function's argument as a `const` reference, not only are you preventing the copying of a potentially huge structure, you also are preventing the function from modifying the contents of that structure. The function can look at the structure and use anything inside of it; it's just not allowed to modify any part of it.

Syntax

The *const* argument modifier

The general syntax for using the `const` modifier in function parameters is

```
returnType functionName(const argType &arg)
```

Example

```
struct userInfo {
   int age;
   char name[150];    // Should be big enough for most names
}

void processUserInfo(const userInfo& ui)
{
   if (ui.age < 18) {
      cout << "You're too young to be using this function." << endl;
      return;
   }
   if (ui.age < 21)
      ui.age = 21;       // -=*> !!!ERROR!!! <*=-
}
```

Note the line with the comment about the error. Whereas the compiler will have absolutely no problems with `processUserInfo` checking to make sure the passed user is old enough, the compiler will stop with an error when it encounters this rogue function trying to arbitrarily change the person's age. So much for getting a fake ID.

Now, after all this argument for passing structures by reference rather than by value, let me just say that there's nothing wrong with passing a smaller structure by value. If there are only a few members in it and it doesn't take up much memory on its own, then there's no reason why you shouldn't just pass it right on in. It can be good, however, to get into the habit of just passing structures by reference all the time.

Recursive Functions

There are many problems that can be solved by breaking them down into simpler and similar problems. Such problems are solved using recursion.

NEW TERM *Recursive functions* are functions that obtain a result and/or perform a task by calling themselves. These recursive calls must be limited in order to avoid exhausting the memory resources of the computer. Consequently, every recursive function must examine a condition that determines the end of the recursion.

NEW TERM A common example of a recursive function is the *factorial function.* A factorial of a number is the product of all the integers from 1 to N, with the exclamation point (!) as the mathematical symbol for the factorial function.

The mathematical equation for a factorial is

N! = 1 * 2 * 3 * ... * (N-2) * (N-1) * N

The recursive version of this equation is

N! =N * (N-1)!
(N-1)! = (N-1) * (N-2)!
(N-2)! = (N-2) * (N-3)!
...
2! = 2 * 1!
1! = 1

Recursion entails looping to obtain a result. Most recursive solutions have alternate non-recursive solutions. In some cases, the recursive solutions are more elegant than the non-recursive ones. The factorial function is an example of a mathematical function that can be implemented using either recursion or a non-recursive straightforward loop.

DO	DON'T

DO include a decision-making statement in a recursive function to end the recursion.

DON'T use recursion unless its advantages significantly outweigh the alternate non-recursive solution.

Look at an example that implements the recursive factorial function. Listing 5.5 shows the source code for the program ADVFUN6.CPP. The program prompts you to enter two positive integers; the first one must be greater than or equal to the second one. The program displays the number of combinations and permutations obtained from the two integers. The number of combinations is given by the following equation:

${}_mC_n = m! / ((m - n)! * n!)$

The number of permutations is given by the following equation:

${}_mP_n = m! / (m - n)!$

Listing 5.5. Source code for the program ADVFUN6.CPP.

```
// C++ program that uses a recursive function

#include <iostream.h>

const int MIN = 4;
const int MAX = 30;

double factorial(int i)
{
  if (i > 1)
    return double(i) * factorial(i - 1);
  else
    return 1;
}

double permutation(int m, int n)
{
  return factorial(m) / factorial(m - n);
}

double combination(int m, int n)
{
  return permutation(m, n) / factorial(n);
}

main()
{
  int m, n;

  do {
    cout << "Enter an integer between "
         << MIN << " and " << MAX << " : ";
    cin >> m;
  } while (m < MIN ¦¦ m > MAX);

  do {
    cout << "Enter an integer between "
         << MIN << " and " << m << ": ";
    cin >> n;
  } while (n < MIN ¦¦[]> m);

  cout << "Permutations(" << m << ", " << n
       << ") = " << permutation(m, n) << "\n";
  cout << "Combinations(" << m << ", " << n
       << ") = " << combination(m, n) << "\n";

  return 0;
}
```

Here is a sample session with the program in Listing 5.5.

```
Enter an integer between 4 and 30 : 10
Enter an integer between 4 and 10 : 5
Permutations(10, 5) = 30240
Combinations(10, 5) = 252
```

The program in Listing 5.5 declares the recursive function `factorial` and the functions `permutation`, `combination`, and `main`. The program also declares the global constants `MIN` and `MAX`, which specify the limits of the first integer you enter.

The function `factorial` has a single parameter—the `int`-typed parameter `i`. The function returns a `double`-typed value. The `if` statement in line 10 compares the value of parameter `i` with 1. This comparison determines whether to make a recursive call, in line 11, or to return the value 1, in line 13. The recursive call in line 11 invokes the function `factorial` with the argument `i - 1`. Thus, the recursive call supplies the function with a smaller (or simpler) argument.

The function `permutation` takes two `int`-typed parameters: `m` and `n`. The function calls the recursive function `factorial` twice—once with the argument `m` and once with the argument `m - n`. The function `permutation` returns the ratio of the two calls to the function `factorial`.

The function `combination` also takes two `int`-typed parameters: `m` and `n`. The function calls the function `permutation` and passes it the arguments `m` and `n`. The function also calls the function `factorial` and passes it the argument `n`. The function `combination` returns the ratio of the values returned by the functions `permutation` and `factorial`.

The function `main` declares the `int`-typed variable `m` and `n`. The function uses two `do-while` loops to prompt you for integer values. The output statement in the first loop prompts you to enter an integer between `MIN` and `MAX`. The statement in line 33 stores your input in variable `m`. The `while` clause of the `do-while` loop validates your input. The clause determines whether your input is less than `MIN` or greater than `MAX`. If this condition is true, then the loop iterates again.

The output statement in the second `do-while` loop prompts you to enter an integer between `m` and `MAX`. The statement in line 39 saves your input in variable `n`. The `while` clause validates your input. The clause determines if your input is less than `MIN` or greater than `m`. If this condition is true, then the loop iterates again.

The output statement in lines 42 and 43 displays the permutations of the values in variables `m` and `n`. The statement calls the function `permutation` and passes it the argument `m` and `n`. The output statement in lines 44 and 45 displays the combinations of the values in variables `m` and `n`. The statement calls function `combination` and passes it the argument `m` and `n`.

Function Overloading

Function overloading is a language feature in C++ that has no parallel in C, Pascal, or BASIC. This new feature enables you to declare multiple functions that have the same name but different

parameter lists. The function's return type is not part of the function signature, because C++ enables you to discard the result type. Consequently, the compiler cannot distinguish between two functions with the same parameters and different return type when these return types are omitted.

NEW TERM A parameter list also is called the *function signature.*

Warning: Using default arguments with overloaded functions may duplicate the signature for some of the functions (when the default arguments are used). The C++ compiler can detect this ambiguity and generate a compile-time error.

DO	DON'T
DO use default arguments to reduce the number of overloaded functions.	
DON'T use overloaded functions to implement different operations.	

The real power of overloaded functions is in the capability to define several versions of the same routine that is capable of acting with different types of data. Look at a simple program that uses overloaded functions. Listing 5.6 contains the source code for the program OVERLOAD.CPP. The program performs the following tasks:

- Declares variables that have the `char`, `int`, and `double` types, and initializes them with values
- Displays the initial values
- Invokes overloaded functions that increment the variables
- Displays the updated values stored in the variables

Listing 5.6. Source code for the program OVERLOAD.CPP.

```
// C++ program that illustrates function overloading

#include <iostream.h>

// inc version for int types
void inc(int& i)
{
  i = i + 1;
}
```

continues

Listing 5.6. continued

```

// inc version for double types
void inc(double& x)
{
  x = x + 1;
}

// inc version for char types
void inc(char& c)
{
  c = c + 1;
}

main()
{
  char c = 'A';
  int i = 10;
  double x = 10.2;

  // display initial values
  cout << "c = " << c << "\n"
       << "i = " << i << "\n"
       << "x = " << x << "\n";
  // invoke the inc functions
  inc(c);
  inc(i);
  inc(x);
  // display updated values
  cout << "After using the overloaded inc function\n";
  cout << "c = " << c << "\n"
       << "i = " << i << "\n"
       << "x = " << x << "\n";

  return 0;
}
```

Here is a sample session with the program in Listing 5.6.

```
c = A
i = 10
x = 10.2
After using the overloaded inc function
c = B
i = 11
x = 11.2
```

The program in Listing 5.6 declares three versions of the overloaded void function `inc`. The first version of function `inc` has an `int`-typed reference parameter, `i`. The function increments the parameter `i` by 1. Because the parameter `i` is a reference to its arguments, the action of function `inc(int&)` affects the argument outside the scope of the function. The second version of function `inc` has a `double`-typed reference parameter, `x`. The function increments the parameter x by 1. Because the parameter x is a reference to its arguments, the action of function inc(double&) affects the argument beyond the scope of the function. The second version of function inc has a char-typed reference parameter, c. The function increments the parameter c by 1. The reference parameter affects its arguments outside the scope of the function.

The function main declares the variables c, i, and x to have the char, int, and double types, respectively. The function also initializes the variables c, i, and x using the values 'A', 10, and 10.2, respectively. The statement in lines 30 through 32 displays the initial values in variables c, i, and x. The function main invokes the overloaded function inc in lines 34 through 36. The call to function inc in line 34 ends up calling the function inc(char&) because the argument used is a char-typed variable. The call to function inc in line 35 results in calling the function inc(int&) because the argument used is an int-typed variable. The call to function inc in line 36 invokes the function inc(double&) because the argument used is a double-typed variable. The output statement in lines 39 through 41 displays the updated values in variable c, i, and x.

Summary

Today's lesson presented the various C++ operators and discussed how to use these operators to manipulate data. You learned the following:

- The general form for defining functions is

```
returnType functionName(parameterList)
{
    <declarations of data items>

    <function body>
    return returnValue;
}
```

  You need to prototype a function if it is used by a client function before the prototyped function is defined. The general form for prototyping functions is

```
returnType functionName(parameterList);
```

  You can omit the name of the parameters from the parameter list.

- Local variables in a function support the implementation of highly independent functions. Declaring local variables is similar to declaring global variables.
- Static variables in functions are declared by placing the keyword static before the data type of the variables. Static variables retain their values between function calls. In most cases, you need to initialize static variables. These initial values are assigned to the static variables the first time the program calls the host function.

- Macros enable you to create simple expressions that are capable of working on many different types of data because of their independence from the actual type-checking parts of the C++ compiler.
- Inline functions enable you to expand their statements in place, similar to macro-based pseudo-functions. Unlike these pseudo-functions, however, inline functions perform type checking.
- You exit functions with the `return` statement. `void` functions do not need to include an expression after the `return` keyword.
- Default arguments enable you to assign default values to the parameters of a function. When you omit the argument of a parameter that has a default argument, that argument is used automatically.
- Passing arguments with references can allow the function to modify the original variables, and it also can allow for smaller amounts of memory to be copied when a structure is passed as an argument.
- The `const` type modifier can be extremely useful in preventing arguments that have been passed by reference from being accidentally modified by a function.
- Recursive functions are functions that obtain a result and/or perform a task by calling themselves. These recursive calls must be limited to avoid exhausting the memory resources of the computer. Consequently, every recursive function must examine a condition that determines the end of the recursion.
- Function overloading enables you to declare multiple functions that have the same name but different parameter lists (the parameter list also is called the function signature). The function's return type is not part of the function signature, because C++ enables you to discard the result type.

Q&A

Q Can C++ functions declare nested functions?

A No. Nested functions actually add a lot of overhead at runtime.

Q When can I use static global variables?

A You can use them whenever you want. When the `static` keyword is applied to a global variable (although I still recommend that you never have any global variables in the first place), it tells the compiler to not make it visible to any other source file. This prevents the same variable from being accessed from different nodes of the same project.

Q What is the memory resource used in managing calls to recursive functions?

A The runtime system uses the stack to store intermediate values, including the ones generated by calls to recursive functions. As with other memory resources, stacks have a limited space. Consequently, recursive calls with long sequence or memory-consuming arguments drain the stack space and cause runtime errors.

NEW TERM A *stack* is a memory location where information is inserted and removed on a last-in-first-out (LIFO) priority.

Workshop

The Workshop provides quiz questions to help you solidify your understanding of the material covered and exercises to provide you with experience in using what you've learned. Try to understand the quiz and exercise answers before continuing on to the next day's lesson. Answers are provided in Appendix A.

Quiz

1. What is the output of the following program? What can you say about the function swap?

```
#include <iostream.h>

void swap(int i, int j)
{
  int temp = i;
  i = j;
  j = temp;
}

int main()
{
  int a = 10, b = 3;
  swap(a, b);
  cout << "a = " << a << " and b = " << b;
  return 0;
}
```

2. What is the output of the following program? What can you say about the function swap?

```
#include <iostream.h>

void swap(int& i, int& j)
{
  int temp = i;
  i = j;
  j = temp;
}

int main()
{
```

```
  int a = 10, b = 3;
  swap(a, b);
  cout << "a = " << a << " and b = " << b;
  return 0;
}
```

3. What is the problem with the following overloaded functions?

```
void inc(int& i)
{
  i = i + 1;
}

void inc(int& i, int diff = 1)
{
  i = i + diff;
}
```

4. Where is the error in the following function?

```
double volume(double length, double width = 1, double
height)
{
  return length * width * height
}
```

5. Where is the error in the following function?

```
void inc(int& i, int diff = 1)
{
  i = I + diff;
}
```

6. What is the error in the following program, and how can you correct it?

```
#include <iostream.h>

int main()
{
  double x = 5.2;

  cout << x << "^2 = " << sqr(x);
  return 0;
}

double sqr(double x)
{ return x * x ; }
```

7. Can you use the conditional operator to write the recursive factorial function?

Exercise

Create the program OVERLOD2.CPP by adding a second parameter with default arguments to the overloaded `inc` functions in the program OVERLOAD.CPP. The new parameter should represent the increment value, with a default argument of `1`.

6

WEEK 1

Arrays

Arrays are among the most utilized data structures. They enable programs to store data for later processing. Most popular programming languages support static arrays. Many languages also support dynamic arrays.

Today, you will learn about the following topics related to static arrays:

- Using single-dimensional arrays
- Initializing single-dimensional arrays
- Declaring single-dimensional arrays as function parameters
- Sorting arrays
- Searching arrays
- Declaring multidimensional arrays
- Using multidimensional arrays
- Initializing multidimensional arrays
- Declaring multidimensional arrays as function parameters

Using Single-Dimensional Arrays

On Day 4, I provided a very simple example of using a single-dimensional array. Today let's look at a slightly more involved example. Listing 6.1 shows the source code for the program ARRAY1.CPP. The program uses a 30-element numeric array to calculate the average for the data in a numeric array. The program performs the following tasks:

- Prompts you to enter the number of actual data points. (This value must lie in the range of valid numbers indicated by the prompting message.)
- Prompts you to enter the data for the array elements
- Calculates the average of the data in the array
- Displays the average value

Listing 6.1. Source code for the program ARRAY1.CPP.

```
/*
  C++ program that demonstrates the use of one-dimensional
  arrays.  The average value of the array is calculated.
*/

#include <iostream.h>

const int MAX = 30;

main()
{

```

```
13:     double x[MAX];
14:     double sum, sumx = 0.0, mean;
15:     int i, n;
16:
17:     do { // obtain number of data points
18:         cout << "Enter number of data points [2 to "
19:              << MAX << "] : ";
20:         cin >> n;
21:         cout << "\n";
22:     } while (n < 2 || n > MAX);
23:
24:     // prompt user for data
25:     for (i = 0; i < n; i++) {
26:         cout << "X[" << i << "] : ";
27:         cin >> x[i];
28:     }
29:
30:     // initialize summations
31:     sum = n;
32:
33:     // calculate sum of observations
34:     for (i = 0; i < n; i++)
35:         sumx += x[i];
36:
37:     mean = sumx / sum; // calculate the mean value
38:     cout << "\nMean = " << mean << "\n\n";
39:     return 0;
40: }
```

Here is a sample session with the program in Listing 6.1.

```
Enter number of data points [2 to 30] : 5

X[0] : 12.5
X[1] : 45.7
X[2] : 25.6
X[3] : 14.1
X[4] : 68.4

Mean = 33.26
```

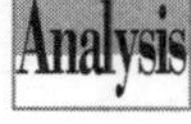

The program in Listing 6.1 declares the global constant `MAX` as the size of the array used in the program. The function `main` declares the `double`-typed array `x`, in line 13, to have `MAX` elements. The function also declares other nonarray variables in lines 14 and 15.

The `do-while` loop, located in lines 17 through 22, obtains the number of data points that you want to store in the array `x`. The output statement in lines 18 and 19 prompts you to enter the number of data points. The output indicates the range of valid numbers, which is `2` to `MAX`. The statement in line 20 obtains your input and stores it in the variable `n`. The `while` clause validates your input. The clause determines if the value in variable `n` is less than `2` or is greater than `MAX`. If this condition is true, the `do-while` loop iterates again to obtain a correct input value.

The `for` loop statement, in lines 25 through 28, prompts you to enter the data. The loop uses the control variable `i` and iterates from `0` to `n-1`, in increments of 1. The output statement in line 26 prompts you to enter the value for the indicated array element. The input statement in line 27 obtains your input and stores it in the element `x[i]`.

The statement in line 31 assigns the integer in variable `n` to the `double`-typed variable `sum`. The `for` loop in lines 34 and 35 adds the values in array `x` to the variable `sumx`. The loop uses the control variable `i` and iterates from `0` to `n-1`, in increments of `1`. The statement in line 35 uses the increment assignment operator to add the value in element `x[i]` to the variable `sumx`.

The statement in line 37 calculates the `mean` value and stores it in variable `mean`. The output statement in line 38 displays the `mean` value.

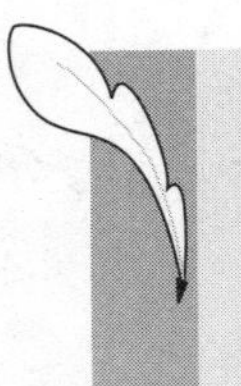

Note: The program in Listing 6.1 shows how to use a `for` loop to process the elements of an array. The loop-continuation test uses the < operator and the value beyond the last valid index. You can use the <= operator followed by the last index. For example, we can write the data-input loop as

```
24:     // prompt user for data
25:     for (i = 0; i <= (n - 1); i++) {
26:         cout << "X[" << i << "] : ";
27:         cin >> x[i];
28:     }
```

This form is not popular, however, because it requires an additional operator, whereas the condition `i < n` does not.

DO	DON'T

DO write the loop-continuation expression so that it uses the minimum number of operators. This approach reduces the code size and speeds up loop execution.

DON'T use the <= operator in the loop-continuation condition, unless using the operator helps you write an expression that minimizes the number of operations.

Initializing Single-Dimensional Arrays

C++ enables you to initialize arrays and is flexible about the initialization. You need to enclose the list of initializing values in a pair of open and close braces (`{ }`). The list is comma-delimited and may continue on multiple lines. If there are fewer items in the initializing list than there are array elements, the compiler assigns 0 to balance the array elements. By contrast, if the list of initializing values has more items than the number of array elements, the compiler flags a compile-time error.

The next program, Listing 6.2, modifies the last program to supply data internally. Consequently, we eliminate the steps that prompt you for the number of data points and the data itself. The program simply displays the array elements (obtained from the initialization list) and the average value for the data. Although this program does not interact with the user, it offers a version that stores data in the source code. You can edit the program periodically to add, edit, and delete data before recalculating a new average value.

Type

Listing 6.2. Source code for the program ARRAY2.CPP.

```
/*
  C++ program that demonstrates the use of single-dimensional
  arrays.  The average value of the array is calculated.
  The array has its values preassigned internally.
*/

#include <iostream.h>

const int MAX = 10;

main()
{

    double x[MAX] = { 12.2, 45.4, 67.2, 12.2, 34.6, 87.4,
                      83.6, 12.3, 14.8, 55.5 };
    double sum = MAX, sumx = 0.0, mean;
    int n = MAX;

    // calculate sum of observations
    cout << "Array is:\n";
    for (int i = 0; i < n; i++) {
        sumx += x[i];
        cout << "x[" << i << "] = " << x[i] << "\n";
    }

    mean = sumx / sum; // calculate the mean value
    cout << "\nMean = " << mean << "\n\n";
    return 0;
}
```

Here is a sample session with the program in Listing 6.2.

```
Array is:
x[0] = 12.2
x[1] = 45.4
x[2] = 67.2
x[3] = 12.2
x[4] = 34.6
x[5] = 87.4
x[6] = 83.6
x[7] = 12.3
```

```
x[8] = 14.8
x[9] = 55.5

Mean = 42.52
```

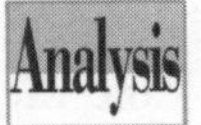

Now we will focus on the initialization of the array `x` in Listing 6.2. Line 14 contains the declaration of array `x` and its initialization. The initializing list, which runs to line 15, is enclosed in a pair of braces and has comma-delimited values. The statement in line 16 declares the variables `sum` and `sumx` and initializes these variables to `MAX` and `0`, respectively. The statement in line 17 declares the `int`-typed variable `n` and initializes it with the value `MAX`. The rest of the program resembles parts of the program in Listing 6.1.

If you are somewhat dismayed by the fact that you have to count the exact number of initializing values, then we have some good news for you: C++ enables you to size an array automatically by using the number of items in the corresponding initializing list. Consequently, you don't need to place a number in the square brackets of the array, and you can let the compiler do the work for you.

DO	DON'T

DO include dummy values in the initializing list, if the initialized array needs to expand later.

DON'T rely on counting the number of items in the initializing list to provide the data for the number of array elements.

Listing 6.3 shows the source code for the program ARRAY3.CPP. This new version uses the feature of automatic array sizing.

Listing 6.3. Source code for the program ARRAY3.CPP.

```
/*
  C++ program that demonstrates the use of single-dimensional
  arrays.  The average value of the array is calculated.
  The array has its values preassigned internally.
*/

#include <iostream.h>

main()
{

    double x[] = { 12.2, 45.4, 67.2, 12.2, 34.6, 87.4,
                   83.6, 12.3, 14.8, 55.5 };
    double sum,  sumx = 0.0, mean;
    int n;

```

```
17:     n = sizeof(x) / sizeof(x[0]);
18:     sum = n;
19:
20:     // calculate sum of observations
21:     cout << "Array is:\n";
22:     for (int i = 0; i < n; i++) {
23:         sumx += x[i];
24:         cout << "x[" << i << "] = " << x[i] << "\n";
25:     }
26:
27:     mean = sumx / sum; // calculate the mean value
28:     cout << "\nNumber of data points = " << n << "\n"
29:          << "Mean = " << mean << "\n";
30:     return 0;
31: }
```

Here is a sample session with the program in Listing 6.3.

```
Array is:
x[0] = 12.2
x[1] = 45.4
x[2] = 67.2
x[3] = 12.2
x[4] = 34.6
x[5] = 87.4
x[6] = 83.6
x[7] = 12.3
x[8] = 14.8
x[9] = 55.5

Number of data points = 10
Mean = 42.52
```

Notice that the program in Listing 6.3 does not declare the constant `MAX`, which appears in the previous version (shown in Listing 6.2). How does the program determine the number of array elements? Line 17 shows that the program calculates the number of elements in array `x` by dividing the size of the array `x` (obtained by using `sizeof(x)`) by the size of the first element (obtained by using `sizeof(x[0])`). You can use this method to obtain the size of any array of any data type.

Array Parameters in Functions

C++ enables you to declare function parameters that are arrays. In fact, C++ permits you to be either specific or general about the size of the array parameter. You can specify the size of the array in the parameter declaration or you can use empty brackets with the array parameter.

A Fixed-Array Parameter

The general syntax for declaring a fixed-array parameter is

```
type parameterName[arraySize]
```

Examples

```
int minArray(int arr[100], int n);
void sort(unsigned dayNum[7]);
```

An Open-Array Parameter

The general syntax for declaring an open-array parameter is

```
type parameterName[]
```

Examples

```
int minArray(int arr[], int n);
void sort(unsigned dayNum[]);
```

DO	DON'T

DO use open-array parameters in functions.

DON'T forget to check the upper bounds of an open-array parameter in general-purpose functions.

Look at a simple example. Listing 6.4 shows the source code for the program ARRAY4.CPP. The program performs the following tasks:

- Prompts you to enter the number of data points, which ranges from 2 to 10
- Prompts you to enter the integer values for the arrays
- Displays the smallest value in the array
- Displays the largest value in the array

Listing 6.4. Source code for the program ARRAY4.CPP.

```
// C++ program that passes arrays as arguments of functions

#include <iostream.h>

const int MAX = 10;

main()
{
  int arr[MAX];
  int n;

  // declare prototypes of functions
```

```
  int getMin(int a[MAX], int size);
  int getMax(int a[], int size);

  do { // obtain number of data points
    cout << "Enter number of data points [2 to "
        << MAX << "] : ";
    cin >> n;
    cout << "\n";
  } while (n < 2 || n > MAX);

  // prompt user for data
  for (int i = 0; i < n; i++) {
    cout << "arr[" << i << "] : ";
    cin >> arr[i];
  }

  cout << "Smallest value in array is "
       << getMin(arr, n) << "\n"
       << "Biggest value in array is "
       << getMax(arr, n) << "\n";
  return 0;
}


int getMin(int a[MAX], int size)
{
  int small = a[0];
  // search for the smallest value in the
  // remaining array elements
  for (int i = 1; i < size; i++)
    if (small > a[i])
      small = a[i];
  return small;
}

int getMax(int a[], int size)
{
  int big = a[0];
  // search for the biggest value in the
  // remaining array elements
  for (int i = 1; i < size; i++)
    if (big < a[i])
      big = a[i];
  return big;
}
```

Here is a sample session with the program in Listing 6.4.

```
Enter number of data points [2 to 10] : 5

arr[0] : 55
arr[1] : 69
arr[2] : 47
arr[3] : 85
arr[4] : 14
Smallest value in array is 14
Biggest value in array is 85
```

Analysis The program in Listing 6.4 declares the global constant `MAX`, in line 5, to size up the array of data. The function `main` declares the `int`-typed array `arr` in line 9. Line 10 contains the declaration of the `int`-typed variable `n`. Lines 13 and 14 declare the prototypes for the functions `getMin` and `getMax`, which return the smallest and largest values in an `int`-typed array, respectively. The prototype of the function `getMin` indicates that it uses a fixed-array parameter. By contrast, the prototype of the function `getMax` indicates that it uses an open-array parameter. We use both types of array parameters for the sake of demonstration.

The `do-while` loop, located in lines 16 through 21, obtains the number of data points you want to store in the array `arr`. The output statement in lines 17 and 18 prompts you to enter the number of data points. The output indicates the range of valid numbers, which runs between `2` and `MAX`. The statement in line 19 obtains your input and stores it in variable `n`. The `while` clause validates your input. The clause determines if the value in variable `n` is less than `2` or is greater than `MAX`. If this condition is true, the `do-while` loop iterates again to obtain a correct input value.

The `for` loop statement in lines 24 through 27 prompts you to enter the data. The loop uses the control variable `i` and iterates from `0` to `n-1`, in increments of 1. The output statement in line 25 prompts you to enter the value for the indicated array element. The statement in line 26 obtains your input and stores it in the element `arr[i]`.

The output statement in lines 29 through 32 displays the smallest and biggest integers in array `arr`. The statement invokes the functions `getMin` and `getMax`, supplying each one of them with the arguments `arr` and `n`.

The program defines the function `getMin` in lines 37 through 46. The function has 2 parameters: the `int`-typed, fixed-array parameter `a`, and the `int`-typed parameter size. The function declares the local variable small and initializes it with `a[0]`, the first element of parameter `a`. The function searches for the smallest value in the parameter `a` using the `for` loop in line 42. This loop declares the control variable `i`, and iterates from `1` to `size-1`, in increments of 1. The loop contains an `if` statement that assigns the value in element `a[i]` to variable `small`, if the latter is greater than element `a[i]`. The function returns the value in variable `small`. The function `getMin` only accepts `int`-typed arrays that have `MAX` elements.

The program defines the function `getMax` in lines 48 through 57. This function, which is similar to the function `getMin`, has 2 parameters: the `int`-typed, open-array parameter `a`, and the `int`-typed parameter size. The function declares the local variable `big` and initializes it with `a[0]`, the first element of parameter `a`. The function searches for the smallest value in the parameter `a`, using the `for` loop in line 53. This loop declares the control variable `i`, and iterates from `1` to `size-1`, in increments of 1. The loop contains an `if` statement that assigns the value in element `a[i]` to the variable `big`, if the latter is less than element `a[i]`. The function returns the value in the variable `big`. The function `getMax` accepts `int`-typed arrays of any size.

Sorting Arrays

Sorting and searching are the most common nonnumerical operations for arrays. Sorting an array typically arranges its elements in ascending order. The process uses parts of or all the value in each element to determine the precedence of the elements in the array. Searching for data in sorted arrays is much easier than in unordered arrays.

Computer scientists have spent much time and effort studying and creating methods for sorting arrays. A comprehensive discussion of these methods is beyond the scope of this book. We only mention that some favorite array-sorting methods include the QuickSort, Shell-Metzner sort, heap sort, and the new Comb sort. The QuickSort method is the fastest method, in general, but requires some operational overhead. The Shell-Metzner and Comb sort methods do not require similar overhead. The example in this section uses the new Comb sort method, which is more efficient than the Shell-Metzner method.

The Comb sort method uses the following steps, given an array, `A`, with `N` elements:

1. Initializes the `Offset` value, used in comparing elements, to `N`.
2. Sets the `Offset` value to either `8*Offset/11` or `1`, whichever is larger.
3. Sets the `InOrder` flag to `true`.
4. Loops for values `0` to `N-Offset`, using the loop control variable `i`:
   - Assigns `I + Offset` to `J`
   - If `A[I]` is greater than `A[J]`, swaps `A[I]` with `A[J]` and sets the `InOrder` flag to `false`
5. Resumes at step 2 if `Offset` is not `1` and `InOrder` is `false`.

Look at a program that sorts an array of integers. Listing 6.5 shows the source code for the program ARRAY5.CPP. The program performs the following tasks:

- Prompts you to enter the number of data points
- Prompts you to enter the integer values for the array
- Displays the elements of the unordered array
- Displays the elements of the sorted array

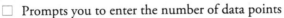

Listing 6.5. Source code for the program ARRAY5.CPP.

```
// C++ program that sorts arrays using the Comb sort method

#include <iostream.h>

const int MAX = 10;
const int TRUE = 1;
const int FALSE = 0;

```

continues

Listing 6.5. continued

```
int obtainNumData()
{
  int m;
  do { // obtain number of data points
    cout << "Enter number of data points [2 to "
        << MAX << "] : ";
    cin >> m;
    cout << "\n";
  } while (m < 2 || m > MAX);
  return m;
}

void inputArray(int intArr[], int n)
{
  // prompt user for data
  for (int i = 0; i < n; i++) {
    cout << "arr[" << i << "] : ";
    cin >> intArr[i];
  }
}

void showArray(int intArr[], int n)
{
  for (int i = 0; i < n; i++) {
    cout.width(5);
    cout << intArr[i] << " ";
  }
  cout << "\n";
}

void sortArray(int intArr[], int n)
{
  int offset, temp, inOrder;

  offset = n;
  do {
    offset = (8 * offset) / 11;
    offset = (offset == 0) ? 1 : offset;
    inOrder = TRUE;
    for (int i = 0, j = offset; i < (n -- offset); i++, j++) {
      if (intArr[i] > intArr[j]) {
        inOrder = FALSE;
        temp = intArr[i];
        intArr[i] = intArr[j];
        intArr[j] = temp;
      }
    }
  } while (!(offset = 1 && inOrder == TRUE));
}

main()
{
  int arr[MAX];
  int n;

  n = obtainNumData();
```

```
65:   inputArray(arr, n);
66:   cout << "Unordered array is:\n";
67:   showArray(arr, n);
68:   sortArray(arr, n);
69:   cout << "\nSorted array is:\n";
70:   showArray(arr, n);
71:   return 0;
72: }
```

Here is a sample session with the program in Listing 6.5.

```
Enter number of data points [2 to 10] : 10
arr[0] : 55
arr[1] : 68
arr[2] : 74
arr[3] : 15
arr[4] : 28
arr[5] : 23
arr[6] : 69
arr[7] : 95
arr[8] : 22
arr[9] : 33
Unordered array is:
55      68      74      15      28      23      69      95      22      33

Sorted array is:
15      22      23      28      33      55      68      69      74      95
```

The program in Listing 6.5 declares the constants `MAX`, `TRUE`, and `FALSE` in lines 5 through 7. The constant `MAX` defines the size of the array used in the program. The constants `TRUE` and `FALSE` define the Boolean values. The program also defines the functions `obtainNumData`, `inputArray`, `showArray`, `sortArray`, and `main`.

The parameterless function `obtainNumData`, defined in lines 9 through 19, prompts you to enter the number of values. The output statement in lines 13 and 14 also specifies the valid range for your input. The statement in line 15 stores your input in the local variable `m`. The function uses a `do-while` loop to ensure that it returns a valid number. The loop iterates as long as the value in variable `m` is less than `2` or greater than `MAX`. The function returns the value in variable `m`.

The function `inputArray`, defined in lines 21 through 28, obtains the data for the tested array. The function has two parameters. The open-array parameter `intArr` passes the input values back to the caller of the function. The parameter `n` specifies how many values to obtain for parameter `intArr`. The function uses a `for` loop, which iterates from `0` to `n-1`, in increments of 1. Each loop iteration prompts you for a value and stores that value in an element of the array `intArr`.

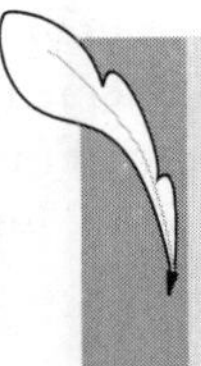

Note: The function `inputArray` illustrates that C++ functions treat array parameters as if they were references to their arguments because these parameters affect the values in the arguments beyond the scope of the functions. In reality, the C++ compiler passes a copy of the address of the array argument to the function when dealing with an array parameter. Armed with the address of the array, C++ functions then can alter the values of the array beyond the scope of these functions. This feature is possible because the function is working with the original array and not a copy.

The function `showArray`, defined in lines 30 through 37, displays the meaningful data in an array. The function has two parameters. The open-array parameter `intArr` passes the array values to be displayed by the function. The parameter `n` specifies how many elements of array `intArr` to display. (Remember that not all the array elements are used to store your data.) The function uses a `for` loop, which iterates from `0` to `n-1`, in increments of 1. Each loop iteration displays the value in an array element. The array elements appear on the same line.

The function `sortArray`, defined in lines 39 through 57, sorts the elements of an array using the Comb sort method. The function has two parameters. The open-array parameter `intArr` passes the array values to be sorted by the function. The parameter `n` specifies how many array elements to sort. The statements in the function `sortArray` implement the Comb sort method outlined earlier.

Note: The function `sortArray` illustrates how array parameters can pass data to and from a function. The function `sortArray` receives an unordered array, sorts it, and passes the ordered array to the function's caller. The compiler supports this feature by passing a copy of the address of the array to the function. Thus, the function need not explicitly return the array because it is working with the original data and not a copy.

The function `main` performs the various program tasks by calling the functions mentioned earlier. The function declares the array `arr` and the simple variable `n` in lines 61 and 62, respectively. The statement in line 64 calls function `obtainNumData` to obtain the number of data points you want to store in the array. The statement assigns the result of the function `obtainNumData` to variable `n`. The statement in line 65 calls the function `inputArray` to prompt you for the data. The function call passes the arguments `arr` and `n`. The output statement in line 66 displays a message indicating that the program is about to display the elements of the unordered array. The statement in line 67 calls `showArray` and passes it the arguments `arr` and `n`. This function call displays the elements of the array `arr` on one line. The statement in line 68 calls the function `sortArray` to sort the first `n` elements in array `arr`. The output statement in line 69 displays a message indicating that the program is about to display the elements of the sorted array. The statement in line 70 calls `showArray` and passes the arguments `arr` and `n`. This function call displays the elements of the ordered array `arr` on one line.

Searching Arrays

Searching arrays is another important nonnumerical operation. Because arrays can be sorted or unordered, there is a general category of search methods for each. The simplest search method for unordered arrays is the *linear search method.* The simplest search method for sorted arrays is the versatile *binary search method.* The search methods for unordered arrays also can be applied to sorted arrays; however, they do not take advantage of the array order.

NEW TERM The *linear search method* sequentially examines the array elements, looking for an element that matches the search value. If the sought value is not in the array, the linear search method examines the entire array's elements.

NEW TERM The *binary search method* takes advantage of the order in the array. The method searches for a matching value by using the shrinking intervals approach. The initial search interval includes all the array elements (which contain meaningful data). The method compares the median element of the interval with the search value. If the two match, the search stops. Otherwise, the method determines which sub-interval to use as the next search interval. Consequently, each search interval is half the size of the previous one. If the search value has no match in the examined array, the binary method makes far fewer examinations than the linear search method. The binary search method is the most efficient general-purpose search method for sorted arrays.

DO	DON'T

DO use the unordered-array search method when you are not sure that the array is sorted.

DON'T use sorted-array search methods with unordered arrays. The results of such searches are not reliable.

Look at a program that sorts an array of integers. Listing 6.6 shows the source code for the program ARRAY6.CPP. We created this program by adding functions and operations to the program ARRAY5.CPP. The program performs the following tasks:

- Prompts you to enter the number of data points
- Prompts you to enter the integer values for the array
- Displays the elements of the unordered array
- Asks you if you want to search for data in the unordered array. (If you type characters other than `Y` or `y`, the program resumes at step 8.)
- Prompts you for a search value

- Displays the search outcome. (If the program finds a matching element, it displays the index of that element; otherwise, the program tells you that it found no match for the search value.)
- Resumes at step 4
- Displays the elements of the sorted array
- Asks you if you want to search for data in the unordered array. (If you type characters other than **Y** or **y** the program ends.)
- Prompts you for a search value
- Displays the search outcome. (If the program finds a matching element, it displays the index of that element; otherwise, the program tells you that it found no match for the search value.)
- Resumes at step 9

Listing 6.6. Source code for the program ARRAY6.CPP.

```
// C++ program that searches arrays using the linear
// and binary searches methods

#include <iostream.h>

const int MAX = 10;
const int TRUE = 1;
const int FALSE = 0;
const int NOT_FOUND = --1;

int obtainNumData()
{
  int m;
  do { // obtain number of data points
    cout << "Enter number of data points [2 to "
        << MAX << "] : ";
    cin >> m;
    cout << "\n";
  } while (m < 2 || m > MAX);
  return m;
}

void inputArray(int intArr[], int n)
{
  // prompt user for data
  for (int i = 0; i < n; i++) {
    cout << "arr[" << i << "] : ";
    cin >> intArr[i];
  }
}

void showArray(int intArr[], int n)
{
  for (int i = 0; i < n; i++) {
    cout.width(5);
    cout << intArr[i] << " ";
```

```
  }
  cout << "\n";
}

void sortArray(int intArr[], int n)
// sort the first n elements of array intArr
// using the Comb sort method
{
  int offset, temp, inOrder;

  offset = n;
  do {
    offset = (8 * offset) / 11;
    offset = (offset == 0) ? 1 : offset;
    inOrder = TRUE;
    for (int i = 0, j = offset; i < (n -- offset); i++, j++) {
      if (intArr[i] > intArr[j]) {
        inOrder = FALSE;
        temp = intArr[i];
        intArr[i] = intArr[j];
        intArr[j] = temp;
      }
    }
  } while (!(offset = 1 && inOrder == TRUE));
}

int linearSearch(int searchVal, int intArr[], int n)
// perform linear search to locate the first
// element in array intArr that matches the value
// of searchVal
{
  int notFound = TRUE;
  int i = 0;
  // search through the array elements
  while (i < n && notFound)
    // no match?
    if (searchVal != intArr[i])
      i++; // increment index to compare the next element
    else
      notFound = FALSE; // found a match
  // return search outcome
  return (notFound == FALSE) ? i : NOT_FOUND;
}

int binarySearch(int searchVal, int intArr[], int n)
// perform binary search to locate the first
// element in array intArr that matches the value
// of searchVal
{
  int median, low, high;

  // initialize the search range
  low = 0;
  high = n - 1;
  // search in array
  do {
    // obtain the median index of the current search range
    median = (low + high) / 2;
```

continues

Listing 6.6. continued

```
   // update search range
   if (searchVal > intArr[median])
     low = median + 1;
   else
     high = median -- 1;
  } while (!(searchVal == intArr[median] ¦¦ low > high));
  // return search outcome
  return (searchVal == intArr[median]) ? median : NOT_FOUND;
}

void searchInUnorderedArray(int intArr[], int n)
// manage the linear search test
{
  int x, i;
  char c;
  // perform linear search
  cout << "Search in unordered array? (Y/N) ";
  cin >> c;
  while (c == 'Y' ¦¦ c == 'y') {
    cout << "Enter search value : ";
    cin >> x;
    i = linearSearch(x, intArr, n);
    if (i != NOT_FOUND)
      cout << "Found matching element at index " << i << "\n";
    else
      cout << "No match found\n";
    cout << "Search in unordered array? (Y/N) ";
    cin >> c;
  }
}

void searchInSortedArray(int intArr[], int n)
// manage the binary search test
{
  int x, i;
  char c;
  // perform binary search
  cout << "Search in sorted array? (Y/N) ";
  cin >> c;
  while (c == 'Y' ¦¦ c == 'y') {
    cout << "Enter search value : ";
    cin >> x;
    i = binarySearch(x, intArr, n);
    if (i != NOT_FOUND)
      cout << "Found matching element at index " << i << "\n";
    else
      cout << "No match found\n";
    cout << "Search in sorted array? (Y/N) ";
    cin >> c;
  }
}

main()
{
  int arr[MAX];
  int n;
```

```
151:
152:    n = obtainNumData();
153:    inputArray(arr, n);
154:    cout << "Unordered array is:\n";
155:    showArray(arr, n);
156:    searchInUnorderedArray(arr, n);
157:    sortArray(arr, n);
158:    cout << "\nSorted array is:\n";
159:    showArray(arr, n);
160:    searchInSortedArray(arr, n);
161:    return 0;
162: }
```

Here is a sample session with the program in Listing 6.6.

```
Enter number of data points [2 to 10] : 5

arr[0] : 85
arr[1] : 41
arr[2] : 55
arr[3] : 67
arr[4] : 48
Unordered array is:
85    41    55    67    48
Search in unordered array? (Y/N) y
Enter search value : 55
Found matching element at index 2
Search in unordered array? (Y/N) y
Enter search value : 41
Found matching element at index 1
Search in unordered array? (Y/N) n

Sorted array is:
41    48    55    67    85
Search in sorted array? (Y/N) y
Enter search value : 55
Found matching element at index 2
Search in sorted array? (Y/N) y
Enter search value : 67
Found matching element at index 3
Search in sorted array? (Y/N) n
```

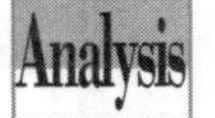

The program in Listing 6.6 declares the functions `obtainNumData`, `inputArray`, `sortArray`, `linearSearch`, `binarySearch`, `searchInUnorderedArray`, `searchInSortedArray`, and `main`. Because the first three functions are identical to those in Listing 6.5, only the remaining functions are discussed.

The `linearSearch` function performs a linear search to find the first element in array `intArr` with a value that matches the one in parameter `searchVal`. The function searches the first `n` elements in array `intArr`. The `linearSearch` function returns the index of the matching element in array `intArr` or yields the value of the global constant `NOT_FOUND` if no match is found. The function uses a `while` loop to examine the elements in array `intArr`. The search loop iterates while the value in variable `i` is less than that in variable `n` and while the local variable `notFound` stores `TRUE`. The statement in line 78 returns the function result using the conditional operator.

The `binarySearch` function has the same parameters as the `linearSearch` function and returns the same type of value. The function uses the local variables `low` and `high` to store the current search interval. The function initializes the variables `low` and `high` using the values `0` and `n-1`, respectively. The `do-while` loop in lines 92 through 100 calculates the index of the median element and compares the median element with the search value. The `if` statement in line 96 performs this comparison, and its clauses update the value of either variable `low` or variable `high`, depending on the outcome of the comparison. The update in either variable shrinks the search interval. The return statement in line 102 yields the function's value based on one last comparison between the search value and the median element of the current search interval.

The function `searchInUnorderedArray` manages the search in the unordered array. The function accesses the unordered array using the open-array parameter `intArr`. The function declares local variables that are used to prompt you for and store the search value. The statement in line 116 calls the function `linearSearch` and passes the argument `x` (the local variable that stores the search value), `intArr`, and `n`. The statement assigns the result of function `linearSearch` to the local variable `i`. The `if` statement in line 117 determines whether the value in variable `i` is not `NOT_FOUND`. If this condition is true, then the output statement in line 118 shows the index of the matching element. Otherwise, the output statement in line 120 displays a `no-match-found` message.

The function `searchInSortedArray` is very similar to the function `searchInUnorderedArray`. The main difference is that the function `searchInSortedArray` deals with ordered arrays and, therefore, calls the `binarySearch` function to conduct a binary search on the ordered array `intArr`.

The function `main` invokes these functions to support the program tasks described earlier.

Multidimensional Arrays

In a *multidimensional array*, each additional dimension provides an additional access attribute. Two-dimensional arrays (or matrices, if you prefer) are the most popular type of multidimensional array. Three-dimensional arrays are used less frequently than matrices, and so on.

NEW TERM *Multidimensional arrays* are supersets of the single-dimensional arrays.

Syntax

Two-Dimensional and Three-Dimensional Arrays

The general syntax for declaring two-dimensional and three-dimensional arrays is

```
type array [size1][size2];
type array [size1][size2][size3];
```

As with simple arrays, each dimension has a lower bound index of 0, and the declaration defines the number of elements in each dimension.

Examples

```
double matrixA[100][10];
char table[41][22][3];
int index[7][12];
```

It is important to understand how C++ stores the elements of a multidimensional array. Most compilers store the elements of a multidimensional array in a contiguous fashion (that is, as one long array). The runtime code calculates where a sought element is located in that long array. To explain the storage scheme of multidimensional arrays, we'll start by employing a convention for referencing the indices of the different dimensions. The following schema specifies the dimension numbering and the concept of high- and low-order dimensions. Following is a six-dimensional array—an extreme case that is a good example:

```
1    2    3    4    5    6   <— dimension number
M [20]  [7]  [5]  [3]  [2]  [2]
higher dimension order —>
```

The first element of the array `M` is `M[0][0][0][0][0][0]` and is stored at the first memory location of array `M`. The array `M` is stored in a contiguous block of 8,400 elements. The location in that contiguous block stores the element at index `1` in the highest dimension number, dimension `6` (that is, `M[0][0][0][0][0][1]`). The location of the next elements in the contiguous block stores the subsequent elements in dimension `6` until the upper limit of dimension `6` is reached. Reaching this limit bumps the index of dimension `5` by `1` and resets the index of dimension `6` to `0`. This process is repeated until every element in a multidimensional array is accessed. You can compare this storage scheme to looking at a gasoline pump meter when refueling your car: the right digits turn the fastest, the left digits turn the slowest.

Here is another example that uses a three-dimensional array, `M[3][2][2]`.

```
M[0][0][0]     <— the starting memory address
M[0][0][1]     <— 3rd dimension is filled
M[0][1][0]
M[0][1][1]     <— 2nd and 3rd dimensions are filled
M[1][0][0]
M[1][0][1]     <— 3rd dimension is filled
M[1][1][0]
M[1][1][1]     <— 2nd and 3rd dimensions are filled
M[2][0][0]
M[2][0][1]     <— 3rd dimension is filled
M[2][1][0]
M[2][1][1]     <— all dimensions are filled
```

Consider an example that illustrates basic matrix manipulation. Listing 6.7 shows the source code for the MAT1.CPP program. The program manages a matrix that contains up to 10 columns and 30 rows and performs the following tasks:

- Prompts you to enter the number of rows; the program validates your input
- Prompts you to enter the number of columns; the program validates your input
- Prompts you to enter the matrix elements
- Calculates and displays the average for each column in the matrix

Type

Listing 6.7. Source code for the program MAT1.CPP.

```
/*
  C++ program that demonstrates the use of two-dimensional arrays.
  The average value of each matrix column is calculated.
*/

#include <iostream.h>

const int MAX_COL = 10;
const int MAX_ROW = 30;

main()
{
    double x[MAX_ROW][MAX_COL];
    double sum, sumx, mean;
    int rows, columns;

    // get the number of rows
    do {
      cout << "Enter number of rows [2 to "
           << MAX_ROW << "] : ";
      cin >> rows;
    } while (rows < 2 || rows > MAX_ROW);

    // get the number of columns
    do {
      cout << "Enter number of columns [1 to "
           << MAX_COL << "] : ";
      cin >> columns;
    } while (columns < 1 || columns > MAX_COL);

    // get the matrix elements
    for (int i = 0; i < rows; i++)  {
      for (int j = 0; j < columns; j++)  {
        cout << "X[" << i << "][" << j << "] : ";
        cin >> x[i][j];
      }
      cout << "\n";
    }

    sum = rows;
    // obtain the sum of each column
    for (int j = 0; j < columns; j++)  {
      // initialize summations
      sumx = 0.0;
      for (i = 0; i < rows; i++)
        sumx += x[i][j];
      mean = sumx / sum;
      cout << "Mean for column " << j
           << " = " << mean << "\n";
    }
    return 0;
}
```

Here is a sample session with the program in Listing 6.7.

```
Enter number of rows [2 to 30] : 3
Enter number of columns [1 to 10] : 3
X[0][0] : 1
X[0][1] : 2
X[0][2] : 3

X[1][0] : 4
X[1][1] : 5
X[1][2] : 6

X[2][0] : 7
X[2][1] : 8
X[2][2] : 9

Mean for column 0 = 4
Mean for column 1 = 5
Mean for column 2 = 6
```

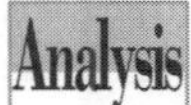

The program in Listing 6.7 declares the global constants `MAX_COL` and `MAX_ROW` in lines 8 and 9, respectively. These constants define the dimensions of the matrix that is created in the program. The function main declares the matrix `x` to have `MAX_ROW` rows and `MAX_COL` columns. The function also declares other nonarray variables.

The `do-while` loop, in lines 18 through 22, prompts you to enter the number of rows of matrix `x` that will contain your data. The output statement in lines 19 and 20 indicates the range of the valid number of rows. The statement in line 21 stores your input in the variable rows.

The second `do-while` loop, in lines 25 through 29, prompts you to enter the number of columns of matrix `x` that will contain your data. The output statement in lines 26 and 27 indicates the range of the valid number of columns. The statement in line 28 saves your input in the variable `columns`.

The nested `for` loops, in lines 32 through 38, prompt you for the matrix elements. The outer `for` loop uses the control variable `i` and iterates from `0` to `rows-1`, in increments of 1. The inner `for` loop uses the control variable `j` and iterates from `0` to `columns-1`, in increments of 1. The output statement in line 34 displays the index of the matrix element that will receive your input. The statement in line 35 stores your input in the matrix element `x[i][j]`.

The process of obtaining the average of each matrix column starts at line 40. The statement in that line assigns the integer in variable `rows` to the `double`-typed variable `sum`. The program uses another pair of nested `for` loops in lines 42 through 50. The outer `for` loop uses the control variable `j` and iterates from `0` to `columns-1`, in increments of 1. This loop processes each column. The first statement inside the outer `for` loop assigns `0` to the variable `sumx`. The inner `for` loop is located at line 45. This loop uses the control variable `i` and iterates from `0` to `rows-1`, in increments of 1. The inner loop uses the statement in line 46 to add the values of elements `x[i][j]` to the variable `sumx`. The statement in line 47 (which is outside the inner `for` loop) calculates the column average and assigns it to the variable `mean`. The output statement in lines 48 and 49 displays the column number and its average value.

Note: The `for` loop in line 42 redeclares its control variable `j`. (This is not the case with the `for` loop in line 45.) Why? The `for` loop in line 33 also declares the control variable `j`. However, the scope of that loop is limited to the scope of the outer `for` loop. Once the first pair of nested loops finishes executing, the loop control variable `j` is removed by the runtime system.

Initializing Multidimensional Arrays

C++ enables you to initialize a multidimensional array in a manner similar to single-dimensional arrays. You need to use a list of values that appear in the same sequence in which the elements of the initialized multidimensional array are stored. Now you realize the importance of understanding how C++ stores the elements of a multidimensional array. We modified the previous C++ program to use an initializing list that internally supplies the program with data. Consequently, the program does not prompt you for any data. Rather, the program displays the values of the matrix and the average for its columns. Listing 6.8. shows the source code for the MAT2.CPP program.

Listing 6.8. Source code for the program MAT2.CPP.

```
/*
  C++ program that demonstrates the use of two-dimensional arrays.
  The average value of each matrix column is calculated.
*/

#include <iostream.h>

const int MAX_COL = 3;
const int MAX_ROW = 3;

main()
{
    double x[MAX_ROW][MAX_COL] = {
                                  { 1, 2, 3 }, // row # 1
                                  { 4, 5, 6 }, // row # 2
                                  { 7, 8, 9 }  // row # 3
                                  };
    double sum, sumx, mean;
    int rows = MAX_ROW, columns = MAX_COL;

    cout << "Matrix is:\n";
    // display the matrix elements
    for (int i = 0; i < rows; i++)  {
      for (int j = 0; j < columns; j++)  {
          cout.width(4);
          cout.precision(1);
          cout << x[i][j] << " ";
```

```
28:       }
29:       cout << "\n";
30:     }
31:     cout << "\n";
32:
33:     sum = rows;
34:     // obtain the sum of each column
35:     for (int j = 0; j < columns; j++)  {
36:       // initialize summations
37:       sumx = 0.0;
38:       for (i = 0; i < rows; i++)
39:         sumx += x[i][j];
40:       mean = sumx / sum;
41:       cout << "Mean for column " << j
42:            << " = " << mean << "\n";
43:     }
44:     return 0;
45: }
```

Here is a sample session with the program in Listing 6.8.

```
Matrix is:
1    2    3
4    5    6
7    8    9

Mean for column 0 = 4
Mean for column 1 = 5
Mean for column 2 = 6
```

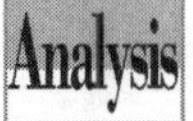

The program in Listing 6.8 declares the matrix `x` and initializes its elements with a list of values. Notice that the program declares the constants `MAX_COL` and `MAX_ROW` with values that match the size of the initialized matrix. The declaration statement in lines 13 through 17 shows the elements assigned to each row. The function `main` also initializes the variables `rows` and `columns` with the constants `MAX_ROW` and `MAX_COL`, respectively. The function performs this initialization for two reasons. First, the program no longer prompts you to enter values for the variables `rows` and `columns`. Second, the program is working with a custom-fit size for matrix `x`.

The program uses the nested `for` loops in lines 21 through 30 to display the elements of the matrix `x`. The second pair of nested `for` loops calculates the average for each matrix column. This nested for loop is identical to the one in Listing 6.7.

Multidimensional Array Parameters

C++ enables you to declare function parameters that are multidimensional arrays. As with single-dimensional arrays, C++ enables you either to be specific or general about the size of the array parameter. In the latter case, however, you can only generalize the first dimension of the array. If you want an array parameter to accept arrays of a fixed dimension, you can specify the size of each dimension of the array in the parameter declaration.

A Fixed-Array Parameter

The general syntax for declaring a fixed-array parameter is

```
type parameterName[dim1Size][dim2Size]...
```

Examples

```
int minMatrix(int intMat[100][20], int rows, int cols);
void sort(unsigned mat[23][55],
int rows, int cols, int colIndex);
```

An Open-Array Parameter

The general syntax for declaring an open-array parameter is

```
type parameterName[][dim2Size]...
```

Examples

```
int minMat(int intMat[][100], int rows, int cols);
void sort(unsigned mat[][55],
int rows, int cols, int colIndex);
```

Look at an example. Listing 6.9 shows the source code for the program MAT3.CPP. The program performs the same tasks as program MAT1.CPP in Listing 6.7. We created program MAT3.CPP by editing program MAT1.CPP and placing each program task in a separate function. Thus, program MAT3.CPP is a highly structured version of program MAT1.CPP.

Listing 6.9. Source code for the program MAT3.CPP.

```
/*
  C++ program that demonstrates the use of two-dimensional arrays.
  The average value of each matrix column is calculated.
*/

#include <iostream.h>

const int MAX_COL = 10;
const int MAX_ROW = 30;

int getRows()
{
  int n;
  // get the number of rows
  do {
    cout << "Enter number of rows [2 to "
         << MAX_ROW << "] : ";
    cin >> n;
  } while (n < 2 || n > MAX_ROW);
  return n;
}

```

```
int getColumns()
{
  int n;
  // get the number of columns
  do {
    cout << "Enter number of columns [1 to "
         << MAX_COL << "] : ";
    cin >> n;
  } while (n < 1 || n > MAX_COL);
  return n;
}

void inputMatrix(double mat[][MAX_COL],
                 int rows, int columns)
{
  // get the matrix elements
  for (int i = 0; i < rows; i++)  {
    for (int j = 0; j < columns; j++)  {
      cout << "X[" << i << "][" << j << "] : ";
      cin >> mat[i][j];
    }
    cout << "\n";
  }
}

void showColumnAverage(double mat[][MAX_COL],
                       int rows, int columns)
{
  double sum, sumx, mean;
  sum = rows;
  // obtain the sum of each column
  for (int j = 0; j < columns; j++)  {
    // initialize summations
    sumx = 0.0;
    for (int i = 0; i < rows; i++)
      sumx += mat[i][j];
    mean = sumx / sum;
    cout << "Mean for column " << j
         << " = " << mean << "\n";
  }
}

main()
{
    double x[MAX_ROW][MAX_COL];
    int rows, columns;
    // get matrix dimensions
    rows = getRows();
    columns = getColumns();
    // get matrix data
    inputMatrix(x, rows, columns);
    // show results
    showColumnAverage(x, rows, columns);
    return 0;
}
```

Here is a sample session with the program in Listing 6.9.

```
Enter number of rows [2 to 30] : 3
Enter number of columns [1 to 10] : 3
X[0][0] : 10
X[0][1] : 20
X[0][2] : 30

X[1][0] : 40
X[1][1] : 50
X[1][2] : 60

X[2][0] : 70
X[2][1] : 80
X[2][2] : 90

Mean for column 0 = 40
Mean for column 1 = 50
Mean for column 2 = 60
```

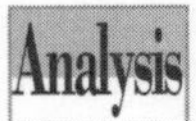

The program in Listing 6.9 declares the functions `getRows`, `getColumns`, `inputMatrix`, `showColumnAverage`, and `main`. The function `getRows` prompts you for the number of matrix rows that you will be using. The function returns your validated input. Similarly, the function `getColumns` returns the validated number of matrix columns.

The function `inputMatrix` obtains the data for the matrix. The function has three parameters. The parameter `mat` specifies the matrix parameter (with an open first dimension). The parameters `rows` and `columns` specify the number of rows and the number of columns of matrix `mat` that will receive input data.

The function `showColumnAverage` calculates and displays the column averages for the matrix parameter `mat`. The parameters `rows` and `columns` specify the number of rows and the number of columns of matrix `mat` that contain meaningful data.

This function contains the same statements that appeared in the program MAT1.CPP. Program MAT3.CPP uses these functions as shells or wrappers for the statements that perform the various tasks. From a structured programming point of view, program MAT3.CPP is superior to program MAT1.CPP.

The function `main` declares the matrix `x` with `MAX_ROW` rows and `MAX_COL` columns. The function calls the functions `getRows` and `getColumns` to obtain the number of working rows and columns, respectively. The statement in line 73 invokes the function `inputMatrix` and supplies it with the arguments `x`, `rows`, and `columns`. The statement in line 75 calls function `showColumnAverage` and passes it the arguments `x`, `rows`, and `columns`.

Summary

Today's lesson covered various topics related to arrays, including single-dimensional and multidimensional arrays. You learned the following:

- The initializing of single-dimensional arrays can be carried out while declaring them. The initializing list of data is enclosed in braces and contains comma-delimited data. C++ enables you to include fewer data than the size of the array. In this case, the compiler automatically assigns zeros to the elements that you do not explicitly initialize. In addition, C++ enables you to omit the explicit size of the initialized array and instead use the number of initializing items as the number of array elements.
- Declaring single-dimensional arrays as function parameters takes two forms. The first one deals with fixed-array parameters, whereas the second one handles open-array parameters. Fixed-array parameters include the size of the array in the parameter. Arguments for this type of parameter must match the type and size of the parameter. Open-array parameters use empty brackets to indicate that the arguments for the parameters can be of any size.
- Sorting arrays is an important nonnumerical array operation. Sorting arranges the elements of an array in either ascending or descending order. Sorted arrays are much easier to search. For sorting arrays, the new Comb sort method is very efficient.
- Searching arrays involves locating an array element that contains the same data as the search value. Searching methods either are geared toward unordered or ordered arrays. The linear search method is used for unordered arrays, and the binary search method is used for sorted arrays.
- Declaring multidimensional arrays requires you to state the data type of the array elements, the name of the array, and the size of each dimension (enclosed in separate brackets). The lower index of each dimension is 0. The upper bound of each dimension in an array is equal to the dimension size minus one.
- Using multidimensional arrays requires you to state the array's name and to include valid indices. Each index must be enclosed in a separate set of brackets.
- The initializing of multidimensional arrays can be carried out while declaring them. The initializing list of data is enclosed in braces and contains comma-delimited data. C++ enables you to include fewer data than the total size of the array. In this case, the compiler automatically assigns zeros to the elements that you do not explicitly initialize.
- Declaring multidimensional arrays as function parameters take two forms. The first one deals with fixed-array parameters, whereas, the second one handles parameters with an open first dimension. Fixed-array parameters include the size of each dimension in the array parameter. Arguments for this type of parameter must match the type and sizes of the parameter. Open-array parameters use empty brackets for only the first dimension to indicate that the arguments for the parameters have varying sizes for the first dimensions. The other dimensions of the arguments must match those of the array parameter.

Q&A

Q Does C++ permit me to alter the size of an array?

A No. C++ does not allow you to redimension arrays.

Q Can I declare arrays with the basic type `void` (for example, `void array[81];`) to create buffers?

A No. C++ does not allow you to use the `void` type with an array, because the `void` type has no defined size. Use the `char` or `unsigned char` type to create an array that works as a buffer.

Q Does C++ allow me to redeclare an array?

A Not really, but C++ enables you to declare a new version of the array in a new statement block in order to change its basic type, the number of dimensions, and its size. Here is an example.

```
#include <iostream.h>
const MAX = 100;
const MAX_ROWS = 100;
const MAX_COLS = 20;

main()
{
  // declare variables here?
  {
    double x[MAX];
    // declare other variables?
    // statements to manipulate the single-dimensional
       array x
  }
  {
    double x[MAX_ROWS][MAX_COLS];
    // declare other variables?
    // statements to manipulate the matrix x
  }
  return 0;
}
```

The function `main` declares the array `x` in the first nested statement block. When program execution reaches the end of that block, the runtime system removes the array `x` and all other variables declared in that block. Then the function redeclares `x` as a matrix in the second block. When program execution reaches the end of the second block, the runtime system removes the matrix `x` and all other variables declared in that block.

Q Are arrays limited to the predefined types?

A Not at all. C++ enables you to create arrays using user-defined types.

Workshop

The Workshop provides quiz questions to help you solidify your understanding of the material covered and exercises to provide you with experience in using what you've learned. Try to understand the quiz and exercise answers before continuing on to the next day's lesson. Answers are provided in Appendix A.

Quiz

1. What is the output of the following program?

```
#include <iostream.h>
const int MAX = 5;
main()
{
  double x[MAX];
  x[0] = 1;
  for (int i = 1; i < MAX; i++)
    x[i] = i * x[i-1];
  for (i = 0; i < MAX; i++)
    cout << "x[" << i << "] = " << x[i] << "\n";
  return 0;
}
```

2. What is the output of the following program?

```
#include <iostream.h>
#include <math.h>
const int MAX = 5;
main()
{
  double x[MAX];
  for (int i = 0; i < MAX; i++)
    x[i] = sqrt(double(i));
  for (i = 0; i < MAX; i++)
    cout << "x[" << i << "] = " << x[i] << "\n";
  return 0;
}
```

3. Where is the error in the following program?

```
#include <iostream.h>
const int MAX = 5;
main()
{
  double x[MAX];
  x[0] = 1;
  for (int i = 0; i < MAX; i++)
     x[i] = i * x[i-1];
  for (i = 0; i < MAX; i++)
     cout << "x[" << i << "] = " << x[i] << "\n";
  return 0;
}
```

Exercise

Write the program ARRAY7.CPP by editing program ARRAY6.CPP and replacing the Comb sort method in the function `sortArray` with an implementation of the Shell-Metzner method.

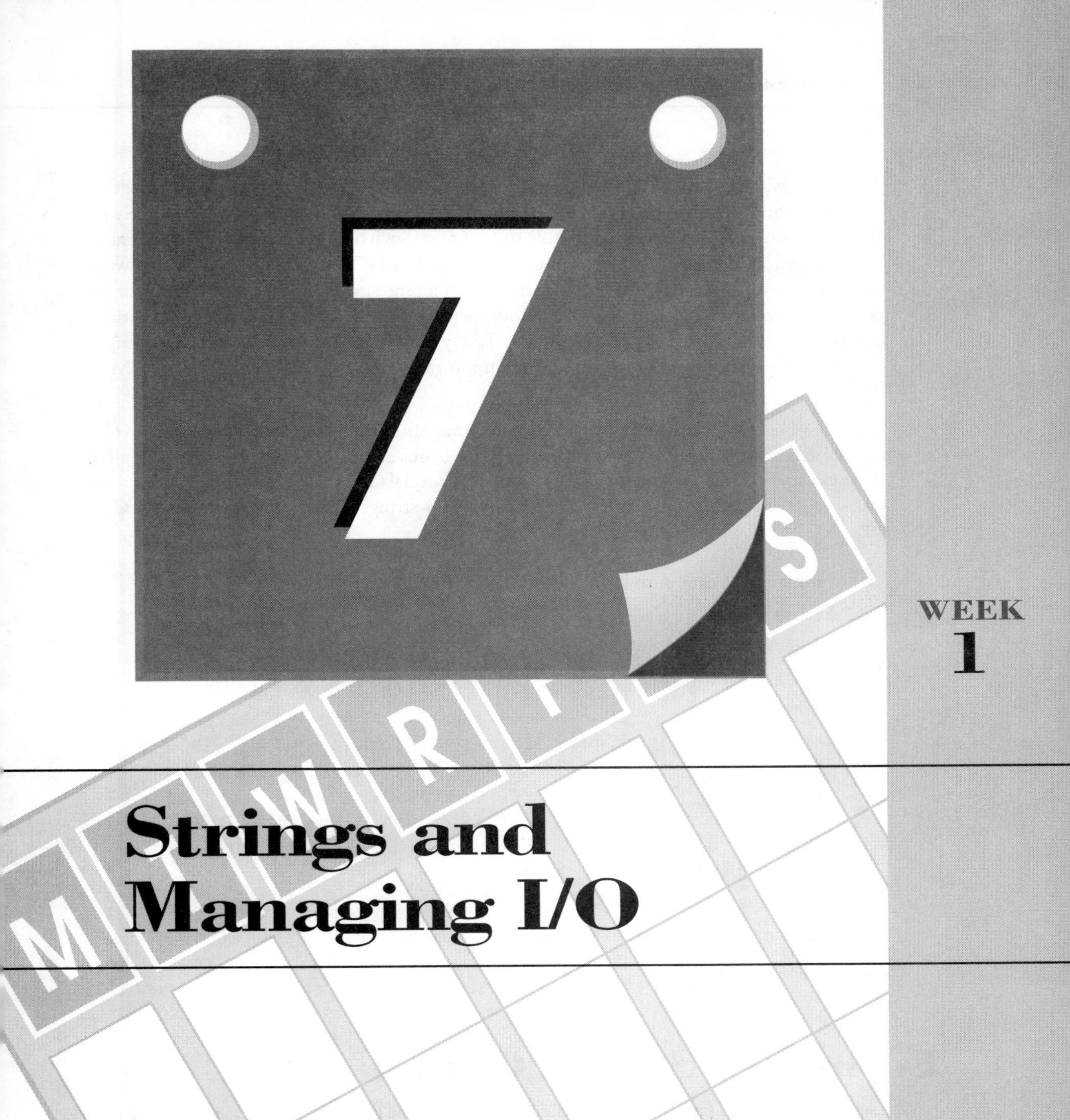

WEEK 1

7

Strings and Managing I/O

Today you will learn about basic console input/output (I/O). C++, like its parent language C, does not define I/O operations that are part of the core language. Instead, C++ and C rely on I/O libraries to provide the needed console I/O support. Such libraries mainly are aimed at non-GUI (graphical user interface) environments such as MS-DOS. These libraries usually work with EasyWin applications, which is why they are of interest in this book. Because our primary goal here is to teach you how to write Windows programs, however, the discussion of these console I/O libraries are kept to a minimum. Today's lesson looks at a small selection of input and output operations and functions that are supported by the STDIO.H and IOSTREAM.H header files.

The examples presented so far have been predominantly numeric, with a few that involve character manipulation. You may have grown suspicious about the absence of strings in all of these examples. On Day 10 you will learn about the special C++ `string` class that makes strings into a more usable type. Today's lesson discusses C++ strings as they are inherited from C.

You will learn about the following topics:

- Formatted stream output
- Stream input
- The `printf` function
- Strings in C++
- String input
- Using the standard string library
- Assigning strings
- Obtaining the length of strings
- Concatenating strings
- Comparing strings
- Converting strings
- Reversing the characters in a string
- Locating characters
- Locating substrings

Formatted Stream Output

C++ brings with it a family of extendable I/O libraries. The language designers recognized that the I/O functions in STDIO.H, inherited from C, have their limitations when dealing with classes. (You learn more about classes in Day 8.) Consequently, C++ extends the notion of streams. Recall that streams, which already exist in C, are a sequence of data flowing from part of a computer to another. In the programs presented thus far, you have seen the extractor operator << working with the standard output stream, `cout`. You also saw the inserter operator >> and the standard input stream, `cin`. In this section, you are introduced to the stream functions `width` and `precision`, which help in formatting the output. The C++ stream libraries have many more functions to additionally fine-tune the output. The `width` function specifies the width of the output. The general form for using this function with the `cout` stream is

```
cout.width(widthOfOutput);
```

The `precision` function specifies the number of digits for floating-point numbers. The general form for using this function with the `cout` stream is

```
cout.precision(numberOfDigits);
```

Look at an example. Listing 7.1 contains the source code for the program OUT1.CPP. (We suggest that you place all of today's programs in the DAY4.IDE project file.) The program, which requires no input, displays formatted integers, floating-point numbers, and characters using the `width` and `precision` stream functions.

Listing 7.1. Source code for the program OUT1.CPP.

```
// Program that illustrates C++ formatted stream output
// using the width and precision functions

#include <iostream.h>

main()
{
  short    aShort      = 4;
  int      anInt       = 67;
  unsigned char aByte  = 128;
  char     aChar       = '@';
  float    aSingle     = 355.0;
  double   aDouble     = 1.130e+002;
  // display sample expressions
  cout.width(3); cout << int(aByte) << " + ";
  cout.width(3); cout << anInt << " = ";
  cout.width(3); cout << (aByte + anInt) << '\n';

  cout.precision(4); cout << aSingle << " / ";
  cout << aDouble << " = ";
  cout.precision(5); cout << (aSingle / aDouble) << '\n';

  cout << "The character in variable aChar is "
       << aChar << '\n';
  return 0;
}
```

Here is a sample session with the program in Listing 7.1.

```
128 +  67 = 195
355 / 113 = 3.1416
The character in variable aChar is @
```

The program in Listing 7.1 declares a set of variables that have different data types. The statements in lines 15 through 17 use the stream function `width` to specify the output width for the next item displayed by a `cout` statement. Notice that it takes six statements to display three integers. In addition, notice that in line 15 the program uses the expression `int(aByte)` to typecast the `unsigned char` type into an `int`. Without this type conversion, the contents of the variable `aByte` appear as a character rather than a number. If you use the stream output to display integers that have default widths, you indeed can replace the six stream-output statements with a single one. Note that the width automatically is reset after each output, which is why you need to set it to the same value multiple times.

Lines 19 through 21 contain the second set of stream-output statements for the floating-point numbers. The statements in these lines contain the stream function `precision` to specify the total number of digits to display. It takes five C++ statements to output three floating-point numbers. Once more, if you use the stream output to display numbers that have default widths, you can replace the five stream-output statements with a single one. Note that the precision is *not* reset after each output, so the output on line 20 is still using a precision of 4.

Stream Input

Like the standard output stream, C++ offers the standard input stream, `cin`. This input stream can read predefined data types, such as `int`, `unsigned`, `long`, and `char`. Typically, you use the inserter operator >> to obtain input for the predefined data types. The programs presented so far use the >> operator to enter a single item. C++ streams enable you to chain the >> operator to enter multiple items. In the case of multiple items, you need to observe the following rules:

1. Enter a space between two consecutive numbers to separate them.
2. Entering a space between two consecutive `char`s is optional.
3. Entering a space between a `char` and a number (or vice versa) is necessary only if the `char` is a digit.
4. The input stream ignores spaces.
5. You can enter multiple items on different lines. The stream-input statements are not fully executed until they obtain all the specified input.

Look at a program that illustrates both the input of multiple items and different combinations of data types. Listing 7.2 shows the source code for the program IN1.CPP. The program performs the following tasks:

- ☐ Prompts you to enter three numbers
- ☐ Calculates the sum of the three numbers
- ☐ Displays the sum and the average of the three numbers you entered
- ☐ Prompts you to type in three characters
- ☐ Displays your input

- ☐ Prompts you to enter a number, a character, and a number
- ☐ Displays your input
- ☐ Prompts you to enter a character, a number, and a character
- ☐ Displays your input

Type

Listing 7.2. Source code for the program IN1.CPP.

```
 1:  // Program that illustrates standard stream input
 2:
 3:  #include <iostream.h>
 4:
 5:  main()
 6:  {
 7:    double x, y, z, sum;
 8:    char c1, c2, c3;
 9:
10:    cout << "Enter three numbers separated by a space : ";
11:    cin >> x >> y >> z;
12:    sum = x + y + z;
13:    cout << "Sum of numbers = " << sum
14:         << "\nAverage of numbers = " << sum / 2 << "\n";
15:    cout << "Enter three characters : ";
16:    cin >> c1 >> c2 >> c3;
17:    cout << "You entered characters '" << c1
18:         << "', '" << c2 << "', and '"
19:         << c3 << "'\n";
20:    cout << "Enter a number, a character, and a number : ";
21:    cin >> x >> c1 >> y;
22:    cout << "You entered " << x << " " << c1 << " " << y << "\n";
23:    cout << "Enter a character, a number, and a character : ";
24:    cin >> c1 >> x >> c2;
25:    cout << "You entered " << c1 << " " << x << " " << c2 << "\n";
26:
27:    return 0;
28:  }
```

Here is a sample session with the program in Listing 7.2.

```
Enter three numbers separated by a space : 1 2 3
Sum of numbers = 6
Average of numbers = 3
Enter three characters : ABC
You entered characters 'A', 'B', and 'C'
Enter a number, a character, and a number : 12A34.4
You entered 12 A 34.4
Enter a character, a number, and a character : A3.14Z
You entered A 3.14 Z
```

The program in Listing 7.2 declares four `double`-typed variables and three `char`-typed variables. The output statement in line 10 prompts you to enter three numbers. The input statement in line 11 obtains your input and stores the numbers in variables `x`, `y`, and `z`. You need to enter a space character between any two numbers. You also can enter each number on a separate line. The statement stores the first number you enter in variable `x`, the second number in variable `y`, and the third one in variable `z`. This sequence is determined by the sequence in which these variables appear in line 11. The statement in line 12 calculates the sum of the values in variables `x`, `y`, and `z`. The output statement in lines 13 and 14 displays the sum and average of the numbers that you entered.

The output statement in line 15 prompts you to enter three characters. The input statement in line 16 obtains your input and sequentially stores the characters in variables `c1`, `c2`, and `c3`. Your input need not separate the characters with a space. Thus, you can type in characters such as `1A2`, `Bob`, and `1    D    d`. The output statement in lines 17 through 19 displays the characters that you type, separated by spaces.

The output statement in line 20 prompts you to enter a number, a character, and a number. The input statement in line 21 sequentially stores your input in variables `x`, `c1`, and `y`. You need to type a space between the character and either of the numbers only if the character can be interpreted as part of either number. For example, if you want to enter the number 12, the dot character, and the number 55, type **`12 . 55`**. The spaces around the dot ensure that the input stream does not consider it as a decimal part of either floating-point number. The output statement in line 22 displays the values you entered, separated by spaces.

The output statement in line 23 prompts you to enter a character, a number, and a character. The input statement in line 24 sequentially stores your input in variables `c1`, `x`, and `c2`. You need to enter a space between the characters and the number only if the characters can be interpreted as part of the number. For example, if you want to enter the character `-`, the number `12`, and the digit `0`, type **`- 12 0`**. The output statement in line 25 displays the values you entered, separated by spaces.

The *printf* Function

As a novice C++ programmer, you have a wealth of I/O functions from which to choose. This section discusses the formatting features of the function `printf`, which is part of the standard I/O of C. The function is prototyped in the header file STDIO.H.

The `printf` function offers much power and presents formatted controls. The general syntax for the individual formatting instruction is

```
% [flags] [width] [.precision] [F ¦[]¦ h ¦ l] <type character>
```

The *`flags`* options indicate the output justification, numeric signs, decimal points, and trailing zeros. In addition, these flags also specify the octal and hexadecimal prefixes. Table 7.1 shows the options for the flags in the format string of the `printf` function.

The *`width`* option indicates the minimum number of displayed characters. The `printf` function uses zeros and blanks to pad the output if needed. When the width number begins with a `0`, the `printf` function uses leading zeros, instead of spaces, for padding. When the `*` character appears

instead of a width number, the `printf` function obtains the actual width number from the function's argument list. The argument that specifies the required width must come before the argument that actually is being formatted. The following is an example that displays the integer 3 using 2 characters, as specified by the third argument of `printf`:

```
printf("%*d", 3, 2);
```

The *`precision`* option specifies the maximum number of displayed characters. If you include an integer, the precision option defines the minimum number of displayed digits. When the `*` character is used in place of a precision number, the `printf` function obtains the actual precision from the argument list. The argument that specifies the required precision must come before the argument that is actually being formatted. The following is an example that displays the floating-point number `3.3244` using 10 characters, as specified by the third argument of `printf`:

```
printf("%7.*f", 10, 3.3244);
```

The `F`, `N`, `h`, and `l` options are sized options used to overrule the argument's default size. The `F` and `[ ]` options are used in conjunction with far and near pointers, respectively. The `h` and `l` options are used to indicate `short int` or `long`, respectively.

Table 7.1. The escape sequence.

Sequence	Decimal Value	Hex Value	Task
`\a`	7	0X07	Bell
`\b`	8	0X08	Backspace
`\f`	12	0X0C	Formfeed
`\n`	10	0X0A	New line
`\r`	13	0X0D	Carriage return
`\t`	9	0X09	Horizontal tab
`\v`	11	0X0B	Vertical tab
`\\`	92	0X5C	Backslash
`\'`	44	0X2C	Single quote
`\"`	34	0X22	Double quote
`\?`	63	0X3F	Question mark
`\000`			1 to 3 digits for octal value
`\Xhhh` and `\xhhh`		0Xhhh	Hexadecimal value

The `printf` function requires that you specify a data type character with each `%` format code. Table 7.2 shows the options for the flags in the format string of `printf`. Table 7.3 shows the data type characters used in the format string of `printf`.

7

Table 7.2. Options for the flags in the format string of the `printf` function.

Format Option	Outcome
-	Justifies to the left within the specified field
+	Displays the plus or minus sign of a value
blank	Displays a leading blank if the value is positive; displays a minus sign if the value is negative
#	No effect on decimal integers; displays a leading `0X` or `0x` for hexadecimal integers; displays a leading zero for octal integers; displays the decimal point for reals

Table 7.3. Data type characters used in the format string of `printf`.

Category	Type Character	Outcome
Character	`c`	Single character
	`d`	Signed decimal `int`
	`i`	Signed decimal `int`
	`o`	Unsigned octal `int`
	`u`	Unsigned decimal `int`
	`x`	Unsigned hexadecimal `int`; the set of numeric characters used is 01234567890abcdef (note the lowercase letters)
	`X`	Unsigned hexadecimal `int`; the set of numeric characters used is 01234567890ABCDEF (note the uppercase letters)
Pointer	`p`	Displays only the offset for `near` pointers as `0000`; displays `far` pointers as `SSSS:0000`
Pointer to `int`	`n`	
Real	`f`	Displays signed value in the format `[-]dddd.dddd`
	`e`	Displays signed scientific value in the format `[-]d.dddde[+¦-]ddd`
	`E`	Displays signed scientific value in the format `[-]d.ddddE[+¦-]ddd`

Category	Type Character	Outcome
	`g`	Displays signed value using either the `f` or `e` formats, depending on the value and the specified precision
	`G`	Displays signed value using either the `f` or `E` formats, depending on the value and the specified precision
String pointer	`s`	Displays characters until the null terminator of the string is reached

Note: Although the function `printf` plays no role in the output of Windows applications, its sister function, `sprintf`, does. The latter function creates a string of characters that contains the formatted image of the output. The `sprintf` function is discussed in a later lesson in which you create a dialog box that contains messages that include numbers.

Consider a simple example. Listing 7.3 shows the source code for the program OUT2.CPP. This program was created by editing the OUT1.CPP in Listing 7.1. The new version displays formatted output using the `printf` function. The program displays the same floating-point numbers using three different sets of format code.

Listing 7.3. Source code for the program OUT2.CPP.

```
// C++ program that uses the printf function for formatted output

#include <stdio.h>

main()
{
   short    aShort     = 4;
   int      anInt      = 67;
   unsigned char aByte = 128;
   char     aChar      = '@';
   float    aSingle    = 355.0;
   double   aDouble    = 1.130e+002;
   // display sample expressions
   printf("%3d %c %2d = %3d\n",
           aByte, '+', anInt, aByte + anInt);

   printf("Output uses the %%lf format\n");
   printf("%6.4f / %6.4lf = %7.5lf\n", aSingle, aDouble,
                                    aSingle / aDouble);
   printf("Output uses the %%le format\n");
```

Listing 7.3. continued

```
21:   printf("%6.4e / %6.4le = %7.5le\n", aSingle, aDouble,
22:                                  aSingle / aDouble);
23:   printf("Output uses the %%lg format\n");
24:   printf("%6.4g / %6.4lg = %7.5lg\n", aSingle, aDouble,
25:                                  aSingle / aDouble);
26:
27:   printf("The character in variable aChar is %c\n", aChar);
28:   printf("The ASCII code of %c is %d\n", aChar, aChar);
29:    return 0;
30: }
```

Here is a sample session with the program in Listing 7.3.

```
128 + 67 = 195
Output uses the %lf format
355.0000 / 113.0000 = 3.14159
Output uses the %le format
3.5500e+002 / 1.1300e+002 = 3.14159e+000
Output uses the %lg format
355 / 113 = 3.1416
The character in variable aChar is @
The ASCII code of @ is 64
```

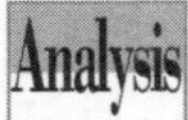

The program in Listing 7.3 declares a collection of variables with different data types. The output statement in lines 14 and 15 displays integers and characters using the `%d` and `%c` format controls. Table 7.4 shows the effect of the various format controls in the `printf` statement at line 14. Notice that the `printf` function converts the first item in output from an `unsigned char` to an `int`.

Table 7.4. Effects of the various format controls in the `printf` statement at line 16.

Format Control	Item	Data Type	Output
`%3d`	`aByte`	`unsigned char`	Integer
`%c`	`'+'`	`char`	Character
`%2d`	`anInt`	`int`	Integer
`%3d`	`aByte + anInt`	`int`	Integer

The output statement in line 18 displays the variable `aSingle`, the variable `aDouble`, and the expression `aSingle / aDouble` using the format controls `%6.4f`, `%6.4lf` and `%7.5lf`. These controls specify precision values of 4, 4, and 5 digits, respectively, and minimum widths of 6, 6, and 7 characters, respectively. The last two format controls indicate that they display a `double`-typed value.

The output statement in line 21 is similar to that in line 18. The main difference is that the `printf` in line 21 uses the `e` format rather than the `f` format. Consequently, the three items in the `printf` statement appear in scientific notation.

The output statement in line 24 is similar to that in line 18. The main difference is that the `printf` in line 24 uses the `g` format instead of the `f` format. Consequently, the first two items in the `printf` statement appear with no decimal places because they are whole numbers.

The output statement in line 27 displays the contents in the variable `aChar` using the `%c` format control. The output statement in line 28 displays the contents of variable `aChar` twice: once as a character and once as an integer (or, to be more exact, the ASCII code of a character). The `printf` function in line 28 performs this task by using the `%c` and `%d` format controls, respectively.

C++ Strings An Overview

C++ (and its parent language C) has no predefined string type. Instead, C++, like C, regards strings as arrays of characters that end with the ASCII 0 null character (`'\0'`).

NEW TERM The `'\0'` character also is called the *null terminator*. Strings that end with the null terminator sometimes are called *ASCIIZ strings*, with the letter Z standing for zero, the ASCII code of the null terminator. You also will see this character referred to as the NUL character as that's the ASCII name for it.

The null terminator *must* be present in all strings and taken into account when declaring space for a string. When you declare a string variable as an array of characters, be sure to reserve an extra character for the null terminator. The advantage of using the null terminator is that you can create strings that are not restricted by any limit imposed by the C++ implementation. In addition, ASCIIZ strings have very simple structures.

Note: The lesson in Day 4 discusses how pointers can access and manipulate the elements of an array. C and C++ make extensive use of this programming feature in manipulating the characters of a string.

7

DO	DON'T

DO include an extra character for the null terminator when specifying the size of a string.

DON'T declare a string variable as a single-character array. Such a variable is useless.

String Input

The programs presented thus far display string literals in output stream statements; C++ supports stream output for strings as a special case for a nonpredefined data type. (You can say the support came by popular demand.) String output using string variables uses the same operator and syntax. With string input, the output operator >> does not work well because strings often contain spaces that are ignored by the output operator. Instead of the output operator, you need to use the `getline` function. This function reads up to a specified number of characters.

Syntax

The *getline* Function

The general syntax for the overloaded `getline` function is

```
istream& getline(signed char* buffer,
int size,
char delimiter = '\n');

istream& getline(unsigned char* buffer,
                 int size,
                 char delimiter = '\n');

istream& getline(char* buffer,
                 int size,
                 char delimiter = '\n');
```

The parameter `buffer` is a pointer to the string receiving the characters from the stream. The parameter `size` specifies the maximum number of characters to read. The parameter `delimiter` specifies the delimiting character that causes the string input to stop before reaching the number of characters specified by parameter `size`. The parameter `delimiter` has the default argument of `'\n'`, which means that input will end when that character is reached; in the case of a person typing, this character will manifest itself when the person presses the Enter key.

Example

```
#include <iostream.h>
main()
{
   char name[80];
   cout << "Enter your name: ";
   cin.getline(name, sizeof(name)-1);
   cout << "Hello " << name << ", how are you";
   return 0;
}
```

Using the STRING.H Library

The community of C programmers has developed the standard string library STRING.H, which contains the most frequently used string-manipulation functions. The STDIO.H and IOSTREAM.H header file prototype functions also support string I/O. The ANSI/ISO C++

committee has also developed a C++-style string class. This class models strings more in line with the way Pascal and BASIC use them. (You learn more about classes on Day 8 and the C++ string class on Day 10.) The next sections present several (but by no means all) of the functions that are prototyped in the STRING.H header file.

Some of the string functions in STRING.H have more than one version. The extra versions that prepend the characters `_f`, `f`, or `_` to the function name work with strings that are specifically accessed using far pointers.

Assigning Strings

C++ supports two methods for assigning strings. You can assign a string literal to a string variable when you initialize it. This method is simple and requires using the = operator and the assigning string.

Syntax

Initializing a String

The general syntax for initializing a string is

```
char stringVar[stringSize] = stringLiteral;
```

Example

```
char aString[81] = "Turbo C++ 4.5 in 21 days";
char name[] = "Rene Kinner";
```

The second method for assigning one ASCIIZ string to another actually is just a function that copies the contents of one array to the other, being mindful of the null character on the end of the string—the function `strcpy`. This function assumes that the copied string ends with null character and stops copying when it's reached.

Syntax

The *strcpy* Function

The prototype for the function `strcpy` is

```
char* strcpy(char* target, const char* source)
```

The function copies the characters from string source to string target. The function *assumes* that the target string has enough space to contain the source string.

Example

```
char name[41];
strcpy(name,"Turbo C++ 4.5");
```

The variable `name` contains the string `"Turbo C++ 4.5"`.

The function `strdup` enables you to copy the characters to another string and allocate required space in the target string.

Syntax

The *strdup* Function

The prototype for the function `strdup` is

```
char* strdup(const char* source)
```

The function copies the characters in the source string and returns a pointer to the duplicate string.

Example

```
char* string1 = "The reign in Spain";
char* string2;

string2 = strdup(string1);
```

This example copies the contents of `string1` into `string2` after allocating the memory space for `string2`.

Note: Because `strdup` allocates memory for the new string, you will have to remember to free it later on. This is a nasty "gotcha" that catches a lot of programmers, both novice and expert.

The string library also offers the function `strncpy` to support copying a specified number of characters from one string to another.

Syntax

The *strncpy* Function

The prototype for the function `strncpy` is

```
char* strncpy(char* target, const char* source, size_t num);
```

The function copies *num* characters from the `source` string to the `target` string. Note that the function doesn't perform any character truncation or padding.

Example

```
char str1[] = "Pascal";
char str2[] = "Hello there";

strncpy(str1, str2, 5);
```

The variable `str1` now contains the string `"Hellol"`. Note how the `'l'` from the original string is still in there after the part that we copied.

Using `strncpy` often is preferred over using `strcpy`. The reason, of course, is to make sure that you don't copy more from the source string than there is room in the target string. If, for example, the target was created with room for only 20 characters and then you do a `strcpy` that moves 40 characters, you run the risk of corrupting memory and causing those nifty Windows GPFs.

Note: Using pointers to manipulate strings is a new idea to many novice C++ programmers. In fact, you can use pointers to manipulate the trailing parts of a string by assigning the address of the first character to manipulate. For example, if we declare the string `str1` as follows:

```
char str1[41] = "Hello World";
char str2[41];
char* p = str1;

p += 6; // p now points to substring "World" in str
strcpy(str2, p);
cout << str2 << "\n";
```

the output statement displays the string `"World"`. This example shows how using pointers can incorporate an offset number of characters.

The Length of a String

Many string operations require information about the number of characters in a string. The STRING.H library offers the function `strlen` to return the number of characters, excluding the null terminator, in a string.

Syntax

The *strlen* Function

The prototype for the function `strlen` is

```
size_t strlen(const char* string)
```

The function `strlen` returns the number of characters in the parameter `string`. The result type `size_t` has a `typedef` of an `unsigned int` type.

Example

```
char str[] = "1234567890";
size_t i;
i = strlen(str);
```

These statements assign `10` to the variable `i`.

Concatenating Strings

Often, you build a string by concatenating two or more strings. The function `strcat` enables you to concatenate one string to another.

NEW TERM When you *concatenate* strings, you join or link them together.

Syntax

The *strcat* Function

The prototype for the function `strcat` is

```
char* strcat(char* target, const char* source)
```

The function appends the contents of the source string to the target string and returns the pointer to the target string. The function *assumes* that the target string can accommodate the characters of the source string.

Example

```
char string[81];
strcpy(string, "Turbo");
strcat(string," C++ 4.5")
```

The variable string now contains `"Turbo C++ 4.5"`.

The function `strncat` concatenates a specified number of characters from the source string to the target strings.

Syntax

The *strncat* Function

The prototype for the function `strncat` is

```
char* strncat(char* target, const char* source, size_t num)
```

The function appends *`num`* characters of the source string to the target string and returns the pointer to the target string.

Example

```
char str1[81] = "Hello I am ";
char str2[41] = "Keith Thompson";

strncat(str1, str2, 5);
```

The variable `str1` now contains `"Hello I am Keith"`.

DO	DON'T

DO use the function `strncat` to control the number of concatenated characters, when you are unsure of the capacity of the target string.

DON'T assume that the target string is always adequate to store the characters in the source string.

Look at a program that uses the `getline`, `strlen`, and `strcat` functions. Listing 7.4 contains the source code for the program STRING1.CPP. The program performs the following tasks:

- Prompts you to enter a string; your input should not exceed 40 characters
- Prompts you to enter a second string; your input should not exceed 40 characters
- Displays the number of characters in each of the strings you enter
- Concatenates the second string to the first one
- Displays the concatenated strings
- Displays the number of characters in the concatenated strings
- Prompts you to enter a search character
- Prompts you to enter a replacement character
- Displays the concatenated string after translating all the occurrences of the search character with the replacement character

Listing 7.4. Source code for the program STRING1.CPP.

```
/*
  C++ program that demonstrates C-style strings
*/

#include <iostream.h>
#include <string.h>

const unsigned MAX1 = 40;
const unsigned MAX2 = 80;

int main()
{

    char smallStr[MAX1+1];
    char bigStr[MAX2+1];
    char findChar, replChar;

    cout << "Enter first string:\n";
    cin.getline(bigStr, MAX2);
    cout << "Enter second string:\n";
    cin.getline(smallStr, MAX1);
    cout << "String 1 has " << strlen(bigStr)
         << " characters\n";
    cout << "String 2 has " << strlen(smallStr)
         << " characters\n";
    // concatenate bigStr to smallStr
    strcat(bigStr, smallStr);
    cout << "Concatenated strings are:\n"
         << bigStr << "\n";
    cout << "New string has " << strlen(bigStr)
         << " characters\n";
    // get the search and replacement characters
    cout << "Enter search character : ";
```

continues

Listing 7.4. continued

```
34:     cin >> findChar;
35:     cout << "Enter replacement character : ";
36:     cin >> replChar;
37:     // replace characters in string bigStr
38:     size_t bigLen = strlen(bigStr);
39:     for (unsigned i = 0; i < bigLen; i++)
40:       if (bigStr[i] == findChar)
41:         bigStr[i] = replChar;
42:     // display the updated string bigStr
43:     cout << "New string is:\n"
44:          << bigStr;
45:     return 0;
46: }
```

Here is a sample session with the program in Listing 7.4.

```
Enter first string:
The rain in Spain stays
Enter second string:
mainly in the plain
String 1 has 23 characters
String 2 has 20 characters
Concatenated strings are:
The rain in Spain stays mainly in the plain
New string has 43 characters
Enter search character : a
Enter replacement character : A
New string is:
The rAin in SpAin stAys mAinly in the plAin
```

The program in Listing 7.4 includes the STRING.H header file for the string manipulation functions. Lines 8 and 9 declare the global constants `MAX1` and `MAX2`, which are used to size a small string and a big string, respectively. The function `main` declares two strings, `smallStr` and `bigStr`. Line 14 declares the variable `smallStr` to store `MAX1+1` characters. (The extra space is for the null character.) Line 15 declares the variable `bigStr` to store `MAX2+1` characters. Line 16 declares the `char`-typed variable `findChar` and `replChar`.

The output statement in line 18 prompts you to enter the first string. The statement in line 19 uses the stream input function `getline` to obtain your input and to store it in variable `bigStr`. The function call specifies that you can enter up to `MAX2` characters. The output statement in line 20 prompts you to enter the second string. The statement in line 21 uses the stream input function `getline` to obtain your input and to store it in the variable `smallStr`. The function call specifies that you can enter up to `MAX1` characters.

The output statements in lines 22 through 25 display the number of characters in variables `bigStr` and `smallStr`, respectively. Each output statement calls function `strlen` and passes it a string variable.

The statement in line 27 concatenates the string in the variable `smallStr` to the variable `bigStr`. The output statement in lines 28 and 29 displays the updated string `bigStr`. The output statement in lines 30 and 31 displays the number of characters in the updated string variable `bigStr`. This statement also uses the function `strlen` to obtain the number of characters.

The statement in line 33 prompts you to enter the search character. The statement in line 34 obtains your input and stores it in variable `findChar`. The statement in line 35 prompts you to enter the replacement character. The statement in line 36 obtains your input and stores it in variable `replChar`.

The `for` loop in lines 38 to 41 translates the characters in string `bigStr`. The loop uses the control variable `i` and iterates, in increments of 1, from `0` to `bigLen-1` (which is set on line 38 to be `strlen(bigstr)`). The `if` statement in line 40 determines whether character number `i` in `bigStr` matches the character in variable `findChar`. If this condition is true, the program executes the statement in line 41. This statement assigns the character in variable `replChar` to character number `i` in variable `bigStr`. This loop shows how you can manipulate the contents of a string variable by accessing each character in that string.

The output statement in lines 43 and 44 displays the updated string `bigStr`.

String Comparison

Because strings are arrays of characters, you can't just simply use the `==` or `!=` operators (or > and <, for that matter) to test for equality. The STRING.H library provides a set of functions to compare strings. These functions compare the characters of two strings using the ASCII value of each character. The functions are `strcmp`, `stricmp`, `strncmp`, and `strnicmp`.

In general, all the comparison functions return `0` if the two strings compare equally, a negative value if the second string in the comparison is greater, or a positive value if the first string is greater.

The function `strcmp` performs a case-sensitive comparison of two strings, using every character possible.

7

Syntax

The *strcmp* Function

The prototype for the function `strcmp` is

```
int strcmp(const char* str1, const char* str2);
```

The function compares strings *str1* and *str2*. The integer result indicates the outcome of the comparison.

```
< 0  when str1 is less than str2
= 0  when str1 is equal to str2
> 0  when str1 is greater than str2
```

Example

```
char string1[] = "Turbo C++ 4.5";
char string2[] = "TURBO C++ 4.5";
int i;

i = strcmp(string1, string2);
```

The last statement assigns a positive number to the variable `i`, because the string in variable `string1` is greater than the string in variable `string2` (lowercase actually is greater than uppercase in ASCII).

The function `stricmp` performs a case-insensitive comparison between two strings, using every character possible.

Syntax

The *stricmp* Function

The prototype for the function `stricmp` is

```
int stricmp(const char* str1, const char* str2);
```

The function compares strings *`str1`* and *`str2`* without making a distinction between upper- and lowercase characters. The integer result indicates the outcome of the comparison.

```
< 0  when str1 is less than str2
= 0  when str1 is equal to str2
> 0  when str1 is greater than str2
```

Example

```
char string1[] = "Turbo C++ 4.5";
char string2[] = "TURBO C++ 4.5";
int i;

i = stricmp(string1, string2);
```

The last statement assigns `0` to the variable `i` because the strings in variables `string1` and `string2` differ only in their cases.

The function `strncmp` performs a case-sensitive comparison on specified leading characters in two strings.

Syntax

The *strncmp* Function

The prototype for the function `strncmp` is

```
int strncmp(const char* str1, const char* str2, size_t num);
```

The function compares the *`num`* leading characters in two strings, *`str1`* and *`str2`*. The integer result indicates the outcome of the comparison, as follows:

```
< 0  when str1 is less than str2
```

```
= 0  when str1 is equal to str2
> 0  when str1 is greater than str2
```

Example

```
char string1[] = "Turbo C++ 4.5";
char string2[] = "Turbo Pascal";
int i;

i = strncmp(string1, string2, 7);
```

This assigns a negative number to the variable `i` because `"Turbo C"` is less than `"Turbo P"`.

The function `strnicmp` performs a case-insensitive comparison on specified leading characters in two strings.

Syntax

The *strnicmp* Function

The prototype for the function `strnicmp` is

```
int strnicmp(const char* str1, const char* str2, size_t num);
```

The function compares the *num* leading characters in two strings, *str1* and *str2*, regardless of the character case. The integer result indicates the outcome of the comparison, as follows:

```
< 0  when str1 is less than str2
= 0  when str1 is equal to str2
> 0  when str1 is greater than str2
```

Example

```
char string1[] = "Turbo C++ 4.5";
char string2[] = "TURBO Pascal";
int i;

i = strnicmp(string1, string2, 5);
```

This assigns `0` to the variable `i` because the strings `"Turbo"` and `"TURBO"` differ only in the case of their characters.

Look at an example that compares strings. Listing 7.5 creates an array of strings and initializes it with data. Then the program displays the unordered array of strings, sorts the array, and displays the sorted array.

Listing 7.5. Source code for the program STRING2.CPP.

```
/*
  C++ program that demonstrates comparing strings
*/

#include <iostream.h>
#include <string.h>

```

continues

Listing 7.5. continued

```
const unsigned STR_SIZE = 40;
const unsigned ARRAY_SIZE = 11;
const int TRUE = 1;
const int FALSE = 0;

main()
{

    char strArr[STR_SIZE][ARRAY_SIZE] =
       { "California", "Virginia", "Alaska", "New York",
         "Michigan", "Nevada", "Ohio", "Florida",
         "Washington", "Oregon", "Arizona" };
    char temp[STR_SIZE];
    unsigned[]= ARRAY_SIZE;
    unsigned offset;
    int inOrder;

    cout << "Unordered array of strings is:\n";
    for (unsigned i = 0; i < ARRAY_SIZE; i++)
      cout << strArr[i] << "\n";

    cout << "\nEnter a non-space character and press Enter";
    cin >> temp[0];
    cout << "\n";

    offset = n;
    do {
      offset = (8 * offset) / 11;
      offset = (offset == 0) ? 1 : offset;
      inOrder = TRUE;
      for (unsigned i = 0, j = offset;
           i <[]- offset; i++, j++)
        if (strcmp(strArr[i], strArr[j]) > 0) {
          strcpy(temp, strArr[i]);
          strcpy(strArr[i], strArr[j]);
          strcpy(strArr[j], temp);
          inOrder = FALSE;
        }
    } while (!(offset == 1 && inOrder));

    cout << "Sorted array of strings is:\n";
    for (i = 0; i < ARRAY_SIZE; i++)
      cout << strArr[i] << "\n";
    return 0;
}
```

Here is a sample session with the program in Listing 7.5.

```
Unordered array of strings is:
California
Virginia
Alaska
New York
```

```
Michigan
Nevada
Ohio
Florida
Washington
Oregon
Arizona
Enter a non-space character and press Enterc
Sorted array of strings is:
Alaska
Arizona
California
Florida
Michigan
Nevada
New York
Ohio
Oregon
Virginia
Washington
```

Analysis The program in Listing 7.5 declares the global constants `STR_SIZE`, `ARRAY_SIZE`, `TRUE`, and `FALSE` in lines 8 through 11. The constant `STR_SIZE` specifies the size of each string. The constant `ARRAY_SIZE` indicates the number of strings in the array used by the program. The constants `TRUE` and `FALSE` represent the Boolean values employed in sorting the array of strings. The function `main` declares the array `strArr` (actually, the variable `strArr` is a matrix of characters) to have `ARRAY_SIZE` elements and `STR_SIZE` characters per elements. Notice that the declaration states the size of each string in the first dimension and the size of the array in the second dimension. The function also initializes the array `strArr`. The function also declares the variable `temp` as a swap buffer. Lines 21 through 23 declare miscellaneous variables.

The output statement in line 25 shows the title before showing the elements of the unordered array `strArr`. The `for` loop in lines 26 and 27 displays the elements. The loop uses the control variable `i` and iterates, in increments of 1, from `0` to `ARRAY_SIZE-1`. The output statement in line 27 displays the string at element `i`, using the expression `strArr[i]`.

The output and input statements in lines 29 and 30 prompt you to enter a nonspace character. This input enables you to examine the unordered array before the program sorts the array and displays its ordered elements.

The statements in lines 33 through 46 implement the Comb sort method. Notice that the `if` statement in line 40 uses the function `strcmp` to compare elements number `i` and `j`, accessed using the expressions `strArr[i]` and `strArr[j]`, respectively. The statements in lines 41 through 43 swap the elements `i` and `j`, using the function `strcpy` and the swap buffer `temp`.

The output statement in line 48 displays the title before showing the elements of the sorted array. The `for` loop in lines 49 and 50 displays these elements. The loop utilizes the control variable `i` and iterates, in increments of 1, from `0` to `ARRAY_SIZE-1`. The output statement in line 50 displays the string at element `i`, using the expression `strArr[i]`.

Converting Strings

The STRING.H library offers the functions `_strlwr` and `_strupr` to convert the characters of a string to lowercase and uppercase, respectively. Note that these functions are more commonly called `strlwr` and `strupr` (without the leading underscore character) in C textbooks. I'm showing it with the leading underscore because it's not an ANSI/ISO standard function (probably because it's so trivial to write it on your own). But it's useful enough to mention here.

Syntax

The *_strlwr* Function

The prototype for the function `_strlwr` is

```
char* _strlwr(char* source)
```

The function converts the uppercase characters in the string *`source`* to lowercase. Other characters are not affected. The function also returns the pointer to the string *`source`*.

Example

```
char str[] = "HELLO THERE";

_strlwr(str);
```

The variable `str` now contains the string `"hello there"`.

Syntax

The *_strupr* Function

The prototype for the function `_strupr` is

```
char* _strupr(char* source)
```

The function converts the lowercase characters in the string *`source`* to uppercase. Other characters are not affected. The function also returns the pointer to the string *`source`*.

Example

```
char str[] = "Turbo C++ 4.5";
_strupr(str);
```

The variable `str` now contains the string `"TURBO C++ 4.5"`.

DO	DON'T

DO make copies for the arguments of functions `_strlwr` and `_strupr` if you need the original arguments later in a program.

DON'T always assume that applying the function `_strlwr` and then the function `_strupr` (or vice versa) to the same variable will succeed in restoring the original characters in that variable.

Reversing Strings

The STRING.H library offers the function `strrev` to reverse the characters in a string.

Syntax

The *strrev* Function

The prototype for the function `strrev` is

```
char* strrev(char* str)
```

The function reverses the order of the characters in string `str` and returns the pointer to the string `str`.

Example

```
char string[] = "Hello";

strrev(string);
cout << string;
```

This displays `"olleH"`.

Look at a program that manipulates the characters in a string. Listing 7.6 shows the source code for the program STRING3.CPP. The program performs the following tasks:

- Prompts you to enter a string
- Displays your input
- Displays the lowercase version of your input
- Displays the uppercase version of your input
- Displays the character you typed, in reverse order
- Displays a message that your input has no uppercase character, if this is true
- Displays a message that your input has no lowercase character, if this is true
- Displays a message that your input has symmetrical characters, if this is true

Listing 7.6. Source code for the program STRING3.CPP.

```
/*
  C++ program that demonstrates manipulating the
  characters in a string
*/

#include <iostream.h>
#include <string.h>

 const unsigned STR_SIZE = 40;
const int TRUE = 1;
const int FALSE = 0;

main()
{
```

7

continues

Listing 7.6. continued

```
15:     char str1[STR_SIZE+1];
16:     char str2[STR_SIZE+1];
17:     int isLowerCase;
18:     int isUpperCase;
19:     int isSymmetrical;
20:
21:
22:     cout << "Enter a string : ";
23:     cin.getline(str1, STR_SIZE);
24:     cout << "Input: " << str1 << "\n";
25:     // copy str1 to str2
26:     strcpy(str2, str1);
27:     // convert to lowercase
28:     strlwr(str2);
29:     isLowerCase = (strcmp(str1, str2) == 0) ? TRUE : FALSE;
30:     cout << "Lowercase: " << str2 << "\n";
31:     // convert to uppercase
32:     strupr(str2);
33:     isUpperCase = (strcmp(str1, str2) == 0) ? TRUE : FALSE;
34:     cout << "Uppercase: " << str2 << "\n";
35:     // copy str1 to str2
36:     strcpy(str2, str1);
37:     // reverse characters
38:     strrev(str2);
39:     isSymmetrical = (strcmp(str1, str2) == 0) ? TRUE : FALSE;
40:     cout << "Reversed: " << str2 << "\n";
41:     if (isLowerCase)
42:       cout << "Your input has no uppercase letters\n";
43:     if (isUpperCase)
44:       cout << "Your input has no lowercase letters\n";
45:     if (isSymmetrical)
46:       cout << "Your input has symmetrical characters\n";
47:     return 0;
48: }
```

Here is a sample session with the program in Listing 7.6.

```
Enter a string : level
Input: level
Lowercase: level
Uppercase: LEVEL
Reversed: level
Your input has no uppercase letters
Your input has symmetrical characters
```

The program in Listing 7.6 declares the string variables `str1` and `str2` in the function `main`. Each string stores `STR_SIZE + 1` characters (including the null terminator). The function also declares the flags `isLowerCase`, `isUpperCase`, and `isSymmetrical`.

The output statement in line 22 prompts you to enter a string. The statement in line 23 uses the string input function `getline` to store your input in variable `str1`. The output statement in line 24 echoes your input.

The statement in line 26 copies the characters in variable `str1` to variable `str2`. The statement in line 26 calls the function `strlwr` to convert the characters in variable `str2`. The program manipulates the characters of variable str2, while maintaining the original input in variable str1. The statement in line 29 calls the function strcmp to compare the characters in str1 and str2. The two strings can be equal only if your input has no uppercase characters. The statement uses the conditional operator to assign the constant TRUE to the flag isLowerCase if the above condition is true. Otherwise, the statement assigns FALSE to the flag isLowerCase. The output statement in line 30 displays the characters in variable str2.

The statement in line 32 calls the function strupr and supplies it the argument str2. This function call converts any lowercase character in variable str2 into uppercase. The statement in line 33 calls the function strcmp to compare the characters in str1 and str2. The two strings can be equal only if your input has no lowercase characters. The statement uses the conditional operator to assign the constant TRUE to the flag isUpperCase if that is true. Otherwise, the statement assigns FALSE to the flag isUpperCase. The output statement in line 34 displays the characters in variable str2.

To display the original input in reverse order, the program calls the function strcpy to copy the characters of variable str1 to variable str2 once more. The statement in line 38 calls the function strrev and passes it the argument str2. The statement in line 39 calls the function strcmp to compare the characters in str1 and str2. The two strings can be equal only if your input has symmetrical characters. The statement uses the conditional operator to assign the constant TRUE to the flag isSymmetrical if the characters in str1 and str2 match. Otherwise, the statement assigns FALSE to the flag isSymmetrical. The output statement in line 40 displays the characters in variable str2.

The program uses the if statements in lines 41, 43, and 45 to indicate that your input has special characteristics. The if statement in line 41 comments on the fact that your input has no uppercase letter when the value in variable isLowerCase is TRUE. The if statement in line 43 comments on the fact that your input has no lowercase letter when the value in variable isUpperCase is TRUE. The if statement in line 45 comments on the fact that your input has symmetrical characters when the value in variable isSymmetrical is TRUE.

Locating Characters

The STRING.H library offers a number of functions for locating characters in strings. These functions include strchr, strrchr, strspn, strcspn, and strpbrk. These functions enable you to search for characters and simple character patterns in strings.

7

The function strchr locates the first occurrence of a character in a string.

Syntax

The *strchr* Function

The prototype for the function strchr is

```
char* strchr(const char* target, int c)
```

The function locates the first occurrence of pattern *c* in the string *target*. The function returns the pointer to the character in string *target* that matches the specified pattern `c`. If character `c` does not occur in the string *target*, the function yields a `NULL`.

Example

```
char str[81] = "Turbo C++ 4.5";
char* strPtr;

strPtr = strchr(str, '+');
```

The pointer `strPtr` points to the substring `"++ 4.5"` in string `str`.

The function `strrchr` locates the last occurrence of a character in a string.

Syntax

The *strrchr* Function

The prototype for the function `strrchr` is

```
char* strrchr(const char* target, int c)
```

The function locates the last occurrence of pattern `c` in the string *target*. The function returns the pointer to the character in string *target* that matches the specified pattern `c`. If character `c` does not occur in the string *target*, the function yields a `NULL`.

Example

```
char str[81] = "Turbo C++ 4.5 is here";
char* strPtr;

strPtr = strrchr(str, '+');
```

The pointer `strPtr` points to the substring `"+ 4.5 is here"` in string `str`.

The function `strspn` yields the number of characters in the leading part of a string that matches any character in a pattern of characters.

Syntax

The *strspn* Function

The prototype for the function `strspn` is

```
size_t strspn(const char* target, const char* pattern)
```

The function returns the number of characters in the leading part of the string *target* that matches any character in the string *pattern*.

Example

```
char str[] = "Turbo C++ 4.5";
char substr[] = "bruTo ";
int index;
```

```
index = strspn(str, substr);
```

This statement assigns 6 to the variable `index` because the characters in `substr` found a match in each of the first six characters of `str`.

The function `strcspn` scans a string and yields the number of leading characters in a string that is totally void of the characters in a substring.

Syntax

The *strcspn* Function

The prototype for the function `strcspn` is

```
size_t strcspn(const char* str1, const char* str2)
```

The function scans *`str1`* and returns the length of the leftmost substring that is totally void of the characters of the substring *`str2`*.

Example

```
char strng[] = "The rain in Spain";
int i;

i = strcspn(strng, " in");
```

This example assigns 3 (the location of the first space) to the variable `i`.

The function `strpbrk` searches a string for the first occurrence of any character in a pattern of characters.

Syntax

The *strpbrk* Function

The prototype for the function `strpbrk` is

```
char* strpbrk(const char* target, const char* pattern)
```

The function searches the *`target`* string for the first occurrence of *any character* among the characters of the string *`pattern`*. If the characters in the pattern do not occur in the string *`target`*, the function yields a `0`.

Example

```
char* str = "Hello there how are you";
char* substr = "hr";
char* ptr;

ptr = strpbrk(str, substr);
cout << ptr << endl;
```

This displays `"here how are you"`, because the `'h'` is encountered in the string before the `'r'`.

Locating Strings

The STRING.H library offers the function `strstr` to locate a substring in a string.

Syntax

The *strstr* Function

The prototype for the function `strstr` is

```
char* strstr(const char* str, const char* substr);
```

The function scans the string *`str`* for the first occurrence of a string *`substr`*. The function yields the pointer to the first character in string *`str`* that matches the parameter *`substr`*. If the string *`substr`* does not occur in the string *`str`*, the function yields a `NULL`.

Example

```
char str[] = "Hello there! how are you";
char substr[] = "how";
char* ptr;

ptr = strstr(str, substr);
cout << ptr << "\n";
```

This displays `"how are you"` because the string search matched `"how"`. The pointer `ptr` points to the rest of the original string, starting with `"how"`.

DO	DON'T

DO use the function `strrev` before calling the function `strstr` if you want to search for the last occurrence of a string.

DON'T forget to reverse both the main and the search strings when using the `strrev` function to locate the last occurrence of the search string.

The string library also provides the function `strtok`, which enables you to break down a string into substrings based on a specified set of delimiting characters.

NEW TERM Substrings are sometimes called *tokens.*

Syntax

The *strtok* Function

The prototype for the function `strtok` is

```
char* strtok(char* target, const char* delimiters);
```

The function searches the target string for tokens. A string supplies the set of delimiter characters. The following example shows how this function works in returning the tokens in a

string. The function strtok modifies the string target by inserting '\0' characters after each token. (Make sure that you store a copy of the original target string in another string variable.)

Example

```
#include <stdio.h>
#include <string.h>

main()
{
   char* str = "(Base_Cost+Profit) * Margin";
   char* tkn = "+* ()";
   char* ptr = str;

   printf("%s\n", str);
   // the first call looks normal
   ptr = strtok(str, tkn);
   printf("\n\nThis is broken into: %s",ptr);
   while (ptr)
      {
      printf(" ,%s",ptr);
      // must make first argument a 0 character
      ptr = strtok(0, tkn);
      }
   printf("\n\n");
}
```

This example displays the following when the program is run:

```
(Base_Cost+Profit) * Margin
```

This is broken into Base_Cost, Profit, Margin.

DO	DON'T

DO remember to supply 0 as the first argument to the function strtok in order to locate the next token.

DON'T forget to store a copy of the target string in the function strtok.

Look at an example that searches for characters and strings. Listing 7.7 shows the source code for the program STRING4.CPP. The program performs the following tasks:

- ☐ Prompts you to enter the main string
- ☐ Prompts you to enter the search string
- ☐ Prompts you to enter the search character
- ☐ Displays a character ruler and the main string
- ☐ Displays the indices where the search string occurs in the main string
- ☐ Displays the indices where the search character occurs in the main string

Listing 7.7. Source code for the program STRING4.CPP.

```
/*
  C++ program that demonstrates searching for the
  characters and strings
*/

#include <iostream.h>
#include <string.h>

const unsigned STR_SIZE = 40;

main()
{
    char mainStr[STR_SIZE+1];
    char subStr[STR_SIZE+1];
    char findChar;
    char *p;
    int index;
    int count;

    cout << "Enter a string : ";
    cin.getline(mainStr, STR_SIZE);
    cout << "Enter a search string : ";
    cin.getline(subStr, STR_SIZE);
    cout << "Enter a search character : ";
    cin >> findChar;

    cout << "          1         2         3         4\n";
    cout << "01234567890123456789012345678901234567890\n";
    cout << mainStr << "\n";
    cout << "Searching for string " << subStr << "\n";
    p = strstr(mainStr, subStr);
    count = 0;
    while (p) {
      count++;
      index = p - mainStr;
      cout << "Match at index " << index << "\n";
      p = strstr(++p, subStr);
    }
    if (count == 0)
      cout << "No match for substring in main string\n";

    cout << "Searching for character " << findChar << "\n";
    p = strchr(mainStr, findChar);
    count = 0;
    while (p) {
      count++;
      index = p - mainStr;
      cout << "Match at index " << index << "\n";
      p = strchr(++p, findChar);
    }
    if (count == 0)
      cout << "No match for search character in main string\n";
    return 0;
}
```

Here is a sample session with the program in Listing 7.7.

```
Enter a string : here, there, and everywhere
Enter a search string : here
Enter a search character : e
          1         2         3         4
01234567890123456789012345678901234567890
here, there, and everywhere
Searching for string here
Match at index 0
Match at index 7
Match at index 23
Searching for character e
Match at index 1
Match at index 3
Match at index 8
Match at index 10
Match at index 17
Match at index 19
Match at index 24
Match at index 26
```

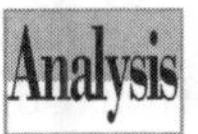

The program in Listing 7.7 declares the strings `mainStr` and `subStr` to represent the main and search strings, respectively. The program also declares the variable `findChar` to store the search character. In addition, the program declares the character pointer `p` and the `int`-typed variables `index` and `count`.

The output statement in line 20 prompts you to enter a string. The statement in line 21 calls the stream input function `getline` and stores your input in variable `mainStr`. The output statement in line 22 prompts you to enter the search string. The statement in line 23 calls the stream input function `getline` and saves your input in variable `subStr`. The output statement in line 24 prompts you to enter the search character. The statement in line 25 obtains your input and stores it in the variable `findChar`.

The output statements in lines 27 through 29 display a ruler, along with your input aligned under the ruler. The output statement in line 30 informs you that the program is searching for the substring you entered. The search begins at the statement in line 31. This statement calls the function `strstr` to locate the first occurrence of string `subStr` in the string `mainStr`. The statement in line 32 assigns `0` to the variable `count`, which keeps track of the number of times the string `mainStr` contains the string `subStr`.

The program uses the `while` loop in lines 33 through 38 to locate all the occurrences of `subStr` in `mainStr`. The condition of the `while` loop examines the address of pointer `p`. If that pointer is not `NULL`, the loop iterates. The first statement inside the loop increments the variable `count`. The statement in line 35 calculates the index of the string `mainStr` where the last match occurs. The statement obtains the sought index by subtracting the address of pointer `p` from the address of the first character in the variable `mainStr`. (Remember that the expression `&mainStr[0]` is equivalent to the simpler expression `mainStr`.) The statement assigns the result to the variable `index`. The output statement in line 36 displays the value in variable `index`.

The statement in line 37 searches for the next occurrence of the string `subStr` in `mainStr`. Notice that this statement calls `strstr` and supplies it the pointer `p` as the first argument. The statement also applies the pre-increment operator to pointer `p` to store the address of the next character. This action ensures that the call to function `strstr` finds the next occurrence, if any, and is not stuck at the last occurrence. The `if` statement outside the `while` loop examines the value in variable `count`. If it contains zero, the program executes the output statement in line 40 to inform you that no match was found for the search string.

The output statement in line 42 informs you that the program is now searching for the character you specified in the main string. The process of searching for the character in `findChar` is very similar to searching for the string `subStr`. The main difference is that searching for a character involves the function `strchr`.

Summary

Today's lesson examined the basic input and output operations and functions that are supported by the IOSTREAM.H and STDIO.H header files as well as the C++ strings and their manipulation by functions that are declared in the STRING.H header file. You learned the following:

- Formatted stream output uses the `precision` and `width` functions to provide some basic formatting output.
- Standard stream input supports the insert operator `>>` to obtain input for the predefined data types in C++.
- The format codes involved in the format string of the `printf` function allow the `printf` function to control the appearance of the output and even perform type conversion.
- Strings in C++ are arrays of characters that end with the null character (the ASCII `0` character).
- String input requires the use of the `getline` stream input function. This function requires that you specify the input variable, the maximum number of input characters, and the optional line delimiter.
- The STRING.H header file contains the standard string library for the C language. This library contains many versatile functions that support copying, concatenating, converting, reversing, and searching for strings.
- C++ supports two methods for assigning strings. The first method assigns a string to another when you declare the latter string. The second method uses the function `strcpy` to assign one string to another at any stage in the program. The string library also offers the function `strdup` to copy a string and allocate the needed space.
- The function `strlen` returns the length of a string.

- The strcat and strncat functions enable you to concatenate two strings. The function strncat enables you to specify the number of characters to concatenate.
- The functions strcmp, stricmp, strncmp, and strnicmp enable you to perform various types of string comparisons. The function strcmp performs a case-insensitive comparison of two strings, using every character possible. The function stricmp is a version of the function strcmp that performs a case-insensitive comparison. The function strncmp is a variant of function strcmp that uses a specified number of characters in comparing the strings. The function strnicmp is a version of function strncmp that also performs a case-insensitive comparison.
- The functions strlwr and strupr convert the characters of a string into lowercase and uppercase, respectively.
- The function strrev reverses the order of characters in a string.
- The functions strchr, strrchr, strspn, strcspn, and strpbrk enable you to search for characters and simple character patterns in strings.
- The function strstr searches for a string in another string. The function strtok enables you to break down a string into smaller strings that are delimited by a set of characters that you specify.

Q&A

Q How can I chain >> or << operators?

A Each of these operators returns a special stream data type that can be the input for another similar stream operator.

Q Why can't I use the console stream I/O operators in Windows applications?

A Windows applications have a fundamentally different way of interacting with you. When an EasyWin program (which emulates a non-GUI MS-DOS application) executes an input statement, it goes into a special mode where it monitors the keyboard input. By contrast, Windows programs (which are GUI applications) are always monitoring the mouse (its movements and its button clicks) and the keyboard and reporting the current status to the part of Windows that monitors such events. The vast differences between GUI and non-GUI applications render non-GUI input functions useless in GUI applications.

Q Can a statement initialize a pointer using a string literal?

A Yes. The compiler stores the characters of the string literal in memory and assigns its address to that pointer. Here is an example.

```
const char* p = "I am a small string";
```

Be aware, however, that some compilers may put these strings into a part of memory that is read-only, so you will not be able to modify them. That's why the example assigns a const char* instead of a regular char*.

Q Can a statement declare a constant pointer to a literal string?

A Yes. This kind of declaration resembles the one mentioned previously. Because the statement declares a constant pointer, however, you cannot overwrite the characters of the initializing string literal (you will get a compile-time error). Here is an example.

```
const char* p = "Version 1.0";
```

Use the `const char*` pointer to store fixed messages and titles.

Q Can a statement declare an array of pointers to a set of string literals?

A Yes. This is the easiest method of using an array of pointers to access a collection of messages, titles, or other types of fixed strings. Here is an example.

```
char* mainMenu[] = { "File", "Edit", "Search", "View",
                     "Debug", "Options", "Windows", "Help"};
```

Thus, the element `mainMenu[0]` accesses the first string, `mainMenu[1]` accesses the second string, and so on.

Q How can I use `strcmp` to compare strings, starting at a specific number of characters?

A Add the offset value to the arguments of the function `strcmp`. Here is an example.

```
char s1[41] = "Turbo C++ 4.5";
char s2[41] = "TURBO Pascal";
int offset = 5;
int i;
i = strcmp(str1 + offset, str2 + offset);
```

Q How can I use `strncmp` to compare a specific number of characters in two strings, starting at a specific character?

A Add the offset value to the arguments of the function `strcmp`. Here is an example.

```
char s1[41] = "Turbo C++ 4.5";
char s2[41] = "TURBO Pascal";
int offset = 5;
int num = 3;
int i;
i = strncmp(str1 + offset, str2 + offset, num);
```

Workshop

The Workshop provides quiz questions to help you solidify your understanding of the material covered and exercises to provide you with experience in using what you've learned. Try to understand the quiz and exercise answers before continuing on to the next day's lesson. Answers are provided in Appendix A.

Quiz

1. What is wrong with the following statement?

```
cout << "Enter a number " >> x;
```

2. What happens in the following statement?

```
cout << "Enter three numbers : ";
cin >> x >> y >> x;
```

3. Where is the error in the following program?

```
#include <iostream.h>
#include <string.h>
const int MAX = 10;
main()
{
  char s1[MAX+1];
  char s2[] = "123456789012345678901234567890";
  strcpy(s1, s2);
  cout << "String 1 is " << s1
       << "\nString 2 is " << s2;
  return 0;
}
```

4. How can you fix the program in the last question using the function `strncpy` instead of `strcpy`?

5. What is the value assigned to variable `i` in the following statements?

```
char s1[] = "Turbo C++";
char s2[] = "Turbo Pascal";
int i;
i = strcmp(s1, s2);
```

6. What is the value assigned to variable `i` in the following statements?

```
char s1[] = "Turbo C++";
char s2[] = "Turbo Pascal";
int offset = strlen("Turbo ");
int i;
i = strcmp(s1 + offset, s2 + offset);
```

7. True or false? The following function correctly returns `1` if a string does not contain lowercase characters, and yields `0` if otherwise.

```
int hasNoLowerCase(const char* s)
{
  char* s2 = new char[strlen(s)+1];
  strcpy(s2, s);
  strupr(s2);
  return (strcmp(s, s2) == 0)? 1 : 0);
}
```

Exercises

1. Write the program OUT3.CPP, which displays a table of square roots for whole numbers in the range of 2 to 10. Use the MATH.H header file to import the `sqrt` function, which calculates the square root of a `double`-typed argument. Because C++ loops have not yet been discussed, use repetitive statements to display the various values. Employ the format controls `%3.0lf` and `%3.4lf`, respectively, to display the number and its square root.
2. Write the program OUT4.CPP, which prompts you for an integer and displays the hexadecimal and octal equivalent forms. Use the `printf` format controls to perform the conversion between decimal, hexadecimal, and octal numbers.
3. Write your own version of the function `strlen`. Use a `while` loop and a character-counting variable to obtain the function result.
4. Write another version of the function `strlen`. This time use a `while` loop and a local pointer to obtain the function result.
5. Write the program STRING5.CPP, which uses the function `strtok` to break down the string `"2*(X+Y)/(X+Z) - (X+10)/(Y-5)"` into three sets of tokens, using the token delimiter strings `"+-*/ ()"`, `"( )"`, and `"+-*/ "`.

WEEK 1 IN REVIEW

Each week in this book is accompanied with a game example to help you get a better idea of how to make use of the lessons learned. Thus far, however, you haven't learned enough to look at the game examples supplied with Turbo C++. For this week, you take a look at a simple example that you can type in. The next two weeks address more interesting fare.

This week's example is a simple number-guessing game (shown in Listing R1.1). The program selects a number at random between 1 and 1,000 and prompts you to enter a number in that range. If your input is greater than the secret number, then the program tells you that your guess was higher. By contrast, if your input is less than the secret number, then the program tells you that your guess was lower. If you guess the secret number, then the game ends with your victory. The program allows you up to 10 guesses.

Week 1 in Review

Listing R1.1. Source code for program GUESS.CPP.

```
#include <ctype.h>
#include <iostream.h>
#include <stdlib.h>

int main()
{
   int guess = 0, number, count;
   char tryagain;

   randomize();
   cout << "The object of the game is to guess a number between" << endl
        << "1 and 1000.  You will be allowed 10 guesses, after" << endl
        << "which you will have lost." << endl;
   do
      {
      number = random(1000) + 1;
      for (count = 1; (guess != number) && (count <= 10); ++count)
         {
         cout << "Please enter try #" << count << ": ";
         cin >> guess;
         if (guess < number)
            cout << "   You're too low." << endl;
         else if (guess > number)
            cout << "   You're too high." << endl;
         else
            cout << "   Congratulations!  Pip pip!  Good show, and all that!" << endl;
         }
      if (count > 10)
         cout << "   Too bad.  The number was " << number << "." << endl;
      cout << "Would you like to try again? ";
      cin >> tryagain;
      cout << endl;
      } while (tolower(tryagain) == 'y');
   return 0;
}
```

Here is a sample session with the program in Listing R1.1.

```
The object of the game is to guess a number between
1 and 1000.  You will be allowed 10 guesses, after
which you will have lost.
Please enter try #1: 500
   You're too low.
Please enter try #2: 750
   You're too high.
Please enter try #3: 625
   You're too high.
Please enter try #4: 570
   You're too high.
Please enter try #5: 530
   You're too low.
Please enter try #6: 550
   You're too low.
```

```
Please enter try #7: 560
   You're too high.
Please enter try #8: 555
   You're too low.
Please enter try #9: 557
   You're too low.
Please enter try #10: 559
   Too bad.  The number was 558.
Would you like to try again? n
```

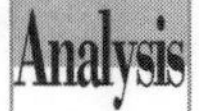

The first thing done by the program in Listing R1.1 is to initialize the random number generator with a call to the `randomize` function. This initializes the random number seed, allowing the program to come up with a different random number each time it's run. (If `randomize` was not called, the program would always use the same secret numbers, and the game would become rather boring.) The program then tells the user the object of the game.

Line 14 is the start of the main `do-while` loop. Lines 30 and 31 ask the user whether he or she wants to play the game again, and the conclusion of the loop on line 33 repeats if the user types `Y`. Note the use of the `tolower` function that enables the user to type the response in either upper- or lowercase. You then do a conversion to the case against which you want to check.

Line 16 sets the secret number via the `random` function. Because the `random` function returns a number from 0 to one less than its argument, you use 1000 for the parameter and then add one immediately afterward to make the range 1 to 1000. The `for` loop that starts on line 17 initializes the `count` variable to 1, and then has a clause that checks two things: that the current guess isn't correct and that the user hasn't run out of guesses. The final clause in the `for` statement increments the count.

Lines 19 and 20 perform the simple task of retrieving a guess from the user. After that, on lines 21 through 26, the program checks the user's guess against the secret number and lets the user know of his or her proximity in rough terms (can't make it too easy!). Note that if the user guesses correctly, the `for` loop will automatically terminate. If the user makes it out of the loop without guessing the number, then the program lets the user know what that secret number was on line 29.

There is a bug in this program, however. It's rather subtle, and you might not find it immediately. Try mentally running through the code in the case where the user is guessing for the last time (`count` is 10) and he or she actually gets the right answer. The `if` statement will print out the congratulatory message, and then the `for` loop will exit. Line 28 is designed to tell if the user has exited the loop because he or she ran out of guesses. This works in most cases as it's written; in this case, however, the program is going to assume that the user failed because the count has run out. In order to fix things, you should change line 28 to read `if (guess != number)`.

WEEK 2

AT A GLANCE

8

9

10

11

12

13

14

This second week continues teaching you about the C++ language. The topics start with the object-oriented programming (OOP) parts of C++. You learn about classes, components, and the rules for using these components. In addition, you learn about basic file I/O using the C++ stream library. Day 10 introduces you to the `string` class, which supports strings using C++ classes; you also learn about templates and how they're used in the Borland class library. Day 11 begins your introduction to the ObjectWindows Library (OWL), which allows you to create full-fledged Windows applications. From there you will be taken through some of the basics of Windows programs, including basic windows, controls, and dialog boxes.

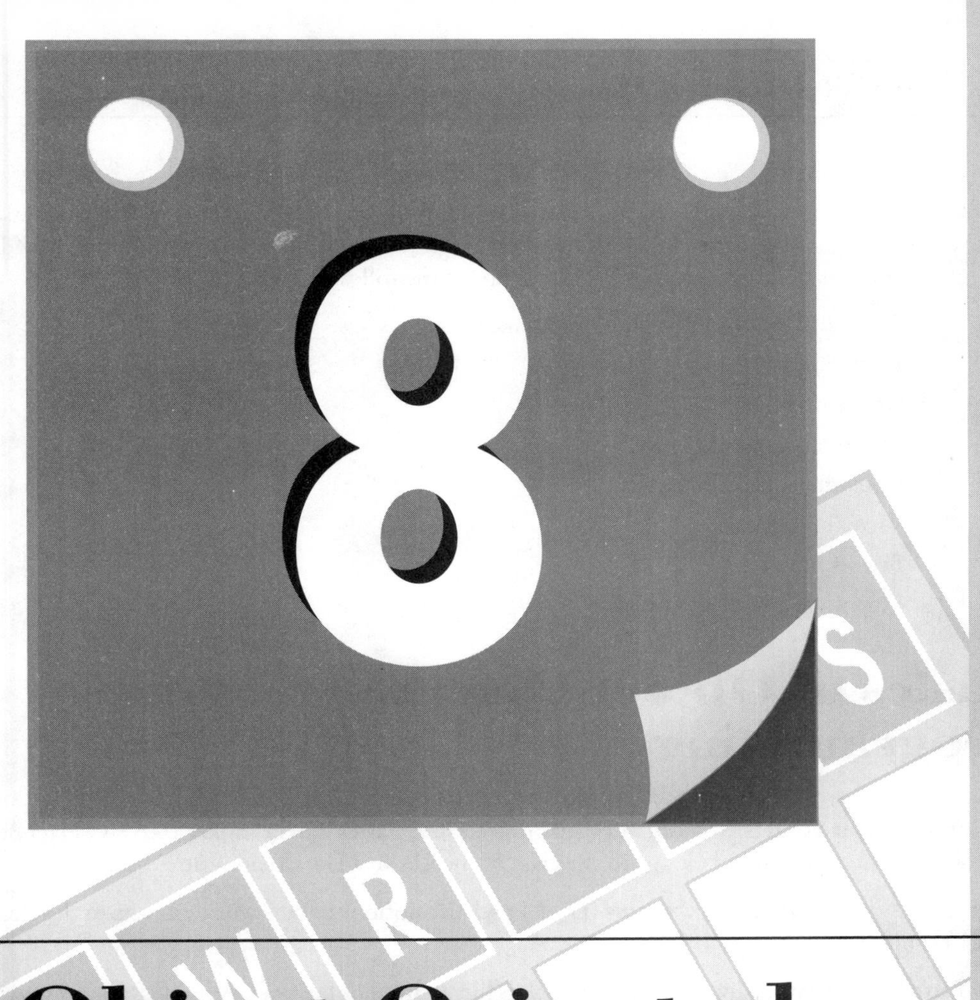

WEEK 2

Object-Oriented Programming and C++ Classes

Classes provide C++ with object-oriented programming (OOP) constructs. Today's lesson, which marks an important milestone for learning C++, introduces you to building individual classes as well as class hierarchy. You learn about the following topics:

- The basics of object-oriented programming
- Declaring base classes
- Constructors
- Destructors
- Declaring a class hierarchy
- Virtual functions
- Friend functions
- Operators and friend operators

Basics of Object-Oriented Programming

We live in a world of objects. Each object has its attributes and operations. Some objects are more animated than others. You can categorize objects into classes. For example, a CASIO Data Bank watch is an object that belongs to the class of the CASIO Data Bank watches.

NEW TERM *Object-oriented programming* (*OOP*) uses the notions of real-world objects to develop applications.

You also can relate individual classes in a class hierarchy. The class of CASIO Data Bank watches is part of the watch class hierarchy. The basics of OOP include classes, objects, methods, inheritance, and polymorphism.

NEW TERM A *class* defines a category of objects. Each *object* is an instance of a class.

Classes and Objects

An object shares the same attributes and functionality of other objects in the same class. Typically, an object has a unique state, defined by the current values of its attributes. The functionality of a class determines the operations that are possible for the class instances. C++ calls the attributes of the class *data members* and calls the operations of the class *member functions*. Classes encapsulate data members and member functions.

Going back to the CASIO watch example, you can note that the buttons in the watch represent the member functions of the class of CASIO watches, whereas the display represents a data member. You can click certain buttons to edit the date and/or time. In OOP terms, the member functions alter the state of the object by changing its data members.

Messages and Methods

Object-oriented programming models the interaction with objects as events where requests are sent to an object or between objects. The object receiving a request responds by invoking the appropriate method (that's the member function in C++). C++ does not explicitly foster the notion of requests and methods as do other OOP languages, such as SmallTalk. However, some find it easier to discuss invoking member functions using the term "request." The terms *methods* and *member functions* are equivalent.

NEW TERM The *request* is what is done to an object. The *method* is how the object responds to the incoming request.

Inheritance

In object-oriented languages, you can derive a class from another one.

NEW TERM With *inheritance*, the derived class (also called the *descendant class*) inherits the data members and member functions of its *parent* and *ancestor classes.*

Deriving a class refines the parent class by appending new attributes and new operations. The derived class typically declares new data members and new member functions. In addition, the derived class also can override inherited member functions when the operations of these functions are not suitable for the derived class.

To apply the concept of inheritance to the CASIO Data Bank watch, consider the following possible scenario. Suppose that the watch manufacturer decides to create a CASIO Data Comm watch that offers the same features as the CASIO Data Bank plus a beeper! Rather than redesigning the new model (that is the new class, in OOP terms) from scratch, the CASIO engineers start with the existing design of the CASIO Data Bank and build on it. This process may well add new attributes and operations to the existing design and alter some existing operations to fit the new design. Thus, the CASIO Data Comm model inherits the attributes and the operations of the CASIO Data Bank model. In OOP terms, the class of CASIO Data Comm watches is a descendant of the class of CASIO Data Bank watches.

Polymorphism

The OOP feature of polymorphism allows the instances of different classes to react in a particular way to a message (or function invocation, in C++ terms). For example, in a hierarchy of graphical shapes (point, line, square, rectangle, circle, ellipse, and so on), each shape has a `Draw` function that is responsible for properly responding to a request to draw that shape.

NEW TERM *Polymorphism* enables the instances of different classes to respond to the same function in ways that are appropriate to each class.

Declaring Base Classes

C++ enables you to declare a class that encapsulates data members and member functions. These functions alter and/or retrieve the values of the data members as well as perform related tasks.

Syntax

A Base Class

The general syntax for declaring a base class is

```
class className
{
private:
   <private data members>
   <private constructors>
   <private member functions>
protected:
   <protected data members>
   <protected constructors>
   <protected member functions>
public:
   <public data members>
   <public constructors>
   <public destructor>
   <public member functions>
};
```

Example

```
class point
{
protected:
   double x;
   double y;
public:
   point(double xVal, double yVal);
   double getX();
   double getY();
   void assign(double xVal, double yVal);
   point& assign(point& pt);
};
```

The Sections of a Class

The previous syntax shows that the declaration involves the keyword `class`. C++ classes offer three levels of visibility for the various members (that is, both data members and member functions).

- The private section
- The protected section
- The public section

NEW TERM In the *private section*, only the member functions of the class can access the private members. Descendant classes are denied access to private members of its base classes. In the *protected section*, only the member functions of the class and its descendant classes can access members. The *public section* specifies members that are visible to the member functions of the class, class instances, member functions of descendant classes, and their instances.

The following rules apply to the various class sections:

1. The class sections can appear in any order.
2. The class sections may appear more than once.
3. If no class section is specified, the C++ compiler treats the members as private.
4. You should avoid placing data members in the public section unless such a declaration significantly simplifies your design. Data members typically are placed in the protected section to allow their access by member functions of descendant classes.
5. Use member functions to set and/or query the values of data members. The members that set the data members assist in performing validation and updating other data members, if need be.
6. The class may have multiple constructors.
7. The class can have only one destructor, which must be declared in the public section.
8. The member functions (as well as the constructors and destructors) that have multiple statements are defined outside the class declaration. The definition may reside in the same file that declares the class.

NEW TERM *Constructors* are special members that must have the same name as the host class, and they're called when class instances are created. *Destructors* are called when class instances are removed.

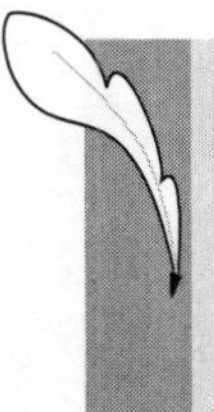

Note: It should be mentioned at this point that classes and structures really are the same with one single difference. In a `class`, without specifying a protection level, it starts out with `private`. A `structure` starts out with `public`. All the rules you are used to for putting data in and manipulating structures applies to classes.

In software libraries, the definition of the member functions referred to in rule 8 typically resides in a separate source file (.H and .CPP files). When you define a member function, you must qualify the function name with the class name. The syntax of such a qualification involves using the class name followed by two colons (::) and then the name of a function. For example, consider the following class:

```
class point
{
protected:
   double x;
   double y;
public:
   point(double xVal, double yVal);
   double getX();
   // other member functions
};
```

The definitions of the constructor and member functions are

```
point::point(double xVal, double yVal)
{
   // statements
}

double point::getX()
{
   // statements
}
```

After you declare a class, you can use the class name as a type identifier to declare class instances. The syntax resembles declaring variables.

Look at an example. Listing 8.1 shows the source code for the program CLASS1.CPP. The program prompts you to enter the length and width of a rectangle (which is an object). The program then displays the length, width, and area of the rectangle you specified.

Type

Listing 8.1. Source code for the program CLASS1.CPP.

```
// C++ program that illustrates a class

#include <iostream.h>

class rectangle
{
  protected:
    double length;
    double width;
  public:
    rectangle() { assign(0, 0); }
    rectangle(double len, double wide) { assign(len, wide); }
    double getLength() { return length; }
    double getWidth() { return width; }
    double getArea() { return length * width; }
```

```
    void assign(double len, double wide);
};

void rectangle::assign(double len, double wide)
{
  length = len;
  width = wide;
}

main()
{
  rectangle rect;
  double len, wide;

  cout << "Enter length of rectangle : ";
  cin >> len;
  cout << "Enter width of rectangle : ";
  cin >> wide;
  rect.assign(len, wide);
  cout << "Rectangle length = " << rect.getLength() << "\n"
       << "          width  = " << rect.getWidth() << "\n"
       << "          area   = " << rect.getArea() << "\n";
  return 0;
}
```

Here is a sample session with the program in Listing 8.1.

```
Enter length of rectangle : 10
Enter width of rectangle : 12
Rectangle length = 10
width  = 12
area   = 120
```

The program in Listing 8.1 declares the class `rectangle`, which models a rectangle. The class has two `double`-typed data members, `length` and `width`, which store the dimensions of a rectangle. In addition, the class has two constructors: the default constructor and the nondefault constructor. The class also defines the member functions `getLength`, `getWidth`, `getArea`, and `assign`.

NEW TERM The *default constructor* creates an instance with 0 dimensions, and the *nondefault constructor* creates an instance with nonzero dimensions.

The function `getLength`, defined in the class declaration, simply returns the value in member `length`. The function `getWidth`, also defined in the class declaration, merely returns the value in member `width`. The function `getArea`, defined in the class declaration, simply returns the value of the result of multiplying the members `length` and `width`.

The member function `assign`, defined outside the class declaration, assigns the arguments for its parameters `len` and `wide` to the data members `length` and `width`, respectively. The implementation of this function is simplified by not checking for negative values.

The function main declares rect as the instance of class rectangle and declares the double-typed variables len and wide. The output statement in line 30 prompts you to enter the length of the rectangle. The statement in line 31 obtains your input and stores it in variable len. The output statement in line 32 prompts you to enter the width of the rectangle. The statement in line 33 obtains your input and stores it in variable wide.

The function main assigns the input values to the instance rect using the assign member function. In OOP terms, we can say that the function main sends the assign message to the object rect. The arguments of the message are variables len and wide. The object rect responds by invoking the method (the member function) rectangle::assign(double, double).

The output statement in lines 35 through 37 displays the length, width, and area of the object rect. This statement sends the messages getLength, getWidth, and getArea to the object rect. In turn, the object rect invokes the appropriate methods (or member functions, if you prefer) to respond to each one of these messages.

Constructors

C++ constructors and destructors work automatically to guarantee the appropriate creation and removal of class instances.

Syntax

Constructors

The general syntax for constructors is

```
class className
{
public:
   className(); // default constructor
   className(const className& c); // copy constructor
   className(<parameter list>); // another constructor
};
```

Example

```
class point
{
protected:
   double x;
   double y;
public:
   point();
   point(double xVal, double yVal);
   point(const point& pt);
   double getX();
   double getY();
   void assign(double xVal, double yVal);
   point& assign(point& pt);
};
```

```
main()
{
   point p1;
   point p2(10, 20);
   point p3(2);
   p1.assign(p2));
   cout << p1.getX() << " " << p1.getY() << "\n";
   cout << p2.getX() << " " << p2.getY() << "\n";
   cout << p3.getX() << " " << p3.getY() << "\n";
   return 0;
}
```

NEW TERM A *copy constructor* enables you to create class instances by copying the data from existing instances.

C++ has the following features and rules regarding constructors:

1. The name of the constructor must be identical to the name of its class.
2. You must not include any return type, not even `void`.
3. A class can have any number of constructors, including none. In the latter case, the compiler automatically creates one for that class.
4. The default constructor is the one that either has no parameters or possesses a parameter list where all the parameters use default arguments. Here are two examples.

```
// class use parameterless constructor
class point1
{
    protected:
         double x;
         double y;
    public:
         point1();
         // other member functions
};

// class use constructor with default arguments
class point2
{
    protected:
         double x;
         double y;
    public:
         point(double xVal = 0, double yVal = 0);
         // other member functions
};
```

5. The *copy constructor* enables you to create a class instance using an existing instance. Here is an example.

```
class point
{
    protected:
        double x;
        double y;
    public:
        point();
        point(double xVal, double yVal);
        point(const point& pt);
        // other member functions
};
```

6. The declaration of a class instance (which includes function parameters and local instances) involves a constructor. Which constructor is called? The answer depends on how many constructors you have declared for the class and how you declared the class instance. For example, consider the following instances of the last version of the class `point`:

```
point p1; // involves the default constructor
point p2(1.1, 1.3); // uses the second constructor
point p3(p2); // uses the copy constructor
```

Because instance `p1` specifies no arguments, the compiler uses the default constructor. The instance `p2` specifies two floating-point arguments. Consequently, the compiler uses the second constructor. The instance `p3` has the instance `p2` as an argument. Therefore, the compiler uses the copy constructor to create instance `p3` from instance `p2`.

DO | **DON'T**

DO declare copy constructors, especially for classes that model dynamic data structures. These constructors perform what is called a *deep copy,* which includes the dynamic data. By default, the compiler creates what are called *shallow copy* constructors, which copy the data members only.

DON'T rely on the shallow copy constructor to copy instances for classes that have members that are pointers.

Destructors

C++ classes may contain destructors that automatically remove class instances.

8

Syntax

Destructors

The general syntax for destructors is

```
class className
{
public:
   className(); // default constructor
   // other constructors
   ~className();
   // other member function
};
```

Example

```
class String
{
protected:
   char *str;
   int len;

public:
   String();
   String(const String& s);
   ~String();
   // other member functions
};
```

C++ has the following features and rules regarding destructors:

1. The name of the destructor must begin with a tilde (~). The rest of the destructor name must be identical to the name of its class.
2. You must not include any return type, not even `void`.
3. A class can have no more than one destructor. In addition, if you omit the destructor, the compiler automatically creates one for you.
4. The destructor cannot have any parameters.
5. The runtime system automatically invokes a class destructor when the instance of that class is out of scope, or when the instance is explicitly deleted.

Examples of Constructors and Destructors

Look at a program that typifies the use of constructors and destructors. Listing 8.2 contains the source code for the CLASS2.CPP program. The program performs the following tasks:

- ☐ Creates a dynamic array (the object)
- ☐ Assigns values to the elements of the dynamic array
- ☐ Displays the values in the dynamic array
- ☐ Removes the dynamic array

Type

Listing 8.2. Source code for the CLASS2.CPP program.

```
// Program demonstrates constructors and destructors

#include <iostream.h>

const unsigned MIN_SIZE = 4;

class Array
{
   protected:
     double *dataPtr;
     unsigned size;

   public:
     Array(unsigned Size = MIN_SIZE);
     Array(const Array& a);
     ~Array()
       { delete [] dataPtr; }
     unsigned getSize() const
       { return size; }
     void store(double x, unsigned index)
       { if (index > 0 && index < size) dataPtr[index] = x; }
     double recall(unsigned index)
       { if (index > 0 and index < size) return dataPtr[index]; }
};

Array::Array(unsigned Size)
{
  size = (Size < MIN_SIZE) ? MIN_SIZE : Size;
  dataPtr = new double[size];
}

Array::Array(const Array& a)
{
  size = a.size;
  dataPtr = new double[size];
  for (int i = 0; i < size; i++)
    dataPtr[i] = a.dataPtr[i];
}

main()
{
  Array Arr(10);
  double x;
  // assign data to array elements
  for (unsigned i = 0; i < Arr.getSize(); i++) {
    x = double(i);
    x = x * x - 5 * x + 10;
    Arr.store(x, i);
  }
  // display data in the array element
  cout << "Array Arr has the following values:\n\n";
  for (i = 0; i < Arr.getSize(); i++)
    cout << "Arr[" << i << "] = " << Arr.recall(i) << "\n";
  return 0;
}
```

Here is a sample session with the program in Listing 8.2.

```
Array Arr has the following values:

Arr[0] = 10
Arr[1] = 6
Arr[2] = 4
Arr[3] = 4
Arr[4] = 6
Arr[5] = 10
Arr[6] = 16
Arr[7] = 24
Arr[8] = 34
Arr[9] = 46
```

The program in Listing 8.2 declares the global constant `MIN_SIZE` in line 5, which specifies the minimum size of dynamic arrays. The program also declares the class `Array` in line 7. The class has two data members, `dataPtr` and `size`. The member `dataPtr` is the pointer to the array's dynamically allocated elements. The member `size` stores the number of elements in an instance of class `Array`.

The class declares a default constructor. (The constructor actually has a parameter with the default value `MIN_SIZE`.) The program defines the default constructor in lines 26 through 30. The arguments for the parameter `Size` specify the number of array elements. The statement in line 28 assigns the greater value of parameter `Size` and the constant `MIN_SIZE` to the data member `size`. The statement in line 29 allocates the dynamic space for the array by using the operator `new`. The statement assigns the base address of the dynamic array to the member `dataPtr`.

The class also declares a copy constructor. Because there is allocated data involved, it's wise to have this constructor in order to make sure the contents of that data are copied properly. Line 35 allocates the same amount of space as the old `Array`, and then proceeds to copy the old contents into the new space on lines 36 and 37.

The destructor `~Array` removes the dynamic space of the array by applying the operator `delete` to the member `dataPtr`.

The member function `getSize`, defined in the class declaration, returns the value in data member `size`.

The function `store`, defined in the class declaration, stores the value passed by parameter `x` at the element number specified by the parameter `index`. The implementation of this function is simplified by eliminating the out-of-range index check.

The function `recall`, defined in the class declaration, returns the value in the element specified by the parameter `index`. The implementation of this function is simplified by eliminating the out-of-range index check.

The function `main` declares the object `Arr` as an instance of class `Array`. The declaration, located in line 42, specifies that the instance has 10 elements. The function also declares the

double-typed variable x. The for loop in lines 45 through 49 stores values in the instance Arr. The loop uses control variable i and iterates from 0 to Arr.getSize()-1, in increments of 1. The loop continuation condition sends the getSize message to instance Arr to obtain the number of elements in the array. The statements in lines 46 and 47 calculate the value to store in an element of instance Arr. The statement in line 48 sends the message store to instance Arr and passes the arguments x and i. The object Arr saves the value in variable x at the element number i.

The output statement in line 51 comments on the output of the for loop in lines 52 and 53. The loop uses the control variable i and iterates from 0 to Arr.getSize() -1, in increments of 1. The output statement in line 53 displays the element in instance Arr by sending the message recall to that instance. The message has the argument i.

Declaring a Class Hierarchy

The power of the OOP features of C++ comes from the fact that you can derive classes from existing ones. A descendant class inherits the members of its ancestor classes (that is, parent class, grandparent class, and so on) and also can override some of the inherited functions. Inheritance enables you to reuse code in descendant classes.

Syntax

A Derived Class

The general syntax for declaring a derived class is

```
class className : [public] parentClass
{
   <friend classes>

private:
   <private data members>
   <private constructors>
   <private member functions>

protected:
   <protected data members>
   <protected constructors>
   <protected member functions>

public:
   <public data members>
   <public constructors>
   <public destructor>
   <public member functions>

   <friend functions and friend operators>
};
```

8

Example

The following example shows the class `cRectangle` and its descendant, the class `cBox`:

```
class cRectangle
{
protected:
   double length;
   double width;
public:
   cRectangle(double len, double wide);
   double getLength() const;
   double getWidth(); const;
   double assign(double len, double wide);
   double calcArea();
};

class cBox : public cRectangle
{
protected:
   double height;

public:
   cBox(double len, double wide, double height);
   double getHeight() const;
   assign(double len, double wide, double height);
   double calcVolume();
};
```

The class lineage is indicated by a colon followed by the optional keyword `public` and then the name of the parent class. When you include the keyword `public`, you allow the instances of the descendant class to access the public members of the parent and other ancestor classes. By contrast, when you omit the keyword `public` or use the private keyword, you deprive the instance of the descendant class from accessing the members of the ancestor classes.

A descendant class inherits the data members of its ancestor classes. C++ has no mechanism for removing unwanted inherited data members—you basically are stuck with them. By contrast, C++ enables you to override inherited member functions. You see more about this topic later in today's lesson. The descendant class declares new data members, new member functions, and overriding member functions. Again, you can place these members in the private, protected, or public sections, as you see fit in your class design.

DO	DON'T

DO reduce the number of constructors by using default argument parameters.

DO use member functions to access the values in the data members. These member functions enable you to control and validate the values in the data members.

DON'T declare all the constructors of a class protected unless you want to force the client programmers (that is, those programs that use the class) to use the class by declaring its descendants with public constructors.

DON'T declare the data members in the public section.

Look at an example that declares a small class hierarchy. Listing 8.3 shows the source code for the CLASS3.CPP program. This program declares classes that contain a hierarchy of two simple geometric shapes: a circle and a cylinder. The program requires no input. Instead, it uses internal data to create the geometric shapes and to display their dimensions, areas, and volume.

Listing 8.3. Source code for the CLASS3.CPP program.

```
// Program that demonstrates a small hierarchy of classes

#include <iostream.h>
#include <math.h>

const double pi = 4 * atan(1);

inline double sqr(double x)
{ return x * x; }

class cCircle
{
  protected:
    double radius;

  public:
    cCircle(double radiusVal = 0) : radius(radiusVal) {}
    void setRadius(double radiusVal)
      { radius = radiusVal; }
    double getRadius() const
      { return radius; }
    double area() const
      { return pi * sqr(radius); }
    void showData();
};

class cCylinder : public cCircle
{
  protected:
    double height;

  public:
     cCylinder(double heightVal = 0, double radiusVal = 0)
       : height(heightVal), cCircle(radiusVal) {}
     void setHeight(double heightVal)
       { height = heightVal; }
     double getHeight() const
```

```
      { return height; }
    double area() const
      { return 2 * cCircle::area() +
               2 * pi * radius * height; }
    void showData();
};

void cCircle::showData()
{
   cout << "Circle radius        = " << getRadius() << "\n"
        << "Circle area          = " << area() << "\n\n";
}

void cCylinder::showData()
{
   cout << "Cylinder radius      = " << getRadius() << "\n"
        << "Cylinder height      = " << getHeight() << "\n"
        << "Cylinder area        = " << area() << "\n\n";
}

main()
{
   cCircle Circle(1);
   cCylinder Cylinder(10, 1);

   Circle.showData();
   Cylinder.showData();
   return 0;
}
```

Here is a sample session with the program in Listing 8.3.

```
Circle radius        = 1
Circle area          = 3.14159

Cylinder radius      = 1
Cylinder height      = 10
Cylinder area        = 69.115
```

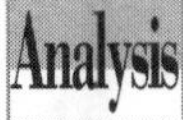

The program in Listing 8.3 declares the classes `cCircle` and `cCylinder`. The class `cCircle` models a circle, whereas the class `cCylinder` models a cylinder.

The `cCircle` class declares a single data member, `radius`, to store the radius of the circle. The class also declares a constructor and a number of member functions. The constructor assigns a value to the data member `radius` when you declare a class instance. Notice that the constructor uses a new syntax to initialize the member `radius`. The functions `setRadius` and `getRadius` serve to set and query the value in member `radius`, respectively. The function `area` returns the area of the circle. The function `showData` displays the radius and area of a class instance.

The class `cCylinder`, a descendant of `cCircle`, declares a single data member, `height`, to store the height of the cylinder. The class inherits the member radius needed to store the radius of the cylinder. The `cCylinder` class declares a constructor and a number of member functions. The constructor assigns values to the radius and height members when creating a class instance. Notice the use of a new syntax to initialize the members—member height is initialized, and member radius is initialized by invoking the constructor of class cCircle with the argument radiusVal. The functions getHeight and setHeight serve to set and query the value in member height, respectively. The class uses the inherited functions setRadius and getRadius to manipulate the inherited member radius. The function area, which overrides the inherited function cCircle::area(), returns the surface area of the cylinder. Notice that this function explicitly invokes the inherited function cCircle::area(). The function showData displays the radius, height, and area of a class instance.

We also would like to point out that the declarations of the functions area, getHeight, and area in lines 22, 37, and 39 end with the keyword const. Using the keyword const in this way tells the compiler that the member function cannot change any data member. This feature mainly is aimed at teams of programmers where the team manager sets the specifications for the class and determines which member functions can alter the values of data members.

The function main declares the instance Circle, of class cCircle, and assigns 1 to the circle's radius. In addition, the function also declares the instance Cylinder, of class cCylinder, and assigns 10 and 1 to the circle's height and radius, respectively. The function then sends the showData message to the instances Circle and Cylinder. Each object responds to this message by invoking the appropriate member function.

Virtual Functions

As mentioned previously, polymorphism is an important object-oriented programming feature. Consider the following simple classes and the function main:

```
#include <iostream.h>
class cA
{
public:
   double A(double x) { return x * x; }
   double B(double x) { return A(x) / 2; }
};

class cB : public cA
{
public:
   double A(double x) { return x * x * x; }
};

main()
{
   cB aB;
   cout << aB.B(3) << "\n";
   return 0;
}
```

Class cA contains functions A and B, where function B calls function A. Class cB, a descendant of class cA, inherits function B, but overrides function A. The intent here is to have the inherited function cA::B call function cB::A in order to support polymorphic behavior. What is the program output? The answer is 4.5 and not 13.5! Why? The answer lies in the fact that the compiler resolves the expression aB.B(3) by using the inherited function cA::B, which in turn calls function cA::A. Therefore, function cB:A is left out and the program fails to support polymorphic behavior.

C++ supports polymorphic behavior by offering virtual functions.

NEW TERM *Virtual functions*, which are bound at runtime, are declared by placing the keyword virtual before the function's return type.

After you declare a function virtual, you can override it only with functions in descendant classes. These overriding functions must have the same parameter list. Virtual functions can override nonvirtual functions in ancestor classes. Note that once a function is declared as virtual in a specific class, all descendants of that class will regard the function as virtual, whether or not the virtual keyword is used.

Syntax

Virtual Functions

The general syntax for declaring virtual functions is

```
class className1
{
   // member functions
   virtual returnType functionName(<parameter list>);
};

class className2 : public className1
{
   // member functions
   virtual returnType functionName(<parameter list>);
};
```

Example

This example shows how virtual functions can successfully implement polymorphic behavior in classes cA and cB:

```
#include <iostream.h>
class cA
{
public:
   virtual double A(double x) { return x * x; }
   double B(double x) { return A(x) / 2; }
};

class cB : public cA
{
public:
```

```
   virtual double A(double x) { return x * x * x; }
};

main()
{
   cB aB;
   cout << aB.B(3) << "\n";
   return 0;
}
```

This example displays 13.5, the correct result, because the call to the inherited function `cA::B` is resolved at runtime by calling `cB::A`.

DO	DON'T

DO use virtual functions when you have a callable function that implements a class-specific behavior. Declaring such a function as virtual ensures that it provides the correct response that is relevant to the associated class.

DON'T declare a member function as virtual by default. Virtual functions have some additional overhead.

Look at an example. Listing 8.4 shows the source code for the program CLASS4.CPP. The program creates a square and a rectangle and displays their dimensions and areas. No input is required.

Type

Listing 8.4. Source code for the program CLASS4.CPP.

```
// Program that demonstrates virtual functions

#include <iostream.h>

class cSquare
{
  protected:
    double length;

  public:
    cSquare(double len) { length = len; }
    double getLength() { return length; }
    virtual double getWidth() { return length; }
    double getArea() { return getLength() * getWidth(); }
};

class cRectangle : public cSquare
{
  protected:
    double width;

```

```
  public:
    cRectangle(double len, double wide) :
       cSquare(len), width(wide) {}
    virtual double getWidth() { return width; }
};

main()
{
   cSquare square(10);
   cRectangle rectangle(10, 12);

   cout << "Square has length = " << square.getLength() << "\n"
        << "       and area   = " << square.getArea() << "\n";
   cout << "Rectangle has length = "
        << rectangle.getLength() << "\n"
        << "          and width  = "
        << rectangle.getWidth() << "\n"
        << "          and area   = "
        << rectangle.getArea() << "\n";
   return 0;
}
```

Here is a sample session with the program in Listing 8.4.

```
Square has length = 10
and area   = 100
Rectangle has length = 10
and width  = 12
and area   = 120
```

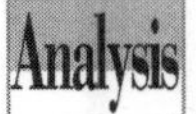

The program in Listing 8.4 declares the classes `cSquare` and `cRectangle` to model squares and rectangles, respectively. The class `cSquare` declares a single data member, `length`, to store the length (and width) of the square. The class declares a constructor with the parameter `len`, which passes arguments to the member `length`. The class also declares the functions `getLength`, `getWidth`, and `getArea`. Both functions `getLength` and `getWidth` return the value in member `length`. Notice that the class declares function `getWidth` as `virtual`. The function `getArea` returns the area of the rectangle, calculated by calling the functions `getLength` and `getWidth`. We choose to invoke these functions rather than use the data member `length` in order to demonstrate how the virtual function `getWidth` works.

The program declares class `cRectangle` as a descendant of class `cSquare`. The class `cRectangle` declares the data member `width` and inherits the member `length`. These members enable the class to store the basic dimensions of a rectangle. The class constructor has the parameters `len` and `wide`. Notice that the constructor invokes the constructor `cSquare` and supplies it with the argument `len`. The constructor initializes the data member `width` with the value of parameter `wide`.

The class `cRectangle` declares the virtual function `getWidth`. This version returns the value in data member `width`. The class inherits the member functions `getLength` and `getArea` because their implementation is adequate for the `cRectangle`.

The function `main` declares the object `square` as an instance of class `cSquare`. The instance `square` has a length of 10. The function `main` also declares the object `rectangle` as an instance of class `cRectangle`. The instance `rectangle` has the length of 10 and the width of 12.

The output statement in lines 33 and 34 displays the length and area of the instance `square`. The statement sends the messages `getLength` and `getArea` to the preceding instance in order to obtain the sought values. The instance `square` invokes the function `getArea`, which in turn calls the functions `cSquare::getLength` and `cSquare::getWidth`.

The output statement in lines 35 through 40 displays the length, width, and area of the instance `rectangle`. The statement sends the messages `getLength`, `getWidth`, and `getArea` to this instance. The instance responds by calling the inherited function `cSquare::getLength`, the virtual function `cRectangle::getWidth`, and the inherited function `cSquare::getArea`. The latter function calls the inherited function `cSquare::getLength` and the virtual function `cRectangle::getWidth` to correctly calculate the area of the rectangle.

DO	DON'T

DO declare your destructor as virtual. This ensures polymorphic behavior in destroying class instances. In addition, I highly recommend that you declare a copy constructor and an assignment operator for each class.

DON'T forget that you inherit virtual functions and destructors in the descendant class. You need not declare shell functions and destructors that simply call the corresponding member of the parent class.

Rule for Virtual Functions

The rule for declaring a virtual function is "once virtual, always virtual." In other words, after you declare a function to be virtual in a class, any descendant class that overrides the virtual function must do so using another function that has the same parameter list. If the descendant class fails to use the same parameter list, the base class's version of the virtual function will be inaccessible to the descendant class (and any of its descendants). At first, this rule seems to lock you in. This limitation certainly is true for object-oriented programming languages that support virtual functions but not overloaded functions. In the case of C++, the work-around is interesting. You can declare nonvirtual and overloaded functions that have the same name as the virtual function, but bear a different parameter list. Moreover, you cannot inherit nonvirtual member functions that share the same name with a virtual function. Here is a simple example that illustrates the point.

```
#include <iostream.h>
class cA
{
public:
   cA() {}
   virtual void foo(char c)
      { cout << "virtual cA::foo() returns " << c << '\n'; }
};

class cB : public cA
{
public:
   cB() {}
   void foo(const char* s)
      { cout << "cB::foo() returns " << s << '\n'; }
   void foo(int i)
      { cout << "cB::foo() returns " << i << '\n'; }
   virtual void foo(char c)
      { cout << "virtual cB::foo() returns " << c << '\n'; }
};

class cC : public cB
{
public:
   cC() {}
   void foo(const char* s)
      { cout << "cC::foo() returns " << s << '\n'; }
   void foo(double x)
      { cout << "cC::foo() returns " << x << '\n'; }
   virtual void foo(char c)
      { cout << "virtual cC::foo() returns " << c << '\n'; }
};

main()
{
   int[]= 100;
   cA Aobj;
   cB Bobj;
   cC Cobj;

   Aobj.foo('A');
   Bobj.foo('B');
   Bobj.foo(10);
   Bobj.foo("Bobj");
   Cobj.foo('C');
   // if you uncomment the next statement, program does not compile
   // Cobj.foo(n);
   Cobj.foo(144.123);
   Cobj.foo("Cobj");
   return 0;
}
```

This code declares three classes—`cA`, `cB`, and `cC`—to form a linear hierarchy of classes. Class `cA` declares function `foo(char)` as virtual. Class `cB` also declares its own version of the virtual function `foo(char)`. In addition, class `cB` declares the nonvirtual overloaded functions `foo(const` char* s) and foo(int). Class cC, the descendant of class cB, declares the virtual function foo(char) and the nonvirtual and overloaded functions foo(const char*) and foo(double). Notice that class cC must declare the foo(const char*) function if it needs the function because it cannot inherit the member function cB::foo(const char*). C++ supports a different function inheritance scheme when an overloaded function and virtual function are involved. The function main creates an instance for each of the three classes and involves the various versions of the member function foo.

Friend Functions

C++ allows member functions to access all the data members of a class. In addition, C++ grants the same privileged access to friend functions. The declaration of friend functions appears in the class and begins with the keyword friend. Other than using the special keyword, friend functions look very much like member functions, except they cannot access the befriended class automatically because that requires the hidden this pointer. Given a pointer to an instance of the befriended class, however, the function can access all parts of the class. When you define friend functions outside the declaration of their befriended class, you need not qualify the function names with the name of the class.

NEW TERM *Friend functions* are ordinary functions that have access to all data members of one or more classes.

Syntax

Friend Functions

The general form of friend functions is

```
class className
{
public:
   className();
   // other constructors

   friend returnType friendFunction(<parameter list>);
};
```

Example

```
class String
{
protected:
   char *str;
   int len;

public:
   String();
   ~String();
   // other member functions
```

```
   friend String& append(String& str1, String& str2);
   friend String& append(const char* str1, String& str2);
   friend String& append(String& str1, const char* str2);
};
```

Friend classes can accomplish tasks that are awkward, difficult, and even impossible with member functions.

Look at a simple example for using friend functions. Listing 8.5 contains the source code for the CLASS5.CPP program. This program internally creates two complex numbers, adds them, stores the result in another complex number, and then displays the operands and resulting complex numbers.

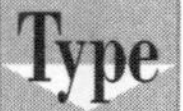

Listing 8.5. Source code for the CLASS5.CPP program.

```
// Program that demonstrates friend functions

#include <iostream.h>

class Complex
{
   protected:
     double x;
     double y;

   public:
     Complex(double real = 0, double imag = 0);
     Complex(Complex& c) { assign(c); }
     void assign(Complex& c);
     double getReal() const { return x; }
     double getImag() const { return y; }
     friend Complex add(Complex& c1, Complex& c2);
};

Complex::Complex(double real, double imag)
{
  x = real;
  y = imag;
}

void Complex::assign(Complex& c)
{
  x = c.x;
  y = c.y;
}

Complex add(Complex& c1, Complex& c2)
{
  Complex result(c1);

  result.x += c2.x;
  result.y += c2.y;
  return result;
}
```

continues

Listing 8.5. continued

```

main()
{
  Complex c1(2, 3);
  Complex c2(5, 7);
  Complex c3;

  c3.assign(add(c1, c2));
  cout << "(" << c1.getReal() << " + i" << c1.getImag() << ")"
       << " + "
       << "(" << c2.getReal() << " + i" << c2.getImag() << ")"
       << " = "
       << "(" << c3.getReal() << " + i" << c3.getImag() << ")"
       << "\n\n";
  return 0;
}
```

Output

Here is a sample session with the program in Listing 8.5.

```
(2 + i3) + (5 + i7) = (7 + i10)
```

The program in Listing 8.5 declares the class `Complex`, which models complex numbers. This class declares two data members, two constructors, a friend function (the highlight of this example), and a set of member functions. The data members `x` and `y` store the real and imaginary components of a complex number, respectively.

The class has two constructors. The first constructor has two parameters (with default arguments) that enable you to build a class instance using the real and imaginary components of a complex number. Because the two parameters have default arguments, the constructor doubles up as the default constructor. The second constructor, `complex(complex&)`, is the copy constructor.

The `Complex` class declares three member functions. The function `assign` copies a class instance into another one. The functions `getReal` and `getImag` return the value stored in the members `real` and `imag`, respectively.

The `Complex` class declares the friend function `add` to add two complex numbers. To make the program short, we do not implement complementary friend functions that subtract, multiply, and divide class instances. What is so special about the friend function `add`? Why not use an ordinary member function to add a class instance? The following declaration of the alternate `add` member function answers these questions:

```
complex& add(complex& c)
```

This declaration states that the function treats the parameter `c` as a second operand. Here is how the member function `add` works.

```
complex c1(3, 4), c2(1.2, 4.5);
c1.add(c2); // adds c2 to c1
```

First, the member function add works as an increment and not as an addition function. Second, the targeted class instance is always the first operand. This is not a problem for operations such as addition and multiplication, but it is a problem for subtraction and division. That is why the friend function add works better by giving you the freedom of choosing how to add the class instances.

The friend function add returns a class instance. The function creates a local instance of class Complex and returns that instance.

The function main uses the member function assign and the friend function add to perform basic complex operations. In addition, the function main invokes the functions getReal and getImag with the various instances of class Complex to display the components of each instance.

Operators and Friend Operators

The last program used a member function and a friend function to implement complex math operations. The approach is typical in C and Pascal because these languages do not support user-defined operators. By contrast, C++ enables you to declare operators and friend operators. These operators include +, -, *, /, %, ==, !=, <=, <, >=, >, +=, -=, *=, /=, %=, [], (), <<, and >>. Consult a C++ language reference book for more details on the rules of using these operators. C++ treats operators and friend operators as special member functions and friend functions.

Syntax

Operators and Friend Operators

The general syntax for declaring operators and friend operators is

```
class className
{
public:
   // constructors and destructor
   // member functions

   // unary operator
   returnType operator operatorSymbol();
   // binary operator
   returnType operator operatorSymbol(operand);
   // unary friend operator
   friend returnType operator operatorSymbol(operand);
   // binary operator
   friend returnType operator operatorSymbol(firstOperand,
         secondOperand);
};
```

Example

```
class String
{
protected:
   char *str;
```

```
    int len;

public:
    String();
    ~String();
    // other member functions
    // assignment operator
    String& operator =(String& s);
    String& operator +=(String& s);
    // concatenation operators
    friend String& operator +(String& s1, String& s2);
    friend String& operator +(const char* s1, String& s2);
    friend String& operator +(String& s1, const char* s2);
    // relational operators
    friend int operator >(String& s1, String& s2);
    friend int operator =>(String& s1, String& s2);
    friend int operator <(String& s1, String& s2);
    friend int operator <=(String& s1, String& s2);
    friend int operator ==(String& s1, String& s2);
    friend int operator !=(String& s1, String& s2);
};
```

The functions you write use the operators and friend operators just like predefined operators. Therefore, you can create operators to support the operations of classes that model, for example, complex numbers, strings, arrays, and matrices. These operators enable you to write expressions that are far more readable than expressions that use named functions.

Look at an example. Listing 8.6 contains the source code for the CLASS6.CPP program. We created this program by modifying and expanding Listing 8.5. The new program performs more additions and displays two sets of operands and results.

Type

Listing 8.6. Source code for the CLASS6.CPP program.

```
// Program that demonstrates operators and friend operators

#include <iostream.h>

class Complex
{
   protected:
     double x;
     double y;

   public:
     Complex(double real = 0, double imag = 0)
       { assign(real, imag); }
     Complex(Complex& c);
     void assign(double real = 0, double imag = 0);
     double getReal() const { return x; }
     double getImag() const { return y; }
     Complex& operator =(Complex& c);
     Complex& operator +=(Complex& c);
     friend Complex operator +(Complex& c1, Complex& c2);
     friend ostream& operator <<(ostream& os, Complex& c);
};
```

```
Complex::Complex(Complex& c)
{
  x = c.x;
  y = c.y;
}

void Complex::assign(double real, double imag)
{
  x = real;
  y = imag;
}

Complex& Complex::operator =(Complex& c)
{
  x = c.x;
  y = c.y;
  return *this;
}

Complex& Complex::operator +=(Complex& c)
{
  x += c.x;
  y += c.y;
  return *this;
}

Complex operator +(Complex& c1, Complex& c2)
{
  Complex result(c1);

  result.x += c2.x;
  result.y += c2.y;
  return result;
}

ostream& operator <<(ostream& os, Complex& c)
{
  os << "(" << c.x << " + i" << c.y << ")";
  return os;
}

main()
{
  Complex c1(3, 5);
  Complex c2(7, 5);
  Complex c3;
  Complex c4(2, 3);

  c3 = c1 + c2;
  cout << c1 << " + " << c2 << " = " << c3 << "\n";
  cout << c3 << " + " << c4 << " = ";
  c3 += c4;
  cout << c3 << "\n";
  return 0;
}
```

Here is a sample session with the program in Listing 8.6.

```
(3 + i5) + (7 + i5) = (10 + i10)
(10 + i10) + (2 + i3) = (12 + i13)
```

The new class `Complex` replaces the `assign(Complex&)` member function with the operator `=`. The class also replaces the friend function `add` with the friend operator `+`.

```
Complex& operator =(Complex& c);
friend Complex operator +(Complex& c1, Complex& c2);
```

The operator `=` has one parameter, a reference to an instance of class `Complex`, and also returns a reference to the same class. The friend operator `+` has two parameters (both are references to instances of class `Complex`) and yields a complex class type.

I also took the opportunity to add two new operators.

```
complex& operator +=(complex& c);
friend ostream& operator <<(ostream& os, complex& c);
```

The operator `+=` is a member of class `Complex`. It takes one parameter, a reference to an instance of class `Complex`, and yields a reference to the same class. The other new operator is the friend operator `<<`, which illustrates how to write a stream extractor operator for a class. The friend operator has two parameters: a reference to class `ostream` (the output stream class) and a reference to class `Complex`. The operator `<<` returns a reference to class `ostream`. This type of value enables you to chain stream output with other predefined types or other classes (assuming these classes have a friend operator `<<`). The definition of friend operator `<<` has two statements. The first one outputs strings and the data members of class `Complex` to the output stream parameter `os`. The friendship status of operator `<<` allows it to access the `real` and `imag` data members of its `Complex`-typed parameter `c`. The second statement in the operator definition returns the first parameter `os`.

The function `main` declares four instances of class `Complex`, `c1`, `c2`, `c3`, and `c4`. The instances `c1`, `c2`, and `c4` are created with nondefault values assigned to the data members `real` and `imag`. The function tests use the operators `=`, `+`, `<<`, `+=`. The program illustrates that you can use operators and friend operators to write code that is more readable and supports a higher level of abstraction.

Summary

Today's lesson introduced you to C++ classes and discussed the following topics:

- The basics of object-oriented programming include classes, objects, messages, methods, inheritance, and polymorphism.
- You declare base classes to specify the various private, protected, and public members. C++ classes contain data members and member functions. The data members store

the state of a class instance, and the member functions query and manipulate that state.

- Constructors and destructors support the automatic creation and removal of class instances. Constructors are special members that must have the same name as the host class. You may declare any number of constructors, or none at all. In the latter case, the compiler creates one for you. Each constructor enables you to create a class instance in a different way. There are two special types of constructors: the default constructor and the copy constructor. In contrast with constructors, C++ enables you to declare only one parameterless destructor. Destructors automatically remove class instances. The runtime system automatically invokes the constructor and destructor when a class instance comes into and goes out of its scope.
- Declaring a class hierarchy enables you to derive classes from existing ones. The descendant classes inherit the members of their ancestor classes. C++ classes are able to override inherited member functions by defining their own versions. If you override a nonvirtual function, you may declare the new version using a different parameter list. By contrast, you cannot alter the parameter list of an inherited virtual function.
- Virtual member functions enable your classes to support polymorphic behavior. Such behavior offers a response that is suitable for each class in a hierarchy. After you declare a function virtual, you can override it only with a virtual function in a descendant class. All versions of a virtual function in a class hierarchy must have the same signature.
- Friend functions are special nonmember functions that may access protected and private data members. These functions enable you to implement operations that are more flexible than those offered by member functions.
- Operators and friend operators enable you to support various operations, such as addition, assignment, and indexing. These operators enable you to offer a level of abstraction for your classes. In addition, they assist in making the expressions that manipulate class instances more readable and more intuitive.

Q&A

Q What happens if I declare the default, copy, and other constructors as protected?

A Client programs are unable to create instances of that class. However, client programs can use that class by declaring descendant classes with public constructors.

Q Can I chain messages to an instance?

A Yes, you can as long as the chained messages invoke member functions that return a reference to the same class that receives the message. For example, if you have a class `String` with the following member functions

```
String& upperCase();
string& reverse();
String& mapChars(char find, char replace);
```

you can write the following statement for the instance of class `String` s:

```
s.upperCase().reverse().mapChar(' ', '+');
```

Q What happens if a class relies on the copy constructor, which is created by the compiler, to copy instances of a class that has pointers?

A These constructors perform a bit-by-bit copy. Consequently, the corresponding pointer members in both instances end up with the address to the same dynamic data. This kind of duplication is a recipe for trouble!

Q Can I create an array of instances?

A Yes, you can; however, the accompanying class must have a default constructor. The instantiation of the array uses the constructor mentioned previously.

Q Can I use a pointer to create an instance of class?

A Yes, you need to use the operators new and `delete` to allocate and deallocate the dynamic space for the instance. Here is an example using the class `Complex`.

```
Complex* pC;
pC = new Complex;
// manipulate the instance accessed by pointer pC
delete pC;
```

or

```
Complex* pC = new Complex;
// manipulate the instance accessed by pointer pC
delete pC;
```

Workshop

The Workshop provides quiz questions to help you solidify your understanding of the material covered and exercises to provide you with experience in using what you've learned. Try to understand the quiz and exercise answers before continuing on to the next day's lesson. Answers are provided in Appendix A.

Quiz

1. Where is the error in the following class declaration?

```
class String {
        char *str;
        unsigned len;
        String();
        String(const String& s);
```

```
        String(unsigned size, char = ' ');
        String(unsigned size);
        String& assign(String& s);
        ~String();
        unsigned getLen() const;
        char* getString();
        // other member functions
};
```

2. Where is the error in the following class declaration?

```
class String {
     protected:
        char *str;
        unsigned len;
     public:
        String();
        String(const char* s);
        String(const String& s);
        String(unsigned size, char = ' ');
        String(unsigned size);
        ~String();
        // other member functions
};
```

3. True or false? The following statement, which creates the instance `s` based on the preceding declaration of class `String`, is correct:

```
s = String("Hello Turbo C++");
```

4. Looking at the program CLASS6.CPP, if you change the declarations of the instances in function `main` to the following, will the program still compile?

```
Complex c1 = Complex(3, 5);
Complex c2 = Complex(7, 5);
Complex c3 = c1;
Complex c4 = Complex(2, 3);
```

Exercise

Create the program CLASS7.CPP from CLASS6.CPP by replacing the individual instances `c1` to `c4` with `c`, an array of instances.

WEEK 2

Basic Stream File I/O

Today's lesson introduces you to file I/O (input/output) operations using the C++ stream library. You have a choice of using file I/O functions in the STDIO.H file or in the C++ stream library. Each of these two I/O libraries offers a lot of power and flexibility. Today's lesson presents basic and practical operations that enable you to read and write data to files. You learn about the following topics:

- Common stream I/O functions
- Sequential stream I/O for text
- Sequential stream I/O for binary data
- Random access stream I/O for binary data

To learn more about the C++ stream library, consult a C++ language reference book, such as Tom Swan's *C++ Primer* (Sams Publishing, 1992).

The C++ Stream Library

The C++ stream I/O library (also known as the iostream library) is made up of a hierarchy of classes that are declared in several header files. The IOSTREAM.H header file used thus far is only one of these. Others include ISTREAM.H, OSTREAM.H, IFSTREAM.H, OFSTREAM.H, and FSTREAM.H. The ISTREAM.H and OSTREAM.H files support the basic input and output stream classes. The IOSTREAM.H combines the operations of the classes in the previous two header files. Similarly, the IFSTREAM.H and OFSTREAM.H files support the basic file input and output stream classes. The FSTREAM.H file combines the operations of the classes in the previous two header files. There are additional stream library files that offer even more specialized stream I/O. The ANSI/ISO C++ committee will define the standard stream I/O library, and the committee's work will end any confusion regarding which classes and header files are part of the standard stream library and which ones are not.

Common Stream I/O Functions

This section presents stream I/O member functions that are common to both sequential and random access I/O. These member functions include `open`, `close`, `good`, and `fail`, in addition to the operator `!`.

The `open` member function enables you to open a file stream for input, output, append, and both input and output. The function also permits you to specify whether the related I/O is binary or text.

Syntax

The *open* Member Function

The prototype for the open function is

```
void open(const char* filename,
          int mode,
          int m = filebuf::openprot);
```

The parameter filename specifies the name of the file to open. The parameter mode indicates the I/O mode. Following is a list of arguments for parameter mode that are exported by the FSTREAM.H header file:

in	Open stream for input
out	Open stream for output
ate	Set stream pointer to the end of the file
app	Open stream for append mode
trunc	Truncate file size to 0 if it already exists
nocreate	Raise an error if the file does not already exist
noreplace	Raise an error if the file already exists
binary	Open in binary mode

Example

```
// open stream for input
fstream f;
f.open("\\AUTOEXEC.BAT", ios::in);

// open stream for output
fstream f;
f.open("\\AUTOEXEC.OLD", ios:out);

// open stream for binary input and output
fstream f;
f.open("INCOME.DAT", ios::in ¦ ios::out ¦ ios::binary);
```

Note: The file stream classes offer constructors that include the action (and have the same parameters) of the member function open.

The close member function closes the stream and recuperates the resources involved. These resources include the memory buffer used in the stream I/O operations.

Syntax

The *close* Member Function

The prototype for the `close` function is

```
void close();
```

Example

```
fstream f;
// open stream
f.open("\\AUTOEXEC.BAT", ios::in);
// process file
// now close stream
f.close();
```

The C++ stream library includes a set of basic functions that check the error status of a stream operation. These functions include the following:

1. The `good()` function returns a nonzero value if there is no error in a stream operation. The declaration of function `good` is

   ```
   int good();
   ```

2. The `fail()` function returns a nonzero value if there is an error in a stream operation. The declaration of function `fail` is

   ```
   int fail();
   ```

3. The overloaded operator `!` is applied to a stream instance to determine the error status.

The C++ stream libraries offer additional functions to set and query other aspects and types of stream errors.

Sequential Text Stream I/O

The functions and operators involved in sequential text I/O are simple. You already have been exposed to most of them in earlier lessons. The functions and operators include the following:

- The stream extractor operator << writes strings and characters to a stream.
- The stream inserter operator >> reads characters from a stream.
- The `getline` function reads strings from a stream.

Syntax

The *getline* Member Function

The prototypes for the member function `getline` are

```
istream& getline(char* buffer,
                 int size,
                 char delimiter = '\n');

istream& getline(signed char* buffer,
                 int size,
                 char delimiter = '\n');
```

```
istream& getline(unsigned char* buffer,
                 int size,
                 char delimiter = '\n');
```

The parameter `buffer` is a pointer to the string receiving the characters from the stream. The parameter `size` specifies the maximum number of characters to read. The parameter `delimiter` specifies the delimiting character, which causes the string input to stop before reaching the number of characters specified by parameter `size`. The parameter delimiter has the default argument of `'\n'`.

Example

```
fstream f;
char textLine[MAX];
f.open("\\CONFIG.SYS", ios::in);
while (!f.eof()) {
f.getline(textLine, MAX);
cout << textLine << "\n";
}
f.close();
```

Look at an example. Listing 9.1 shows the source code for the program IO1.CPP. The program performs the following tasks:

- Prompts you to enter the name of an input text file.
- Prompts you to enter the name of an output text file. (The program detects if the names of the input and output files are the same, and if so, reprompts you for a different output filename.)
- Reads the lines from the input files and removes any trailing spaces in these lines.
- Writes the lines to the output file and also to the standard output window.

Listing 9.1. Source code for the IO1.CPP program.

```
// C++ program that demonstrates sequential file I/O

#include <iostream.h>
#include <fstream.h>
#include <string.h>

enum boolean { false, true };

const unsigned LINE_SIZE = 128;
const unsigned NAME_SIZE = 64;

void trimStr(char* s)
{
  int i = strlen(s) - 1;
  // locate the character where the trailing spaces begin
```

continued

Listing 9.1. continued

```
  while (i >= 0 && s[i] == ' ')
    i--;
  // truncate string
  s[i+1] = '\0';
}

void getInputFilename(char* inFile, fstream& f)
{
  boolean ok;

  do {
    ok = true;
    cout << "Enter input file : ";
    cin.getline(inFile, NAME_SIZE);
    f.open(inFile, ios::in);
    if (!f) {
      cout << "Cannot open file " << inFile << "\n\n";
      ok = false;
    }
  } while (!ok);

}

void getOutputFilename(char* outFile, const char* inFile,
                       fstream& f)
{
  boolean ok;

  do {
    ok = true;
    cout << "Enter output file : ";
    cin.getline(outFile, NAME_SIZE);
    if (stricmp(inFile, outFile) != 0) {
      f.open(outFile, ios::out);
      if (!f) {
        cout << "File " << outFile << " is invalid\n\n";
        ok = false;
      }
    }
    else {
      cout << "Input and output files must be different!\n";
      ok = false;
    }
  } while (!ok);
}

void processLines(fstream& fin, fstream& fout)
{
  char line[LINE_SIZE + 1];

  // loop to trim trailing spaces
  while (fin.getline(line, LINE_SIZE)) {
    trimStr(line);
    // write line to the output file
    fout << line << "\n";
    // echo updated line to the output window
```

```
72:     cout << line << "\n";
73:   }
74:
75: }
76: main()
77: {
78:
79:   fstream fin, fout;
80:   char inFile[NAME_SIZE + 1], outFile[NAME_SIZE + 1];
81:
82:   getInputFilename(inFile, fin);
83:   getOutputFilename(outFile, inFile, fout);
84:   processLines(fin, fout);
85:   // close streams
86:   fin.close();
87:   fout.close();
88:   return 0;
89: }
```

Here is a sample session with the program in Listing 9.1.

```
Enter input file : sample.txt
Enter output file : sample.out
This is line 1
This is line 2
This is line 3
This is line 4
```

The program in Listing 9.1 declares no classes and, instead, focuses on using file streams to input and output text. The program declares the functions `trimStr`, `getInputFilename`, `getOutputFilename`, `processLines`, and `main`.

The function `trimStr` shaves the trailing spaces in the strings passed by parameter `s`. The function declares the local variable `i` and assigns it the index of the character just before the null terminator. The function uses the `while` loop in line 13 to perform a backward scan of the characters in string `s` for the first nonspace character. The statement at line 16 assigns the null terminator character to the character located right after the last nonspace character in the string `s`.

The function `getInputFilename` obtains the input filename and opens its corresponding input file stream. The parameter `inFile` passes the name of the input file to the function `caller`. The reference parameter `f` passes the opened input stream to the function `caller`. The function `getInputFilename` declares the local flag `ok`. The function uses the `do-while` loop in lines 26 through 35 to obtain a valid filename and to open that file for input. Line 27 contains the first statement inside the loop, which assigns the enumerated value `true` to the local variable `ok`. The output statement in line 28 prompts you for the input filename. The statement in line 29 calls the stream input function `getline` to obtain your input and to store it in the parameter `inFile`. The statement in line 30 opens the input file using the stream parameter `f`. The open statement uses the `ios::in` value to indicate that the stream is opened for text input. The `if` statement in line 31 determines whether the stream `f` is successfully opened. If not, the function executes the statements in lines 32 and 33. These statements display an error message and assign the

enumerated value `false` to the local variable `ok`. The loop's `while` clause in line 35 examines the condition `!ok`. The loop iterates until you supply it a valid filename, which must successfully be opened for input.

The function `getOutputFilename` complements the function `getInputFilename` and has three parameters. The parameter `outFile` passes the output filename of the function caller. The parameter `inFile` supplies the function with the input filename. The function uses this parameter to ensure that the input and output filenames are not the same. The parameter `f` passes the output stream to the function caller. The implementation of function `getOutputFilename` is very similar to that of function `getInputFilename`. The main difference is that the function `getOutputFilename` calls the function `stricmp` to compare the values in parameter `inFile` and `outFile`. The function uses the result of `stricmp` to determine whether the names of the input and output files are identical. If so, the function executes the statements in the `else` clause at lines 57 and 58. These statements display an error message and assign `false` to the local variable `ok`.

The function `processLines` reads the lines from the input file stream, trims them, and writes them to the output file stream. The parameters `fin` and `fout` pass the input and output file streams, respectively. The function declares the local string variable `line` and uses the `while` loop in lines 67 through 73 to process the text lines. The `while` clause contains the call to function `getline`, which reads the next line in the input stream `fin` and assigns the input line to variable `line`. The result of function `getline` causes the `while` loop to stop iterating when there are no more input lines. The first statement inside the loop, located at line 68, calls the function `trimStr` and passes it the argument `line`. This function call prunes any existing trailing spaces in the local variable `line`. The statement in line 70 writes the string in variable `line` to the output file stream. The statement in line 72 echoes the string in `line` to the standard output window. (We placed this statement in the program so that you can monitor the progress of the program.)

The function `main` declares the file streams `fin` and `fout`, and the string variables `inFile` and `outFile`. The statement in line 82 calls function `getInputFilename` and passes it the arguments `inFile` and `fin`. This call obtains the name of the input file and the input stream through the arguments `inFile` and `fin`, respectively. The statement in line 83 calls the function `getOutputFilename` and passes it the arguments `outFile`, `inFile`, and `fout`. This call obtains the name of the output file and the output stream through the arguments `outFile` and `fout`, respectively. The statement in line 84 calls function `processLines` and passes it the arguments `fin` and `fout`. This call processes the lines in the input file stream `fin` and writes the results to the output file stream `fout`. The statements in lines 86 and 87 close the input and output file streams, respectively.

Sequential Binary File Stream I/O

The C++ stream library offers the overloaded stream member functions `write` and `read` for sequential binary file stream I/O. The member function `write` sends multiple bytes to an output stream. This function can write any variable or instance to a stream.

Syntax

The *write* Member Function

The prototypes for the overloaded member function `write` are

```
ostream& write(const char* buff, int num);
ostream& write(const signed char* buff, int num);
ostream& write(const unsigned char* buff, int num);
```

The parameter `buff` is the pointer to the buffer that contains the data to be sent to the output stream. The parameter `num` indicates the number of bytes in the buffer that are sent to the stream.

Example

```
const MAX = 80;
char buff[MAX+1] = "Hello World!";
int len = strlen(buffer) + 1;
fstream f;
f.open("CALC.DAT", ios::out ¦ ios::binary);
f.write((const unsigned char*)&len, sizeof(len));
f.write((const unsigned char*)buff, len);
f.close();
```

The member function `read` receives multiple bytes from an input stream. This function can read any variable or can read from a stream.

Syntax

The *read* Member Function

The prototypes for the overloaded member function `read` are

```
istream& read(char* buff, int num);
istream& read(signed char* buff, int num);
istream& read(unsigned char* buff, int num);
```

The parameter `buff` is the pointer to the buffer that receives the data from the input stream. The parameter `num` indicates the number of bytes to read from the stream.

Example

```
const MAX = 80;
char buff[MAX+1];
int len;
fstream f;
f.open("CALC.DAT", ios::in ¦ ios::binary);
f.read((const unsigned char*)&len, sizeof(len));
f.read((const unsigned char*)buff, len);
f.close();
```

Look at an example that performs sequential binary stream I/O. Listing 9.2 shows the source code for the program IO2.CPP. The program declares a class that models dynamic numerical arrays. The stream I/O operations enable the program to read and write both the individual array elements and an entire array in binary files. The program creates the arrays `arr1`, `arr2`, and `arr3` and then performs the following tasks:

- ☐ Assigns values to the elements of array `arr1`. (This array has 10 elements.)
- ☐ Assigns values to the elements of array `arr3`. (This array has 20 elements.)
- ☐ Displays the values in array `arr1`.
- ☐ Writes the elements of array `arr1` to the file ARR1.DAT, one element at a time.
- ☐ Reads the elements of `arr1` from the file into the array `arr2`. (The array `arr2` has 10 elements—the same size as array `arr1`.)
- ☐ Displays the values in array `arr2`.
- ☐ Displays the values in array `arr3`.
- ☐ Writes the elements of array `arr3` to file ARR3.DAT in one swoop.
- ☐ Reads, in one swoop, the data in file ARR3.DAT and stores them in array `arr1`.
- ☐ Displays the values in array `arr1`. (The output shows that array `arr1` has the same size and data as array `arr3`.)

Type

Listing 9.2. Source code for the IO2.CPP program.

```
/*
   C++ program that demonstrates sequential binary file I/O
*/

#include <iostream.h>
#include <fstream.h>

const unsigned MIN_SIZE = 10;
const double BAD_VALUE = -1.0e+30;
enum boolean { false, true };

class Array
{
     Array(const Array&);  //prevent copy const. getting called
   protected:
     double *dataPtr;
     unsigned size;
     double badIndex;
   public:
     Array(unsigned Size = MIN_SIZE);
     ~Array()
       { delete [] dataPtr; }
     unsigned getSize() const { return size; }
     double& operator [](unsigned index)
     { return (index < size) ? *(dataPtr + index) : badIndex; }
     boolean writeElem(fstream& os, unsigned index);
     boolean readElem(fstream& is, unsigned index);
     boolean writeArray(const char* filename);
     boolean readArray(const char* filename);
};

Array::Array(unsigned Size)
```

```
{
  size = (Size < MIN_SIZE) ? MIN_SIZE : Size;
  badIndex = BAD_VALUE;
  dataPtr = new double[size];
}

boolean Array::writeElem(fstream& os, unsigned index)
{
   if (index < size) {
     os.write((unsigned char*)(dataPtr + index), sizeof(double));
     return (os.good()) ? true : false;
   }
   else
     return false;
}

boolean Array::readElem(fstream& is, unsigned index)
{
   if (index < size) {
     is.read((unsigned char*)(dataPtr + index), sizeof(double));
     return (is.good()) ? true : false;
    }
    else
      return false;
 }

 boolean Array::writeArray(const char* filename)
 {
    fstream f(filename, ios::out | ios::binary);

    if (f.fail())
      return false;
    f.write((unsigned char*) &size, sizeof(size));
    f.write((unsigned char*)dataPtr, size * sizeof(double));
    f.close();
    return (f.good()) ? true : false;
 }

 boolean Array::readArray(const char* filename)
 {
    fstream f(filename, ios::in | ios::binary);
    unsigned sz;

    if (f.fail())
      return false;
    f.read((unsigned char*) &sz, sizeof(sz));
    // need to expand the array
    if (sz != size) {
      delete [] dataPtr;
      dataPtr = new double[sz];
      size = sz;
    }
    f.read((unsigned char*)dataPtr, size * sizeof(double));
    f.close();
    return (f.good()) ? true : false;
 }
```

continued

Listing 9.2. continued

```
main()
{
  const unsigned SIZE1 = 10;
  const unsigned SIZE2 = 20;
  char* filename1 = "array1.dat";
  char* filename2 = "array3.dat";
  Array arr1(SIZE1), arr2(SIZE1), arr3(SIZE2);
  fstream f(filename1, ios::out | ios::binary);

  // assign values to array arr1
  for (unsigned i = 0; i < arr1.getSize(); i++)
    arr1[i] = 10 * i;

  // assign values to array arr3
  for (i = 0; i < SIZE2; i++)
    arr3[i] = i;

  cout << "Array arr1 has the following values:\n";
  for (i = 0; i < arr1.getSize(); i++)
    cout << arr1[i] << "  ";
  cout << "\n\n";

  // write elements of array arr1 to the stream
  for (i = 0; i < arr1.getSize(); i++)
    arr1.writeElem(f, i);
  f.close();

  // reopen the stream for input
  f.open(filename1, ios::in | ios::binary);

  for (i = 0; i < arr1.getSize(); i++)
    arr2.readElem(f, i);
  f.close();

  // display the elements of array arr2
  cout << "Array arr2 has the following values:\n";
  for (i = 0; i < arr2.getSize(); i++)
    cout << arr2[i] << "  ";
  cout << "\n\n";

  // display the elements of array arr3
  cout << "Array arr3 has the following values:\n";
  for (i = 0; i < arr3.getSize(); i++)
    cout << arr3[i] << "  ";
  cout << "\n\n";

  // write the array arr3 to file ARRAY3.DAT
  arr3.writeArray(filename2);
  // read the array arr1 from file ARRAY3.DAT
  arr1.readArray(filename2);

```

```
141:    // display the elements of array arr1
142:    cout << "Array arr1 now has the following values:\n";
143:    for (i = 0; i < arr1.getSize(); i++)
144:      cout << arr1[i] << "  ";
145:    cout << "\n\n";
146:    return 0;
147: }
```

Here is a sample session with the program in Listing 9.2.

```
Array arr1 has the following values:
0  10  20  30  40  50  60  70  80  90

Array arr2 has the following values:
0  10  20  30  40  50  60  70  80  90

Array arr3 has the following values:
0  1  2  3  4  5  6  7  8  9  10  11  12  13  14  15  16  17  18  19

Array arr1 now has the following values:
0  1  2  3  4  5  6  7  8  9  10  11  12  13  14  15  16  17  18  19
```

The program in Listing 9.2 declares a version of class `Array` that resembles the one in Day 8, Listing 8.2. The main difference is that here we use the `operator [ ]` to replace both the member functions `store` and `recall`. This operator checks for valid indices and returns the value in member `badIndex` if the argument is out of range. In addition to `operator [ ]`, we added the member functions `writeElem`, `readElem`, `writeArray`, and `readArray` to perform sequential binary file stream I/O.

Also note the copy constructor on line 14, and especially that it isn't actually defined anywhere. This is a trick that can be used to prevent other functions or classes from automatically copying it when you know that it would be a Bad Thing (in this case because of the dynamic data, the contents of which would need to be copied).

The function `writeElem`, defined in lines 39 through 47, writes a single array element to an output stream. The parameter `os` represents the output stream. The parameter `index` specifies the array element to write. The function `writeElem` yields true if the argument for the index is valid and if the stream output proceeds without any error. After `writeElem` writes an array element, the internal stream pointer advances to the next location.

The function `readElem`, defined in lines 49 through 57, reads a single array element from an input stream. The parameter `is` represents the input stream. The parameter index specifies the array element to read. The function `readElem` returns true if the argument for the index is valid and if the stream input proceeds without any error. After the `readElem` reads an array element, the internal stream pointer advances to the next location.

The functions `writeElem` and `readElem` permit the same class instance to write and read data elements, respectively, from multiple streams.

The function `writeArray`, defined in lines 59 through 69, writes the entire elements of the array to a binary file. The parameter `filename` specifies the name of the output file. The function opens an output stream and writes the value of the data member `size` and then writes the elements of the dynamic array. The `writeArray` function returns true if it successfully writes the array to the stream. Otherwise, it yields false. The function opens a local output stream by using the stream function `open` and supplying it with the filename and I/O mode argument. The I/O mode argument is the expression `ios::out | ios::binary`, which specifies that the stream is opened for binary output only. The function makes two calls to the stream function `write`—the first to write the data member `size`, and the second to write the elements of the dynamic array.

The function `readArray`, defined in lines 71 through 88, reads the entire elements of the array from a binary file. The parameter `filename` specifies the name of the input file. The function opens an input stream and reads the value of the data member `size` and then reads the elements of the dynamic array. The `readArray` function returns true if it successfully reads the array to the stream. Otherwise, the function yields false. The function opens a local input stream by using the stream function `open` and supplying it the filename and I/O mode arguments. The I/O mode argument is the expression `ios::in | ios::binary`, which specifies that the stream is opened for binary input only. The function makes two calls to the stream function `read`—the first to read the data member `size`, and the second to read the elements of the dynamic array. Another feature of function `readArray` is that it resizes the instance of class `Array` to accommodate the data from the binary file. This means that a dynamic array accessed by the class instance may either shrink or expand, depending on the size of the array stored on file.

The member functions in Listing 9.2 indicate that the program performs two types of sequential binary stream I/O. The first type of I/O, implemented in functions `readElem` and `writeElem`, involves items that have the same data type. The second type of I/O, implemented in the functions `readArray` and `writeArray`, involves items that have different data types.

In Listing 9.2, the function `main` performs the following relevant tasks:

- ☐ Declares, in line 96, three instances of class `Array`, namely, `arr1`, `arr2`, and `arr3`. (The first two instances have the same dynamic array size, specified by the constant `SIZE1`, whereas instance `arr3` has a larger size, specified by the constant `SIZE2`.)
- ☐ Declares, in line 97, the file stream `f` and opens it (using a stream constructor) to access file ARR1.DAT in binary output mode.
- ☐ Uses the `for` loops in lines 100 and 104 to arbitrarily assign values to the instance `arr1` and `arr3`, respectively.
- ☐ Displays the elements of instance `arr1` using the `for` loop in line 108.
- ☐ Writes the elements of array `arr1` to the output file stream `f`, using the `for` loop in line 113 to send the `writeElem` message to instance `arr1` and to supply the message with the output file stream `f` and the loop control variable `i`.

- Closes the output file stream by sending the close message to the output file stream `f`.
- Opens, in line 118, the file stream `f` to access the data file ARR1.DAT. (This time, the message `open` specifies a binary input mode.)
- Reads the elements of instance `arr2` (which has not yet been assigned any values) from the input file stream `f`, using the `for` loop in line 120 to send the message `readElem` to instance `arr2` and to supply the message with the arguments `f`, the file stream, and `i`, the loop control variable.
- Closes the input file stream, in line 122, by sending the message `close` to the input file stream `f`.
- Displays the elements of instance `arr2` using the `for` loop in line 126. (These elements match those of instance `arr1`.)
- Displays the elements of instance `arr3` by using the `for` loop in line 132.
- Writes the entire instance `arr3` by sending the message `writeArray` to instance `arr3`. (The message `writeArray` has the filename argument of ARR3.DAT.)
- Reads the array in file ARR3.DAT into instance `arr1`, sending the message `readArray` to instance `arr1` and supplying the message with the filename argument of ARR3.DAT.
- Displays the new elements of instance `arr1` using the `for` loop in line 143.

Random Access File Stream I/O

Random access file stream operations also use the stream member functions `read` and `write` that were presented in the preceding section. The stream library offers a number of stream-seeking functions to enable you to move the stream pointer to any valid location. The member function `seekg` is one of such functions.

Syntax

The *seekg* Member Function

The prototypes for the overloaded member function `seekg` are

```
istream& seekg(long pos);
istream& seekg(long pos, seek_dir dir);
```

The parameter `pos` in the first version specifies the absolute byte position in the stream. In the second version, the parameter `pos` specifies a relative offset, based on the argument for parameter `dir`. Following are the arguments for the latter parameter:

`ios::beg`From the beginning of the file
`ios::cur`From the current position of the file
`ios::end`From the end of the file

Example

```
const BLOCK_SIZE = 80;
char buff[BLOCK_SIZE] = "Hello World!";
fstream f("CALC.DAT", ios::in ¦ ios::out ¦ ios::binary);
f.seekg(3 * BLOCK_SIZE); // seek block # 4
f.read((const unsigned char*)buff, BLOCK_SIZE);
cout << buff <<< "\n";
f.close();
```

NEW TERM A *virtual array* is a disk-based array that stores fixed-size strings on disk.

Look at an example that uses random access file stream I/O. Listing 9.3 shows the source code for the program IO3.CPP and implements a virtual array. The program performs the following tasks:

- Uses an internal list of names to create a virtual array object
- Displays the elements in the unordered virtual array object
- Prompts you to enter a character and press the Return key
- Sorts the elements of the virtual array object; this process requires random access I/O
- Displays the elements in the sorted virtual array object

Type

Listing 9.3. Source code for the IO3.CPP program.

```
/*
   C++ program that demonstrates random-access binary file I/O
*/

#include <iostream.h>
#include <fstream.h>
#include <stdlib.h>
#include <string.h>

const unsigned MIN_SIZE = 5;
const unsigned STR_SIZE = 31;
const double BAD_VALUE = -1.0e+30;
enum boolean { false, true };

class VmArray
{
   protected:
     fstream f;
     unsigned size;
     double badIndex;

   public:
     VmArray(unsigned Size, const char* filename);
     ~VmArray()
       { f.close(); }
     unsigned getSize() const
       { return size; }
```

```
        boolean writeElem(const char* str, unsigned index);
        boolean readElem(char* str, unsigned index);
        void Combsort();
};

VmArray::VmArray(unsigned Size, const char* filename)
{
    char s[STR_SIZE+1];
    size = (Size < MIN_SIZE) ? MIN_SIZE : Size;
    badIndex = BAD_VALUE;
    f.open(filename, ios::in | ios::out | ios::binary);
    if (f.good()) {
      // fill the file stream with empty strings
      strcpy(s, "");;
      f.seekg(0);
      for (unsigned i = 0; i < size; i++)
        f.write((unsigned char*)s, sizeof(s));
    }
}

boolean VmArray::writeElem(const char* str, unsigned index)
{
     if (index < size) {
       f.seekg(index * (STR_SIZE+1));
       f.write((unsigned char*)str, (STR_SIZE+1));
       return (f.good()) ? true : false;
     }
     else
       return false;
}

boolean VmArray::readElem(char* str, unsigned index)
{
     if (index < size) {
       f.seekg(index * (STR_SIZE+1));
       f.read((unsigned char*)str, (STR_SIZE+1));
       return (f.good()) ? true : false;
     }
     else
       return false;
}

void VmArray::Combsort()
{
     unsigned i, j, gap = size;
     boolean inOrder;
     char strI[STR_SIZE+1], strJ[STR_SIZE+1];

     do {
       gap = (gap * 8) / 11;
       if (gap < 1)
         gap = 1;
       inOrder = true;
       for (i = 0, j = gap; i < (size - gap); i++, j++) {
         readElem(strI, i);
         readElem(strJ, j);
         if (strcmp(strI, strJ) > 0) {
```

Listing 9.3. continued

```
        inOrder = false;
        writeElem(strI, j);
        writeElem(strJ, i);
      }
    }
  } while (!(inOrder && gap == 1));
}

main()
{
  char* data[] = { "Michigan", "California", "Virginia", "Maine",
                   "New York", "Florida", "Nevada", "Alaska",
                   "Ohio", "Maryland" };
  VmArray arr(10, "arr.dat");
  char str[STR_SIZE+1];
  char c;

  // assign values to array arr
  for (unsigned i = 0; i < arr.getSize(); i++) {
    strcpy(str, data[i]);
    arr.writeElem(str, i);
  }
  // display unordered array
  cout << "Unsorted arrays is:\n";
  for (i = 0; i < arr.getSize(); i++) {
    arr.readElem(str, i);
    cout << str << "\n";
  }
  // pause
  cout << "\nPress any key and then Return to sort the array...";
  cin >> c;
  // sort the array
  arr.Combsort();
  // display sorted array
  cout << "Sorted arrays is:\n";
  for (i = 0; i < arr.getSize(); i++) {
    arr.readElem(str, i);
    cout << str << "\n";
  }
  return 0;
}
```

Here is a sample session with the program in Listing 9.3.

```
Unsorted arrays is:
Michigan
California
Virginia
Maine
New York
Florida
Nevada
Alaska
Ohio
Maryland
```

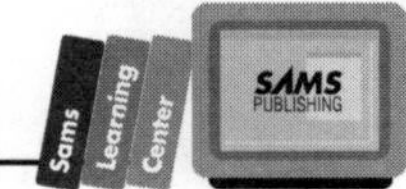

```
Press any key and then Return to sort the array...d
Sorted arrays is:
Alaska
California
Florida
Maine
Maryland
Michigan
Nevada
New York
Ohio
Virginia
```

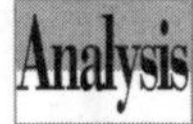

The program in Listing 9.3 declares the class `VmArray`. This class models a disk-based dynamic array that stores all its elements in a random access binary file. Notice that the class declares an instance of class `fstream` and that there is no pointer to a dynamic array. The class declares a constructor, a destructor, and a number of member functions.

The class constructor has two parameters, namely, `Size` and `filename`. The parameter `Size` specifies the size of the virtual array. The parameter `filename` names the binary file that stores the elements of a class instance. The constructor opens the stream `f` using the stream function `open` and supplies it the argument of parameter `filename` and the I/O mode expression `ios::in | ios::out | ios::binary`. This expression specifies that the stream is opened for binary input and output mode (that is, random access mode). If the constructor successfully opens the file stream, it proceeds to fill the file with zeros. The class destructor performs the simple task of closing the file stream `f`.

The functions `writeElem` and `readElem` support the random access of array elements. These functions use the stream function `seekg` to position the stream pointer at the appropriate array element. The `writeElem` then calls the stream function `write` to store an array element (supplied by the parameter `str`). By contrast, the function `readElem` calls the stream function `read` to retrieve an array element (returned by the parameter `str`). Both functions return Boolean results that indicate the success of the I/O operation.

The `VmArray` class also declares the `Combsort` function to sort the elements of the virtual array. This function uses the `readElem` and `writeElem` member functions to access and swap the array elements.

The function `main` performs the following relevant tasks:

- ☐ Declares the instance `arr`, of class `VmArray`. (This instance stores 10 strings in the binary file ARR.DAT.)
- ☐ Assigns random values to the elements of instance `arr`, using the `for` loop in lines 103 through 106, to assign strings accessed by `data[i]` to the variable `str` and then to write the value in `str` to the instance `arr` by sending it the message `writeElem`. (The arguments for the message `writeElem` are the string variable `str` and the loop control variable `i`.)

- Displays the unsorted elements of instance `arr` using the `for` loop in line 109. (The statement in line 110 sends the message `readElem` to the instance `arr` to obtain an element in the virtual array.)
- Sorts the array by sending the message `Combsort` to the instance `arr`.
- Displays the sorted elements of instance `arr` using the `for` loop in line 120. (The statement in line 121 sends the message `readElem` to the instance `arr` to obtain an element in the virtual array.)

Summary

Today's lesson provided a brief introduction to the C++ stream I/O library and discussed the following topics:

- Common stream functions include `open`, `close`, `good`, `fail`, and the operator `!`. The function `open` opens a file for stream I/O and supports alternate and multiple I/O modes. The function `close` shuts down a file stream. The functions `good` and `fail` indicate the success or failure, respectively, of a stream I/O operation.
- C++ enables you to perform sequential stream I/O for text, using the operators `<<` and `>>` as well as the stream function `getline`. The operator `<<` is able to write characters and strings (as well as the other predefined data types). The operator `>>` is suitable for obtaining characters. The function `getline` enables your applications to read strings from the keyboard or from a text file.
- Sequential stream I/O for binary data uses the stream functions `write` and `read` to write and read data from any types of variables.
- Random access stream I/O for binary data uses the `seekg` function in conjunction with the functions `read` and `write`. The `seekg` function enables you to move the stream pointer to either absolute or relative byte locations in the stream.

Q&A

Q How can I emulate the random access of lines in a text file?

A First, read the lines in the file as text, obtain the length of the lines (plus the two characters for the end of each line), and store the cumulative length in a special array. (Call it `lineIndex`.) This array stores the byte location where each line starts. The last array element should store the size of the file. To access line number `i`, use the `seek` or `seekg` function to locate the offset value in `lineIndex[i]`. The size of line number `i` is equal to `lineIndex[i+1]-lineIndex[i]`.

Q How do I write a general-purpose routine to copy between an input and an output file stream?

A You need to use the stream function `gcount()` to obtain the number of bytes actually read in the last unformatted stream input. The following is the function `copyStream`:

```
void copyStream(fstream& fin, fstream& fout,
                unsigned char* buffer, int buffSize)
{
  int n;
  while (fin.read(buffer, buffSize) {
    n = fin.gcount();
    fout.write(buffer, n);
  }
}
```

Q Why declare data members in classes that support exceptions?

A These data members help the catch blocks to pass information related to the cause and state that lead to the exception. The simplest example is that the exception class has a string-typed data member that passes the error message text.

Workshop

The Workshop provides quiz questions to help you solidify your understanding of the material covered and exercises to provide you with experience in using what you've learned. Try to understand the quiz and exercise answers before continuing on to the next day's lesson. Answers are provided in Appendix A.

Quiz

1. True or false? The stream I/O functions `read` and `write` are able to correctly read and write any data type.
2. True or false? The stream I/O functions `read` and `write` are able to correctly read and write any data type, as long as the type has no pointer members.
3. True or false? The `seek` and `seekg` functions expand the file when you supply them an index that is one byte beyond the current end of file.
4. True or false? The arguments of the functions `seek` and `seekg` require no range checking.

Exercise

Create the program IO4.CPP by modifying the program IO3.CPP. The class `VmArray` in IO4.CPP should have the function `binSearch`, which conducts a binary search on the members of the sorted array. Add a loop at the end of the function `main` to search in the array `arr`, using the unordered data of the initializing list. (The members of this list are accessed using the pointer data.)

WEEK
2

The C++ *string* Class, Templates, and the Class Library

On Day 7, you learned about strings and the functions in STRING.H that work with them. Turbo C++ 4.5 provides a more powerful method of dealing with strings—the `string` class. This class conforms to the `string` class from the ANSI/ISO C++ standards committee and is prototyped in the header file CSTRING.H.

Note: ANSI is American National Standards Institute and ISO is the International Standards Organization. ANSI and ISO are jointly developing a standard for the C++ language.

C-style strings are powerful but require control of many low-level items such as allocation sizes and pointer offsets. The C++ `string` class is designed to increase the power available above that of C strings, but without need for low-level concerns.

Today you also will learn about templates, the C++ version of a type-checking macro. Hand in hand with templates, you also learn about the class library that comes with Turbo C++ 4.5, which is a useful set of classes for manipulating collections of data.

At the end of today's lesson, you will be familiar with the following:

- Benefits of the C++ `string` class
- I/O with the C++ `string` class
- Comparing strings
- Searching for "tokens"
- Controlling how string class comparisons are done
- Searching for substrings inside of larger strings
- Mixed operations with C/C++ style strings and the `string` class
- Templates
- The Turbo C++ class libraries

Benefits of the C++ *string* Class

The programmer can design a class that inherits from the `string` class. The newly designed class can use all the power of the `string` class, as well as whatever else needs to be added.

The result is an object-oriented program design, which is easier to write and maintain. The following shows how the C++ `string` class provides solutions to C-string difficulties.

Table 10.1. C String difficulties and C ++ class solutions.

C String Difficulty	C++ `string` Class Solution

C string functions have obscure names, which makes it difficult to find the function you want.	Operators such as `!=` or `=` are used when possible. When function names are used, they sound like what they do, such as the following:
	`strcmp` versus `==`
	`strcpy` versus `=`
	`strstr` versus `find`
	`strlwr` versus `to_lower`

No variable or function reports the allocated size of a C string. When copying to a string, the programmer must remember the allocated size or allocate a new string large enough to hold the string or strings that he or she wants to store.	The C++ `string` class handles allocations and knows the allowed size. Operations are checked against the current size, and the allocated size is increased when necessary.
When allocating memory for a string, an additional byte must be allocated for the terminating `\0` character. Forgetting to do this is a common error.	String terminating characters are automatically provided.
Comparisons using C-style strings must be done with a call to a function such as `strcmp`. A frequent error is when the programmer uses logical operators, such as `=` or `<`, for C strings, receiving a result that tells of the relationship between the address of the strings in memory rather than of the strings themselves.	Source code to compare C++ strings can be written as if comparing integers, because familiar comparison operators (such as `==`, `!=`, and so on) are provided. An explicit function call is not needed to do a comparison.
Parsing strings into words or finding substrings in C-style strings involves many lines of code with calls to functions such as `strtok`, the use of which are complicated and detail-intensive.	This work and the consequent debugging are now unnecessary. Powerful functions are in the `string` class to do such common tasks. For example, read-next word (token) from the keyboard, a file, or from another string is done with a call to `read_token`. It can be set to skip leading spaces or leave them in the string.

continues

Table 10.1. continued

C String Difficulty	C++ `string` Class Solution
When an allocation error is made, other memory outside the string array is altered. When that memory is a critical area, it often will cause the program to crash or the computer to lock up.	Exception handling is done by the class. It traps allocation failures and errors, terminating the program safely.

The *string* Class Header File CSTRING.H

The `string` class uses three other classes. Those classes are as follows:

`TStringRef` — The `string` class uses this class in reserving and managing memory. Normally the programmer needs not access or use anything from this class. The `string` class is declared a friend within `TStringRef`. The `string` class declares `TStringRef` as a friend as well.

`TSubString` — This is a class that handles the operations on substrings. Both the `string` and `TSubString` classes declare each other as friends. Many of the operations done with a `string` class actually are performed by `TSubString`.

`TReference` — A base class used in copy and access operations, `TReference` is shown in the header file REF.H.

Note: All programs that use the `string` class must include the header file CSTRING.H.

`NPOS` is used as a value to indicate that no position is specified. It is declared as follows:

```
const size_t NPOS = size_t(-1);
```

Constructors and Copy Constructors

What follows is a list of the public constructors for the `string` class that can be used to create a new `string` object instance:

```
string();
string( const string& s);
string( const string& s,  size_t startIndex,
        size_t numChars = NPOS);

string( const char   *cp);
string( const char   *cp, size_t startIndex,
        size_t numChars = NPOS);

string( char          c);
string( char          c,  size_t numChars);
string( signed char   c);
string( signed char   c,  size_t numChars);
string( unsigned char c);
string( unsigned char c,  size_t numChars);

string( const TSubString& ss);

string copy() const; // Note: There are other copy() functions below

string&     operator = (const string& s);
TSubString& operator = (const string& s);
```

The following constructor is only valid for Windows applications. It creates a string object that is loaded directly from the application's string resources.

```
string( HINSTANCE instance, UINT id, int numChars = 255);
```

Comparing

As stated earlier, the `string` class provides easier methods of comparison than the `strcmp` style functions. The following are the comparison operators defined by the `string` class:

```
friend int operator == ( const string& s1, const string& s2 );
friend int operator == ( const string& s,  const char   *cp );
friend int operator == ( const char   *cp, const string& s );
int operator == ( const char   *cp );
int operator == ( const string& s );

friend int operator != ( const string& s1, const string& s2 );
friend int operator != ( const string& s,  const char   *cp );
friend int operator != ( const char   *cp, const string& s );
int operator != ( const char   *cp );
int operator != ( const string& s );

friend int operator >  ( const string& s1, const string& s2 );
friend int operator >  ( const string& s,  const char   *cp );
friend int operator >  ( const char   *cp, const string& s );

friend int operator <  ( const string& s1, const string& s2 );
friend int operator <  ( const string& s,  const char   *cp );
friend int operator <  ( const char   *cp, const string& s );


friend int operator <= ( const string& s1, const string& s2 );
friend int operator <= ( const string& s,  const char   *cp );
```

```
friend int operator <= ( const char   *cp, const string& s );


friend int operator >= ( const string& s1, const string& s2 );
friend int operator >= ( const string& s,  const char   *cp );
friend int operator >= ( const char   *cp, const string& s );

int compare ( const string& s) const;
int compare ( const string& s, size_t startIndex,
              size_t numChars = NPOS ) const;
```

Concatenating Strings

The `string` class provides simpler methods of concatenating strings than using the `strcat` style of functions. Several of these are implemented as operators, whereas others are implemented with the `append` member function for adding on to the end of a string and the `prepend` member function for adding on to the beginning of a string.

```
friend string operator + (  const string& s, const char *cp );

string& operator += ( const string& s );
string& operator += ( const char   *cp );

string& append( const string& s );
string& append( const string&& s, size_t startIndex,
                size_t numChars = NPOS );

string& prepend( const string& s );
string& prepend( const string& s, size_t startIndex,
                 size_t numChars = NPOS )

string& prepend( const char *cp );
string& prepend( const char *cp, size_t startIndex,
                 size_t numChars = NPOS );
```

Inserting Characters into a String

The `insert` member function enables you to insert other strings into the middle of a `string` object.

```
string& insert( size_t startInsertAt, const string& s );
string& insert( size_t startInsertAt, const string& s,
                size_t startFrom, size_t numChars = NPOS );
```

Removing Characters from Within a String

There are two member functions for removing characters from within a string. The `replace` member function replaces characters in a string with the contents of another string. The `strip` member function removes characters from either the beginning, the ending, or both sides of a string.

```
string& replace( size_t removeFrom, size_t removeCount,
                 const string& s );
string& replace( size_t removeFrom, size_t removeCount,
                 const string& s,   size_t startReplacePosition,
                 size_t replaceCount = NPOS );

TSubString strip( StripType s = Trailing, char c = ' ' );

// Note: strip uses this enum which is defined within the class
//       enum StripType { Leading, Trailing, Both };
//
//       The programmer accesses it as one of
//         string::Leading  string::Trailing  string::Both
```

Addressing Individual Characters in a String

When dealing with regular C-string arrays, it's possible to manipulate single characters within the string by using the array operators `[ ]`. The C++ `string` object defines the bracket operators to perform the same function, as well as supplying parentheses operators.

Note in the following syntax that these operators return a reference to the specified character rather than just the character itself. This means that you can assign new characters to that position in the string in the same way you would with a C-string array.

In addition to the bracket and parentheses operators, `get_at` and `put_at` are provided for a more primitive method of getting and changing characters in a `string` object.

```
char& operator [] ( size_t index ); // Note: [] and () both
char& operator () ( size_t index ); //       do the same thing

char operator  [] ( size_t index ) const;
char operator  () ( size_t index ) const;

char get_at( size_t index ) const;
void put_at( size_t index, char c ) const;
```

Getting a Substring from Within a String

The `string` class provides methods for obtaining substrings from a string. There are two sets of these functions: functions that return results that can be modified and functions that can only be examined. For a result that can be examined, but won't be modified, see the following:

```
const TSubString operator()( size_t startIndex, size_t numChars );

const TSubString substring( const char *cp ) const;
const TSubString substring( const char *cp, size_t start ) const;
```

For a copy that can be examined and modified, see the following:

```
string substr( size_t startIndex ) const;
string substr( size_t startIndex, size_t numChars ) const;

TSubString substring( const char *cp );
TSubString substring( const char *cp, size_t startIndex );
```

Searching within a String

Some of the more useful features of the `string` class are its member functions that enable you to search the contents of a string. The basic member functions are `find_first_of`, `find_first_not_of`, `find_last_of`, and `find_last_not_of`. One of the most powerful searching functions, however, is in the overloaded parentheses operators, which allows you to supply a regular expression as the search parameter.

```
const TSubString operator()( const TRegexp& pattern ) const;
const TSubString operator()( const TRegexp& pattern,
                             size_t startIndex );

size_t find_first_of     ( const string& s ) const;
size_t find_first_of     ( const string& s, size_t startIndex ) const;
size_t find_first_not_of ( const string& s ) const;
size_t find_first_not_of ( const string& s, size_t startIndex ) const;
size_t find_last_of      ( const string& s ) const;
size_t find_last_of      ( const string& s, size_t startIndex ) const;
size_t find_last_not_of  ( const string& s ) const;
size_t find_last_not_of  ( const string& s, size_t startIndex );
```

Reading the Length

In order to get the length of a C-style string, you use the `strlen` function. The `string` class supplies the `length` member function to obtain the length of the string.

```
size_t length() const;
```

Copying to a C-Style String

Although using the `string` class is very useful, occasionally it still may be necessary to use a C-style string array. The `copy` member function copies the contents of a `string` object into a standard character array.

```
size_t copy( char *cb, size_t numChars );
size_t copy( char *cb, size_t numChars, size_t startIndex );
```

Reading and Setting Parameters for a Single String

A number of internal parameters affect how the `string` class acts. The `reserve` member function alternately sets or returns the number of characters reserved for the string; `hash` returns a hash value that can be used during sorting. The `is_null` member function can be used to inquire as to whether the string is empty, and `resize` can either contract or expand a string, appending spaces as necessary.

```
size_t   reserve();
void     reserve( size_t numChars );
unsigned hash() const;
int      is_null() const;
void     resize( size_t numChars );
```

I/O Operations

There are a number of functions for getting strings to interact with input and output streams. Some of these are member functions of the string class (read_token, read_file, read_string, read_line, and read_to_delim), whereas others are just globally declared (operator >>, operator <<, and getline).

```
istream& read_token( istream& is );
istream& read_file( istream& is );
istream& read_string( istream& is );
istream& read_line( istream& is );
istream& read_to_delim( istream& is, char delim = '\n' );

ostream& operator << ( ostream& os, const string& s );
istream& operator >> ( istream& is, string& s );

istream& getline( istream& is, string& s );
istream& getline( istream& is, string& s, char c ); **check**
```

Character Set Conversion

Several functions are available for manipulating such things as the case or the character set of a string. The case manipulators are to_lower and to_upper. There are two versions of these functions: member functions and globally declared functions. The globally declared functions return a copy of the converted string, whereas the member functions modify the string itself.

```
string to_lower( const string &s );
string to_upper( const string &s );

void to_lower();
void to_upper();
```

In the Windows environment, the string can be represented in either the ANSI character set or an OEM character set. The ansi_to_oem and oem_to_ansi member functions convert the string between the two sets.

```
void _RTLENTRY ansi_to_oem();
void _RTLENTRY oem_to_ansi();
```

Reading and Setting Parameters for the Whole Class

The following member functions set internal parameters that affect all string objects as opposed to just a particular instance. Most the parameters affect such things as how searches are undertaken and the initial space reserved for characters when strings are created.

```
static int    set_case_sensitive ( int onOff = 1 );
static int    set_paranoid_check ( int onOff = 1 );
static int    skip_whitespace    ( int onOff = 1 );
static size_t initial_capacity   ( size_t numChars = 63 );
```

```
static size_t resize_increment   ( size_t numChars = 64 );
static size_t max_waste          ( size_t numChars = 63 );

static int    get_case_sensitive_flag();
static int    get_paranoid_check_flag();
static int    get_skip_whitespace_flag();
static size_t get_initial_capacity();
static size_t get_resize_increment();
static size_t get_max_waste();
```

Protected Items (Accessible Only in an Inherited Class)

The following member functions are declared as `protected`, which means that they can only be accessed from friends or from derived classes.

```
int  valid_element  ( size_t pos ) const;
int  valid_index    ( size_t pos ) const;

void assert_element ( size_t pos ) const;
void assert_index   ( size_t pos ) const;

string( const string& s, const char *cb );

void cow();     // Note: "cow" = "copy on write"
```

Syntax

Declaring a String

You can declare variables of `string` class type (called *instances of the class* or *class instances*). You also can declare pointers or references to a class instance. Any of these can be initialized in the same statement that declares the variable. A string can be declared with an optional initial value.

```
string Str1;
string Str2 = "String 2";
string Str3("String 3");
```

A string pointer or reference also can be allocated with an optional initial value.

```
string *pStr4 = new string;
string *pStr5 = new string("String 5");
string *pStr6;
string &rStr7 = * new string("String Reference");

pStr6 = new string("A New String Is Constructed");
```

`Str1`, `Str2`, and `Str3` are strings. `Str1` has not been given an initial value so it begins as an empty string (as `""`). `Str2` is set to a value, but the initialization is done with an assignment statement on the same line; it also begins life as an empty string, but that is changed immediately. `Str3` takes advantage of the class constructor argument to set the initial value without the additional step of assigning it.

The pStr4, pStr5, and pStr6 are not strings. They are pointers to strings; they each can hold the address of a string.

The pStr4 and pStr5 are assigned the address of a string by a call to the function new. The string to which pStr4 points is empty, and the one to which pStr5 points contains String 5.

The pStr6 begins as pointing to nothing in particular. The assignment statement creates a string with new, initializes it to the given value, and places the address into pStr6.

Bug Busters

Be careful not to use items such as pStr6 until they have been assigned a valid address. Forgetting this is a common programming mistake that can be difficult to track down. Always check that all pointers have been initialized before being used.

10

The rStr7 is a reference to a string. You can think of it as a pointer to a string, which can be handled in source code as if it were a string.

When new is called to initialize pStr7, a * is placed before it. As new returns a pointer and a reference is treated as an actual string, the * indicates to use the item at the address contained in the pointer.

Reading and Comparing Strings

In C, to copy the contents of one string to another, you place the addresses of the source and destination C strings as calling arguments to the strcpy() function. The string class defines an = operator, so you need only do an assignment, just as with an integer.

Syntax

Assigning Strings

You can assign one string to another using the equals sign (=).

```
string str = initialString;
```

Example

```
string string_1 = "First String";
string string_2 = "Second String";

string_2 = string_1;
```

This places the characters "First String" into string_2. The old contents of string_2 are lost.

As was the case with an assignment statement, the class provides familiar operators for use in performing comparisons. Operators such as == and < free you from calling and interpreting the results of the `strcmp` function used for C-style strings. In cases where you want to save the comparison results, a `strcmp`-like function that returns the same kind of positive integer, zero, or negative integer is available. The name is a bit easier to remember than `strcmp`. It's called `compare`.

Syntax

Comparing Strings

Strings can be compared directly as if comparing an integer. Old-style strings can also be compared to C++ strings in this fashion.

The following comparison operators are supplied for strings:

```
==   <=   >=   <   >   !=
```

Example

```
char oldstyle[] = "OLD STYLE STRING";
string newstyle = "new style string";

if (oldstyle < newstyle)
   cout << "oldstyle is lower in value than newstyle" << endl;
```

The message will be displayed because capital letters have smaller values than lowercase letters. The line

```
int compare(const string &compareTo);
```

returns a positive value if the string is greater than `compareTo`, and a negative value if it is less. If the two strings are equal, then zero is returned. Although using < > and == to compare strings is easy, `compare` provides a value that can be saved for use later.

Another version of the same function enables you to indicate at what position from the start of the string the comparison should begin, and to specify a maximum number of characters to compare. Although these extra features are more specialized, it is not uncommon to need them.

```
int compare(const string& s,
size_t startIndex, size_t numChars = NPOS);
```

The familiar `cin >>`, `getline`, and `cout <<` syntax works well with C++ strings. Because the streams classes also handle file I/O, this works with disk files as well.

Syntax

Reading and Writing Strings

Normal iostreams functions are provided for the C++ string class. The `cin`, `cout`, and file I/O are supported.

Example

```
string textLine;

cin >> textLine;    // Get input from stdin.
```

```
// If "the word" is entered, textLine will become "the"

getline(cin, textLine);
// If "the word" is entered, textLine will become "the word"


ifstream inputFile;
ofstream outputFile;

inputFile.open("FileName.Txt");
outputFile.open("FileName.Out");

getline(inputFile, textLine);
// textLine now contains the first line from the file

outputFile << textLine << endl;
// the string is now stored in the output disk file
```


Just as with C style strings, a C++ string can be addressed as if it were an array with an index within square brackets. Readers who have migrated from BASIC or FORTRAN might be pleased to learn that parentheses also can be used.

Examining Individual Characters

C++ strings can be accessed as arrays just as is done with C strings. Remember that the first element is `stringName[0]`. If the value contained in `stringVar` is "0123456789", then `cout << stringVar[7];` will print a 7 to the screen.

For those of you whose first love was FORTRAN or another language that uses parentheses for array subscripts, you can use them as well: `cout << stringVar(7);` would also print a 7.

This example is a small program using some of the previously mentioned syntax. References are used so that the code is more readable.

Three references to string are created. The program reads strings from the keyboard and reports on how they compare. Entering a string of `end` ends the program. Because comparison defaults to being case-sensitive, a value of `END` will not end the program.

Listing 10.1 contains a program that reads and compares C++ `string` class strings.

Listing 10.1. Source code for the program CSTRING1.CPP.

```
#include <iostream.h>
#include <cstring.h>

int main()
  {
  int result;

  string &s1 = * new string; // create 2 references to string
  string &s2 = * new string;
```

continues

Listing 10.1. continued

```
   string message;             // create an instance of a string

   while (1)     // run this loop forever
     {
     cout << "Enter two lines of text, \"end\" to end program\n";
     getline(cin, s1);    // read a line into s1 from the keyboard

     if (s1 == "end")     // If ending the program is requested
       break;             // break out of the loop

     getline(cin, s2);    // read a line into s2

     if (s2 == "end")     // If ending the program is requested
       break;             // break out of the loop

     result = s1.compare(s2); // get and save comparison result

     if (result == 0)         // save what we've found in "message"
       message = "The strings are equal";
     else if (result > 0)
       message = "The first string is greater";
     else
       message = "The second string is greater";

     cout << message << endl << endl; // report the result
     }

  delete &s1;  // References are handled in source code as if they
  delete &s2;  // were actual items. This is why the '&' operator
  return 0;         // is used to get their address for use by
  }                 // delete.
```

Here is a sample session with the example program.

```
Enter two lines of text, "end" to end program
this
that
The first string is greater

Enter two lines of text, "end" to end program
that
this
The second string is greater

Enter two lines of text, "end" to end program
those
those
The strings are equal

Enter two lines of text, "end" to end program
end
```

Analysis In lines 8, 9, and 10, the string reference variables `s1`, `s2`, and the string variable `message` are declared, and instances of two of them are allocated by the call to `new`. The `*` in front of the `new` is said to "dereference the pointer." This means that it refers to the value at the address returned by `new` rather than the address itself. By using reference variables instead of pointers, the variables can be used in the following source lines without the special handling needed when using pointers.

On lines 15 and 20, a full line of text is read into a string. Remember that the `getline` function removes the end of line character from the input.

On line 22, a string is compared to another with only the `==` operator. With C-style strings, a call to `strcmp` would have been necessary. Line 25 uses the `string` class `compare` member function to return a value that will be tested on lines 27 and 29. Because it is done this way, the computer only examines the variable `result` rather than performing a second full-string comparison.

Assigning a new value to a string class item need not call `strcpy` or `strdup`. Lines 28, 30, and 32 show `message` being assigned a value with a simple assignment statement.

Lines 37 through 39 discard the strings you have allocated. Although this program will end and the memory will be recovered by the operating system, in a true application program memory management is of great concern, and objects that have been allocated should be discarded when they are no longer of use. The string variable `message` is not deleted because it was not created with `new`. When `main` ends, `message` automatically will be destroyed by the compiler's code.

String Search, Substitution, and File I/O

The `string` class provides powerful tools for searching within strings and substituting parts of strings (substrings). CSTRING2.CPP manipulates the text in a file, substituting alternative text for words and placing this new text in an output file. Listing 10.2 contains the source code for the program CSTRING2.CPP.

Listing 10.2. Source code for the program CSTRING2.CPP.

```
#include <fstream.h>
#include <cstring.h>

const short True = 1;
const short False = 0;

string    toFind;
string    replaceWith;
char      lineBuf[81];
```

continues

Listing 10.2. continued

```
ifstream  inFile;
ofstream  outFile;

short GetFindReplace()
  {
  char caseFlag;

  cout << "Enter the word to find: ";
  cin >> toFind;

  cout << endl << "Enter replacement word: ";
  cin >> replaceWith;

  while (1)
    {
    cout  << "Case sensitive [Y/N]? ";
    cin >> caseFlag;
    caseFlag = toupper(caseFlag);

    if ((caseFlag == 'Y') || (caseFlag == 'N'))
      {
      string::set_case_sensitive(caseFlag == 'Y');
      break;
      }
    }

  return (toFind != replaceWith) ? True : False;
  } // end GetFindReplace()

short ProcessFile()
  {
  short  findLen;      // Number of characters to find
  size_t foundPos;     // Position in string where found
  string buffer;       // Holds a line of input data from the file
  short  startPos;     // Position in string to start search
  short  replaced;     // Set to True if replacement has been done
  short  numFound = 0; // Number of replacements that were made

  inFile.open("\\TCWINC45\\README.TXT");
  outFile.open("README.NEW");
  findLen = toFind.length();     // get # char's in string to find
  buffer.skip_whitespace(False); // don't skip leading spaces

  while (inFile)                 // while data left in input file
    {
    getline(inFile, buffer);     // read one line
    replaced = False;            // init flag and position
    startPos = 0;

    do
      {
```

```
61:       foundPos = buffer.find(toFind, startPos);
62:
63:       if (foundPos != NPOS)      // if a match is found
64:         {
65:         buffer.replace(foundPos, findLen, replaceWith);
66:         ++numFound;
67:         replaced = True;
68:         startPos = foundPos + replaceWith.length();
69:         }
70:       } while (foundPos != NPOS);
71:
72:     outFile << buffer << endl;   // copy line to the output file
73:
74:     if (replaced)
75:       cout << buffer << endl;    // show modified lines on screen
76:     }
77:
78:   inFile.close();
79:   outFile.close();
80:   cout << endl;
81:   return numFound;
82:   } // end ProcessFile()
83:
84: int main()
85:   {
86:   if (GetFindReplace())
87:     cout << ProcessFile() << " words were replaced\n";
88:   else
89:     cout << "Error: Find and Replace words are the same\n";
90:
91:   return 0;
92:   }
```

Here is an example session with the CSTRING2 application.

```
Enter the word to find: important

Enter replacement word: unimportant
Case sensitive [Y/N]? y
This README file contains unimportant information about
  Turbo C++.

1 words were replaced
```

This program uses the C++ string class to take the README.TXT file, which came with Turbo C++ 4.5, and to create a new file, README.NEW, in which it has substituted some words. When run, it asks for the word to find, the word to replace it, and whether the search is to be case-sensitive.

Constants are declared for `True` and `False` on lines 4 and 5 to make the program more readable.

Note: Windows declares `#define` macros for `TRUE` and `FALSE` in its header file WINDOWS.H. If you declare constants with these names, they will be replaced with `1` and `0`, respectively, and could generate an error. To avoid this, `True` and `False` are used here instead of `TRUE` and `FALSE`.

The main program is small. It calls `GetFindReplace` on line 86, and if the user's input is valid, it calls `ProcessFile` on line 87, printing out the number of changes that were made. If the find and replace words are the same, no substitutions would be made, so `GetFindReplace` returns `False`, the program prints an error message, and ends.

`GetFindReplace`, starting on line 13, uses two instances of the C++ `string` class: `toFind` and `replaceWith`. The `string` class provides overloaded `input >>` and `output >>` operators, thus, values to and from the console are handled on lines 18 and 21 just as is done with C-style strings. On line 31, the case-sensitive flag for the string class is adjusted to control the type of comparisons made. In line 36, the function returns `True` if the two words compare differently.

Syntax

Case Sensitivity

The following is a member function of the `string` class. It sets how comparisons will be done.

```
static string::set_case_sensitive(int tf = 1);
```

The calling argument defaults to `true`. If called with a `0` or `false` value, it causes all comparisons to ignore uppercase versus lowercase.

Example

```
string s1("THIS IS A STRING")
string s2("this is a string")

string::set_case_sensitive(0);

if (s1 == s2)
cout << "the strings are equal\n"; /* this is printed */

string::set_case_sensitive();

if (s1 != s2)
cout << "the strings are not equal\n"; /* this is printed */
```

Note: There is only one case-sensitive flag for the entire string class. When you change it, *all* instances of the class will have their style of comparisons changed.

If `GetFindReplace` returns `True`, then on line 87 `main` calls `ProcessFile` and prints the returned count of replaced words. That function opens the README.TXT file in the \BC4 directory and creates a README.NEW file in the current directory to receive the program output. On line 50, the `ProcessFile` function uses the `length` member function to have `toFind` report how many characters long the string is.

Syntax

Number of Characters in a String

Each `string` class variable has a member function called `length` that reports the length of the string in characters. The return value is an `unsigned`. The name `size_t` is defined by the language standards groups, so that it can be set to whatever is appropriate for the current machine. With Turbo C++ 4.5, `size_t` is defined as an `unsigned`. The `stringVar.length();` returns the same value as `strlen(stringVar.c_str());`.

10

The loop that starts on line 53 and ends on line 76 is where the real work of `ProcessFile` is done. With each pass through the loop, a line of text is read from the input file into the string variable `buffer` (line 55).

Because the string class `skip-whitespace` flag was cleared on line 51, leading spaces are preserved. The variable `replaced` acts as a detector to remember if any words have been replaced on a line and is set to `False`. The `startPos` is the starting position for searching the line and is set to the beginning of the line (to zero).

Syntax

Searching within a String

The following `string` member functions search for a match with the `toFind` string. The return value is the index of where the match occurred, or `NPOS` if no match is found.

```
size_t find(const string &toFind);
size_t find(const string &toFind, size_t startAt);
```

The second version of the function specifies that, instead of beginning at the start of the string, the search will begin at position `startAt` in the string. Remember that the first character of an array in C or C++ is array index zero. Because of that, if `startAt` were 2, then the third character is where the search would begin.

The `do-while` loop from lines 59 through 70 processes a single line of text from the input file. Starting in character position `startPos`, it searches the string for a match with the `toFind` string. If successful, the `find` function returns the starting character position in `buffer` of the matching characters. In line 63, the position found is compared against the predefined symbol `NPOS`, whose value is used to indicate that no position in the string matches the search string.

Lines 64 through 69 only execute if a match is found. The call to `replace` causes `findLen` characters beginning at position `foundPos` to be deleted and the contents of the string `replaceWith` to be inserted in their place.

Syntax

String Class I/O

The `getline` member functions using the C++ `string` class are declared for input and output file streams. The >> and << input and output operators also are provided for file operations with this class.

```
istream &getline(istream &is, string &s);
ostream &getline(istream &is, string &s);
operators >> and <<
```

Syntax

Controlling Whether Spaces Are Skipped

The following two functions enable you to modify the `skip_whitespace` flag internal to the `string` class:

```
static int skip_whitespace(int skip = 1);
static int get_skip_whitespace_flag();
```

The `skip_whitespace` determines if whitespace will be skipped during read operations. The default value is to skip spaces and tabs on input operations such as `getline`, `>>`, and `read_token`. By calling `get_skip_whitespace`, you can read the current setting of the flag.

Example

```
string   myString;
ifstream myFile("\\TCWIN45\\DOC\\UTILS.TXT");

myString.skip_whitespace(0);
getline(myFile, myString);
```

The string `myString` will contain `"UTILS.TXT"`.

The string `myString` would have been `"UTILS.TXT"` had `skip_whitespace` not been called. There is only one whitespace setting for the entire `string` class. Any call to `skip_whitespace` changes the setting for all.

Syntax

Changing Part of a C++ String

The `replace` function, a member function of the C++ `string` class, is overloaded to have two forms.

```
string &replace(size_t       startPos,
                size_t       deleteLen,
                const string &replaceWith);

string &replace(size_t       startPos,
                size_t       deleteLength,
                const string &replaceWith,
                size_t       replaceFrom,
                size_t       replaceLength);
```

The first form will search the string, starting at the index given in `startPos`, until it finds a match to the string `replaceWith`. It then will delete `deleteLen` characters from the string and insert the characters from `replaceWith` in that position.

If the string to be modified is too short to remove the requested number of characters, then the characters from `startPos` to the end of the string are removed.

The second form adds two additional arguments: `replaceFrom` and `replaceLength`. The `replaceLength` indicates how many characters from the replacement string will be inserted into the modified one.

`"Steven Smith"`, for example, could be searched for and `"Steven"` replaced with `"George"` from the string `"George Jones"`.

The `replaceFrom` argument specifies the starting position in the replacement string to begin in substituting characters. If there are no `replaceLength` characters in the replacement string, then the number found in the string is used.

The `replaceLength` can be given the value `NPOS` and will use all remaining characters in the string if that value is given.

The following two lines, for example, perform the same function:

```
replace(startPos, deleteLen, replaceWith, 0, NPOS);
replace(startPos, deleteLen, replaceWith);
```

Line 72 executes independently of having done any replacements and writes the possibly altered string to the new file. Lines 74 and 75 detect whether any replacements have been done and, if so, writes the changed string to the console.

Lines 78 through 81 perform the clean-up actions of closing files and returning the number of replacements that have been made.

There also are more useful functions in the `string` class.

Other C++ *string* Class Functions

The following `append` member function adds characters to the end of a string:

```
string& append(const string &fromStr);
```

This places the characters from `fromStr` to the end of the string.

Example

```
string firstString("ABC");
string secondString("DEF");

firstString.append(secondString); // firstString is now "ABCDEF"
```

Note that another way to append characters to the end of a string is to use the += operator. The same appending operations could have been done with the following:

```
firstString += secondString;
```

Often it will be necessary to just pass a string object as if it were a C-style string array. The string class provides the c_str member function, which simply returns a const char* to a C-style version of the string.

The contains member function is used to determine whether a particular substring can be found in a string object.

```
int contains(const char *cStyleStr);
```

The member function returns either 1 or 0, depending on whether cStyleStr is found in the string.

After you determine that a substring exists within a string object, it can be useful to determine where in that string the substring can be found. This is done with the find_first_of function.

```
size_t find_first_of(const string &s);
size_t find_first_of(const string &s, size_t startAt);
```

These return the position of the first character found in the string, which is one of the characters in the string s passed to the function. The second overloaded form starts the search at startAt. If nothing is found, then these return NPOS.

In addition to finding the first position in a string at which another string begins, it also is possible to find the first position that isn't a part of another string. This is done with the find_first_not_of member function.

```
xsize_t find_first_not_of(const string &s);
size_t find_first_not_of(const string &s, size_t startAt);
```

These return the first character *not* in the calling argument, or NPOS if nothing is found.

The find_last_of and find_last_not_of member functions are very similar to their find_first equivalents, except that they search starting at the end of the string and work backward.

```
size_t find_last_of(const string &s);
size_t find_last_of(const string &s, size_t startAt);
size_t find_last_not_of(const string &s);
size_t find_last_not_of(const string &s, size_t startAt);
```

These are called in exactly the same manner as the corresponding find_first type functions, and they return the same type of information, except that they work backwards.

When you want to delete characters from a string, you use the remove member function.

```
string &remove(size_t startAt);
string &remove(size_t startAt, size_t howMany);
```

These delete `howMany` characters from a string, starting at position `startAt`. The version with only one argument removes all the remaining characters in the string. The `stringVar.remove(4);` statement is the same as `stringVar[4] = '\0';`.

Templates

It is common for a language to have many functions, each of which does the same thing but for different data types. Wouldn't it be nice if you could tell the compiler "Here's what I want to do; you figure out how to do it."? C++ has a feature that can do this. It's called a *template*.

Note: AT&T, the original developers of C++, originally added templates to version 2.0 of the C++ specification. That specification currently is at version 3.0 and this is the version used by Turbo C++ 4.5. Templates also have been accepted by the ANSI/ISO committee.

10

NEW TERM A *template* is a method for telling the compiler the algorithm to use to perform a function. The compiler handles the details of the function for the data type being used. Both global functions and classes can be programmed as templates.

When programming a template, you provide a name to use as the symbol for the unknown data type and write the code using that symbol.

Here is a function defined as a template.

```
// return the lowest of 3 values
template <class T> const T& Low(const T& a, const T& b, const T& c)
{
   if (a < b)
      {
      if (a < c)
         return a;
      }
   else if (b < c)
      return b;
   return c;
}
```

The first line of the function is what identifies it as a template (see Figure 10.1).

The word `template` in the function definition is followed by the characters `<class`, a symbol to use for the type, and then by a `>`. Although a single character is most often used for the symbol, it can be any legal C++ name.

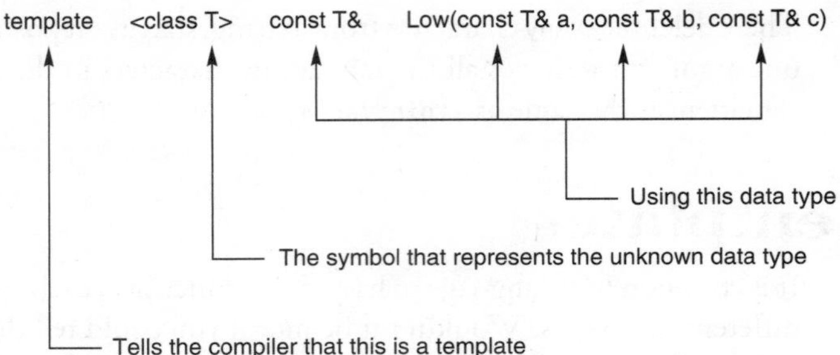

Figure 10.1.
A template function's declaration.

This template function is used as any other function would be. For example, this returns the lowest of three C++ string items.

```
string s1("6543");
string s2("5432");
string s3("4321");
cout << Low(s1, s2, s3) << endl;
```

Although use of the word `class` is required when defining a template, templates are not limited to having classes as arguments. They can be used as fundamental data types also. `Low(1, 2, 3);`, for example, uses integers and is a valid call of the `Low` function.

A class can be defined in terms of templates. The syntax for doing this is the same as with the preceding function, but some changes are required when declaring instances of the class.

```
template <class TypeSymbol> class ArrayType
{
protected:
   TypeSymbol *items;
   int        numItems;
public:
   ArrayType(const TypeSymbol& firstItem);
   ~ArrayType();
   int AddItem(TypeSymbol& toAdd);
   TypeSymbol& operator [] (int index);
};
```

When you declare an instance of this class, the compiler must know what data type is to be used with this class. The declaration for `iArray` shows this, as the angle brackets enclose the type to use.

```
ArrayType<int> iArray(1);
```

Look at Listing 10.3, which is an example of using templates. It implements a template class that can hold up to five items, gives them values, and prints them to the screen. Versions of the class are used for float and integer types. It also uses a template function that is not in a class. That function reports the size of the data type.

Listing 10.3. An example that uses templates.

```
#include <iostream.h>


const int True = 1;
const int False = 0;


template <class X> class ArrayType
   {
protected:
  int maxItems; // maximum number of items this will hold
  int numItems; // number of items it is holding now
  X  *items;    // array of items

public:
  ArrayType(int capacity);
  ~ArrayType()       { delete [] items; }

  int InRange(int n) { return((n >= 0) && (n < numItems)); }
  int Capacity()     { return maxItems; }
  int AddItem(X& toAdd);
  X& operator [] (int index) { return items[index]; }
  }


template <class X> ArrayType<X>::ArrayType(int capacity)
  {
  maxItems = capacity;
  items = new X[capacity];
  numItems = 0;
  } // end ArrayType::ArrayType()


template <class a> int ArrayType<a>::AddItem(a& toAdd)
  {
  if (numItems < maxItems)
    {
    items[numItems++] = toAdd;
    return True;
    }

  return False;
  } // end ArrayType::AddItem()


template <class SomeType> size_t Size(const SomeType&)
  {
  return sizeof(SomeType);
  } // end Size()


template <class D, class X> void Report(const char *s, D& d, X& x)
```

continues

Listing 10.3. continued

```
53:   {
54:   cout << endl << s << "has space for " << d.Capacity()
55:        << " items.  Each item uses " << Size(x) << " bytes.\n";
56:
57:   for (int i = 0; d.InRange(i); i++)
58:     cout << "\t" << s << "[" << i << "] " << d[i] << endl;
59:   } // end Report()
60:
61:
62: int main()
63:   {
64:   int                 iVal;
65:   float               fVal;
66:   ArrayType <int>     iArray(3);
67:   ArrayType <float> fArray(5);
68:
69:   for (iVal = 0, fVal = 0.0; iVal < 10; ++iVal, fVal += 1.11)
70:     {
71:     iArray.AddItem(iVal);
72:     fArray.AddItem(fVal);
73:     }
74:
75:   Report("iArray: ", iArray, iArray[0]);
76:   Report("fArray: ", fArray, fArray[0]);
77:
78:   return 0;
79:   }
```

When you run this example, the results are as follows:

```
iArray: has space for 3 items. Each item uses 2 bytes.
iArray: [0] 0
iArray: [1] 1
iArray: [2] 2

fArray: has space for 5 items. Each item uses 4 bytes.
fArray: [0] 0
fArray: [1] 1.11
fArray: [2] 2.22
fArray: [3] 3.33
fArray: [4] 4.44
```

Beginning with line 8, the template class is defined. The symbol `X` is declared to be used for the type and is used within the body of the definition wherever the type name is needed.

The `X` is only valid within the block to which the `template` word refers. It is not related to what is used in other blocks. In line 34, a is used as the symbol for the type, and although the `AddItem()` function with which it is used is a member of the `ArrayType` class that uses an `X` in its template, there is no confusion. The compiler is content to use a for the function block.

The inline functions `InRange()`, `Capacity()`, operator `[ ]`, and `~ArrayType()` don't need a separate `template` word applied to them, because they are contained in the same one that is used for the class.

Both `ArrayType()` (line 26) and `AddItem()` (line 34) need `template` in their definition, because the lines of code for them are not located within the class and are not covered by the class use of the word `template`.

Line 46 has a template function that is neither a class nor a class member. The syntax of C++ still requires the word `class` in the function header. `SomeType` is used as the type symbol, but `X` or any other valid C++ name would work as well. The calling argument to `Size()` is described as a type without a variable name applied to it. Unlike C, C++ does not require that a variable name be placed there; the `Size()` function only needs to know the type, not an actual variable.

10

The function `Report()` (line 52) has an interesting variation on the template system. Two dummy type names are provided, and both types are used by the function. When called from lines 75 and 76, the function makes calls to `Capacity()` and `InRange()`. If the data type for the `d` calling argument in `Report()` did not have functions with those names, an error would be generated.

The `main()` function is in line 62. In lines 66 and 67 it declares two instances of `ArrayType`: one that will hold up to three items of type `int` and one that will hold up to three items of type `float`.

Between lines 69 and 73, the items in the two classes are initialized. Ten initializations are done for each, relying on the `AddItem()` function to detect and ignore initializations following those that have already filled the class to capacity.

Lines 75 and 76 call the `Report()` function to tell some things about the classes. `Report()` uses the `Capacity()` member function of the class to print the maximum number of items it can hold. It also calls `Size()` (line 55) to show the number of bytes used for each member.

Lines 57 through 59 then perform a `for` loop to display the data members of each class, stopping when the `InRange()` function returns `False`.

This example is a bit contrived in order to illustrate using templates. For container classes that you can use for general arrays and so on, the Turbo C++ 4.5 class library provides a multitude of better choices.

The Class Libraries

There are a number of data structures for holding on to data that have been developed over the years. These various structures are referred to as *containers*, and Borland supplies a set of these called the Class Libraries. Table 10.2 shows the types of containers provided with the Turbo C++ compiler.

Table 10.2. Turbo C++ Class Library Containers.

Container	Header File	Usage
Array	arrays.h	Mimics the standard C++ arrays in which objects are contained in a contiguous block of memory, but with the addition of being expandable in size after they already have been declared.
Association	assoc.h	Stores a key value with each object, allowing you to use the key to locate and retrieve the object.
Bag	bags.h	This is the least structured of all the containers in that it just stores objects in any order.
Binary search tree	binimp.h	Binary trees are a method of storing sorted data in an easy to search way. Objects are stored in such a way that each object can have up to two children. The child on the "left" of the parent must be less than the parent, and the "right" child greater than the parent.
Dequeue	deques.h	Contains a "train" of objects; you store objects at either end of the container and then access them in the order in which they were stored. As you access either end of the container, the objects are removed.
Dictionary	dict.h	Simple storage of objects as they're added to the container.
Double-linked list	dlistimp.h	A double-linked list contains objects in non-contiguous memory. Traversing the list involves following pointers in each entry that point to the previous and next entries in the list.
Hash table	hashimp.h	This is similar to an association container, except that the associated keys (the hash values) are calculated based on the object being stored rather than specified directly.
Queue	queues.h	Queus allow objects to be stored in one end and retrieved from the other end. This sometimes is referred to as a FIFO (First In, First Out) container.
Set	sets.h	Sets are similar to bags in that they store objects in an unordered format, but sets can contain only one of any object.

Container	Header File	Usage
Single-linked list	listimp.h	Single-linked lists, like double-linked lists, contain objects that aren't stored in contiguous memory. Single-linked list entries, however, only contain a pointer to the next entry and no pointer to the previous.
Stack	stacks.h	A stack is a way of storing objects one on top of each other, so that the most recently added object will be the one that can be retrieved. This sometimes is referred to as a LIFO (Last In, First Out) container.
Vector	vectimp.h	Vectors contain objects in contiguous memory. It usually is used simply as a storage method for the other classes.

Each of these types of classes has several different versions. These different versions are created to reflect the differing conditions in which they are used. In order to help the programmer distinguish between the different versions of each class, there is a standard set of characters that are used at the beginning of class names (see Table 10.3). By looking at the classes provided and decoding the abbreviation characters, you can deduce the differences of the container.

Table 10.3. Container class name abbreviations.

Abbreviation	Meaning	Description
T	Class Library Prefix	All Borland-supplied classes (including OWL, which is described on Day 11) start with this letter.
M	User-supplied mem-mgt.	The programmer must supply to the container a class that will handle the memory management for the contained objects.
I	Indirect	The container holds a pointer to the object rather than to the object itself.
C	Counted	The container keeps a running count of the number of objects stored within it.
S	Sorted	The container sorts its objects. In order to achieve this, the objects must have valid comparison operators.

Each container has specific iterators associated with it. These iterators act much in the same way as the simple integers you have used before in `for` loops, except that they are written specifically for manipulating and accessing the data of a container. While each iterator can have any number of functions, there are a few that are common amongst all the iterators (see Table 10.4).

Table 10.4. Common container iterator member-functions.

Function	Description
`constructor`	The constructor typically takes one argument: a reference to the specific container for which it is to manipulate. The constructor initializes the iterator to point at the "beginning" of the container. (Note that the term "beginning" doesn't apply very well to some containers.)
`Current`	This returns the object currently being pointed to by the iterator.
`Restart`	This restarts the iterator to point at the "beginning" of the list.
`operator int`	When you need to know whether a container has been completely traversed, you can just compare it to `0`, which will invoke a conversion operator. If the iterator is equal to `0`, then the "end" of the container has been reached.
`operator ++`	Obviously, traversing a container involves incrementing its iterator, and this is the function that does it. Just use the regular `++` increment operator.

Space constraints prevent me from providing a full list of all the various classes in the class libraries; there are a great deal of them. Instead, I will present one example that goes through using a double-linked list for storing strings in Listing 10.4.

Listing 10.4. A demonstration of double-linked lists.

```
#include <cstring.h>
#include <classlib\dlistimp.h>
#include <iostream.h>

// Create some typedefs to make things easier
// later on when we create the list and its
// iterator.
//
typedef TDoubleListImp<string> strList;
typedef TDoubleListIteratorImp<string> strIter;

int main()
{
   strList list;

```

```
16:         // Add some strings
17:         //
18:         list.Add("first");
19:         list.Add("second");
20:         list.Add("third");
21:         list.Add("fourth");
22:         list.Add("fifth");
23:         list.AddAtHead("Head");    // Add at Head
24:         list.AddAtTail("Tail");    // Add at Tail
25:
26:         // Print out the list
27:         //
28:         strIter i(list);
29:         while (i != 0)
30:            {
31:            cout << i.Current() << endl;
32:            ++i;
33:            }
34:         cout << endl;             // Add a blank line
35:
36:         // Get rid of one of the entries
37:         //
38:         list.Detach("third");
39:
40:         // Now show what's left in reverse
41:         //
42:         for (i.RestartAtTail(); i != 0; --i)
43:            cout << i.Current() << endl;
44:
45:         return 0;
46:      }
```

Here is the output produced by Listing 10.4.

```
Head
fifth
fourth
third
second
first
Tail

Tail
first
second
fourth
fifth
Head
```

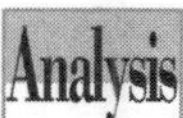

Taking a look at the program, you can see that on lines 9 and 10 that two `typedefs` are used to create easy access to the new template list and iterator. The names for these template classes can become rather long, so it's a common practice to create shorter `typedefs` of the more complicated names for easier typing and identification during programming.

On line 14 is a declaration for the list itself. As you can see, it's a fairly simple line with no special parameters needed for the constructor. Immediately following this are some calls to the class member functions `Add`, `AddAtHead`, and `AddAtTail`. These are passing literal strings which are, in turn, being passed to the `string` constructor, which then is passed to the various add routines. The template nature of the class libraries means that each container class is specially made to match the type of its contained objects, so the add functions take `string` parameters and passing a literal string just creates a `string` object to be added to the container.

Note the `AddAtHead` and `AddAtTail` functions on lines 23 and 24. The normal `Add` function actually adds items to the head of the list by default, as you can see in the output where the `"Head"` string is displayed next to the `"fifth"` string. Using `AddAtHead` and `AddAtTail` allows for finer control of where objects are placed in the list.

NEW TERM The *head* and *tail* of a linked list are the beginning and ending, respectively. Since there's no real sense of a 0 index or a maximum size, it's necessary to keep track of the beginning and ending of the list differently.

Next, on line 28, you can see how an iterator is instantiated with the list to which it should be associated. Following this, you can see how the iterator is used to traverse the list, displaying each item in turn, and then displaying an additional blank line in preparation for the next list.

On line 38, the string `"third"` is removed from the list. Note that it isn't necessary to search for the item before detaching it; the container automatically searches for the requested item and then removes it.

Starting on line 42, another method of traversing the list is shown: a `for` loop. Here you use the initializing portion of the `for` loop expression to restart the iterator at the list's tail, and you then decrement the iterator as you traverse the list backwards. Note how the output shows the contents of the list in reverse order from which its contents were initially added.

Altogether, the class libraries provide for a very easy method of using powerful data structures. Many versions of these will automatically sort items as they are added to the containers, and some provide very fast searching mechanisms. Take some time to read the documentation for a full list of the various containers provided by the class libraries.

Summary

This chapter presented the C++ string class, templates, and a glimpse at the class library. You should now be familiar with the following:

- The `string` class handles allocation and manipulation of strings without need for the low-level issues necessary when working with C-style strings.

- When declaring a string variable, the initial value can be placed in parentheses immediately after (as in `string myStr("Init Value");`). When you assign a new value to it, any necessary size adjustment is handled for you.
- Simple comparison operators can be used with the `string` class. There is no need to call functions such as `strcmp` or `strncmp`.
- C++ templates can be used with functions and classes to work with any kind of data type. You define a template with "generic" arguments and use a template giving specific arguments. The compiler generates code appropriate to the actual argument types.
- Creating an instance of a template class requires that you specify the type(s) as part of the class name.
- The class libraries provide a rich set of easy-to-use classes for creating containers. These containers can store objects in a variety of useful formats.

Q&A

Q Can I get the value of a character in a string as I can in C?

A Yes, and in the same way. If `strC` is a C-style array and `strCpp` is a C++ string class and both are set to `"ABC"`, then both `strC[1]` and `strCpp[1]` are equal to the character `'B'`.

Q What happens if I assign a `char` to a string index that is beyond the end of an array?

A In C, when you write to a character that is past the end of an array, the character is stored in the position where it would have been, had the array been large enough. If that memory contains critical information, then the computer could lock up, but only after it has run further, destroying the symptoms of where the problem occurred.

With a C++ string when you write past the end of the array, the over-write is detected and the exception handling system is called. If running a DOS program, the program ends with an `Abnormal program termination` error. If you were stepping through the program with Turbo Debugger, the error would be displayed at the line where it occurred, not elsewhere.

Q What happens if I copy to a string and the size is larger than has been allocated?

A The C++ string class detects that and expands the array to fit. If you were using C-style strings, a DOS Abnormal Termination would be presented or an equivalent complaint would be shown by Windows. If debugging, Turbo Debugger would stop at the line where the problem occurred, telling you of the problem.

Q I found a function that operates on C-style strings and does what I want. How can I use it with C++ string class items?

A Use the `c_str` function. For example, if `strCpp` is a C++ string, then `strlen(strCpp.c_str());` will find the length of the string.

Q Can I use templates with my own structures and classes, or am I limited to using C++'s built-in types?

A Templates can use any type, as in the following example:

```
template <class T> const T& Dump(const T& objectToDump);

int a = 100;

struct {
  int p;
  long q;
  double r;
} b;

Dump(a);
Dump(b);
```

Q Can I create a template with more than one type?

A Yes. Just separate the types with commas, as in the following example:

```
template <class Form, class Printer> class SpecialFormPrinter
{
  ...
};

InsuranceFormLaserPrinter = new SpecialFormPrinter<InsuranceForm,
LaserPrinter>;
```

Q Can I create a double-linked list that automatically sorts the items added to it?

A Yes. Use the `TSDoubleListImp` and `TSDoubleListIteratorImp` classes to create and traverse such a list.

Workshop

The Workshop provides quiz questions to help you solidify your understanding of the material covered and exercises to provide you with experience in using what you've learned. Try to understand the quiz and exercise answers before continuing on to the next day's lesson. Answers are provided in Appendix A.

Quiz

1. What header file must be included to use the C++ string class?
2. How is a C++ string class variable declared?
3. How do you compare a string to a C-style string?
4. What string class function will find and replace text in one call?
5. To read the second character in a string, what array index is used?
6. Declare a string named `myString` with an initial value of `12`.
7. Assuming that you have two string class variables, `s1` and `s2`, and that `s1` contains `"11"` and `s2` contains `"2112"`, what is the result of the following code lines?
    a. `s1 + s2;`
    b. `s2.contains(s1);`
    c. `s1 > s2`
    d. `s2.find(s1, 0);`
8. True or false? Templates let you use any type, including your own classes, without ever having to provide any extra code.

Exercises

1. Write a line of code that declares a C-style string of value `12`, and another that declares a C++ string class variable with the same value.
2. Write a function that accepts a reference to a string as its calling argument and writes that string to the computer screen.
3. Modify the function written for the previous exercise to perform a loop, writing all the characters from the string, one per pass through the loop, and to return the size of the string.
4. Write a line of code that uses the function `strrev`, which reverses the characters in a C-style string, to reverse the characters contained in a C++ string class variable.

Tip: If `myCStr` is a C-style string, a would do this.

WEEK
2

Programming Windows with OWL 2.5

ObjectWindows version 2.5 (or OWL 2.5) is included with Turbo C++ 4.5. It is a C++ library that shortens the time and effort needed to develop a Windows program. OWL uses a feature of the C++ language called *templates*. Today, you will learn about the following:

- OWL and basic Windows issues
- Hungarian notation
- The basic structure of OWL
- Windows messages and OWL
- Developing a real OWL program, complete with resources, menus, screen writing

OWL and Windows Issues

Although using OWL means that you need not worry about many of the details of Windows, you still need some knowledge of how Windows does things and especially of some of the symbols used in Windows programs.

Under DOS, there can only be one program running at a time (with the exception of TSR programs, such as Print). That program owns the screen, keyboard, and mouse. Under Windows, several programs can be running at a time, and normally each one has screen, keyboard, and mouse I/O capability. To force these programs to cooperate, Windows enforces strict conditions on program structure, handling each task almost as if it were a function in a larger application of which Windows itself is the main program.

Windows administers a communication channel called the *message loop*, which acts as a type of "party line" by which it communicates with all the executing tasks. When a task writes to the screen or the user provides some keyboard or mouse input, Windows gathers up the information and calls a function in whichever task it has decided should receive the appropriate message.

The complexity of having independently executing functions for each of your program's screen windows, along with a main program that never calls any of them directly, is what OWL addresses. The problem is that no interface library can totally hide what is underneath. Windows uses an extensive set of macros that substitute for data types and other items. Table 11.1 is a list of some of the more important ones. You might want to put a bookmark at this page so that you can refer back to it.

Table 11.1. Some common Windows MACRO names.

Macro	Meaning	Equivalent
`TRUE`	Used for function return values	`1`
`FALSE`	Used for function return values	`0`
`NULL`	A null pointer, as in the C language	`0`

Macro	Meaning	Equivalent
`UINT`	An unsigned 16-bit integer value	`unsigned int`
`BYTE`	An unsigned 8-bit value	`unsigned char`
`WORD`	An unsigned 16-bit value	`unsigned short`
`DWORD`	An unsigned 32-bit value	`unsigned long`
`LONG`	A signed 32-bit value	`long`
`VOID`	As a function return, it means that it returns nothing; as a pointer, it means that the data type it points to is not specified	`void`
`LPSTR`	Long pointer to a string	`char far *`
`LPCSTR`	Long pointer to a constant string	`const char far *`

Type	Meaning
`HANDLE`	A generic handle to some form of Windows item
`HWND`	A handle to a window
`PASCAL`	Specifies that the function to which it applies uses the Pascal calling method. Most Windows API functions use this calling convention because it allows Pascal programs to use the API and because it is a slightly more efficient method of passing parameters to a function (the reasons for which are beyond the scope of this book).
`WPARAM`	A word parameter, used to define a data type as a calling argument to a function; defined as a `UINT`
`LPARAM`	A long parameter, used to define a data type as a calling argument to a function; defined as a `LONG LRESULT` used to define the data type a function returns
`HINSTANCE`	Handle to the instance or copy of the program that is currently running

Hungarian Notation

Microsoft has been developing Windows since the early 1980s. At its inception, the ANSI standard for C compilers did not exist and type-checking was minimal. Microsoft programmers adopted a naming convention for variables that had the data type indicated as the first few characters of the variable name. It was called *Hungarian notation* because its inventor was from Hungary.

11

With the introduction of the ANSI C standard with its stronger type-checking, and especially with C++, a strongly typed language, Hungarian notation is no longer needed; still, it is not uncommon.

In a variable name such as `lpszFilename`, the `lpsz` means long pointer to zero-terminated string. Many programmers feel confident that they would know a variable called `Filename` is a string without having to add `lpsz` to the name. Because Windows documentation uses Hungarian notation, however, it is important to have some feel for what the leading characters in the names are, so Table 11.2 shows the prefixes used in Hungarian notation. Nonetheless, your program will run as well without them as with them.

Table 11.2. Hungarian notation prefixes.

Prefix	Data Type
`c`	`char`
`by`	`BYTE` (unsigned `char`)
`n`	`short` or `int`
`i`	`int`
`x, y`	`short` (used as x-coordinate or y-coordinate)
`cx, cy`	`short` (used as x or y length; the `c` stands for `"count"`)
`b`	`BOOL` (`int`)
`w`	`UINT` (unsigned `int`) or `WORD` (unsigned `short`)
`l`	`LONG` (`long`)
`dw`	`DWORD` (unsigned `long`)
`fn`	function
`s`	C string
`sz`	C string terminated by `0` byte

The Basic Structure of OWL

OWL has groups of classes, each of which addresses a certain phase of Windows programming. The structure uses multiple inheritance to allow classes to encapsulate those combinations of functionality they need.

Event Handling, *TEventHandler*

The programmer does little with this directly. The functions it provides are available in many of the other program groups because of C++ inheritance. It manages the messages that constantly flow in a Windows program.

Streamable or Persistent Objects, *TStreamableBase*

This actually is part of the regular class library and not an OWL class. It allows a class to be viewed as a stream and saved to memory or disk for later use in the current run of the program or at another time that the program is run. This is exotic for small programs but is of great value in more advanced programs, such as those using the document-view architecture.

Module Management, *TModule* and *TApplication*

`TModule` and `TApplication` are in the module management group. `TModule` is responsible for loading and unloading DLLs while `TApplication` is responsible for initializing the program, managing it while it runs, and handling the tasks that are needed when the program ends.

Window Management, *TWindow*

`TWindow` is the base window class and inherits from `TEventHandler` and `TStreamableBase`. There are various types of windows that you might want to use in your program, and they all build on `TWindow`.

- `TFrameWindow` is a simple framed window with menu capability.
- `TDecoratedFrame` adds capabilities to use other items, such as status bars and tool bars.
- `TMDIFrame`, `TMDIChild`, and `TDecoratedMDIFrame` are Multiple Document Interface (MDI) classes used to present multiple windows in a single application.

Other functional groups are provided for the graphics, menu handling, dialog boxes, printing, and exception handling.

A Sample OWL Program

Our first OWL program only displays a window with a title. You have to press Alt+F4 or open the system menu and select Close to end it.

This program has two elements: a class to manage the window and a class to manage the application.

A class called `MainApp` is derived from `TApplication`, the class that manages the startup, the continuing message handling, and the ending tasks. `TApplication` has a virtual function called `InitMainWindow()`. In `MainApp`, you overload that function and provide your own. Within the function, you make a call setting the main window to a frame window with your window title.

Windows applications normally do not start with a function called `main()`. Instead they use a function that is declared as follows:

```
int PASCAL WinMain(HINSTANCE hInstance, HINSTANCE hPrevInstance,
                   LPSTR lpszCmdLine, int cmdShow);
```

OWL allows a `main()` function similar to what you're used to with other C and C++ programs, as follows:

```
int OwlMain(int argc, char *argv[]);
```

Note: On the first day, when EasyWin was described, it was mentioned that when a so-called real Windows program was created, the `EasyWin` flag needed to be turned off in the IDE's option screens. Because OWL applications are considered real Windows applications, you will need to access the IDE's TargetExpert by clicking the right mouse button and selecting the option from the pop-up menu. A dialog box will appear with a list box titled Target Type. You need to select the Application [.exe] item in this list box and then click the OK button.

Type

Listing 11.1. FIRST.CPP, a first OWL program.

```
#include <owl\framewin.h>
#include <owl\applicat.h>

class MainApp : public TApplication
{
public:
   MainApp() : TApplication() {}
   void InitMainWindow();        // overload TApplication function
};

void MainApp::InitMainWindow()
{
   SetMainWindow(new TFrameWindow(0, "First OWL Program"));
}

int OwlMain(int, char **)
{
   return MainApp().Run();
}
```

Figure 11.1 shows what the first OWL program does.

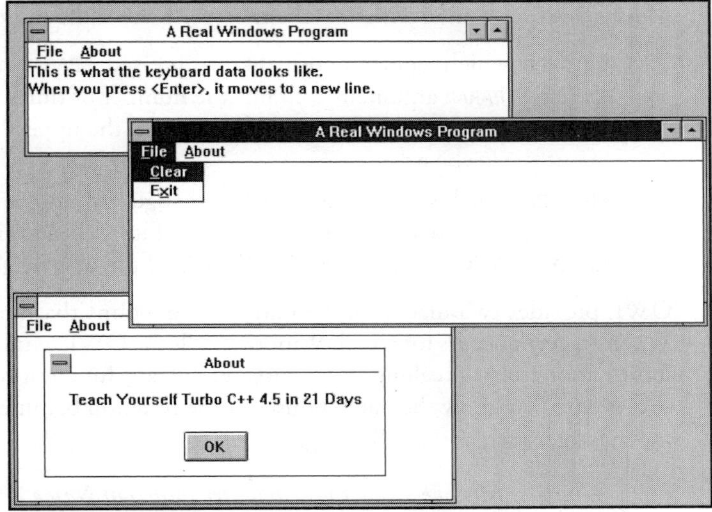

Figure 11.1.
The minimalist OWL program.

`OwlMain` begins in line 16. It calls the `Run()` function, and OWL's default processing does the rest. (`Run()` is a function within `TApplication`.)

The "magic" of how this operates is hidden in how the classes are set up. `MainApp` calls the constructor for `TApplication` on line 7, inside of its own constructor. That triggers default processing for all maintenance functions except the `InitMainWindow()` function, which has been overloaded by declaring a member function of the same name in line 8.

In line 13, the `InitMainWindow()` function calls `SetMainWindow()` to allocate a `TFrameWindow` and link the application with this window object. The same line allocates the `TFrameWindow` by calling `new` for it and passes the window caption to it in the constructor call.

The two header files that are included are for `TFrameWindow` (framewin.H) and `TApplication` (applicat.H). A Windows program should have a .DEF file to tell the linker what to do with the segments and stack. Turbo C++ supplies one for you, \TCWIN45\LIB\DEFAULT.DEF, and it was used for this program. It should be added to the list in your project file by following the instructions for project management on Day 1.

Windows Messages and OWL

The Windows system calls the function in your program that it has logged as the handling function for an open window. Several calling arguments are passed to the function, one of which is called the message. The other calling parameters are `WPARAM` and `LPARAM`. What they mean varies depending upon what the message was.

Messages are all named with `#define` macros. Two of the more common ones are

`WM_CHAR`, which reports a normal key is pressed. `WPARAM` argument contains the value of the key. `LPARAM` argument contains the number of times it has been pressed in the lower 16 bits, and has an array of bit flags in the upper 16 bits to indicate other data about the keyboard.

`WM_SIZE`, which says window size has changed. `WPARAM` argument contains a value defining the type of size change, such as if it has been minimized. `LPARAM` argument has the new width in the lower 16 bits and the new height in the upper 16 bits.

OWL provides two macros and an array of functions that know about Windows messages. When an event occurs for which Windows calls the OWL window procedure, OWL parses the information from the calling arguments and calls any function you may have provided to handle that event. You know the name to use for the function because it is derived from the name of the message, such as the following:

Windows Message	*Event-handler Function Name*
`WM_CHAR`	`void EvChar(UINT key, UINT repeat, UINT flags);`
`WM_SIZE`	`void EvSize(UINT sizeType, TSize& newSize); TSize` is a structure with an `x` and a `y` member called `cx` and `cy`, respectively. It holds the new dimensions of the window.

In the OWL handlers, the other calling parameters are said to be "cracked"—broken down into more easily understood parameters and not buried into the middle of a parameter value. The cracking of messages avoids many common code bugs. OWL's handling of the repetitive overhead needed by each message avoids many more bugs.

The way you tell OWL that you have supplied an event handler is done with two macros and a declaration. Within your class derived from `TWindow`, you declare the function itself. Also within the class definition, you place a macro to tell it that the overloading of functions is being done. In a typical class definition, those lines would look like the following:

```
class BaseWindow : public TWindow
{
protected:
   void EvChar(UINT key, UINT repeatCount, UINT flags);
   :
public:
   :
DECLARE_RESPONSE_TABLE(BaseWindow);
};
```

Later in the code, you define the response table with one entry for each function that you need.

```
DEFINE_RESPONSE_TABLE1(BaseWindow, TWindow)
   EV_WM_CHAR,
   EV_WM_SIZE,
END_RESPONSE_TABLE;
```

The macro used here is DEFINE_RESPONSE_TABLE1 because there is only one immediate class from which BaseWindow inherits. Were there to be two classes, then DEFINE_RESPONSE_TABLE2 would be used and the second class also would be listed as an argument to the macro. Macros are available for up to three inherited classes.

The Windows message name has EV_ placed in front of it to help in the macro parsing, but otherwise it is the same name as the message.

As described on Day 1, a helpful feature of the Turbo C++ IDE is that if the cursor is placed on a name such as EvChar and Ctrl+F1 is pressed, the online Help will display the function, its calling arguments, and an explanation of what each argument means.

A Real OWL Program Resources, Menus, Screen Writing

A demo that only puts a window on the screen is not very useful. Menus and screen writing have been added to the next example. It demonstrates techniques for handling normal Windows messages and messages from menus.

Menus are a feature that you can add to a window. The Windows system runs them for you, returning a number corresponding to the user selection. The message that Windows sends in response to a menu selection is WM_COMMAND, with the WPARAM parameter set to the value of the selected item. Because the selections in a menu that you create would not be part of the operating system, OWL has no built-in detection for them. What it does have is an EV_COMMAND macro that enables you to specify response functions for nonstandard events.

There are three source files involved in adding a menu to an application. The source file for the program is involved, but you also need a resource file.

Resources are predefined items that will be added to the executable as a last step. As the program is already compiled and linked when they are added, this arrangement enables resources to be more easily changed—a great advantage when changing a menu from English to German, for example. Because a resource file normally has the file extension .RC, they often are called .RC files.

The third file involved is a header file listing the macros used for menu selections, along with their number equivalents. By including the same header file in the source code and the .RC file, any changes in the selection numbers will track through to the C++ compilation as well as to the resource compiler's handling of the .RC file. As you did with DEFAULT.DEF, add the name REAL.RC to the IDE project file list. Listing 11.2 shows a resource file.

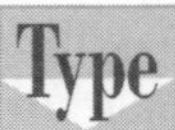

Listing 11.2. REAL.RC, a resource file.

```
1:  #include "real.rh"
2:
3:  MENU_1 MENU
4:    {
5:    POPUP "&File"
6:      {
7:      MENUITEM "&Clear", CM_CLEAR
8:      MENUITEM "E&xit",  CM_FILEEXIT
9:      }
10:
11:   MENUITEM "&About",  CM_ABOUT
12:   }
```

Figure 11.2 shows what it looks like.

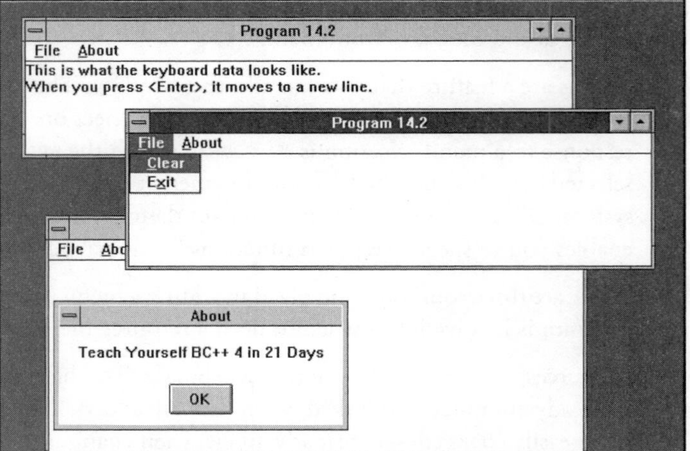

Figure 11.2.
From REAL.RC, a resource file.

Later you will use Resource Workshop to create .RC files containing menus and other items. For now, there is little value in using that tool unless you have some feel for what is being created with it, so this text file is what you will use instead.

On line 3, the `MENU_1` item is not referenced in the header file or the source file. With the available information, the resource compiler will make it a text string. You can take advantage of this name string in the program when you load a menu identified as MENU_1.

Line 5 starts defining a pop-up menu. A *pop-up* is a menu that, when selected, opens to display more menu selections. It does not return a value, although the newly shown selections often do.

The first pop-up item in the menu is given the name `&File`. The `&` character flags the `F` as special. In the menu it will be shown underlined, and pressing Alt+F will cause it to be selected.

The pop-up contains two menu items on lines 7 and 8. A menu item does return a value to the program. In this, case the displayed names for the menu items are **C**lear and E**x**it with the **C** and **x** underlined. You can use Alt+C and Alt+X to select these items when the pop-up is opened. If **C**lear is selected, `CM_CLEAR` is returned. The following header file assigns the number 1125 to `CM_CLEAR`, but the program doesn't care what that number is. All it cares about is if it receives a message with the `WPARAM` set equal to whatever the macro `CM_CLEAR` stands for.

On line 9, the curly brace after `E&xit` ends the pop-up. Following that on line 10 is another menu item selection for About. If selected, the value `CM_ABOUT` will be sent to the program, which will display an About box that tells the name of the program.

When the program is running, OWL doesn't have any knowledge of what the `CM_CLEAR`, `CM_FILEEXIT` or `CM_ABOUT` values accompanying a `WM_COMMAND` message are, so it ignores them. You can change this with additions to the response table, which tells OWL what to do with those messages.

Along with predefined messages such as `WM_SIZE` and `WM_CHAR`, you can use the `EV_COMMAND` macro to say that you have a command message that you want OWL to handle. It is used as follows:

```
DEFINE_RESPONSE_TABLE1(BaseWindow, TWindow)
   EV_WM_CHAR,
   EV_WM_SIZE,
   EV_COMMAND( CM_ABOUT, CmAbout),
END_RESPONSE_TABLE;
```

The function is expected to take no parameters and return no value—in other words, `void CmAbout()`. OWL programmers commonly use a certain way of naming such functions, and if you follow that convention, your code will be more understandable to others and you will be getting used to the same type of naming that is used in the documentation that came with Turbo C++. To name the function, delete any underscores and capitalize the first letter of each word. For example, `CM_ABOUT` becomes `CmAbout()`. Windows event handlers drop the `WM_` entirely and put `Ev` at the beginning of the name; thus `WM_CHAR` becomes `EvChar`. Remember that event handlers usually take some parameters. When you use one, look it up in the online Help to check that you have the arguments correct.

REAL.CPP writes to the screen what you have typed. OWL provides an entire class, called `TEdit`, which can edit and capture your input far better than REAL.CPP does. This and other controls will be covered in later chapters. This example's writing to the screen is meant to illustrate how one paints a window under Windows—which is very different than under DOS.

NEW TERM Windows uses an item called a *device context*, also called a *DC*. A DC is a structure containing information about a device such as a screen, a printer, or a block of memory.

You can write to anything for which you have asked Windows to provide a DC. Windows only has a limited number of DC blocks, so they are handled by requesting one, using it, and then calling Windows to free it for other uses. Forgetting to release DCs can result in Windows apparently stopping. With OWL, you needn't worry unless requesting a DC yourself. OWL automatically checks out a DC when it's time to paint the screen and returns it afterward. OWL expands upon this by placing the device context into a class called `TDC` along with functions that use DCs. Those functions already know what device you are writing to when you call them. Listing 11.3 shows a header file.

Type

Listing 11.3. REAL.RH, a header file.

```
#define CM_CLEAR    1125
#define CM_FILEEXIT 1126
#define CM_ABOUT    1127
```

REAL.RH does not get listed in the compiler's project file. The compiler will discover what header files are used by itself.

Listing 11.4 shows a program that uses a menu, accepts keyboard input, and writes the input to the screen.

Listing 11.4. REAL.CPP, a real OWL program.

```
#include <owl\framewin.h>
#include <owl\applicat.h>
#include <owl\dc.h>
#include <mem.h>

#pragma hdrstop

#include "real.rh"

const int maxLines = 25;
const int maxWidth = 80;
const int maxData = maxLines * (maxWidth + 1);

class BaseWindow : public TWindow
{
protected:
  int   currentLine;         // line being typed in now
  int   lineLen[maxLines];   // length of each line
  char *linePtrs[maxLines];  // string for each line
  BOOL  isMinimized;         // TRUE if window is an icon
  TSize windowSize;          // structure with size in pixels

  void EvChar(UINT key, UINT repeatCount, UINT flags);
  void Paint(TDC& dc, BOOL, TRect&);
  void EvSize(UINT sizeType, TSize& size);

  void CmAbout();
  void CmClear();
```

```

  // Menu choice, end the program
  void CmFileExit() { PostQuitMessage(0); }

public:
  BaseWindow(TWindow *parent = 0);
  ~BaseWindow() {}
  DECLARE_RESPONSE_TABLE(BaseWindow); // says we'll have a
};                                    // response table

DEFINE_RESPONSE_TABLE1(BaseWindow, TWindow)
  EV_WM_CHAR,
  EV_WM_SIZE,
  EV_COMMAND( CM_ABOUT,    CmAbout),
  EV_COMMAND( CM_FILEEXIT, CmFileExit),
  EV_COMMAND( CM_CLEAR,    CmClear),
END_RESPONSE_TABLE;

class MyApp : public TApplication
{
public:
  MyApp() : TApplication() {}

  void InitMainWindow();
};

BaseWindow::BaseWindow(TWindow *parent)
{
  int lineNum;

  Init(parent, 0, 0);
  linePtrs[0] = new char[maxData]; // allocate edit buffer
  lineLen[0] = currentLine = 0;

  // apportion the buffer out to the line pointer array
  for (lineNum = 1; lineNum < maxLines; ++lineNum)
     {
     linePtrs[lineNum] = linePtrs[lineNum - 1] + maxWidth;
     lineLen[lineNum] = 0;
     }
}

// Menu choice, display an About box, use a message box to do it
void BaseWindow::CmAbout()
{
  MessageBox("Teach Yourself Turbo C++ 4.5 in 21 Days", "About");
}

// Menu choice, clear the display
void BaseWindow::CmClear()
{
  for (int lineNum = 0; lineNum < maxLines; ++lineNum)
     lineLen[lineNum] = 0;    // empty all lines

  currentLine = 0;            // move back to top line
  Invalidate();               // window is invalid, repaint
```

continues

Listing 11.4. continued

```
}

// this is called whenever the window changes size
void BaseWindow::EvSize(UINT sizeType, TSize& size)
{
  if (sizeType == SIZE_MINIMIZED) // if shrunk to icon
     isMinimized = TRUE;
  else
     {
     windowSize = size;              // save window size
     isMinimized = FALSE;
     }
}

// called when time to update (paint) the screen
void BaseWindow::Paint(TDC& dc, BOOL, TRect&)
{
  int   lineNum;          // line number to write
  int   yPos;             // vertical position on screen
  int   displayedLines;   // number of linePtrs in this window
  TSize textSize;         // used to get char height in pixels

  if (isMinimized)        // don't write to an icon
     return;

  // get char sizes so that height is saved
  textSize = dc.GetTextExtent("W", 1);
  displayedLines = windowSize.cy / textSize.cy;

  if (displayedLines > maxLines)
     displayedLines = maxLines;

  for (lineNum = yPos = 0; lineNum < displayedLines; ++lineNum)
     {
     if (lineLen[lineNum] > 0)  // if any text on the line
        dc.TextOut(0, yPos, linePtrs[lineNum], lineLen[lineNum]);

     yPos += textSize.cy;   // adjust screen line position
     }
}

// called when a normal key is pressed
void BaseWindow::EvChar(UINT key, UINT repeatCount, UINT)
{
  BOOL invalidDisplay = FALSE;
  BOOL eraseBackground = FALSE;

  while (repeatCount—)
     {
     if ((key >= ' ') && (key <= '~')) // if a printable key
        {
        if (currentLine >= maxLines)   // if buffer full
           {
           MessageBeep(-1);            //   complain
           break;
           }
```

```
141:         else                              // else
142:            {                              //   add char
143:            linePtrs[currentLine][lineLen[currentLine]] = (char)key;
144:
145:            if (++lineLen[currentLine] >= maxWidth)
146:              ++currentLine;
147:
148:            invalidDisplay = TRUE;
149:            }
150:         }
151:      else if (key == '\b')  // rubout, delete char
152:         {
153:         if (currentLine >= maxLines)
154:            break;
155:         else if (lineLen[currentLine] == 0)
156:            {
157:            if (currentLine > 0)
158:               --currentLine;
159:            }
160:         else
161:            --lineLen[currentLine];
162:
163:         invalidDisplay = eraseBackground = TRUE;
164:         }
165:      else if (key == '\r') // if carriage return (Enter key)
166:         ++currentLine;
167:      }
168:
169:   if (currentLine >= maxLines)
170:      currentLine = maxLines - 1;
171:
172:   if (invalidDisplay)              // if buffer has changed
173:      Invalidate(eraseBackground); //   force window repaint
174: }
175:
176: void MyApp::InitMainWindow()
177: {
178:   SetMainWindow(new TFrameWindow(0, "A Real Windows Program",
179:                                 new BaseWindow()));
180:   GetMainWindow()->AssignMenu("MENU_1");
181: }
182:
183:
184: int OwlMain(int, char **)
185: {
186:   return MyApp().Run();
187: }
```

Before running this application, you may want to get a feel for how it looks by examining Figure 11.1. Three instances of this program are shown on-screen, one each for an About box displayed, data typed in, and the pop-up menu opened.

As with the first program, this begins in `OwlMain()`. Line 186 calls the constructor for `MyApp`, and then calls `Run()`.

The constructor is declared on line 52. It in turn calls the constructor for `TApplication`. Line 54 has a function called `InitMainWindow()` that overloads the virtual function of the same name in the inherited class.

`TApplication`'s constructor calls `InitMainWindow()` (lines 176 through 181). That function makes two calls to `new`, creating a base window and then a frame window to handle the items on the base window's borders. The `GetMainWindow()` call on the next line assigns the menu to the main window. From then on, the application runs on its own, with Windows driving it by way of messages about menu selections and keyboard events.

The response table on lines 39 through 45 declared response functions for a character being entered, a window size change, and any of the three menu selections. Also, `BaseWindow`'s inheritance chain includes a virtual function called `Paint()`, which has been overloaded.

The data in the `BaseWindow` class is for keyboard input. Such input causes `EvChar()` on line 127 to be called. The calling arguments are the value of the key, the number of times it has been entered since you were last called, and a flag's variable that you don't use. The repeat count is important because a long process such as saving a disk file could allow the keyboard to insert several keys into the keyboard buffer.

This function passes through a loop as many times as the repeat count directs, adding keys to the keyboard buffer. When a line is full, it skips to the next line and begins entering there. If the buffer is full, the computer beeps at you (line 138).

If the user chooses the Backspace button, it deletes the last character entered (if one exists). The end of the function calls `Invalidate()`, a function that tells Windows that the whole window must be updated. The `eraseBackground` variable is only set to `TRUE` if a character is deleted. This minimizes screen blinking.

In response to the `Invalidate()` call, Windows sends the window procedure a message to paint the window. In the process, it sets things up and calls `Paint()`.

`Paint()` gets the text size. Fonts in Windows often are of variable width, but the measurement you are interested in is the vertical, which doesn't vary. You also calculate the number of displayable lines. It's a waste of time to paint more than that, because additional lines won't be placed on the screen.

A loop starting on line 118 passes through each line, writing any data in it to the screen. Note that `linePtrs[lineNum]` is an array of characters, not a string. No `'\0'` has been placed at the end. It relies on the `lineLen` array to handle how long the string is.

Note the `TDC` argument to `Paint()`. That is the device context you are to use in writing the screen. OWL has assigned it and will delete it after your function ends.

If you grab the corner of the window with the mouse cursor and resize it, `EvSize()` from line 88 will be called. If the application is minimized (shrunk to an icon), it merely sets a flag and returns.

If it is not minimized, it captures the window dimensions into the `TSize` structure called `windowSize` for later use by the `Paint()` function.

Menu operation is straightforward. Select any menu item and OWL calls the corresponding function. The `CMClear()` function (starting on line 78) sets the line length for all strings to zero and moves the current line number to point at the first line (`linePtrs[0]`). It then invalidates the window so that `Paint()` will be called. When called with no arguments, `Invalidate()` defaults to `TRUE` so the background will also be erased.

`CmAbout` calls a message box—a built-in Windows function—to show the name of the book.

`CmFileExit()` on line 31 calls a true Windows function, `PostQuitMessage()`. This function ends the program, and the return value (which Windows ignores in version 3.1) is the function argument.

Summary

Today's lesson introduced you to Borland's ObjectWindows application framework/class library and discussed the following topics:

- Windows requires special programming techniques because it allows multiple programs to run at the same time (unlike DOS).
- Windows communicates with programs via messages, and programs receive and process these messages in their message loop.
- Windows defines several shorthand names for common types of variables.
- Hungarian notation is a style of naming variables to indicate the type of data they hold and it helps in preventing bugs caused by mixing incompatible types. It's somewhat old-fashioned, as Turbo C++ implements very strong C++ type checking, but Windows still uses some of its notations.
- OWL consists of groups of classes used to represent Windows structures, including event handling, module management, and window management.
- OWL processes Windows messages by executing the appropriate functions found in a window object's response table. OWL also "cracks" the parameters that Windows sends into more meaningful values.
- Adding a menu to a window requires that you create a menu resource, tell OWL to load it, and process the menu items using the `EV_COMMAND` macro.

Q&A

Q I have a DOS program I'd like to port to Windows. Do I have to rewrite it to use Windows techniques like message loops?

A Yes. It won't be a Windows program if it doesn't follow Windows rules. However, you can use Turbo C++'s EasyWin library, which enables you to use DOS-style input and output functions. The result is a Windows program that looks like a DOS program.

Q The shorthand type names like DWORD and LPCSTR are confusing; can't I just use the normal C++ types?

A Yes, you can, but you have to make sure you do everything exactly the same. For example, everywhere you would normally use `LPCSTR`, make sure you use `const char far *`. Although learning the types takes some time, it usually is worth the extra effort, if only in saving the time it takes to type!

Q What function in my program is called first?

A DOS programs start at the `main()` function, which has arguments for the command-line parameters. Windows instead looks for a `WinMain()` function, with several arguments for instance handles, command-line parameters, and main window sizes. OWL simplifies it by providing an `OwlMain()` function that takes the same parameters as `main()` does.

Q Do I have to use a resource editor like Resource Workshop to create my resources?

A No. Resource files (with a .RC extension) are text files, so you can create and edit them with any text editor. However, Resource Workshop greatly simplifies editing resources, especially graphical ones.

Workshop

The Workshop provides quiz questions to help you solidify your understanding of the material covered and exercises to provide you with experience in using what you've learned. Try to understand the answers before continuing on to the next day's lesson. Answers are provided in Appendix A.

Quiz

1. True or false? The underlying types of Windows types like `WORD` and `UINT` will never change.
2. True or false? Even though an OWL program is quite different from a program written in C, it still is a normal Windows program.

Exercise

Create the program REAL2.CPP by using the `TWindow::MessageBox` function to display a message when the user types an invalid key.

WEEK
2

Basic Windows

The most relevant aspect of the Windows environment, as the name suggests, is the use of windows. Windows are the holders of information. The application is responsible for maintaining information when you resize, move, or use existing scroll bars. In today's lesson, you learn about the following:

- Creating read-only text windows
- Scrolling through text using scroll bars
- Changing the scroll bar metrics (units, line size, page size, and ranges)
- Optimizing the `Paint` member function

Creating a Read-Only Text Window

Day 11 presented a number of menu-driven OWL applications. However, there was very little explanation concerning how information was displayed in windows. This section presents an OWL application that displays read-only text in its windows. The basic notion of the application is similar to that of the read-only online Help windows.

The purpose of the program is to demonstrate how to display text and maintain that text after one or more of the following has occurred:

- Resizing the window
- Minimizing, restoring, or maximizing the window
- Moving a window or dialog box over the text area

The main tools to implement the application's features are the member functions `TDC::TextOut` and `TWindow::Paint`. The function `TDC::TextOut` draws a character string on the specified display. The text appears in the currently selected font and at the specified window coordinates.

Syntax

The *TextOut* Function

The declarations for the overloaded `TDC` member function `TextOut` are

```
bool TextOut(int x, int y, const char far* str, int count = -1);
bool TextOut(const TPoint& p, const char far* str, int count = -1);
```

The `x` and `y` parameters identify the window location where the first character appears. The `str` parameter points to the string to be displayed in the window. The `count` parameter indicates the leading number of characters of `str` to display. The argument for the last parameter is usually the size of the displayed string argument. Note that this has a default of `-1`, which means to display all the characters of `str`. In the second version of the function `TextOut`, the `x` and `y` parameters are replaced by a reference to a `TPoint` structure. The function returns a nonzero value when successful and `0` when it fails.

Example

```
char s[81] = "Hello";
string str("Guten Tag!");
TPoint pt(10, 20);
dc.TextOut(20, 10, s);
dc.TextOut(pt, str.c_str());
```

As expected, the function `TDC::TextOut` displays text once. This means that altering the viewing area of the window or moving another window over the displayed text erases that text. What is needed is a mechanism that updates the display of text in the window. Enter the member function `TWindow::Paint`. This function enables you to display and maintain the contents of a window (both text and graphics). The versatility of the function `TWindow::Paint` comes from the fact that it responds to a `WM_PAINT` message whenever Windows determines that the window needs repainting. This repainting feature includes the initial creation of the window. Consequently, the versatility of `TWindow::Paint` includes setting the initial display as well as maintaining it.

Note: You need to declare your own version of the `Paint` member function in your derived window class. The code you place inside your version of the `Paint` function determines what information appears, remains, and disappears.

12

In the case of this OWL application, the same information is displayed from start to finish. The general form of the `Paint` member function is

```
void MyWindow::Paint(TDC& dc, bool erase, TRect& rect)
{
   // declarations

   // statements using the TextOut member function
   // e.g.
   //      dc.TextOut(x, y, s, strlen(s));
}
```

The parameter `dc` that is passed to the `Paint` member function is referred to as the device context, and it's the link to the display of the window. The `dc.TextOut` function can be used as needed to place text on the window. Interestingly, if you come across a C-coded Windows application that uses the `TextOut` API function, you note that a similar text output requires initializing the device-context object and then promptly releasing it once it has finished its task. These steps are performed automatically by the `TWindow::EvPaint` function, which in turn calls the `Paint` function.

NEW TERM A *device context* (or DC for short) is the place in which all output goes. Anything that needs to be painted, such as text or graphics, must go onto DCs. These DCs can directly represent physical pixels on the screen, or they can be *memory DCs*. These memory DCs typically are used as temporary space in which to create such things as bitmaps before actually putting them on the screen by copying to another DC.

Now look at the code for the OWL application. Listing 12.1 contains the script for the resource file WINDOW1.RC. This resource file defines a menu with a single menu item, Exit, to exit the application. Listing 12.2 shows the source code for the WINDOW1.CPP program.

Create the directory WINDOW1 as a subdirectory of \TCWIN45\TC21DAY and store all the project's files in the new directory. The project's IDE file should contain the files WINDOW1.CPP and WINDOW1.RC.

Compile and run the application. Notice that the lines of text appear when the window is created. Alter the window by resizing it, minimizing it, and then restoring it to normal. The lines of text are always visible (or at least a portion of them) as long as the upper-left portion of the screen is not obscured by another window. You also can click the left mouse button to display a message box. Drag that message box over the text lines and release the mouse. Then, drag the message box away from the text location. What do you see? The text lines reappear; `Paint` is constantly at work.

Listing 12.1. Script code for WINDOW1.RC.

```
#include <windows.h>
#include <owl\window.rh>

EXITMENU MENU LOADONCALL MOVEABLE PURE DISCARDABLE
BEGIN
  MENUITEM "E&xit", CM_EXIT
END
```

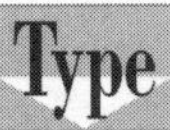

Listing 12.2. Source code for WINDOW1.CPP.

```
#include <owl\applicat.h>
#include <owl\dc.h>
#include <owl\framewin.h>
#include <owl\window.h>
#include <owl\window.rh>
#include <stdio.h>

const MAX_LINES = 30;

class TMyWindow : public TWindow
{
public:
   TMyWindow(TWindow* parent = 0);

protected:
   bool CanClose();

   void CmExit();
```

```
   void EvLButtonDown(UINT, TPoint &);

   void Paint(TDC &, bool, TRect &);

   DECLARE_RESPONSE_TABLE(TMyWindow);
};
DEFINE_RESPONSE_TABLE1(TMyWindow, TWindow)
   EV_WM_LBUTTONDOWN,
   EV_COMMAND(CM_EXIT, CmExit),
END_RESPONSE_TABLE;

class TMyApp : public TApplication
{
public:
   TMyApp() : TApplication() {}

   void InitMainWindow()
      {
      SetMainWindow(new TFrameWindow(  0,
                            "A Simple Read-Only Text Window",
                            new TMyWindow ));
      GetMainWindow()->AssignMenu("EXITMENU");
      }
};

TMyWindow::TMyWindow(TWindow* parent)
{
   Init(parent, 0, 0);
}

bool TMyWindow::CanClose()
{
   return IDYES == MessageBox("Want to close this application?",
                              "Query",
                              MB_YESNO | MB_ICONQUESTION );
}

void TMyWindow::CmExit()
{
   SendMessage(WM_CLOSE);
}

void TMyWindow::EvLButtonDown(UINT, TPoint &)
{
   MessageBox( "You clicked the left button!",
               "Mouse Click Event",
               MB_OK );
}

void TMyWindow::Paint(TDC& dc, bool /*erase*/, TRect& /*rect*/)
{
   char s[81];
   bool ok = true;
   int y = 0;

   for (int i = 0; i < MAX_LINES && ok; ++i)
```


continues

Listing 12.2. continued

```
75:        {
76:        sprintf(s, "This is line number %d", i);
77:        ok = dc.TextOut(0, y, s);
78:        y += dc.GetTextExtent(s, lstrlen(s)).cy;
79:        }
80: }
81:
82: int OwlMain(int, char *[])
83: {
84:    return TMyApp().Run();
85: }
```

Figure 12.1 shows a sample session with the program WINDOW1.EXE.

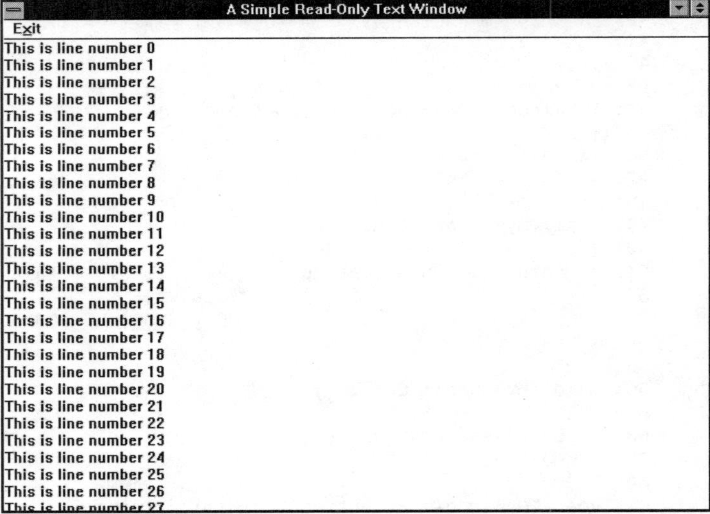

Figure 12.1.
A sample session with the program WINDOW1.EXE.

Analysis

Listing 12.2 shows the source code for the WINDOW1.CPP program file. The part of the program that is relevant to this application is the `TMyWindow` class and its member functions, declared on lines 10 through 28. The window class declares a constructor and three member functions, namely `EvLButtonDown`, `CmClose`, and `Paint`. The constructor creates a window on line 37 with the title `"A Simple Read-Only Text Window"` that has default size and location, and that uses the EXITMENU menu resource.

The main point of interest is the `Paint` function that starts on line 68. The function declares the constant `MAX_LINES`, the string variable `s`, and the `bool`-typed variable `ok`. The `Paint` function

displays the lines using the `for` loop on lines 74 through 79. Each loop iteration executes two statements. The first statement calls the `sprintf` function (prototyped in the STDIO.H header file) to create the image of a formatted output and store it in the variable `s`. The next statement calls the `dc`'s `TextOut` member function, which places the formatted output on the window. Notice the first two arguments of the `TextOut` function. They are `0` (for parameter `X`) and `y`. These values result in displaying the text, starting with the left margin of the window. The next function called is the `dc`'s `GetTextExtent` member function. This is used to determine the height of the text and any line spacing and to use that information by adding it to the `y` variable so that the next time through the loop, the next line is placed appropriately below the previous line.

Scrolling Through Text

One of the versatile features of windows is the capability to scroll information, if that information cannot be contained in the current viewing portion of the window. The scroll bars are the visual components of a window that assist in scrolling through the window's contents. Recall that a window can have a vertical scroll bar, horizontal scroll bar, or both. A scroll bar has an arrow box at each end and a scroll thumb. The arrow boxes enable you to scroll the window's contents to either end or to either side. In today's lesson, you learn about scrolling windows that contain text drawn using device-context objects.

NEW TERM The *scroll thumb* serves two purposes. First, it shows where you are relative to the entire width or length of the viewed information. Second, when you drag the thumb with the mouse, you can move to a specific portion of the viewed information.

12

The scrolling effect mentioned at the beginning of today's lesson is supported by a visual interface and an internal "engine." You can easily include the visual scroll bars in a window by incorporating the `WS_VSCROLL` and `WS_HSCROLL` styles in the `Attr.Style` member data from the window's constructor. To create a window with both vertical and horizontal scroll bars, for example, use the following statement:

```
// both vertical and horizontal scroll bars
Attr.Style |= WS_VSCROLL | WS_HSCROLL;
```

The `WS_VSCROLL` and `WS_HSCROLL` constants add the visual aspect of the scroll bars. The functionality is supported by overriding the `EvVScroll`, `EvHScroll`, and `EvSize` functions, and then adjusting your Paint function to take advantage of any scrolling changes. OWL provides an integrated class that does just this, called `TScroller`. An object of this class, when assigned the `TWindow`'s `Scroller` member function, provides scrolling by working with the `TWindow` class to automatically sense the setting of the scroll bars and adjusts the window's viewport accordingly.

NEW TERM The *viewport* is that portion of the window that is visible at any one time. It is possible to paint on a window outside of the visible portion, but that will be *clipped* from view. By adjusting the viewport's origin, the clipped region will change, and offsets within the window will be adjusted accordingly. For example, given a standard window, when a string of text is drawn at (10,10), the text will appear offset down and to the right of the upper-left corner of the window. By adjusting the viewport origin to begin at (10,10), drawing that same text at the same location now will make it appear in the upper-left corner.

The constructor for the TScroller class looks like this.

```
TScroller(TWindow* window, int xUnit, int yUnit,
long xRange, long yRange);
```

The window parameter is a pointer to the window for which the TScroller object is being created. The xUnit and yUnit parameters specify how many device units to scroll in each direction. In the case of textual information, this usually is going to be the size of a single character, so that scrolling goes by lines. Note, however, that because most fonts in Windows are variable (each of the characters are of differing widths), the horizontal unit tends to be the average width of all the characters. Finally, the xRange and yRange parameters specify how many scrolling positions exist. For example, a yRange of 20 would mean that the down arrow on the scroll bar could be clicked 20 times.

It is easy to add an additional include file at the top,

```
#include <owl\scroller.h>
```

and the following two lines to the constructor of the TMyWindow class from the last example:

```
Attr.Style |= WS_VSCROLL | WS_HSCROLL;
Scroller = new TScroller(7, 16, 20, MAX_LINES - 1);
```

If you add those two lines and recompile, you will find that your window now has scroll bars on the bottom and right side, and you can scroll to the right 20 columns and down as many lines as are drawn (minus one, so at least one of the lines stays on-screen). The two more interesting functions of the TScroller class are the VScroll and HScroll member functions.

Syntax

Manually Scrolling with *TScroller*

The declarations of TScroller's VScroll and HScroll member functions are

```
void VScroll(UINT scrollEvent, int thumbPos);
void HScroll(UINT scrollEvent, int thumbPos);
```

The scrollEvent specifies the scrolling request. Table 12.1 shows the predefined constants for the various scrolling requests. The thumbPos parameter specifies the position of the thumb box when the argument for scrollEvent is either SB_THUMBPOSITION or SB_THUMBTRACK.

Example

```
Scroller->VScroll(SB_LINEDOWN, 0);
Scroller->HScroll(SB_THUMBPOSITION, 23);
```

Table 12.1. Predefined constants for vertical scrolling requests.

Value	Meaning
`SB_BOTTOM`	Scroll to the bottom
`SB_ENDSCROLL`	End scroll
`SB_LINEDOWN`	Scroll one line down
`SB_LINEUP`	Scroll one line up
`SB_PAGEDOWN`	Scroll one page down
`SB_PAGEUP`	Scroll one page up
`SB_THUMBPOSITION`	Scroll to the `nPos` position
`SB_THUMBTRACK`	Drag the scroll thumb box to the `nPos` position
`SB_TOP`	Scroll to the top

In the preceding short example, the 7 and 16 are approximations of a character's width and height. They will work when using the default font on most standard VGA screens, but you will run into problems when you try to use different fonts or when you run on screens that use a smaller font (such as an 800×600 or 1024×768 screen). The solution is to figure out the size of the font beforehand and set the scroll units accordingly.

A Scrolling Window

12

This section presents a program that defines general scrollable windows. WINDOW2.EXE has two main menu items: Exit and Char Sets. The second menu item is a pop-up menu that has three selections: Set 1, Set 2, and Set 3. These options produce text lines that have a different line spacing and different maximum number of lines. The text fonts are the same for all three sets. Initially, the client area of the application window is clear. Therefore, you must select one of the three character sets. The application also supports the cursor movement keys to scroll the text. The <Home> and <End> keys scroll vertically to the top and bottom, respectively. Similarly, the <PgUp> and <PgDn> keys scroll up and down one page. The up- and down-arrow keys scroll one line at a time. The left- and right-arrow keys scroll horizontally by pages.

This program illustrates two main aspects of scrolling windows:

- ☐ Declaring a scrolling window class with additional member functions that manage the assignment, access, and use of scrolling-related data
- ☐ Using assigned values to control vertical scrolling, and relying on the current window metrics to control the horizontal scrolling

Look at the code for the general text scroller window application. Listings 12.3 and 12.4 show the header file WINDOW2.H and the resource file WINDOW2.RC, respectively. Listing 12.5 contains the source code for the WINDOW2.CPP program.

Create the directory WINDOW2 as a subdirectory of \TCWIN45\TC21DAY and store all the project's files in the new directory. The project should contain the files WINDOW2.CPP and WINDOW2.RC.

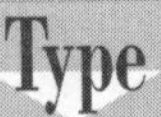

Listing 12.3. Source code for WINDOW2.H.

```
#define  CM_HEIGHT8     (WM_USER + 100)
#define  CM_HEIGHT10    (WM_USER + 101)
#define  CM_HEIGHT14    (WM_USER + 102)
#define  CM_HEIGHT20    (WM_USER + 103)
#define  CM_HEIGHT26    (WM_USER + 104)
```

Listing 12.4. Script code for WINDOW2.RC.

```
#include <windows.h>
#include <owl\window.rh>
#include "window2.h"

EXITMENU MENU LOADONCALL MOVEABLE PURE DISCARDABLE
BEGIN
   MENUITEM "E&xit", CM_EXIT
   POPUP "&Char Heights"
   BEGIN
      MENUITEM "&8", CM_HEIGHT8
      MENUITEM "1&0", CM_HEIGHT10
      MENUITEM "1&4", CM_HEIGHT14
      MENUITEM "&20", CM_HEIGHT20
      MENUITEM "2&6", CM_HEIGHT26
   END
END
```

Listing 12.5. Source code for WINDOW2.CPP.

```
#include <owl\applicat.h>
#include <owl\dc.h>
#include <owl\framewin.h>
#include <owl\scroller.h>
#include <owl\window.h>
#include <owl\window.rh>
#include <stdio.h>

#include "window2.h"

const MAX_LINES = 30;

class TMyWindow : public TWindow
{
public:
   TMyWindow(TWindow* parent = 0);
   ~TMyWindow();

protected:
```

```
   virtual void SetupWindow();

   bool CanClose();

   void CmExit();
   void CmHeight8();
   void CmHeight10();
   void CmHeight14();
   void CmHeight20();
   void CmHeight26();
   void EvKeyDown(UINT, UINT, UINT);
   void EvLButtonDown(UINT, TPoint &);

   void Paint(TDC &, bool, TRect &);

private:
   TFont* pFont;

   void NewFont(int);

   DECLARE_RESPONSE_TABLE(TMyWindow);
};
DEFINE_RESPONSE_TABLE1(TMyWindow, TWindow)
   EV_WM_KEYDOWN,
   EV_WM_LBUTTONDOWN,
   EV_COMMAND(CM_EXIT, CmExit),
   EV_COMMAND(CM_HEIGHT8, CmHeight8),
   EV_COMMAND(CM_HEIGHT10, CmHeight10),
   EV_COMMAND(CM_HEIGHT14, CmHeight14),
   EV_COMMAND(CM_HEIGHT20, CmHeight20),
   EV_COMMAND(CM_HEIGHT26, CmHeight26),
END_RESPONSE_TABLE;

class TMyApp : public TApplication
{
public:
   TMyApp() : TApplication() {}

   void InitMainWindow()
      {
      SetMainWindow(new TFrameWindow(  0,
                              "A Simple Read-Only Text Window",
                              new TMyWindow ));
      GetMainWindow()->AssignMenu("EXITMENU");
      }
};

TMyWindow::TMyWindow(TWindow* parent)
{
   Init(parent, 0, 0);
   Attr.Style |= WS_VSCROLL | WS_HSCROLL;    // Add scroll bars
   pFont = NULL;
}

TMyWindow::~TMyWindow()
{
   if (pFont)
```

continues

Listing 12.5. continued

```
      delete pFont;
}

void TMyWindow::SetupWindow()
{
   TWindow::SetupWindow();

   // Set up the scroller and font.  Note that
   // dummy values of 7 and 16 are used for the
   // scroll bar's units, but they'll be reset
   // as soon as the font is set.
   //
   Scroller = new TScroller(this, 7, 16, 20, MAX_LINES - 1);
   NewFont(8);                            // Initialize our font
}

bool TMyWindow::CanClose()
{
   return IDYES == MessageBox("Want to close this application?",
                              "Query",
                              MB_YESNO ¦ MB_ICONQUESTION );
}

void TMyWindow::CmExit()
{
   SendMessage(WM_CLOSE);
}

void TMyWindow::CmHeight8()
{
   NewFont(8);
}

void TMyWindow::CmHeight10()
{
   NewFont(10);
}

void TMyWindow::CmHeight14()
{
   NewFont(14);
}

void TMyWindow::CmHeight20()
{
   NewFont(20);
}

void TMyWindow::CmHeight26()
{
   NewFont(26);
}

void TMyWindow::EvKeyDown( UINT key,
                           UINT /*repeatCount*/,
```

```
                           UINT /*flags*/ )
{
   if (Scroller)        // Can't scroll if it ain't there!
      switch (key)
         {
         case VK_HOME:
            Scroller->VScroll(SB_TOP, 0);
            break;
         case VK_END:
            Scroller->VScroll(SB_BOTTOM, 0);
            break;
         case VK_PRIOR:
            Scroller->VScroll(SB_PAGEUP, 0);
            break;
         case VK_NEXT:
            Scroller->VScroll(SB_PAGEDOWN, 0);
            break;
         case VK_UP:
            Scroller->VScroll(SB_LINEUP, 0);
            break;
         case VK_DOWN:
            Scroller->VScroll(SB_LINEDOWN, 0);
            break;
         }
}

void TMyWindow::EvLButtonDown(UINT, TPoint &)
{
   MessageBox( "You clicked the left button!",
               "Mouse Click Event",
               MB_OK );
}

void TMyWindow::Paint(TDC& dc, bool /*erase*/, TRect& /*rect*/)
{
   char s[81];
   bool ok = true;
   int y = 0;

   for (int i = 0; i < MAX_LINES && ok; ++i)
      {
      if (pFont)
         dc.SelectObject(*pFont);
      sprintf(s, "This is line number %d", i);
      ok = dc.TextOut(0, y, s);
      y += dc.GetTextExtent(s, lstrlen(s)).cy;
      if (pFont)
         dc.RestoreFont();
      }
}

void TMyWindow::NewFont(int nHeight)
{
   if (pFont)
      delete pFont;
   pFont = new TFont("Arial", nHeight);

```

12

continues

Listing 12.5. continued

```
    // Now reset the scroller's units
    if (pFont && Scroller)
       {
       TClientDC dc(*this);
       TEXTMETRIC tm;

       dc.SelectObject(*pFont);
       dc.GetTextMetrics(tm);
       dc.RestoreFont();

       Scroller->SetUnits(  tm.tmAveCharWidth,
                            tm.tmHeight + tm.tmExternalLeading );

       Invalidate();
       }
}

int OwlMain(int, char *[])
{
   return TMyApp().Run();
}
```

Figure 12.2 shows a sample session with the program WINDOW2.EXE.

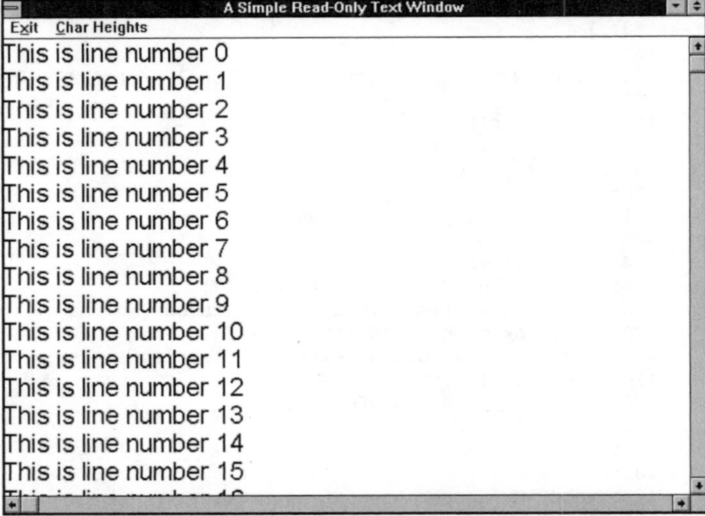

Figure 12.2.
A sample session with the program WINDOW2.EXE.

This program is very similar to the first one presented in this chapter. The major differences are the addition of the scroll bars on the right and bottom of the window and the new menu item enabling the user to change the font as it is displayed on-screen.

NEW TERM A *font* is a description of the type of characters used to display text. This description includes what the characters look like, called the *typeface*, as well as their size, referred to as their *point size*. Some common typefaces are *Arial* and *Times New Roman*, both of which come with Windows. Also, such things as italics and bold characters are described by fonts.

The `TMyWindow` class on lines 13 through 51 declares a new data member and a new function member, both private, for use in displaying using different point-sized fonts:

- The `pFont` member on line 36 stores a pointer to the font used to display the text. This variable is preset to `NULL` in the class's constructor on line 71 and initialized in the `SetupWindow` function on line 90. It then is reset by the user via the menus.
- The `NewFont` function starting on line 183 is used to change the font. It takes an integer value that is used as the point size, and it then creates a `TFont` object, assigning it to the `pFont` data member.
- The `Paint` function starting on line 165 first selects the `pFont` object into the device context before writing to the window. After it's done, it reselects the original font back into the window.

Note: When dealing with windows and selecting objects into device contexts such as fonts or text colors, it's always a good idea to make sure you leave the DC in the same condition as you found it. If you change the font, make sure you change it back to whatever it might have been before you modified it.

Note that the `pFont` is only preset to `NULL` in the constructor, but the real initialization occurs in the `SetupWindow` member function. This is a very important distinction, as creating the font requires the existence of a window.

The *SetupWindow* Member Function

Although the `TWindow` class has the usual constructor where things can be initialized as in any other class, it also has the member function `SetupWindow` for all initializations that rely on an actual window to be there. The `SetupWindow` function looks like this.

```
void SetupWindow(void);
```

When the `TWindow` class is first created, all that exists is the interface object or C++ object. For many initializations, an actual interface element or Windows object (a window) may need to exist. During the course of the window's initialization, the `SetupWindow` will be called. This function does the actual initialization of the Windows object to which the C++ object is to be connected; this includes the creation of any child windows contained within the window. This is why it is vitally important for any derived versions of `SetupWindow` to call the parent's version. Until the actual `TWindow::SetupWindow` function is called, there will be no Windows object.

This program enables the user to use the keyboard to scroll the window. It does this through a single member function `EvKeyDown` starting on line 130. In this function is a switch statement that checks for the keys on the keypad. For each of these, it sends the `Scroller` object the appropriate command (refer to Table 12.1) to scroll the window. The `Scroller` object is closely tied to the `TWindow` object, of which `TMyWindow` is directly descended, so it handles all the dirty work of changing the scroll bars and telling the window to update itself, which then calls `Paint` to paint the right portions of the screen.

In order to enable the user to change the font, the Char Heights pop-up menu item has been added with various selections, enabling the user to select specific point sizes for the fonts. The program responds to these menu selections through the various `CmHeightXX` member functions on lines 105 through 128. These functions serve only to call the `NewFont` member function with the appropriate point size, as specified by the user.

Finally, the `NewFont` member function, starting on line 183, handles the creation of the fonts used in painting the window:

- First, it checks to see if the `pFont` data member has been set yet. If so, it deletes the old one in preparation for replacing the old one with a new version, which it does immediately. It allocates a new `TFont` object with the typeface *Arial* and a point size of `nHeight`.

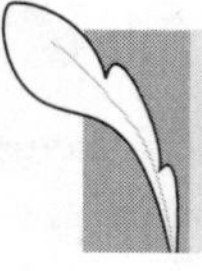

Note: Although it is safe to delete a `NULL` pointer in Turbo C++, it still is a good idea to check first, because not all compilers are as safe.

- Assuming that the `Scroller` object exists and the creation of `pFont` succeeded, the function proceeds to set the `Scroller` with new values to let it know how big the characters are now. To do this, it first gets a device context from the window and selects the new `pFont` into it. The font's attributes are placed into the `TEXTMETRIC` object and that information is used in the `TScroller`'s `SetUnits` function.
- Finally, because the font you use to paint the window has changed, you need to tell the window to update itself with the new font. This is done with the `Invalidate` function, which tells the window that its contents are no longer valid and need repainting. Windows automatically tells the window to repaint itself, at which time the `Paint` function will be entered.

Summary

Today's lesson discussed the mechanics of creating windows that show fixed and scrollable text. The lesson included the following topics:

- Read-only text windows that display information are the basis of help screens
- You can write text in a window using the versatile `TDC::TextOut` member function.
- You can create scrollable windows with vertical and horizontal scroll bars. These windows scroll using either the mouse or the cursor-control keys. The classes of scrollable windows use the `TScroller` class assigned to the `TWindow`'s `Scroller` data member, as well as other functions to manage the text metrics.

Q&A

Q Is the member function `Paint` needed to maintain windows with visual controls such as command buttons?

A No. You need only to write the function `Paint` to maintain windows that draw text and graphics. In the case of windows with controls, you do not need to declare your own version of function `Paint`.

Workshop

The Workshop provides quiz questions to help you solidify your understanding of the material covered and exercises to provide you with experience in using what you've learned. Try to understand the quiz and exercise answers before continuing on to the next day's lesson. Answers are provided in Appendix A.

Quiz

1. True or false? The member function `Paint` redraws the window only when needed.
2. True or false? The `TWindow::Scroller` data member offers default scrolling features.
3. True or false? Omitting the `EvKeyDown` member function in program WINDOW2.CPP disables the vertical scrolling feature altogether.

Exercise

Experiment with modifying the WINDOW2.CPP program by adding cases to the `EvKeyDown` function that will enable the window to scroll horizontally in response to the right- and left-arrow keys being pressed. In addition, you can experiment with adding more `CmHeightXX` member functions and the corresponding menu selections.

WEEK 2

OWL Controls

Interacting with Windows applications often involves dialog boxes that contain various types of controls, such as the list box, the edit control (also called edit box), and the pushbutton. These controls can be included in windows or, more frequently, in dialog boxes. Today's lesson and the next three look at the controls as they appear in windows and focus on the basic properties of these controls. Day 14 presents dialog boxes and views how the controls work with these boxes. Today, you learn about the following topics:

- The `TControl` object
- Static text control
- Edit control
- Pushbutton control

Understanding the various controls and mastering how they behave and interact enables you to implement highly interactive Windows applications. Today's lesson and the two that follow discuss the constructors and relevant member functions for the control classes.

The *TControl* Object

To learn about OWL controls, it's best to start with the `TControl` object. This object is the base from which all other control objects are derived. Note that you will never have any need to create a `TControl` object directly, but a discussion of it here helps you to understand the control objects derived from it.

The `TControl` object is derived from the `TWindow` class, which means that it has much of the same functionality as the `TWindow` class. This actually is a direct mapping of the Windows environment where controls are, indeed, just specialized child windows. Because the `TControl` class merely is meant as a common base class for the rest of the control classes, the only public function is the constructor.

Syntax

The *TControl* Constructor

The constructor of the `TControl` class is

```
TControl(TWindow*          parent,
         int               id,
         const char far*   title,
         int               x,
         int               y,
         int               w,
         int               h,
         TModule*          module = 0);
```

The `parent` parameter is a pointer to the parent window in which the control will be placed. The `id` represents the control's ID, which is used in communication between the parent window and the control itself (more on this later, when specific controls are discussed). Next comes the title of the control. This parameter isn't always displayed by the particular control created, but it's always set. The four parameters `x`, `y`, `w`, and `h` describe the position and size of the control to be created. Finally, the `module` parameter specifies the DLL with which the control is associated. This has a default value of `0`, and you will rarely find a need to override that.

You will see the parameters to this class duplicated repeatedly in the various control classes derived from `TControl`. Added on to these standard parameters will be other parameters specific to the particular class being created.

The Static Text Control

The static text control provides a window or a dialog box with static text. The `TStatic` class implements the static text control. Look at the class constructor and members.

NEW TERM *Static text* is text that the application user cannot easily and readily change. Static text does not necessarily mean text etched in stone! In fact, static text controls allow your OWL applications to alter the text at any time, or you still can specify that the text be permanent and unchangeable. The choice ultimately is yours.

The `TStatic` class, a descendant of `TControl` (which, in turn, is descended from `TWindow`), offers static text that is defined by a display area, text to display, and text attributes. Of these three components, you can alter only the displayed text during runtime.

Syntax

The *TStatic* Constructor

The constructor of the `TStatic` control is

```
TStatic(TWindow*        parent,
        int             id,
        const char far *title,
        int             x,
        int             y,
        int             w,
        int             h,
        uint            textLen = 0,
        TModule*        module = 0 );
TStatic(TWindow*        parent,
        int             resourceId,
        uint            textLen = 0,
        TModule*        module = 0 );
```

Example

```
pText = new TStatic(this, -1, "Sample Text", 10, 10, 75, 25);
pText->Attr.Style &=~SS_LEFT;
pText->Attr.Style !=SS_SIMPLE;
```

The `parent` parameter specifies the parent window into which the static control will be placed. The `id` is used to give the static control a unique identifier. A control's ID typically is used when the static text needs to be changed by the application. In the case of a static control, this is a very rare occasion, so the `id` parameter is usually set to `-1`. The `title` sets an initial text string that will appear within the control. The next four parameters—x, y, w, and h—describe the location and size of the control as it will appear within its parent window. The textLen parameter is used for advanced transfer and streaming capabilities, and the module pointer is used for specifying the DLL with which the static control is associated. Note that these last two both have default values of 0, and you rarely will find a need to override that.

The second constructor is used when connecting a TStatic object with a static control that has been loaded from a resource (in a dialog box). In this case, the resourceId must be the same as the one specified in the resource. Dialog boxes and how this constructor is used are discussed on Day 14.

In addition to the usual WS_CHILD and WS_VISIBLE styles that go along with all controls, static controls have their own special set of SS_XXX styles, as shown in Table 13.1. Note that the TStatic class automatically includes the SS_LEFT style.

Table 13.1. Values for static text styles.

Value	Meaning
SS_BLACKFRAME	Designates a box with a frame drawn with the color matching that of the window frame (black, in the default Windows color scheme).
SS_BLACKRECT	Specifies a rectangle filled with the color matching that of the window frame (black, in the default Windows color scheme).
SS_CENTER	Centers the static text characters; text is wrappable.
SS_GRAYFRAME	Specifies a box with a frame that has the same color as the screen background (gray, in the default Windows color scheme).
SS_GRAYRECT	Selects a rectangle filled with the same color as the screen background (gray, in the default Windows color scheme).
SS_ICON	Specifies an icon that is to be displayed in the control. The text is interpreted as the resource name of the icon. (Note that the width and height of the control are ignored as the icon automatically is sized.)
SS_LEFT	Indicates left-justified text; text is wrappable.
SS_LEFTNOWORDWRAP	Indicates left-justified text that cannot be wrapped.
SS_NOPREFIX	Specifies that the ampersand character (&) in the static text string should not be a hot key designator character, but rather part of the static text character.

Value	Meaning
`SS_RIGHT`	Selects right-justified text that is wrappable.
`SS_SIMPLE`	Indicates that the static text characters cannot be altered at runtime and that the static text is displayed on a single line with line breaks ignored.
`SS_WHITEFRAME`	Specifies a box with a frame that has the same color as the window background (white, in the default Windows color scheme).
`SS_WHITERECT`	Selects a rectangle filled with the same color as the window background (white, in the default Windows color scheme).

The string accessed by the `title` pointer in the constructor may include the ampersand (`&`) character to visually specify a hot key. The hot-key character appears as an underlined character. The ampersand should be placed before the hot key character. If the string contains more than one ampersand character, only the last occurrence is effective. The other occurrences of the ampersand are not displayed and are ignored. To display the `&` character, you need to specify the `SS_NOPREFIX` style. The price you pay for using this style is the inability to display a hot key character.

Now focus on the component of the static text control that you can change during runtime, namely, the text itself. If you specify the `SS_SIMPLE` style in the control's `Attr.Style` data member, you cannot alter its text. In this sense, the instance of `TStatic` is, indeed, etched in stone. The `TStatic` class enables you to set, query, and clear the characters of the static text using the `GetTextLen`, `GetText`, `SetText`, and `Clear` functions.

Syntax

The *GetTextLen* Function

The parameterless `GetTextLen` member function returns the length of the control's text.

```
int GetTextLen()
```

Example

```
int nLen = pText->GetTextLen();
```

Syntax

The *GetText* Function

The `GetText` member function enables you to access the static text characters. The declaration of the function is

```
int GetText(char far* text, int maxChars);
```

The text parameter is a pointer to the string that receives a copy of the static text characters. The maxChars parameter specifies the maximum number of static text characters to copy. The function result returns the actual number of characters copied to the string accessed by the pointer text.

Example

```
char s[128];
pText->GetText(s, sizeof(s) - 1);
```

Syntax

The *SetText* Function

The SetText member function overwrites the current static text characters with those of a new string. The declaration of the function is

```
void SetText(const char far* str);
```

The str parameter is the pointer to the new text for the control. If the new text is an empty string, the SetText function call simply clears the text in the static text control instance.

Example

```
pText->SetText("New Text");
```

Syntax

The *Clear* Function

The Clear member function is simply a wrapper that passes an empty string to the SetText member function. The declaration of the function is

```
void Clear();
```

Its existence is there to make code look a little cleaner by enabling you to call the Clear function rather than SetText("");.

The Edit Control

The ObjectWindows Library offers the TEdit class that implements an edit control. The edit control enables the user to type in and edit the text in the input dialog box. This section discusses the functionality of class TEdit in more detail, because implementing customized text editors in your OWL application requires you to become quite familiar with the TEdit member functions.

The *TEdit* Class

The TEdit class is derived from the TStatic class and implements a versatile edit control that supports single-line and multiline text, as well as the capability to cut, paste, copy, delete, and clear text. The edit control also can undo the last text changes and exchange text with the Clipboard.

Syntax

The *TEdit* Constructor

The declaration of the `TEdit` constructor is

```
TEdit(TWindow*        parent,
      int             id,
      const char far* text,
      int             x,
      int             y,
      int             w,
      int             h,
      uint            textLen = 0,
      bool            multiline = false,
      TModule*        module = 0 );
TEdit(TWindow*        parent,
      int             resourceId,
      uint            textLen = 0,
      TModule*        module = 0 );
```

The parameters to the first constructor are almost identical to the ones for the `TStatic` constructor. The only difference is the addition of a `multiline` parameter. This tells whether the edit control should have more than one input line, like a text editor. Unlike the `TStatic` control, however, it never makes sense to use an invalid number in the `id` parameter of the `TEdit` control, as the `TEdit` control will need to send notification messages back to its parent window.

The second constructor is identical in usage to the second constructor for the `TStatic` control. It is used to associate a C++ class object with a control loaded with a dialog resource. Again, this will be discussed on Day 14.

Example

```
const IDE_INPUT = 101;
pInput = new TEdit(this, IDE_INPUT, "", 10, 10, 100, 25);
```

The `TEdit` control also has its own set of special styles, `ES_XXX`, that can be used to modify its behavior (see Table 13.2). When you create a `TEdit` object, the `ES_LEFT` and `ES_AUTOHSCROLL` automatically are added in. If the `multiline` parameter is set, then the `ES_MULTILINE` and `ES_AUTOVSCROLL` also are automatically set.

Table 13.2. Values for edit control styles.

Value	Meaning
`ES_AUTOHSCROLL`	Allows the text to automatically scroll to the right by 10 characters when the user enters a character at the end of the line; when the user presses the Enter key, text scrolls back to the left.
`ES_AUTOVSCROLL`	Permits the text to scroll up by one page when the user presses the Enter key on the last visible line.
`ES_CENTER`	Centers the text in a multiline edit control.

continues

Table 13.2. continued

Value	Meaning
`ES_LEFT`	Justifies the text to the left.
`ES_LOWERCASE`	Converts into lowercase all the letters that the user types.
`ES_MULTILINE`	Specifies a multiline edit control that recognizes line breaks (designated by the sequence of carriage return and line feed characters).
`ES_NOHIDESEL`	By default, hides the selected text when it loses focus and shows the selection when it gains focus again; prevents edit control from restoring the selected text.
`ES_OEMCONVERT`	Converts the entered text from the Windows character set to the OEM character set and back again. This is useful for controls that receive filenames.
`ES_PASSWORD`	Displays all characters as asterisks (*) as they are typed. Note that this only affects the display; what the user types is stored accurately in the control.
`ES_READONLY`	Prevents the user from modifying the contents of the control, although it is still possible to select text in the control.
`ES_RIGHT`	Justifies the text to the right in multiline edit controls.
`ES_UPPERCASE`	Converts into uppercase all the letters that the user types.
`ES_WANTRETURN`	Normally, the Enter key will click the default button. When this style is set in an edit control, however, pressing Enter while editing text will insert a new line. This applies only to multiline edit controls.

Clipboard-Related Editing Functions

The `TEdit` class includes a set of member functions that handle Clipboard-related text editing commands. These commands are available in typical menu options: Cut, Copy, Paste, Clear, Undo, and Delete. Table 13.3 shows the `TEdit` member functions and their purpose. These functions work with the Clipboard in the `CF_TEXT` format.

Table 13.3. `TEdit` member functions that support Clipboard-related editing menu commands.

Member Function	Purpose
`CanUndo`	Returns whether an undo operation is possible at the moment. It is used to enable and disable the Undo menu item accordingly.
`Cut`	Deletes the current selection in the edit control and copies the text to the Clipboard.
`Copy`	Copies the current selection to the Clipboard.
`Paste`	Inserts the text from the Clipboard to the current cursor position in the edit control.
`Clear`	Deletes all the text in the control; this does not affect the Clipboard.
`Undo`	Undoes the last change made to the text of the edit control.

Query of Edit Controls

The `TEdit` class has a family of text query member functions. These functions enable you to retrieve either the entire control text or parts of it, or they permit you to obtain information on the text statistics (number of lines, length of lines, and so on). Two of these functions are inherited directly from the `TStatic` class. They are `GetTextLen` and `GetText`. They are used to retrieve the contents of edit controls and are declared and used in the same way as they are in the `TStatic` class.

Because edit controls allow for both multiple lines and user manipulation, additional functions are used to get text from different lines and for manipulating the selection.

Syntax

The *GetNumLines* Function

The `GetNumLines` member function returns the number of lines in the edit control. The declaration is

```
int GetNumLines() const;
```

Example

```
nLineCount = pEdit->GetNumLines();
```

Note: In the case of `multiline` edit controls, you should take into account the characters involved in either the soft or hard line breaks.

Hard line breaks use pairs of carriage return and line feed characters (`"\r\n"`) at the end of each line. Soft line breaks use two carriage returns and a line feed at line breaks (`"\r\r\n"`).

This information is relevant when you are counting the number of characters to process.

Syntax

The *GetLineFromPos* Function

The `GetLineFromPos` member function returns the line number of a specified character index. Its declaration is

```
int GetLineFromPos(uint charPos) const;
```

If the `charPos` argument is `-1`, then the function will return either of the following two values:

- If there is selected text, the function yields the line number where the first selected character is located.
- If there is no selected text, the function returns the line number where the caret is, where character insertion occurs.

Example

```
nLineNum = pEdit->GetLineFromPos(-1);
```

Syntax

The *GetLineIndex* Function

The `GetLineIndex` member function returns the character index of a specific line. The character index also is the size of the text in the edit control up to the specified line number. Its declaration is

```
uint GetLineIndex(int lineNumber) const;
```

The `lineNumber` parameter specifies the line index. If it is `-1`, then it represents the current line as represented by the caret, which marks the user's current position. The function returns the number of characters from the first line through to the specified line. If the argument of `lineNumber` is greater than the actual number of lines, then the function will return `-1`.

Example

```
nCharIndex = pEdit->GetLineIndex(-1);
```

Syntax

The *GetLineLength* Function

The `GetLineLength` member function returns the length of a line for a specific line number. Its declaration is

```
int GetLineLength(int lineNumber) const;
```

The `lineNumber` parameter specifies the line number from which to get the length. If `lineNumber` is `-1`, then the function will return one of the following:

- If no text is selected, the length of the current line is returned.
- If text is selected, the length of the line, minus the length of the currently selected text, is returned.

Example

```
nLen = pEdit->GetLineLength(1);
```

Syntax

The *GetSelection* Function

The `GetSelection` member function returns the starting and ending character positions of the selected text. The starting character position is the index of the first selected character. The ending position is the index of the first character *after* the selected text. The declaration of the function is

```
void GetSelection(uint& startPos, uint& endPos) const;
```

The function fills in the passed `startPos` and `endPos` with the corresponding selection locations. If these two values are equal, there is no selected text, because both `uint`s are the character indices to the current position.

Example

```
pEdit->GetSelection(start, end);
```


Syntax

The *GetLine* Function

The `GetLine` member function returns a line from a multiline edit control. Its declaration is

```
bool GetLine(char far* str, int strSize, int lineNumber) const;
```

The `str` parameter points to a buffer that is to receive the text of the line; `strSize` is the number of characters to receive; and `lineNumber` is the line to retrieve. If there is a problem copying the line or if the line is longer than `strSize`, the function will return `false`; otherwise it will return `true`.

Example

```
char s[128];
pEdit->GetLine(s, sizeof(s) - 1, 22);
```

Altering the Edit Controls

Now focus on the member functions of TEdit that alter the edit control text. The operations of these member functions include writing new text to the control, selecting text, and replacing the selected text.

- The SetText member function that is inherited from the parent TStatic class acts in the same manner; it overwrites the current edit control characters with those of a new string.
- The SetSelection member function defines a block of characters as the new selected text.
- The Insert member function replaces the selected text with new characters.

Syntax

The *SetSelection* Function

The declaration of the SetSelection function is

```
bool SetSelection(uint startPos, uint endPos);
```

The startPos and endPos parameters define the range of characters that make up the new selected text. If the starting and ending positions are 0 and -1, respectively, then the entire text in the edit control is selected. If startPos is -1, then any selection is removed. The current position is placed at the greater of the two parameters.

Example

```
pEdit->SetSelection(0, -1);
```

Syntax

The *Insert* Function

The declaration of the Insert function is

```
void Insert(const char far* str);
```

The str parameter is the pointer to the new selected text that replaces the current selection. If there is no selected text, the function simply inserts the text accessed by str at the current insertion point.

Example

```
pEdit->Insert("New Text");
```

Note: You can use the Insert function to delete parts of the edit control text by first selecting that part and then replacing it with an empty string.

The Pushbutton Control

The *pushbutton control* is, perhaps, psychologically the most powerful control (you never hear about the nuclear list box or the nuclear check box). In a sense, the pushbutton control represents the fundamental notion of a control—you click on the control and something happens. The rest of today's lesson focuses on the aspects of the class `TButton` that deal with the pushbutton controls.

NEW TERM There basically are two types of pushbutton controls: *default buttons* and *nondefault buttons.* Default buttons have slightly thicker edges than nondefault buttons. Pressing the Enter key is equivalent to clicking the default button in a dialog box. There can be only one default button in a dialog box. You can select a new default button by pressing the Tab key. This feature works only when the buttons are in a dialog box. If a nondialog box window owns a pushbutton control, it can only visually display a default button—the functionality is not supported.

The *TButton* Class

The `TButton` class, a descendant of `TControl`, does not declare any public member functions other than its constructors.

Syntax

The *Tbutton* Constructor

The declaration for the `TButton` constructor is

```
TButton(TWindow*        parent,
        int             id,
        const char far* text,
        int             X,
        int             Y,
        int             W,
        int             H,
        bool            isDefault = false,
        TModule*        module = 0 );
TButton(TWindow* parent, int resourceId, TModule* module = 0);
```

The first seven parameters to this function now should be relatively familiar to you, as they're identical to the ones in both the `TStatic` and `TEdit` controls. In fact, you'll find that most of these controls are descendants of the `TControl` class; the parameters virtually will be the same across the control classes. In this case, the difference is the addition of an `isDefault` parameter. This parameter specifies whether or not the button is default.

Example

```
pOk = new TButton(this, IDOK, "&OK", 10, 10, 50, 25, true);
pCancel = new TButton(this, IDCANCEL, "&Cancel", 70, 10, 50, 25);
```

Handling Button Messages

When you click a button, the control sends the BN_CLICKED notification message to its parent window. The parent window responds to this message by invoking a message response member function based on the ID of the button. If you have a button that was created with an ID of IDB_EXIT, for example, the message handler function is

```
// Other declarations
void HandleExitBtn();
// Other declarations

DEFINE_RESPONSE_TABLE1(TMyWindow, TWindow)
    // Other possible message mapping macros
    EV_BN_CLICKED(IDB_EXIT, HandleExitBtn),
    // Other possible message mapping macros
END_RESPONSE_TABLE;
```

This example shows that the message map macro EV_BN_CLICKED is used to map the IDB_EXIT notification message with the HandleExitBtn member function.

Manipulating Buttons

You can disable and enable a button by using the EnableWindow function, which is inherited from the TWindow ancestor. A disabled button has a faded gray caption and does not respond to mouse clicks or keyboard input. The TWindow::EnableWindow function enables you to enable or disable a button. The function accepts a single argument, a Boolean argument that specifies whether the button is enabled (when the argument is true) or disabled (when the argument is false). Sample calls to the EnableWindow member function are

```
pOk->EnableWindow(false);
pCalculate->EnableWindow(true);
```

You can query the enabled state of a button by using the Boolean IsWindowEnabled function, which takes no arguments. A sample call to IsWindowEnabled is

```
// Toggle the enabled state of a button
pButton->EnableWindow(!pButton->IsWindowEnabled());
```

You also can hide and show a button using the ShowWindow function. The function takes one argument, either the SW_HIDE constant to hide the button or the SW_SHOW constant to show the button. Other constant values are defined for this function, but the SW_HIDE and SW_SHOW are the only two that apply to pushbuttons. The Boolean IsWindowVisible function queries the visibility of a button. This function takes no arguments. A sample call to the ShowWindow and IsWindowVisible functions is

```
// Toggle the visibility of a button
pButton->ShowWindow(pButton->IsWindowVisible() ? SW_HIDE : SW_SHOW);
```

Mr. Calculator

Look at an application that uses static text, single-line edit controls, multiline edit controls, and pushbuttons—*Mr. Calculator*. This nontrivial application implements a floating-point calculator that uses edit controls rather than buttons. This type of interface is somewhat visually inferior to the typical button-populated calculator Windows applications. This interface, however, can support more mathematical functions without requiring the addition of the buttons for those extra functions. In Mr. Calculator, the calculator is made up of the following controls:

- Two edit controls for the first and second operands to accept integers, floating-point numbers, and the names of single-letter variables, `A` to `Z`
- One edit control for the operator supports the calculator's four basic math operations and the exponentiation (using a caret, `^`)
- One edit control displays the result of the math operation
- One edit control displays any error messages
- One multiline edit control that enables you to store a number in the Result edit control in one of 26 single-letter variables, `A` to `Z`. The multiline edit displays the current values stored in these variables and enables you to view and edit these numbers. You can use the vertical scroll bar to inspect the values in the different variables.
- Multiple static text controls serve to label the various edit controls. Of particular interest is the static control for the Error Message box. If you click the accompanying static text, the Error Message is cleared of any text.
- A menu has the single Exit option.
- A pushbutton with the caption "Calc" performs the operation specified in the Operator edit control, using the operands in the operand edit controls.
- A pushbutton with the caption "Store" stores the contents of the result edit control in the currently selected line of the multiline edit control.
- A pushbutton with the caption "Exit" exits the application.

13

The program supports the following special features for the Store button control:

- The Store pushbutton is disabled if the application attempts to execute an invalid operator. This feature illustrates an example of disabling a pushbutton when a certain condition arises (in this case, a specific calculation error).
- The Store pushbutton is enabled if you click the Error Message static text. The same button is enabled when you successfully execute a math operation.

The calculator application demonstrates the following tasks:

- Using single-line edit controls for simple input
- Using a multiline edit control to view and edit information
- Accessing and editing line-oriented text
- Simulating static text that responds to mouse clicks
- Using pushbuttons
- Disabling and enabling pushbuttons

Create the directory MRCALC as a subdirectory of \TCWIN45\TC21DAY and store all the project's files in the new directory. The project's .IDE file should contain the files MRCALC.CPP and MRCALC.RC.

First, compile and run the application to get a good sense for how the calculator application works. Experiment with typing different numeric operands and the supported operators and click the Calc button. Each time, the result appears in the Result box, overwriting the previous result. Try dividing a number by zero to experiment with the error handling features.

Using the single-letter variables is easy. All these variables are initialized with `0`. Therefore, the first step to using them is to store a nonzero value. Perform an operation and then click inside the Variables edit box. Select the first line that contains the variable `A`. Now click the Store button and watch the number in the Result box appear in the first line of the Variables edit box. The name of the variable and the colon and space characters that follow reappear with the new text line. Now replace the contents of the Operand1 edit box with the variable `A`, and then click the Calc button. The Result edit box displays the result of the latest operation.

Listing 13.1 shows the source code for the MRCALC.H header file. The header file declares the command constants for the menu item and the various controls. Listing 13.2 contains the script for the MRCALC.RC resource file. Listing 13.3 contains the source code for the MRCALC.CPP program file.

Listing 13.1. Source code for the MRCALC.H header file.

```
#define IDB_CALC     101
#define IDB_STORE    102
#define IDB_EXIT     103
#define IDE_OPERAND1 104
#define IDE_OPERATOR 105
#define IDE_OPERAND2 106
#define IDE_RESULT   107
#define IDE_ERRMSG   108
#define IDE_VARIABLE 109
```

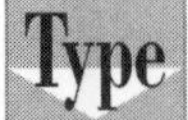

Listing 13.2. Script for the MRCALC.RC resource file.

```
#include <windows.h>
#include <owl\window.rh>

EXITMENU MENU LOADONCALL MOVEABLE PURE DISCARDABLE
BEGIN
   MENUITEM "E&xit", CM_EXIT
END
```

Listing 13.3. Source code for the MRCALC.CPP program file.

```
#include <ctype.h>
#include <math.h>
#include <stdio.h>
#include <owl\applicat.h>
#include <owl\button.h>
#include <owl\edit.h>
#include <owl\framewin.h>
#include <owl\static.h>
#include <owl\window.h>
#include <owl\window.rh>

#include "mrcalc.h"

class TCalcWindow : public TWindow
{
public:
   TCalcWindow(TWindow* parent = 0);
   ~TCalcWindow();

protected:
   virtual void SetupWindow();
   virtual void EvLButtonDown(uint modKeys, TPoint &point);

   void CmCalc();
   void CmStore();
   void CmExit();

private:
   TStatic  *ErrMsgLabel;
   TEdit    *Operand1, *Operator, *Operand2, *Result,
            *ErrMsg, *Variable;
   TButton  *Store;

   double get_number(TEdit* edit);
   double get_var(int line);
   void put_var(double val);

   DECLARE_RESPONSE_TABLE(TCalcWindow);
};
DEFINE_RESPONSE_TABLE1(TCalcWindow, TWindow)
   EV_WM_LBUTTONDOWN,
   EV_COMMAND(CM_EXIT, CmExit),
```

Listing 13.3. continued

```
   EV_BN_CLICKED(IDB_CALC, CmCalc),
   EV_BN_CLICKED(IDB_STORE, CmStore),
   EV_BN_CLICKED(IDB_EXIT, CmExit),
END_RESPONSE_TABLE;

TCalcWindow::TCalcWindow(TWindow* parent)
{
   Init(parent, 0, 0);

   int   wlblspacing = 40,
         hlblspacing = 5,
         wlbl = 100,
         hlbl = 20,
         wbox = 100,
         hbox = 30,
         wboxspacing = 40,
         hboxspacing = 40,
         wbtn = 80,
         hbtn = 30,
         wbtnspacing = 30;
   int   wlongbox = 4 * (wbox + wboxspacing);
   int   wvarbox = 2 * wbox,
         hvarbox = 3 * hbox;
   int   x0 = 20, y0 = 30;
   int   x, y;

   // First, create the labels for the edit text boxes.
   //
   x = x0;
   y = y0;
   new TStatic(this, -1, "Operand1", x, y, wlbl, hlbl);
   x += wlbl + wlblspacing;
   new TStatic(this, -1, "Operator", x, y, wlbl, hlbl);
   x += wlbl + wlblspacing;
   new TStatic(this, -1, "Operand2", x, y, wlbl, hlbl);
   x += wlbl + wlblspacing;
   new TStatic(this, -1, "Result", x, y, wlbl, hlbl);
   x += wlbl + wlblspacing;

   // Now create the edit text boxes
   //
   x = x0;
   y += hlbl + hlblspacing;
   if (NULL != (Operand1 = new TEdit(this, IDE_OPERAND1, "",
                                             x, y, wbox, hbox)))
      Operand1->Attr.Style |= ES_UPPERCASE;
   x += wbox + wboxspacing;
   if (NULL != (Operator = new TEdit(this, IDE_OPERATOR, "",
                                             x, y, wbox, hbox)))
      Operator->Attr.Style |= ES_UPPERCASE;
   x += wbox + wboxspacing;
   if (NULL != (Operand2 = new TEdit(this, IDE_OPERAND2, "",
                                             x, y, wbox, hbox)))
      Operand2->Attr.Style |= ES_UPPERCASE;
   x += wbox + wboxspacing;
   Result = new TEdit(this, IDE_RESULT, "", x, y, wbox, hbox);
   x += wbox + wboxspacing;
```

```
   // Now create the label and box for the error message
   //
   x = x0;
   y += hbox + hboxspacing;
   ErrMsgLabel = new TStatic( this, -1, "Error Message", x, y,
                              wlbl, hlbl );
   y += hlbl + hlblspacing;
   ErrMsg = new TEdit(this, IDE_ERRMSG, "", x, y, wlongbox, hbox);

   // Create the label and box for the single-letter
   // variable selection
   //
   y += hbox + hboxspacing;
   new TStatic(this, -1, "Variables", x, y, wlbl, hlbl);
   y += hlbl + hlblspacing;
   char str[6 * ('Z' - 'A' + 1) + 1];
   char *p = str;
   for (char ch = 'A'; ch <= 'Z'; ++ch)
      p += sprintf(p, "%c: 0\r\n", ch);
   Variable = new TEdit(this, IDE_VARIABLE, str, x, y,
                           wvarbox, hvarbox, 0, true );

   // Finally create some buttons
   //
   x += wvarbox + wbtnspacing;
   new TButton(this, IDB_CALC, "Calc", x, y, wbtn, hbtn);
   x += wbtn + wbtnspacing;
   Store = new TButton(this, IDB_STORE, "Store", x, y, wbtn, hbtn);
   x += wbtn + wbtnspacing;
   new TButton(this, IDB_EXIT, "Exit", x, y, wbtn, hbtn);
}

TCalcWindow::~TCalcWindow()
{
}

void TCalcWindow::SetupWindow()
{
   TWindow::SetupWindow();    // Initialize the visual element

   // Keep the users out of the destination areas.
   //
   if (Result)
      Result->SetReadOnly(true);
   if (ErrMsg)
      ErrMsg->SetReadOnly(true);
   if (Variable)
      Variable->SetReadOnly(true);
}

void TCalcWindow::EvLButtonDown(uint /*modKeys*/, TPoint& point)
{
   if (     ErrMsgLabel
        && (ErrMsgLabel->HWindow == ChildWindowFromPoint(point)) )
      {
      if (ErrMsg)
```

Listing 13.3. continued

```
            ErrMsg->Clear();
         if (Store)
            Store->EnableWindow(true);
         }
}

double TCalcWindow::get_number(TEdit *edit)
{
   double rslt;
   char *str;
   int size;

   if (edit)
      {
      str = new char[size = edit->GetWindowTextLength() + 1];
      if (str)
         {
         edit->GetWindowText(str, size);
         if (isalpha(str[0]))
            rslt = get_var(tolower(str[0]) - 'a');
         else
            rslt = atof(str);
         delete str;
         }
      }
   return rslt;
}

double TCalcWindow::get_var(int line)
{
   double rslt = 0;

   if (Variable)
      {
      int size = Variable->GetLineLength(line) + 1;
      char *str = new char[size];
      if (str)
         {
         Variable->GetLine(str, size, line);
         rslt = atof(str + 3);      // Don't want first 3 chars
         delete str;
         }
      }
   return rslt;
}

void TCalcWindow::put_var(double var)
{
   if (Variable)
      {
      uint start, end;
      Variable->GetSelection(start, end);
      if (start != end)
         Variable->SetSelection(start, start);
      int line = Variable->GetLineFromPos(-1);
      int size = Variable->GetLineLength(line) + 1;
      char *str = new char[size];
```

```
      if (str)
         {
         Variable->GetLine(str, size, line);
         sprintf(str, "%c: %g", str[0], var);
         start = Variable->GetLineIndex(-1);
         end = start + Variable->GetLineLength(-1);
         Variable->SetSelection(start, end);
         Variable->Insert(str);
         delete str;
         }
      }

}

void TCalcWindow::CmCalc()
{
   double x, y, z = 0;
   char  *str, *err = NULL;
   int   size;

   x = get_number(Operand1);
   y = get_number(Operand2);

   if (Operator)
      {
      str = new char[size = Operator->GetWindowTextLength() + 1];
      if (str)
         {
         Operator->GetWindowText(str, size);
         if (str[1] != '\0')
            err = "Invalid operator";
         else
            switch (str[0])
               {
               case '+':
                  z = x + y;
                  break;
               case '-':
                  z = x - y;
                  break;
               case '*':
                  z = x * y;
                  break;
               case '/':
                  if (y)
                     z = x / y;
                  else
                     err = "Division by zero error";
                  break;
               case '^':
                  if (x > 0)
                     z = exp(y * log(x));
                  else
                     err = "Can't raise power of negative numbers";
                  break;
               default:
                  err = "Invalid operator";
```

Listing 13.3. continued

```
                  break;
               }
            if (ErrMsg)
               if (!err)
                  ErrMsg->Clear();
               else
                  ErrMsg->SetWindowText(err);
            if (Store)
               Store->EnableWindow(!err);
            if (!err && Result)
               {
               char dest[81];
               sprintf(dest, "%g", z);
               Result->SetWindowText(dest);
               }
         delete str;
         }
      }
}

void TCalcWindow::CmStore()
{
   if (Result)
      {
      int size = Result->GetWindowTextLength() + 1;
      char *str = new char[size];
      if (str)
         {
         Result->GetWindowText(str, size);
         put_var(atof(str));
         delete str;
         }
      }
}

void TCalcWindow::CmExit()
{
   SendMessage(WM_CLOSE);
}

class TCalcApp : public TApplication
{
public:
   TCalcApp() : TApplication()
      { nCmdShow = SW_SHOWMAXIMIZED; }

   void InitMainWindow()
      {
      SetMainWindow(new TFrameWindow(  0,
                              "Mr. Calculator",
                              new TCalcWindow ));
      GetMainWindow()->AssignMenu("EXITMENU");
      }
};

int OwlMain(int, char *[])
```

```
327: {
328:     return TCalcApp().Run();
329: }
330:
```

Figure 13.1 shows a sample session with the Mr. Calculator program.

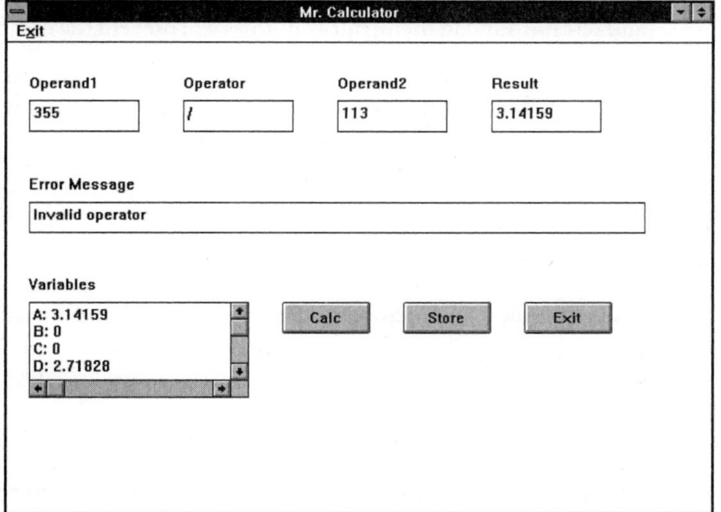

Figure 13.1.
A sample session with MRCALC.EXE.

The program in Listing 13.3 contains a number of data members in the `TCalcWindow` class, each of which is a pointer to a control class. These are the `TStatic`, `TEdit`, and `TButton` controls, declared on lines 29 through 32. In general, there is no real need to keep track of these controls because OWL will automatically take care of deleting these controls when their corresponding Windows elements are destroyed. If you have some need to access them during the duration of their existence, however, you will need a pointer in order to affect them.

Note that as the operand and operator edit boxes are created on lines 82 through 96, they are given the style of `ES_UPPERCASE`. This style results in automatically converting into uppercase the single-letter variable names that you type in these edit controls.

Usually, controls such as `TButton` and especially `TStatic` can be created without bothering to keep a pointer to them; a button will automatically send notifications to its parent and, because static text controls are usually used as labels, there rarely is a need to keep track of them. In this case, however, you need to keep track of the Store button so that you can enable and disable it according to error conditions. You also need to keep track of the Error Message label so that you can tell when the user has clicked it, at which point you need to clear the error message and re-enable the Store button.

In the constructor of `TCalcWindow` are a number of declarations between lines 52 and 57. These are used when placing the controls as they are created. The declarations define the various widths and heights of the controls as well as the space in between them. As the controls are created, the local variables `x` and `y` are updated to the location of the next control.

In the `SetupWindow` member function of `TCalcWindow` starting on line 37, the `Result`, `ErrMsg`, and `Variable` edit controls are set to read-only by calling the `TEdit::SetReadOnly` member function. This is done to prevent the user from modifying the parts of the screen that should be updated only by the program itself. The user can still place the caret in these edit controls, even select text and scroll around in them, but Windows will prevent the user from changing any of the contents.

On lines 110 through 121, the `Variable` edit box is created somewhat differently from the other edit boxes. First, an elaborate initializing string is made up for it. This string consists of 26 letters (`'A'` through `'Z'`), each followed by a colon, a space, the number `0`, and finally the characters `"\r\n"`. This makes up the format of the list box and later will be changed dynamically by the user clicking the Store button.

Secondly, the `Variable` edit box constructor receives two extra parameters on lines 120 through 121. The first of the two extra parameters, `0`, is the same as the default parameter that is used whenever the constructor is called without passing anything for that argument. The next parameter, however, is the one stating that you want a multiline edit control. This automatically sets the control to allowing for multiple lines, as well as adding the horizontal and vertical scroll bars.

The `EvLButtonDown` member function starting on line 151 performs a simple task. It checks whether the mouse click occurs in the rectangle occupied by the error message static text control. If this condition is true, then the function performs the following tasks:

- Uses the `ChildWindowFromPoint` function starting on line 154 to determine in which window the mouse was clicked, and then checks that against the window of `ErrMsgLabel`
- Clears the error message box by invoking the function `Clear` on line 157
- Enables the Store button by invoking the function `EnableWindow` on line 159

Because you will have two edit boxes from which you will want to get either a number or a value associated with a variable, it makes sense to have only one function that performs this action and is called for in each edit box. This is the purpose of the `get_number` private member function starting on line 163. Its single parameter is a pointer to a `TEdit` object. From this, the function obtains the text that is stored in that edit box on line 174. If the first character in that edit box is an alphabetic character (checked through the ANSI C function `isalpha` on line 175), then the private `get_var` function is called on line 176; otherwise, the contents are converted to a floating point number with the `atof` function on line 178.

The get_var function starting on line 185 is used to obtain the value associated with a specific variable in the Variable edit control. Given a line number, it gets the text from that line in the edit control, and then passes that line, skipping the first three characters (the variable letter, the colon, and the space), to the atof function for conversion to a floating point number.

The put_var function starting on line 203 changes a variable in the Variable edit box. It does so with the following steps:

1. Check for a selection in the Variable edit box on lines 208 and 209. If there is one, then you remove that selection and set the current insertion point to the beginning of the selection.
2. Using the GetLineFromPos function, you get the line of the insertion point on line 211.
3. After creating a string large enough to hold the line, you get the line and then change it to include the new value on lines 212 through 217.
4. By passing -1 to the GetLineIndex function on line 218, you obtain the character location of the start of the current line. Adding the length of the line, you get the start of the next line.
5. Using the SetSelection function on line 220, you select the current line. You then Insert the new string on line 221, replacing the current selection.

The CmCalc member function starting on line 228 responds to the notification message emitted by the Calc button. You told the window to have the function called by using the EV_BN_CLICKED macro during the TCalcWindow's response table declaration on line 43. The function performs the following tasks:

1. Obtains the two operands from the Operand1 and Operand2 edit boxes with the get_number private member function on lines 234 and 235
2. Copies the text in the Operator edit box into the local variable str on line 242
3. Determines and performs the requested operation by using a switch statement on lines 246 through 272, checking the first character of the string for the supported operators +, –, *, / and ^ (power)
4. If at any time an error is detected, the err local variable is set to a string describing the error, and at the end on line 273, if this variable is non-NULL, its value is placed in the Error Message edit box, and the Store button is disabled.

13

The CmStore member function, starting on line 291, stores the contents of the Result box in a single-letter variable. The function first obtains the string from the Result edit box by calling the GetWindowText function on line 299. Then, the function invokes the private member function put_var on line 300 to actually store the result string at the current insertion point in the Variables edit box.

The `CmExit` member function, starting on line 306, responds to the notification message of both the Exit button and the Exit menu item. It sends a `WM_CLOSE` message to the window, which effectively terminates the program.

Summary

Today's lesson looked at the static text, edit box, and pushbutton controls. Using these and other controls animates the Windows applications and provides a more consistent user interface. You learned about the following topics:

- You can create static text controls and manipulate their text at runtime.
- Single-line and multiline edit box controls enable you to type in and edit the text in the input dialog box.

Day 15 presents the grouped controls, the classes for group, check box, and radio controls. These controls are used to fine-tune the execution of a specified task, such as searching and replacing text in a text editor.

Q&A

Q How do I create a string for a multiline static text control?

A You build a multiline string, such as "This is\r\na multiline" (notice the embedded \r\n characters, which break the line) and pass it as the third argument to the `TStatic` class's constructor.

Q Why does program MRCALC.CPP use local variables such as `x` and `y` to specify the location of a control? Why not replace these variables with numeric constants?

A Using variables, such as `x` and `y`, enables you to specify the location of the controls relative to one another. This method enables you to shift controls very easily. By contrast, using numeric constants specifies the absolute values for the control locations. Shifting controls, in this case, means plugging in a new set of numbers.

Q What do .RC resource files compile into?

A The .RC resource files are compiled into .RES files. Also, note that the Resource Workshop is quite capable of saving your various dialog boxes and other resources in an .RES file as well as an .RC file. This precompiled file then could be included in your .IDE file instead of the .RC.

Workshop

The Workshop provides quiz questions to help you solidify your understanding of the material covered and exercises to provide you with experience in using what you've learned. Try to understand the quiz and exercise answers before continuing on to the next day's lesson. Answers are provided in Appendix A.

Quiz

1. True or false? The text for all static text controls is unchangeable.
2. True or false? The `SS_CENTER` style centers each line of a multiline static text control.
3. True or false? A static text control needs an accompanying pointer for access only when the program needs to set or query the text in the control.
4. True or false? Every edit control needs an accompanying pointer for access.
5. True or false? The API Windows function `EnableWindow` can disable any control.
6. True or false? The Windows messages emitted by a pushbutton can be mapped using the `EV_COMMAND` map.

Exercises

1. Experiment with the program MRCALC.CPP to add trigonometric functions, inverse trigonometric functions, hyperbolic functions, and inverse hyperbolic functions.
2. Experiment with a copy of the program MRCALC.CPP by changing values assigned to the constants that specify the size and spacing of the various controls.

WEEK 2

Dialog Boxes

Dialog boxes are special pop-up windows that contain controls serving to display information or to input data. Windows applications use dialog boxes to exchange information with the user. The nicest feature of dialog boxes is that they can be created with all their controls by using a screen painter (the resource workshop), and then accessed simply by loading them in from resources.

Today's lesson looks at the modal and modeless dialog boxes supported by Windows.

NEW TERM *Modal dialog boxes* require you to close them before you can proceed any further with the application because they are meant to perform a critical exchange of data. In fact, modal dialog boxes disable their parent windows while they have the focus. Modeless dialog boxes do not need to be closed to continue using the application. You need merely to click on another of the application's windows to continue.

Today you learn about the following topics:

- ☐ Constructing instances of the class `TDialog`
- ☐ Executing a modal dialog box
- ☐ Transferring control data
- ☐ Transferring data for modal dialog boxes
- ☐ Transferring data for modeless dialog boxes

Constructing Dialog Boxes

OWL declares the `TDialog` class to support both modeless and modal dialog boxes. The `TDialog` class, a descendant of `TWindow`, has a class constructor and a number of member functions, including the `Create` and `Execute` functions. The `TDialog` constructor is declared as follows:

```
TDialog(TWindow* parent, TResId resId, TModule* module = 0);
```

The `parent` parameter is a pointer to the parent window. The `resId` parameter describes the dialog box's resource name or ID. The `module` parameter, which normally is left out of calls to the constructor, can be used to specify different locations from which to load the resource (for example, loading from a separate DLL).

The `TResId` class is a method used by OWL to encapsulate the different ways that a resource can be named in an application's resources. For example, one could specify a dialog template as having either a number or a name. The useful `TResId` class has three overloaded constructors. The first one, the default constructor, takes no arguments and initializes the class to a `0` value. The other two constructors look like the following:

```
TResId(LPCSTR resString);
TResId(int resNum);
```

This means that you can easily create a `TResId` by simply passing the appropriate value for the constructor. Also, if you use it as a temporary object, you can have `TDialog` constructors that look something like this.

```
TDialog* errdlg = new TDialog(this, "ErrorDlg");
TDialog* newdlg = new TDialog(this, 101);
```

Note: Using resources to define dialog boxes and their controls enables you to define the location, dimensions, style, and caption of a control outside the Windows application source code. Thus, you can change the resource file, recompile it, and then incorporate it in the .EXE application file without recompiling the source file itself. This approach enables you to develop different resource versions with varying colors, styles, and even languages while maintaining a single copy of the application code. Furthermore, this approach does away with the need to write all that complicated code for creating and placing controls in the constructor of a `TWindow` class.

The Turbo C++ package includes the *Resource Workshop*, which enables you to create dialog boxes by drawing the controls in the dialog boxes. The Resource Workshop creates .RC resource files that then are bound in your Windows applications. If you are a novice Windows programmer, first learn about the .RC file and its script. Using the Resource Workshop is easy and intuitive. Knowing about the .RC resource script makes working with the output of the Resource Workshop even easier.

Creating Dialog Boxes

Typically, modal dialog boxes are created and removed more frequently than modeless dialog boxes and much more frequently than windows. Executing modal dialog boxes involves the following steps:

14

1. Create a dialog box object by using `TDialog` constructor.
2. Call the `Execute` member function, declared in the class `TDialog`, to display the dialog box. Typically, dialog boxes contain the OK and Cancel pushbuttons, with the OK button as the default button. The OK and Cancel buttons have the predefined IDs of `IDOK` and `IDCANCEL`, respectively. You can use pushbutton controls with different captions other than OK and Cancel; however, you still should use the `IDOK` and `IDCANCEL` with these renamed buttons. Using these IDs enable you to take advantage of the automatic response to `IDOK` and `IDCANCEL` provided by the `CmOk` and `CmCancel` member functions defined in the `TDialog` class. Clicking OK or pressing the Enter

key usually signals your acceptance of the current (that is, the default or edited) data in the dialog box. By contrast, clicking the Cancel button signals your dissatisfaction with the current data. Following is the declaration of the `Execute` function:

```
int Execute();
```

The function returns an integer that represents the outcome. This typically is the value of a pushbutton ID, such as `IDOK` and `IDCANCEL`.

3. Compare the result of the `Execute` function with `IDOK` (or, less frequently, `IDCANCEL`). The outcome of this comparison determines the steps to take. Such steps usually involve accessing data that you entered in the dialog box controls.

Creating modeless dialog boxes takes only a little more effort. First, they must be created on the heap with a call to `new`. Then its `Create` and `ShowWindow` member functions must be called, as in the following:

```
TDialog* pdlg = new TDialog(this, "My Dialog");
pdlg -> Create();
pdlg -> ShowWindow(SW_SHOW);
```

Unlike with modal dialog boxes, the modeless dialog object will not be deleted automatically when the dialog box is closed. Be sure to delete the object when you know the dialog box is gone. This *can* be done automatically, however, if you set the `wfDeleteOnClose` flag in the window with the following member-function call:

```
pdlg->SetFlag(wfDeleteOnClose);
```

Like the `TWindow` class, from which much of `TDialog`'s functionality is inherited, the `SetupWindow`, `CanClose`, and `Destroy` member functions support the execution of both modal and modeless dialog boxes. The `SetupWindow` member function serves to initialize the dialog box and its controls. The declaration of the `SetupWindow` function is as follows:

```
virtual void SetupWindow();
```

Typically, the `SetupWindow` function initializes the controls of the dialog box. This initialization usually involves copying data from buffers or data members.

The `CanClose` function is called whenever the user presses the OK button. Following is the declaration of the `CanClose` function:

```
virtual bool CanClose();
```

The `CanClose` acts to copy data from the dialog box controls to data members or buffers after deciding whether it's all right to close the dialog. This function returns either `true` or `false`, depending on whether the user is allowed to close the dialog box, given the data entered.

The `Destroy` member function handles the closing of the dialog box. Following is the declaration of the `Destroy`:

```
virtual void Destroy(int retValue = IDCANCEL);
```

The `Destroy` function serves to clean up before the dialog box is closed, which may involve closing data files, for example. Usually, the last statement in the `Destroy` member function definition is a call to the `Destroy` function of its parent class.

The next example is a simple OWL program that uses a dialog box defined in resource files. It also uses resource files to create alternate forms of the same dialog box; the first uses modern English and the second uses old English. The application is simple and is made up of an empty window with a single menu item, Exit. When you click the Exit menu item (or press the Alt+X keys), a dialog box appears and asks you whether you want to exit the application. The dialog box has a title, a message, and the two buttons (in fact, we purposely made it so that it resembles the dialog boxes spawned by the `MessageBox` function). The program alternates between the two versions of the dialog box. When you first click the Exit menu, you get the modern English version (with OK and Cancel buttons), shown in Figure 14.1. If you click the Cancel button and then click the Exit menu again, you get the old English version of the dialog box (with Yea and Nay buttons), shown in Figure 14.2. Every time you select the Cancel or Nay button and then click the Exit menu, you toggle between the two versions of the dialog box. To exit the application, click the OK or Yea button, depending on the current dialog box version.

Listing 14.1 shows the DIALOG1.RC resource file. Listing 14.2 shows the source code for the DIALOG1.CPP program.

Type

Listing 14.1. Script for the DIALOG1.RC resource file.

```
#include <windows.h>
#include <owl\window.rh>

EXITMENU MENU LOADONCALL MOVEABLE PURE DISCARDABLE
BEGIN
  MENUITEM "E&xit", CM_EXIT
END

ModernEnglish DIALOG DISCARDABLE LOADONCALL PURE MOVEABLE 20, 50, 200, 100
STYLE WS_POP-UP ¦ DS_MODALFRAME
CAPTION "Message"
BEGIN
   CTEXT "Exit the application?", -1, 10, 10, 170, 15
   DEFPUSHBUTTON "OK", IDOK, 20, 50, 70, 15, WS_VISIBLE ¦ WS_TABSTOP
   PUSHBUTTON "Cancel", IDCANCEL, 110, 50, 70, 15, WS_VISIBLE ¦ WS_TABSTOP
END

OldeEnglish DIALOG DISCARDABLE LOADONCALL PURE MOVEABLE 20, 50, 200, 100
STYLE WS_POP-UP ¦ DS_MODALFRAME
CAPTION "Message"
BEGIN
   CTEXT "Leavest thou now?", -1, 10, 10, 170, 15
   DEFPUSHBUTTON "Yea", IDOK, 20, 50, 70, 15, WS_VISIBLE ¦  WS_TABSTOP
   PUSHBUTTON "Nay", IDCANCEL, 110, 50, 70, 15, WS_VISIBLE ¦  WS_TABSTOP
END
```

Listing 14.2. Source code for the DIALOG1.CPP program file.

```
#include <windows.h>
#include <owl\applicat.h>
#include <owl\dialog.h>
#include <owl\framewin.h>
#include <owl\window.h>
#include <owl\window.rh>

class TMyWindow : public TWindow
{
public:
   TMyWindow(TWindow* parent = 0);

   virtual bool CanClose();

protected:
   void CmExit();

   DECLARE_RESPONSE_TABLE(TMyWindow);
};
DEFINE_RESPONSE_TABLE1(TMyWindow, TWindow)
   EV_COMMAND(CM_EXIT, CmExit),
END_RESPONSE_TABLE;

TMyWindow::TMyWindow(TWindow* parent)
   : TWindow(parent)
{
}

bool TMyWindow::CanClose()
{
   static bool bFlag = false;

   bFlag = !bFlag;
   if (bFlag)
      return TDialog(this, "ModernEnglish").Execute() == IDOK;
   else
      return TDialog(this, "OldeEnglish").Execute() == IDOK;
}

void TMyWindow::CmExit()
{
   SendMessage(WM_CLOSE);
}

class TDialogApp : public TApplication
{
public:
   TDialogApp() : TApplication()
      { nCmdShow = SW_SHOWMAXIMIZED; }

```

```
    void InitMainWindow()
      {
      SetMainWindow(new TFrameWindow(  0,
                           "Simple Dialog Box Tester Application",
                           new TMyWindow ));
      GetMainWindow()->AssignMenu("EXITMENU");
      }
};

int OwlMain(int, char *[])
{
    return TDialogApp().Run();
}
```

Figure 14.1 shows a sample session.

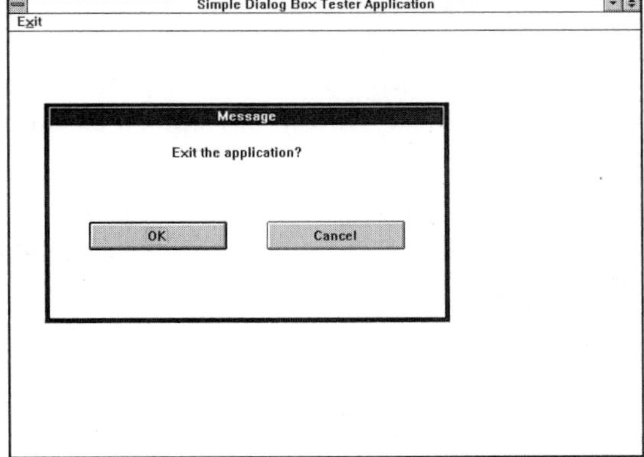

Figure 14.1.
A sample session with the DIALOG1.EXE application showing the dialog box with modern English wording.

Listing 14.1 shows the script for the DIALOG1.RC resource file, which defines the following resources:

- The menu resource, `EXITMENU`, which displays a single menu with the single item Exit
- The dialog box resource starting on line 9, `ModernEnglish`, which has a defined style, caption, and list of child controls. The specified style indicates that the dialog box is a modal pop-up child window. The caption specified on line 11 is the string `Message`. The dialog box contains three controls: a centered static text (for the dialog box message), a default OK pushbutton, and an ordinary Cancel button. The OK button has the resource ID of the predefined `IDOK` constant, and the Cancel button has the resource ID of the predefined `IDCANCEL` constant.

Figure 14.2 shows a sample session.

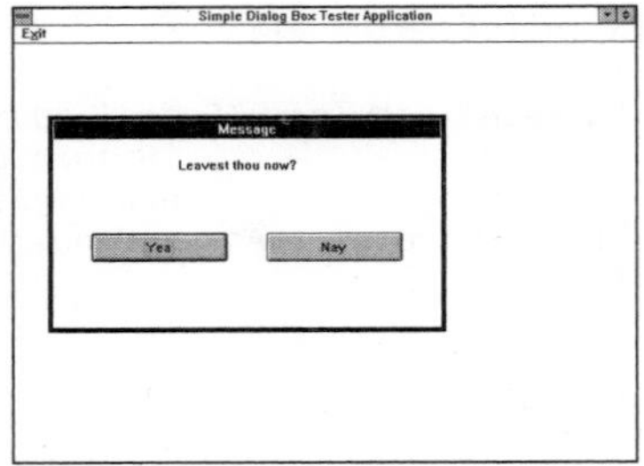

Figure 14.2.
A sample session with the DIALOG1.EXE application showing the dialog box with the old English wording.

- The dialog box resource starting on line 18, `OldeEnglish`, which is similar to the `ModernEnglish` dialog box resource, except that it uses old English wording. The Yea button has the resource ID of the predefined `IDOK` constant. The Nay button has the resource ID of the predefined `IDCANCEL` constant. These buttons are examples of exit buttons with atypical captions.

The `CTEXT` keyword specifies centered text. The `DEFPUSHBUTTON` keyword enables you to define any control and requires the caption, ID, location, dimensions, and control style of the control. The `PUSHBUTTON` definition is identical to the `DEFPUSHBUTTON` keyword's definition, but it describes an ordinary button instead of a default pushbutton.

Until now, you have been creating resources by manually creating the .RC file. When making dialog boxes, it is far easier to use the Resource Workshop. This provides an easy interface by which dialog boxes can be painted on-screen exactly the way you want them to appear when your application is run.

Listing 14.2 shows the source code for the DIALOG1.CPP program file. The source code declares two classes: an application class starting on line 45 and a window class starting on line 8. The application uses the standard `TDialog` class; it does not derive a specialized descendant, because no additional dialog box functionality is required.

The most relevant member function is `CanClose` starting on line 29, which responds to the user's request to close the window (triggered by the `CmExit` function on line 40, which in turn is triggered by the Exit menu choice). The function uses the Boolean static local variable, `bFlag`, to toggle between the two dialog box resources `ModernEnglish` and `OldeEnglish`. The modern English dialog box is invoked in the following statement:

```
return TDialog(this, "ModernEnglish").Execute() == IDOK;
```

The dialog box object is executed using the `Execute` function, disabling the parent window until you click either pushbutton control. The value returned by the `Execute` member function is compared with the `IDOK` constant, and the result is returned to the caller to let it know what the user selected, and whether to close the application window.

The instance of the old English version of the dialog box is similarly created, as shown in the following statement:

```
return TDialog(this, "OldeEnglish").Execute() == IDOK;
```

Connecting OWL Objects with Windows Controls

Until now, the constructors for the various controls you have learned have had the same general look of the constructor of the TControl class from which they are descendants.

```
TControl( TWindow* parent,
          int id,
          const char far* title,
          int x,
          int y,
          int w,
          int h,
          TModule* module = 0 );
```

Occasionally, there have been additional parameters after the h and before the module parameters, as the various controls needed. These all assume that the controls needed to be created from scratch, including their positions in their parent window.

When creating a dialog box from a resource file, however, these controls will be created automatically from the resource script at the same time as the dialog box. In order to have access to the controls from an OWL object, there is a second constructor for each control class that enables you to create an object that has a direct correspondence with the actual Windows control. They're all based on the following constructor for the TControl class.

```
TControl(TWindow* parent, int resourceId, TModule* module = 0);
```

The following are the constructors for creating the various controls that have already been introduced:

```
TStatic( TWindow* parent, int resourceId, uint textLen = 0,
         TModule* module = 0);
TEdit( TWindow* parent, int resourceId, uint textLen = 0,
       TModule* module = 0 );
TButton(TWindow* parent, int resourceId, TModule* module = 0);
```

In addition, there are a number of other controls that will be introduced formally in the next few days. Since I am assuming you are at least marginally familiar with the controls themselves, I will introduce their constructors here so that you can easily create them in your dialog boxes.

```
TCheckBox( TWindow* parent, int resourceId, TGroupBox* group = 0,
           TModule* module = 0 );
TRadioButton( TWindow* parent, int resourceId, TGroupBox* group = 0,
              TModule* module = 0 );
TGroupBox(TWindow* parent, int resourceId, TModule* module = 0);
TListBox(TWindow* parent, int resourceId, TModule* module = 0);
TComboBox( TWindow* parent, int resourceId, uint textLen = 0,
           TModule* module = 0 );
TScrollBar(TWindow* parent, int resourceId, TModule* module = 0);
```

The control objects, as with the full versions, should be created in a dialog's constructor. The following is an example of creating an OWL object to interface with a window's Cancel button:

```
cancel = new TButton(this, IDCANCEL);
```

Transferring Control Data

Dialog boxes serve mainly as pop-up windows to request input from the application user. This input often includes a variety of settings that use radio buttons, check boxes, and edit boxes. Because dialog boxes are frequently created, it makes sense to preserve the latest values in the dialog's controls for the next time it appears. The Search and Replace dialog boxes that are found in many Windows editors are typical examples. These dialog boxes remember the settings of all or some of their controls from the last time the dialog box was executed. You also can use the transfer mechanism as an easy way to set and retrieve data in the dialog box for simple initialization and retrieval purposes.

To implement this feature in dialog boxes, you need a data transfer mechanism between the dialog box and a buffer. This buffer usually is a data member of the parent window. Therefore, the first step in supporting data transfer is to define a transfer buffer type. The buffer declares the data fields to buffer the controls that transfer their data. These controls typically include the edit box, list box, combo box, scroll bar, check box, and radio button. The static text, group box, and pushbutton controls usually have no data to transfer and, therefore, do not enter in the declaration of the data transfer buffer type because OWL has them disabled by default. Following is a sample data buffer type that includes a single instance of each allowable control:

```
struct TAppTransferBuffer
{
   char EditBox[MaxEditLen];
   TListBoxData ListBoxData;
   TComboBoxData ComboBoxData;
   TScrollBarData ScrollBarData;
   uint CheckBox;
   uint RadioButton;
};
```

The buffer structure needs only to include the controls that actually transfer data. You do not need to declare the fields of the buffer structure in any particular order, so long as the controls they match are created in the same order. This sample buffer type includes three special classes that transfer data between dialog boxes and list boxes, combo boxes, and scroll bars. You will see more about these classes later in this section.

Look at the various members of the data transfer buffer type.

- The `EditBox` member assists in moving data between the edit control and the data buffer. The data member defines a character array that should be equal to or greater than the number of characters in the edit control.
- The `ListBoxData` member helps to transfer data between a list box control and the data buffer. The `ListBoxData` is an instance of the `TListBoxData` class that OWL provides for keeping track of the contents of a list box, including any selections.

- The `ComboBoxData` member helps to move data between a combo box control and the data buffer. The `ComboBoxData` is an instance of the `TComboBoxData` class. This, too, is provided by OWL to keep track of the contents and state of a combo box.
- The `ScrollBarData` member is an instance of the `TScrollBarData` class that assists in transferring data between a scroll bar control and the data buffer.
- The `CheckBox` member stores the current check state of a check box in a `uint` type.
- The `RadioButton` member stores the current check state of a radio button in a `uint` type.

Data Transfer for Modal Dialog Boxes

The next application is a simple example of transferring data between the controls of a modal dialog box and a buffer. It creates a typical dialog box that is used in replacing characters in a text editor. The dialog box contains the following controls:

- Find edit box
- Replace edit box
- Scope group box that contains the Global and Selected Text radio button controls
- Case-Sensitive check box
- The Whole Word check box
- The OK pushbutton control
- The Cancel pushbutton control

The application has a main menu with the Exit and Dialog menu items. To invoke the dialog box, click the Dialog menu item or press Alt+D. When you invoke the dialog box for the first time, the controls have the following initial values and states:

- The Find edit box contains the string DOS.
- The Replace edit box has the string Windows.
- The Global radio button is checked.
- The Case-Sensitive check box is checked.
- The Whole Word check box is checked.

Type new strings in the edit box and alter the check states of the radio buttons and check boxes. Now, click the OK button (or press Alt+O) to close the dialog box. Invoke the Dialog menu item again to pop up the dialog box. Notice that the controls of the dialog box have the same values and states as when you last closed the dialog box.

Listing 14.3 shows the source code for the DIALOG2.H header file. Listing 14.4 contains the script for the DIALOG2.RC resource file. Listing 14.5 shows the source code for the DIALOG2.CPP program file.

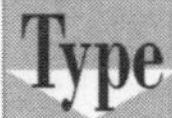

Listing 14.3. Source code for the DIALOG2.H header file.

```
#define CM_DIALOG (WM_USER + 100)

#define IDE_FIND        101
#define IDE_REPLACE     102
#define IDR_GLOBAL      103
#define IDR_SELTEXT     104
#define IDC_CASE        105
#define IDC_WHOLEWORD   106
```

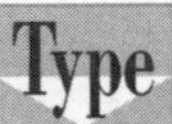

Listing 14.4. Script for the DIALOG2.RC resource file.

```
#include <windows.h>
#include <owl\window.rh>
#include "dialog2.h"

Search DIALOG DISCARDABLE LOADONCALL PURE MOVEABLE 10, 10, 200, 150
STYLE DS_MODALFRAME ¦ WS_POP-UP ¦ WS_VISIBLE ¦ WS_CAPTION ¦
  WS_SYSMENU
CAPTION "Controls Demo"
BEGIN
  LTEXT "Find", -1, 20, 10, 100, 15, NOT WS_GROUP
   EDITTEXT IDE_FIND, 20, 25, 100, 15
   LTEXT "Replace", -1, 20, 45, 100, 15, NOT WS_GROUP
   EDITTEXT IDE_REPLACE, 20, 60, 100, 15
   GROUPBOX " Scope ", -1, 20, 80, 90, 50, BS_GROUPBOX
   RADIOBUTTON "Global", IDR_GLOBAL, 30, 90, 50, 15,
      BS_AUTORADIOBUTTON
   RADIOBUTTON "Selected Text", IDR_SELTEXT, 30, 105, 60, 15,
       BS_AUTORADIOBUTTON
   CHECKBOX "Case Sensitive", IDC_CASE, 20, 130, 80, 15,
      BS_AUTOCHECKBOX ¦
       WS_TABSTOP
   CHECKBOX "Whole Word", IDC_WHOLEWORD, 100, 130, 80, 15,
      BS_AUTOCHECKBOX
       ¦ WS_TABSTOP
   DEFPUSHBUTTON "&OK", IDOK, 120, 90, 30, 20
   PUSHBUTTON "&Cancel", IDCANCEL, 160, 90, 30, 20
END

MainMenu MENU LOADONCALL MOVEABLE PURE DISCARDABLE
BEGIN
   MENUITEM "E&xit", CM_EXIT
   MENUITEM "&Dialog", CM_DIALOG
END
```

Listing 14.5. Source code for the DIALOG2.CPP program file.

```
#include <cstring.h>
#include <windows.h>
#include <owl\applicat.h>
```

```
#include <owl\checkbox.h>
#include <owl\dialog.h>
#include <owl\edit.h>
#include <owl\framewin.h>
#include <owl\radiobut.h>
#include <owl\window.h>
#include <owl\window.rh>

#include "dialog2.h"

const MaxEditLen = 30;

struct TTransferBuffer
{
   char find[MaxEditLen];
   char replace[MaxEditLen];
   uint global, seltext, csensitive, wholeword;
};

class TSearchDialog : public TDialog
{
public:
   TSearchDialog( TWindow* parent,
                  TTransferBuffer* xfer,
                  TModule* module = 0);

};

TSearchDialog::TSearchDialog( TWindow* parent,
                              TTransferBuffer* xfer,
                              TModule* module)
   : TDialog(parent, "Search", module)
{
   new TEdit(this, IDE_FIND, MaxEditLen);
   new TEdit(this, IDE_REPLACE, MaxEditLen);
   new TRadioButton(this, IDR_GLOBAL);
   new TRadioButton(this, IDR_SELTEXT);
   new TCheckBox(this, IDC_CASE);
   new TCheckBox(this, IDC_WHOLEWORD);
   SetTransferBuffer(xfer);
}

class TMyWindow : public TWindow
{
public:
   TMyWindow(TWindow* parent = 0);

protected:
   void CmExit();
   void CmDialog();

private:
   TTransferBuffer xfer;

   DECLARE_RESPONSE_TABLE(TMyWindow);
};
DEFINE_RESPONSE_TABLE1(TMyWindow, TWindow)
```

Listing 14.5. continued

```
   EV_COMMAND(CM_EXIT, CmExit),
   EV_COMMAND(CM_DIALOG, CmDialog),
END_RESPONSE_TABLE;

TMyWindow::TMyWindow(TWindow* parent)
   : TWindow(parent)
{
   memset(&xfer, 0, sizeof(xfer));
   lstrcpy(xfer.find, "DOS");
   lstrcpy(xfer.replace, "Replace");
   xfer.global = BF_CHECKED;
   xfer.csensitive = BF_CHECKED;
   xfer.wholeword = BF_CHECKED;
}

void TMyWindow::CmExit()
{
   SendMessage(WM_CLOSE);
}

void TMyWindow::CmDialog()
{
   if (TSearchDialog(this, &xfer).Execute() == IDOK)
     {
      string msg("Find String: ");
      msg += xfer.find;
      msg += "\n\nReplace String: ";
      msg += xfer.replace;
      MessageBox(msg.c_str(), "Dialog Box Data");
      }
 }

 class TDialogApp : public TApplication
 {
 public:
    TDialogApp() : TApplication()
       { nCmdShow = SW_SHOWMAXIMIZED; }

    void InitMainWindow()
       {
       SetMainWindow(new TFrameWindow(  0,
                             "Modal Dialog Box Data Transfer Tester",
                             new TMyWindow ));
       GetMainWindow()->AssignMenu("MainMenu");
       }
};

int OwlMain(int, char *[])
{
   return TDialogApp().Run();
}
```

Figure 14.3 shows a sample session with the DIALOG2.EXE application.

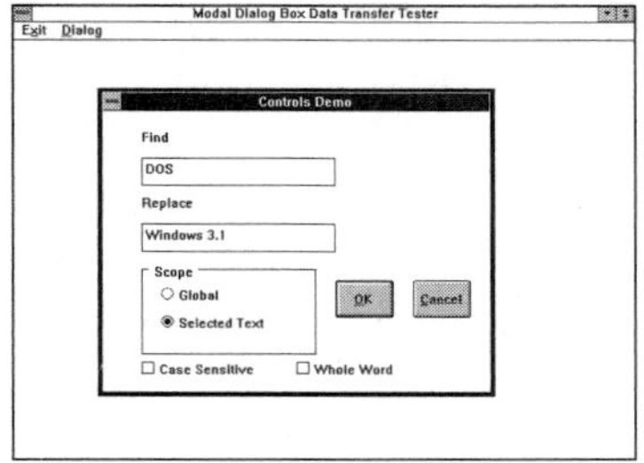

Figure 14.3.
A sample session with the DIALOG2.EXE application.

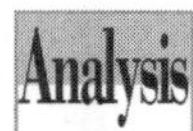

Listing 14.4 contains the script for the DIALOG2.RC resource file. This file defines the resources for the menu and the dialog box, including its controls. In the dialog box resource definition on lines 21 and 22, the OK and Cancel pushbuttons have the predefined `IDOK` and `IDCANCEL` IDs, respectively.

Listing 14.5 shows the source code for the DIALOG2.CPP program file. The program declares the data transfer type `TTransferBuffer` starting on line 16 and includes members for the edit boxes, radio buttons, and check boxes.

Starting on line 23, the application declares the `TSearchDialog` class as a descendant of the `TDialog` class. Notice that it doesn't have any member data, and the only function declared is its constructor. This constructor starts on line 32 and, in turn, does nothing more than create some OWL interface objects to be associated with the various controls created from the dialog resource. The constructor then makes a call to the `SetTransferBuffer` function on line 43, passing the `xfer` parameter along. OWL takes over from here and performs automatically all the transfers between `xfer` and the actual controls.

Starting on line 43, the `TMyWindow` class declares its constructor, two functions to respond to the menu, and a data member of type `TTransferBuffer`. This data member is initialized in the constructor, first with a call to the `memset` function on line 68. This call fills the `xfer` data member with zeros. We recommend that you systematically call the `memset` function to perform a basic initialization of buffers and structures before assigning specific values to them. Then the `xfer`'s data members are set to some initial values. Another way to ensure an empty structure is to provide it with a default constructor that clears all the data members.

14

Starting on line 81, the `CmDialog` function, which responds to the Dialog menu item, creates a modal dialog of type `TSearchDialog` on line 83, passing the `xfer` data member as a parameter. If the user clicks the OK button to exit this dialog box, it will return `IDOK`, and the `CmDialog` function then will build and display a message string that reflects the current Find and Replace text on lines 85 through 89.

Transferring Data for Modeless Dialog Boxes

The method of transferring data from modeless dialog boxes almost is the same as that used for modal dialog boxes. The main difference is that the mechanism that automatically transfers the data between the controls, and the transfer buffer is only called when the dialog window is modal. The programmer needs to make the call, explicitly in the case of a modeless dialog box. This can be done by overriding the `CloseWindow` member function in the dialog box's descendant class.

```
void TMyDialog::CloseWindow(int retValue)
{
   TransferData(tdGetData);
   TDialog::CloseWindow(retValue);
}
```

At this point, all the control data will be transferred to the buffer that was sent to the `SetTransferBuffer` in the dialog box's constructor.

Another possible action might be to have a Send button in the dialog box, with a response function that looks similar to the following:

```
void TMyDialog::CmSend()
{
   TransferData(tdGetData);
   Parent->HandleMessage(WM_COMMAND, IDB_SEND);
}
```

Then, in the dialog box's parent's window class, add a member function to handle the Send button in the same way you did for the dialog class. This function will be called automatically when the dialog box simulates the press of the Send button via the call to its parent's `HandleMessage` function.

Summary

Today's lesson presented you with powerful dialog boxes that serve as input tools. You learned about the following topics:

- ☐ You can construct instances of class `TDialog` to create modeless or modal dialog boxes.
- ☐ You can construct instances of the various control classes that give access to the controls created automatically from the dialog resource.
- ☐ Modal dialog boxes are executed with the `Execute` member function.
- ☐ The basics of transferring control data include declaring the data transfer buffer type, declaring the buffer, creating the controls in a sequence that matches their buffers, and establishing the buffer link with the `SetTransferBuffer` member function.
- ☐ The first step in supporting data transfer is to define a transfer buffer type. You can transfer data for modal dialog boxes and modeless dialog boxes.

Q&A

Q Does OWL support specialized dialog boxes?

A Yes. OWL has a set of classes that implement dialog boxes for selecting files, selecting colors, selecting fonts, printing, and searching/replacing text. The classes that model these dialog boxes are all descendants of the class `TDialog` and display the common dialog boxes.

Q Is the data transfer buffer necessary for modeless dialog boxes?

A Not always. You can have an application that pops up multiple modeless dialog boxes and have them communicate with each other directly, without the need of a data transfer buffer.

Workshop

The Workshop provides quiz questions to help you solidify your understanding of the material covered and exercises to provide you with experience in using what you've learned. Try to understand the quiz and exercise answers before continuing on to the next day's lesson. Answers are provided in Appendix A.

Quiz

1. True or false? You must compile all the .RC files into .RES files before or during the creation of the application.
2. True or false? The OK and Cancel buttons in a dialog box are optional.
3. True or false? You can create a dialog box with buttons labeled Yes and No.
4. True or false? Nested dialog boxes are not allowed by Windows.
5. True or false? Dialog boxes must always have a nondialog window parent.

Exercises

1. Create a version of the MrCalc application (from Day 13) that uses a dialog box as a stand-alone window.
2. Use the Resource Workshop to create the dialog box resource for the DIALOG2 program.

WEEK 2 IN REVIEW

8 9 10 11 12 13 14

As you end the second week of learning to program with Turbo C++ 4.5, look at the Turbo Blocks example provided with the package. This is a Tetris clone, and it can be found in the TCWIN45\EXAMPLES\OWL\GAMES\BLOCKS directory. The file of most importance, the one with all the C++ source code, is BLOCKS.CPP. Accompanying this example also is a BLOCKS.RC file, which contains the program's menu, an About dialog box, and the program's icon. To run this program, open the BLOCKS.IDE file with Turbo C++. You'll be able to see the files that make up the project, and you'll be able to build and run the application.

One of the first items in the file is the declaration and definition of the `TBlock` structure. Notice that, although this is declared as a `struct`, it includes a member function. You'll remember from Day 8 that structures are really just classes, except a structure's member starts out with the `public` default, while classes start out as `private`. The `TBlock` structure declares two items of member data, `size` and `elements`. The first of these two is an indicator of just how large the block is, and the second holds an array of characters that are used to define the actual shape of the block. The `rotate` member function is used to rotate the shape 90 degrees to the left. Note that four rotations will bring the block back to its initial state, so there's no real need for a function that will rotate to the right: just rotate it to the left three times.

Immediately following the rotate member function is the declaration of the global variable `blocks`. This holds the definition of all the blocks that will be used in the game. There also are the global variables `pen` and `brush`, which will be used to draw the blocks in the window. We'll get to those in a bit. Notice, however, that there is one more entry in each of `pen` and `brush` than there is in `blocks`. Next is the enumeration GameState, which provides values for the different states in which the game can be at any one time: an idle state (no game running), a block dropping (game in progress), paused (the user needs a break), and when lines are flashing or being removed.

Now we start to get into the meat of the program with the `TBlocksWindow` class. This class is a descendant of `TWindow`, and so inherits all the functionality thereof. The first members of the new class are data items, each of which is labeled quite well, so I'll skip their descriptions here, and instead mention them as they're used.

An interesting member function is `EvEraseBkgnd`. All it does is return `true`, but that has a lot of significance in the Windows world. Normally, when Windows goes to redraw a window (just before sending the `WM_PAINT` message, which triggers the OWL `Paint` member function), it sends the `WM_ERASEBKGND` message. The default response to this message is to completely erase the background of the window. This is normally a "good thing," but when you're trying to do animation, you don't want the flicker this action creates; the window would briefly clear before being redrawn. So, in order to prevent Windows from performing its default action, you return `true`, thus keeping the window's painting all to yourself.

You'll notice that the `SetupWindow` is rather simple, in that it merely calls the base class's version (a requirement) then proceeds to set up a timer. Timers are discussed more completely on Day 17, but suffice it to say that this call sets up a Windows timer that will call us back every hundredth of a second with a message that triggers the `EvTimer` member function. The timer is destroyed by the `CleanupWindow` member function, which is called when the window is closed.

The `PauseEnabler` member function is called whenever the user tries to use the program's menu. This function allows the program to enable or change the text of the menu item for which it's associated. This association occurs in the response table definition on the line that reads `EV_COMMAND_ENABLE(CM_GAMEPAUSE, PauseEnabler)`. The `PauseEnabler` function disables the menu item if there's no game in progress, and it sets the text of the menu item to reflect whether the user can pause or resume the game in progress.

The constructor simply resets the size of the window to the size of the board before clearing the board and initializing various member data. The `RemoveLines` member function is sort of interesting to look at. It initializes one counter to the bottom line of the board, then checks each line to see if it's full of blocks. If so, the function removes that line by copying the contents of all the lines above down by one line, and then clears the top. There's no need to actually remove the full line because the copy operation will cover it up. Note that the `while` loop doesn't iterate to the previous line if there was a copy operation; if it did, it might skip a full line that had just been copied from its old location down to the current line. Instead, the next iteration of the loop looks at the very same line.

The `NewGame` member function is a little less interesting. It simply clears the board before creating a new falling block at random. It then sets the game state to that of one in progress and invalidates the window. This last action tells Windows that the window needs to be repainted, and the `Paint` function will get called in short order. Similarly uninteresting is the `ClearBoard` member function. It just goes through all the blocks and sets them to `0` while setting the invisible borders to `-1` (the latter action is done so it will be easy to tell when a falling block hits it).

The `EvTimer` function, which is called intermittently by Windows, performs different actions depending on the current game state. If no game is going on, or the if current game is paused, or if the game is in the process of removing lines, the function does nothing. If, however, the game is in progress and a block is dropping, then the timer function must act to animate the block. First it increments the `dropCount` data member, which is used to further subdivide the timer intervals. If either `dropCount` has reached its maximum value or if the user has asked to drop the current block (signified by the `dropping` data member), then the function needs to move the block down a line. First, `dropCount` is reset for the next run-through with the timer. Then, the block's location is moved down a line by incrementing its `y` component. If the `HitTest` function returns `true`, then it signifies that the block has hit something and must be placed onto the board. This is done with the `PlaceBlock` function. After that, you make sure to remove lines and start a new block falling. Finally, the window is invalidated to make sure everything gets redrawn properly.

The `EvKeyUp` and `EvKeyDown` functions handle keypresses. Rather than wait for the standard keypress that results in an `EvChar` message, you want to watch as the keys are actually pressed and held down, and then watch them be released. This allows the player to press a key and have it affect the game for the duration of time it is pressed. The various keys do some rather obvious things, such as move the block over to the left or right, if possible, or rotate the block. With the matching sections of both `EvKeyDown` and `EvKeyUp`, the `dropping` data member is set to `true` as long as the down arrow key is pressed, and then is reset to `false` the moment it's released.

The `HitTest` function actually is quite simple. It first sets up a pair of nested loops that runs through the contents of the current block, and then performs a series of three `if` statements. The first statement checks to make sure that the part block it's about to check actually is in range on the board; because pieces don't always take up the whole space of the block, there could be parts that extend off the board. The second test is to see if something already is on the board in the selected location. If so, then you check the block itself to see if there's a piece of it there as well. If all of these conditions are `true`, then the function returns that condition.

The `NewBlock` function sets the `currentBlock` according to the `blockType` parameter and the current `color` accordingly. Because the player could be about to lose, it also checks to see if the new block is hitting something at the top of the screen. If so, it then places the block and ends the game. `PlaceBlock` simply copies the contents of the current block to the board and then removes any full lines that might exist.

`DrawBlock` actually paints a block on-screen. First it selects a brush and pen of the appropriate color into the supplied device context. For objects such as rectangles (which is what this function draws), you use the pen to draw the outline, and use the brush to fill that in. This makes it quite easy to create those nice-looking segmented squares of which each block is made. After selecting the drawing objects, a pair of nested loops goes through all the elements of the block and puts a rectangle on the DC for each occupied element.

Finally you get to the `Paint` function—the workhorse function that is responsible for all the drawing on the window. First it creates a memory DC and then selects a new bitmap in it. The reasoning behind this is to minimize any flicker on-screen and make the drawing as smooth as possible. If you were to draw to the screen DC directly, the user might be able to see the drawing process as it happened. By drawing to the memory DC instead, and then copying that memory DC directly to the screen, you make the whole screen-drawing process happen in one quick step.

Next, `Paint` takes care of the case in which the game is paused. If you allowed users to pause the game and study the screen, the game would become a little easier, and consequently less fair. So, in this case, the DC is cleared with a call to `FillRect` and then the string `" * * P A U S E D * * "` is written in the middle. The resulting DC is copied to the screen with the `BitBlt` function and `Paint` returns.

If the game isn't paused, `Paint` goes through the process of drawing the board. It draws a square for each position on the board, doing so in the color that had been assigned to it either during initialization or in the `PlaceBlock` function. Finally, if the game is in progress, it calls `DrawBlock` to show the currently falling block. When all this is done, `Paint` copies the memory DC to the screen.

The rest of the program should look quite familiar to you by now. A `TApplication` descendant is defined that creates a frame window with our specially defined window as its client. This `TBlocksApp` object then is instantiated in the `OwlMain` function and run.

WEEK 3 AT A GLANCE

15

16

17

18

19

20

21

This last week presents topics that cover more aspects of creating Windows applications using various classes in the OWL library. You will learn about more complicated Windows controls, including check boxes, radio buttons, list boxes, combo boxes, and scroll bars. You also will learn how to include Visual Basic Controls (VBXs) in your application. These controls make up most of the visual controls that are common to Windows applications. You then will be introduced to MDI windows and OLE 2 applications.

Along with this basic information on Windows programming, you also will be introduced to the Application and Class Experts, features of the Turbo C++ IDE that enable you to quickly and easily generate and maintain complex Windows programs. After that will be a chapter with a walk-through of a debugging session, giving you some useful tips on fixing a broken program.

WEEK 3

Grouped Controls

Windows supports check box and radio button controls that act as software switches. These controls appear in typical Search and Replace dialog boxes and influence certain aspects of the text search or replacement. These aspects include the scope, direction, and case-sensitivity of searching or replacing text. In today's lesson, you learn about the following topics:

- The check box control
- The radio button control
- The group control

Today's lesson also shows you how to respond to the messages emitted by these controls as well as how to use the `ForEach` iterators to manipulate the check box and radio button controls.

NEW TERM The *group box control* is a special control that visually and logically groups the check box and radio button controls.

The Check Box Control

The check box control is a special button that toggles a check mark. The control instances appear with a small rectangular button and a title that appears, by default, to the right side of the square. When you click the square, you toggle the control's check mark. Think of the check box as a binary digit that can be either set or cleared. The instances of a check box can appear inside or outside a group box and are not mutually exclusive—toggling any check box does not affect the check state of other check boxes.

Note: Placing check boxes inside groups (inside a dialog box) serves two purposes. First, the group box provides a visual grouping that clarifies the purpose of the check boxes to the application user. Second, you can streamline the notification messages emitted by the check boxes in a group to detect any change in the checked state of the check boxes.

NEW TERM Windows enables you to specify a check box that can have one of three states: checked, unchecked, and *grayed*. The grayed state fills the control's rectangular button with a gray color. This third state can serve to indicate that the check box control is in an indeterminate (or "don't care") state.

The *TCheckBox* Class

The ObjectWindows Library offers the `TCheckBox` class, a descendant of `TButton`, as the class that provides the instances of check box controls. Day 13 introduced you to the `TButton` class and discussed the aspects of that class that are related to the pushbutton controls. Because check boxes really are just specialized buttons, much of what applies to buttons also applies to check boxes. By deriving the TCheckBox class from the TButton class, you ensure that TCheckBox inherits much of the parent's functionality. The check box styles shown in Table 15.1 indicate that there are two basic modes for managing the check state of a check box control: automatic and nonautomatic (manual, if you prefer). In automatic mode (specified by BS_AUTOCHECKBOX and BS_AUTO3STATE), Windows toggles the check state when you click the control. In manual mode, your application code is responsible for managing the check state of the check box.

Table 15.1. Check box control styles.

Style	Meaning
BS_CHECKBOX	Specifies a check box with the title to the right of the rectangular button
BS_AUTOCHECKBOX	Same as BS_CHECKBOX, except the button is automatically toggled when you click it. This is the default setting for the TCheckBox class.
BS_3STATE	Same as BS_CHECKBOX, except that the control has three states: checked, unchecked, and grayed
BS_AUTO3STATE	Same as BS_3STATE, except the button is automatically toggled when you click it
BS_LEFTTEXT	Sets the control's title to the left of the button. Note that this is the only style that can be ORed into the style.

The TCheckBox class provides member functions to set and query the state of the check box. The GetCheck member function returns a state of the check box control and is declared as follows:

```
uint GetCheck() const;
```

The function returns a uint-typed value that represents the check state. A value of BF_UNCHECKED indicates that the control is not checked. A value of BF_CHECKED signals that the control is checked. A value of BF_GRAYED indicates that the control is in an indeterminate state. The latter value is valid for the BS_3STATE and BS_AUTO3STATE styles.

The SetCheck member function enables you to set the check state of a check box control. The declaration of the SetCheck function is

```
void SetCheck(uint check);
```

The check parameter specifies the new state of the check box control and should be one of the BF_XXX values.

Responding to Check Box Messages

Because check boxes are descendants of `TButton` with a `BS_CHECKBOX` or `BS_AUTOCHECKBOX` style, your OWL application responds to the messages emitted by check boxes in a manner similar to the pushbuttons. The `EV_BN_CLICKED` macro maps the message sent by the check box control with the member function that responds to that message.

The Radio Button Control

Radio buttons typically enable you to select an option from two or more options. This type of control comes with a circular button and a title that appears, by default, to the right of the button. When you check a radio button, a tiny, filled circle appears inside the circular button. Radio buttons need to be placed in group boxes that visually and logically group them. In each group of radio buttons, only one button can be selected. Therefore, radio buttons are mutually exclusive.

The *TRadioButton* Class

OWL applications use the `TRadioButton` class, a descendant of `TCheckBox`, to create radio button controls by specifying `BS_RADIOBUTTON` or `BS_AUTORADIOBUTTON`. Table 15.2 contains the radio button styles. The constructor creates a radio button with the `BS_AUTORADIOBUTTON` style. Like the check box controls, the radio buttons use the `GetCheck` and `SetCheck` member functions to query and set the state. Unlike the check box, the radio button has only two states: checked and unchecked.

Table 15.2. Radio button control styles.

Style	Meaning
`BS_RADIOBUTTON`	Specifies a radio button with the title to the right of the circular button
`BS_AUTORADIOBUTTON`	Same as `BS_RADIOBUTTON`, except the button is automatically toggled when you click it. This is the default style for the `TRadioButton` class.
`BS_LEFTTEXT`	Sets the control's title to the left of the button. This is the only style that can be `OR`ed into the style.

The radio button controls send the same type of notification messages to their parent windows as do the check box controls. Handling these messages for radio buttons is identical to that of check box and pushbutton controls.

The Group Control

The group box control encloses radio buttons and check boxes. The group box performs the following tasks:

- Visually groups radio buttons or check boxes, which makes relating these controls to each other clearer for the application user, by placing a box around them. Note that you don't necessarily need controls in a box to get the visual effect.
- Logically groups multiple radio buttons so that when you select one radio button, the other buttons in the same group are automatically deselected.

NEW TERM The group box control is a special type of control known as a *container control.*

You can code your OWL application so that the controls inside a group box notify the parent of the group box that you have changed the state of its controls.

The *TGroupBox* Class

Your OWL applications can create group boxes with the `TGroupBox` class, descended from `TControl`. This automatically creates the visual element and provides access via its `SelectionChanged` member function. The declaration of the `SelectionChanged` function is

```
void SelectionChanged(int controlId);
```

When an item in the group is changed, this function is called. By default, the `SelectionChanged` function checks the `TGroupBox`'s `NotifyParent` data member. If it's `TRUE`, then the function notifies the parent window of the group box that one of its selections has changed by sending it a child-ID-based message. By deriving your own version of `TGroupBox` and redefining `SelectionChanged`, you can handle selection changes from the group box itself.

The Widget Selection Application

Here's a short application that demonstrates a possible use for the controls introduced in this chapter. The program shows a sample order form for the World-Wide Widget Weilders company. On it, the user can select one each of Type A, Type B, and Type C widgets. For each of those widget types, there are several different models from which the user can choose. In each case, the different models are disabled so long as the widget type is not checked.

This program illustrates the following:

- The basic use of check box controls
- The basic use of radio buttons

- Responding to check box notification messages
- Overriding a group box to keep track of changes in radio button selections
- Making initial radio button selections

Listing 15.1 contains the source code for the WIDGETS.H header file, listing 15.2 shows the source code for the WIDGETS.RC resource file, and listing 15.3 shows the WIDGETS.CPP program file. Create the directory WIDGETS as a subdirectory of \TCWIN45\TC21DAY and store all the project's files in the new directory. The project's .IDE file should contain the file WIDGETS.CPP and WIDGETS.RC.

Listing 15.1. Source code for the WIDGETS.H header file.

```
#define IDC_TYPEA       101
#define IDC_TYPEB       102
#define IDC_TYPEC       103
#define IDR_ETCHED      104
#define IDR_POLISHED    105
#define IDR_WOODGRAIN   106
#define IDR_VARNISHED   107
#define IDR_ENGRAVED    108
#define IDR_MEDIOCRE    109
#define IDR_DELUXE      110
#define IDG_TYPEA       111
#define IDG_TYPEB       112
#define IDG_TYPEC       113
```

Listing 15.2. Source code for the WIDGETS.RC resource file.

```
/****************************************************************************


WIDGETS.RC

produced by Borland Resource Workshop


*****************************************************************************/

        #include "widgets.h"

        WWWW DIALOG 8, 15, 241, 165
        STYLE DS_MODALFRAME | WS_POPUP | WS_VISIBLE | WS_CAPTION | WS_SYSMENU
        CAPTION "World-Wide Widget Weilders"
        FONT 8, "MS Sans Serif"
        {
         CHECKBOX "Type A", IDC_TYPEA, 10, 12, 40, 12, BS_AUTOCHECKBOX |
         WS_TABSTOP
         CONTROL "", IDG_TYPEA, "static", SS_BLACKFRAME | WS_GROUP, 67, 6, 160,
25
```

```
        CONTROL "Etched", IDR_ETCHED, "BUTTON", BS_AUTORADIOBUTTON, 77, 12, 60, 12
        CONTROL "Polished", IDR_POLISHED, "BUTTON", BS_AUTORADIOBUTTON, 147, 12, 60, 12
        CHECKBOX "Type B", IDC_TYPEB, 10, 59, 40, 12, BS_AUTOCHECKBOX | WS_TABSTOP
        CONTROL "", IDG_TYPEB, "static", SS_BLACKFRAME | WS_GROUP, 67, 48, 160, 34
        CONTROL "Wood-Grain", IDR_WOODGRAIN, "BUTTON", BS_AUTORADIOBUTTON, 77, 49, 60, 12
        CONTROL "Varnished", IDR_VARNISHED, "BUTTON", BS_AUTORADIOBUTTON, 150, 49, 60, 12
        CONTROL "Engraved", IDR_ENGRAVED, "BUTTON", BS_AUTORADIOBUTTON, 77, 68, 60, 12
        CHECKBOX "Type C", IDC_TYPEC, 10, 105, 40, 12, BS_AUTOCHECKBOX | WS_TABSTOP
        CONTROL "", IDG_TYPEC, "static", SS_BLACKFRAME | WS_GROUP, 67, 97, 160, 28
        CONTROL "Mediocre", IDR_MEDIOCRE, "BUTTON", BS_AUTORADIOBUTTON, 77, 105, 60, 12
        CONTROL "Deluxe", IDR_DELUXE, "BUTTON", BS_AUTORADIOBUTTON, 153, 105, 60, 12
        DEFPUSHBUTTON "Done", IDOK, 47, 134, 50, 14
        PUSHBUTTON "Cancel", IDCANCEL, 144, 134, 50, 14
       }
```

Type

Listing 15.3. Source code for the WIDGETS.CPP program file.

```
#include <stdio.h>
#include <owl\applicat.h>
#include <owl\button.h>
#include <owl\checkbox.h>
#include <owl\dialog.h>
#include <owl\framewin.h>
#include <owl\groupbox.h>
#include <owl\radiobut.h>
#include <owl\window.h>
#include <owl\window.rh>

#include "widgets.h"

class TMyGroup : public TGroupBox
{
public:
   TMyGroup(TWindow*       parent,
            int            id,
            TModule*       module = 0 )
      : TGroupBox(parent, id, module), cur(-1)
      { }

   LPCSTR GetCurCheck();
```

continues

Listing 15.3. continued

```
   virtual void SelectionChanged(int controlId)
      { TGroupBox::SelectionChanged(cur = controlId); }

private:
   int cur;
};

LPCSTR TMyGroup::GetCurCheck()
{
   TWindow* w = Parent->ChildWithId(cur);
   return w ? w->Title : NULL;
}

class TWidgetDialog : public TDialog
{
public:
   TWidgetDialog(TWindow* parent = 0, TModule* module = 0);

protected:
   virtual void SetupWindow();

   void EnableGroupA(bool enable);
   void EnableGroupB(bool enable);
   void EnableGroupC(bool enable);

   bool BuildStr( LPSTR str,
                  LPCSTR name,
                  TCheckBox* check,
                  TMyGroup* group );

   void CmDone();
   void CmCancel();
   void CmTypeA();
   void CmTypeB();
   void CmTypeC();

private:
   TCheckBox      *TypeA, *TypeB, *TypeC;
   TMyGroup       *GroupA, *GroupB, *GroupC;
   TRadioButton   *Etched, *Polished,
                  *WoodGrain, *Varnished, *Engraved,
                  *Mediocre, *Deluxe;

   DECLARE_RESPONSE_TABLE(TWidgetDialog);
};
DEFINE_RESPONSE_TABLE1(TWidgetDialog, TDialog)
   EV_BN_CLICKED(IDOK, CmDone),
   EV_BN_CLICKED(IDCANCEL, CmCancel),
   EV_BN_CLICKED(IDC_TYPEA, CmTypeA),
   EV_BN_CLICKED(IDC_TYPEB, CmTypeB),
   EV_BN_CLICKED(IDC_TYPEC, CmTypeC),
END_RESPONSE_TABLE;
```

```
TWidgetDialog::TWidgetDialog(TWindow* parent, TModule* module)
   : TDialog(parent, "WWWW", module)
{
   TypeA = new TCheckBox(this, IDC_TYPEA);
   GroupA = new TMyGroup(this, IDG_TYPEA);
   Etched = new TRadioButton(this, IDR_ETCHED);
   Polished = new TRadioButton(this, IDR_POLISHED);

   TypeB = new TCheckBox(this, IDC_TYPEB);
   GroupB = new TMyGroup(this, IDG_TYPEB);
   WoodGrain = new TRadioButton(this, IDR_WOODGRAIN);
   Varnished = new TRadioButton(this, IDR_VARNISHED);
   Engraved = new TRadioButton(this, IDR_ENGRAVED);

   TypeC = new TCheckBox(this, IDC_TYPEC);
   GroupC = new TMyGroup(this, IDG_TYPEC);
   Mediocre = new TRadioButton(this, IDR_MEDIOCRE);
   Deluxe = new TRadioButton(this, IDR_DELUXE);
}

void TWidgetDialog::SetupWindow()
{
   TDialog::SetupWindow();    // Initialize the visual element

   EnableGroupA(false);
   EnableGroupB(false);
   EnableGroupC(false);
}

void TWidgetDialog::EnableGroupA(bool enable)
{
   if (Etched)
      Etched->EnableWindow(enable);
   if (Polished)
      Polished->EnableWindow(enable);
}

void TWidgetDialog::EnableGroupB(bool enable)
{
   if (WoodGrain)
      WoodGrain->EnableWindow(enable);
   if (Varnished)
      Varnished->EnableWindow(enable);
   if (Engraved)
      Engraved->EnableWindow(enable);
}

void TWidgetDialog::EnableGroupC(bool enable)
{
   if (Mediocre)
      Mediocre->EnableWindow(enable);
   if (Deluxe)
      Deluxe->EnableWindow(enable);
}
```

continues

Listing 15.3. continued

```
bool TWidgetDialog::BuildStr( LPSTR str,
                              LPCSTR name,
                              TCheckBox* check,
                              TMyGroup* group )
{
   bool rslt = false;
   if (str && check && check->GetCheck())
      {
      rslt = true;
      LPCSTR groupname;

      str += lstrlen(str);    // point to end of str
      sprintf(str, "\n    %s: ", name);
      if (group && (NULL != (groupname = group->GetCurCheck())))
         strcat(str, groupname);
      }
   return rslt;
}

void TWidgetDialog::CmDone()
{
   char           str[256] = "";
   int            sels = 0;

   strcpy(str, "You have selected the following:");
   sels += BuildStr(str, "Widget A", TypeA, GroupA);
   sels += BuildStr(str, "Widget B", TypeB, GroupB);
   sels += BuildStr(str, "Widget C", TypeC, GroupC);
   if (!sels)
      strcat(str, "\n   << No selections >>");
   MessageBox(str, "Widget Selection", MB_OK);
   SendMessage(WM_CLOSE);
}

void TWidgetDialog::CmCancel()
{
   SendMessage(WM_CLOSE);
}

void TWidgetDialog::CmTypeA()
{
   if (TypeA)
      EnableGroupA(TypeA->GetCheck());
   if (GroupA && !GroupA->GetCurCheck() && Etched)
      Etched->Check();
}

void TWidgetDialog::CmTypeB()
{
   if (TypeB)
      EnableGroupB(TypeB->GetCheck());
   if (GroupB && !GroupB->GetCurCheck() && WoodGrain)
      WoodGrain->Check();
}
```

```
void TWidgetDialog::CmTypeC()
{
   if (TypeC)
      EnableGroupC(TypeC->GetCheck());
   if (GroupC && !GroupC->GetCurCheck() && Mediocre)
      Mediocre->Check();
}

class TWidgetApp : public TApplication
{
public:
   TWidgetApp() : TApplication()
      { nCmdShow = SW_SHOWMAXIMIZED; }

   void InitMainWindow()
   {
      SetMainWindow(new TFrameWindow(  0,
              "World-Wide Widget Weilders",
              new TWidgetDialog ));
   }
};

int OwlMain(int, char *[])
{
   return TWidgetApp().Run();
}
```

Figure 15.1 shows a sample session with the WIDGETS.EXE program.

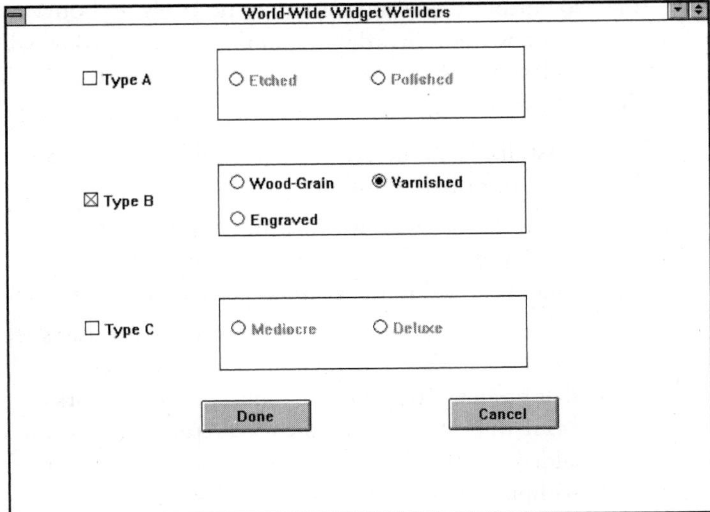

Figure 15.1.
A sample session with program WIDGETS.EXE.

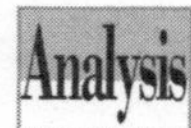

Analysis The program starts off on line 14 of Listing 15.3 by declaring a descendant of `TGroupBox` called `TMyGroup`. The purpose of this is to keep track of the selections made by the controls contained within it. The class initializes its `cur` data member to `-1` in the constructor on line 20. This signifies that no control has yet been selected inside the group. This value is changed in the overridden `SelectionChanged` member function on line 26. This function, as described earlier, is called whenever a control inside the group is selected. Our version of the function simply passes the single parameter along to the parent's version of the function while assigning the value of that parameter to our `cur` data member. Finally, the `TMyGroup` class defines the `GetCurCheck` member function starting on line 32. This function uses the parent window's `ChildWithId` function to obtain a `TWindow` pointer to the control with the ID recorded in `cur`. If a control was found, then its `Title` data member is returned.

The main dialog `TWidgetDialog` then is declared, starting on line 38. As usual, there is a constructor and a `SetupWindow` member function. The constructor creates all the various controls that are to appear on the screen, starting on line 78: three check boxes, each with a group next to it, and then between two and three radio buttons inside that group. The `SetupWindow` member function that starts on line 98, after calling its parent's version of the function, makes calls to three functions to initially disable the various groups of radio buttons.

Next are the helper functions `EnableGroupA`, `EnableGroupB`, and `EnableGroupC` on lines 107 through 131. These are used to enable and disable whole groups of controls via `TDialog`'s `EnableWindow` member function. They each take a single `bool`-typed `enable` parameter that determines whether the controls are to be enabled or disabled. This parameter is passed directly on to the individual control's `EnableWindow` function.

The two functions `CmDone` and `CmCancel` on lines 152 through 170 come next. They respond to the two buttons Done and Cancel, respectively. In both cases, they send the `WM_CLOSE` message to the main window in order to shut the application down, but the `CmDone` function first creates and displays a message box informing the user of the selections made. It builds this string by doing the following:

- First, it fills in the `str` variable on line 157 with an initial string, letting the user know what information follows.
- Next, the `BuildStr` member function (discussed next) is called for each of the three check boxes and group boxes on lines 158 through 160. The return values of these calls are added to the `sels` variable and `BuildStr` modifies `str`.
- After filling up the string with results of the user's selections, the `sels` variable is checked. If it's still `0`, then nothing was selected, and the `str` variable is filled to reflect that on lines 161 and 162. This bit of code works because `true` is defined to be `1` and `false` to be `0`. So, when the `bool` return values from multiple calls to `BuildStr` are added together in `sels`, we're checking to see if any of the return values were `true` without actually caring about which one.

- The `str` variable is then sent to the `MessageBox` function on line 163 for display to the user.
- Finally, the `WM_CLOSE` message is sent to the window via the `SendMessage` function on line 164 to effectively terminate the window and, thus, the program.

The `BuildStr` member function, starting on line 133, works by taking a destination string in its `str` parameter, the name of the check box to be reported to the user in the `name` parameter, and the pointers to the check box and group box controls in the `check` and `group` parameters, respectively. The function does the following things:

- First, it checks on line 139 to make sure it received valid `str` and `check` parameters. It's always a good idea to check parameters before trying to use them to help prevent unwanted bugs in the program. In the same statement, it also calls `check`'s `GetCheck` function. If that returns `true`, then the check box has been checked, and you need to start filling in the `str` parameter.
- In order to keep from overwriting the previous contents of the `str` parameter, `str` is made to point at its end by adding the value obtained from the `lstrlen` function on line 144.
- The name of the check box is printed into the `str`, along with some formatting characters on line 145.
- If you have a valid `group` parameter and you are able to get the title of its selected radio button, then that title is concatenated to the `str` parameter on line 147.
- Finally, the result of whether anything was actually added to `str` is returned on line 149.

The last functions of interest are the `CmTypeA`, `CmTypeB`, and `CmTypeC` member functions on lines 172 through 194. These each respond, in turn, to the Type A, Type B, and Type C check boxes respectively. In each one, first the appropriate `EnableGroupX` is called with the check box's check state to either enable or disable the appropriate group's radio buttons. The function then attempts to find out the title of the currently selected radio button. If this value isn't set, then you know that this is the first time the check box has been set, so you initialize the radio buttons by setting the first one with its `Check` member function.

Summary

Today's lesson discussed the special switch controls: group box, check box, and radio button. You learned about the following:

- Check box and radio button controls act as software switches.
- You can set and query the check state for the check box and radio button controls.

- ☐ Notification messages can be sent by these controls to their parent window.
- ☐ Group box controls enclose radio buttons and check boxes.
- ☐ Switch controls can be selectively manipulated.

Day 16 presents the list box, and Day 17 presents the scroll bar and combo box controls. These controls are value selectors because they enable you to select from a list or range of values.

Q&A

Q The check box has the states `BF_UNCHECKED`, `BF_CHECKED`, and `BF_GRAYED`. What can I use the third state for?

A You can use the `BF_GRAYED` state as a "don't care" or as an undetermined state.

Q Does it make any difference if I place check box controls in a group control?

A Placing check box controls in a group control affects the logical grouping of such controls as the user sees it. Consequently, this can enhance the interface for the user.

Workshop

The Workshop provides quiz questions to help you solidify your understanding of the material covered and exercises to provide you with experience in using what you've learned. Try to understand the quiz and exercise answers before continuing on to the next day's lesson. Answers are provided in Appendix A.

Quiz

1. True or false? A check box can replace any two radio buttons in a group control.
2. True or false? You should use radio buttons in a group control when you have three or more options.
3. True or false? A set of check boxes parallels the bits in a byte or word.
4. True or false? Radio buttons, in a group control, are mutually nonexclusive.

Exercise

Expand on program WIDGETS.CPP by adding more widget types and more design types for each widget.

WEEK
3

List Box Controls

List box controls are input tools that conveniently provide you with items from which to choose. This feature makes list box controls popular because they absolve you from remembering the list members—especially when computer programs expect exact spelling. Experience with DOS programs has shown that the various DOS utilities that display lists of files and directories are far easier and friendlier to use than their counterparts that assume the user knows all the names of the files and directories. Using list box controls gradually has become a routine method for retrieving information. Today's lesson discusses the single-selection and multiple-selection list boxes. You will learn about the following topics:

- The list box control
- Handling single-selection list boxes
- Handling multiple-selection list boxes

The List Box Control

List boxes typically are framed and include a vertical scroll bar. When you select an item by clicking it, the selection is highlighted. Microsoft suggests the following guidelines for making a selection:

- Use a single mouse click to select a new or an additional item. A separate button control retrieves the selected item.
- Use a double-click as a shortcut for selecting an item and retrieving it.

NEW TERM The *list box* is an input control that permits the application user to select from a list of items.

A list box control supports multiple selections only if you specify the multiple-selection style when you create the control. Making multiple selections is convenient when you want to process the selected items in a similar manner. For example, selecting multiple files for deletion speeds up the process and reduces the effort you have to make.

The *TListBox* Class

The Borland ObjectWindows Library offers the `TListBox` class, a descendant of `TControl`, to implement list box controls. The `TListBox` class has a set of member functions that enable you to easily manipulate and query both the contents of the list box and the selected item. As with many other classes in OWL, the class `TListBox` uses a default constructor to create list box instances.

Syntax

The *TListBox* Constructor

The declarations of the `TListBox` constructors are

```
TListBox(TWindow* parent,
         int      id,
         int      x,
         int      y,
         int      w,
         int      h,
         TModule* module = 0 );
TListBox(TWindow* parent, int resourceId, TModule* module = 0);
```

Notice that the `TListBox` class constructor looks very much like the other controls descended from `TControl` (such as `TEdit`, `TButton`, and so on). You specify the control's parent window, its control ID, and its dimensions within that window, or you specify its id in the dialog box as loaded from a resource file.

Example

```
TListBox* pFiles = new TListBox(this, IDL_FILES, 10, 10, 75, 250);
TListBox* pFolders = new TListBox(this, IDL_FOLDERS);
```

Along with the regular `WS_XXX` styles, the list box makes use of the special `LBS_XXX` styles (see Table 16.1). The `TListBox` class, by default, sets the `LBS_STANDARD` style. This is equivalent to the `WS_BORDER`, `WS_VSCROLL`, `LBS_SORT`, and `LBS_NOTIFY` styles. You can remove the `LBS_SORT` style from the list box controls to maintain a list of items that is not automatically sorted. Such a list enables you to maintain items in a chronological fashion. You also can use this type of list to maintain the items sorted in descending order (you are responsible for maintaining the list items in that order). Removing the `WS_VSCROLL` style gives you a list box without the vertical scroll bar. The next section presents a demonstration program that uses this type of list box to implement the synchronized scrolling of multiple list boxes.

Table 16.1. List box control styles.

Style	Meaning
`LBS_DISABLENOSCROLL`	Specifies that the list box is to always have a scroll bar that is gray when there is nothing to scroll. Normally, the scroll bar disappears when not needed.
`LBS_EXTENDEDSEL`	Allows the extension of multiple-selections in the list box by using the Shift key.
`LBS_HASSTRINGS`	Used in owner-drawn list boxes to have the control maintain a copy of the strings added.
`LBS_MULTICOLUMN`	Designates a multicolumn list box that scrolls horizontally.
`LBS_MULTIPLESEL`	Supports multiple selections in a list box.

continues

Table 16.1. continued

Style	Meaning
`LBS_NOINTEGRALHEIGHT`	Allows showing parts of an item if it doesn't fit within the displayed portion of the list box.
`LBS_NOREDRAW`	Prevents the list box from being updated when the selection is changed. (You can use the `SetRedraw` member function to change this at will.)
`LBS_NOTIFY`	Notifies the parent window when you click or double-click in the list box.
`LBS_OWNERDRAWFIXED`	Used to specify an owner-drawn list box (a list box for which the application is responsible for drawing, instead of the automatic Windows functions). Specifies that the list box items all will be the same height.
`LBS_OWNERDRAWVARIABLE`	Specifies an owner-drawn list box that contains items of differing heights.
`LBS_SORT`	Specifies that the items inserted in the list box be automatically sorted in ascending alphanumeric order.
`LBS_STANDARD`	Sets the `WS_BORDER`, `WS_VSCROLL`, `LBS_SORT`, and `LBS_NOTIFY` styles.
`LBS_USETABSTOPS`	Allows the tab character to be expanded within the list box control.
`LBS_WANTKEYBOARDINPUT`	Permits the list box owner to receive `WM_VKEYTOITEM` or `WM_CHARTOITEM` messages when a key is pressed while the list box has the focus (allows the application to manipulate the items in the list box).

The `TListBox` class enables you to refer to the items in a list box by index. The index of the first item is 0. The `TListBox` class offers the following member functions to set and query ordinary and selected list members:

- The `AddString` member function adds a string to the list box.
- The `DeleteString` member function removes a list member from a specified position.
- The parameterless `ClearList` member function clears the list of strings in the list box control in one swoop. This function serves to reset the contents of a list box before building up a new list.
- The `FindExactString` and `FindString` member functions perform case-insensitive searches for items in the list box. The first searches the list box for an exact match to a string, whereas the second searches for a list box entry that begins with a string.

- The parameterless `GetCount` member function returns the number of items in the list box. The function returns a negative number if there is an error.
- The parameterless `GetSelIndex` member function returns the position of the selected item in a single-selection list box. If there is no selected item, the function yields a negative value. This function is aimed at single-selection list boxes only.
- The `GetSel` member function returns the selection state of a list box item, specified by an index.
- The parameterless `GetSelCount` member function returns the number of selected items in the list box. For single-selection list boxes, the number will be either 0 or 1.
- The `GetSelIndexes` member function returns the number and positions of the selected items in a multiple-selection list box.
- The `GetString` member function obtains an item in a list box by specifying its index.
- The `GetStringLen` member function returns the length of a list item specified by its position in the list.
- The `GetTopIndex` member function returns the index of the first visible list box item.
- The `InsertString` member function inserts a string in a list box.
- The `SetSelString` member function selects a list box item that matches a search string.
- The `SetSelItemRange` member function enables you to select a range of items in one call.
- The `SetSelIndex` member function chooses a list item as the new selection in a single-selection list box.
- The `SetSel` member function makes or clears a selection in a multiple-selection list box.
- The `SetTopIndex` member function selects the list box entry that becomes the first visible item in the list box control.
- The `DirectoryList` member function is a special member function that enables you to automatically insert filenames in a list box.

Note: Many of the `TListBox` functions return either `LB_ERR` or `LB_ERRSPACE`. Note that both of these values are negative, so just checking a return value to see if it's less than `0` is often enough.

Syntax

The *AddString* Function

The declaration of the `AddString` member function is

```
int AddString(const char far* str);
```

The `str` parameter is the pointer to the added string. The function returns the position of the added string in the control. If there is any error in adding the string, the function yields an `LB_ERR` or `LB_ERRSPACE` value (out-of-memory error). If the `LBS_SORT` style is set, then the string is inserted so that the list order is maintained. If the `LBS_SORT` style is not set, then the added string is inserted at the end of the list.

Example

```
pList->AddString("MS-DOS");
```

Syntax

The *DeleteString* Function

The declaration of the `DeleteString` member function is

```
int DeleteString(int index);
```

The `index` parameter specifies the position of the item to delete. The function returns the number of remaining list members. If errors occur, then `DeleteString` yields the value `LB_ERR`.

Example

```
pList->DeleteString(0); //Deletes item 0
```

Syntax

The *FindExactString* and *FindString* Functions

The declarations of the `FindExactString` and `FindString` functions are

```
int FindExactString(const char far* str, int searchIndex) const;
int FindString(const char far* str, int searchIndex) const;
```

In both cases, the `searchIndex` parameter specifies the index of the first list box member to be searched, and the `str` parameter is the pointer to the searched string. The functions search the entire list, beginning with position `searchIndex` and resuming at the beginning of the list, if needed. The search stops when either a list member matches the search string or the entire list is searched. Passing an argument of `1` to `searchIndex` forces the functions to start searching from the beginning. The functions return the position of the matching list item, or they yield the `LB_ERR` value if no match is found or when an error occurs.

The difference between the two functions is that, although `FindExactString` looks for an exact match of the parameter `str` to an entry in the list box, `FindString` will stop as soon as it finds an entry that begins with `str`.

Example

```
int msdos = pList->FindString("MS-DOS", -1);
int anti = pList->FindString("anti", -1);
```

Note: The interesting search method used by `FindExactString` and `FindString` enables you to speed up the search by specifying a position that comes closely before the most likely location for a match. For example, if you happen to know where the first item starting with an `s` is located, and you're searching for something that begins with the same character, you can specify that initial index in an attempt to speed up the search.

The beauty of this method is that if you specify a position that actually is beyond that of the string you seek, you cannot miss finding that string because the function resumes searching at the beginning of the list. Another benefit of `FindExactString` and `FindString` is their capability to find duplicate strings.

Syntax

The *GetSel* Function

The declaration of the function `GetSel` is

```
bool GetSel(int index) const;
```

The `index` parameter specifies the index of the queried list box item. The function returns a `TRUE` if the item is selected, `FALSE` if the item is not selected.

Example

```
pList->SetSel(0, !pList->GetSel(0)); //toggles sel state of item 0
```

Syntax

The *GetSelIndexes* Function

The declaration of the `GetSelIndexes` function is

```
int GetSelIndexes(int* indexes, int maxCount) const;
```

The `maxCount` parameter specifies the size of the array accessed by the `indexes` pointer. The `indexes` parameter is the pointer to an array of integers that stores the positions of the selected items. The function returns the current number of selections. The function yields `LB_ERR` with single-selection list boxes.

Example

```
int num_items = pList->GetSelCount();
int* items = new int[num_items];
pList->GetSelIndexes(items, num_items);
```

Syntax

The *GetString* Function

The declaration for the `GetString` function is

```
int GetString(char far* str, int index) const;
```

The `index` parameter specifies the index of the retrieved item. The first list box item has the index of 0. The `str` parameter points to a buffer that receives the retrieved item.

You are responsible for ensuring that the buffer has enough space for the retrieved item (for example, using `GetStringLen` when allocating a receiving buffer). The function returns the number of characters retrieved from the list box.

Example

```
char* s = NULL;
int size = pList->GetStringLen(ix);
if ((size > 0) && (NULL != (s = new char[size + 1])))
   pList->GetString(s, ix);
```

Syntax

The *GetStringLen* Function

The declaration of the `GetStringLen` function is

```
int GetStringLen(int index) const;
```

The parameter `index` specifies the index of the target list item. The function returns the length of the target item, or the `LB_ERR` result if an error occurs.

Example

See the example for `GetString`.

Syntax

The *InsertString* Function

The declaration of the `InsertString` function is

```
int InsertString(const char far* str, int index);
```

The `index` parameter specifies the requested insertion position. The `str` parameter is the pointer to the inserted string. The function returns the actual insertion position, or it yields the `LB_ERR` value if an error occurs. If the argument for `index` is `1`, then the string is simply appended to the end of the list.

Example

```
pList->InsertString("Windows", 0);
```

Warning: In general, do not use the `InsertString` member function with list boxes that have the `LBS_SORT` style set. Using this function with ordered list boxes will most likely corrupt the sort order of the list.

Syntax

The *SetSelString* Function

The declaration of the `SetSelString` function is

```
int SetSelString(const char far* str, int searchIndex);
```

The parameters and search mechanism of `SetSelString` are identical to those of `FindString`. The difference is that `SetSelString` selects the list box item that matches the string accessed by parameter `str`.

Example

```
int ix = pList->SetSelString("MS-DOS", -1);
```

Syntax

The *SetSelItemRange* Function

The declaration of the `SetSelItemRange` function is

```
int SetSelItemRange(bool select, int first, int last);
```

The `select` parameter acts as a switch used to select or deselect the range of list box items defined by parameters of `first` and `last`. The number returned is the number of items actually selected between and including `first` and `last`.

Example

```
pList->SetSelItemRange(TRUE, 0, 10);
```

Syntax

The *SetSelIndex* Function

The declaration of the `SetSelIndex` function is

```
int SetSelIndex(int index);
```

The parameter `index` specifies the position of the new selection. To clear a list box from any selection, pass a `1` argument as the `select` parameter. The function returns `LB_ERR` if an error occurs. This is used for single-selection list boxes.

Example

```
pList-SetSelIndex(-1);      // clear current selection
```

Syntax

The *SetSel* Function

The declaration of the `SetSel` function is

```
int SetSel(int index, bool select);
```

The `index` parameter specifies the list box item to either select, if `select` is `TRUE`, or deselect, if `select` is `FALSE`. The function returns `LB_ERR` if an error occurs. The function result serves only to flag a selection/deselection error. You can use the `SetSel` function to toggle the selection of multiple items in a multiple-selection list box, one at a time.

Example

```
pList->SetSel(0, TRUE);      // select first item in list
```

Syntax

The *SetTopIndex* Function

The declaration of the function `SetTopIndex` is

```
int SetTopIndex(int index);
```

The `index` parameter specifies the index of the list box item that becomes the first visible item. This selection scrolls the list box, unless the item `index` is already the first visible item. The function returns `LB_ERR` if an error occurs. Otherwise, the result is meaningless.

Example

```
pList->SetTopIndex(10);
```

Syntax

The *DirectoryList* Function

The declaration of the `DirectoryList` function is

```
int DirectoryList(uint attrs, const char far* fileSpec);
```

The `attrs` parameter specifies the combination of attributes, as shown in Table 16.2. The table also shows the equivalent file attribute constants that are declared in the DOS.H header file. The `fileSpec` parameter is the pointer to the filename specification, such as `*.*`, `L*.EXE`, or `A???.CPP`. The return value is the number of files added to the list box.

Example

```
int numFiles = pList->DirectoryList(DDL_ARCHIVE, "CTL*.CPP");
```

Table 16.2. Attributes for the `attrs` parameter in the `TListbox::DirectoryList` member function.

Attribute Value	Equivalent Constant in DOS.H Header File	Meaning
DDL_READWRITE	FA_NORMAL or _A_NORMAL	File can be used for input and output.
DDL_READONLY	FA_RDONLY or _A_RDONLY	File is read only.
DDL_HIDDEN	FA_HIDDEN or _A_HIDDEN	File is hidden.
DDL_SYSTEM	FA_SYSTEM or _A_SYSTEM	File is system file.
DDL_DIRECTORY	FA_DIREC or _A_SUBDIR	Name indicated by parameter `fileSpec` also supplies the directory.
DDL_ARCHIVE	FA_ARCH or _A_ARCH	File has the archive bit set.
DDL_POSTMSGS		Posts messages to the application instead of sending them directly to the list box.
DDL_DRIVES		Includes all the drives that match the filename supplied by `fileSpec`.
DDL_EXCLUSIVE		Exclusive flag (prevents normal files from being included with specified files).

Note that in the preceding table, there are two constants defined in the DOS.H header file for each item. The first is the value defined by Borland. The second is the one defined for the Microsoft compiler. Borland defines these to help with compatibility to make programs more easily portable between the two compilers.

Responding to List Box Notification Messages

The list box control emits various types of messages, as shown in Table 16.3. The table also shows the message-mapping macros that are associated with the various command and notification messages. Each type of command or notification message requires a separate member function declared in the control's parent window class.

Table 16.3. List box notification messages.

Message	Macro	Meaning
`WM_COMMAND`	`EV_COMMAND`	The Windows command message through which all the `LBN_XXX` sub-commands are passed; they're specified in the `wParam` parameter.
`LBN_DBLCLK`	`EV_LBN_DBLCLK`	A list item is selected with a mouse double-click.
`LBN_ERRSPACE`	`EV_LBN_ERRSPACE`	The list box cannot allocate more dynamic memory to accommodate new list items.
`LBN_KILLFOCUS`	`EV_LBN_KILLFOCUS`	The list box has lost focus.
`LBN_SELCHANGE`	`EV_LBN_SELCHANGE`	A list item is selected with a mouse click.
`LBN_SETFOCUS`	`EV_LBN_SETFOCUS`	The list box has gained focus.

The List Manipulation Tester

The next program demonstrates how to set and query normal and selected strings, and how to set and query the current selection in a single-selection list box—a simple list manipulation tester. This program focuses on illustrating how to use most of the `TListBox` member functions presented earlier in this section. The program contains the following controls that offer the indicated test features:

- A list box control
- A String Box edit control that enables you to type in and retrieve a list member
- An Index Box edit control that enables you to key in and retrieve the position of the current selection
- An Add String pushbutton to add the contents of the String Box to the list box (the program does not enable you to add duplicate names, and, if you attempt to do so, the program displays a warning message)
- A Delete String pushbutton to delete the current selection in the list box (the program automatically selects another list member)
- The Get Selected String pushbutton that copies the current list selection to the String Box
- The Set Selected String pushbutton that overwrites the current selection with the string in the String Box
- The Get Selected Index pushbutton that writes the position of the current selection in the Index Box
- The Set Selected Index pushbutton that uses the integer value in the Index Box as the position of the new list box selection

- The Get String button that copies the string whose position appears in the Index Box into the String Box
- The Exit pushbutton

These controls exercise various aspects of manipulating a sorted list box and its members. The program is coded to retain a current selection and to prevent the insertion of duplicate names.

Listings 16.1, 16.2, and 16.3 show the header file CTLLST.H, the script for the CTLLST.RC resource file, and the source code for the CTLLST.CPP program file, respectively. The resource file contains a single-item menu resource.

Create the directory CTLLST as a subdirectory of TCWIN45\TC21DAY and store all the project's files in the new directory. The project's IDE file should contain the files CTLLST.CPP and the CTLLST.RC.

Compile and run the program. When the program starts running, it places a set of names in the list box. Experiment with the various pushbutton controls to add, delete, and obtain strings. The program is straightforward and easy to run.

Listing 16.1. Source code for the CTLLST.H header file.

```
#define IDL_STRINGS     101
#define IDE_STRING      102
#define IDE_INDEX       103
#define IDB_ADD         104
#define IDB_DEL         105
#define IDB_GETSELSTR   106
#define IDB_SETSELSTR   107
#define IDB_GETSELIDX   108
#define IDB_SETSELIDX   109
#define IDB_GETSTR      110
#define IDB_EXIT        111
```

Listing 16.2. Script for the CTLLST.RC resource file.

```
#include <windows.h>
#include <owl\window.rh>
#include "ctllst.h"

EXITMENU MENU LOADONCALL MOVEABLE PURE DISCARDABLE
BEGIN
   MENUITEM "E&xit", CM_EXIT
END

   CTLLST DIALOG 7, 18, 288, 209
STYLE DS_MODALFRAME | WS_POPUP | WS_VISIBLE | WS_CAPTION | WS_SYSMENU
CAPTION "Simple List Box Tester Application"
FONT 8, "MS Sans Serif"
{
LTEXT "List Box", -1, 10, 20, 60, 8
```

Listing 16.2. continued

```
LISTBOX IDL_STRINGS, 10, 31, 74, 137, LBS_STANDARD
LTEXT "String Box", -1, 100, 20, 60, 8
EDITTEXT IDE_STRING, 100, 31, 180, 12
LTEXT "Index Box", -1, 100, 63, 62, 8
EDITTEXT IDE_INDEX, 100, 74, 180, 12
PUSHBUTTON "Add String", IDB_ADD, 100, 111, 80, 14
PUSHBUTTON "Delete String", IDB_DEL, 100, 136, 80, 14
PUSHBUTTON "Get Selected String", IDB_GETSELSTR, 100, 161, 80, 14
PUSHBUTTON "Set Selected String", IDB_SETSELSTR, 100, 186, 80, 14
PUSHBUTTON "Get Selected Index", IDB_GETSELIDX, 200, 111, 80, 14
PUSHBUTTON "Set Selected Index", IDB_SETSELIDX, 200, 136, 80, 14
PUSHBUTTON "Get String by Index", IDB_GETSTR, 200, 161, 80, 14
PUSHBUTTON "Exit", IDB_EXIT, 200, 186, 80, 14
}
```

Type

Listing 16.3. Source code for the CTLLST.CPP program file.

```
#include <stdio.h>
#include <owl\applicat.h>
#include <owl\button.h>
#include <owl\dialog.h>
#include <owl\edit.h>
#include <owl\framewin.h>
#include <owl\listbox.h>
#include <owl\static.h>
#include <owl\window.h>
#include <owl\window.rh>

#include "ctllst.h"

class TMyDialog : public TDialog
{
public:
   TMyDialog(TWindow* parent = 0, TModule* module = 0);
   virtual ~TMyDialog();

protected:
   virtual void SetupWindow();

   void CbAdd();
   void CbDel();
   void CbGetSelStr();
   void CbSetSelStr();
   void CbGetSelIdx();
   void CbSetSelIdx();
   void CbGetStr();
   void CmExit();

private:
   TListBox *list;
   TEdit *strbox, *idxbox;

   DECLARE_RESPONSE_TABLE(TMyDialog);
};
```

```
DEFINE_RESPONSE_TABLE1(TMyDialog, TDialog)
   EV_COMMAND(CM_EXIT, CmExit),
   EV_BN_CLICKED(IDB_ADD, CbAdd),
   EV_BN_CLICKED(IDB_DEL, CbDel),
   EV_BN_CLICKED(IDB_GETSELSTR, CbGetSelStr),
   EV_BN_CLICKED(IDB_SETSELSTR, CbSetSelStr),
   EV_BN_CLICKED(IDB_GETSELIDX, CbGetSelIdx),
   EV_BN_CLICKED(IDB_SETSELIDX, CbSetSelIdx),
   EV_BN_CLICKED(IDB_GETSTR, CbGetStr),
   EV_BN_CLICKED(IDB_EXIT, CmExit),
END_RESPONSE_TABLE;

TMyDialog::TMyDialog(TWindow* parent, TModule* module)
   : TDialog(parent, "CTLLST", module)
{
   list = new TListBox(this, IDL_STRINGS);
   strbox = new TEdit(this, IDE_STRING);
   idxbox = new TEdit(this, IDE_INDEX);
}

TMyDialog::~TMyDialog()
{
}

void TMyDialog::SetupWindow()
{
   TDialog::SetupWindow();    // Initialize the visual element

   // Initialize the list box with some data and
   // select the second item
   //
   if (list)
      {
      list->AddString("Keith");
      list->AddString("Kevin");
      list->AddString("Ingrid");
      list->AddString("Roger");
      list->AddString("Rick");
      list->AddString("Beth");
      list->AddString("Kate");
      list->AddString("James");
      list->SetSelIndex(1);
      }
}

void TMyDialog::CbAdd()
{
   if (strbox && list)
      {
      char* str;
      int size = strbox->GetWindowTextLength() + 1;
      if ((size > 1) && (NULL != (str = new char[size])))
         {
         strbox->GetWindowText(str, size);
         if (list->FindExactString(str, -1) >= 0)
            MessageBox("Cannot add duplicate names", "Bad Data");
         else
```

Listing 16.3. continued

```
            {
            int ix = list->AddString(str);
            list->SetSelIndex(ix);
            }
         delete str;
        }
     }
 }

void TMyDialog::CbDel()
{
   if (list)
      {
      int ix = list->GetSelIndex();
      list->DeleteString(ix);
      list->SetSelIndex((ix > 0) ? (ix - 1) : 0);
      }
}

void TMyDialog::CbGetSelStr()
{
   if (list && strbox)
      {
      char* str;
      int ix = list->GetSelIndex();
      if (ix >= 0)
         {
         if (NULL != (str = new char[list->GetStringLen(ix) + 1]))
            {
            list->GetString(str, ix);
            strbox->SetWindowText(str);
            delete str;
            }
         }
      }
}

void TMyDialog::CbSetSelStr()
{
   if (list && strbox)
      {
      int ix = list->GetSelIndex();

      char* str;
      int size = strbox->GetWindowTextLength() + 1;
      if ((size > 1) && (NULL != (str = new char[size])))
         {
         strbox->GetWindowText(str, size);
         if (list->FindExactString(str, -1) >= 0)
            MessageBox("Cannot add duplicate names", "Bad Data");
         else
            {
            list->DeleteString(ix);
            ix = list->AddString(str);
            list->SetSelIndex(ix);
```

16

```
            }
         delete str;
         }
      }
}

void TMyDialog::CbGetSelIdx()
{
   if (list && idxbox)
      {
      char str[15];
      sprintf(str, "%d", list->GetSelIndex());
      idxbox->SetWindowText(str);
      }
}

void TMyDialog::CbSetSelIdx()
{
   if (list && idxbox)
      {
      char* str;
      int size = idxbox->GetWindowTextLength() + 1;
      if ((size > 1) && (NULL != (str = new char[size])))
         {
         idxbox->GetWindowText(str, size);
         list->SetSelIndex(atoi(str));
         delete str;
         }
      }
}

void TMyDialog::CbGetStr()
{
   if (list && idxbox && strbox)
      {
      char* str;
      int ix = -1;
      int size = idxbox->GetWindowTextLength() + 1;
      if ((size > 1) && (NULL != (str = new char[size])))
         {
         idxbox->GetWindowText(str, size);
         ix = atoi(str);
         delete str;
         }
      if ((ix >= 0) && (NULL != (str = new char[list->GetStringLen(ix) +
         ➥ 1])))
         {
         list->GetString(str, ix);
         strbox->SetWindowText(str);
         delete str;
         }
      }
}

void TMyDialog::CmExit()
{
```

continues

Listing 16.3. continued

```
205:      SendMessage(WM_CLOSE);
206:  }
207:
208:  class TListApp : public TApplication
209:  {
210:  public:
211:      TListApp() : TApplication()
212:         { nCmdShow = SW_SHOWMAXIMIZED; }
213:
214:      void InitMainWindow()
215:         {
216:         SetMainWindow(new TFrameWindow(  0,
217:                  "Simple List Box Tester Application",
218:                  new TMyDialog ));
219:         GetMainWindow()->AssignMenu("EXITMENU");
220:         }
221:  };
222:
223:  int OwlMain(int, char *[])
224:  {
225:    return TListApp().Run();
226:  }
```

Figure 16.1 shows a sample session with the CTLLST.EXE application.

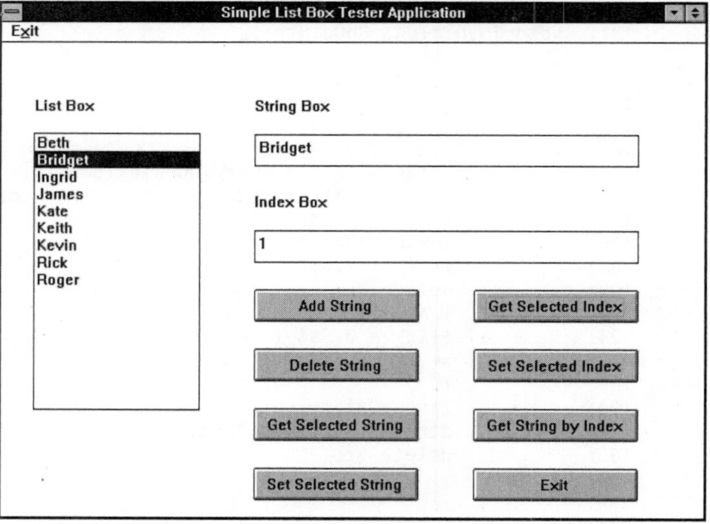

Figure 16.1.
A sample session with the CTLLST.EXE application.

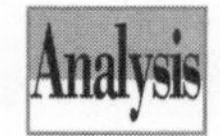

The program in Listing 16.3 declares the dialog class `TMyDialog`, starting on line 14, which contains a number of data members that are pointers to the controls owned by the main dialog. The class also declares a `SetupWindow` member function and several member functions that respond to the notification messages emitted by the various pushbutton controls.

The `TMyDialog` constructor, starting on line 50, performs the creation of interface elements that can connect with the resources loaded in the dialog box. Then the `SetupWindow` member function initializes the list box, starting on line 62.

The member function `CbAdd`, starting on line 83, adds the string of the String Box in the list box control. The function performs the following tasks:

- Ensures that the list box and edit box were created properly on line 85.
- If the String Box edit control isn't empty, then the function creates room for copying the contents of the edit control and then places those contents in the `str` variable on lines 87 through 91.
- Verifies that the added string does not already exist in the list box, using the `FindExactString` function on line 92 to detect an attempt to add duplicate strings, and complains with a message box on line 93 if a duplicate is found.
- Adds the string in `str` to the list box and assigns the position of the string to the local variable `ix` using the `AddString` function on line 96.
- Makes the added string the current selection by invoking the `SetSelIndex` function with the argument `ix` on line 97.

16

The member function `CbDel`, starting on line 104, deletes the current selection by carrying out the following tasks:

- After ensuring the `list` pointer was created properly on line 106, obtains the position of the current selection by invoking the `GetSelIndex` function on line 108, and stores the selection position in the local variable `ix`
- Deletes the selection by calling the `DeleteString` function and supplying it the argument `ix` on line 109
- Selects another list item on line 110 as the new selection at position `ix - 1` (if the variable `ix` already contains `0`, the new first list item becomes the new selection)

The member function `CbGetSelStr` starting on line 114 copies the current selection to the String Box edit control. The function performs the following tasks:

- Creates room for and copies the contents of the list box's current selection using the `GetSelIndex`, `GetStringLen`, and `GetString` functions on lines 118 through 124
- Overwrites the contents of the String Box with the characters retrieved from the list box on line 125

The member function `CbSetSelStr`, starting on line 132, overwrites the current selection with the string in the String Box edit control. Because the list maintains sorted items, the replacement string likely has a different position from the original selection. The function performs the following tasks:

- Obtains the position of the current selection, using the `GetSelIndex` function, and assigns that value to the local variable `ix` on line 136.

- Copies the text in the String Box to the newly allocated `str` variable on line 142.
- Verifies that the string in `str` does not already exist in the list box, using the `FindExactString` function on line 143, displaying a message box if the string already exists on line 144.
- If the string is new to the list, then the function uses the `DeleteString` function to delete the current selection on line 147, uses the `AddString` function to add the string on line 198, and then uses `SetSelIndex` to select the added string on line 149.

If the string has a matching list item, the function displays a message informing you that you cannot add duplicate strings in the list box. This warning also appears if you attempt to overwrite the current selection with the same string.

The member function `CbGetSelIdx`, starting on line 156, writes the position of the current selection to the Index Box edit box on line 162. The function uses the `GetSelIndex` function to obtain the sought position on line 161.

The member function `CbSetSelIdx`, starting on line 166, reads the value in the Index Box edit control and uses that value to set the new current selection. The function uses the `SetSelIndex` function to make the new selection on line 175.

The member function `CbGetStr`, starting on line 181, enables you to retrieve the list item whose position appears in the Index Box edit control. The function performs the following tasks:

- Copies the characters of the Index Box to an allocated string in the `str` data member on line 190
- Converts the string in `str` to the `int`-typed local variable `ix` on line 191
- Copies the characters of the list item at position `ix` to a reallocated `str` on line 196
- Writes the characters of `str` to the String Box edit control on line 197

Handling Multiple-Selection Lists

This section demonstrates the use of multiple-selection lists and focuses on getting and setting the selection strings and their indices. There are two modes for making multiple selections in a list box. These modes depend on whether you set the `LBS_EXTENDEDSEL` style when you create a `TListBox` instance. Setting this style enables you to quickly extend the range of selected items by holding down the Shift key and clicking the mouse. The disadvantage of this style is that you are committed to selecting blocks of contiguous items in the list box manually (that is, using the mouse or cursor keys). Using the `SetSel` or `SetSelItemRange` member functions, you can make your program select noncontiguous items. However, this approach requires extra effort on behalf of the application user and a few extra controls. By contrast, if you do not set the `LBS_EXTENDEDSEL` style, then you can make dispersed selections easily by clicking the mouse button on the individual items that you want to select. The disadvantage of this selection mode is that you must click every item to select it, including neighboring items. Choose the selection mode that you feel best meets the user-interface requirements for your OWL applications.

The Multiple-Selection List Tester

Figure 16.2 shows a sample session with the XFERLIST.EXE application—a program that demonstrates how to query multiple selections in a list box—and also shows the controls used by that application. Following are the controls used by the test program and the operations they support:

- Two multiple-selection list boxes that have the `LBS_MULTIPLESEL` style selected, but not the `LBS_EXTENDEDSEL` style
- Two pushbuttons, one with the caption "<" and the other with the caption ">", that transfer the selected items of one list box to the other
- Static text controls that label the list boxes

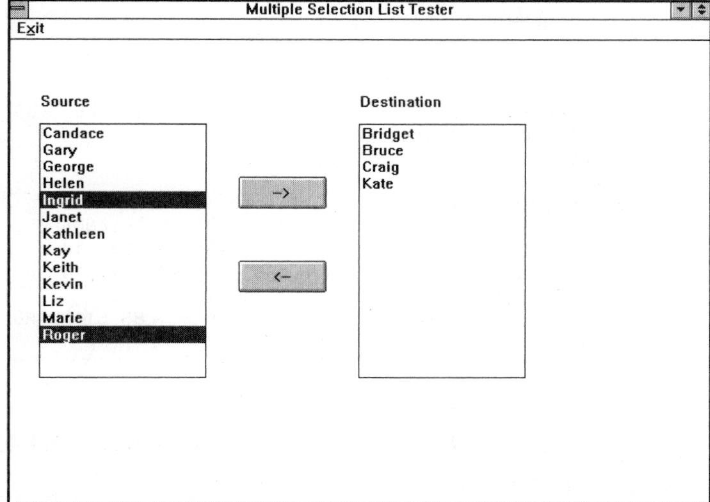

Figure 16.2.
A sample session with the XFERLIST.EXE application.

The multiple-selection list tester application basically enables the user to transfer the contents of one list box to the other and then back again. Listings 16.4, 16.5, and 16.6 contain the source code for the XFERLIST.H, XFERLIST.RC, and XFERLIST.CPP files, respectively.

Create the directory XFERLIST as a subdirectory of \TCWIN45\TC21DAY and store all the project's files in the new directory. As before, the project's IDE file should contain the files XFERLIST.CPP and XFERLIST.RC.

Compile and run the program. The application initializes the list box with many names. Select a few list items in the Source list box and click the > pushbutton. The selected strings appear in the Destination list box and disappear from the Source list box. Now select a few names in the Destination list box and click the < pushbutton. The names move over to the Source list box. When you have finished experimenting with the program, click the Exit menu item or press Alt+X.

Listing 16.4. Source code for the XFERLIST.H header file.

```
#define IDL_SRC   101
#define IDL_DST   102
#define IDB_TOSRC 103
#define IDB_TODST 104
```

Listing 16.5. Script for the XFERLIST.RC resource file.

```
#include <windows.h>
#include <owl\window.rh>
#include "xferlist.h"

EXITMENU MENU LOADONCALL MOVEABLE PURE DISCARDABLE
BEGIN
   MENUITEM "E&xit", CM_EXIT
END

XFERLIST DIALOG 6, 15, 219, 170
STYLE DS_MODALFRAME ¦ WS_POPUP ¦ WS_VISIBLE ¦ WS_CAPTION ¦ WS_SYSMENU
CAPTION "Multiple Selection List Tester"
FONT 8, "MS Sans Serif"
{
 LTEXT "Source", -1, 9, 15, 60, 8
 LISTBOX IDL_SRC, 9, 27, 78, 130, LBS_STANDARD ¦ LBS_MULTIPLESEL
 PUSHBUTTON "—>", IDB_TODST, 95, 62, 30, 14
 PUSHBUTTON "<—", IDB_TOSRC, 95, 92, 30, 14
 LTEXT "Destination", -1, 135, 15, 60, 8
 LISTBOX IDL_DST, 135, 27, 78, 130, LBS_STANDARD ¦ LBS_MULTIPLESEL
}
```

Listing 16.6. Source code for the XFERLIST.CPP program file.

```
#include <owl\applicat.h>
#include <owl\button.h>
#include <owl\dialog.h>
#include <owl\framewin.h>
#include <owl\listbox.h>
#include <owl\static.h>
#include <owl\window.h>
#include <owl\window.rh>

#include "xferlist.h"

class TMyDialog : public TDialog
{
public:
   TMyDialog(TWindow* parent = 0, TModule* module = 0);
   virtual ~TMyDialog();

protected:
   virtual void SetupWindow();
```

```
   void CbToDst();
   void CbToSrc();
   void CmExit();

private:
   TListBox *src, *dst;

   void MoveSels(TListBox* src, TListBox* dst);

   DECLARE_RESPONSE_TABLE(TMyDialog);
};
DEFINE_RESPONSE_TABLE1(TMyDialog, TDialog)
   EV_COMMAND(CM_EXIT, CmExit),
   EV_BN_CLICKED(IDB_TODST, CbToDst),
   EV_BN_CLICKED(IDB_TOSRC, CbToSrc),
END_RESPONSE_TABLE;

TMyDialog::TMyDialog(TWindow* parent, TModule* module)
   : TDialog(parent, "XFERLIST", module)
{
   src = new TListBox(this, IDL_SRC);
   dst = new TListBox(this, IDL_DST);
}

TMyDialog::~TMyDialog()
{
}

void TMyDialog::SetupWindow()
{
   static char *names[] =
      {  "Keith", "Bruce", "Kevin", "Bridget", "Kate",
         "Kay", "Roger", "Marie", "Kathleen", "Liz",
         "Ingrid", "Craig", "George", "Janet", "Gary",
         "Helen", "Candace",
         NULL };

   TWindow::SetupWindow();

   if (src)
      for (int ix = 0; names[ix]; ++ix)
         src->AddString(names[ix]);
}

void TMyDialog::MoveSels(TListBox* src, TListBox* dst)
{
   if (src && dst)
      {
      int *sels, numsels = src->GetSelCount();
      if ((numsels > 0) && (NULL != (sels = new int[numsels])))
         {
         int ix;

         src->GetSelIndexes(sels, numsels);
         for (ix = 0; ix < numsels; ++ix)
            {
```

Listing 16.6. continued

```
76:             char* str;
77:             int size = src->GetStringLen(sels[ix]) + 1;
78:             if ((size > 1) && (NULL != (str = new char[size])))
79:                {
80:                src->GetString(str, sels[ix]);
81:                dst->AddString(str);
82:                delete str;
83:                }
84:             }
85:          for (ix = numsels - 1; ix >= 0; —ix)
86:             src->DeleteString(sels[ix]);
87:
88:          delete sels;
89:          }
90:       }
91: }
92:
93: void TMyDialog::CbToDst()
94: {
95:    MoveSels(src, dst);
96: }
97:
98: void TMyDialog::CbToSrc()
99: {
100:   MoveSels(dst, src);
101: }
102:
103: void TMyDialog::CmExit()
104: {
105:    SendMessage(WM_CLOSE);
106: }
107:
108: class TXferApp : public TApplication
109: {
110: public:
111:    TXferApp() : TApplication()
112:       { nCmdShow = SW_SHOWMAXIMIZED; }
113:
114:    void InitMainWindow()
115:       {
116:       SetMainWindow(new TFrameWindow(  0,
117:              "Multiple Selection List Tester",
118:              new TMyDialog ));
119:       GetMainWindow()->AssignMenu("EXITMENU");
120:       }
121: };
122:
123: int OwlMain(int, char *[])
124: {
125:    return TXferApp().Run();
126: }
```

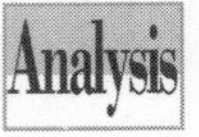

The program in Listing 16.6 works similarly to the other programs presented so far. It declares an application class `TXferApp` on line 108 and a dialog class `TMyDialog` on line 11.

The dialog class creates a couple of interface controls in its constructor and then does its initialization in the `SetupWindow` member function.

The `TMyDialog` dialog class declares two data members, `src` and `dst` on line 25, which are pointers to class objects of type `TListBox`. These are used to access the source and destination list boxes after they are created.

16

The function `MoveSels`, starting on line 64, is the main workhorse of the program. It does the following:

- It takes two parameters: the source list box `src` and the destination list box `dst`.
- After making sure it was given valid `TListBox` pointers, it obtains the number of selections from the source list box on line 68 and creates an array to hold those indices on line 69. It then retrieves those indices and stores them in the newly created `sels` array on line 73.
- The function iterates through the list of selections on lines 74 through 84 and gets a string for each entry with the `GetString` function on line 80. It then adds this string to the destination list box with the `AddString` function on line 81.
- Finally, the function iterates through the list of selections again, this time backwards, and deletes them from the source list box with the `DeleteString` function on lines 85 and 86.

Note that when the `MoveSels` function deletes the selections from the source list box, it does so in reverse order. The reason for this is that, as the function deletes an entry, every item after the now-deleted one in the list box has its index decreased by one. If the function were to delete the strings forwards, then all but the first selection would be incorrect, because the retrieved list became out of sync with the list box itself.

The two functions that respond to the buttons, `CbToDst` on line 93 and `CbToSrc` on line 98, both call the `MoveSels` function, and they both pass the same arguments; however, they each pass them in a different order. By doing this, you can use the `MoveSels` function for both buttons, but have it move the selections between opposite list boxes as the parameters are switched.

Summary

Today's lesson presented the list box control, which enables an application user to choose from a collection of values. You learned about the following topics:

- The single-selection list box control provides you with a list of items from which to select. This type of list box enables you to select only one item at a time.
- The multiple-selection list box enables you to select multiple items in a list box for collective processing. Setting the `LBS_EXTENDEDSEL` style when you create the list box enables you to quickly extend the range of selected items by holding down the Shift key and clicking the mouse.

Q&A

Q Can the argument for the `fileSpec` parameter in function `TListBox::DirectoryList` contain multiple wildcards, such as `"*.CPP *.H"`?

A No, the argument list for `fileSpec` is limited to one filename wildcard.

Q Does OWL support intercepting the messages related to the movement of the thumb box in a list box control?

A Yes, but the standard `ListBox` control doesn't have any default notifications for these events. You can intercept the `WM_HSCROLL` and `WM_VSCROLL` messages to track the thumb. You'll learn a bit more about scroll bars on Day 17.

Q What is the general approach to implementing a program with two list boxes that scroll simultaneously?

A The general approach is to intercept the `WM_HSCROLL` and `WM_VSCROLL` messages in each list box and then adjust the other accordingly. Again, you learn more about handling scroll bars on Day 17.

Q Should I use `InsertString` in a list box created with the `LBS_SORT` style?

A No, you shouldn't because the `LBS_SORT` style maintains the list box items in order. Using `InsertString` corrupts the order in the list box. Instead, use the `AddString` member function.

Workshop

The Workshop provides quiz questions to help you solidify your understanding of the material covered and exercises to provide you with experience in using what you've learned. Try to understand the quiz and exercise answers before continuing on to the next day's lesson. Answers are provided in Appendix A.

Quiz

1. True or false? The list box notification message `LBN_SETFOCUS` is suitable for optional initializing related to selecting a list box control.
2. True or false? The list box notification message `LBN_KILLFOCUS` is suitable for optional validation after you deselect a list box control.
3. True or false? The list box enables you to detect only the final selection, using the `LBN_KILLFOCUS` notification.

4. True or false? You should use `LBN_SELCHANGE` with a special flag to detect mouse double-clicks on a list box item.
5. True or false? `LBS_STANDARD` creates a list box control with unordered items.

Exercise

Modify the XFERLIST program to initialize the source list box with a directory listing, and then have it enable and disable the appropriate pushbuttons depending on whether there is anything selected in the corresponding list boxes.

WEEK
3

Scroll Bars, Combo Boxes, and VBX Controls

Day 16 presented list box controls. Today's lesson presents two somewhat similar controls: the scroll bar and the combo box. The scroll bar control enables you to select a numeric value quickly, usually in a wide range of values. The combo box control combines the edit control and the list box, enabling the user to select a value from the list box component or to enter a new value in the edit control part.

Today, you also will learn about the Visual Basic Controls (VBXs). The VBX interface was designed to allow for a standard method of creating custom controls for Visual Basic, allowing third-party vendors to supply interesting, original controls in addition to those supplied by standard Windows. VBXs are wide and varied, and Borland supplies a set of classes to allow the programmer to implement them easily.

You will learn about the following topics:

- The scroll bar control
- The combo box control in its various styles
- VBX controls

The Scroll Bar Control

Windows allows the scroll bar to exist as a separate control as well as to be incorporated in windows, lists, and combo boxes. The scroll bar control appears and behaves much like the scroll bar of a window. The control has a thumb box that keeps track of the current value; when the user clicks and drags the thumb box, the display can be changed with a fine control. This thumb box mechanism is supported by the `EvVScroll` or `EvHScroll` member functions. In addition, the scroll bar responds to cursor control keys, such as Home, End, PageUp, and PageDown. This feature is supported by the `EvKeyDown` member function. The main purpose of the scroll bar control is to enable you to quickly and efficiently select an integer value in a predefined range of values. Windows, for example, uses scroll bars to fine-tune the color palette, the keyboard rate, and the mouse sensitivity.

The *TScrollBar* Class

The ObjectWindows Library offers the `TScrollBar` class, a descendant of `TControl`, as the class that models the scroll bar controls. The `TScrollBar` class declares a class constructor and a number of member functions to set and query the control's current position and range of values.

The class constructors appear similar to all the other classes derived from `TControl`.

Syntax

The *TScrollBar* Constructor

The declaration of the `TScrollBar` constructor is

```
TScrollBar( TWindow* parent,
            int id,
            int x,
            int y,
            int w,
            int h,
            bool isHScrollBar,
            TModule* module = 0 );
TScrollBar(TWindow* parent, int resourceId, TModule* module = 0);
```

As with the other control class constructors, the `parent` refers to the parent window that contains the control, and `id` is the identifier used in differentiating the control from others. The `x`, `y`, `w`, and `h` parameters describe the location and size of the scroll bar control. The `isHScrollBar` parameter is used to specify in which direction the scroll bar will be. If the parameter is `true`, then the scroll bar will extend horizontally; `false` will mean a vertical scroll bar. The `resourceId` parameter is used to associate the OWL object with a dialog box's interface element.

17

Note that the type of scroll bar that appears will be the same regardless of the values specified in the `w` and `h` parameters. If you specify a width and height for a vertical scroll bar, but specify `true` for the `isHScrollBar` parameter, you'll end up with a very oddly shaped horizontal scroll bar. For this reason, the constructor will automatically set either the width or height of the control if the appropriate parameter is set to `0`. When creating a horizontal scroll bar, for example, specifying `0` for the `h` parameter will give the control a standard height.

There are several styles, described in Table 17.1, that can be used to control the display of the scroll bar with respect to the rectangle you define in the constructor. Only two of them, the `SBS_HORZ` and `SBS_VERT` styles, are automatically set, depending on the state of the `isHScrollBar` parameter.

Example

```
TScrollBar* pThermometer = TScrollBar( this,
                                       IDSB_THERMOMETER,
                                       10, 10, 180, 0,
                                       true );
```

Table 17.1. `SBS_XXX` styles for the scroll bar control.

Value	Meaning
`SBS_BOTTOMALIGN`	Specifies a style used with `SBS_HORZ` to align the bottom of the scroll bar with the bottom edge of the rectangle specified in the `TScrollBar` constructor.
`SBS_HORZ`	Specifies a horizontal scroll bar whose location, width, and height are specified by the parameters in the constructor, if neither `SBS_BOTTOMALIGN` nor `SBS_TOPALIGN`.

continues

Table 17.1. continued

Value	Meaning
SBS_LEFTALIGN	Specifies a style used with the SBS_VERT to align the left edge of the scroll bar with the left edge of the rectangle specified in the constructor.
SBS_RIGHTALIGN	Specifies a style used with SBS_VERT to align the right edge of the scroll bar with the right edge of the rectangle specified in the constructor.
SBS_SIZEBOX	Specifies a size box whose location, width, and height are specified by the parameters in the constructor, if neither one of the next two SBS_XXX styles is specified.
SBS_SIZEBOXBOTTOMRIGHTALIGN	Specifies a style used with SBS_SIZEBOX to align the lower right corner of the size box with the lower right corner of the rectangle specified in the constructor.
SBS_SIZEBOXTOPLEFTALIGN	Specifies a style used with the SBS_SIZEBOX style to align the upper left corner of the size box with the upper left corner of the rectangle specified in the constructor.
SBS_TOPALIGN	Specifies a style used with SBS_HORZ to align the top of the scroll bar with the top edge of the rectangle specified in the constructor.
SBS_VERT	Specifies a vertical scroll bar whose location, width, and height are specified by the parameters in the constructor, if neither SBS_RIGHTALIGN nor SBS_LEFTALIGN is specified.

The TScrollBar class declares a number of member functions. The following are some of the more useful functions:

- The first member function that you will most likely use after creating a TScrollBar instance is SetRange. This function enables you to set the range of values for the scroll bar.
- The GetRange member function enables you to query the current range of values for the scroll bar.
- The parameterless GetPosition member function returns the current position of the thumb box.
- The SetPosition member function moves the thumb box to the specified position. You are responsible for ensuring that the new thumb position is within the current scroll bar range.

Syntax

The *SetRange* Function

The declaration of the `SetRange` function is

```
void SetRange(int min, int max);
```

The arguments for the `min` and `max` parameters designate the new range of values for the scroll bar control.

Example

```
pThermometer->SetRange(32,212);      // Freezing to boiling
```

Syntax

The *GetRange* Function

The declaration of the `GetRange` function is

```
void GetRange(int& min, int& max) const;
```

The parameters `min` and `max` are filled in by the `GetRange` member function with the minimum and maximum of the current range values for the scroll bar control.

Example

```
int freezing, boiling;
pThermometer->GetRange(freezing, boiling);
```

Syntax

The *SetPosition* Function

The declaration of the member function `SetPosition` is

```
void SetPosition(int thumbPos);
```

The parameter `thumbPos` specifies the new thumb box position.

Example

```
pThermometer->SetPosition(72);     // a comfortable temp
```

Responding to Scroll Bar Notification Messages

There are several methods by which a program can handle scroll bar notifications. The first is by creating a descendant class of the `TScrollBar` class, and then overriding the various member functions that are called in response to the `SB_XXX` notification messages as listed in Day 15's lesson. The following table associates the notification messages with their corresponding `TScrollBar` member functions:

Table 17.2. SBS_XXX and TScrollBar member functions.

Notification Message	TScrollBar member function
SB_LINEUP	SBLineUp
SB_LINEDOWN	SBLineDown
SB_PAGEUP	SBPageUp
SB_PAGEDOWN	SBPageDown
SB_THUMBPOSITION	SBThumbPosition
SB_THUMBTRACK	SBThumbTrack
SB_TOP	SBTop
SB_BOTTOM	SBBottom

You must remember, however, that when overriding a descendant class's version of a response function, the parent's version must be called first. It is that version that keeps the scroll bar updated. Consider the following example:

```
void TMyScrollBar::SBTop()
{
   TScrollBar::SBTop();      // Make sure our parent gets a chance
   sndPlaySound("TOP.WAV", SND_ASYNC);    // Play a sound
}
```

Another method of responding to scroll bar notification messages is by intercepting the `EvHScroll` or `EvVScroll` member functions in the scroll bar's parent class. There, you can interrogate the scroll bar as to its current position and then act accordingly.

```
void TMyWindow::EvVScroll(uint code, uint pos, HWND hwnd)
{
   TWindow::EvVScroll(code, pos, hwnd);  // Give our parent a chance
   int newpos = scrollbar->GetPosition(); // get the updated position
   switch (code)
      {
      case SB_TOP:
         sndPlaySound("TOP.WAV", SND_ASYNC);
         break;
      }
}
```

Finally, if one uses the `EV_CHILD_NOTIFY_ALL_CODES` macro when defining the response table to assign a function response to the scroll bar's ID, the assigned function will be called for all notification messages coming from the scroll bar. The response function looks and acts similarly to the `EvXScroll` functions, but in this case it isn't necessary to call the parent's version of the function.

```
DEFINE_RESPONSE_TABLE1(TMyWindow, TWindow)
   EV_CHILD_NOTIFY_ALL_CODES(IDSC_THERMOMETER, EvScrollBar),
END_RESPONSE_TABLE;
```

```
void TMyWindow::EvScrollBar(uint code)
{
   switch (code)
      {
      case SB_TOP:
         sndPlaySound("TOP.WAV", SND_ASYNC);
         break;
      }
}
```

The Count Down Timer

17

The *count down timer* application contains the following controls:

- A timer scroll bar control that has a default range of 0 to 60 seconds
- Two static text controls that label the range of values for the timer scroll bar
- A static text control to show the current setting of the scroll bar
- Start and Exit buttons

You can set the number of seconds by using the scroll bar. When you move the scroll bar thumb box, the current thumb position appears in a static box. To trigger the countdown process, click the Start button. During the countdown, the application decrements the number of seconds in the edit box and moves the scroll bar's thumb box upward. When the countdown ends, the program sounds a beep and restores the scroll bar to its starting value.

The countdown timer application illustrates the following scroll bar manipulations:

- Setting and altering the scroll bar range of values
- Moving and changing the scroll bar thumb box position (the program illustrates how these tasks are performed internally or with the mouse)
- Using the scroll bar to supply a value

Listing 17.1 shows the source code for the COUNTDN.H header file, Listing 17.2 shows the source code for the COUNTDN.RC resource file, and Listing 17.3 shows the source code for the COUNTDN.CPP program file.

Listing 17.1. Source code for the COUNTDN.H header file.

```
#define IDB_START    101
#define IDB_EXIT     102
#define IDS_STATUS   103
#define IDSC_TIMER   104
```

Listing 17.2. Source code for the COUNTDN.RC resource file.

```
/****************************************************************************


COUNTDN.RC

produced by Borland Resource Workshop


****************************************************************************/

        #include "countdn.h"

        COUNTDN DIALOG 6, 15, 272, 182
        STYLE DS_MODALFRAME ¦ WS_POPUP ¦ WS_VISIBLE ¦ WS_CAPTION ¦ WS_SYSMENU
        CAPTION "Count Down Timer"
        FONT 8, "MS Sans Serif"
        {
         RTEXT "Countdown: ", -1, 42, 20, 52, 8
         LTEXT "50", IDS_STATUS, 94, 20, 29, 8
         PUSHBUTTON "Start", IDB_START, 19, 65, 30, 20
         PUSHBUTTON "Exit", IDB_EXIT, 62, 65, 30, 20
         SCROLLBAR IDSC_TIMER, 131, 32, 9, 100, SBS_VERT
         LTEXT "0", -1, 145, 33, 13, 8
         LTEXT "60", -1, 145, 124, 13, 8
        }
```

Listing 17.3. Source code for the COUNTDN.CPP program file.

```
#include <stdio.h>
#include <owl\applicat.h>
#include <owl\button.h>
#include <owl\dialog.h>
#include <owl\framewin.h>
#include <owl\scrollba.h>
#include <owl\static.h>
#include <owl\window.h>
#include <owl\window.rh>

        #include "countdn.h"

        class TMyDialog : public TDialog
        {
        public:
           TMyDialog(TWindow *parent = 0, TModule* module = 0);

        protected:
           virtual void SetupWindow();

           void EvTimerBar(uint code);
           void CbStart();
```

```
      void CbExit();

   private:
      TScrollBar  *timerbar;
      TStatic     *status;

      DECLARE_RESPONSE_TABLE(TMyDialog);
   };
   DEFINE_RESPONSE_TABLE1(TMyDialog, TDialog)
      EV_CHILD_NOTIFY_ALL_CODES(IDSC_TIMER, EvTimerBar),
      EV_BN_CLICKED(IDB_START, CbStart),
      EV_BN_CLICKED(IDB_EXIT, CbExit),
   END_RESPONSE_TABLE;

   TMyDialog::TMyDialog(TWindow *parent, TModule* module)
      : TDialog(parent, "COUNTDN", module)
   {
      status = new TStatic(this, IDS_STATUS);
      timerbar = new TScrollBar(this, IDSC_TIMER);
   }

   void TMyDialog::SetupWindow()
   {
      TWindow::SetupWindow();    // Initialize the visual element

      if (timerbar)
         {
         timerbar->SetRange(0, 60);
         timerbar->SetPosition(15);
         EvTimerBar(SB_THUMBPOSITION);
         }
   }

   void TMyDialog::EvTimerBar(uint /*code*/)
   {
      if (status)
         {
         char text[25];
         sprintf(text, "%d", timerbar ? timerbar->GetPosition() : 0);
         status->SetText(text);
         }
   }

   void DelaySecs(DWORD dwSecs)
   {
      DWORD dwTime = GetTickCount() + (dwSecs * 1000L);
      while (GetTickCount() < dwTime)
        /* Just wait a while. */;
   }

   void TMyDialog::CbStart()
   {
      if (timerbar)
         {
         // First, let the user know that we're stopping the
         // system for a time.
         //
```

continues

Listing 17.3. continued

```
79:                 ::SetCursor(::LoadCursor(NULL, IDC_WAIT));
80:
81:                 int start = timerbar->GetPosition();
82:                 for (int ix = start - 1; ix >= 0; —ix)
83:                    {
84:                    timerbar->SetPosition(ix);
85:                    EvTimerBar(SB_THUMBPOSITION);
86:                    DelaySecs(1);
87:                    }
88:                 timerbar->SetPosition(start);
89:                 EvTimerBar(SB_THUMBPOSITION);
90:                 }
91:           }
92:
93:           void TMyDialog::CbExit()
94:           {
95:              SendMessage(WM_CLOSE);
96:           }
97:
98:           class TCountDownApp : public TApplication
99:           {
100:          public:
101:             TCountDownApp() : TApplication()
102:                { nCmdShow = SW_SHOWMAXIMIZED; }
103:
104:             void InitMainWindow()
105:                {
106:                SetMainWindow(new TFrameWindow(   0,
107:                       "Count Down Timer",
108:                       new TMyDialog ));
109:                }
110:          };
111:
112:          int OwlMain(int, char *[])
113:          {
114:             return TCountDownApp().Run();
115:          }
```

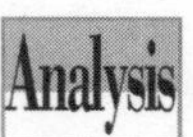

The interesting parts of the program in Listing 17.3 on line 92 start with the `SetupWindow` member function starting on line 43. First make sure to call the parent's version to create the actual visual elements. After making sure you can create the `timerbar` object, its range and position are initialized on lines 49 and 50, and the `EvTimerBar` member function is called with the parameter `SB_THUMBPOSITION` on line 51. Although `EvTimerBar` doesn't actually make use of the parameter it's passed, you should be sure that you send an accurate value, just in case some future version of this program *does* make use of the parameter.

The `EvTimerBar` member function that starts on line 55 responds to any notification message that might be sent by the scroll bar, as well as the various times it's called explicitly by the program itself. Its sole purpose at this point is to keep the `status` static text box updated with the current position of the scroll bar.

Figure 17.1 shows a sample session with the COUNTDN.EXE application.

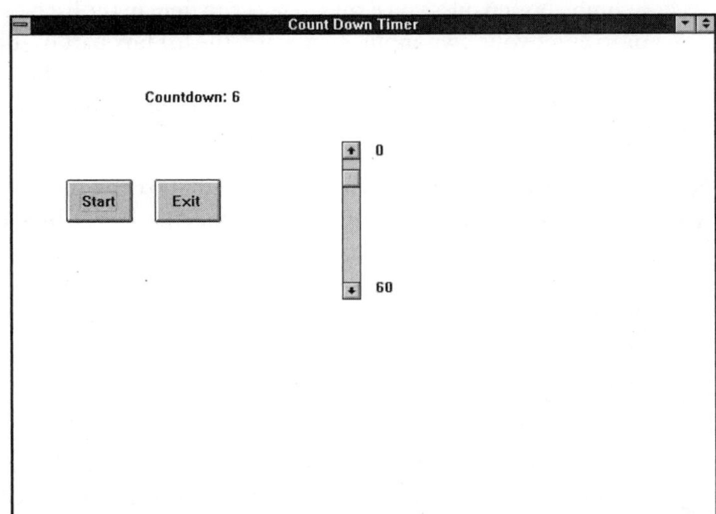

Figure 17.1.
A sample session with the COUNTDN.EXE application.

The next function is the nonmember function `DelaySecs` starting on line 65. This simply sits on its laurels for the number of seconds specified in the `dwSecs` parameter. It does this by calling the Windows `GetTickCount` function. This function returns the number of milliseconds elapsed since Windows was started. By multiplying `dwSecs` by `1000L` and then adding that to the result of the `GetTickCount` call on line 67, you get the end time. From there, all that's needed is a small loop that keeps calling the `GetTickCount` function as long as its result is less than the end time.

It's the `CbStart` function that provides the real meat of the program starting on line 72. After ensuring on line 74 that you have a valid pointer to the `timerbar` object, you set the cursor to the hourglass on line 79. Because you'll be delaying the entire Windows system for the duration of the countdown, it's polite to let the user know that you are taking over for a while by changing the cursor to the hourglass. As soon as you exit the loop and go back to Windows, the cursor will automatically be changed back to the regular arrow. Note the use of the scope modifier on the calls to `SetCursor` and `LoadCursor`. This is used to make sure we get the original Windows functions instead of the `TWindow` member functions, which behave slightly differently.

On line 81 you initialize the `start` variable with the current position of the scroll bar and start a countdown to 0 from there. As you count down, you set the scroll bar's position, update the static text box, and then call the `DelaySecs` function on lines 94 through 86. Once the loop is finished, you reset the scroll bar to its original position on line 88 and update the static text control on line 89.

The Combo Box Control

Windows supports the combo box control, which combines an edit box with a list box. Thus, a combo box enables you either to select an item in the list box component (or part, if you prefer) or to enter your own input. In a sense, the list box part of the combo box contains convenient or frequently used selections. A combo box, unlike a list box, does not confine you to choosing items in the list box. There are three types of combo boxes: simple, drop-down, and drop-down list.

NEW TERM The *simple combo box* includes the edit box and the list box that are always displayed. The *drop-down combo box* differs from the simple type by the fact that the list box appears only when you click the down scroll arrow. The *drop-down list combo box* provides a drop-down list that appears when you click the down scroll arrow. There is no edit box in this type of combo box.

Syntax

The *TComboBox* Class

OWL offers the `TComboBox` class, a descendant of `TListBox`, to support the combo box controls. The `TComboBox` class declares a constructor and a rich set of member functions to support both the edit control components, in addition to all the inherited list box member functions.

The declaration of the constructor is

```
TComboBox( TWindow* parent,
           int      id,
           int      x, int y, int w, in h,
           uint32   style,
           uint     textLen,
           TModule* module = 0 );
TComboBox(TWindow* parent, int resourceId, uint testLen, TModule* module = 0);
```

The new parameters to this control class are the `style` and `textLen` parameter. The `TComboBox` control is the only control class whose constructor takes a parameter for specifying the style. This is because it is the one class in which you will most often want to modify the style. These styles are described in Table 17.3, and only the `CBS_SORT` and `CBS_AUTOHSCROLL` styles are set automatically; anything else you might want must be passed via the `style` parameter. The `textLen` parameter works similarly to the one sent to the `TEdit` class from Day 13. When the combo box has an edit box at the top, this parameter specifies the text length for that box to be `textLen - 1`. Specifying 0 for `textLen` will allow up to 64K of text in the edit box.

Example

```
pcb = new TComboBox(this, 101, 10, 10, 100, 150, CBS_DROPDOWN, 0);
```

The `style` parameter may include either `CBS_SIMPLE` for a simple combo box, `CBS_DROPDOWN` for a drop-down combo box, or `CBS_DROPDOWNLIST` for a drop-down list combo box.

Table 17.3. Combo box control styles.

Style	Meaning
`CBS_AUTOHSCROLL`	Automatically scrolls the text in the edit control to the right when you enter a character at the end of the line (removing this style limits the text to the characters that fit inside the rectangular boundary of the edit control).
`CBS_DISABLENOSCROLL`	Causes the scroll bar of the dropped-down list box portion of the combo box simply to become disabled and gray when scrolling is not allowed. By default, the scroll bar disappears.
`CBS_DROPDOWN`	Specifies a drop-down combo box.
`CBS_DROPDOWNLIST`	Specifies a drop-down list combo box.
`CBS_HASSTRINGS`	When used with an owner-drawn combo box, it causes the strings added to the combo box to be copied internally by the standard Windows routines. This always is the case when Windows does the drawing of the combo box.
`CBS_NOINTEGRALHEIGHT`	Tells the combo box that its drop-down list box portion need not be truncated to fit the height of its items; partial displays of items may be displayed.
`CBS_OEMCONVERT`	Allows Windows to convert the character sets as appropriate (useful for filenames).
`CBS_OWNERDRAWFIXED`	Creates an owner-drawn combo box; the programmer must create routines to display the items in the combo box. All items in the drop-down list box portion will be the same height.
`CBS_OWNERDRAWVARIABLE`	Exactly the same as `CBS_OWNERDRAWFIXED`, except the display items may be of differing heights.
`CBS_SIMPLE`	Specifies a simple combo box.
`CBS_SORT`	Automatically sorts the items in the list box.

The `TComboBox` class declares member functions to manage the edit box component and overrides member functions to manage the list box components. Most of these functions are similar to the corresponding members of the `TEdit` and `TListBox` classes.

In addition to the inherited `TListBox` member functions, the `TComboBox` class declares some extra member functions to handle the drop-down specifics of the combo box control. Among these are the following:

- The parameterless `ShowList` and `HideList` functions to drop down and roll up the combo box, respectively. Note that these are just wrapper functions that call the version of the `ShowList` function that takes a `bool` parameter, `ShowList` passing `TRUE` and `HideList` passing `FALSE`.
- The `GetDroppedControlRect` member function to obtain the size of the dropped-down control
- The parameterless `GetDroppedState` member function that returns a `bool` to tell whether the combo box is currently dropped down
- The pair of member functions `GetExtendedUI` and `SetExtendedUI` that get and set the extended user interface for the combo box

Syntax

The *GetDroppedControlRect* Function

The declaration of the `GetDroppedControlRect` function is

```
void GetDroppedControlRect(TRect& Rect) const;
```

When this function is called, the `Rect` parameter is filled with the screen coordinates of the dropped-down list box.

Example

```
TRect rct;
pcb->GetDroppedControlRect(rct);
```

Although the `TComboBox` class isn't directly derived from the `TEdit` class, it has member functions to manipulate the edit control that comes as part of the combo box:

- The parameterless `GetTextLen` member function that returns an integer specifying the length of the text in the edit box
- The `GetText` and `SetText` member functions for modifying the edit text
- The `GetEditSel` and `SetEditSel` member functions that allow the manipulation of the starting and ending character position (that is, the index of the first selected character and the index of the first selected character that is not in the selected text)
- The parameterless `Clear` member function that clears the selected text

Syntax

The *GetText* Function

The declaration of the `GetText` function is

```
int GetText(char far* str, int maxChars) const;
```

The parameter `str` is a pointer to a buffer into which `GetText` will copy the contents of the edit box, and `maxChars` is the maximum number of characters to copy (the size of the input buffer).

Example

```
int len = pcb->GetTextLen() + 1;
char* str = new char[len];
if (str)
   pcb->GetText(str, len);
```

Responding to Combo Box Notification Messages

The combo box control emits various types of messages (see Table 17.4). The table also shows the message-mapping macros that are associated with the various command and notification messages. Each type of command or notification message requires a separate member function declared in the control's parent window class.

17

Table 17.4. Combo box notification messages.

Message	Macro	Meaning
CBN_CLOSEUP	EV_CBN_CLOSEUP	The combo box has been closed up.
CBN_DBLCLK	EV_CBN_DBLCLK	A combo item is selected with a mouse double-click.
CBN_DROPDOWN	EV_CBN_DROPDOWN	The combo box has been dropped down.
CBN_EDITCHANGE	EV_CBN_EDITCHANGE	The contents of the edit box are changed.
CBN_EDITUPDATE	EV_CBN_EDITUPDATE	The contents of the edit box are updated.
CBN_ERRSPACE	EV_CBN_ERRSPACE	The combo box cannot allocate more dynamic memory to accommodate new list items.
CBN_KILLFOCUS	EV_CBN_KILLFOCUS	The combo box has lost focus.
CBN_SELCHANGE	EV_CBN_SELCHANGE	A combo item is selected or deselected with a mouse click.
CBN_SELENDCANCEL	EV_CBN_SELENDCANCEL	The user has just selected an item and then selected another control or closed the window.
CBN_SELENDOK	EV_CBN_SELENDOK	The user has just clicked a list item or selected an item and closed the list. This is sent before every CBN_SELCHANGE message.
CBN_SETFOCUS	EV_CBN_SETFOCUS	The combo box has gained focus.

Combo Boxes as History List Boxes

A combo box also can be a history list box. History list boxes typically follow these rules of operation.

- The combo list box removes the `CBS_SORT` style to insert the list items in a chronological fashion. New items are inserted at position `0`, pushing the older items farther down the list. The oldest item is the one at the bottom of the list.
- History boxes usually have a limit on the number of items you can insert, to prevent bleeding memory. This conservation scheme requires that oldest list items be removed after the number of list items reaches a maximum limit.
- If the edit control contains a string that does not have an exact match in the accompanying list box, the edit control string is inserted as a new member at position `0`.
- If the edit control contains a string that has an exact match in the accompanying list box, the matching list member is moved to position `0`, the top of the list. This process involves first deleting the matching list member from its current position and then reinserting it at position `0`.

A history list box is really a combo box that manipulates its edit control and list box items in a certain way. There is no need to derive a descendant of `TComboBox` to add new member functions, although if you use a history list box enough, it might make sense to create a descendant class that automates the functionality. Furthermore, for additional functionality, the descendant class could save the history list to disk for future invocations of the program.

The Son of Mr. Calculator Application

This section presents an updated version of the calculator application—*Son of Mr. Calculator.* This new version adds functionality to Day 13's version by using history combo boxes for the operands and result, instead of the standard edit boxes, and uses a simple combo box that contains the list of supported operators and functions. Figure 17.2 shows a sample session with the CALCJR.EXE application and indicates the controls that are used.

Compile and run the program. Experiment with entering and executing numbers and operators or functions. Notice that combo boxes for the operands and the result fill in their accompanying list boxes in a chronological order. The Operand and Result combo boxes remember the last 30 different operands you entered. In a way, the Result combo box acts as temporary memory.

Listing 17.4 shows the source code for the CALCJR.H header file, Listing 17.5 contains the source code for the CALCJR.RC resource file, and Listing 17.6 contains the source code for the CALCJR.CPP program file. The resource file defines the accelerator keys and menu resources.

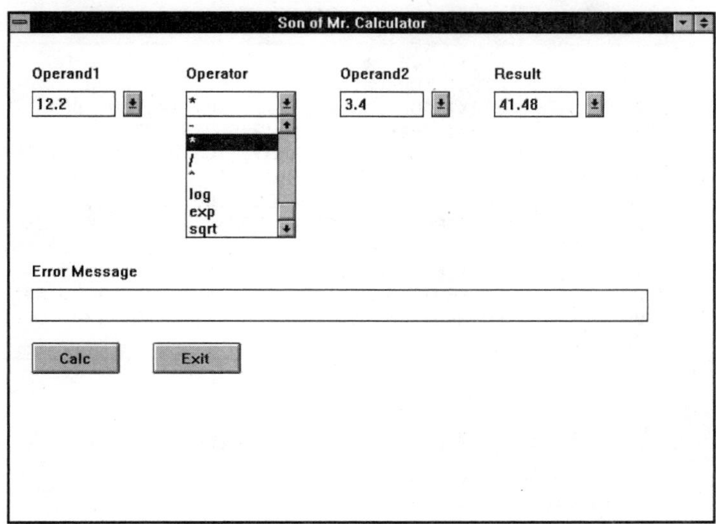

Figure 17.2.
A sample session with the CALCJR.EXE application.

Listing 17.4. Source code for the CALCJR.H header file.

```
#define IDB_CALC      101
#define IDB_EXIT      102
#define IDC_OPERAND1 103
#define IDC_OPERATOR 104
#define IDC_OPERAND2 105
#define IDC_RESULT   106
#define IDE_ERRMSG   107
```

Listing 17.5. Source code for the CALCJR.RC resource file.

```
/****************************************************************************


CALCJR.RC

produced by Borland Resource Workshop


*****************************************************************************/

        #include "calcjr.h"

        CALCJR DIALOG 6, 19, 326, 205
        STYLE DS_MODALFRAME ¦ WS_POPUP ¦ WS_VISIBLE ¦ WS_CAPTION ¦ WS_SYSMENU
        CAPTION "Son of Mr. Calculator"
        FONT 8, "MS Sans Serif"
        {
```

continues

Listing 17.5. continued

```
    LTEXT "Operand1", -1, 10, 15, 60, 8
    LTEXT "Operator", -1, 85, 15, 60, 8
    LTEXT "Operand2", -1, 160, 14, 60, 8
    LTEXT "Result", -1, 235, 15, 60, 8
    COMBOBOX IDC_OPERAND1, 10, 27, 60, 95, CBS_DROPDOWN ¦ WS_TABSTOP
    COMBOBOX IDC_OPERATOR, 85, 27, 60, 95, CBS_DROPDOWNLIST ¦ WS_TABSTOP
    COMBOBOX IDC_OPERAND2, 160, 26, 60, 95, CBS_DROPDOWN ¦ WS_TABSTOP
    COMBOBOX IDC_RESULT, 235, 27, 60, 95, CBS_DROPDOWN ¦ WS_TABSTOP
    LTEXT "Error Message", -1, 10, 133, 60, 8
    EDITTEXT IDE_ERRMSG, 10, 145, 301, 12
    PUSHBUTTON "Calc", IDB_CALC, 10, 169, 50, 15
    PUSHBUTTON "Exit", IDB_EXIT, 76, 169, 50, 15
}
```

Type

Listing 17.6. Source code for the CALCJR.CPP program file.

```
#include <ctype.h>
#include <math.h>
#include <stdio.h>
#include <owl\applicat.h>
#include <owl\button.h>
#include <owl\dialog.h>
#include <owl\combobox.h>
#include <owl\edit.h>
#include <owl\framewin.h>
#include <owl\static.h>
#include <owl\window.h>
#include <owl\window.rh>

#include "calcjr.h"

class THistoryBox : public TComboBox
{
public:
   THistoryBox(TWindow* parent,
               int      id,
               int x, int y, int w, int h,
               int      historyLen,
               uint     textLen = 0,
               TModule* module = 0);
   THistoryBox(TWindow* parent,
               int      resourceId,
               int      historyLen,
               uint     textLen = 0,
               TModule* module = 0);

   void EvKillFocus(HWND);

private:
   int history;

   DECLARE_RESPONSE_TABLE(THistoryBox);
};
```

```
DEFINE_RESPONSE_TABLE1(THistoryBox, TComboBox)
   EV_WM_KILLFOCUS,
END_RESPONSE_TABLE;

THistoryBox::THistoryBox(  TWindow* parent,
                           int      id,
                           int x, int y, int w, int h,
                           int      historyLen,
                           uint     textLen,
                           TModule* module )
   : TComboBox(parent, id, x, y, w, h, CBS_DROPDOWN, textLen, module)
{
   Attr.Style &= ~CBS_SORT;      // We don't want to sort
   history = historyLen;
}

THistoryBox::THistoryBox(TWindow* parent,
                          int      resourceId,
                          int      historyLen,
                          uint     textLen,
                          TModule* module )
   : TComboBox(parent, resourceId, textLen, module)
{
   Attr.Style |= CBS_DROPDOWN;   // Make sure it's a drop-down
   Attr.Style &= ~CBS_SORT;             // We don't want to sort
   history = historyLen;
}

void THistoryBox::EvKillFocus(HWND)
{
   int len = GetTextLen() + 1;
   char* str = new char[len];
   if (str)
      {
      GetText(str, len);
      int ix = FindExactString(str, -1);
      if (ix < 0)
         {
         InsertString(str, 0);
         while (GetCount() >= history)
            DeleteString(GetCount() - 1);
         }
      else if (ix > 0)
         {
         DeleteString(ix);
         InsertString(str, 0);
         SetSelIndex(0);
         }
      delete str;
      }
}

class TCalcJrDialog : public TDialog
{
public:
   TCalcJrDialog(TWindow* parent = 0, TModule* module = 0);

```

continues

Listing 17.6. continued

```
protected:
   virtual void SetupWindow();

   void CmCalc();
   void CmExit();

private:
   TComboBox   *Operator;
   THistoryBox *Operand1, *Operand2, *Result;
   TEdit       *ErrMsg;

   DECLARE_RESPONSE_TABLE(TCalcJrDialog);
};
DEFINE_RESPONSE_TABLE1(TCalcJrDialog, TDialog)
   EV_BN_CLICKED(IDB_CALC, CmCalc),
   EV_BN_CLICKED(IDB_EXIT, CmExit),
END_RESPONSE_TABLE;

TCalcJrDialog::TCalcJrDialog(TWindow* parent, TModule* module)
   : TDialog(parent, "CALCJR", module)
{
   Operand1 = new THistoryBox(this, IDC_OPERAND1, 30);
   Operator = new TComboBox(this, IDC_OPERATOR);
   Operand2 = new THistoryBox(this, IDC_OPERAND2, 30);
   Result = new THistoryBox(this, IDC_RESULT, 30);
   ErrMsg = new TEdit(this, IDE_ERRMSG);
}

void TCalcJrDialog::SetupWindow()
{
   TWindow::SetupWindow();    // Initialize the visual element

   // Fill up out Operator combo box with a variety
   // of operators for our users compuational pleasure.
   //
   if (Operator)
      {
      static char* p[] =
         { "+", "-", "*", "/", "^", "log", "exp", "sqrt", NULL };
      for (int ix = 0; p[ix]; ++ix)
         Operator->AddString(p[ix]);
      }

   // Keep the users out of the error box.
   //
   if (ErrMsg)
      ErrMsg->SetReadOnly(TRUE);
}

double get_number(TComboBox *numbox)
{
   double rslt = 0;        // default to 0
   char* str;
   int size;

```

```
   if (numbox)
      {
      str = new char[size = numbox->GetTextLen() + 1];
      if (str)
         {
         numbox->GetText(str, size);
         rslt = atof(str);
         delete str;
         }
      }
   return rslt;
}

void TCalcJrDialog::CmCalc()
{
   double x, y, z = 0;

   x = get_number(Operand1);
   y = get_number(Operand2);

   if (Operator)
      {
      int   ix = Operator->GetSelIndex();
      if (ix >= 0)
         {
         char* err = 0;

         switch (ix)
            {
            case 0:     // + operator
               z = x + y;
               break;
            case 1:     // - operator
               z = x - y;
               break;
            case 2:     // * operator
               z = x * y;
               break;
            case 3:     // / operator
               if (y)
                  z = x / y;
               else
                  err = "Can't divide by zero.";
               break;
            case 4:     // ^ operator
               if (x > 0)
                  z = exp(y * log(x));
               else
                  err = "Need positive number to raise power.";
               break;
            case 5:     // log function
               if (x > 0)
                  z = log(x);
               else
                  err = "Need positive number for log.";
               break;
            case 6:     // exp function
```

continues

Listing 17.6. continued

```
               if (x < 230)
                  z = exp(x);
               else
                  err = "Need a smaller number for exp.";
               break;
            case 7:     // sqrt function
               if (x >= 0)
                  z = sqrt(x);
               else
                  err = "Can't do sqrt of negative number.";
               break;
            default:
               err = "Unknown operator";
               break;
            }

         if (ErrMsg)
            if (!err)
               ErrMsg->Clear();
            else
               ErrMsg->SetWindowText(err);
         if (!err && Result)
            {
            char dest[81];
            sprintf(dest, "%g", z);
            Result->SetWindowText(dest);
            Result->EvKillFocus(NULL);    // Force history addition
            }
         }
      }
}

void TCalcJrDialog::CmExit()
{
   SendMessage(WM_CLOSE);
}

class TCalcJrApp : public TApplication
{
public:
   TCalcJrApp() : TApplication()
      { nCmdShow = SW_SHOWMAXIMIZED; }

   void InitMainWindow()
      {
      SetMainWindow(new TFrameWindow(  0,
             "Son of Mr. Calulator",
             new TCalcJrDialog ));
      }
};

int OwlMain(int, char *[])
{
   return TCalcJrApp().Run();
}
```

Analysis

The program in Listing 17.6 begins by declaring, starting on line 16, a descendant of `TComboBox` called `THistoryBox`. This descendant declares its constructors, a single member function, and a single data member. The constructor that creates a brand new control specifies the `CBS_DROPDOWN` style when calling the parent `TComboBox` constructor on line 48, and then turns off the `CBS_SORT` style and initializes the `history` member data with the `historyLen` parameter on lines 50 and 51.

The constructor that simply associates the OWL object with the pre-existing dialog control works similarly to the other constructor, except this needs to move the `CBS_DROPDOWN` setting into the constructor's body, rather than the call to the base class' constructor.

The `EvKillFocus` member function of `THistoryBox` that starts on line 66 is called in response to the `WM_KILLFOCUS` Windows message. At this time, the function inserts the string of the edit control part in the list box part. This insertion occurs only if the string is not already in the list box part. In this case, the string is inserted at index `0` and becomes the new top-of-the-list item. If the targeted string already is in the list box part, then the function deletes the existing item in the list box and reinserts it at index `0`. Thus, the targeted string appears to have moved up to the top of the list box part.

17

The `TCalcJrDialog`'s constructor that starts on line 113 does the usual creation of controls. The `SetupWindow` member function then initializes the Operator combo box by filling its list box component with the supported operators and functions on lines 130 through 136.

The `get_number` function, starting on line 144, is used, as in Day 13, to obtain a `double` value from a control. This time, it receives a `TComboBox` pointer, gets the contents of its edit box, then uses the `atof` function to obtain the `double` value that is returned.

The Calc button causes the `CmCalc` member function, starting on line 163, to be called. This is the function that does all the following work of the application:

- Retrieves the values from the Operand1 and Operand2 combo boxes and places their values in the `x` and `y` variables, respectively, on lines 167 and 168.
- Obtains the index of the selected operator in the Operator combo box on line 172.
- If something is actually selected, a `switch` statement is used to determine the requested operation or math function, then the `case` statement performs the requested task and assigns the result to variable `z`, or sets the `err` pointer to an appropriate error string.
- Sets the Error Message edit box if an error occurred or clears that same edit box if no error was detected on lines 223 through 227.
- If no error occurred, displays the result of the operation or function evaluation in the edit control box of the Result combo box, then calls its `EvKillFocus` function directly to have that value inserted into its list box component on lines 228 through 234.

VBX Controls

VBX is an acronym for *Visual Basic eXchange* and describes the host of controls written to the Visual Basic control format. The VBX interface is rather complex, but OWL makes it easy to use with support classes that can be mixed in to the standard ones you've been using so far. There really are just a few simple steps to using VBX controls:

- Declare an instance of the class `TBIVbxLibrary`. This initializes the VBX subsystem that is required to interface with the VBX controls, and is usually done in the `OwlMain` function.
- Use the mixin class `TVbxEventHandler`, multiply inheriting from it and the regular interface class (such as `TWindow` or `TDialog`) and specifying it when defining the response table.
- Use the `EV_VBXEVENTNAME` macro when defining a response table for your interface.
- Create OWL objects to connect with the VBX interface elements that appear on the screen.

Initializing the VBX Subsystem

The initialization and termination of the VBX subsystem occurs with calls to two simple functions: `VBXInit` and `VBXTerm`. Here is a sample `OwlMain` function in which these functions are called.

```
int OwlMain(int argc, char* argv[])
{
   TBIVbxLibrary vbxLib;
   return TApplication().Run();
}
```

As you can see, there really isn't all that much to it. The `TBIVbxLibrary`'s constructor does the initialization, and its destructor shuts down the system when the program closes.

Using the VBX Mixin Class

Mixin classes are ones that can add functionality to a base class simply by being co-declared as multiply-inherited base class. For example, the following code snippet adds VBX control functionality to a descendent dialog class by simply adding `TVbxEventHandler` to the list of base classes:

```
class MyVbxDialog : public TDialog, public TVbxEventHandler
{
   // ... member functions and data go here ...
DECLARE_RESPONSE_TABLE(MyVbxDialog);
}
```

Defining a VBX Response Table

The response table for a dialog box that uses VBX controls looks very much like the ones you've already created, except for a few additions.

```
DEFINE_RESPONSE_TABLE2(MyVbxDialog, TDialog, TVbxEventHandler)
   // ... other response functions go here ...
   EV_VBX_EVENTNAME(ID_CONTROL1, "DragDrop", EvControl1),
   EV_VBX_EVENTINDEX(ID_CONTROL1, 1, EvControl1),
END_RESPONSE_TABLE;
```

Take careful note of the `DEFINE_RESPONSE_TABLE2` line. So far, your response tables have been defined with a `1`, but because this is multiply-inherited from two separate classes, you need to specify this when defining the response table by using a `2`. (Note that if this were for a `TWindow` descendant, then `TWindow` would have been used in place of `TDialog`.) Then the response table entries themselves use the `EV_VBX_EVENTNAME` or `EV_VBX_EVENTINDEX` macros, which have the following basic definitions:

17

```
EV_VBX_EVENTNAME(controlID, eventName, EvHandler)
EV_VBX_EVENTINDEX(controlID, eventIndex, EvHandler)
```

The `controlId` parameter is the typical control ID parameter used in defining other response-table entries; it refers to the ID assigned to the control when it's created by Windows, typically the ID used in the resource file describing the dialog in which the control resides. `eventName` is a string holding the name of the event itself. VBX controls identify their separate events with both indexes and with string labels; these are what belong here. Finally, the `EvHandler` is the name of the member function to be called whenever the event occurs, much like you've already defined in earlier response tables.

The response function for a VBX event is rather simple and looks like the following:

```
void EvHandler(VBXEVENT far* event);
```

Because the VBX events have so much information associated with them, they're passed in a structure rather than as individual arguments to the function. Here is the definition of the `VBXEVENT` structure.

```
struct VBXEVENT
{
   HCTL   Control;
   HWND   Window;
   int    ID;
   int    EventIndex;
   LPCSTR EventName;
   int    NumParams;
   LPVOID ParamList;
};
```

Following is the breakdown of the various items in the structure:

- `Control` is the handle of the sending VBX control. Be careful not to confuse this with a window control; this is a special handle used to refer to the VBX control alone.

- `Window` is a handle to the control window itself.
- `ID` is the ID of the VBX control, the same one defined in the resource file, and so on.
- `EventIndex` is the event index. All VBX controls have their individual events numbered, and this is the number associated with this particular VBX control's event.
- `EventName` is the name of the event. The name is provided, mainly, for the programmer's convenience so the VBX control authors can more easily communicate the purpose of the event.
- `NumParams` is the number of parameters for this event. Each event can have a number of different parameters (`VBXEVENT` is just a wrapper that describes the event itself) that are encoded in the next structure item.
- `ParamList` is a pointer to an array containing the pointers to the parameter values for this event. The number of parameters is defined by the previous parameter, and they are indexed from `0` to `NumParams - 1`. You need to know the details of the VBX control itself to be able to identify the types of the parameters. These are supplied by the VBX control vendor.

There are two macros that can be used to access the parameters passed in `ParamList`. Both of them require the parameters up to the one accessed be the same as the one accessed. Here are the two macros.

```
VBX_EVENTARGNUM(event, type, index)
VBX_EVENTARGSTR(event, index)
```

The `event` parameter is the same as the one passed to an event handler of the type `VBXEVENT far*`. The `type` parameter in the first macro should be the type of the argument to retrieve. `index` is the 0-based number of the argument. Since strings are such a common item to retrieve, `VBX_EVENTARGSTR` is provided which already knows the type of argument to access. The types are all based upon Visual Basic types, and have C++ equivalents as shown in Table 17.5.

Table 17.5. VBX argument types.

Basic	C++
Boolean	`bool`
Control	`HCTL`
Double	`double`
Enum	`short`
Integer	`short`
Long	`long`
Single	`float`
String	`HLSTR`

Note that the string is referred to as an `HLSTR`. This is not a standard C++ character array or even a reference to the C++ `string` class. These are handles to Visual Basic strings, and they need to be accessed with the following special functions:

```
HLSTR  VBXCreateBasicString(LPVOID buffer, USHORT len);
VOID   VBXDestroyBasicString(HLSTR string);
int    VBXGetBasicStringBuf(HLSTR string, LPSTR buffer, int len);
USHORT VBXGetBasicStringLength(HLSTR string);
ERR    VBXSetBasicString(HLSTR far *string, LPVOID buffer, USHORT len);
```

Based on your previous experiences in this book, I would imagine the functions and how they're used are fairly obvious after reading just the function names. In order, they create strings, destroy them, copy them to a character array, obtain a string's length, and copy a character array into a string. If you need more information, you can check out the online help provided with Turbo C++.

17

The *TVbxControl* OWL Interface Class

When it finally comes time to instantiate an interface object to communicate with the VBX control, you need to use the `TVbxControl` class. The following are the two constructors for this object:

```
TVbxControl(TWindow*         parent,
            int              id,
            const char far*  vbxName,
            const char far*  vbxClass,
            const char far*  title,
            int              x,
            int              y,
            int              w,
            int              h,
            long             initLen = 0,
            void far*        initData = 0,
            TModule*         module = 0);
TVbxControl(TWindow* parent, int resourceId, TModule* module = 0);
```

Notice that the second constructor looks just like all the other constructors used to associate an OWL class with a resource control, and that's just exactly what it is. Looking back at the first constructor, you'll see that many of the parameters are the same as those used to create other controls (`parent`, `id`, `title`, `x`, `y`, `w`, `h`, and `module`). The `vbxName` parameter specifies the filename of the VBX control library and the `vbxClass` parameter specifies the class name of the control (libraries can contain multiple controls, and the class name enables you to select the particular one in which you're interested).

There are two additional parameters towards the end of the list called `initLen` and `initData`, both of which have default values of `0`. These are used to supply specific information to the VBX control as it is being initialized. This information is control-specific, and its exact makeup needs to be defined by the author of the VBX control.

Unlike the other controls, however, VBX controls have a number of properties which describe their appearance and actions. These properties, like the response functions, are defined by the VBX control author and you will need to consult the documentation for the specific control you want to use.

Once you know which properties you want to manipulate, you can do so with a variety of `GetProp` and `SetProp` functions. There are a substantial number of these overloaded functions, enabling you to access properties of varying types, either by index or name.

Note: As you might have noticed before with the response functions, all VBX controls use both indexes and names together to provide easier access to the programmer.

Here are the general formats of the property manipulation functions.

```
bool GetProp(int propIndex, type& value, int arrayIndex = -1);
bool GetProp(const char far* name, type& value, int arrayIndex = -1);
bool SetProp(int propIndex, type value, int arrayIndex = -1);
bool SetProp(const char far* name, type value, int arrayIndex = -1);
```

Note that I didn't specify a particular type for each of these functions. As stated earlier, these functions are overloaded to accept a number of different types: `int`, `long`, `bool`, `ENUM`, `HPIC`, `float`, `string`, and `COLORREF`. The `arrayIndex` parameter can be used to access different elements of an array property. By default, you access the first property, whether or not there are any more to access.

In addition to the functions for changing the different properties, you can ask the VBX to tell you which properties it contains, and even what the property types are.

```
int GetNumProps();
int GetPropIndex(const char far* name);
void GetPropName(int propIndex, string& str);
int GetPropType(int propIndex);
int GetPropType(char far* name);
bool IsArrayProp(int propIndex);
bool IsArrayProp(char far* name);
```

The `GetNumProps` function returns the number of properties associated with the control, while `GetPropName` will supply the name of the indexed control. `GetPropIndex` will search the control's properties for the supplied name and return the associated index. You can determine a property's type by using the `GetPropType` function. This returns a value that can be checked against one of the macros described in Table 17.6. Checking the `IsArrayProp` function tells you whether or not the specified property is stored as an array.

Table 17.6. VBX Property Types

Property Type	Equivalent C++ Type
PTYPE_CSTRING	HSZ
PTYPE_SHORT	short
PTYPE_LONG	LONG
PTYPE_BOOL	bool
PTYPE_COLOR	DWORD or COLORREF
PTYPE_ENUM	BYTE or ENUM
PTYPE_REAL	float
PTYPE_XPOS	LONG (Twips)
PTYPE_XSIZE	LONG (Twips)
PTYPE_YPOS	LONG (Twips)
PTYPE_YSIZE	LONG (Twips)
PTYPE_PICTURE	HPIC
PTYPE_BSTRING	HLSTR

While this listing of and inquiry of the various properties of a VBX control can be useful, you probably won't have much call for it. Usually you will need to determine the properties beforehand by reading the VBX's documentation and then make use of the properties as described.

Summary

Today's lesson presented the scroll bar and combo box controls. These controls share the common factor of being input objects. You learned about the following topics:

- The scroll bar control enables you to select quickly from a wide range of integers.
- There are various types of combo box controls: simple, drop-down, and drop-down list.
- You can make a history list box out of a drop-down combo box.
- VBX controls can be easily controlled with OWL classes and, with a few minor differences, can be treated like ordinary Windows controls.

Q&A

Q Do the scroll bars strictly select integers?

A Yes. However, these integers can be indices to arrays, items in list box controls, and other integer codes to various attributes such as colors. Therefore, in a sense, the scroll bar can be used to select nonintegers.

Q Can I create a scroll bar control with an excluded subrange of values?

A No. You may want to use a list box control instead and have that control list the value numbers.

Workshop

The Workshop provides quiz questions to help you solidify your understanding of the material covered and exercises to provide you with experience in using what you've learned. Try to understand the quiz and exercise answers before continuing on to the next day's lesson. Answers are provided in Appendix A.

Quiz

1. True or false? If you do not include the `CBS_AUTOHSCROLL` style in creating a combo list box, you limit the text to the characters that fit inside the rectangular boundary of the edit control.
2. True or false? You can handle the `CBN_SELCHANGE` notification message to monitor every keystroke in the edit control of a combo box.
3. True or false? Setting `CBS_SORT` creates a combo box whose list box items are sorted and unique.
4. True or false? To emulate a history list box, a combo box must be created without the `CBS_SORT` style.
5. True or false? A history list may have duplicate items.
6. True or false? COUNTDN.CPP demonstrates how to implement a two-way connection between the current value of a scroll bar control and the numeric value in a text box.
7. True or false? The range of values for a scroll bar control are fixed when you create the control.

Exercise

Modify the CALCJR.CPP program by adding a Variables multiline box and a Store pushbutton.

Write a wrapper class to simulate the VBX `HLSTR` object, allowing programmers to act on it like it was a C++ string.

WEEK 3

MDI Windows

The *Multiple Document Interface* (*MDI*) is a standard Windows interface used by many popular Windows applications and utilities, such as the Windows Program Manager, the Windows File Manager, and even the Turbo C++ IDE. The MDI interface also is part of the Common User Access (CUA) standard set by IBM. Each MDI-compliant application enables you to open child windows for file-specific tasks such as editing text, managing a database, or working with a spreadsheet. Today, you will learn the following topics on managing MDI windows and objects:

- The basic features and components of an MDI-compliant application
- Basics of building an MDI-compliant application
- The class `TMDIFrame`
- The class `TMDIClient`
- Building MDI client windows
- The class `TMDIChild`
- Building MDI child windows
- Managing messages in an MDI-compliant application

The MDI Application Features and Components

An MDI-compliant application is made up of the following objects:

- The visible *MDI frame window* that contains all other MDI objects. The MDI frame window is an instance of the class `TMDIFrame` or its descendants. Each MDI application has one MDI frame window.
- The invisible *MDI client window* that performs underlying management of the MDI child windows that are dynamically created and removed. The MDI client window is an instance of the class `TMDIClient`. Each MDI application has one MDI client window.
- The dynamic and visible *MDI child window*. An MDI application dynamically creates and removes multiple instances of MDI child windows. An MDI child window is an instance of `TMDIChild` or its descendant. These windows are located, moved, resized, maximized, and minimized inside the area defined by the MDI frame window. At any given time (and while there is at least one MDI child window), there is only one active MDI child window.

When you maximize an MDI child window, it occupies the area defined by the client area of the MDI frame window. When you minimize an MDI child window, the icon of that window appears at the bottom area of the MDI frame window.

Note: The MDI frame window has a menu that manipulates the MDI child windows and their contents. The MDI child windows cannot have a menu, but they may contain controls. In any other respect, you can think of an MDI child window as an instance of `TFrameWindow` or its descendants.

Basics of Building an MDI Application

Before discussing in more detail the creation of the various components that make up an MDI application, focus on the basic strategy involved. In the last section, you learned that the basic ingredients for an MDI application are the `TMDIFrame`, `TMDIClient`, and `TMDIChild` (or a `TMDIChild` descendant) classes. The `TMDIFrame` class supports the creation and handling of the MDI client window as well as menu management.

The `MDIClient` class focuses on the creation and underlying management of MDI child windows. The `TMDIChild` class offers the functionality for the MDI child windows.

At this stage you might ask, "Do I typically derive descendants for all three classes to create an MDI application?" The answer is no. You normally need to derive descendants only for the `TMDIFrame` and `TWindow` classes. The functionality of the `TMDIClient` class is adequate for most MDI-compliant applications.

The *TMDIFrame* Class

ObjectWindows offers the `TMDIFrame` class, a descendant of `TFrameWindow`, to implement the MDI frame window of an MDI application. The declaration of the `TMDIFrame` class is as follows:

```
class _OWLCLASS TMDIFrame : virtual public TFrameWindow {
public:
   TMDIFrame(const char far* title,
             TResId          menuResId,
             TMDIClient&     clientWnd = *new TMDIClient,
             TModule*        module = 0);


   TMDIFrame(HWND hWindow, HWND clientHWnd, TModule* module = 0);

   //
   // override virtual functions defined by TFrameWindow
   //
   bool         SetMenu(HMENU);
   TMDIClient*  GetClientWindow();
   virtual HWND GetCommandTarget();
   void         PerformCreate(int menuOrId);
```

```
    //
    // find & return the child menu of an MDI frame's (or anyone's) menu
    // bar.
    //
    static HMENU FindChildMenu(HMENU);

protected:
    //
    // call ::DefFrameProc() instead of ::DefWindowProc()
    //
    LRESULT DefWindowProc(uint message, WPARAM wParam, LPARAM lParam);

private:
    //
    // hidden to prevent accidental copying or assignment
    //
    TMDIFrame(const TMDIFrame&);
    TMDIFrame& operator=(const TMDIFrame&);

    DECLARE_RESPONSE_TABLE(TMDIFrame);
    DECLARE_STREAMABLE(_OWLCLASS, TMDIFrame, 1);
};
```

The TMDIFrame class has public, protected, and private members. The MDI frame window class has three constructors, one of which is private. The first constructor creates a class instance by specifying the title, associated menu resource ID, and reference to the associated MDI client window. The second constructor creates a class instance from an existing non-OWL window. The third constructor, which is declared private and thus is used only internally in the class, creates an instance of class TMDIFrame using another existing instance.

The class TMDIFrame declares the public member functions SetMenu, GetClientWindow, and FindChildMenu. The function SetMenu looks for the MDI submenu in the new menu bar and updates member ChildMenuPos if the menu is found. The function searches for the MDI submenu in the menu bar and updates the position in the MDI window's top-level menu of the child window submenu. The function GetClientWindow returns a pointer to the associated MDI client window. The function FindChildMenu searches for the child menu of an MDI frame's menu bar.

The class TMDIFrame declares the single protected member function DefWindowProc. This function overrides the inherited function TWindow::DefWindowProc and invokes the Windows API function DefFrameProc. The API function provides the default processing for any incoming Windows message that is not handled by the MDI frame window.

Building MDI Frame Windows

The usual approach for creating the objects that make up an ObjectWindows application starts with creating the application instance and then its main window instance. In the case of an MDI-compliant application, the application's main window is typically a descendant of class TMDIFrame. The InitMainWindow member function of the application class creates this window.

Looking at the first two TMDIFrame constructors, you can tell that creating the main MDI window involves a title and menu resource—there is no pointer to a parent window because MDI frame windows have no parent windows. The MDI frame window, unlike most descendants of class TWindow, must have a menu associated with it. This menu typically includes the items shown in Table 18.1, needed to manipulate the MDI children. In addition, the menu of the MDI frame window is dynamically and automatically updated to include the current MDI children.

The constructor of the descendant of TMDIFrame (call it the application frame class) can, in many cases, simply invoke the parent class constructor. This invocation occurs if the steps taken by the parent class are adequate for creating the MDI frame window instance. In the case in which you want to modify the behavior of the application frame class, you need to include the required statements. Such statements might assign initial values to data members declared in the application frame class.

The SetupWindow member function invokes the InitClientWindow to create the TMDIClient instance. You can modify the SetupWindow function to automatically create the first child MDI window, for example.

The *TMDIClient* Class

ObjectWindows offers the TMDIClient class, a descendant of TWindow, to implement the MDI client window. The declaration of the TMDIClient class is as follows:

```
class _OWLCLASS TMDIClient : public virtual TWindow {
public:
   LPCLIENTCREATESTRUCT  ClientAttr;

   TMDIClient(TModule* module = 0);
   ~TMDIClient();

   virtual bool CloseChildren();

   TMDIChild* GetActiveMDIChild();

   //
   // member functions to arrange the MDI children
   //
   virtual void ArrangeIcons();
   virtual void CascadeChildren();
   virtual void TileChildren(int tile = MDITILE_VERTICAL);

   //
   // override member functions defined by TWindow
   //
   bool PreProcessMsg(MSG& msg);
   bool Create();

   virtual TWindow* CreateChild();
```

```
    //
    // constructs a new MDI child window object. By default, constructs
    // an instance of TWindow as an MDI child window object
    //
    // will almost always be overridden by derived classes to construct
    // an instance of a user-defined TWindow derived class as an MDI
    // child window object
    //
    virtual TMDIChild* InitChild();

protected:
    char far* GetClassName();

    //
    // menu command handlers & enabler
    //
    void CmCreateChild()
       { CreateChild(); }  // CM_CREATECHILD
    void CmTileChildren()
       { TileChildren(); }  // CM_TILECHILDREN
    void CmTileChildrenHoriz()
       { TileChildren(MDITILE_HORIZONTAL); }  // CM_TILECHILDREN
    void CmCascadeChildren()
       { CascadeChildren(); }  // CM_CASCADECHILDREN
    void CmArrangeIcons()
       { ArrangeIcons(); }  // CM_ARRANGEICONS
    void CmCloseChildren()
       { CloseChildren(); }  // CM_CLOSECHILDREN
    void CmChildActionEnable(TCommandEnabler& commandEnabler);

    LRESULT EvMDICreate(MDICREATESTRUCT far& createStruct);
    void    EvMDIDestroy(hwnd hWnd);

private:
    friend class TMDIFrame;
    TMDIClient(HWND hWnd, TModule* module = 0);

    //
    // hidden to prevent accidental copying or assignment
    //
    TMDIClient(const TMDIClient&);
    TMDIClient& operator =(const TMDIClient&);

    DECLARE_RESPONSE_TABLE(TMDIClient);
    DECLARE_STREAMABLE(_OWLCLASS, TMDIClient, 1);
};
```

The class `TMDIClient` declares a public constructor and destructor. The MDI client class declares a number of member functions that handle Windows and menu command messages for activating an MDI child window; arranging the MDI child icons; cascading and tiling MDI children; closing MDI children; and creating an MDI child window. These message response functions use sibling member functions. Table 18.1 shows the predefined menu ID constants and the `TMDIClient` member functions that respond to them.

Table 18.1. The predefined menu command messages for manipulating MDI children.

Action	Menu ID Constant	Responding TMDIClient Member Function
Tile	CM_TILECHILDREN	CmTileChildren
Tile Horizon	CM_TILECHILDRENHORIZ	CmTileChildrenHoriz
Cascade	CM_CASCASDECHILDREN	CmCascadeChildren
Arrange Icons	CM_ARRANGEICONS	CmArrangeIcons
Close All	CM_CLOSECHILDREN	CmCloseChildren

There are a number of member functions in the class `TMDIClient` that you may want to modify when you create class descendants. The list of such member functions includes `CreateChild`, `SetupWindow`, `CanClose`, and `CloseChildren`. These functions enable you to modify how to create, set up, and close MDI children.

The MDI Child Window Class

18

The class `TMDIChild` models the basic operations of all MDI child windows. The declaration for the class `TMDIChild` is as follows:

```
class _OWLCLASS TMDIChild : virtual public TFrameWindow {
public:
   TMDIChild(TMDIClient&      parent,
             const char far* title = 0,
             TWindow*        clientWnd = 0,
             bool            shrinkToClient = false,
             TModule*        module = 0);

             TMDIChild(HWND hWnd, TModule* module = 0);

             ~TMDIChild() {}

   //
   // override method defined by TWindow
   //
   bool PreProcessMsg(MSG& msg);
   bool ShowWindow(int cmdShow);
   bool EnableWindow(bool enable);
   void Destroy(int retVal = 0);

protected:
   void PerformCreate(int menuOrId);
   LRESULT DefWindowProc(uint msg, WPARAM wParam, LPARAM lParam);
   void EvMDIActivate(HWND hWndActivated,
                      HWND hWndDeactivated);
   bool EvNCActivate(bool active);
```

```
private:
   //
   // hidden to prevent accidental copying or assignment
   //
   TMDIChild(const TMDIChild&);
   TMDIChild& operator =(const TMDIChild&);

   DECLARE_RESPONSE_TABLE(TMDIChild);
   DECLARE_STREAMABLE(_OWLCLASS, TMDIChild, 1);
};
```

The class `TMDIChild` declares three constructors (one of which is private) and a destructor. The first constructor enables you to create a class instance by specifying the parent MDI client window, MDI child window title, the client window, and whether the MDI child window shrinks to fit the client window. The second constructor creates a class instance using an existing non-OWL MDI child window. The third constructor, which is declared private and used only internally within the class, creates a `TMDIChild` class instance using an existing instance.

The MDI child window class declares the single public member function `PreProcessMsg`. This function preprocesses the Windows messages sent to the MDI child windows. The class `TMDIChild` offers a set of protected functions that create, destroy, and activate MDI child windows. In addition, the class provides its own version of function `DefWindowProc` to handle default Windows message processing.

Building MDI Child Windows

Building MDI child windows is very similar to building application windows in the programs presented earlier. Following are the differences:

- An MDI child window cannot have its own menu. The menu of the MDI frame window is the one that manipulates the currently active MDI child window or all of the MDI children.

Note: The keyboard handler must not be enabled. It actually causes the reverse effect in the MDI children and antagonizes the proper operations of the MDI application.

- An MDI child window can have controls—this is unusual but certainly allowed.

Managing MDI Messages

The message loop directs the command messages first to the current focus window, and then after that to the active MDI child window to allow it to respond. If that window does not respond, then the message is sent to the parent MDI frame window. The active MDI child window responds to the notification messages sent by its controls, just as any window or dialog box would.

Simple Text Viewer

Look at a simple MDI-compliant application. Because MDI applications frequently are used as text viewer and text editors, we present the next application that emulates a simple text viewer. We say "emulates" because the application actually displays random text rather than text that you can retrieve from a file. This approach keeps the program simple and helps you to focus on implementing the various MDI objects. Figure 18.1, which appears after Listing 18.4, shows a sample session with the MDI1.EXE program. The MDI application has a simple menu containing the Exit and MDI Children items.

Compile and run the application. Experiment with creating MDI children. Notice that the text in odd-numbered MDI child windows is static, whereas the text in even-numbered windows can be edited. This feature is implemented to illustrate how to create a simple form of text viewer and text editor (with no Save option, to keep the example short). Try to tile, cascade, maximize, and minimize these windows. Also test closing individual MDI child windows as well as closing all of the MDI children.

Examine the code that implements this simple MDI application. Listing 18.1 shows the contents of the MDI1.DEF definition file. Listing 18.2 shows the source code for the MDI1.H header file. This file declares the command message constants and a control ID constant. Listing 18.3 contains the script for the MDI1.RC resource file. The file defines the menu resource required by the MDI frame window. The menu has two menu items, Exit and MDI Children. The latter menu item is a pop-up menu with several options. The commands, except the option Count Children, use predefined command message constants. Listing 18.4 shows the source code for the MDI1.CPP program file.

Type

Listing 18.1. The contents of the MDI1.DEF definition file.

```
NAME           MDI1
DESCRIPTION    'An OWL Windows Application'
EXETYPE        WINDOWS
CODE           PRELOAD MOVEABLE DISCARDABLE
DATA           PRELOAD MOVEABLE MULTIPLE
HEAPSIZE       1024
STACKSIZE      8192
```

Listing 18.2. The source code for the MDI1.H header file.

```
#define CM_COUNTCHILDREN 101
#define ID_TEXT_EDIT     102
#define IDM_COMMANDS     400
```

Listing 18.3. The script for the MDI1.RC resource file.

```
#include <windows.h>
#include <owl\window.rh>
#include <owl\mdi.rh>
#include "mdi1.h"
IDM_COMMANDS MENU LOADONCALL MOVEABLE PURE DISCARDABLE
BEGIN
  MENUITEM "E&xit", CM_EXIT
  POPUP "&MDI Children"
  BEGIN
    MENUITEM  "C&reate", CM_CREATECHILD
    MENUITEM  "&Cascade", CM_CASCADECHILDREN
    MENUITEM  "&Tile", CM_TILECHILDREN
    MENUITEM  "Arrange &Icons", CM_ARRANGEICONS
    MENUITEM  "C&lose All", CM_CLOSECHILDREN
    MENUITEM  "C&ount Children", CM_COUNTCHILDREN
  END
END
```

Listing 18.4. The source code for the MDI1.CPP program file.

```
/*
  Program to illustrate simple MDI windows
*/
#include <owl\mdi.rh>
#include <owl\applicat.h>
#include <owl\framewin.h>
#include <owl\mdi.h>
#include <owl\static.h>
#include <owl\edit.h>
#include <owl\scroller.h>
#include "mdi1.h"
#include <stdio.h>
#include <string.h>

const MaxWords = 100;
const WordsPerLine = 12;
const NumWords = 10;
char* Words[NumWords] = { "The ", "friend ", "saw ", "the ",
                          "girl ", "drink ", "milk ", "boy ",
                          "cake ", "bread " };

bool ExpressClose = false;
int NumMDIChild = 0;
```

```
int HighMDIindex = 0;

class TWinApp : public TApplication
{
public:
  TWinApp() : TApplication() {}

protected:
  virtual void InitMainWindow();
};

class TAppMDIChild : public TMDIChild
{
public:
  // pointer to the edit box control
  TEdit* TextBox;
  TStatic* TextTxt;

  TAppMDIChild(TMDIClient& parent, int ChildNum);

protected:

  // handle closing the MDI child window
  virtual bool CanClose();
};

class TAppMDIClient : public TMDIClient
{
public:

  TAppMDIClient() : TMDIClient() {}

 protected:

  // create a new child
  virtual TMDIChild* InitChild();

  // close all MDI children
  virtual bool CloseChildren();

  // handle the command for counting the MDI children
  void CMCountChildren();

  // handle closing the MDI frame window
  virtual bool CanClose();

  // declare response table
  DECLARE_RESPONSE_TABLE(TAppMDIClient);
};

DEFINE_RESPONSE_TABLE1(TAppMDIClient, TMDIClient)
  EV_COMMAND(CM_COUNTCHILDREN, CMCountChildren),
 END_RESPONSE_TABLE;

 TAppMDIChild::TAppMDIChild(TMDIClient& parent, int ChildNum)
   : TMDIChild(parent),
```

continues

Listing 18.4. continued

```
     TFrameWindow(&parent),
     TWindow(&parent)
{
  char s[1024];

  // set the scrollers in the window
  Attr.Style |= WS_VSCROLL | WS_HSCROLL;
  // create the TScroller instance
  Scroller = new TScroller(this, 200, 15, 10, 50);

  // set MDI child window title
  sprintf(s, "%s%i", "MDI Child #", ChildNum);
  Title = _fstrdup(s);

  // randomize the seed for the random-number generator
  randomize();

  // assign a null string to the variable s
  strcpy(s, "");
  // build the list of random words
  for (int i = 0; i < MaxWords; i++) {
      if (i > 0 && i % WordsPerLine == 0)
         strcat(s, "\r\n");
      strcat(s, Words[random(NumWords)]);
  }
  // create a static text object in the child window if the
  // ChildNum variable stores an odd number. Otherwise,
  // create an edit box control
  if (ChildNum % 2 == 0) {
     // create the edit box
     TextBox = new TEdit(this, ID_TEXT_EDIT, s,
              10, 10, 300, 400, 0, true);
     // remove borders and scroll bars
     TextBox->Attr.Style &= ~WS_BORDER;
     TextBox->Attr.Style &= ~WS_VSCROLL;
     TextBox->Attr.Style &= ~WS_HSCROLL;
  }
  else
     // create static text
     TextTxt = new TStatic(this, -1, s, 10, 10, 300, 400,
                           strlen(s));
}

bool TAppMDIChild::CanClose()
{
  // return true if the ExpressClose member of the
  // parent MDI frame window is true
  if (ExpressClose == true) {
    NumMDIChild--;
    return true;
  }
  else
    // prompt the user and return the prompt result
     if (MessageBox("Close this MDI window?",
         "Query", MB_YESNO | MB_ICONQUESTION) == IDYES) {
```

```
      NumMDIChild--;
      return true;
    }
    else
      return false;
}

TMDIChild* TAppMDIClient::InitChild()
{
  ++NumMDIChild;
  return new TAppMDIChild(*this, ++HighMDIindex);
}

bool TAppMDIClient::CloseChildren()
{
  bool result;
  // set the ExpressClose flag
  ExpressClose = true;
  // invoke the parent class CloseChildren() member function
  result = TMDIClient::CloseChildren();
  // clear the ExpressClose flag
  ExpressClose = false;
  NumMDIChild = 0;
  HighMDIindex = 0;
  return result;
}

//  display a message box that shows the number of children
void TAppMDIClient::CMCountChildren()
{
  char msgStr[81];

  sprintf(msgStr, "There are %i MDI child windows", NumMDIChild);
  MessageBox(msgStr, "Information", MB_OK | MB_ICONINFORMATION);
}

bool TAppMDIClient::CanClose()
{
  return MessageBox("Close this application?", "Query",
                    MB_YESNO | MB_ICONQUESTION) == IDYES;
}

void TWinApp::InitMainWindow()
{
  MainWindow = new TMDIFrame("Simple MDI Text Viewer",
                      TResID(IDM_COMMANDS),
                      *new TAppMDIClient);
}

int OwlMain(int /* argc */, char** /*argv[] */)
{
  TWinApp app;
  return app.Run();
}
```

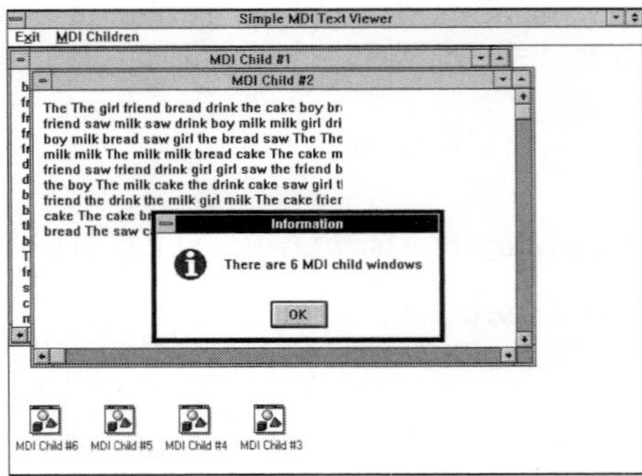

Figure 18.1.
A sample session with the MDI1.EXE program.

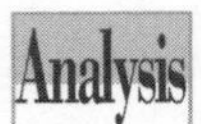

The program in Listing 18.4 declares a set of global constants used in generating the random text in each MDI child window. The global array of pointer `Words` contains the program's somewhat restricted vocabulary. The listing also declares the global variables `ExpressClose`, `NumMDIChild`, and `HighMDIindex`. These variables provide a simple solution for sharing information between the descendants of branched-out OWL classes. The variable `ExpressClose` assists in closing all of the child MDI windows in one swoop. The variable `NumMDIChild` maintains the actual number of MDI child windows. The variable `HighMDIindex` stores the index of the last MDI child window created.

The program listing declares three classes: the application class, `TWinApp`, in line 26; the MDI client class, `TAppMDIClient`, in line 50; and the MDI child window class, `TAppMDIChild`, in line 35. We will discuss these classes in order.

The code for the application class looks very much like the ones in previous programs, with one exception. The `InitMainWindow` member function, defined in lines 177 to 182, creates an instance of the stock MDI frame class, `TMDIFrame`. The `TMDIFrame` constructor call has the following arguments: title of the application; the name of the menu resource, `COMMANDS`; and the pointer to the dynamically allocated instances of `TAppMDIClient`.

The `TAppMDIClient` class declares a constructor and a group of protected member functions. The member functions are as follows:

- The member function `InitChild` (defined in lines 142 to 146) initializes an MDI child window. The function increments the global variable `NumMDIChild` and then returns a dynamically allocated instance of `TAppMDIChild`. The arguments of creating this instance are `*this` (a reference to the object itself) and `++HighMDIindex`. The second argument pre-increments the global variable `HighMDIindex`, which keeps track of the highest index for an MDI child window.
- The member function `CloseChildren` (defined in lines 148 to 160) alters the behavior of the inherited `CloseChildren` function. The new version performs the following tasks:
    - Assigns `true` to the global variable `ExpressClose` (see line 152)

- Invokes the parent class version of `CloseChildren` and stores the result of that function call in the local variable result
- Assigns `false` to the variable `ExpressClose` in line 156
- Assigns `0` to the global variable `NumMDIChild` in line 157
- Assigns `0` to the global variable `HighMDIindex` in line 157. This task resets the value in variable `HighMDIindex` when you close all of the MDI child windows.
- Returns the value stored in the variable result

- The member function `CMCountChildren` (defined in lines 163 to 168) responds to the Windows command message `CM_COUNTCHILDREN` generated by the menu option Count Children. The function displays the number of MDI child windows in a message dialog box. The function first builds the string `msgStr` to contain the formatted image of the global variable `NumMDIChild`. Then, the function invokes the member function `MessageBox` to display the sought information.
- The virtual member function `CanClose` (defined in lines 171 to 175) prompts you to confirm closing the MDI-compliant application.

18

The MDI child window class, `TAppMDIChild`, declares the `TextBox` and `TextTxt` data members, a constructor, and the `CanClose` member function. The member `TextBox` is the pointer to the `TEdit` instance created to store the random text in one kind of the MDI child windows. The member `TextTxt` is the pointer to the `TStatic` instance created to store random text in the other type of MDI child windows.

The `TAppMDIChild` constructor (defined in lines 78 to 121) performs a variety of tasks, as follows:

- Sets the window style to include the vertical and horizontal scroll bars (see line 86).
- Creates an instance of `TScroller` to animate the window's scroll bars (see line 88).
- Sets the window title to include the MDI child window number, using the statements in lines 91 and 92.
- Randomizes the seed for the random-number generator function, `random`.
- Creates the random text and stores it in the local string variable `s`. This task uses the `for` loop in lines 100 to 104.
- If the MDI child window number is even, creates a multiline instance of `TEdit` in lines 110 and 111. This instance contains a copy of the text stored in variable `s`. In addition, the constructor disables the border, vertical scroll bar, and horizontal scroll bar styles (see the statements in lines 113 to 115). These scroll bars are not needed because the MDI child window itself has scroll bars. In the case of an odd-numbered MDI child window number, the constructor creates static text using the characters in variable `s` (see the statement in lines 119 and 120).

The `CanClose` member function regulates closing an MDI child window. When you close such a window using the Close option in its own system menu, the function requires your confirmation. If the request to close comes from the Close All menu command in the parent window, the MDI child window closes without confirmation. The function decrements the global variable `NumMDIChild` in two cases: first, when the global variable `ExpressClose` is `true`; and second, when the function `MessageBox`, which prompts you to confirm closing the window, returns `IDYES`.

Revised Text Viewer

Let's expand on the MDI1.EXE program to illustrate other aspects of managing MDI windows. The next application also creates MDI children that contain edit box controls with random text. However, each MDI child window has the following additional controls:

- An UpperCase pushbutton control that converts the text in the MDI child window into uppercase.
- A LowerCase pushbutton control that converts the text in the MDI child window into lowercase.
- A Can Close check box. Using this box replaces using the confirmation dialog box that appears when you want to close the MDI child window. The check box enables you to predetermine whether the MDI child window can be closed.

The application menu adds a new pop-up menu item, Current MDI Child. This menu item has options that work on the current MDI child window. The commands enable you to clear, convert to uppercase, convert to lowercase, or rewrite the characters in the MDI child window. The new pop-up menu shows how you can manipulate MDI children with custom menus.

Compile and run the application. Create a few MDI children and use their pushbutton controls to toggle the case of characters in these windows. Also use the Current MDI Child commands to further manipulate the text in the currently active MDI child window. Try to close the MDI children with the Can Close check box marked and unmarked. Only the MDI children with the Can Close control checked close individually. Use the Close All option in the MDI Children pop-up menu and watch all of the MDI children close, regardless of the check state of the Can Close control. Figure 18.2, which appears after Listing 18.8, shows a sample session with the MDI2.EXE program.

Listing 18.5 shows the contents of the MDI2.DEF definition file. Listing 18.6 shows the source code for the MDI2.H header file. The file contains the constants for the menu commands and the control IDs. Listing 18.7 contains the script for the MDI2.RC resource file and shows the resource for the expanded menu. Listing 18.8 contains the source code for the MDI2.CPP program file.

Listing 18.5. The contents of the MDI2.DEF definition file.

```
NAME         MDI2
DESCRIPTION  'An OWL Windows Application'
EXETYPE      WINDOWS
CODE         PRELOAD MOVEABLE DISCARDABLE
```

```
DATA         PRELOAD MOVEABLE MULTIPLE
HEAPSIZE     1024
STACKSIZE    8192
```

Listing 18.6. The source code for the MDI2.H header file.

```
#define CM_COUNTCHILDREN 101
#define CM_CLEAR         102
#define CM_UPPERCASE     103
#define CM_LOWERCASE     104
#define CM_RESET         105
#define ID_TEXT_EDIT     106
#define ID_CANCLOSE_CHK  107
#define ID_UPPERCASE_BTN 108
#define ID_LOWERCASE_BTN 109
#define IDM_COMMANDS     400
```


Listing 18.7. The script for the MDI2.RC resource file.

```
#include <windows.h>
#include <owl\window.rh>
#include <owl\mdi.rh>
#include "mdi2.h"
IDM_COMMANDS MENU LOADONCALL MOVEABLE PURE DISCARDABLE
BEGIN
  MENUITEM "E&xit", CM_EXIT
  POPUP "&MDI Children"
  BEGIN
    MENUITEM  "C&reate", CM_CREATECHILD
    MENUITEM  "&Cascade", CM_CASCADECHILDREN
    MENUITEM  "&Tile", CM_TILECHILDREN
    MENUITEM  "Arrange &Icons", CM_ARRANGEICONS
    MENUITEM  "C&lose All", CM_CLOSECHILDREN
    MENUITEM  "C&ount Children", CM_COUNTCHILDREN
  END
  POPUP "&Current MDI Child"
  BEGIN
    MENUITEM  "&Clear", CM_CLEAR
    MENUITEM  "&Uppercase", CM_UPPERCASE
    MENUITEM  "&Lowercase", CM_LOWERCASE
    MENUITEM  "&Reset", CM_RESET
  END
END
```

Listing 18.8. The source code for the MDI2.CPP program file.

```
/*
  Program to demonstrate MDI windows with controls
*/
```

continues

Listing 18.8. continued

```
#include <owl\mdi.rh>
#include <owl\applicat.h>
#include <owl\framewin.h>
#include <owl\button.h>
#include <owl\edit.h>
#include <owl\checkbox.h>
#include <owl\scroller.h>
#include <owl\mdi.h>
#include "mdi2.h"
#include <stdio.h>
#include <string.h>

// declare constants for sizing and spacing the controls
// in the MDI child window
const Wbtn = 50 * 3;
const Hbtn = 30;
const BtnHorzSpacing = 20;
const BtnVertSpacing = 10;
const Wchk = 200 * 3;
const Hchk = 20;
const ChkVertSpacing = 10;
const Wbox = 400 * 3;
const Hbox = 200 * 3;

// declare the constants for the random text that appears
// in the MDI child window
const MaxWords = 200;
const WordsPerLine = 10;
const NumWords = 10;
const BufferSize = 1024;
char AppBuffer[BufferSize];
char* Words[NumWords] = { "The ", "friend ", "saw ", "the ",
                "girl ", "drink ", "milk ", "boy ",
                "cake ", "bread " };


bool ExpressClose = false;
int NumMDIChild = 0;
int HighMDIindex = 0;

class TWinApp : public TApplication
{
public:
  TWinApp() : TApplication() {}

protected:
  virtual void InitMainWindow();
};

class TAppMDIChild : public TMDIChild
{
public:


  TAppMDIChild(TMDIClient& parent, int ChildNum);
```

```

 protected:

   TEdit* TextBox;
   TCheckBox* CanCloseChk;

   // handle the UpperCase button
   void HandleUpperCaseBtn()
     { CMUpperCase(); }

   // handle the LowerCase button
   void HandleLowerCaseBtn()
     { CMLowerCase(); }

   // handle clear the active MDI child
   void CMClear()
     { TextBox->Clear(); }

   // handle converting the text of the active
   // MDI child to uppercase
   void CMUpperCase();

   // handle converting the text of the active
   // MDI child to lowercase
   void CMLowerCase();

   // handle resetting the text of the active MDI child
   void CMReset();

   // reset the text in an MDI child window
   void InitText();

    // handle closing the MDI child window
    virtual bool CanClose();

    // declare response table
    DECLARE_RESPONSE_TABLE(TAppMDIChild);
  };

  DEFINE_RESPONSE_TABLE1(TAppMDIChild, TMDIChild)
    EV_COMMAND(ID_UPPERCASE_BTN, HandleUpperCaseBtn),
    EV_COMMAND(ID_LOWERCASE_BTN, HandleLowerCaseBtn),
    EV_COMMAND(CM_CLEAR, CMClear),
    EV_COMMAND(CM_UPPERCASE, CMUpperCase),
    EV_COMMAND(CM_LOWERCASE, CMLowerCase),
    EV_COMMAND(CM_RESET, CMReset),
  END_RESPONSE_TABLE;

  class TAppMDIClient : public TMDIClient
  {
  public:

   TAppMDIClient() : TMDIClient() {}

   protected:

```

continues

Listing 18.8. continued

```
  // create a new child
  virtual TMDIChild* InitChild();

  // close all MDI children
  virtual bool CloseChildren();

  // handle the command for counting the MDI children
  void CMCountChildren();

  // handle closing the MDI frame window
  virtual bool CanClose();

  // declare response table
  DECLARE_RESPONSE_TABLE(TAppMDIClient);
};

DEFINE_RESPONSE_TABLE1(TAppMDIClient, TMDIClient)
  EV_COMMAND(CM_COUNTCHILDREN, CMCountChildren),
END_RESPONSE_TABLE;

TAppMDIChild::TAppMDIChild(TMDIClient& parent, int ChildNum)
  : TMDIChild(parent),
    TFrameWindow(&parent),
    TWindow(&parent)
{
  char s[41];
  int x0 = 10;
  int y0 = 10;
  int x = x0;
  int y = y0;

  // set the scrollers in the window
  Attr.Style |= WS_VSCROLL | WS_HSCROLL;
  // create the TScroller instance
  Scroller = new TScroller(this, 200, 15, 10, 50);

  // set MDI child window title
  sprintf(s, "%s%i", "Child #", ChildNum);
  Title = _fstrdup(s);

  // create the push button controls
  new TButton(this, ID_UPPERCASE_BTN, "->UpperCase",
              x, y, Wbtn, Hbtn, true);
  x += Wbtn + BtnHorzSpacing;
  new TButton(this, ID_LOWERCASE_BTN, "->LowerCase",
              x, y, Wbtn, Hbtn, false);

  x = x0;
  y += Hbtn + BtnVertSpacing;
  CanCloseChk = new TCheckBox(this, ID_CANCLOSE_CHK, "Can Close",
                              x, y, Wchk, Hchk, NULL);
  y += Hchk + ChkVertSpacing;
  InitText();
  // create the edit box
  TextBox = new TEdit(this, ID_TEXT_EDIT, AppBuffer,
                      x, y, Wbox, Hbox, 0, true);
```

```
  // remove borders and scroll bars
  TextBox->Attr.Style &= ~WS_BORDER;
  TextBox->Attr.Style &= ~WS_VSCROLL;
  TextBox->Attr.Style &= ~WS_HSCROLL;
}

void TAppMDIChild::CMUpperCase()
{
  TextBox->GetText(AppBuffer, BufferSize);
  strupr(AppBuffer);
  TextBox->SetText(AppBuffer);
}

void TAppMDIChild::CMLowerCase()
{
  TextBox->GetText(AppBuffer, BufferSize);
  strlwr(AppBuffer);
  TextBox->SetText(AppBuffer);
}

void TAppMDIChild::CMReset()
{
  InitText();
  TextBox->SetText(AppBuffer);
}

bool TAppMDIChild::CanClose()
{
  // return true if the ExpressClose member of the
  // parent MDI frame window is true
  if (ExpressClose == true) {
    NumMDIChild—;
    return true;
  }
  else
  // do not close the MDi child window if the Can Close is
  // not checked
  if (CanCloseChk->GetCheck() == BF_UNCHECKED)
    return false;
  else {
    NumMDIChild—;
     return true;
  }
}

void TAppMDIChild::InitText()
{
  // randomize the seed for the random-number generator
  randomize();

  // assign a null string to the buffer
  AppBuffer[0] = '\0';
  // build the list of random words
  for (int i = 0;
       i < MaxWords && strlen(AppBuffer) <= (BufferSize - 10);
       i++) {
```

18

Listing 18.8. continued

```
    if (i > 0 && i % WordsPerLine == 0)
      strcat(AppBuffer, "\r\n");
    strcat(AppBuffer, Words[random(NumWords)]);
  }
}

TMDIChild* TAppMDIClient::InitChild()
{
  ++NumMDIChild;
  return new TAppMDIChild(*this, ++HighMDIindex);
}

bool TAppMDIClient::CloseChildren()
{
  bool result;
  // set the ExpressClose flag
  ExpressClose = true;
  // invoke the parent class CloseChildren() member function
  result = TMDIClient::CloseChildren();
  // clear the ExpressClose flag
  ExpressClose = false;
  NumMDIChild = 0;
  HighMDIindex = 0;
  return result;
}

//  display a message box that shows the number of children
void TAppMDIClient::CMCountChildren()
{
  char msgStr[81];

  sprintf(msgStr, "There are %i MDI children", NumMDIChild);
  MessageBox(msgStr, "Information", MB_OK ¦ MB_ICONINFORMATION);
}

bool TAppMDIClient::CanClose()
{
  return MessageBox("Close this application?",
             "Query", MB_YESNO ¦ MB_ICONQUESTION) == IDYES;
}

void TWinApp::InitMainWindow()
{
  MainWindow = new TMDIFrame("Simple MDI Text Viewer (version 2)",
                   TResID(IDM_COMMANDS),
                   *new TAppMDIClient);
}

int OwlMain(int /* argc */, char** /*argv[] */)
{
  TWinApp app;
  return app.Run();
}
```

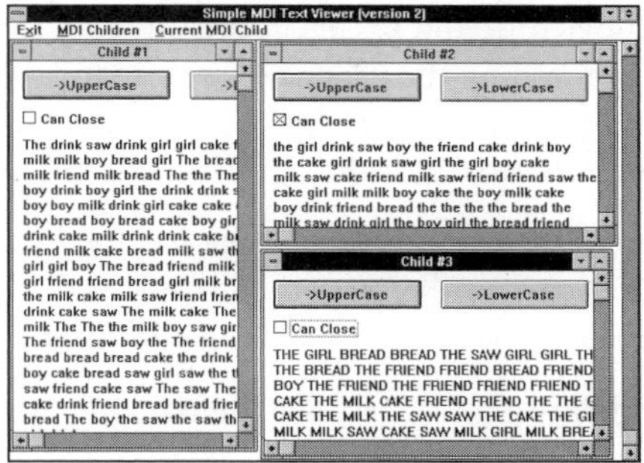

Figure 18.2.
A sample session with the MDI2.EXE program.

Analysis

The program in Listing 18.8 declares two sets of constants. The first set is used for sizing and spacing the controls of each MDI child window. The second set of constants is used to manage the random text. The program also declares variable `AppBuffer` as a single 1KB text buffer. We chose to make the buffer global instead of a class data member mainly to reduce the buffer space—the application classes need only one shared buffer at any time. The program listing also declares the global variables `ExpressClose`, `NumMDIChild`, and `HighMDIindex`—another set of components carried over from the program in file MDI1.CPP.

18

The new application maintains the same three classes described in the last program. However, the MDI child class has different members in this program. The new members manage the response to the control notification messages as well as the Current MDI Child menu command messages.

The `TAppMDIChild` constructor (defined in lines 135 to 175) performs the following tasks:

- Sets the window style to include the vertical and horizontal scroll bars, using the statement in line 147
- Creates an instance of `TScroller` to animate the window's scroll bars, using the statement in line 149
- Sets the window title to include the MDI child window number using the statements in lines 152 and 153
- Creates the LowerCase and UpperCase pushbutton controls using the statements in lines 156 to 160
- Creates the Can Close check box control using the statements in lines 162 to 165
- Calls the `InitText` member function to generate random text in the application buffer `AppBuffer`
- Creates a multiline instance of `TEdit` in statement located in lines 169 and 170. This instance contains a copy of the text stored in the application buffer.
- Disables the border, vertical scroll bar, and horizontal scroll bar styles of the edit control. This task uses the statements in lines 172 to 174.

The member function `CMUpperCase` (defined in lines 177 to 182) responds to the command message emitted by the `UpperCase` command. The function copies the text in the MDI child window to the application's buffer, converts the characters in the buffer to uppercase, and then writes the buffer back to the MDI child window.

The member function `CMLowerCase` (defined in lines 184 to 189) responds to the command message emitted by the `LowerCase` command. The function performs similar steps to those in `CMUpperCase`—except the text is converted into lowercase.

The member function `CanClose` (defined in lines 197 to 214) responds to the `WM_CLOSE` message emitted by the Close option in the system menu available in each MDI child window. If the MDI frame window's `ExpressClose` variable is `true`, then the function decrements the global variable `NumMDIChild` and returns `true`. Otherwise, the function returns `false` if the Can Close check box is unchecked, or it decrements the global variable `NumMDIChild` and then returns `false` if the control is not checked.

The member function `InitText` (defined in lines 233 to 237) is an auxiliary routine that fills the application buffer with random text. The function creates up to `MaxWords` words or enough that the buffer limit is closely reached (within 10 bytes). Checking the number of characters in the buffer ensures that the program does not corrupt the memory while attempting to add `MaxWords` words to the buffer.

The member functions `HandleUpperCaseBtn` and `HandleLowerCase` respond to the notification messages sent by the pushbuttons of an MDI child window. These functions perform the same tasks of `CMUpperCase` and `CMLowerCase`, respectively. Therefore, the notification response functions call their respective command-message response member functions.

The member function `CMClear` (defined in lines 74 and 75) responds to the command message emitted by the Clear command in the Current MDI Child menu item. The function simply invokes the `TextBox->Clear()` function call.

The member function `CMReset` (defined in lines 191 to 195) responds to the command message emitted by the Reset command in the Current MDI Child menu item. The function calls the `InitText` member function to create a new batch of random text and then copies the buffer's text to the edit control of the MDI child window.

Note: The Current MDI Child pop-up menu has four options that manipulate the currently active MDI child window. The command messages emitted by these options are handled by the MDI child window instances and not the MDI frame instance—which is what a window instance normally does regarding its own menu commands. This order of handling the command messages is preferred and makes use of the fact that the menu-based messages do reach the currently active MDI

child window first. You can rewrite the program such that the functions `CMClear`, `CMUpperCase`, `CMLowerCase`, and `CMReset` appear as member functions of class `TAppMDIFrame`.

Summary

This chapter presented the Multiple Document Interface (MDI), which is an interface standard in Windows. The chapter discussed the following subjects:

- The basic features and components of an MDI-compliant application. These components include the MDI frame window, the invisible MDI client window, and the dynamically created MDI child windows.
- Basics of building an MDI application
- The `TMDIFrame` class, which manages the MDI client window, the MDI child windows, and the execution of the menu commands
- Building MDI frame windows as objects that are owned by the application and that own the MDI client window
- The `TMDIClient` class, which owns the MDI child windows
- Building MDI child windows as an instance of a `TMDIChild` descendant and using customized client windows as instances of `TWindow` descendants
- Managing messages in an MDI-compliant application. The currently active MDI child window has a higher priority for handling menu-based command messages than its parent, the MDI client window

18

Q&A

Q Should each MDI child window have an ID?

A Yes. Associating each MDI child window with an ID gives you more control over managing these windows, especially if they vary in relevance. Thus, you can use the ID to exclude special MDI child windows from collective operations.

Q Can I hide MDI child windows?

A Yes. You can use the inherited member function `TWindow::ShowWindow` to show and hide one MDI child window or more.

Workshop

The Workshop provides quiz questions to help you solidify your understanding of the material covered and exercises to provide you with experience in using what you've learned. Try to understand the quiz and exercise answers before continuing on to the bonus chapters. Answers are provided in Appendix A.

Quiz

1. True or false? MDI child windows can have their own menus.
2. True or false? MDI child windows can be moved outside the area of the frame window.
3. True or false? The MFC library supports nested MDI child windows.

Exercises

1. Experiment with the expanding vocabulary of programs MDI1.EXE and MDI2.EXE.
2. Add a control that inserts the date and time in MDI child windows of program MDI1.EXE.

WEEK 3

The Application and Class Experts

The AppExpert utility is a versatile tool that helps you create project source code files quickly and systematically. The utility generates functioning skeleton-code that you then can customize to meet the needs of your Windows applications. Thus, rather than starting from scratch or from adapting similar existing code, you can rely on the AppExpert utility to do much of the systematic work for you, freeing you to concentrate on implementing the code that supports your application's special features. It's like having a consultant inside Turbo C++! This chapter focuses on the following topics:

- Using the AppExpert utility
- Examining the source code output that is generated by selecting some project options in AppExpert
- Using the ClassExpert utility to modify the AppExpert output

Note: The listings generated by AppExpert were edited to better fit the pages in this book.

Using the AppExpert Utility

To use the *AppExpert utility*, invoke the AppExpert option in the Project menu. The IDE brings up the project file-selection dialog box. This dialog box is very similar to the Open A File dialog box. Select an .IDE filename or type in the name of a new .IDE file and then click the OK button. If you type in the name of a new .IDE file, the AppExpert utility creates a new project file. On the other hand, if you choose an existing .IDE file, the AppExpert utility merely adds the new target to that project file. Next, the AppExpert utility displays the AppExpert Application Generation Options dialog box (called the AppExpert dialog box for short), as shown in Figure 19.1. This dialog box has three topics in its left hand list box: Application, Main Window, and MDI Child/View.

Note: It is important to know that the AppExpert dialog box hides and shows different controls based on the currently selected topic or subtopic in the same way as the options dialog box. As you select different items in the left hand list box, the options on the right side of the dialog will change.

The Application Topic

Figure 19.1 shows the options of the *Application topic*. You will be working with these options in this chapter and the following chapter to generate projects with the AppExpert utility. The options of the Application topic are as follows:

- The choice between an application that supports SDI or MDI child windows, or one that supports a dialog client
- The use of document and view classes in the text editor
- The inclusion of a toolbar
- The inclusion of a status line
- The support for the drag-and-drop feature
- The support for printing and print-previewing features

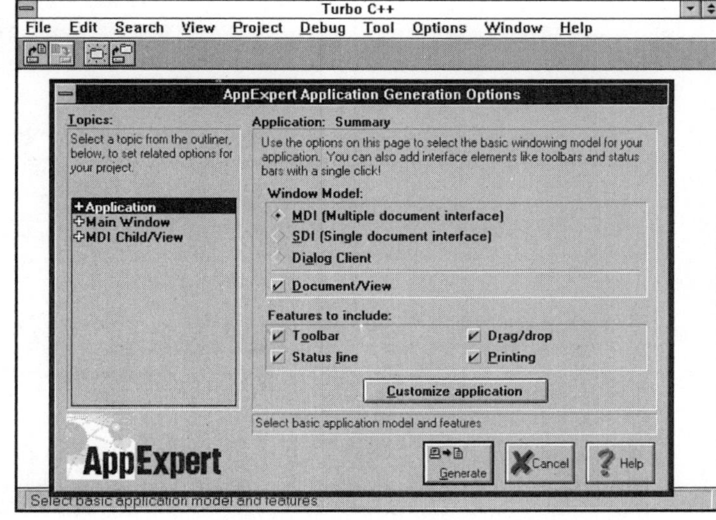

Figure 19.1.
The AppExpert Application Generation Options dialog box.

If you click the + sign located to the left of the Application topic (or double-click the Application topic itself), you expand the Application subtopics. Figure 19.2 shows the options offered by the Application subtopics:

- Basic Options
- OLE 2 Options
- Code Gen Control
- Admin Options

19

The Basic Options Subtopic

Figure 19.2 shows the options offered by the *Basic Options subtopic*. The option choices include the following:

- The name of the target
- The base directory for the target
- The option to provide online help with its corresponding help file
- The application's startup state
- The control styles

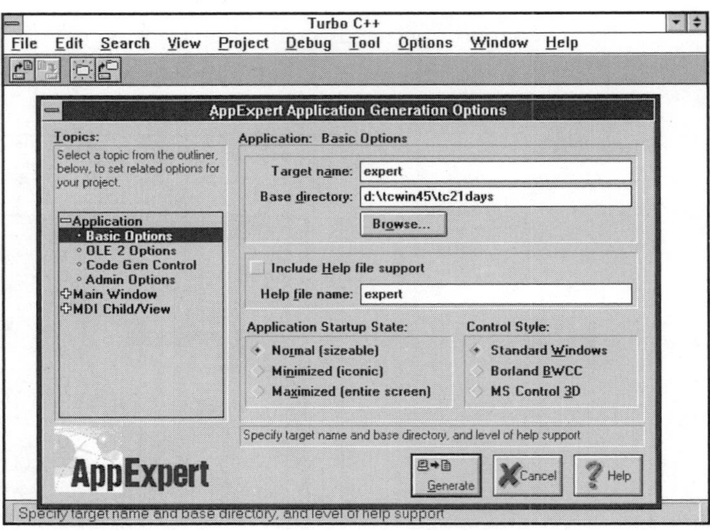

Figure 19.2.
The AppExpert dialog box showing the Basic Options subtopic in the Application topic.

The dialog box offers three edit box controls for you to enter the preceding information. In addition, the dialog box shows a Browse pushbutton, which enables you to invoke a dialog box for selecting a new base directory. As for the help file, the AppExpert dialog box contains a check box that enables you to either support or prevent the creation of the help file.

The radio buttons for setting the startup options allow you to have the application automatically minimized or maximized when it starts up, or to start up in the normal manner. The radio buttons for the control styles default to the standard Windows setting, which shows a white background on dialog boxes. The BWCC style refers to Borland's set of "chiseled steel" dialog boxes with the mottled background and controls with a more three-dimensional appearance. The MS Control 3D appearance is used in standard Microsoft applications.

The OLE 2 Options Subtopic

The *OLE 2 Options* offered by the Application Generator are shown in figure 19.3. They include the following:

- Whether an application is an OLE 2 container
- Whether an application is an OLE 2 server, and whether it's an EXE or a DLL server
- Whether the application should be automated
- The server ID to be used in registering the application

The first option is obvious; an application either is or isn't an OLE 2 container. With the server, however, an application may have the OLE 2 server routines reside in either an EXE or a DLL, and the application generator will handle both cases. The automation routines allow one application to be controlled from another. Finally, the server ID is a unique number, guaranteed to be different from all other IDs that might exist. OLE 2 is described in more detail on Day 20.

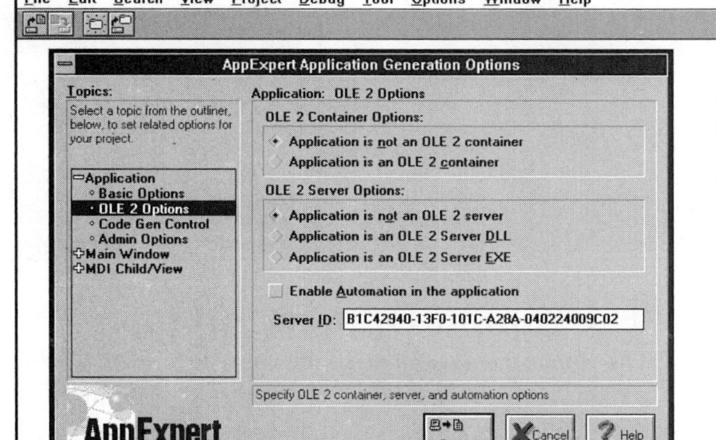

Figure 19.3. *The AppExpert dialog box showing the OLE 2 Options subtopic in the Application topic.*

The Code Gen Control Subtopic

The *Code Gen Control subtopic* offers the options shown in Figure 19.4. When you select this subtopic, the AppExpert dialog box displays the target name and the base directory. In addition, the dialog box offers edit-box controls to select the following:

- The source directory
- The header directory

19

- The main source file
- The main header file
- The application class
- The About dialog class

The dialog box offers browse buttons for the preceding source and header directory options. In addition, the dialog box presents a frame with two radio buttons that enable you to select between verbose or terse comments. The default setting enables verbose comments.

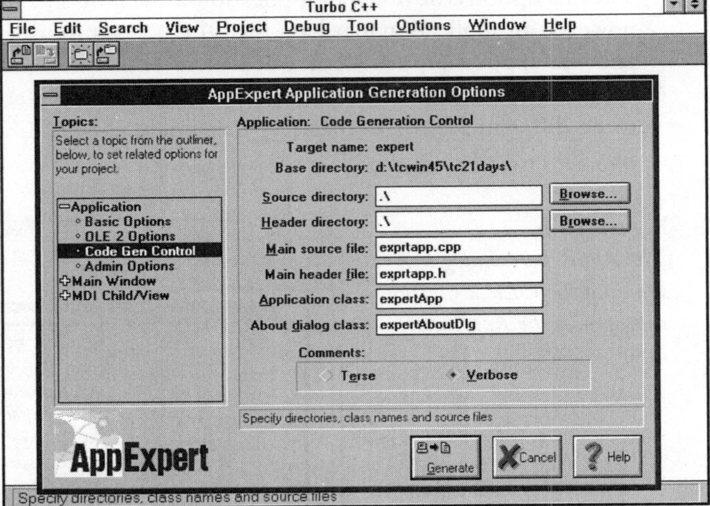

Figure 19.4.
The AppExpert dialog box showing the Code Generation Control subtopic.

The Admin Options Subtopic

The *Admin Options subtopic*, shown in Figure 19.5, handles the administrative side of the project. The AppExpert dialog box provides you with edit box controls to enter the following information:

- The version number (the default is 1.0)
- The copyright notice (the dialog box offers a default wording for the copyright notice)
- The description (the default description is the target name)
- The name of the target author
- The name of the company

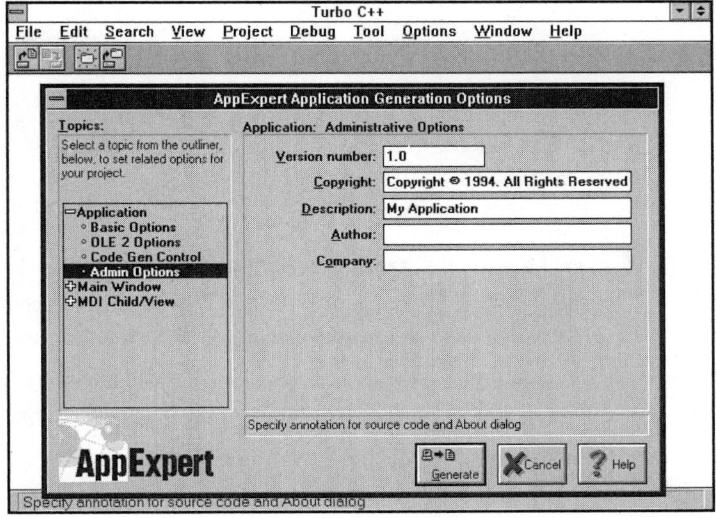

Figure 19.5.
The AppExpert dialog box showing the Administrative Options subtopic.

The Main Window Topic

The *Main Window topic*alters the AppExpert dialog box to offer you options that set the window title and background (see Figure 19.6). The dialog box also presents a Set background color pushbutton for altering the background color.

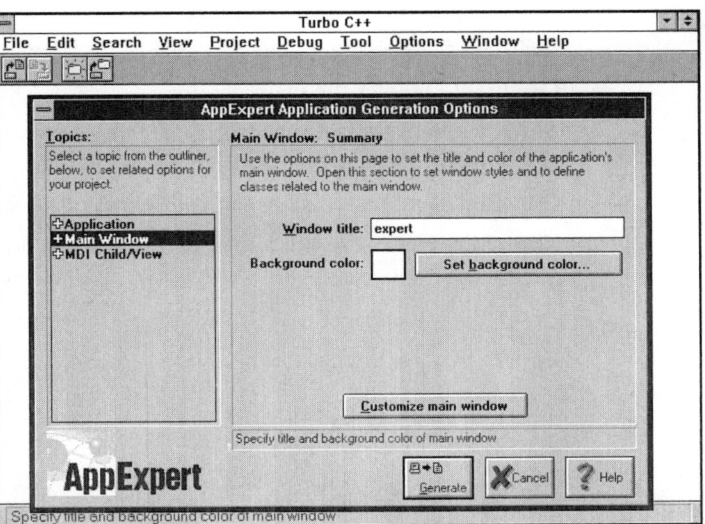

Figure 19.6.
The AppExpert dialog box showing the Main Window topic.

The Main Window topic has the following subtopics:

- Basic Options
- SDI Client
- MDI Client
- Dialog Client

The Basic Options Subtopic

The *Basic Options subtopic* in the Main Window topic permits you to select the window style. Figure 19.7 shows the options offered by this subtopic, as follows:

- **Caption:** Creates a single thin border and a title bar that can display a caption.
- **Border:** Creates a single thin border that has no title bar.
- **Max box:** Adds a maximize button to the right side of the title bar that belongs to the application's main window.
- **Min box:** Adds a minimize button to the right side of the title bar that belongs to the application's main window.
- **Vertical scroll:** Includes a vertical scroll on the right side of the main window.
- **Horizontal scroll:** Includes a horizontal scroll on the bottom of the main window.
- **System menu:** Includes the system-menu button located to the left side of the title bar in the main window. The Caption option must be selected to make this option available.
- **Visible:** Makes the main window visible.
- **Disabled:** Disables the main window.
- **Thick frame:** Displays the main window as a dialog box, with a double border. Consequently, you cannot resize the main window.
- **Clip siblings:** Protects the sibling windows of the main window.
- **Clip children:** Ensures that the main window is not painted over by the child windows.

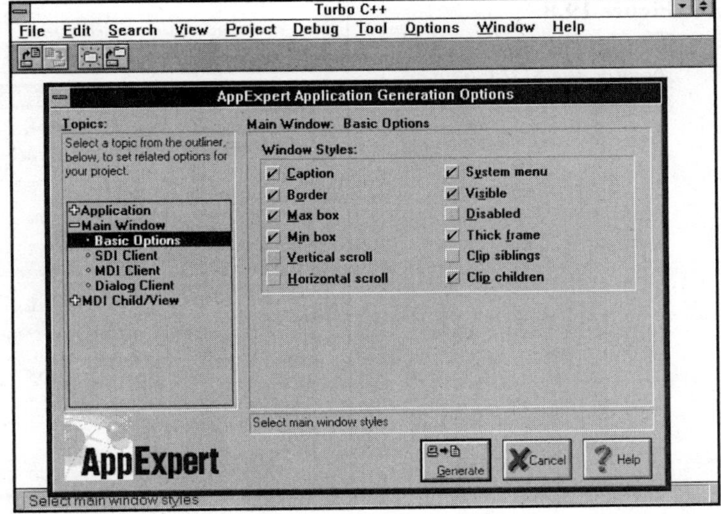

Figure 19.7.
The AppExpert dialog box showing the Basic Options subtopic in the Main Window topic.

The SDI Client Subtopic

The *SDI Client subtopic* offers options that define the class, which in turn models the client area of an SDI-compliant main window. These options are effective only if you select the Single Document Interface option in the opening AppExpert dialog box. Figure 19.8 shows the AppExpert dialog box displaying the SDI Client subtopic with the following options:

- The drop-down combo box that enables you to select the Client/View class
- The drop-down combo box that permits you to select the Document class
- The three edit boxes to enter the file-type filters. These controls accept the file description, filters, and default extensions.
- An edit box allowing you to set the name of the SDI view class
- Two edit boxes to set the names of the header file and the source file for the SDI class

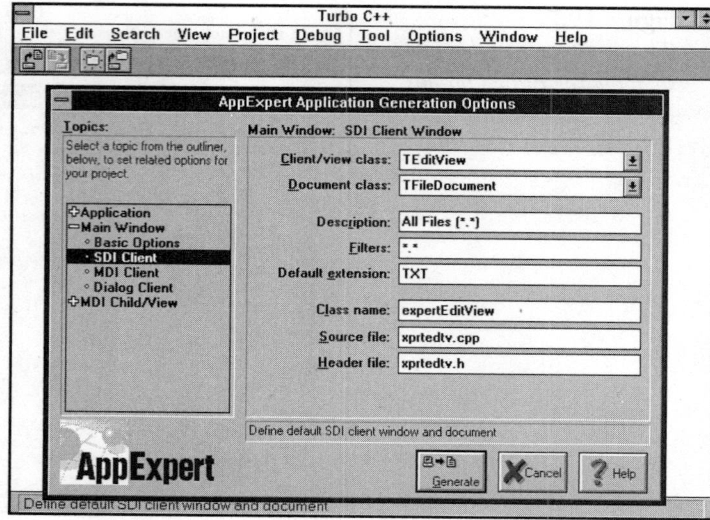

Figure 19.8.
The AppExpert dialog box showing the SDI Client subtopic.

The MDI Client Subtopic

The *MDI Client subtopic* offers options to define the class that models the client area of an MDI-compliant frame window. These options are effective only if you select the Multiple Document Interface option in the opening AppExpert dialog box. Figure 19.9 shows the AppExpert dialog box displaying the MDI Client subtopic with the following options:

- The name of the MDI client window class
- The source (which we are calling *implementation* in this book, because we mean *source* in a broad sense) filename
- The header filename

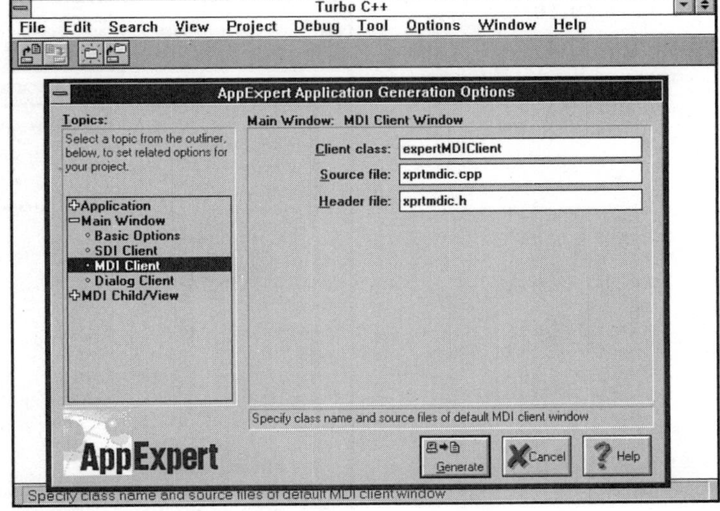

Figure 19.9.
The AppExpert dialog box showing the MDI Client subtopic.

The Dialog Client Subtopic

The *Dialog Client subtopic* offers options to define the class that models the client area of a dialog frame window. You can select the resource ID of the dialog box to load, and you can select whether to include a menu bar. These options are effective only if you select the Dialog Client option in the opening AppExpert dialog box. Figure 19.10 shows the AppExpert dialog box displaying the MDI Client subtopic with the following options:

- The name of the MDI client window class
- The source (which we are calling *implementation* in this book, because we mean source in a broad sense) filename
- The header filename
- The resource ID of the dialog box to load into the client
- Whether to include a menu bar in the frame

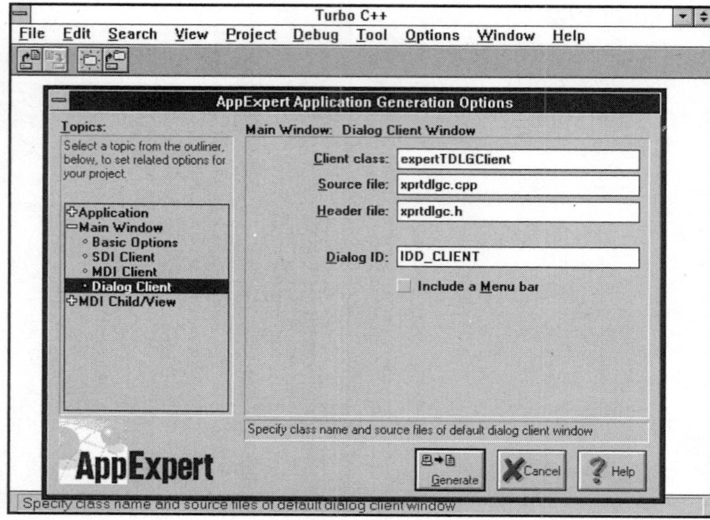

Figure 19.10. *The AppExpert dialog box showing the MDI Client subtopic.*

The MDI Child/View Topic

The MDI Child/View topic, shown in Figure 19.11, has options that enable you to specify the following:

- The name of the MDI child-window class
- The source file that contains the implementation of the MDI child-window class
- The header file that contains the declaration of the MDI child-window class

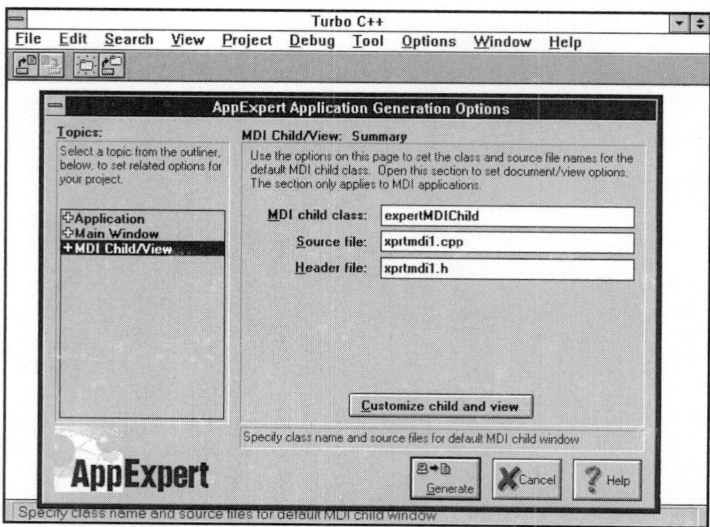

Figure 19.11. *The AppExpert dialog box showing the MDI Child/View topic.*

The AppExpert dialog box offers the Customize child and view pushbutton control, which simply invokes the Basic Options subtopic that is discussed next.

The Basic Options Subtopic

The *Basic Options subtopic* offers options to define the class that models the client area of an MDI child window. These options are effective only if you select the Multiple Document Interface option in the opening AppExpert dialog box. Figure 19.12 shows the AppExpert dialog box displaying the Basic Options subtopic with the following options:

- The drop-down combo box that enables you to select the MDI Client/view class.
- The drop-down combo box that enables you to select the Document class.
- The three edit boxes to enter the file-type filters. These controls accept the file description, filters, and default extensions.
- The class name, header file, and source file.

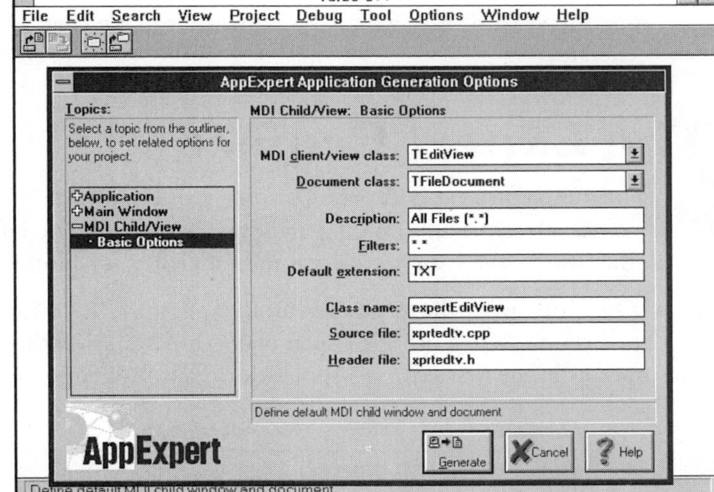

Figure 19.12.
The AppExpert dialog box showing the Basic Options subtopic in the MDI Child/View topic.

19

Studying the AppExpert Output

You've just seen that the AppExpert utility offers many options to determine the kind of source code files that can be generated. Now I present an SDI-compliant project generated by altering the AppExpert options. Because the total number of possible source-code listings is rather large, we will focus on a selection of source-code files generated by AppExpert.

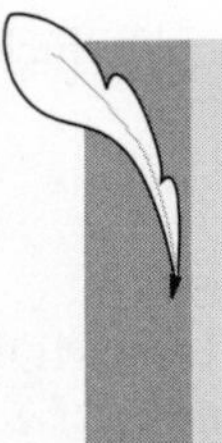

Note: Although the AppExpert creates a sizable amount of source code very quickly, you should nonetheless study the output. Acquainting yourself with the output enables you to quickly and efficiently customize the AppExpert output. This approach shortens the overall process of developing your applications. By contrast, not becoming familiar with the emitted source code will cost you extra time in debugging your programs.

The ideal study of the source-code files generated by AppExpert would include varying each of the AppExpert options, one at a time, and covering all of the possible combinations. Because the total number of these combinations is relatively large, we will examine just one set of the possible output source-code that is generated. The AppExpert generates a minimally functioning text editor. Please do not interpret the words *minimally functioning* to mean that it's a real dud. In fact, the generated text editors offer an acceptable level of operations, because the various OWL classes used in these editors support these operations. I would like to point out that working with all the different combinations is a good independent exercise. I suggest that you experiment with these various combinations to see what kind of program each combination generates.

The *Expert* Project

The sample project is *Expert.* This project generates an SDI-compliant text editor with no toolbar, no status line, no drag-and-drop feature support, and no printing-related features. In other words, the Expert project is the simplest text editor generated by AppExpert.

When you invoke the AppExpert utility from the IDE Project menu, set the name of the project to "Expert." When the AppExpert dialog appears, select the SDI option and turn off the other options in the first section "Application." The utility generates the following set of files.

Filename	*Size*	*Description*
`applsdi.ico`	1,086	Application icon
`expert.apx`	18,572	AppExpert reference file
`expert.ide`	27,138	IDE project file
`exprtapp.rc`	13,331	Resource source
`exprtapp.rh`	4,404	Resource header
`exprtapp.def`	503	Application definition file
`exprtapp.cpp`	4,325	Main application source
`exprtapp.h`	1,533	Main application header
`xprtabtd.cpp`	4,974	About box source
`xprtabtd.h`	1,480	About box header
`xprtedtf.cpp`	1,137	`TEditFile` descendant class source
`xprtedtf.h`	1,010	`TEditFile` descendant class header

The preceding files contains icon, header, definition, resource header, resource, implementation, and IDE files. Look at the .DEF, .H, .RH, .RC, and .CPP files. Build the EXPERT project and experiment with its text-editing features.

Listing 19.1. The contents of the EXPRTAPP.DEF definition file.

```
;----------------------------------------------
;   Project expert
;
;   Copyright © 1994. All Rights Reserved.
;
;   SUBSYSTEM:    expert.exe Module Defintion File
;   FILE:         exprtapp.def
;   AUTHOR:
;
;----------------------------------------------

NAME expert

DESCRIPTION 'expert Application - Copyright © 1994. All Rights Reserved.'
EXETYPE     WINDOWS
CODE        PRELOAD MOVEABLE DISCARDABLE
DATA        PRELOAD MOVEABLE
HEAPSIZE    4096
STACKSIZE   8192
```

Listing 19.2. The source code for the EXPRTAPP.RH resource header file.

```
//#if !defined(__exprtapp_rh)              // Sentry use file only if it's not
➥already included.
//#define __exprtapp_rh

/*  Project expert

Copyright © 1994. All Rights Reserved.

SUBSYSTEM:    expert.exe Application
FILE:         exprtapp.h
AUTHOR:


OVERVIEW
========
Constant definitions for all resources defined in exprtapp.rc.
*/


//
// IDHELP BorButton for BWCC dialogs.
//
#define IDHELP                    998              // Id of help button
```

continues

Listing 19.2. continued

```
//
// Application specific definitions:
//
#define IDI_SDIAPPLICATION          1001            // Application icon

#define SDI_MENU                    100             // Menu resource ID and Accelerator
➥IDs

//
// CM_FILEnnnn commands (include\owl\editfile.rh except for CM_FILEPRINTPREVIEW)
//
#define CM_FILENEW                  24331           // SDI New
#define CM_FILEOPEN                 24332           // SDI Open
#define CM_FILECLOSE                24339
#define CM_FILESAVE                 24333
#define CM_FILESAVEAS               24334


//
// Window commands (include\owl\window.rh)
//
#define CM_EXIT                     24310


//
// CM_EDITnnnn commands (include\owl\window.rh)
//
#define CM_EDITUNDO                 24321
#define CM_EDITCUT                  24322
#define CM_EDITCOPY                 24323
#define CM_EDITPASTE                24324
#define CM_EDITDELETE               24325
#define CM_EDITCLEAR                24326
#define CM_EDITADD                  24327
#define CM_EDITEDIT                 24328


//
// Search menu commands (include\owl\editsear.rh)
//
#define CM_EDITFIND                 24351
#define CM_EDITREPLACE              24352
#define CM_EDITFINDNEXT             24353


//
// Help menu commands.
//
#define CM_HELPABOUT                2009


//
// About Dialogs
//
```

```
#define IDD_ABOUT                22000
#define IDC_VERSION              22001
#define IDC_COPYRIGHT            22002
#define IDC_DEBUG                22003


//
// OWL defined strings
//

// Statusbar
#define IDS_MODES                32530
#define IDS_MODESOFF             32531


// EditFile
#define IDS_UNTITLED             32550
#define IDS_UNABLEREAD           32551
#define IDS_UNABLEWRITE          32552
#define IDS_FILECHANGED          32553
#define IDS_FILEFILTER           32554

// EditSearch
#define IDS_CANNOTFIND           32540


//
// General & application exception messages (include\owl\except.rh)
//
#define IDS_UNKNOWNEXCEPTION     32767
#define IDS_OWLEXCEPTION         32766
#define IDS_OKTORESUME           32765
#define IDS_UNHANDLEDXMSG        32764
#define IDS_UNKNOWNERROR         32763
#define IDS_NOAPP                32762
#define IDS_OUTOFMEMORY          32761
#define IDS_INVALIDMODULE        32760
#define IDS_INVALIDMAINWINDOW    32759
#define IDS_VBXLIBRARYFAIL       32758

//
// Owl 1 compatibility messages
//
#define IDS_INVALIDWINDOW        32756
#define IDS_INVALIDCHILDWINDOW   32755
#define IDS_INVALIDCLIENTWINDOW  32754

//
// TXWindow messages
//
#define IDS_CLASSREGISTERFAIL    32749
#define IDS_CHILDREGISTERFAIL    32748
#define IDS_WINDOWCREATEFAIL     32747
#define IDS_WINDOWEXECUTEFAIL    32746
#define IDS_CHILDCREATEFAIL      32745
```

continues

Listing 19.2. continued

```
#define IDS_MENUFAILURE          32744
#define IDS_VALIDATORSYNTAX      32743
#define IDS_PRINTERERROR         32742

#define IDS_LAYOUTINCOMPLETE     32741
#define IDS_LAYOUTBADRELWIN      32740

//
// TXGdi messages
//
#define IDS_GDIFAILURE           32739
#define IDS_GDIALLOCFAIL         32738
#define IDS_GDICREATEFAIL        32737
#define IDS_GDIRESLOADFAIL       32736
#define IDS_GDIFILEREADFAIL      32735
#define IDS_GDIDELETEFAIL        32734
#define IDS_GDIDESTROYFAIL       32733
#define IDS_INVALIDDIBHANDLE     32732


// TInputDialog DIALOG resource (include\owl\inputdia.rh)
#define IDD_INPUTDIALOG          32514
#define ID_PROMPT                4091
#define ID_INPUT                 4090


// TSlider bitmaps (horizontal and vertical) (include\owl\slider.rh)
#define IDB_HSLIDERTHUMB         32000
#define IDB_VSLIDERTHUMB         32001


// Validation messages (include\owl\validate.rh)
#define IDS_VALPXPCONFORM        32520
#define IDS_VALINVALIDCHAR       32521
#define IDS_VALNOTINRANGE        32522
#define IDS_VALNOTINLIST         32523

//#endif         // __exprtapp_rh sentry.
```

Listing 19.2 shows the source code for the EXPRTAPP.RH resource header file. The file contains the definitions of constants used to manage the following menu commands and resources:

- The File menu options
- The Edit menu options
- The Help menu options
- The About dialog box
- The edit file messages
- The general and application exception messages

- The GDI exception messages
- The input dialog box resources
- The slider bitmaps
- The validation messages

Listing 19.3. The source code for the EXPRTAPP.H header file.

```
#if !defined(__exprtapp_h)              // Sentry, use file only if it's not
➥already included.
#define __exprtapp_h

/*  Project expert

Copyright © 1994. All Rights Reserved.

SUBSYSTEM:    expert.exe Application
FILE:         exprtapp.h
AUTHOR:


OVERVIEW
========
Class definition for expertApp (TApplication).
*/


#include <owl\owlpch.h>
#pragma hdrstop


#include "exprtapp.rh"            // Definition of all resources.


//
// FrameWindow must be derived to override Paint for Preview and Print.
//
//{{TDecoratedFrame = SDIDecFrame}}
class SDIDecFrame : public TDecoratedFrame {
public:
SDIDecFrame (TWindow *parent, const char far *title, TWindow *clientWnd, bool
➥trackMenuSelection = false, TModule *module = 0);
~SDIDecFrame ();
};    //{{SDIDecFrame}}


//{{TApplication = expertApp}}
class expertApp : public TApplication {
private:

public:
expertApp ();
virtual ~expertApp ();
```

continues

Listing 19.3. continued

```
TOpenSaveDialog::TData FileData;                           // Data to control open/saveas
➥standard dialog.
void OpenFile (const char *fileName = 0);
//{{expertAppVIRTUAL_BEGIN}}
public:
virtual void InitMainWindow();
//{{expertAppVIRTUAL_END}}

//{{expertAppRSP_TBL_BEGIN}}
protected:
void CmFileNew ();
void CmFileOpen ();
void CmHelpAbout ();
//{{expertAppRSP_TBL_END}}
DECLARE_RESPONSE_TABLE(expertApp);
};    //{{expertApp}}


#endif                                               // __exprtapp_h sentry.
```

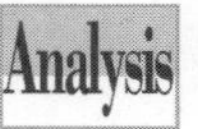

Listing 19.3 shows the source code for the EXPRTAPP.H header file. This file declares the text-editor application class `expertApp` as a descendant of `TApplication`. The class has public, protected, and private members. The public members include the constructor, destructor, and member function `InitMainWindow`. The protected members include the `Cm`*`XXXX`* functions that respond to various menu commands. Note the data member `FileData`, an instance of class `TOpenSaveDialog::TData`, which stores the data for the File Open and File Save dialog boxes.

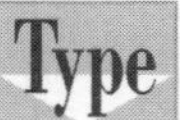

Listing 19.4. The source code for the XPRTABTD.H header file.

```
#if !defined(__xprtabtd_h)               // Sentry, use file only if it's not
➥already included.
#define __xprtabtd_h

/*  Project expert

Copyright © 1994. All Rights Reserved.

SUBSYSTEM:    expert.exe Application
FILE:         xprtabtd.h
AUTHOR:


OVERVIEW
========
Class definition for expertAboutDlg (TDialog).
*/
```

```
#include <owl\owlpch.h>
#pragma hdrstop

#include "exprtapp.rh"                    // Definition of all resources.


//{{TDialog = expertAboutDlg}}
class expertAboutDlg : public TDialog {
public:
expertAboutDlg (TWindow *parent, TResId resId = IDD_ABOUT, TModule *module = 0);
virtual ~expertAboutDlg ();

//{{expertAboutDlgVIRTUAL_BEGIN}}
public:
void SetupWindow ();
//{{expertAboutDlgVIRTUAL_END}}
};    //{{expertAboutDlg}}


// Reading the VERSIONINFO resource.
class ProjectRCVersion {
public:
ProjectRCVersion (TModule *module);
virtual ~ProjectRCVersion ();

bool GetProductName (LPSTR &prodName);
bool GetProductVersion (LPSTR &prodVersion);
bool GetCopyright (LPSTR &copyright);
bool GetDebug (LPSTR &debug);

protected:
LPBYTE      TransBlock;
void FAR    *FVData;

private:
// Don't allow this object to be copied.
ProjectRCVersion (const ProjectRCVersion &);
ProjectRCVersion & operator =(const ProjectRCVersion &);
};

#endif                                   // __xprtabtd_h sentry.
```

Analysis Listing 19.4. shows the source code for the XPRTABTD.H header file. This header file contains the declaration of the About dialog box class, `expertAboutDlg`. This class is a descendant of the class `TDialog` and declares a constructor, destructor, and the member function `SetupWindow`. Whereas many of the generated files will change from project to project, the About dialog source code will remain fairly constant. The only real difference will be in the name of the dialog box class, which is derived from the project name.

19

Listing 19.5. The script for the EXPRTAPP.RC resource file.

```
/*  Project expert

Copyright © 1994. All Rights Reserved.

SUBSYSTEM:    expert.exe Application
FILE:         exprtapp.rc
AUTHOR:


OVERVIEW
========
All resources defined here.
*/

#if !defined(WORKSHOP_INVOKED)
#include <windows.h>
#endif
#include "exprtapp.rh"

SDI_MENU MENU
BEGIN
POPUP "&File"
BEGIN
MENUITEM "&New", CM_FILENEW
MENUITEM "&Open...", CM_FILEOPEN
MENUITEM SEPARATOR
MENUITEM "&Save", CM_FILESAVE, GRAYED
MENUITEM "Save &As...", CM_FILESAVEAS, GRAYED
MENUITEM SEPARATOR
MENUITEM "E&xit\tAlt+F4", CM_EXIT
END

MENUITEM SEPARATOR

POPUP "&Edit"
BEGIN
MENUITEM "&Undo\tAlt+BkSp", CM_EDITUNDO, GRAYED
MENUITEM SEPARATOR
MENUITEM "Cu&t\tShift+Del", CM_EDITCUT, GRAYED
MENUITEM "&Copy\tCtrl+Ins", CM_EDITCOPY, GRAYED
MENUITEM "&Paste\tShift+Ins", CM_EDITPASTE, GRAYED
MENUITEM SEPARATOR
MENUITEM "Clear &All\tCtrl+Del", CM_EDITCLEAR, GRAYED
MENUITEM "&Delete\tDel", CM_EDITDELETE, GRAYED
END

POPUP "&Search"
BEGIN
MENUITEM "&Find...", CM_EDITFIND, GRAYED
MENUITEM "&Replace...", CM_EDITREPLACE, GRAYED
MENUITEM "&Next\aF3", CM_EDITFINDNEXT, GRAYED
END

MENUITEM SEPARATOR
```

```
MENUITEM SEPARATOR

MENUITEM SEPARATOR


MENUITEM SEPARATOR

POPUP "&Help"
BEGIN
MENUITEM "&About...", CM_HELPABOUT
END

END


// Accelerator table for short-cut to menu commands. (include\owl\editfile.rc)
SDI_MENU ACCELERATORS
BEGIN
VK_DELETE, CM_EDITDELETE, VIRTKEY
VK_DELETE, CM_EDITCUT, VIRTKEY, SHIFT
VK_INSERT, CM_EDITCOPY, VIRTKEY, CONTROL
VK_INSERT, CM_EDITPASTE, VIRTKEY, SHIFT
VK_DELETE, CM_EDITCLEAR, VIRTKEY, CONTROL
VK_BACK,   CM_EDITUNDO, VIRTKEY, ALT
VK_F3,     CM_EDITFINDNEXT, VIRTKEY
END


//
// Table of help hints displayed in the status bar.
//
STRINGTABLE
BEGIN
                        "File/document operations"
CM_FILENEW,                 "Creates a new window"
CM_FILEOPEN,                "Opens a window"
CM_FILECLOSE,               "Close this document"
CM_FILESAVE,                "Saves this document"
CM_FILESAVEAS,              "Saves this document with a new name"
CM_EXIT,                    "Quits expertApp and prompts to save the documents"
CM_EDITUNDO-1,              "Edit operations"
CM_EDITUNDO,                "Reverses the last operation"
CM_EDITCUT,                 "Cuts the selection and puts it on the Clipboard"
CM_EDITCOPY,                "Copies the selection and puts it on the Clipboard"
CM_EDITPASTE,               "Inserts the clipboard contents at the insertion point"
CM_EDITDELETE,              "Deletes the selection"
CM_EDITCLEAR,               "Clear the document"
CM_EDITADD,                 "Insert a new line"
CM_EDITEDIT,                "Edit the current line"
CM_EDITFIND-1,              "Search/replace operations"
CM_EDITFIND,                "Finds the specified text"
CM_EDITREPLACE,             "Finds the specified text and changes it"
CM_EDITFINDNEXT,            "Finds the next match"
CM_HELPABOUT-1,             "Access About"
CM_HELPABOUT,               "About the expert application"
END
```

continues

Listing 19.5. continued

```
//
// OWL string table
//

// EditFile (include\owl\editfile.rc and include\owl\editsear.rc)
STRINGTABLE LOADONCALL MOVEABLE DISCARDABLE
BEGIN
IDS_CANNOTFIND,             "Cannot find ""%s""."
IDS_UNTITLED,               "Document"
IDS_UNABLEREAD,             "Unable to read file %s from disk."
IDS_UNABLEWRITE,            "Unable to write file %s to disk."
IDS_FILECHANGED,            "The text in the %s file has changed.\n\nDo you want to
➥save the changes?"
IDS_FILEFILTER,             "Text files (*.TXT)¦*.TXT¦AllFiles (*.*)¦*.*¦"
END


// Exception string resources (include\owl\except.rc)
STRINGTABLE LOADONCALL MOVEABLE DISCARDABLE
BEGIN
IDS_OWLEXCEPTION,           "ObjectWindows Exception"
IDS_UNHANDLEDXMSG,          "Unhandled Exception"
IDS_OKTORESUME,             "OK to resume?"
IDS_UNKNOWNEXCEPTION,       "Unknown exception"

IDS_UNKNOWNERROR,           "Unknown error"
IDS_NOAPP,                  "No application object"
IDS_OUTOFMEMORY,            "Out of memory"
IDS_INVALIDMODULE,          "Invalid module specified for window"
IDS_INVALIDMAINWINDOW,      "Invalid MainWindow"
IDS_VBXLIBRARYFAIL,         "VBX Library init failure"

IDS_INVALIDWINDOW,          "Invalid window %s"
IDS_INVALIDCHILDWINDOW,     "Invalid child window %s"
IDS_INVALIDCLIENTWINDOW,    "Invalid client window %s"

IDS_CLASSREGISTERFAIL,      "Class registration fail for window %s"
IDS_CHILDREGISTERFAIL,      "Child class registration fail for window %s"
IDS_WINDOWCREATEFAIL,       "Create fail for window %s"
IDS_WINDOWEXECUTEFAIL,      "Execute fail for window %s"
IDS_CHILDCREATEFAIL,        "Child create fail for window %s"

IDS_MENUFAILURE,            "Menu creation failure"
IDS_VALIDATORSYNTAX,        "Validator syntax error"
IDS_PRINTERERROR,           "Printer error"

IDS_LAYOUTINCOMPLETE,       "Incomplete layout constraints specified in window %s"
IDS_LAYOUTBADRELWIN,        "Invalid relative window specified in layout constraint
➥in window %s"

IDS_GDIFAILURE,             "GDI failure"
IDS_GDIALLOCFAIL,           "GDI allocate failure"
IDS_GDICREATEFAIL,          "GDI creation failure"
IDS_GDIRESLOADFAIL,         "GDI resource load failure"
```

```
IDS_GDIFILEREADFAIL,        "GDI file read failure"
IDS_GDIDELETEFAIL,          "GDI object %X delete failure"
IDS_GDIDESTROYFAIL,         "GDI object %X destroy failure"
IDS_INVALIDDIBHANDLE,       "Invalid DIB handle %X"
END


// General Window's status bar messages. (include\owl\statusba.rc)
STRINGTABLE
BEGIN
IDS_MODES                   "EXT¦CAPS¦NUM¦SCRL¦OVR¦REC"
IDS_MODESOFF                "   ¦    ¦   ¦    ¦   ¦   "
SC_SIZE,                    "Changes the size of the window"
SC_MOVE,                    "Moves the window to another position"
SC_MINIMIZE,                "Reduces the window to an icon"
SC_MAXIMIZE,                "Enlarges the window to its maximum size"
SC_RESTORE,                 "Restores the window to its previous size"
SC_CLOSE,                   "Closes the window"
SC_TASKLIST,                "Opens task list"
SC_NEXTWINDOW,              "Switches to next window"
END


// Validator messages (include\owl\validate.rc)
STRINGTABLE LOADONCALL MOVEABLE DISCARDABLE
BEGIN
IDS_VALPXPCONFORM          "Input does not conform to picture:\n""%s"""
IDS_VALINVALIDCHAR         "Invalid character in input"
IDS_VALNOTINRANGE          "Value is not in the range %ld to %ld."
IDS_VALNOTINLIST           "Input is not in valid-list"
END


//
// Misc application definitions
//

// Application ICON
IDI_SDIAPPLICATION ICON "applsdi.ico"


// About box.
IDD_ABOUT DIALOG 12, 17, 204, 65
STYLE DS_MODALFRAME ¦ WS_POPUP ¦ WS_CAPTION ¦ WS_SYSMENU
CAPTION "About expert"
FONT 8, "MS Sans Serif"
BEGIN
CTEXT "Version", IDC_VERSION, 2, 14, 200, 8, SS_NOPREFIX
CTEXT "My Application", -1, 2, 4, 200, 8, SS_NOPREFIX
CTEXT "", IDC_COPYRIGHT, 2, 27, 200, 17, SS_NOPREFIX
RTEXT "", IDC_DEBUG, 136, 55, 66, 8, SS_NOPREFIX
ICON IDI_SDIAPPLICATION, -1, 2, 2, 34, 34
DEFPUSHBUTTON "OK", IDOK, 82, 48, 40, 14
END
```

continues

Listing 19.5. continued

```
// TInputDialog class dialog box.
IDD_INPUTDIALOG DIALOG 20, 24, 180, 64
STYLE WS_POPUP ¦ WS_CAPTION ¦ DS_SETFONT
FONT 8, "Helv"
BEGIN
LTEXT "", ID_PROMPT, 10, 8, 160, 10, SS_NOPREFIX
CONTROL "", ID_INPUT, "EDIT", WS_CHILD ¦ WS_VISIBLE ¦ WS_BORDER ¦ WS_TABSTOP ¦
➥ES_AUTOHSCROLL, 10, 20, 160, 12
DEFPUSHBUTTON "&OK", IDOK, 47, 42, 40, 14
PUSHBUTTON "&Cancel", IDCANCEL, 93, 42, 40, 14
END


// Horizontal slider thumb bitmap for TSlider and VSlider (include\owl\slider.rc)
IDB_HSLIDERTHUMB BITMAP PRELOAD MOVEABLE DISCARDABLE
BEGIN
'42 4D 66 01 00 00 00 00 00 00 76 00 00 00 28 00'
'00 00 12 00 00 00 14 00 00 00 01 00 04 00 00 00'
'00 00 F0 00 00 00 00 00 00 00 00 00 00 00 00 00'
'00 00 10 00 00 00 00 00 00 00 00 C0 00 00 C0'
'00 00 00 C0 C0 00 C0 00 00 00 C0 00 C0 00 C0 C0'
'00 00 C0 C0 C0 00 80 80 80 00 00 00 FF 00 00 FF'
'00 00 00 FF FF 00 FF 00 00 00 FF 00 FF 00 FF FF'
'00 00 FF FF FF 00 BB BB 0B BB BB BB B0 BB BB 00'
'00 00 BB B0 80 BB BB BB 08 0B BB 00 00 00 BB 08'
'F8 0B BB B0 87 70 BB 00 00 00 B0 8F F8 80 BB 08'
'77 77 0B 00 00 00 08 F8 88 88 00 88 88 87 70 00'
'00 00 0F F7 77 88 00 88 77 77 70 00 00 00 0F F8'
'88 88 00 88 88 87 70 00 00 00 0F F7 77 88 00 88'
'77 77 70 00 00 00 0F F8 88 88 00 88 88 87 70 00'
'00 00 0F F7 77 88 00 88 77 77 70 00 00 00 0F F8'
'88 88 00 88 88 87 70 00 00 00 0F F7 77 88 00 88'
'77 77 70 00 00 00 0F F8 88 88 00 88 88 87 70 00'
'00 00 0F F7 77 88 00 88 77 77 70 00 00 00 0F F8'
'88 88 00 88 88 87 70 00 00 00 0F F7 77 88 00 88'
'77 77 70 00 00 00 0F F8 88 88 00 88 88 87 70 00'
'00 00 0F F7 77 78 00 88 77 77 70 00 00 00 0F FF'
'FF FF 00 88 88 88 80 00 00 00 B0 00 00 00 BB 00'
'00 00 0B 00 00 00'
END


// Vertical slider thumb bitmap for TSlider and HSlider (include\owl\slider.rc)
IDB_VSLIDERTHUMB BITMAP PRELOAD MOVEABLE DISCARDABLE
BEGIN
'42 4D 2A 01 00 00 00 00 00 00 76 00 00 00 28 00'
'00 00 28 00 00 00 09 00 00 00 01 00 04 00 00 00'
'00 00 B4 00 00 00 00 00 00 00 00 00 00 00 00 00'
'00 00 10 00 00 00 00 00 00 00 00 C0 00 00 C0'
'00 00 00 C0 C0 00 C0 00 00 00 C0 00 C0 00 C0 C0'
'00 00 C0 C0 C0 00 80 80 80 00 00 00 FF 00 00 FF'
'00 00 00 FF FF 00 FF 00 00 00 FF 00 FF 00 FF FF'
'00 00 FF FF FF 00 B0 00 00 00 00 00 00 00 00 0B'
'B0 00 00 00 00 00 00 00 00 0B 0F 88 88 88 88 88'
'88 88 88 80 08 88 88 88 88 88 88 88 88 80 0F 77'
'77 77 77 77 77 77 77 80 08 77 77 77 77 77 77 77'
```

```
'77 80 0F 77 FF FF FF FF FF FF F7 80 08 77 FF FF'
'FF FF FF FF F7 80 0F 70 00 00 00 00 00 00 77 80'
'08 70 00 00 00 00 00 00 77 80 0F 77 77 77 77 77'
'77 77 77 80 08 77 77 77 77 77 77 77 77 80 0F 77'
'77 77 77 77 77 77 77 80 08 77 77 77 77 77 77 77'
'77 80 0F FF FF FF FF FF FF FF FF F0 08 88 88 88'
'88 88 88 88 88 80 B0 00 00 00 00 00 00 00 00 0B'
'B0 00 00 00 00 00 00 00 00 0B'
END


// Version info.
//
#if !defined(__DEBUG_)
// Non-Debug VERSIONINFO
VERSIONINFO LOADONCALL MOVEABLE
FILEVERSION 1, 0, 0, 0
PRODUCTVERSION 1, 0, 0, 0
FILEFLAGSMASK 0
FILEFLAGS VS_FFI_FILEFLAGSMASK
FILEOS VOS__WINDOWS16
FILETYPE VFT_APP
BEGIN
BLOCK "StringFileInfo"
BEGIN
// Language type = U.S. English (0x0409) and Character Set = Windows,
Multilingual(0x04e4)
BLOCK "040904E4"                              // Matches VarFileInfo Translation hex
➥value.
BEGIN
VALUE "CompanyName", "\000"
VALUE "FileDescription", "expert for Windows\000"
VALUE "FileVersion", "1.0\000"
VALUE "InternalName", "expert\000"
VALUE "LegalCopyright", "Copyright © 1994. All Rights Reserved.\000"
VALUE "LegalTrademarks", "Windows (TM) is a trademark of Microsoft Corporation\000"
VALUE "OriginalFilename", "expert.EXE\000"
VALUE "ProductName", "expert\000"
VALUE "ProductVersion", "1.0\000"
END
END

BLOCK "VarFileInfo"
BEGIN
VALUE "Translation", 0x0409, 0x04e4        // U.S. English(0x0409) & Windows
➥Multilingual(0x04e4) 1252
END

END
#else

// Debug VERSIONINFO
VERSIONINFO LOADONCALL MOVEABLE
FILEVERSION 1, 0, 0, 0
PRODUCTVERSION 1, 0, 0, 0
FILEFLAGSMASK VS_FF_DEBUG ¦ VS_FF_PRERELEASE ¦ VS_FF_PATCHED ¦ VS_FF_PRIVATEBUILD ¦
➥VS_FF_SPECIALBUILD
```

continues

Listing 19.5. continued

```
FILEFLAGS VS_FFI_FILEFLAGSMASK
FILEOS VOS__WINDOWS16
FILETYPE VFT_APP
BEGIN
BLOCK "StringFileInfo"
BEGIN
// Language type = U.S. English (0x0409) and Character Set = Windows,
Multilingual(0x04e4)
BLOCK "040904E4"                              // Matches VarFileInfo Translation hex
➥value.
BEGIN
VALUE "CompanyName", "\000"
VALUE "FileDescription", "expert for Windows\000"
VALUE "FileVersion", "1.0\000"
VALUE "InternalName", "expert\000"
VALUE "LegalCopyright", "Copyright © 1994. All Rights Reserved.\000"
VALUE "LegalTrademarks", "Windows (TM) is a trademark of Microsoft Corporation\000"
VALUE "OriginalFilename", "expert.EXE\000"
VALUE "ProductName", "expert\000"
VALUE "ProductVersion", "1.0\000"
VALUE "SpecialBuild", "Debug Version\000"
VALUE "PrivateBuild", "Built by \000"
END
END

BLOCK "VarFileInfo"
BEGIN
VALUE "Translation", 0x0409, 0x04e4       // U.S. English(0x0409) & Windows
Multilingual(0x04e4) 1252
END

END
#endif
```

Listing 19.5 contains the script for the EXPRTAPP.RC resource file. This file contains the definition of the various menu, accelerator, string, icon, and dialog box resources.

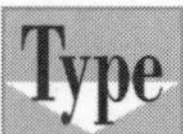

Listing 19.6. The source code for the XPRTABTD.CPP implementation file.

```
/*  Project expert

Copyright © 1994. All Rights Reserved.

SUBSYSTEM:    expert.exe Application
FILE:         xprtabtd.cpp
AUTHOR:


OVERVIEW
========
Source file for implementation of expertAboutDlg (TDialog).
*/
```

```
#include <owl\owlpch.h>
#pragma hdrstop

#if !defined(__FLAT__)
#include <ver.h>
#endif

#include "exprtapp.h"
#include "xprtabtd.h"


ProjectRCVersion::ProjectRCVersion (TModule *module)
{
char    appFName[255];
char    subBlockName[255];
DWORD   fvHandle;
UINT    vSize;

FVData = 0;

module->GetModuleFileName(appFName, sizeof(appFName));
OemToAnsi(appFName, appFName);
DWORD dwSize = ::GetFileVersionInfoSize(appFName, &fvHandle);
if (dwSize) {
FVData  = (void FAR *)new char[(UINT)dwSize];
if (::GetFileVersionInfo(appFName, fvHandle, dwSize, FVData)) {
// Copy string to buffer so if the -dc compiler switch (Put constant strings in
➥code segments)
// is on VerQueryValue will work under Win16.  This works around a problem in
➥Microsoft's ver.dll
// which writes to the string pointed to by subBlockName.
strcpy(subBlockName, "\\VarFileInfo\\Translation");
if (!::VerQueryValue(FVData, subBlockName, (void FAR* FAR*)&TransBlock, &vSize)) {
delete FVData;
FVData = 0;
} else
// Swap the words so wsprintf will print the lang-charset in the correct format.
*(DWORD *)TransBlock = MAKELONG(HIWORD(*(DWORD *)TransBlock), LOWORD(*(DWORD
➥*)TransBlock));
}
}
}


ProjectRCVersion::~ProjectRCVersion ()
{
if (FVData)
delete FVData;
}


bool ProjectRCVersion::GetProductName (LPSTR &prodName)
{
UINT    vSize;
char    subBlockName[255];
```

continues

Listing 19.6. continued

```
wsprintf(subBlockName, "\\StringFileInfo\\%08lx\\%s", *(DWORD *)TransBlock,
➥(LPSTR)"ProductName");
return FVData ? ::VerQueryValue(FVData, subBlockName, (void FAR* FAR*)&prodName,
➥&vSize) : false;
}


bool ProjectRCVersion::GetProductVersion (LPSTR &prodVersion)
{
UINT    vSize;
char    subBlockName[255];

wsprintf(subBlockName, "\\StringFileInfo\\%08lx\\%s", *(DWORD *)TransBlock,
➥(LPSTR)"ProductVersion");
return FVData ? ::VerQueryValue(FVData, subBlockName, (void FAR* FAR*)&prodVersion,
➥&vSize) : false;
}


bool ProjectRCVersion::GetCopyright (LPSTR &copyright)
{
UINT    vSize;
char    subBlockName[255];

wsprintf(subBlockName, "\\StringFileInfo\\%08lx\\%s", *(DWORD *)TransBlock,
➥(LPSTR)"LegalCopyright");
return FVData ? ::VerQueryValue(FVData, subBlockName, (void FAR* FAR*)&copyright,
➥&vSize) : false;
}


bool ProjectRCVersion::GetDebug (LPSTR &debug)
{
UINT    vSize;
char    subBlockName[255];

wsprintf(subBlockName, "\\StringFileInfo\\%08lx\\%s", *(DWORD *)TransBlock,
➥(LPSTR)"SpecialBuild");
return FVData ? ::VerQueryValue(FVData, subBlockName, (void FAR* FAR*)&debug,
➥&vSize) : false;
}


//{{expertAboutDlg Implementation}}


//////////////////////////////////////////////////////////
// expertAboutDlg
// ==========
// Construction/Destruction handling.
expertAboutDlg::expertAboutDlg (TWindow *parent, TResId resId, TModule *module)
: TDialog(parent, resId, module)
{
// INSERT>> Your constructor code here.
}
```

```
expertAboutDlg::~expertAboutDlg ()
{
Destroy();

// INSERT>> Your destructor code here.
}


void expertAboutDlg::SetupWindow ()
{
LPSTR prodName = 0, prodVersion = 0, copyright = 0, debug = 0;

// Get the static text for the value based on VERSIONINFO.
TStatic *versionCtrl = new TStatic(this, IDC_VERSION, 255);
TStatic *copyrightCtrl = new TStatic(this, IDC_COPYRIGHT, 255);
TStatic *debugCtrl = new TStatic(this, IDC_DEBUG, 255);

TDialog::SetupWindow();

// Process the VERSIONINFO.
ProjectRCVersion applVersion(GetModule());

// Get the product name and product version strings.
if (applVersion.GetProductName(prodName) &&
➥applVersion.GetProductVersion(prodVersion)) {
// IDC_VERSION is the product name and version number, the initial value of
➥IDC_VERSION is
// the word Version (in whatever language) product name VERSION product version.
char    buffer[255];
char    versionName[128];

buffer[0] = '\0';
versionName[0] = '\0';

versionCtrl->GetText(versionName, sizeof(versionName));
wsprintf(buffer, "%s %s %s", prodName, versionName, prodVersion);

versionCtrl->SetText(buffer);
}

//Get the legal copyright string.
if (applVersion.GetCopyright(copyright))
copyrightCtrl->SetText(copyright);

// Only get the SpecialBuild text if the VERSIONINFO resource is there.
if (applVersion.GetDebug(debug))
debugCtrl->SetText(debug);
}
```

19

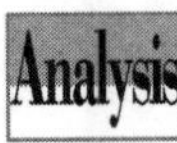

Listing 19.6 shows the source code for the XPRTABTD.CPP implementation file. This file defines the class `expertAboutDlg`, which implements the About dialog box. In addition, the file declares and defines the project resource version class, `ProjectRCVersion`. Look

briefly at this class first. The class defines a constructor, destructor, a set of public member functions, and two protected data members. The class `ProjectRCVersion` supports operations that extract the information about the product name, version, and copyright.

The About dialog box class defines the following members:

- The constructor simply invokes the constructor of the parent class `TDialog`. The constructor has no executable statements and contains a comment that indicates where to place your code to support additional initialization.
- The destructor simply calls the inherited member function `Destroy`. The definition contains a comment that indicates where to place your code to support additional cleanup.
- The member function `SetupWindow` is a bit more interesting; it sets up the About dialog box by carrying out the following tasks:
  - Creates three static text control objects for the version, copyright, and debug information. The function assigns the addresses of these controls to the local pointers `versionCtrl`, `copyrightCtrl`, and `debugCtrl`. These objects are surrogate objects for the statics created in the dialog resource.
  - Invokes the `SetupWindow` member function of the parent dialog box class.
  - Creates the instance `applVersion` of the class `ProjectRCVersion`.
  - Calls `applVersion`'s `GetProductName` and `GetProductVersion` to obtain the product name and version. If successful in getting these, the function then sets the `versionCtrl` static text box with the names.
  - Calls `applVersion`'s `GetCopyright` to obtain the copyright information from the dialog box resource. If successful, it then sets the corresponding static text box.
  - Assigns the debug information to the debug static text control if `applVersion`'s `GetDebug` function returns a nonzero value.

Type **Listing 19.7. The source code for the EXPRTAPP.CPP implementation file.**

```
/*  Project expert

Copyright © 1994. All Rights Reserved.

SUBSYSTEM:    expert.exe Application
FILE:         exprtapp.cpp
AUTHOR:


OVERVIEW
========
Source file for implementation of expertApp (TApplication).
*/
```

```
#include <owl\owlpch.h>
#pragma hdrstop


#include "exprtapp.h"
#include "xprtedtf.h"                           // Definition of client class.
#include "xprtabtd.h"                           // Definition of about dialog.


//{{expertApp Implementation}}


//
// Build a response table for all messages/commands handled
// by the application.
//
DEFINE_RESPONSE_TABLE1(expertApp, TApplication)
//{{expertAppRSP_TBL_BEGIN}}
EV_COMMAND(CM_FILENEW, CmFileNew),
EV_COMMAND(CM_FILEOPEN, CmFileOpen),
EV_COMMAND(CM_HELPABOUT, CmHelpAbout),
//{{expertAppRSP_TBL_END}}
END_RESPONSE_TABLE;


//////////////////////////////////////////////////////////
// expertApp
// =====
//
expertApp::expertApp () : TApplication("expert")
{

// Common file file flags and filters for Open/Save As dialogs.  Filename and
➥directory are
// computed in the member functions CmFileOpen, and CmFileSaveAs.
FileData.Flags = OFN_FILEMUSTEXIST ¦ OFN_HIDEREADONLY ¦ OFN_OVERWRITEPROMPT;
FileData.SetFilter("All Files (*.*)¦*.*¦");

// INSERT>> Your constructor code here.
}


expertApp::~expertApp ()
{
// INSERT>> Your destructor code here.
}


//////////////////////////////////////////////////////////
// expertApp
// =====
// Application intialization.
//
void expertApp::InitMainWindow ()
```

19

Listing 19.7. continued

```
{
if (nCmdShow != SW_HIDE)
nCmdShow = (nCmdShow != SW_SHOWMINNOACTIVE) ? SW_SHOWNORMAL : nCmdShow;

SDIDecFrame *frame = new SDIDecFrame(0, GetName(), 0, false);

//
// Assign ICON w/ this application.
//
frame->SetIcon(this, IDI_SDIAPPLICATION);

//
// Menu associated with window and accelerator table associated with table.
//
frame->AssignMenu(SDI_MENU);

//
// Associate with the accelerator table.
//
frame->Attr.AccelTable = SDI_MENU;


SetMainWindow(frame);

frame->SetMenuDescr(TMenuDescr(SDI_MENU));
}


//////////////////////////////////////////////////////////
// expertApp
// ===========
// Menu File New command
void expertApp::CmFileNew ()
{
expertEditFile *client = TYPESAFE_DOWNCAST(GetMainWindow()->GetClientWindow(),
➥expertEditFile);     // Client window for the frame.
client->NewFile();
}


//////////////////////////////////////////////////////////
// expertApp
// ===========
// Menu File Open command
void expertApp::CmFileOpen ()
{
//
// Display standard Open dialog box to select a file name.
//
*FileData.FileName = 0;

expertEditFile *client = TYPESAFE_DOWNCAST(GetMainWindow()->GetClientWindow(),
➥expertEditFile);     // Client window for the frame.
if (client->CanClose())
if (TFileOpenDialog(GetMainWindow(), FileData).Execute() == IDOK)
```

```
OpenFile();
}


void expertApp::OpenFile (const char *fileName)
{
if (fileName)
strcpy(FileData.FileName, fileName);

expertEditFile *client = TYPESAFE_DOWNCAST(GetMainWindow()->GetClientWindow(),
➥expertEditFile);     // Client window for the frame.
client->ReplaceWith(FileData.FileName);
}


//{{SDIDecFrame Implementation}}


SDIDecFrame::SDIDecFrame (TWindow *parent, const char far *title, TWindow
➥*clientWnd, bool trackMenuSelection, TModule *module)
: TDecoratedFrame(parent, title, clientWnd == 0 ? new expertEditFile(0, 0, 0) :
➥clientWnd, trackMenuSelection, module)
{
// INSERT>> Your constructor code here.

}


SDIDecFrame::~SDIDecFrame ()
{
// INSERT>> Your destructor code here.

}


/////////////////////////////////////////////////////////////
// expertApp
// ===========
// Menu Help About expert.exe command
void expertApp::CmHelpAbout ()
{
//
// Show the modal dialog.
//
expertAboutDlg(MainWindow).Execute();
}
int OwlMain (int , char* [])
{
try {
expertApp    app;
return app.Run();
}
catch (xmsg& x) {
::MessageBox(0, x.why().c_str(), "Exception", MB_OK);
}

return -1;
}
```

Analysis

Listing 19.7 shows the source code for the EXPRTAPP.CPP implementation file. The listing includes the XPRTABTD.H header file to access the definition of the application and About dialog box classes. In addition, the listing contains the declaration of a class that models a decorated SDI window frame.

The listing contains the definition of the message-response table for the application class `expertApp`. The table includes a set of `EV_COMMAND` macros to map the various `CM_XXXX` commands with their respective `CmXXXX` member functions.

The listing contains the definitions of the following members:

- The constructor, which performs the following minimal initialization:
  - Assigns an expression of bitwise `ORed` `OFN_XXXX` constants to the `Flags` member of the data member `FileData`.
  - Calls the data member `FileData`'s `SetFilter` member function with a string literal argument that assigns the file-type filters to the member `FileData`.

    The preceding assignments initialize the data member `FileData` to prepare it for the dialog boxes that open and save files. The constructor contains a comment that indicates where to place statements for additional initialization.
- The destructor merely contains a comment that indicates where to place statements for application clean-up.
- The member function `InitMainWindow` initializes the main window by carrying out the following tasks:
  - Assigns a value to the inherited data member `nCmdShow` such that the window appears in its normal state.
  - Creates a new decorated SDI frame window by allocating an instance of class `SDIDecFrame`. The function assigns the address of this instance to the local pointer `frame`.
  - Assigns the application's icon using the icon resource `IDI_SDIAPPLICATION`. This involves calling the member function `SetIcon` of the SDI window accessed by the pointer `frame`.
  - Assigns the application's menu using the menu resource `SDI_MENU` using the `frame`'s `AssignMenu` member function.
  - Assigns the accelerator table `SDI_MENU` to the frame window.
  - Uses the `SetMainWindow` member function to set the main window to `frame`.
  - Sets the menu descriptor to the `SDI_MENU` resource.
- The member function `CmFileNew` responds to the New menu option by sending the C++ message `NewFile` to the window client area accessed by pointer `client`.

- The member function `CmFileOpen` responds to the Open menu option. The function contains nested `if` statements. The outer `if` statement sends the C++ message `CanClose` to the client area. If this message returns a nonzero value, the function `CmFileOpen` executes the nested `if` statement. This statement creates a dynamic instance of the class `TFileOpenDialog` and sends it the C++ message `Execute`. The `if` statement compares the result of the message with the predefined constant `IDOK`. If the two values match, the function invokes the member function `OpenFile`.
- The member function `OpenFile` performs two simple tasks. The first task assigns the string in the parameter `fileName` to the member `FileName` of data member `FileData`. The second task updates the title of the window with the name of the newly opened file. The function performs this task by sending the C++ message `ReplaceWith` to the window client area object. The argument of this message is the member `FileName` of the data member `FileData`.
- The listing offers the definition of class `SDIDecFrame`. This class, a descendant of class `TDecoratedFrame`, models the decorated SDI frame window. The AppExpert comments remind you that this class needs to override the member functions that support the printing and print-previewing features. The class declares a constructor and a dummy destructor.
- The `expertApp`'s member function `CmHelpAbout` responds to the Help | About menu option. The function creates a new instance of class `expertAboutDlg` to invoke the About dialog box. The function invokes this modal dialog box by sending it the C++ message `Execute`.

19

Finally, the typical `OwlMain` is presented in which an `expertApp` object is created and run. Note that this is enclosed automatically in a `try/catch` block to keep exceptions from getting out of hand.

Altering AppExpert's Options

As mentioned before, the potential output from the AppExpert is varied. I go over some different output on Day 20 when I use the AppExpert to jump-start the creation of an OLE2 application. In the meantime, you really need to experiment with all the various options.

For one thing, letting the AppExpert generate code for you, and then studying that output is a great way of figuring out how to get certain things done with Turbo C++, such as generating an application that uses a toolbar (there's a check box on the first AppExpert option screen). You see many extra files generated, particularly .BMP files with bitmaps, that will be displayed on the buttons in the toolbar. You also will see how the toolbar is set up and used.

Invoking ClassExpert

To use the *ClassExpert*, invoke the ClassExpert menu option in the View menu selection. Figure 19.13 shows a sample session with the ClassExpert utility in a project created by AppExpert. The ClassExpert window contains three panes: the Classes pane, the Events pane, and the editor pane. The Classes pane lists the classes in the current project. If there are too many classes to fit in this pane, the ClassExpert window displays vertical scroll bars. The Events pane shows an outline of the various messages for the selected class in the Classes pane. These messages include command notifications, control notifications, virtual functions, and Windows messages. The thick + symbol indicates that an outline item is hiding sub-items. The thick – symbol indicates that the item is expanded. The editor pane is supported by a BRIEF-like smart editor that enables you to enter, edit, and delete statements.

When you select a different class in the Class pane, the contents of the Events pane automatically change to reflect the events available for the newly selected class.

When you expand the outlines in the Events pane, notice check marks to the left of certain outline items. These check marks indicate that the event has a handler in the project's source code.

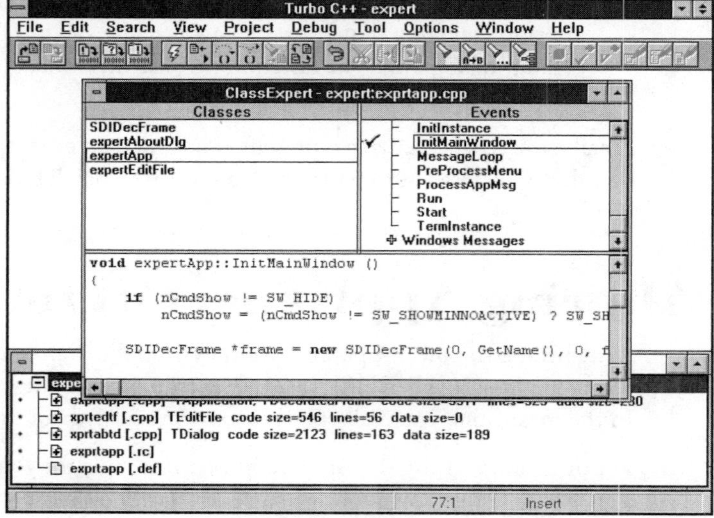

Figure 19.13.
A sample session with the ClassExpert utility.

Note: The right mouse button offers versatile, context-sensitive pop-up menus that enable you to perform various tasks. (The pop-up menus are so context-sensitive that they vary not only from one pane to another, but also between one type of selection and another in the same pane.)

The following sections describe how to add new member functions and classes.

Adding New Member Functions

Use the simple SDI-compliant text editor you just finished. First, add an additional menu in the Resource Workshop. This new menu should support the following features:

- Converting the selected text or the entire contents of the file (if there is no selected text) to lowercase characters
- Converting the selected text or the entire contents of the file (if there is no selected text) to uppercase characters
- Reversing the characters of the selected text or the entire contents of the file (if there is no selected text)
- Inserting the current date
- Inserting the current time
- Inserting the current date and time

Each of the preceding features is supported by a menu option. Each menu option has an event-handler member function. To create the new application, follow these general steps:

1. Use the Resource Workshop to add the menu selection Special and its nested menu options Lowercase, UpperCase, Reverse, Insert Date, Insert Time, and Insert Date/Time. (Consult Part II of the *Turbo C++ User's Guide* manual to learn more about using this utility.) Use the identifiers `CM_LOWERCASE`, `CM_UPPERCASE`, `CM_REVERSE`, `CM_INSDATE`, `CM_INSTIME`, and `CM_INSDATETIME`, respectively, for the menu options. Insert a separator menu item between the first three and last three menu options in the menu selection. The targeted menu resource is the one with the ID `SDI_MENU`. When you finish adding the preceding menu items, save the updated resources.
2. Use the ClassExpert utility to add the member functions needed to handle the six new menu options. Click on `expertApp` in the Classes pane, and then on the plus sign of the Command Notifications item in the Events pane to expand that outline item.
3. Search for the `CM_LOWERCASE` identifier, which represents the commands for the new menu option Lowercase.
4. Click in the + symbol located to the left of the identifier `CM_LOWERCASE`. This action reveals two nested outline items: Command and Command Enable.
5. Select the Command outline and click the right mouse button to access the pop-up menu.
6. Select and invoke the Add Handler menu option. This option prompts you with a simple input dialog box, which requests that you enter the name of the handler

member function. Type **`CMLowerCase`** and then click the OK button of the dialog box. The ClassExpert responds by creating the following:

- ☐ The declaration of member function `CMLowerCase` in the declaration of class `expertApp` (located in the header file EXPRTAPP.H)
- ☐ The event response-table macro that links the command `CM_LOWERCASE` with the member function `CMLowerCase` (located in the implementation file EXPRTAPP.CPP)
- ☐ The empty definition of member function `CMLowerCase` (located in the implementation file EXPRTAPP.CPP)

7. Repeat steps 4 through 7 for the other `CM_XXXX` constants that handle the remaining new menu options. Specify the member functions `CmUppercase`, `CmInsertDate`, `CmInsertTime`, `CmInsertDateTime`, and `CmReverse` to handle the Windows commands `CM_UPPERCASE`, `CM_INSDATE`, `CM_INSTIME`, `CM_INSDATETIME`, and `CM_REVERSE`, respectively.
8. Add the header files STDIO.H, STRING.H, and DOS.H, along with the statements for the member function `CmXXXX` in file EXPRTAPP.CPP. (More about these statements later.)
9. Add the functionality for each of these new member functions by double-clicking on the appropriate Command members for each of the new events. You then can use the editor window on the bottom of the ClassExpert window to modify the empty member-function stubs.

If you take a look at EXPRTAPP.RH, you'll see the new `CM_XXXX` identifiers, and EXPRTAPP.RC contains an updated menu. EXPRTAPP.H has the new `CmXXXX` member functions added to the `expertApp` class, and EXPRTAPP.CPP now has the new code for those member functions. Listing 19.8 shows the new version of EXPRTAPP.CPP with the new member functions that implement the text manipulation.

Type

Listing 19.8. The new source code for the EXPRTAPP.CPP implementation file.

```
/*  Project expert

Copyright © 1994. All Rights Reserved.

SUBSYSTEM:    expert.exe Application
FILE:         exprtapp.cpp
AUTHOR:


OVERVIEW
========
Source file for implementation of expertApp (TApplication).
*/


```

```
#include <owl\owlpch.h>
#pragma hdrstop

#include <dos.h>
#include <stdio.h>
#include <string.h>

#include "exprtapp.h"
#include "xprtedtf.h"                    // Definition of client class.
#include "xprtabtd.h"                    // Definition of about dialog.


//{{expertApp Implementation}}



//
// Build a response table for all messages/commands handled
// by the application.
//
DEFINE_RESPONSE_TABLE1(expertApp, TApplication)
//{{expertAppRSP_TBL_BEGIN}}
EV_COMMAND(CM_FILENEW, CmFileNew),
EV_COMMAND(CM_FILEOPEN, CmFileOpen),
EV_COMMAND(CM_HELPABOUT, CmHelpAbout),
EV_COMMAND(CM_LOWERCASE, CmLowercase),
EV_COMMAND(CM_UPPERCASE, CmUppercase),
EV_COMMAND(CM_REVERSE, CmReverse),
EV_COMMAND(CM_INSDATE, CmInsertDate),
EV_COMMAND(CM_INSTIME, CmInsertTime),
EV_COMMAND(CM_INSDATETIME, CmInsertDateTime),
//{{expertAppRSP_TBL_END}}
END_RESPONSE_TABLE;


//////////////////////////////////////////////////////////
// expertApp
// =====
//
expertApp::expertApp () : TApplication("expert")
{

// Common file file flags and filters for Open/Save As dialogs.
   ➥Filename and directory are
// computed in the member functions CmFileOpen, and CmFileSaveAs.
FileData.Flags = OFN_FILEMUSTEXIST ¦ OFN_HIDEREADONLY ¦
➥OFN_OVERWRITEPROMPT;
FileData.SetFilter("All Files (*.*)¦*.*¦");

// INSERT>> Your constructor code here.
}


expertApp::~expertApp ()
{
// INSERT>> Your destructor code here.
}

```

19

Listing 19.8. continued

```

//////////////////////////////////////////////////////////////
// expertApp
// =====
// Application intialization.
//
void expertApp::InitMainWindow ()
{
if (nCmdShow != SW_HIDE)
nCmdShow = (nCmdShow != SW_SHOWMINNOACTIVE) ? SW_SHOWNORMAL : nCmdShow;

SDIDecFrame *frame = new SDIDecFrame(0, GetName(), 0, false);

//
// Assign ICON w/ this application.
//
frame->SetIcon(this, IDI_SDIAPPLICATION);

//
// Menu associated with window and accelerator table associated with
➥table.
//
frame->AssignMenu(SDI_MENU);

//
// Associate with the accelerator table.
//
frame->Attr.AccelTable = SDI_MENU;


SetMainWindow(frame);

frame->SetMenuDescr(TMenuDescr(SDI_MENU));
}


//////////////////////////////////////////////////////////////
// expertApp
// ===========
// Menu File New command
void expertApp::CmFileNew ()
{
expertEditFile *client = TYPESAFE_DOWNCAST(GetMainWindow()->
➥GetClientWindow(), expertEditFile);     // Client window for the frame.
client->NewFile();
}


//////////////////////////////////////////////////////////////
// expertApp
// ===========
// Menu File Open command
void expertApp::CmFileOpen ()
{
//
```

```
// Display standard Open dialog box to select a file name.
//
*FileData.FileName = 0;

expertEditFile *client = TYPESAFE_DOWNCAST(GetMainWindow()->
➥GetClientWindow(), expertEditFile);     // Client window for the frame.
if (client->CanClose())
if (TFileOpenDialog(GetMainWindow(), FileData).Execute() == IDOK)
OpenFile();
}


void expertApp::OpenFile (const char *fileName)
{
if (fileName)
strcpy(FileData.FileName, fileName);

expertEditFile *client = TYPESAFE_DOWNCAST(GetMainWindow()->
➥GetClientWindow(), expertEditFile);     // Client window for the frame.
client->ReplaceWith(FileData.FileName);
}


//{{SDIDecFrame Implementation}}


SDIDecFrame::SDIDecFrame (TWindow *parent, const char far *title,
➥TWindow *clientWnd, bool trackMenuSelection, TModule *module)
: TDecoratedFrame(parent, title, clientWnd == 0 ? new expertEditFile(0,
➥ 0, 0) : clientWnd, trackMenuSelection, module)
{
// INSERT>> Your constructor code here.

}


SDIDecFrame::~SDIDecFrame ()
{
// INSERT>> Your destructor code here.

}


////////////////////////////////////////////////////////////
// expertApp
// ===========
// Menu Help About expert.exe command
void expertApp::CmHelpAbout ()
{
//
// Show the modal dialog.
//
expertAboutDlg(MainWindow).Execute();
}
int OwlMain (int , char* [])
```


continues

Listing 19.8. continued

```
{
try {
expertApp    app;
return app.Run();
}
catch (xmsg& x) {
::MessageBox(0, x.why().c_str(), "Exception", MB_OK);
}

return -1;
}

void expertApp::CmLowercase ()
{
uint startPos, endPos;
int numChars;
char* str;
expertEditFile *client = TYPESAFE_DOWNCAST(GetMainWindow()->
➥GetClientWindow(), expertEditFile);     // Client window for the frame.

client->GetSelection(startPos, endPos);
if (startPos < endPos)
{
numChars = endPos - startPos + 1;
str = new char[numChars + 1];
client->GetSubText(str, startPos, endPos);
strlwr(str);
client->Insert(str);
client->SetSelection(startPos, endPos);
delete[] str;
}
else
{
numChars = client->GetWindowTextLength();
str = new char[numChars + 1];
client->GetSubText(str, 0, (uint)numChars);
strlwr(str);
client->DeleteSubText(0, (uint)numChars);
client->SetSelection(0, 0);
client->Insert(str);
delete[] str;
}
}


void expertApp::CmUppercase ()
{
uint startPos, endPos;
int numChars;
char* str;
expertEditFile *client = TYPESAFE_DOWNCAST(GetMainWindow()->
➥GetClientWindow(), expertEditFile);     // Client window for the frame.

client->GetSelection(startPos, endPos);
if (startPos < endPos)
```

```
{
numChars = endPos - startPos + 1;
str = new char[numChars + 1];
client->GetSubText(str, startPos, endPos);
strupr(str);
client->Insert(str);
client->SetSelection(startPos, endPos);
delete[] str;
}
else
{
numChars = client->GetWindowTextLength();
str = new char[numChars + 1];
client->GetSubText(str, 0, (uint)numChars);
strupr(str);
client->DeleteSubText(0, (uint)numChars);
client->SetSelection(0, 0);
client->Insert(str);
delete[] str;
}
}


void expertApp::CmReverse ()
{
uint startPos, endPos;
int numChars;
char swap, *str;
expertEditFile *client = TYPESAFE_DOWNCAST(GetMainWindow()->
➥GetClientWindow(), expertEditFile);     // Client window for the frame.

client->GetSelection(startPos, endPos);
if (startPos < endPos)
{
numChars = endPos - startPos + 1;
str = new char[numChars + 1];
client->GetSubText(str, startPos, endPos);
for (int i = 0, j = strlen(str) - 1; i < j; ++i, --j)
{
swap = str[i];
str[i] = str[j];
str[j] = swap;
}
client->Insert(str);
client->SetSelection(startPos, endPos);
delete[] str;
}
else
{
numChars = client->GetWindowTextLength();
str = new char[numChars + 1];
client->GetSubText(str, 0, (uint)numChars);
for (int i = 0, j = strlen(str) - 1; i < j; ++i, --j)
{
swap = str[i];
str[i] = str[j];
```


continues

Listing 19.8. continued

```
283:        str[j] = swap;
284:        }
285:        client->DeleteSubText(0, (uint)numChars);
286:        client->SetSelection(0, 0);
287:        client->Insert(str);
288:        delete[] str;
289:        }
290:        }
291:
292:
293:        void expertApp::CmInsertDate ()
294:        {
295:        struct date dt;
296:        char str[41];
297:        expertEditFile *client = TYPESAFE_DOWNCAST(GetMainWindow()->
           ➥GetClientWindow(), expertEditFile);     // Client window for the frame.
298:
299:        getdate(&dt);
300:        sprintf(str, "%02d/%02d/%02d",
301:        dt.da_mon, dt.da_day, dt.da_year % 100 );
302:        client->Insert(str);
303:        }
304:
305:        void expertApp::CmInsertTime ()
306:        {
307:        struct time tm;
308:        char str[41];
309:        expertEditFile *client = TYPESAFE_DOWNCAST(GetMainWindow()->
           ➥GetClientWindow(), expertEditFile);     // Client window for the frame.
310:
311:        gettime(&tm);
312:        sprintf(str, "%02d:%02d:%02d",
313:        tm.ti_hour, tm.ti_min, tm.ti_sec );
314:        client->Insert(str);
315:        }
316:
317:
318:        void expertApp::CmInsertDateTime ()
319:        {
320:        expertEditFile *client = TYPESAFE_DOWNCAST(GetMainWindow()->
           ➥GetClientWindow(), expertEditFile);     // Client window for the frame.
321:        CmInsertDate();
322:        client->Insert(" ");
323:        CmInsertTime();
324:        }
```

The implementation file in Listing 19.8 shows the definitions of the `CmXXXX` member functions that handle the new menu options. The file contains the `#include` statements that we added to include the header files STDIO.H, STRING.H, and DOS.H. Also, notice the response table macros that were inserted by the ClassExpert utility. We added the code for the following member functions:

1. The member function `CMLowerCase` (defined on lines 187 to 216) responds to the Lowercase menu option by performing the following tasks:

- Obtains the currently selected text (if any). This task involves sending the C++ message `GetSelection` (on line 194) to the client. The arguments for this message are the local variables `startPos` and `endPos`.
- Performs the following sequence of subtasks (found on lines 197 to 203) if the value in variable `startPos` is less than that in `endPos` (which indicates that there is selected text):
  - Calculates the number of characters in the selected text and assigns this number to the local variable `numChars`
  - Creates a dynamic string with `numChars+1` characters and assigns the address of that string to the local pointer `str`
  - Copies the selected text into the dynamic string. This task involves sending the C++ message `GetSubText` to the client window. The arguments for this message are `str`, `startPos`, and `endPos`.
  - Converts the characters of the dynamic string to lowercase by using the string function `strlwr`
  - Replaces the selected text with the contents of the dynamic string. This task involves sending the C++ message `Insert` to the client window. The argument for this message is the pointer `str`.
  - Selects the newly inserted text by sending the C++ message `SetSelection` to the client window. The arguments for this message are the local variables `startPos` and `endPos`.
  - Deletes the dynamic string accessed by pointer `str`
- If there is no selection, the function converts all of the characters in the file to lowercase by performing the following subtasks (using the statements in lines 207 to 214):
  - Obtains the size of the edited text by sending the C++ message `GetWindowTextLength` to the client window. This task assigns the result of the message to the local variable `numChars`.
  - Creates a dynamic string with `numChars+1` characters and assigns the address of that string to the local pointer `str`
  - Obtains the entire edited text by sending the C++ message `GetSubText` to the client area. The arguments for this message are `str` (the text copy buffer), `0`, and `(uint)numChars`.
  - Converts the characters of the dynamic string to lowercase by using the string function `strlwr`
  - Deletes the entire edited text by sending the C++ message `DeleteSubText` to the client window. The arguments for this message are `0` and `(uint)numChars`.

- Selects the start of the file as the insertion point by sending the C++ message `SetSelection` to the client window. The arguments for this message are the integers `0` and `0`.
- Inserts the characters of the dynamic string into the client window. This task involves sending the C++ message `Insert` to the client area. The argument for this message is the pointer `str`.
- Deletes the dynamic string accessed by pointer `str`.

Note: The program implements the various text-edit operations using the data member `client`, which is a pointer to the class `expertEditFile`. This class includes `TEdit` as one of its base classes. This lineage enables the pointer `client` to receive C++ editing messages implemented by the member functions of class `TEdit`.

2. The member function `CmUppercase` (defined on lines 219 to 248) responds to the menu option UpperCase. The function is very similar to the function `CMLowerCase` and differs only by its use of the string function `strupr` instead of the function `strlwr`.
3. The member function `CmInsertDate` (defined on lines 293 to 303) responds to the Insert Date menu option by performing the following options:
   - Obtains the current system date by calling the function `getdate` (prototyped in the DOS.H header file). The argument for this function call is the address of the structured variable `dt`. This variable has the date structure.
   - Creates a formatted string image of the month number, day number, and year number. This task uses the function `sprintf` and assigns the formatted string to the local string variable `str`.
   - Inserts the string image into the client window by sending that window the C++ message `Insert`. The argument for this message is the variable `str`.
4. The member function `CmInsertTime` (defined in lines 305 to 315) responds to the Insert Time menu option by performing the following options:
   - Obtains the current system time by calling the function `gettime` (prototyped in the DOS.H header file). The argument for this function call is the address of the structured variable `tm`. This variable has the time structure.
   - Creates a formatted string image of the hour, minute, and second. This task uses the function `sprintf` and assigns the formatted string to the local string variable `str`.
   - Inserts the string image into the client window by sending that window the C++ message `Insert`. The argument for this message is the variable `str`.

5. The member function `CmInsertDateTime` responds to the Insert Date/Time menu option. This function simply calls the `CmInsertDate` and `CmInsertTime` functions, inserting a space in between them.
6. The member function `CmReverse` (defined on lines 251 to 290) responds to the Reverse menu option. This function performs the following tasks:
   - Obtains the currently selected text (if any). This task involves sending the C++ message `GetSelection` to the client window. The arguments for this message are the local variables `startPos` and `endPos`.
   - Performs the following sequence of subtasks (in lines 261 to 272) if the value in variable `startPos` is less than that in `endPos` (which indicates that there is selected text):
     - Calculates the number of characters in the selected text and assigns this number to the local variable `numChars`.
     - Creates a dynamic string with `numChars+1` characters and assigns the address of that string to the local pointer `str`.
     - Copies the selected text into the dynamic string. This task involves sending the C++ message `GetSubText` to the client window. The arguments for this message are `str`, `startPos`, and `endPos`.
     - Reverses the characters in the dynamic string. This task involves using a `for` loop with two control variables: `i` and `j`. The loop statements swap characters using the local variable `swap`. The loop initializes the variable `i` and `j` to `0` and `strlen(str)-1`, respectively, and iterates until variable `i` is equal to or is greater than variable `j`.
     - Replaces the selected text with the contents of the dynamic string. This task involves sending the C++ message `Insert` to the client window. The argument for this message is the pointer `str`.
     - Selects the newly inserted text by sending the C++ message `SetSelection` to the client window. The arguments for this message are the local variables `startPos` and `endPos`.
     - Deletes the dynamic string accessed by pointer `str`.
   - If there is no selection, the function converts all the characters in the file to uppercase by performing the following subtasks (using the statements on lines 276 to 288):
     - Obtains the size of the edited text by sending the C++ message `GetWindowTextLength` to the client window. This task assigns the result of the message to the local variable `numChars`.
     - Creates a dynamic string with `numChars+1` characters and assigns the address of that string to the local pointer `str`.

- Obtains the entire edited text by sending the C++ message `GetSubText` to the client area. The arguments for this message are `str` (the text copy buffer), `0`, and `(uint)numChars`.
- Reverses the characters in the dynamic string. This task involves using a `for` loop with two control variables: `i` and `j`. The loop statements swap characters using the local variable `swap`. The loop initializes the variable `i` and `j` to `0` and `strlen(str)-1`, respectively, and iterates until variable `i` is equal to or is greater than variable `j`.
- Deletes the entire edited text by sending the C++ message `DeleteSubText` to the client window. The arguments for this message are `0` and `(uint)numChars`.
- Selects the start of the file as the insertion point by sending the C++ message `SetSelection` to the client window. The arguments for this message are the integers `0` and `1`.
- Inserts the characters of the dynamic string into the client window. This task involves sending the C++ message `Insert` to the client area. The argument for this message is the pointer `str`.
- Deletes the dynamic string accessed by pointer `str`

Compile and run the program EXPERT.EXE. Load a small text file and experiment with converting and reversing the characters of selected text and of the entire file. In addition, experiment with inserting the date, the time, or both. When you are done experimenting, exit the file without saving it. Figure 19.14 shows a sample session with the EXPERT.EXE program.

Figure 19.14.
A sample session with the EXPERT.EXE program.

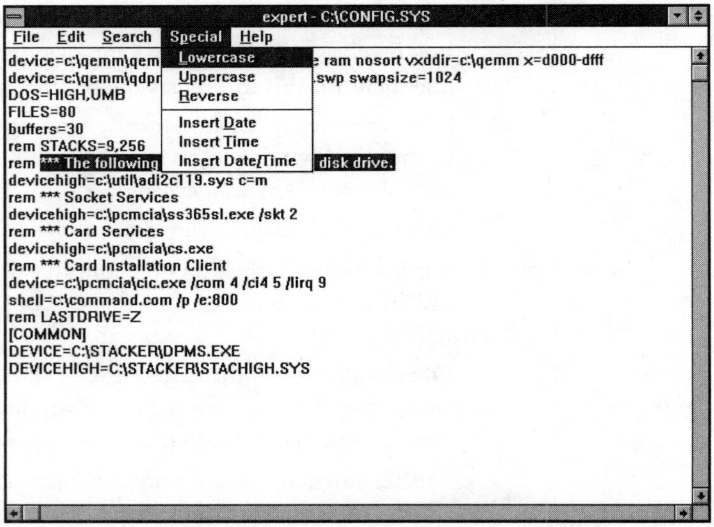

Summary

This chapter introduced you to using the AppExpert utility and offered sample SDI-compliant, text-editor applications generated by that utility. You learned about the following topics:

- Working with the AppExpert utility, which you invoke from inside the IDE.
- The Application topics in AppExpert, which enable you to make main selections about the type of application you want AppExpert to generate.
- The Main Window topics in AppExpert, which enable you to fine-tune the window styles and the SDI or MDI client windows.
- The MDI Child/View options in AppExpert, which enable you to control the creation of the MDI child windows.
- The EXPERT project, which implements an SDI-compliant, minimally functioning text editor generated by the AppExpert utility. The project implements the simplest type of text editor that you can create with the AppExpert utility.

Q&A

Q How does the ClassExpert utility complement the source code generated by AppExpert?

A The ClassExpert enables you to fine-tune the source code of AppExpert by adding new classes and/or member functions that support custom operations of your program.

Q Can I customize the code generated by AppExpert without using ClassExpert?

A Yes. However, depending on how you manually customize the code, it may be difficult to use ClassExpert later for further customization.

Q How can I change the menus and other resources?

A Use the Resource Workshop utility.

Exercises

1. Use the AppExpert utility to create a text editor that supports the drag/drop and printing features. Compare the output code with the listings in this chapter.
2. Use the AppExpert utility to create a text editor that supports the speed bar, status line, drag/drop, and printing features. Compare the output code with the listings in this chapter.
3. Use the AppExpert utility to create a text editor that uses the document/view feature. Compare the output code with the listings in this chapter.

WEEK 3

OLE 2

Object Linking and Embedding (OLE) is the Windows system for enabling several programs to work together, and OLE 2 represents a further degree of refinement and increase in function over the original OLE system. With Turbo C++ 4.5, new classes have been provided to support OLE 2. Today, you explore the following topics:

- The Borland solution to implementing OLE 2
- Embedding objects the OWL way
- Passing data between programs—OLE Automation

What Is OLE 2?

NEW TERM With *object linking and embedding*, objects can be linked together. Thus, a document or other object can be composed of many objects from different applications, and the data that represents the objects can be embedded into the document.

A *linked* object holds sufficient information in the client to invoke another application with the reference for the data to be operated on.

An *embedded* object has the data of the object held in the client.

Before going into detail, let's examine why a user would want linking and embedding. From the early days of PC programs, users wanted the capability of joining information from different applications. For example, every word-processed sales report needs that sales-up-in-the-third-quarter pie chart. The original solutions of integration, such as Lotus Symphony, tried to do everything in one large application. Similarly, most of the industry-standard word processors, spreadsheets, and presentation graphics programs have a tremendous overlap of function—in Excel, you can draw on your spreadsheet; in Word, you can make a simple spreadsheet in a word processing table. Of course, the user does not want cut-down functionality in these add-on features. The solution in Windows is to provide the capability of inserting the output from other applications into documents.

OLE 2 is not just about providing the user with desktop publishing, however. The question could better be phrased "What *are* OLE 2?" OLE 2 comes in two forms:

- A system of data exchange called *Automation* that enables programs to pass data between themselves
- A system of joining programs and data together to create a compound document

NEW TERM Throughout the rest of the day, the term *OLE* means OLE 2 unless explicit reference is made to OLE 1.

There is a significant difference between the two activities. With Automation, the two programs must have a defined interface and know about the data that is being passed between them, as with DDEML. The client transaction processes the data provided by the Automation server.

With object linking and embedding, the principle is that the container knows nothing about the object being contained; rather, it interacts with the OLE system only. However, an OLE container must provide certain features to enable an object to cohabit.

NEW TERM The correct terminology for the user of an OLE object is a *container*. The provider of an OLE object is a *server*.

To the user, OLE means being able to edit a document or graphic and place other objects on the screen. An object is inserted into a container either by an Insert Object command, the Clipboard using the special OLE options, or drag-and-drop. The container is responsible for providing the space for the object; the object's server is responsible for drawing it. Similarly, when saving an embedded object, the server is responsible for writing the object to the file provided by the container.

Note: Once an OLE object has been linked or embedded, the server is no longer required. The OLE container keeps an image of the object (drawn using a Windows metafile) so it can reproduce the object. This includes scaling to fit the page and printing it—true WYSIWYG fashion.

There are two different processes. In linking, the container stores a reference to another application with instructions as to how to access the server. One linked document can be shared among several containers. A change to a linked document can be updated across several containers—and, if the document is moved to another machine, the linked document needs to go with it and the links may need to be reestablished. In embedding, all the data is held in the container document. This means that the object is safely owned by the document, and it can be copied from one place to another without losing the embedded data. Only one document owns the data, however—other documents are not kept up to date. The appropriate method for linking is a user decision, depending on why the object is being inserted.

OLE gets in everywhere. OLE 2 defines a standard for the format for storing objects. The storage is divided into compartments, which can contain other compartments. The main document contains a subcompartment for each embedded object. The advantages of the standardization of the storage are that containers can identify the server data mixed in with its own data and that the container can use the OLE file structure so that it reads only objects that are needed. For example, if the object is a 24-bit screen print that is displayed on the second page of a document, it may not be necessary to read the picture when opening a document to view the first page. More importantly, the storage structure is hierarchical and can be used by an object to contain other objects. Finally, the storage concept is independent of the medium in which the objects are saved; a storage can be on disk or in memory or held in a blob on a Paradox database, for example.

NEW TERM The OLE name for a compartment is a *storage*.

An OLE object is made of two separate components: the data and the view. As you have seen, the data can be stored separately from the application that displays the object. An object also can be viewed in a number of different ways, as with Clipboard formats. So, for an extreme (but actual) example, an embedded wave file may provide a visual "view" for its representation in a document and a sound "view" to play it.

The level of integration in OLE is very high. A true OLE 2 container embedding or linking an OLE object enables its menu, toolbar, and status bar to be taken over by the server for in-place editing, effectively appearing to be the server application. The object, when activated (when it has focus, rather than being edited), can add options to menus, provides for pop-up menus over the object, and can be moved and sized within a document. Originally, OLE 1 enabled embedded objects, but, to edit them, a separate application window had to be opened. Figure 20.1 shows an ancient Word 2 processor doing simple embedding.

Figure 20.1.
The WordArt object opens as a separate application from Word 2.

OLE applications can work as containers, servers, or both. Even more confusing is that an OLE embedded object with in-place editing can itself open an in-place edited object, as in Figure 20.2. OLE 2 provides backwards compatibility with OLE 1 so that you can embed OLE 2 objects in an OLE 1 application (without in-place editing). Similarly, OLE 2 can insert OLE 1 objects; they just cannot provide in-place editing.

There are two ways you can provide an OLE server: as an executable and as a DLL. Even as an executable, you may not want to provide your object as a stand-alone application—to save implementing the stand-alone requirements of printing and file management, for example. Providing a server as a DLL has large performance improvements. This enables OLE to call server functions directly. With an OLE executable, OLE has a problem. Because OLE is

designed for true multitasking systems, it has to organize calls between tasks properly; it cannot simply send messages. Therefore, OLE has to convert its commands into task-independent messages to ensure that it can edit the object without having the container aware of the object implementation. Furthermore, the intention is that the OLE implementation can be extended to enable objects to be implemented across networks so that the OLE tasks might run on different computers—all transparent to the user and the programmer.

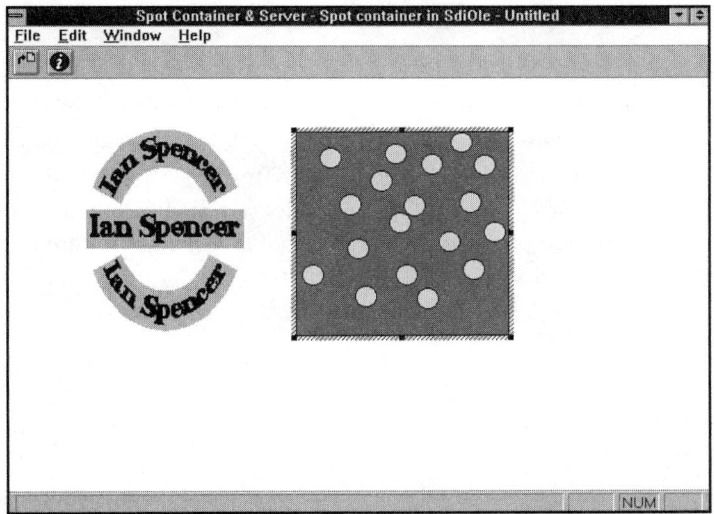

Figure 20.2. *The OLE 2 way of embedding.*

How Does Borland Implement OLE 2?

NEW TERM *OCF* stands for *Object Components Framework.* This is Borland's high-level C++ wrapper around OLE, which converts between a simplified C++ OOP interface and the OLE API. It is similar to the ObjectWindows Library that acts as a wrapper around the standard Windows API.

20

OLE contains many features. However, "there ain't no such thing as a free lunch." To provide all these features, a container application must provide the correct interaction with OLE. This, as you might imagine, is hard work, considering the tremendous number of different situations with which the application has to cope. OCF simplifies the work required by providing a number of classes that support the basic function in the same way that OWL supports the Windows API. Aside from the classes, OCF provides a number of macros to simplify the definition of the OLE registration data and class definitions. It does so in a way similar to the way that OWL uses macros for the response tables, and it also defines its own special messages to enable a simplified OCF event to be handled.

Note: OCF is a separate set of classes from OWL. OWL 2.5 provides classes that make use of OCF to build OLE applications, but OCF does not require the use of OWL.

OCF provides class support for OLE servers, OLE containers, and OLE Automation. OCF helps implement the following:

- *Linking and embedding.* OCF provides support for both server and container.
- *The Clipboard.* OCF provides all the cut-and-paste options.
- *Drag-and-drop.* This is the capability of dragging an object and, when placed in a drag-and-drop enabled window, placing the object in that window.
- *OLE interface.* OCF provides standard components to build OLE dialog boxes, and also provides the capability of modifying the container window if it is written to conform to OCF's requirements.
- OLE compound files

OCF places a layer of abstraction over the standard Microsoft OLE interface. If you were to program in straight C++ without OWL, OCF would provide a simplified way of programming OLE. For OLE Automation, OCF provides all the function required to pass data between a client and server object. OCF also provides additional help to the application to enable it to handle the command line correctly, which is used to instruct an OLE application as to the mode in which it should run. However, there still is a lot of work to do in managing a linking and embedding application.

Building on the OCF classes, OWL then provides a number of classes to ease the programming of OLE via OCF. There are OLE-enabled frames, `TOleFrame` and `TOleMDIFrame`, and OLE container windows—for example, `TOleWindow`. `TOleDocument` and `TOleView` represent the container and views of the container. There also have been some modifications to the `TApplication` class to enable it to run in the different ways required by OLE.

OWL provides support for these OCF functions, but wraps them further still to the point that you need very little code in your program to support OLE.

AppExpert (discussed on Day 19) has been revised to support the OLE classes and you can quickly generate the framework of an OLE application for both an OLE container and server.

OLE *Doc/View*

For the rest of the look at OLE linking and embedding, you study the `TOleDocument` and `TOleView` implementation of OLE. The `Doc/View` model has been present in OWL 2 since its original release. The principle of the `Doc/View` model is that the storing of data and the presentation of data are two different tasks.

NEW TERM For simplicity, *Doc/View* refers to `TOleDocument` and `TOleView` throughout the rest of today's lesson.

Defining a *TOleDocument* Class

There are several steps to follow in defining a `TOleDocument` class.

Step 1: Define the Document Storage

`TOleDocument` understands how to store OLE documents and provides the container with access to the storage medium so that the programmer can easily add specific data to the document.

OWL Note: Transparently, you write to the special OLE storage format. This means that you do not need to do anything special to store data in either embedded or stand-alone file format.

Normally, you derive a class and provide `Open` and `Commit` functions to enable the document to read and write its data. You also provide a `Close` function to clear the document, and you may want to provide a `Revert` function to reset your document to a cleared or as-originally-read state. In each of these, you need to call the base `TOleDocument` function. You access the file by using the `Instream` function to return a `TInStream` for reading and the `OutStream` function for getting a `TOutStream`. When writing the file, you should place markers or read a fixed number of objects, which you note before writing so that you can safely reread the data.

Warning: At the end of writing out data in the `Commit` function, make sure you call `TOleDocument::CommitTransactedStorage`, which updates the storage to disk. If you do not do this, the file you write will be incomplete and cannot be opened.

Step 2: Define Notifications to Tell Views to Update Themselves

You are likely to need some notifications to tell the document views of any changes to the document that might affect them. At any time, a document may have several views open, although only one will be active. When a document changes, it uses the `NotifyViews` function, which sends the notification to all the views that are open; it does this via the standard message response table. There are a number of standard notifications. Additionally, you can define your own document-specific notifications for which you need to define a notification value, a response function signature (via a macro that OWL provides), and a response table entry. This code snippet, for example, defines document notifications for when the document has been added to or been cleared:

```
//
// Custom Doc/View notifications
//
const int vnDrawAppend = vnCustomBase+0;
const int vnDrawClear = vnCustomBase+1;
//
// Custom Doc/View signatures
//
NOTIFY_SIG(vnDrawAppend, uint)
NOTIFY_SIG(vnDrawClear, void)
//
// Response table macros
//
#define EV_VN_DRAWAPPEND  VN_DEFINE(vnDrawAppend,  VnAppend,  int)
#define EV_VN_DRAWCLEAR  VN_DEFINE(vnDrawClear,  VnClear,  void)
```

Step 3 is to provide data access functions for views.

Defining a *TOleView* Class

Next, you need to provide access functions so that the various views can get at the data. Their exact form is up to you, but normally, you require at least something to add data and to get the data from the document. More sophisticated applications provide more functions.

Creating a `TOleView` class requires a bit more work. How much work depends on whether the view is intended to contain OLE objects (remember that an OLE server can itself contain objects if you want). `TOleView` contains all the work to contain objects.

OWL Note: When building your `TOleView` class, you should store a pointer or reference to your document class. There already is such a pointer, but it is of the generic `TOleDocument` type and needs down-casting to use.

Step 1: Define the Presentation

Defining the presentation is based on accessing data from the document. Generally, this consists of having the `Paint` function retrieve data from the document. You may have more than one method of presenting the data. If so, you can either create separate `TOleView` classes or, more likely, derive further classes from a common class of your own devising. The special trick to an

OLE server is that the view may not be presented in device units. OWL looks after the scaling, but it means that any interaction you have with the screen needs to be managed in logical window units—not pixels as you would expect.

Step 2: Add Data Editing Methods

How the view accepts data is up to the view. However, because there may be several views open on the document at once, take care as to how you handle this. The general approach is to handle the editing in the view, and when the object is complete, store it in the document, using the document access functions you provide. The document accepts the data and sends a notification message. In a PaintBrush example, you might type text on the picture only in the active view and when the text is accepted by the user, add the text to the document. Then, in the notification response, invalidate the window to ensure that the screen is redisplayed. By using custom notifications, you can refine the process so that when adding data, all the views can, if possible, modify their screen rather than entirely redrawing it.

Step 3: Add Notification Responses

The view should handle all document notifications to ensure that the display matches the document data. The normal response often is to invalidate the screen (by calling `Invalidate`), but, if the object is a server, the view should also call `InvalidatePart` to ensure that the container is kept in step with the editing.

Note: It's important to remember that if you edit an OLE object (rather than opening for in-place editing), you can observe your embedded object being updated as you edit the object in a separate application.

Step 4: Support Embedded Objects, if Required

OWL supports embedded objects for you in `TOleView`; however, you need to avoid interfering with how it works. Essentially, OWL provides a default place to dump new objects, then uses `EvLButtonDown`, `EvMouseMove`, and `EvLButtonUp` to manage moving and sizing the embedded objects. There are a few traps to mouse handling.

- You need to enable the mouse messages to be responded to by the base class to enable contained objects to be handled.

- The `EvLButtonDown` and `EvMouseMove` messages convert the `TPoint` mouse position parameter into logical units, dependent on the view. The DC view is provided by the `DragDC` member of the view. The mouse down always creates a `DragDC` for you. If you are drawing on the view, you need to use the `DragDC` to get the correct scaling for an embedded edit. If you are storing the position of the object based on the `EvLButtonUp`, you need to convert the mouse coordinates to logical units yourself.
- You should use the mouse only if the mouse hasn't selected an embedded object. You can test for this by testing whether a `DragDC` exists (it will unless your mouse has been moved over the window, having first been pressed outside). Then you should check whether the mouse is holding the object. You do this by calling `SelectEmbedded`, which returns `true` if the `TOleView` is currently handling an embedded object.

By default, you have no control over the placement of the objects (which is normal for many embedding applications). You can provide a current position for insertion by providing a `GetInsertPosition` function (for example, this might return the current cursor position in a word processor).

You provide the rest of the OLE container functionality by giving the appropriate menu options—all the OLE function is built in whether you are building a server or a container.

As you can see, the steps using the `Doc/View` model are nearly identical for a container or server.

The OLE Registry

The first thing an OLE application does when it starts up is to register itself with Windows, letting the operating system know just what parts of OLE the program can handle. The standard method has been to fill in all sorts of long complicated parameters to all manner of OLE API functions. With OCF, however, the information still can be rather complicated; the information is created in a structure with the aid of special registration macros. The structure then is passed into the OCF object constructors, which make sure that your application's program is registered properly with the operating system.

Note: The actual registry information is stored in the REG.DAT file in Windows 3.1. In Windows NT and Windows 95, the information is stored in the system registry.

Although there are several registry functions, the most common ones—the ones in which you're interested—are listed in Table 20.1. These are used to build the registration structures that describe both the application and the various document formats.

Table 20.1. OCF registry macros.

Macro	Meaning
`BEGIN_REGISTRATION`	This is used to start defining a structure. This is similar to the `DEFINE_RESPONSE_TABLEx` macro used in OWL. The single parameter to this macro is the name of the structure to be defined.
`END_REGISTRATION`	This is used to end the definition of a structure. It is similar to OWL's `END_RESPONSE_TABLE` macro.
`REGDATA`	This is the main workhorse macro that adds a keyed entry to the structure. The first parameter to this macro is the key. The second parameter is a value to associate with the key.
`REGDOCFLAGS`	This adds an entry containing flags for a document template. These flags are used in the `Doc/View` model of OLE programming. The parameter is an `OR`ed together bunch of `dt`*`XXX`* flags.
`REGFORMAT`	Each document needs to let the OLE registry know what formats, such as metafiles, bitmaps, and so on, it can handle. This adds information regarding a document's capabilities to the structure.
`REGISTRATION_FORMAT_BUFFER`	Some of the macros used to create the registration structure require some temporary space in order to properly expand. This macro provides that temporary space, the size of which is based on its single parameter.

In the description of the `REGDATA` macro, I mentioned that it registers keyed entries. There are quite a number of keys available to be registered, some of which are required for various structures. Table 20.2 describes some of the keys.

Table 20.2. OCF registry keys.

Key Name	Entry Value
`clsid`	This defines the Globally Unique Identifier (GUID) needed to differentiate each OLE application from one another. The GUIDs are generated automatically by the IDE's AppExpert. If you create an OLE application on your own, you can use the GUIDGEN.EXE program supplied with the compiler to generate a GUID for this field.

continues

Table 20.2. continued

Key Name	Entry Value
`progid`	This is a string that identifies the structure. This is used for both documents and for applications, and it typically consists of three parts: a program name, an object name, and a version number.
`description`	When OLE puts up a string for the user to see, it shows the contents of this entry, which can be up to 40 characters long.
`cmdline`	This describes the arguments that OLE should place on the program's command line when OLE starts the application. It's often just an empty string.
`appname`	This usually is the title that shows up in the application's main window.
`docfilter`	This is represented as a file mask, such as *.SPT, and generally uses the same letters as in the document's `extension`. That file mask is used in the common dialogs, along with a file type (see `menuname` and `description`) when OLE asks the user to open or save files.
`usage`	This is a flag that lets OLE know whether it should start up a new instance of the application server for each client that requests it. If `ocrSingleUse` is used here, the application will be started once for each OLE client that needs it. `ocrMultipleUse` means that the server application will be opened only once, no matter how many clients ask for it.
`insertable`	The key for this entry is always an empty string; its presence is used in a structure to identify a document as one that can be inserted into other container documents. It will appear in the list of available documents when the user selects the `Insert Object` menu item.
`menuname`	This is a short name that shows up as a menu item in container programs. In order to keep menu sizes short and readable, the suggested maximum length for this entry is 15 characters.
`verb`*`N`*	This describes the verbs used for documents, ones that will appear in pop-up menus. *N* represents a number that should begin with 0 and go no further than 7. Typical entries are &Edit and &Open.
`extension`	This is used to identify filename extensions for OLE documents. When OLE is asked to open a file, it matches the extension of the file with the various servers associated with extensions and then uses the matching one.

It's important to note that this list is by no means complete. There are a number of other keys that can be used, but the ones listed so far are enough to get a program up and running with full OLE functionality.

Creating an OLE Application

The previous discussion has created only the Doc/View components and described the registry in general terms, but this has not explained how documents and views are managed. OWL provides a document manager, called TDocManager. It is this class (which you normally don't need to amend in any way) that looks after documents and views. There are a few simple steps that you take to enable the document manager to understand your class.

Step 1: Declare a *Doc/View* Template and Register its Details

You do not need to worry about the internals of declaring a Doc/View template. There are three components you need to define. (You don't use these yourself, they are used by the TDocManager.) The DEFINE_DOC_TEMPLATE_CLASS macro associates the documents and the views. You declare one of these for each combination:

```
DEFINE_DOC_TEMPLATE_CLASS(SpotDoc, SpotView, SpotTemplate);
```

Then you need to declare some important OLE registration details for each document.

```
BEGIN_REGISTRATION(__SpotRegistration)
    REGDATA(progid, "Spot.Container.1")
    REGDATA(description, "Spot Container Version 1")
    REGDATA(extension, "SPT")
    REGDATA(docfilter, "*.SPT")
    REGDOCFLAGS(dtAutoDelete | dtUpdateDir
                | dtAutoOpen | dtRegisterExt)
    REGDATA(menuname, "Spot container")
    REGDATA(insertable, "")
    REGDATA(verb0, "&Edit")
    REGDATA(verb1, "&Open")
    REGFORMAT(0, ocrEmbedSource,  ocrContent,
                 ocrIStorage, ocrGet)
    REGFORMAT(1, ocrMetafilePict, ocrContent,
                 ocrMfPict | ocrStaticMed, ocrGet)
    REGFORMAT(2, ocrBitmap, ocrContent,
                 ocrGDI | ocrStaticMed, ocrGet)
    REGFORMAT(3, ocrDib, ocrContent,  ocrHGlobal
                 | ocrStaticMed, ocrGet)
    REGFORMAT(4, ocrLinkSource, ocrContent,
                 ocrIStream, ocrGet)
END_REGISTRATION
```

This table is passed to Windows so that your application is entered into the system. This enables other applications to know of your existence. Important entries (well, they are all important!) are the progid and description, which appear when the user accesses the object (for example, via Insert Object). insertable is a placeholder to indicate that this object can be inserted—that is, the document is an OLE server. extension, docfilter, and the REGDOCFLAGS line all tell the document manager (and OLE) what files can be handled by the Doc/View combination. The REGFORMATs tell OLE what formats the server can produce for linking and embedding. OWL Doc/View can provide all these formats for you.

Having created this information, you then declare a global static instance of the `Doc/View` template. The instance looks after associating itself with the manager, so you can call it what you like. It takes the registration information as a parameter (you pass the registration details even if you decide not to provide OLE support).

```
SpotTemplate __spotTemplate(__SpotRegistration);
```

You now have created your `Doc/View` classes.

Step 2: Add the Application Registration Details

Next, you need to sort out the application. There are a number of new features for this. First, you need a static `TAppDictionary`. This manages OWL internal information. This must be called `AppDictionary` to ensure that certain OWL features work.

Second, you need to register the application (by the way, place this before your `Doc/View` registration).

```
//
// Ole 2 linking and embedding apps need a TOcRegistrar
//
static TPointer<TOcRegistrar> Registrar;

REGISTRATION_FORMAT_BUFFER(100)

BEGIN_REGISTRATION(ApplicationReg)
//
// The following must be unique per Ole 2 application
//
    REGDATA(clsid, "{FE91A8E0-DBDA-101B-A585-040224007802}")
    REGDATA(appname, "Spot Container & Server")
    REGDATA(description, "Spot Container & Server Application")
    REGDATA(cmdline, "")
    REGDATA(usage, ocrMultipleUse)
END_REGISTRATION
```

Create a `TOcRegistrar` pointer, which must be called `Registrar`. OCF uses templates that rely on this. You will set up the `Registrar` in `OwlMain`.

Note: The `TPointer` class is a cunning ruse to ensure that dynamically allocated objects get cleaned up. It accepts a pointer of the type of the object specified and deletes the object if the instance goes out of scope, a new object is assigned to it, or zero is assigned to it. This improves the capability of cleaning up objects if something goes wrong. You can use this class yourself. Typically, you use it where you would declare a variable, but, because of size, you want to declare it using `new`. One

place it works well is where an exception may be thrown—objects declared on the stack are cleaned up, but dynamically allocated objects are not. By wrapping the pointer in an object, dynamically allocatable objects can now be cleaned up.

Next, create the application registration. `appname` and `description` are self-explanatory. `usage` enables multiple clients to use the same application, and `cmdline` indicates that there are no arguments needed on the command line. The important one is `clsid`.

Warning: The class `id` must be absolutely unique to ensure that OLE starts the correct program. The Globally Unique Identifier is unique around the world, and you should never copy someone else's—especially if you are going to distribute your application.

This horrible long number can easily be generated. Merely run GUIDGEN (which lives in your Turbo C++ BIN directory). This places a new GUID in your Clipboard and you can then paste it into your code.

Step 3: Implement the Application Class

You now can move and look at the class. A `Doc/View` application handles a couple of responses for the document manager:

```
DEFINE_RESPONSE_TABLE1(SpotApp, TApplication)
    EV_OWLVIEW(dnCreate, EvNewView),
    EV_OWLVIEW(dnClose,  EvCloseView),
    EV_COMMAND(CM_HELPABOUT, CmHelpAbout),
END_RESPONSE_TABLE;
```

20

The application itself is multi-derived from `TApplication` and `TOcModule`. The `TOcModule` is transparent, but you do need to use a special `TApplication` constructor:

```
SpotApp::SpotApp () : TApplication
   (::ApplicationReg["description"], ::Module, &::AppDictionary)
{
    SetDocManager(new TDocManager(dmSDI | dmMenu, this));
}
```

The constructor is identical for any OLE application you write, using the global objects you created earlier. In the constructor, set up the document manager. This needs to be set for whether you are using SDI or MDI (it controls whether multiple documents can be open).

`InitMainWindow` is fairly standard, except that you cannot create a client at this point; OLE is not yet ready. You use a `TOleFrame`, which is a special `TDecoratedFrame` that can handle the OLE toolbar interface. You would create your toolbar for a stand-alone application here, setting the toolbar's `Attr.Id` to `IDW_TOOLBAR`. This enables OWL to swap it if another application takes over your application.

In `TApplication::InitInstance`, the application can now have its client window set up if required. If the application is not embedding, you can open the file based on the command line, or you can open a blank document. To open files, you ask the document manager. In the following snippet, if not embedding, the application finds out whether the document manager recognizes the filename that has been sent via `MatchTemplate`. If so, it attempts to open the file by creating a document. It uses the document template to construct an empty document, then uses the document manager to initialize it, which, in turn, opens a view. Similarly, if there is no document, the application merely opens a new view.

```
if (!::Registrar->IsOptionSet(amEmbedding))
  {
    TDocTemplate* tpl = GetDocManager()
        ->MatchTemplate(GetCmdLine().c_str());
    if (tpl)
      {
        TDocument* doc = tpl->ConstructDoc();
        if (doc)
          {
            doc->SetTemplate(tpl);
            GetDocManager()->InitDoc(doc,
                  GetCmdLine().c_str(), 0);
            return;
          }
      }
    GetDocManager()->CreateAnyDoc(0, dtNewDoc);
  }
```

The document manager opens the view. Recall that the application response table defined two document notifications. Once a view has been created, it has to be associated with a window. Because the application may operate in an embedded mode, this view may be a window in the container document. So, to handle the notification, the application needs to test whether the document is embedded. If the document is embedded, it creates a view parented to a special window; otherwise, the view is created as a standard client (in this case, an SDI client).

```
TOleView* ov = dynamic_cast<TOleView*>(&view);
if (ov && view.GetDocument().IsEmbedded() &&
    !ov->GetOcRemView()->IsOpenEditing())
  {
    //
    // Embedded view window
    //
    TWindow* vw = view.GetWindow();
    vw->SetParent(dynamic_cast<TOleFrame*>(GetMainWindow())
                 ->GetRemViewBucket());
    vw->Create();
  }
else
  {
    //
```

```
    // Normal window - associate with MainWindow
    //
    GetMainWindow()->SetClientWindow(view.GetWindow());
    if (!view.IsOK())
      GetMainWindow()->SetClientWindow(0);
    else
       if (view.GetViewMenu())
          GetMainWindow()->MergeMenu(*view.GetViewMenu());
  }
```

Note: In `Doc/View` menu merging is used even in an SDI application, because different views can be placed as a client.

Step 4: Implement an OLE *OwlMain*

The `OwlMain` is changed around. This is to enable the OLE system to call your application correctly. When you run an OLE application, it receives a variety of command-line options. It is responsible for registering and unregistering itself, and also for interpreting the command-line options that OLE might have passed. OWL strips these out for you, leaving a simplified command line with only non-OLE information. This saves you from having to decode the flags yourself. You can interrogate the flags by calling `TRegistrar::IsOptionSet`. This tests for any flags you send, which are enumerated. The main test you need is to decide whether your application is operating in embedded mode. Normally, the command line can contain the filename to enable File Manager to start your application via its associations. It also normally passes the filename and a flag to request printing a document.

```
int OwlMain (int , char* [])
{
    try
      {
        ::Registrar = new TOcRegistrar(::ApplicationReg,
                            TOleDocViewFactory<SpotApp>(),
                            TApplication::GetCmdLine(),
                            ::DocTemplateStaticHead);
        if (!::Registrar->IsOptionSet(amAnyRegOption))
          ::Registrar->Run();
        ::Registrar = 0;
        return 0;
      }
    catch (xmsg& x)
      {
        ::MessageBox(0, x.why().c_str(), "Exception", MB_OK);
      }
    return -1;
}
```

The main trick here is the use of the `::Registrar` object. For an OLE application that does linking and embedding, you need a `TOcRegistrar` object. The `::ApplicationReg` and

TApplication::GetCommandLine() are all standard objects that you use. ::DocTemplateStaticHead represents a special link for the registration to find the document template registration details. The special part is the TOleDocViewFactory. This is a template class that generates a hidden callback function. This callback function is what actually is called by the ::Registrar->Run() call. OWL provides a number of different callbacks depending on the sort of application you are building. The name Factory implies that this is the OLE object generator. When building an OLE application, your target needs to include the OCF libraries. (When distributing an OLE application, you also need to distribute the OLE libraries.)

Put all that together, and then run your application. However, before you run an OLE-enabled server, you should run it in register mode. The proper way to do this is to run it with a -RegServer command line. The IDE makes this easy for you; there are two special commands on the SpeedMenu for a target node. Choose SpeedMenu | Special | Register or Unregister, and the IDE will run your application in registration mode. In this mode, it does not create windows; it merely performs the registration and then immediately exits.

Creating OLE Applications with AppExpert

The following application initially was generated using AppExpert, although it has been substantially tidied up. With Turbo C++ 4.5, AppExpert is OLE-enabled. You can create Doc/View servers or containers with all the usual features that you would expect to be able to generate. ClassExpert understands the OLE Doc/View model. You are familiar with AppExpert, so you will find it simple to amend OLE applications. At the time of writing, AppExpert gives a derived TOleView object to work with, but does not provide a derived TOleDocument class. This always is required for all but trivial examples. This can easily be derived by using ClassExpert. (Remember to use the SpeedMenu from the class pane; this enables you to derive from any class that the ClassExpert knows about.)

Another suggestion is to amend the derived TOleView class manually so that it accepts a derived TOleDocument as a parameter rather than the TOleDocument set as the parameter. This saves down-casting the document each time you access it.

If you want to create an OLE container to play with, press the generate button and compile the result. You will find that you can make an application that provides a nearly complete OLE implementation. AppExpert is useful, because an OLE application normally needs to support toolbars and status bars, and it will generate all the different menus and registration tables.

Note: Do not select Automation support in the OLE 2 options yet. This option is covered in the second part of today's lesson.

Listings 20.1 through 20.12, SPOT.EXE, provide a practical and stimulating example.

Listing 20.1. Source code for the SPOTAPP.H header file.

```
#if !defined(__spotapp_h)
#define __spotapp_h

//    Class definition for SpotApp (TApplication).

#include <owl\owlpch.h>
#pragma hdrstop


#include "spotapp.rh"
//
// For OLE2 linking & embedding, need TOcModule,
// which coordinates with OCF
//
class SpotApp : public TApplication, public TOcModule
  {
    public:
      SpotApp ();
      virtual void InitMainWindow ();
      virtual void InitInstance ();
    protected:
      void EvNewView (TView& view);
      void EvCloseView (TView& view);
      void CmHelpAbout ();
    DECLARE_RESPONSE_TABLE(SpotApp);
};

#endif
```

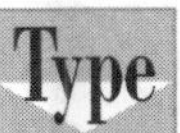

Listing 20.2. Source code for the SPOTAPP.CPP program file.

```
#include <owl\owlpch.h>
#pragma hdrstop
#include "spotdoc.h"
#include "spotapp.h"
#include "spotview.h"
#include "sptabtdl.h"
//
// Ole 2 linking & embedding apps (may need to) use a special
// dictionary.
//
DEFINE_APP_DICTIONARY(AppDictionary);
//
// Ole 2 linking and embedding apps need a TOcRegistrar
//
static TPointer<TOcRegistrar> Registrar;

REGISTRATION_FORMAT_BUFFER(100)
```

continues

Listing 20.2. continued

```
BEGIN_REGISTRATION(ApplicationReg)
//
// The following must be unique per Ole 2 application
// Use GUIDGEN to make one.
//
    REGDATA(clsid, "{FE91A8E0-DBDA-101B-A585-040224007802}")
    REGDATA(appname, "Spot Container & Server")
    REGDATA(description, "Spot Container & Server Application")
    REGDATA(cmdline, "")
    REGDATA(usage, ocrMultipleUse)
END_REGISTRATION

//
// This builds the relationship between the document
// and the view.
//
DEFINE_DOC_TEMPLATE_CLASS(SpotDoc, SpotView, SpotTemplate);

BEGIN_REGISTRATION(__SpotRegistration)
    REGDATA(progid, "Spot.Container.1")
    REGDATA(description, "Spot Container Version 1")
    REGDATA(extension, "SPT")
    REGDATA(docfilter, "*.SPT")
    REGDOCFLAGS(dtAutoDelete ¦ dtUpdateDir ¦ dtAutoOpen ¦
                dtRegisterExt)
    REGDATA(menuname, "Spot container")
    REGDATA(insertable, "")
    REGDATA(verb0, "&Edit")
    REGDATA(verb1, "&Open")
    REGFORMAT(0, ocrEmbedSource,  ocrContent,  ocrIStorage,
              ocrGet)
    REGFORMAT(1, ocrMetafilePict, ocrContent,  ocrMfPict ¦
              ocrStaticMed, ocrGet)
    REGFORMAT(2, ocrBitmap, ocrContent,  ocrGDI ¦ ocrStaticMed,
              ocrGet)
    REGFORMAT(3, ocrDib, ocrContent,  ocrHGlobal ¦ ocrStaticMed,
              ocrGet)
    REGFORMAT(4, ocrLinkSource, ocrContent,  ocrIStream, ocrGet)
END_REGISTRATION
SpotTemplate __spotTemplate(__SpotRegistration);


//
// Build a response table for all messages/commands handled
// by the application.
//
DEFINE_RESPONSE_TABLE1(SpotApp, TApplication)
    EV_OWLVIEW(dnCreate, EvNewView),
    EV_OWLVIEW(dnClose,  EvCloseView),
    EV_COMMAND(CM_HELPABOUT, CmHelpAbout),
END_RESPONSE_TABLE;

//
// Note the special constructor
//
SpotApp::SpotApp () : TApplication
```

```
   (::ApplicationReg["description"], ::Module, &::AppDictionary)
{
    //
    // Tell the doc manager what sort of application it is
    // dealing with - SDI in this case
    //
    SetDocManager(new TDocManager(dmSDI | dmMenu, this));
}


//
// Application intialization.
//
void SpotApp::InitMainWindow ()
{
//
// AppExpert likes to set this in a complicated way...
//
    if (nCmdShow != SW_HIDE)
      nCmdShow = (nCmdShow != SW_SHOWMINNOACTIVE) ?
                             SW_SHOWNORMAL : nCmdShow;

    TOleFrame *frame = new TOleFrame(GetName(), 0, false, this);
    //
    // Assign ICON w/ this application.
    //
    frame->SetIcon(this, IDI_SDIAPPLICATION);
    //
    //  Menu and accelerator
    //
    frame->AssignMenu(SDI_MENU);
    frame->Attr.AccelTable = SDI_MENU;

    SetMainWindow(frame);
    //
    // OLE 2 needs to use menu descriptors for
    // easy merging of menus
    //
    frame->SetMenuDescr(TMenuDescr(SDI_MENU));
    EnableCtl3d(true);
    }
void SpotApp::InitInstance ()
{
    TApplication::InitInstance();

    if (!::Registrar->IsOptionSet(amEmbedding))
      {
          TDocTemplate* tpl = GetDocManager()
            ->MatchTemplate(GetCmdLine().c_str());
          if (tpl)
            {
              TDocument* doc = tpl->ConstructDoc();
              if (doc)
                {
                  doc->SetTemplate(tpl);
                  GetDocManager()->InitDoc(doc,
                         GetCmdLine().c_str(), 0);
                  return;
```


continues

Listing 20.2. continued

```
                }
              }
            GetDocManager()->CreateAnyDoc(0, dtNewDoc);
        }

}
// Response Table handlers:
//
void SpotApp::EvNewView (TView& view)
{
    //
    // When a new view is opened - need to associate with
    // correct window. If the object is embedded and is
    // using in-place editing - get the in-place window.
    // (Can be embedded and do full-screen editing)
    //
    // Only OLE servers need this test
    //
    TOleView* ov = dynamic_cast<TOleView*>(&view);
    if (ov && view.GetDocument().IsEmbedded() &&
        !ov->GetOcRemView()->IsOpenEditing())
      {
        //
        // Embedded view window
        //
        TWindow* vw = view.GetWindow();
        vw->SetParent(dynamic_cast<TOleFrame*>(GetMainWindow())
                   ->GetRemViewBucket());
        vw->Create();
      }
    else
      {
        //
        // Normal window - associate with application
        // main window frame.
        //
        GetMainWindow()->SetClientWindow(view.GetWindow());
        if (!view.IsOK())
          GetMainWindow()->SetClientWindow(0);
        else
          if (view.GetViewMenu())
            GetMainWindow()->MergeMenu(*view.GetViewMenu());
      }
}


void SpotApp::EvCloseView (TView&)
{
    GetMainWindow()->SetClientWindow(0);
    //
    // Set caption back to just title
    //
    GetMainWindow()->SetCaption("Spot");
}
//
// Menu Help About spot.exe command
```

```
void SpotApp::CmHelpAbout ()
{
    //
    // Show the modal dialog.
    //
    // Note the special parenting command
    //
    SpotAboutDlg(&TWindow(GetMainWindow()->
         GetCommandTarget())).Execute();
}


int OwlMain (int , char* [])
{
    try
      {
        ::Registrar = new TOcRegistrar(::ApplicationReg,
                            TOleDocViewFactory<SpotApp>(),
                            TApplication::GetCmdLine(),
                            ::DocTemplateStaticHead);
        if (!::Registrar->IsOptionSet(amAnyRegOption))
        // If this is an exe server normal run, run the app now.
          ::Registrar->Run();
        ::Registrar = 0; // Explicitly free registrar
        return 0;
      }
    catch (xmsg& x)
      {
        ::MessageBox(0, x.why().c_str(), "Exception", MB_OK);
      }
    return -1;
}
```

Type

Listing 20.3. Source code for the SPOTDOC.H header file.

```
#if !defined(__spotdoc_h)
#define __spotdoc_h

//    Class definition for SpotDoc (TOleDocument).

#include <owl\owlpch.h>
#pragma hdrstop
#include "spotapp.rh"
//
// Custom Doc/View notifications
//
const int vnDrawAppend = vnCustomBase+0;
const int vnDrawClear  = vnCustomBase+1;
//
// Custom Doc/View signatures
//
NOTIFY_SIG(vnDrawAppend, uint)
NOTIFY_SIG(vnDrawClear, void)
//
// Response table macros
```

Listing 20.3. continued

```
//
#define EV_VN_DRAWAPPEND VN_DEFINE(vnDrawAppend,  VnAppend,  int)
#define EV_VN_DRAWCLEAR  VN_DEFINE(vnDrawClear,  VnClear,  void)

typedef TArray<TPoint> Points;
//
// Underlying OLE-capable document - uses OLE2 storage
// format
//
class SpotDoc : public TOleDocument
  {
    public:
      SpotDoc (TDocument* parent = 0);
      virtual ~SpotDoc ();
//
// SpotView helper functions
//
      TPoint* GetSpot(uint index);
      void    AddSpot(TPoint& point);
      void    Clear();
//
// Document manager functions
//
      virtual bool Open (int mode, const char far* path = 0);
      virtual bool Commit (bool force);
      virtual bool Close ();
    protected:
      Points* points;
  };
#endif
```

Type **Listing 20.4. Source code for the SPOTDOC.CPP program file.**

```
#include <owl\owlpch.h>
#pragma hdrstop
#include "spotdoc.h"
SpotDoc::SpotDoc (TDocument* parent):
    TOleDocument(parent)
{
    points = new Points(10,0,10);
}


SpotDoc::~SpotDoc ()
{
    delete points;
}
//
// Warning! Open is called and path is never
// populated!
//
bool SpotDoc::Open (int mode, const char far* path)
{
```

```
    points->Flush();
    //
    // If new - GetDocPath() will return 0
    //
    if (GetDocPath())
      {
        //
        // Read base storage for any contained
        // objects
        //
        TOleDocument::Open(mode,path);
        //
        // Get the file stream
        //
        TInStream* is = (TInStream*)InStream(ofRead);
        //
        // If cannot open file, will be zero
        //
        if (!is)
          return false;
        // reference for convenience
        TInStream& in = *is;
        //
        // Check how many points to read
        //
        //
        uint pointCount;
        in >> pointCount;
        //
        // Read specified number of points
        //
        TPoint p;
        for (int i = 0; i < pointCount; i++)
         {
           in >> p;
           points->Add(p); // Add to container
         }
        delete is;
      }
     SetDirty(false);       // Mark as unchanged
     return true;
   }
bool SpotDoc::Commit (bool force)
{
    bool result;
    //
    // Write out contained objects
    //
    result = TOleDocument::Commit(force);
    //
    // Get output stream to write own data
    //
    TOutStream* os = OutStream(ofWrite);
    if (!os)
      return false;
    TOutStream& out = *os; // reference for convenience
    //
    // Write out number of points
```

continues

Listing 20.4. continued

```
    //
    out << points->GetItemsInContainer();
    //
    // For each point, write out to stream
    //
    for (int i = 0; i < points->GetItemsInContainer();i++)
      out << (*points)[i];
    delete os;
    //
    // Mark document as matching
    //
    SetDirty(false);
    //
    // Very important line! This forces write to disk;
    // without this, the file IS created but is corrupt.
    //
    TOleDocument::CommitTransactedStorage();
    return true;
}

//
// Close document
//
bool SpotDoc::Close()
  {
    points->Flush();
    return TOleDocument::Close();
  }
//
// View service functions
//
//  GetSpot returns a point at index
//
TPoint* SpotDoc::GetSpot(uint index)
  {
    if (points && index < points->GetItemsInContainer())
      return &(*points)[index];
    else
      return 0;
  }
//
// Add spot to collection
//
void SpotDoc::AddSpot(TPoint& point)
  {
    points->Add(point);
    // Picture has changed - set dirty flag
    SetDirty(true);
    //
    // Notify all views that the view has changed
    // Pass the index of the new point so that the
    // views can draw the new spot without redrawing
    // the entire screen.
    //
    // vnDrawAppend is defined in the header
    //
    NotifyViews(vnDrawAppend, points->GetItemsInContainer() - 1);
```

```
  }
//
// Entirely clear document
//
void SpotDoc::Clear()
  {
    //
    // Clear the document data
    //
    points->Flush();
    SetDirty(true);
    //
    // Tell view to empty container
    //

    NotifyViews(vnDrawClear,0);
   }
```

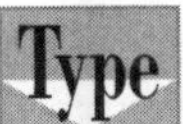

Listing 20.5. Source code for the SPOTVIEW.H header file.

```
#if !defined(__spotview_h)
#define __spotview_h
#include <owl\owlpch.h>
#pragma hdrstop


#include "spotapp.rh"            // Definition of all resources.
#include "spotdoc.h"
//
// View class (may be several instances of this per
// document)
//
class SpotView : public TOleView
  {
    public:
      SpotView (SpotDoc& doc, TWindow* parent = 0);
      virtual ~SpotView ();
      virtual void Paint (TDC& dc, bool erase, TRect& rect);
      virtual const char far* GetViewName ();
      static const char far* StaticName ();
    protected:
      SpotDoc& spotDoc;  // Parent document
      TBrush* backBrush;
      TBrush* spotBrush;
      TPoint storePoint;
      TControlBar * toolBar;
      //
      // Draw a spot from a view
      //
      void SpotView::DrawSpot(TDC& dc, const TPoint& point);
      void EvLButtonDown (uint modKeys, TPoint& point);
      void EvMouseMove (uint modKeys, TPoint& point);
      void EvLButtonUp (uint modKeys, TPoint& point);
      void CmClear ();
      void CmEditCopy ();
      void CmEditCut ();
```

continues

Listing 20.5. continued

```
        bool EvOcViewPartSize(TOcPartSize far& ps);
        bool EvOcViewShowTools(TOcToolBarInfo far& tbi);

      // Document notifications
        bool VnCommit(bool force); // Document saved
        bool VnRevert(bool clear); // Document restored
        bool VnAppend(uint index); // Document amended
        bool VnClear();            // document blanked
        DECLARE_RESPONSE_TABLE(SpotView);
};

#endif
```

Type **Listing 20.6. Source code for the SPOTVIEW.CPP program file.**

```
#include <owl\owlpch.h>
#pragma hdrstop

#include "sptabtdl.h"
#include "spotapp.h"
#include "spotview.h"
#include "spotapp.rh"
#include <stdio.h>

const int spotRadius = 10; // Spot size
//
// Build a response table for all messages/commands handled
// by the application.
//
DEFINE_RESPONSE_TABLE1(SpotView, TOleView)
  //
  // Standard messages
  //
  EV_WM_LBUTTONDOWN,
  EV_WM_MOUSEMOVE,
  EV_WM_LBUTTONUP,
  EV_COMMAND(CM_EDITCLEAR, CmClear),
  EV_COMMAND(CM_EDITCOPY, CmEditCopy),
  EV_COMMAND(CM_EDITCUT, CmEditCut),
  //
  // View notifications
  //
  EV_VN_COMMIT,
  EV_VN_REVERT,
  EV_VN_DRAWAPPEND,
  EV_VN_DRAWCLEAR,
  //
  // OCF notifications
  //
  EV_OC_VIEWPARTSIZE,
  EV_OC_VIEWSHOWTOOLS,
END_RESPONSE_TABLE;
```

```
// SpotView
// ==========
// Construction/Destruction handling.
SpotView::SpotView (SpotDoc& doc, TWindow* parent)
    : TOleView(doc, parent),
      spotDoc(doc)
{
    backBrush = new TBrush(TColor::LtMagenta);
    spotBrush = new TBrush(TColor::LtYellow);
    toolBar = 0;
}


SpotView::~SpotView ()
{
    delete backBrush;
    delete spotBrush;
    delete toolbar;    // Just in case
}
//
// Class and View names
//
const char far* SpotView::GetViewName ()
{
    return "SpotViewClass";
}
const char far* SpotView::StaticName ()
{
    return "Spot View";
}
//
// Paint is not only called for window, but also to update
// OLE2 metafile
//
void SpotView::Paint (TDC& dc, bool erase, TRect& rect)
{
    TPoint* spot;
    //
    TRect clientRect(0,0,GetSystemMetrics(SM_CXSCREEN),
                         GetSystemMetrics(SM_CYSCREEN));
    dc.FillRect(clientRect,*backBrush);

    //
    // This line paints the OLE embedded objects
    // (note: OLE objects are painted from a metafile and
    // do not require the server to be present)
    //
    TOleView::Paint(dc, false, rect);
    //
    // Spots before your eyes...
    //
    dc.SelectObject(*spotBrush);
    int i = 0;
    do
      {
        spot = spotDoc.GetSpot(i++);
        if (spot)
          DrawSpot(dc,*spot);
```

20

continues

Listing 20.6. continued

```
        }
    while (spot);

    dc.RestoreBrush();
}
void SpotView::DrawSpot(TDC& dc, const TPoint& point)
  {
    int radius = spotRadius;
    TRect spotRect(point.x - radius,
                   point.y - radius,
                   point.x + radius,
                   point.y + radius);
    dc.Ellipse(spotRect);

  }


void SpotView::EvLButtonDown (uint modKeys, TPoint& point)
{
    //
    // Base call sets up DragDC - it also modifies point
    // to be in logical units. This enables in-place editing
    // to work when the window has been stretched
    //
    TOleView::EvLButtonDown(modKeys, point);
    if (DragDC && !SelectEmbedded())
      {
        //
        // If haven't hit an OLE object -
        // capture mouse and draw temporary spot
        //
        SetCapture();
        DragDC->SetROP2(R2_XORPEN);     // Invert drawing
        storePoint = point;             // store point
        DragDC->SelectObject(*spotBrush);
        DrawSpot(*DragDC,storePoint);  // Draw spot inverted
      }
  }


void SpotView::EvMouseMove (uint modKeys, TPoint& point)
{
    TOleView::EvMouseMove(modKeys, point); // point modified
    if (DragDC&& !SelectEmbedded())  // If not dragging OLE object
      {
         DrawSpot(*DragDC,storePoint); // Clear up spot
         storePoint = point;
         DrawSpot(*DragDC,storePoint); // Spot breaks out again
      }

}


void SpotView::EvLButtonUp (uint modKeys, TPoint& point)
{
    if (DragDC && !SelectEmbedded()) // Not OLE2 object
```

```
        {
          DrawSpot(*DragDC,storePoint); // Clear up spot
          storePoint = point;           // Store point
          DragDC->DPtoLP(&storePoint);  // Convert to LPs
          ReleaseCapture();
          spotDoc.AddSpot(storePoint);
        }
                                       // Inconsistent:
      TOleView::EvLButtonUp(modKeys, point);
                                       // Does not convert point
                                       // except if using itself
}
//
// Let container know about the server view size in pixels
//
bool
SpotView::EvOcViewPartSize(TOcPartSize far& ps)
{
  TClientDC dc(*this);
  // Set minimum size...
  TRect rect(0, 0, 0, 0);
  // a 2" x 2" extent for server
  //
  rect.right  = dc.GetDeviceCaps(LOGPIXELSX) * 2;
  rect.bottom = dc.GetDeviceCaps(LOGPIXELSY) * 2;
  //
  // Note: this would be better calculated on open of
  // view and when data changed - but for simplicity, I have
  // just done it a nasty way.
  //
  // Declare picture size to be a minimum of 2" x 2"
  // but enable user to add more points for scaling
  //
  // Iterate through all the points and calculate the
  // most extreme
  //
  uint i = 0;
  TPoint* point = spotDoc.GetSpot(i++);
  while (point)
    {
      if (point->x > rect.bottom)
        rect.bottom = point->x;
      if (point->y > rect.right)
        rect.right = point->y;
      point = spotDoc.GetSpot(i++);
    }
  ps.PartRect = rect;
  return true;
}
//
// Give toolbar to container application.
// Note: to emphasize the point, when executing, the
// server does not have a toolbar - only when embedding.
// For the application, create a toolbar in the standard
// fashion. (Give it an Attr.Id of IDW_TOOLBAR)
//
bool
SpotView::EvOcViewShowTools(TOcToolBarInfo far& tbi)
```

continues

Listing 20.6. continued

```
{
  //
  // Construct & create a control bar for show;
  // destroy our bar for hide
  //
  if (tbi.Show)
    {
      if (!toolBar)
        {
          toolBar = new TControlBar(this);
          toolBar->Insert(*new TButtonGadget(CM_EDITCLEAR,
                      CM_EDITCLEAR, TButtonGadget::Command));
          toolBar->Insert(*new TSeparatorGadget);
          toolBar->Insert(*new TButtonGadget(CM_HELPABOUT,
                      CM_HELPABOUT, TButtonGadget::Command));
        }
    toolBar->Create();
    tbi.HTopTB = (HWND)*toolBar;
  }
  else
    {
      if (toolBar)
        {
          toolBar->Destroy();
          delete toolBar;
          toolBar = 0;
        }
    }
  return true;
}


bool SpotView::VnCommit(bool /*force*/)
{
  // nothing to do here; no data held in view
  return true;
}

bool SpotView::VnRevert(bool /*clear*/)
{
  Invalidate();  // force full repaint
  return true;
}
//
// View notification that the document has been
// emptied
//
bool SpotView::VnClear()
  {
  Invalidate();  // force full repaint
  //
  // Component parts are held in a collection
  // iterate the collection to remove the data
  //
  for (TOcPartCollectionIter i(GetOcDoc()->GetParts()); i; i++)
    {
```

```
      TOcPart* p = i.Current();
      TOcPartChangeInfo changeInfo(p, invData¦invView);
      EvOcViewPartInvalid(changeInfo);
      GetOcDoc()->GetParts().Detach(p,true);
    }
  InvalidatePart(invData¦invView);
  return true;
}
//
// View notiification that the document has been added to
//
bool SpotView::VnAppend(uint index)
{
  //
  // Append a spot onto current views - could be a metafile
  //
  // Get a dc for the view window
  TClientDC dc(*this);
  //
  // Get the spot notified at index
  //
  const TPoint* spot = spotDoc.GetSpot(index);
  bool metafile = dc.GetDeviceCaps(TECHNOLOGY) == DT_METAFILE;
  //
  // If drawing to metafile, need to scale
  //
  SetupDC(dc, !metafile);
  dc.SelectObject(*spotBrush);
  DrawSpot(dc,*spot);
  //
  // Tell container to redraw
  //
  InvalidatePart(invView);
  return true;
}


void SpotView::CmClear ()
{
    //
    // Tell document to clear down
    //
    spotDoc.Clear();
}


void SpotView::CmEditCopy ()
{
  //
  // Supposed to be able to copy view to Clipboard
  //
  // Not implemented at time of writing
  //
    TOcRemView* orv = GetOcRemView();
  //  if (orv)
  //     orv->Copy();
}
```

continues

Listing 20.6. continued

```
void SpotView::CmEditCut ()
{
    // Do nothing... nothing sensible to do
}
```

Listing 20.7. Source code for the SPOTAB.H header file.

```
#if !defined(__sptab_h)
#define __sptab_h

#include <owl\owlpch.h>
#pragma hdrstop

#include "spotapp.rh"
class SpotAboutDlg : public TDialog
 {
  public:
    SpotAboutDlg (TWindow *parent, TResId resId = IDD_ABOUT,
                  TModule *module = 0);
    virtual ~SpotAboutDlg ();
  public:
    void SetupWindow ();
};
// Reading the VERSIONINFO resource.
class ProjectRCVersion
  {
    public:
      ProjectRCVersion (TModule *module);
      virtual ~ProjectRCVersion ();

      bool GetProductName (LPSTR &prodName);
      bool GetProductVersion (LPSTR &prodVersion);
      bool GetCopyright (LPSTR &copyright);
      bool GetDebug (LPSTR &debug);

    protected:
      LPBYTE      TransBlock;
      void FAR    *FVData;

    private:
    // Don't enable this object to be copied.
    ProjectRCVersion (const ProjectRCVersion &);
    ProjectRCVersion & operator =(const ProjectRCVersion &);
  };

#endif
```

Listing 20.8. Source code for the SPOTAB.CPP program file.

```
#include <owl\owlpch.h>
#pragma hdrstop

#if !defined(__FLAT__)
#include <ver.h>
#endif

#include "spotapp.h"
#include "spotab.h"
//
// AppExpert generated About box
//
ProjectRCVersion::ProjectRCVersion (TModule *module)
{
    char    appFName[255];
    char    subBlockName[255];
    DWORD   fvHandle;
    uint    vSize;

    FVData = 0;

    module->GetModuleFileName(appFName, sizeof(appFName));
    DWORD dwSize = ::GetFileVersionInfoSize(appFName,&fvHandle);
    if (dwSize)
     {
        FVData  = (void FAR *)new char[(uint)dwSize];
        if (::GetFileVersionInfo(appFName, fvHandle, dwSize,
                                 FVData))
          {
            strcpy(subBlockName, "\\VarFileInfo\\Translation");
            if (!::VerQueryValue(FVData, subBlockName,
                          (void FAR* FAR*)&TransBlock, &vSize))
              {
                delete FVData;
                FVData = 0;
              }
            else
                *(DWORD *)TransBlock =
                            MAKELONG(HIWORD(*(DWORD *)TransBlock),
                            LOWORD(*(DWORD *)TransBlock));
          }
     }
  }


ProjectRCVersion::~ProjectRCVersion ()
  {
    if (FVData)
        delete FVData;
  }


bool ProjectRCVersion::GetProductName (LPSTR &prodName)
```

continues

Listing 20.8. continued

```
  {
    uint    vSize;
    char    subBlockName[255];

    wsprintf(subBlockName, "\\StringFileInfo\\%08lx\\%s",
      *(DWORD *)TransBlock, (LPSTR)"ProductName");
    return FVData ? ::VerQueryValue(FVData, subBlockName,
                   (void FAR* FAR*)&prodName, &vSize) : false;
  }


bool ProjectRCVersion::GetProductVersion (LPSTR &prodVersion)
  {
    uint    vSize;
    char    subBlockName[255];

    wsprintf(subBlockName, "\\StringFileInfo\\%08lx\\%s",
             *(DWORD *)TransBlock, (LPSTR)"ProductVersion");
    return FVData ? ::VerQueryValue(FVData, subBlockName,
           (void FAR* FAR*)&prodVersion, &vSize) : false;
  }


bool ProjectRCVersion::GetCopyright (LPSTR &copyright)
  {
    uint    vSize;
    char    subBlockName[255];

    wsprintf(subBlockName, "\\StringFileInfo\\%08lx\\%s",
            *(DWORD *)TransBlock, (LPSTR)"LegalCopyright");
    return FVData ? ::VerQueryValue(FVData, subBlockName,
           (void FAR* FAR*)&copyright, &vSize) : false;
  }


bool ProjectRCVersion::GetDebug (LPSTR &debug)
{
    uint    vSize;
    char    subBlockName[255];

    wsprintf(subBlockName, "\\StringFileInfo\\%08lx\\%s",
            *(DWORD *)TransBlock, (LPSTR)"SpecialBuild");
    return FVData ? ::VerQueryValue(FVData, subBlockName,
           (void FAR* FAR*)&debug, &vSize) : false;
}


SpotAboutDlg::SpotAboutDlg (TWindow *parent, TResId resId,
                            TModule *module)
    : TDialog(parent, resId, module)
 {
 }

SpotAboutDlg::~SpotAboutDlg ()
  {
    Destroy();
```

```
  }

void SpotAboutDlg::SetupWindow ()
{
    LPSTR prodName = 0, prodVersion = 0, copyright = 0, debug = 0;

    // Get the static text for the value based on VERSIONINFO.
    TStatic *versionCtrl = new TStatic(this, IDC_VERSION, 255);
    TStatic *copyrightCtrl = new TStatic(this, IDC_COPYRIGHT,
                                         255);
    TStatic *debugCtrl = new TStatic(this, IDC_DEBUG, 255);
    TDialog::SetupWindow();
    // Process the VERSIONINFO.
    ProjectRCVersion applVersion(GetModule());
    // Get the product name and product version strings.
    if (applVersion.GetProductName(prodName) &&
        applVersion.GetProductVersion(prodVersion)) {
        char    buffer[255];
        char    versionName[128];
        buffer[0] = '\0';
        versionName[0] = '\0';
        versionCtrl->GetText(versionName, sizeof(versionName));
        wsprintf(buffer, "%s %s %s", prodName,
                 versionName, prodVersion);
        versionCtrl->SetText(buffer);
    }
    //Get the legal copyright string.
    if (applVersion.GetCopyright(copyright))
        copyrightCtrl->SetText(copyright);
    if (applVersion.GetDebug(debug))
        debugCtrl->SetText(debug);
  }
```

Type

Listing 20.9. Source code for the SPOTAPP.RH resource header file.

```
//#if !defined(__spotapp_rh)
//#define __spotapp_rh
//
// IDHELP BorButton for BWCC dialogs.
//
#define IDHELP      998             // Id of help button


//
// Application-specific definitions:
//
#define IDI_SDIAPPLICATION      1001  // Application icon

#define SDI_MENU                100   // Menu and Accelerator IDs

#define IDM_DOCMANAGERFILE      32401
                               // Menu for DocManager merging.

//
```

20

continues

Listing 20.9. continued

```
// OleView merged menus (include\owl\oleview.rh)
//
#define IDM_OLEPOPUP            32405
#define IDM_OLEVIEW             32406


//
// CM_FILEnnnn commands
//  (include\owl\editfile.rh except for CM_FILEPRINTPREVIEW)
//
#define CM_FILENEW              24331          // SDI New
#define CM_FILEOPEN             24332          // SDI Open
#define CM_FILECLOSE            24339
#define CM_FILESAVE             24333
#define CM_FILESAVEAS           24334
#define CM_FILEREVERT           24335
#define CM_VIEWCREATE           24341


//
// Window commands (include\owl\window.rh)
//
#define CM_EXIT                 24310


//
// CM_EDITnnnn commands (include\owl\window.rh)
//
#define CM_EDITUNDO             24321
#define CM_EDITCUT              24322
#define CM_EDITCOPY             24323
#define CM_EDITPASTE            24324
#define CM_EDITDELETE           24325
#define CM_EDITCLEAR            24326
#define CM_EDITADD              24327
#define CM_EDITEDIT             24328
#define CM_EDITPASTESPECIAL     24311
#define CM_EDITPASTELINK         24312
#define CM_EDITINSERTOBJECT     24313
#define CM_EDITLINKS            24314

#define CM_EDITOBJECT           24370
#define CM_EDITFIRSTVERB        24371       // 20 verbs at most
#define CM_EDITLASTVERB         24390

#define CM_EDITCONVERT          24391
#define CM_EDITSHOWOBJECTS      24392


//
// Search menu commands (include\owl\editsear.rh)
//
#define CM_EDITFIND             24351
#define CM_EDITREPLACE          24352
#define CM_EDITFINDNEXT         24353
```

```
//
// Help menu commands.
//
#define CM_HELPABOUT            2009


//
// About Dialogs
//
#define IDD_ABOUT               22000
#define IDC_VERSION             22001
#define IDC_COPYRIGHT           22002
#define IDC_DEBUG               22003


//
// OWL defined strings
//

// Status bar
#define IDS_MODES               32530
#define IDS_MODESOFF            32531


// EditFile
#define IDS_UNABLEREAD          32551
#define IDS_UNABLEWRITE         32552
#define IDS_FILECHANGED         32553
#define IDS_FILEFILTER          32554

// EditSearch
#define IDS_CANNOTFIND          32540


//
// General & application exception messages
//  (include\owl\except.rh)
//
#define IDS_UNKNOWNEXCEPTION    32767
#define IDS_OWLEXCEPTION        32766
#define IDS_OKTORESUME          32765
#define IDS_UNHANDLEDXMSG       32764
#define IDS_UNKNOWNERROR        32763
#define IDS_NOAPP               32762
#define IDS_OUTOFMEMORY         32761
#define IDS_INVALIDMODULE       32760
#define IDS_INVALIDMAINWINDOW   32759
#define IDS_VBXLIBRARYFAIL      32758

//
// Owl 1 compatibility messages
//
#define IDS_INVALIDWINDOW       32756
#define IDS_INVALIDCHILDWINDOW  32755
#define IDS_INVALIDCLIENTWINDOW 32754

//
```

Listing 20.9. continued

```
// TXWindow messages
//
#define IDS_CLASSREGISTERFAIL   32749
#define IDS_CHILDREGISTERFAIL   32748
#define IDS_WINDOWCREATEFAIL    32747
#define IDS_WINDOWEXECUTEFAIL   32746
#define IDS_CHILDCREATEFAIL     32745

#define IDS_MENUFAILURE         32744
#define IDS_VALIDATORSYNTAX     32743
#define IDS_PRINTERERROR        32742

#define IDS_LAYOUTINCOMPLETE    32741
#define IDS_LAYOUTBADRELWIN     32740

//
// TXGdi messages
//
#define IDS_GDIFAILURE          32739
#define IDS_GDIALLOCFAIL        32738
#define IDS_GDICREATEFAIL       32737
#define IDS_GDIRESLOADFAIL      32736
#define IDS_GDIFILEREADFAIL     32735
#define IDS_GDIDELETEFAIL       32734
#define IDS_GDIDESTROYFAIL      32733
#define IDS_INVALIDDIBHANDLE    32732


// ListView (include\owl\listview.rh)
#define IDS_LISTNUM             32584


// DocView (include\owl\docview.rh)
#define IDS_DOCMANAGERFILE      32500
#define IDS_DOCLIST             32501
#define IDS_VIEWLIST            32502
#define IDS_UNTITLED            32503
#define IDS_UNABLEOPEN          32504
#define IDS_UNABLECLOSE         32505
#define IDS_READERROR           32506
#define IDS_WRITEERROR          32507
#define IDS_DOCCHANGED          32508
#define IDS_NOTCHANGED          32509
#define IDS_NODOCMANAGER        32510
#define IDS_NOMEMORYFORVIEW     32511
#define IDS_DUPLICATEDOC        32512
#define IDS_EDITOBJECT          32600
#define IDS_EDITCONVERT         32601
#define IDS_CLOSESERVER         32602
#define IDS_EXITSERVER          32603

// Text for Clipboard format names
#define IDS_CFTEXT              32610
#define IDS_CFBITMAP            32611
#define IDS_CFMETAFILE          32612
#define IDS_CFSYLK              32613
```

```
#define IDS_CFDIF                   32614
#define IDS_CFTIFF                  32615
#define IDS_CFOEMTEXT               32616
#define IDS_CFDIB                   32617
#define IDS_CFPALETTE               32618
#define IDS_CFPENDATA               32619
#define IDS_CFRIFF                  32620
#define IDS_CFWAVE                  32621
#define IDS_CFUNICODETEXT           32622
#define IDS_CFENHMETAFILE           32623

#define IDS_IN             32700


//#endif
```

Type

Listing 20.10. Script for the SPOTAPP.RC resource file.

```
#if !defined(WORKSHOP_INVOKED)
#include <windows.h>
#endif
#include "spotapp.rh"
//
// Standard application menu
//
SDI_MENU MENU
{
 POPUP "&File"
 {
  MENUITEM "&New", CM_FILENEW
  MENUITEM "&Open...", CM_FILEOPEN
  MENUITEM SEPARATOR
  MENUITEM "&Save", CM_FILESAVE, GRAYED
  MENUITEM "Save &As...", CM_FILESAVEAS, GRAYED
  MENUITEM SEPARATOR
  MENUITEM "E&xit\tAlt+F4", CM_EXIT
 }

 MENUITEM SEPARATOR
 POPUP "&Edit"
 {
  MENUITEM "&Undo\tAlt+BkSp", CM_EDITUNDO, GRAYED
  MENUITEM SEPARATOR
  MENUITEM "Cu&t\tShift+Del", CM_EDITCUT, GRAYED
  MENUITEM "&Copy\tCtrl+Ins", CM_EDITCOPY, GRAYED
  MENUITEM "&Paste\tShift+Ins", CM_EDITPASTE, GRAYED
  MENUITEM "Paste &Special...",    CM_EDITPASTESPECIAL
  MENUITEM "Paste &Link",          CM_EDITPASTELINK
  MENUITEM SEPARATOR
  MENUITEM "Clear &All\tCtrl+Del", CM_EDITCLEAR, GRAYED
  MENUITEM Separator
  MENUITEM "&Insert Object...",    CM_EDITINSERTOBJECT
  MENUITEM "&Links...",            CM_EDITLINKS
  MENUITEM "&Object",              CM_EDITOBJECT
  MENUITEM Separator
```

20

continues

Listing 20.10. continued

```
     MENUITEM "&Show Objects",       CM_EDITSHOWOBJECTS
     }

     MENUITEM SEPARATOR
     MENUITEM SEPARATOR
     MENUITEM SEPARATOR
     MENUITEM SEPARATOR
     POPUP "&Help"
     {
      MENUITEM "&About...", CM_HELPABOUT
     }

    }


    // Accelerator table for short-cut to menu commands. (include\owl\editfile.rc)
    SDI_MENU ACCELERATORS
    BEGIN
      VK_DELETE, CM_EDITDELETE, VIRTKEY
      VK_DELETE, CM_EDITCUT, VIRTKEY, SHIFT
      VK_INSERT, CM_EDITCOPY, VIRTKEY, CONTROL
      VK_INSERT, CM_EDITPASTE, VIRTKEY, SHIFT
      VK_DELETE, CM_EDITCLEAR, VIRTKEY, CONTROL
      VK_BACK,   CM_EDITUNDO, VIRTKEY, ALT
      VK_F3,     CM_EDITFINDNEXT, VIRTKEY
    END


    // DocManager File menu

    IDM_DOCMANAGERFILE MENU LOADONCALL MOVEABLE PURE DISCARDABLE
    BEGIN
        MENUITEM "&New", CM_FILENEW
        MENUITEM "&Open...", CM_FILEOPEN
        MENUITEM "&Close", CM_FILECLOSE
        MENUITEM SEPARATOR
        MENUITEM "&Save", CM_FILESAVE, GRAYED
        MENUITEM "Save &As...", CM_FILESAVEAS, GRAYED
        MENUITEM SEPARATOR
        MENUITEM "E&xit\tAlt+F4", CM_EXIT
    END


    // Menu merged in when TOleView is active;
    // notice the extra MENUITEM SEPARATORs, which are
    // for menu negotation.  These separators are used as group
    // markers by OWL.
    IDM_OLEVIEW MENU
    {
     MENUITEM SEPARATOR
     POPUP "&Edit"
     {
      MENUITEM "&Undo\aCtrl+Z", CM_EDITUNDO
      MENUITEM SEPARATOR
      MENUITEM "&Cut\aCtrl+X", CM_EDITCUT
      MENUITEM "C&opy\aCtrl+C", CM_EDITCOPY
```

```
  MENUITEM "&Paste\aCtrl+V", CM_EDITPASTE
  MENUITEM "Paste &Special...", CM_EDITPASTESPECIAL
  MENUITEM "Paste &Link", CM_EDITPASTELINK
  MENUITEM "Clear &All\aCtrl+Del", CM_EDITCLEAR
  MENUITEM Separator
  MENUITEM "&Insert Object...",    CM_EDITINSERTOBJECT
  MENUITEM "&Links...",            CM_EDITLINKS
  MENUITEM "&Object",              CM_EDITOBJECT
  MENUITEM Separator
  MENUITEM "&Show Objects",        CM_EDITSHOWOBJECTS

 }

 MENUITEM SEPARATOR
 MENUITEM SEPARATOR
 MENUITEM SEPARATOR
 MENUITEM SEPARATOR
 POPUP "&Help"
 {
  MENUITEM "&About...", CM_HELPABOUT
 }

}
//
// OLE pop-up
//

IDM_OLEPOPUP MENU LOADONCALL MOVEABLE PURE DISCARDABLE
BEGIN
    POPUP "OLE"
    BEGIN
        MENUITEM "&Cut\aCtrl+X", CM_EDITCUT
        MENUITEM "C&opy\aCtrl+C", CM_EDITCOPY
        MENUITEM "&Delete\aDel", CM_EDITDELETE
        MENUITEM SEPARATOR
        MENUITEM "&Object", CM_EDITOBJECT
    END
END


//
// Table of help hints displayed in the status bar.
//
STRINGTABLE
BEGIN
    -1,              "File/document operations"
    CM_FILENEW,      "Creates a new document"
    CM_FILEOPEN,     "Opens an existing document"
    CM_VIEWCREATE,   "Create a new view for this document"
    CM_FILEREVERT,   "Reverts changes to last document save"
    CM_FILECLOSE,    "Close this document"
    CM_FILESAVE,     "Saves this document"
    CM_FILESAVEAS,   "Saves this document with a new name"
    CM_EXIT,         "Quits Spot and prompts to save the documents"
    CM_EDITUNDO-1,   "Edit operations"
    CM_EDITUNDO,     "Reverses the last operation"
    CM_EDITCUT,  "Cuts the selection and puts it on the Clipboard"
```

20

continues

Listing 20.10. continued

```
    CM_EDITCOPY,  "Copies selection and puts it on the Clipboard"
    CM_EDITPASTE, "Inserts clipboard contents at insertion point"
    CM_EDITPASTESPECIAL, "Select paste option and format"
    CM_EDITPASTELINK,    "Link with object on the clipboard"
    CM_EDITDELETE,  "Deletes the selection"
    CM_EDITCLEAR,   "Clear the document"
    CM_EDITLINKS,   "Edit links to the document"
    CM_EDITINSERTOBJECT,      "Insert an object into the document"
    CM_EDITOBJECT,  "Ask the selected object to perform an action"
    CM_EDITSHOWOBJECTS,       "Hilight selected object"
    CM_EDITADD,     "Insert a new line"
    CM_EDITEDIT,    "Edit the current line"
    CM_EDITFIND-1,  "Search/replace operations"
    CM_EDITFIND,    "Finds the specified text"
    CM_EDITREPLACE, "Finds the specified text and changes it"
    CM_EDITFINDNEXT,"Finds the next match"
    CM_HELPABOUT-1, "Access About"
    CM_HELPABOUT,   "About the Spot application"
END

//
// OWL string table
//

// EditFile (include\owl\editfile.rc and include\owl\editsear.rc)
STRINGTABLE LOADONCALL MOVEABLE DISCARDABLE
BEGIN
    IDS_CANNOTFIND,  "Cannot find ""%s""."
    IDS_UNABLEREAD,  "Unable to read file %s from disk."
    IDS_UNABLEWRITE, "Unable to write file %s to disk."
    IDS_FILECHANGED, "The text in the %s file has changed."
                     "\n\nDo you want to save the changes?"
    IDS_FILEFILTER,  "Text files (*.TXT)¦*.TXT¦AllFiles
                     "(*.*)¦*.*¦"
END


// ListView (include\owl\listview.rc)
STRINGTABLE LOADONCALL MOVEABLE DISCARDABLE
BEGIN
  IDS_LISTNUM,  "Line number %d"
END


// Doc/View (include\owl\docview.rc)
STRINGTABLE LOADONCALL MOVEABLE DISCARDABLE
BEGIN
    IDS_DOCMANAGERFILE,          "&File"
    IDS_DOCLIST,                 "--Document Type--"
    IDS_VIEWLIST,                "--View Type--"
    IDS_UNTITLED,                "Document"
    IDS_UNABLEOPEN,              "Unable to open document."
    IDS_UNABLECLOSE,             "Unable to close document."
    IDS_READERROR,               "Document read error."
    IDS_WRITEERROR,              "Document write error."
    IDS_DOCCHANGED,              "The document has been"
             "changed.\n\nDo you want to save the changes?"
```

```
    IDS_NOTCHANGED,       "The document has not been changed."
    IDS_NODOCMANAGER,           "Document Manager not present."
    IDS_NOMEMORYFORVIEW,        "Insufficient memory for view."
    IDS_DUPLICATEDOC,           "Document already loaded."
END


// OLEView (include\owl\oleview.rc)
STRINGTABLE LOADONCALL MOVEABLE DISCARDABLE
BEGIN
     IDS_EDITOBJECT,            "&Object"
     IDS_EDITCONVERT,           "Convert..."
     IDS_CLOSESERVER,           "Close and Return to "
     IDS_EXITSERVER,            "Exit and Return to "
END

STRINGTABLE LOADONCALL MOVEABLE DISCARDABLE
BEGIN
    IDS_CFTEXT,                 "Text\nplain text"
    IDS_CFBITMAP,               "Bitmap\na bitmap image"
    IDS_CFMETAFILE,             "Metafile Picture\na static picture"
    IDS_CFSYLK,                 "Sylk\na spreadsheet"
    IDS_CFDIF,                  "DIF\na document"
    IDS_CFTIFF,                 "Tagged Image File Format\na "
                                "TIFF image file"
    IDS_CFOEMTEXT,              "OEM Text\nan OEM text"
    IDS_CFDIB,                  "DIB\na device independent bitmap"
                                "image"
    IDS_CFPALETTE,              "Palette\na color palette"
    IDS_CFPENDATA,              "Pen Data\npen data"
    IDS_CFRIFF,                 "RIFF\na RIFF media file"
    IDS_CFWAVE,                 "Wave\na sound wave file"
    IDS_CFUNICODETEXT,          "UniCode Text\nUnicode text"
    IDS_CFENHMETAFILE,          "Enhanced Metafile\nan "
                                "enhanced metafile picture"
    IDS_IN,                     " in "
END


// Exception string resources (include\owl\except.rc)
STRINGTABLE LOADONCALL MOVEABLE DISCARDABLE
BEGIN
    IDS_OWLEXCEPTION,           "ObjectWindows Exception"
    IDS_UNHANDLEDXMSG,          "Unhandled Exception"
    IDS_OKTORESUME,             "OK to resume?"
    IDS_UNKNOWNEXCEPTION,       "Unknown exception"

    IDS_UNKNOWNERROR,           "Unknown error"
    IDS_NOAPP,                  "No application object"
    IDS_OUTOFMEMORY,            "Out of memory"
    IDS_INVALIDMODULE,      "Invalid module specified for window"
    IDS_INVALIDMAINWINDOW,      "Invalid MainWindow"
    IDS_VBXLIBRARYFAIL,         "VBX Library init failure"

    IDS_INVALIDWINDOW,          "Invalid window %s"
    IDS_INVALIDCHILDWINDOW,     "Invalid child window %s"
    IDS_INVALIDCLIENTWINDOW,    "Invalid client window %s"
```

continues

Listing 20.10. continued

```
    IDS_CLASSREGISTERFAIL,
             "Class registration fail for window %s"
    IDS_CHILDREGISTERFAIL,
             "Child class registration fail for window %s"
    IDS_WINDOWCREATEFAIL,          "Create fail for window %s"
    IDS_WINDOWEXECUTEFAIL,         "Execute fail for window %s"
    IDS_CHILDCREATEFAIL,           "Child create fail for window %s"

    IDS_MENUFAILURE,               "Menu creation failure"
    IDS_VALIDATORSYNTAX,           "Validator syntax error"
    IDS_PRINTERERROR,              "Printer error"

    IDS_LAYOUTINCOMPLETE,
         "Incomplete layout constraints specified in window %s"
    IDS_LAYOUTBADRELWIN,
        "Invalid relative window specified in layout constraint
         in window %s"

    IDS_GDIFAILURE,                "GDI failure"
    IDS_GDIALLOCFAIL,              "GDI allocate failure"
    IDS_GDICREATEFAIL,             "GDI creation failure"
    IDS_GDIRESLOADFAIL,            "GDI resource load failure"
    IDS_GDIFILEREADFAIL,           "GDI file read failure"
    IDS_GDIDELETEFAIL,             "GDI object %X delete failure"
    IDS_GDIDESTROYFAIL,            "GDI object %X destroy failure"
    IDS_INVALIDDIBHANDLE,          "Invalid DIB handle %X"
END


// General Window's status bar messages. (include\owl\statusba.rc)
STRINGTABLE
BEGIN
    IDS_MODES                      "EXT¦CAPS¦NUM¦SCRL¦OVR¦REC"
    IDS_MODESOFF                   "   ¦    ¦   ¦    ¦   ¦   "
    SC_SIZE,               "Changes the size of the window"
    SC_MOVE,               "Moves the window to another position"
    SC_MINIMIZE,           "Reduces the window to an icon"
    SC_MAXIMIZE,           "Enlarges the window to it maximum size"
    SC_RESTORE,            "Restores the window to its previous size"
    SC_CLOSE,                      "Closes the window"
    SC_TASKLIST,                   "Opens task list"
    SC_NEXTWINDOW,                 "Switches to next window"
END


//
// Misc application definitions
//

// Application ICON
IDI_SDIAPPLICATION ICON "applsdi.ico"


// About box.
IDD_ABOUT DIALOG 12, 17, 204, 65
STYLE DS_MODALFRAME ¦ WS_POPUP ¦ WS_CAPTION ¦ WS_SYSMENU
```

```
CAPTION "About Spot"
FONT 8, "MS Sans Serif"
BEGIN
    CTEXT "Version", IDC_VERSION, 2, 14, 200, 8, SS_NOPREFIX
    CTEXT "Expert OWL Application", -1, 2, 4, 200, 8, SS_NOPREFIX
    CTEXT "", IDC_COPYRIGHT, 2, 27, 200, 17, SS_NOPREFIX
    RTEXT "", IDC_DEBUG, 136, 55, 66, 8, SS_NOPREFIX
    ICON IDI_SDIAPPLICATION, -1, 2, 2, 34, 34
    DEFPUSHBUTTON "OK", IDOK, 82, 48, 40, 14
END

CM_EDITCLEAR BITMAP LOADONCALL MOVEABLE
{
  '42 4D 66 01 00 00 00 00 00 00 76 00 00 00 28 00'
 '00 00 14 00 00 00 14 00 00 00 01 00 04 00 00 00'
 '00 00 F0 00 00 00 00 00 00 00 00 00 00 00 00 00'
 '00 00 00 00 00 00 00 00 00 00 00 00 80 00 00 80'
 '00 00 00 80 80 00 80 00 00 00 80 00 80 00 80 80'
 '00 00 80 80 80 00 C0 C0 C0 00 00 00 FF 00 00 FF'
 '00 00 00 FF FF 00 FF 00 00 00 FF 00 FF 00 FF FF'
 '00 00 FF FF FF 00 88 88 88 88 88 88 88 88 88 88'
 '40 00 88 88 88 88 88 88 88 88 88 88 90 00 88 88'
 '88 88 88 88 88 88 88 88 20 00 88 88 88 88 88 88'
 '88 88 88 88 40 18 88 88 88 88 88 88 88 88 88 88'
 '00 00 88 88 88 88 88 88 88 88 88 88 00 00 88 88'
 '88 88 88 88 88 88 88 88 00 00 88 88 88 88 88 88'
 '88 88 88 88 0B 00 88 80 08 88 88 88 88 88 88 88'
 '00 00 88 80 08 88 88 88 88 88 88 88 00 00 88 80'
 '08 88 88 84 44 44 44 48 00 00 88 80 08 80 88 84'
 'EF EF EF 48 0B 00 88 80 07 80 08 84 FE FE FE 48'
 '00 00 88 87 00 00 00 84 EF EF EF 48 00 00 88 88'
 '70 00 00 84 FE FE FE 48 00 00 88 88 88 80 08 84'
 'EF EF EF 48 0B 00 88 88 88 80 88 84 FE FE 44 48'
 'FF FF 88 88 88 88 88 84 EF EF 44 88 FF FF 88 88'
 '88 88 88 84 44 44 48 88 00 00 88 88 88 88 88 88'
 '88 88 88 88 0B 00'
}
CM_HELPABOUT BITMAP
{
'42 4D 66 01 00 00 00 00 00 00 76 00 00 00 28 00'
'00 00 14 00 00 00 14 00 00 00 01 00 04 00 00 00'
'00 00 F0 00 00 00 00 00 00 00 00 00 00 00 00 00'
'00 00 00 00 00 00 00 00 00 00 00 00 80 00 00 80'
'00 00 00 80 80 00 80 00 00 00 80 00 80 00 80 80'
'00 00 80 80 80 00 C0 C0 C0 00 00 00 FF 00 00 FF'
'00 00 00 FF FF 00 FF 00 00 00 FF 00 FF 00 FF FF'
'00 00 FF FF FF 00 88 88 88 88 88 88 88 88 88 88'
'00 00 88 88 88 84 44 44 48 88 88 88 00 00 88 88'
'84 44 44 44 44 48 88 88 00 00 88 88 44 46 FF 64'
'44 44 88 88 00 00 88 84 44 4F FF F6 44 44 48 88'
'00 00 88 44 44 4F F6 48 44 44 44 88 00 00 88 44'
'44 46 FF 44 44 44 44 88 01 01 84 44 44 44 FF 64'
'44 44 44 48 08 33 84 44 44 44 6F F4 44 44 44 48'
'00 00 84 44 44 44 4F F6 44 44 44 48 00 00 84 44'
'44 48 46 FF 44 44 44 48 00 00 84 44 44 46 FF FF'
'44 44 44 48 00 00 84 44 44 44 6F F6 44 44 44 48'
'00 00 88 44 44 44 44 44 44 44 44 88 00 00 88 44'
'44 44 44 66 44 44 44 88 00 00 88 84 44 44 46 FF'
```

20

Listing 20.10. continued

```
'64 44 48 88 00 00 88 88 44 44 46 FF 64 44 88 88'
'00 00 88 88 84 44 44 66 44 48 88 88 00 00 88 88'
'88 84 44 44 48 88 88 88 00 00 88 88 88 88 88 88'
'88 88 88 88 00 00'
}
// Version info.
//
#if !defined(__DEBUG_)
// Non-Debug VERSIONINFO
1 VERSIONINFO LOADONCALL MOVEABLE
FILEVERSION 1, 0, 0, 0
PRODUCTVERSION 1, 0, 0, 0
FILEFLAGSMASK 0
FILEFLAGS VS_FFI_FILEFLAGSMASK
FILEOS VOS__WINDOWS16
FILETYPE VFT_APP
BEGIN
    BLOCK "StringFileInfo"
    BEGIN
        // Language type = U.S. English (0x0409) and
        // Character Set = Windows, Multilingual(0x04e4)
        BLOCK "040904E4"
            // Matches VarFileInfo Translation hex value.
        BEGIN
            VALUE "CompanyName", "Honor Oak Systems\000"
            VALUE "FileDescription", "Spot for Windows\000"
            VALUE "FileVersion", "1.0\000"
            VALUE "InternalName", "Spot\000"
            VALUE "LegalCopyright",
              "Copyright   1994 by Honor Oak Systems. \000"
            VALUE "LegalTrademarks", "Windows (TM)\000"
            VALUE "OriginalFilename", "Spot.EXE\000"
            VALUE "ProductName", "Spot\000"
            VALUE "ProductVersion", "1.0\000"
        END
    END

    BLOCK "VarFileInfo"
    BEGIN
        VALUE "Translation", 0x0409, 0x04e4
   // U.S. English(0x0409) & Windows Multilingual(0x04e4) 1252
    END

END
#else

// Debug VERSIONINFO
1 VERSIONINFO LOADONCALL MOVEABLE
FILEVERSION 1, 0, 0, 0
PRODUCTVERSION 1, 0, 0, 0
FILEFLAGSMASK VS_FF_DEBUG ¦ VS_FF_PRERELEASE ¦ VS_FF_PATCHED ¦
VS_FF_PRIVATEBUILD ¦ VS_FF_SPECIALBUILD
FILEFLAGS VS_FFI_FILEFLAGSMASK
FILEOS VOS__WINDOWS16
FILETYPE VFT_APP
BEGIN
```

```
    BLOCK "StringFileInfo"
    BEGIN
        // Language type = U.S. English (0x0409)
        // and Character Set = Windows, Multilingual(0x04e4)
        BLOCK "040904E4"
        // Matches VarFileInfo Translation hex value.
        BEGIN
            VALUE "CompanyName", "Honor Oak Systems\000"
            VALUE "FileDescription", "Spot for Windows\000"
            VALUE "FileVersion", "1.0\000"
            VALUE "InternalName", "Spot\000"
            VALUE "LegalCopyright",
               "Copyright 1994 by Honor Oak Systems.  \000"
            VALUE "LegalTrademarks", "Windows (TM)\000"
            VALUE "OriginalFilename", "Spot.EXE\000"
            VALUE "ProductName", "Spot\000"
            VALUE "ProductVersion", "1.0\000"
            VALUE "SpecialBuild", "Debug Version\000"
            VALUE "PrivateBuild", "Built by Ian Spencer\000"
        END
    END

    BLOCK "VarFileInfo"
    BEGIN
        VALUE "Translation", 0x0409, 0x04e4
    // U.S. English(0x0409) & Windows Multilingual(0x04e4) 1252
    END

END
#endif

IDM_OLEVIEW ACCELERATORS
{
 VK_DELETE, CM_EDITDELETE, VIRTKEY, CONTROL
}
```

Listing 20.11. Source code for the SPOTAPP.DEF definition file.

```
NAME spot

DESCRIPTION 'Spot - Copyright 1994 by Honor Oak Systems.'
EXETYPE      WINDOWS
CODE         PRELOAD MOVEABLE DISCARDABLE
DATA         PRELOAD MOVEABLE
HEAPSIZE     4096
STACKSIZE    20000
```

Listing 20.12. Contents of the SPOT.IDE project file.

```
SPOT[.EXE] OWL + OCF LIBRARIES
  SPOTAPP[.CPP]
  SPOTDOC[.CPP]
  SPOTVIEW[.CPP]
```

continues

Listing 20.12. continued

```
SPOTAB[.CPP]
SPOTAPP[.RC]
SPOTAPP[.DEF]
```

Analysis First, ensure that you have registered the server. You may want to build some of the OLE samples in the EXAMPLES directory to give you a test bed, unless you have a modern application. Running it as a stand-alone application might give you a result like the one in Figure 20.3. Running in another OLE application, STEP14.EXE (provided as an example in the OWL tutorial directory), gives the appearance shown in Figure 20.4.

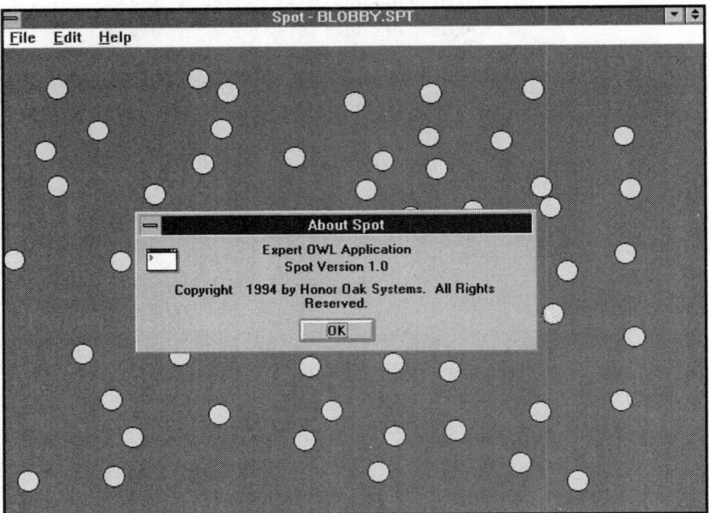

Figure 20.3.
The SPOT application running as a stand-alone application.

Analysis Looking first to the application class in Listing 20.2 (SPOTAPP.CPP), you see that there was no toolbar created in the `InitMainWindow`. This emphasizes that, when running as an in-place editor, you provide a toolbar specifically for the application. In fact, if you can guarantee that the instance will be only single-use (set by the registration option `usage` for the application), you can borrow the control bar for your main application. OWL `TOleView` does this by default in response to `EvOcShowTools`. You should always provide a toolbar—if you don't, the screen jumps about while switching in the container application as the client window is repositioned.

Note also that OWL expects to use menu merging even for an SDI application. For OWL to manage the menus for you, you merely need to create menus of the correct identity. OWL creates the `TMenuDescr` objects for you, except for the main menu, as long as you use the predefined menu identifiers.

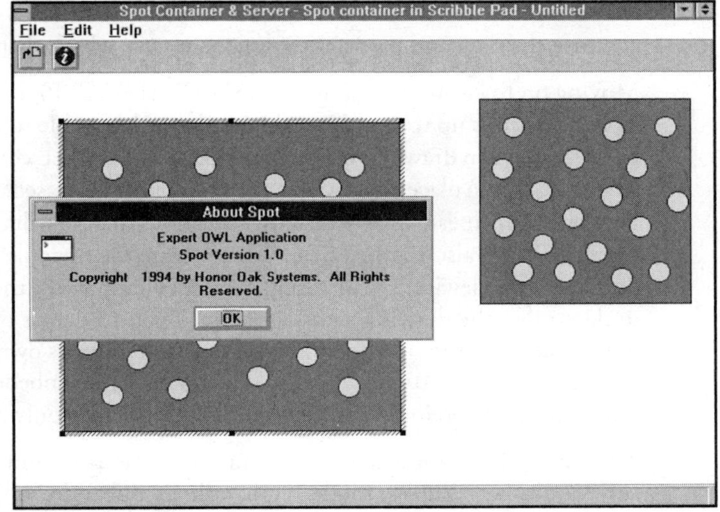

Figure 20.4.
The SPOT application running with in-place editing.

Take a look at the `InitInstance`. If the application starts as an embedding application, OWL looks after creating the view. In this SDI application, there should always be a client view by first attempting to open a command-line document (this could be optimized to avoid opening for obviously invalid command lines).

The trivialities of the About box bring out an important point about embedded objects. You may want to bring up dialog boxes. `GetCommandTarget` can be used to provide a suitable parent in place of `GetMainWindow`, which may, in fact, be hidden during embedding. This should ensure that the dialog stays modal over the container application.

In Listing 20.4 (SPOTDOC.CPP), the first catch is in writing the `Open` function. Although the path appears to be passed in as a parameter, it is not used. You should use `GetDocPath`, which is filled in before `Open` is called in `TOleDocument::InitDoc`.

You can detect a failure to open a file by using the result of the `InStream` function. In `SpotDoc`, the spots are held in a `TArray` container. They can easily be read in from and out to this container.

Warning: Failure to read a document can occur because the document was improperly written. Check that the `Commit` function is properly structured and ends with a call to `TOleDocument::CommitTransactedStorage`.

`AddSpot` uses a custom notification to get the views updated. This is a good optimization, because, for this application, the views need to add the item to their current display, rather than redrawing the entire screen. Note the interaction of the view and the document. The view captures the data and passes it to the document, which then tells the view to draw it.

Moving on to `Paint` in Listing 20.6 (SPOTVIEW.CPP), the drawing here requires care. Your `Paint` functions up to now have almost always been able to rely on having the mapping mode be `MM_TEXT` when drawing to a window. Because the OLE container may have scaled the image, when you edit in place, your window may not be pixel-based. OWL sorts out the scaling for you. However, this means that you must be careful that you draw in logical units, not pixels. The `Paint` function also is called by OWL to create the metafile that OLE stores in the embedded document for viewing and printing. This does not provide the usual functions you might expect to determine the drawing area—it is up to you to define the drawing area. The view always obtains its data from the document; it does not store its own data. The other unusual thing to note is the call to `TOleView::Paint`. This is how the embedded objects that are not active get redisplayed. (Therefore, it is not required for a server-only application.)

The mouse handling needs consideration. `TOleView` handles matching the mouse with the current display mapping mode. To handle its embedded objects, it provides a DC to enable it to draw and to scale its mouse movements. The tricky part is in the use of the `EvLButtonUp` response. Unlike the other two mouse events, `TOleView` does not scale the mouse coordinates. Also, unlike the other two responses, your code needs to happen before the base class processing so that you can test for the presence of the DC. (Again, if the application is not a container, it does not need to worry about the base class processing.)

There are two OCF events you might like to handle, which are specific for an OLE server.

The first is declaring the size of your view to OLE with `EvOcViewPartSize`. The implementation here is quick and dirty. Normally, good programming practice dictates avoiding recalculating the view size each time the message is called. In this case, the view expands if data is placed outside the declared bounds. To avoid problems, the minimum view is declared to be a two-inch square.

NEW TERM In OCF, the embedded objects are known as *parts.*

Second, there is the placing of the toolbar. This is requested when OLE opens the object for in-place editing. You create a standard toolbar. (By default, `TOleView` assumes that it can borrow the application `MainWindow` toolbar on the assumption that the application instance is single-use.) This toolbar is likely to be slightly different from a normal stand-alone application toolbar, leaving out File Save and other items. Hidden away is the OWL processing, which updates the menu and manages the status bar. Much of the processing is enabled merely by placing the correct options on the menu and toolbar.

There is a whole raft of functions that OWL provides. You should spend some time experimenting with the effects of the different embedding options. Try dragging objects around, resizing their borders when selected, resizing when open for editing, pasting links and so on. It is worth remembering that, in OWL, most of the `Doc/View` control is provided by the document

manager (`TDocManager`). The controlling of the window is mainly provided by `TOleView` through `TOleWindow`. With luck, investigating these classes should provide you with the information you need to go beyond this quick look at OLE linking and embedding.

Consider what the changes would be to take away the container functionality—a very few statements, removing a few menu items and a few base class calls. Consider what it would take to take away server function—some registration options and some spare notifications. Finally, compare that with a stand-alone application—using the `Doc/View` model. OLE `Doc/View` provides a surprisingly high degree of implementation independence. It is possible to write OWL OLE applications without the `Doc/View` model; however, your application needs to be quite specialized to make it worthwhile.

There is a wealth of issues not covered here. OLE 2 provides language independence for the interface. `Doc/View` is a very high-level abstraction—OWL does enable closer control of the OLE process. You can go on to explore enabling your application to control object positioning or laying out objects around the embedded parts. Finally, don't get so involved with providing OLE support that you forget to develop a useful application. There already are a lot of container applications out there—what is needed are useful servers.

OLE Automation

As the final part of your tour of OLE, you look at OLE Automation. OLE Automation provides a method of linking application data across the OLE interface. This acts as a replacement for DDEML. When you study Automation, the most noticeable thing you find in the OCF implementation is the ease of use of these objects—unlike the low level of DDEML. The big difference is that Automation understands classes. Using OCF, your server provides a C++ class that can use all the usual features. The client uses another C++ class that maps onto the server class behind the scenes, using OCF magic. In both applications, the class is handled the same way as a normal C++ class. An Automation object interface is not limited in the same way as VBX. You can call functions and pass data, which includes your own C++ classes.

20

NEW TERM Under Automation, you provide an *Automation server* to supply services and an *Automation controller* to ask for them.

A server can provide methods (or callable functions), properties (data members accessed by function), direct access to data members, or even automated objects it is accessing from another server.

NEW TERM Declaring a member, function, or class to be visible via Automation is called *exposing*.

Using Automation is surprisingly simple. Just follow a few simple steps.

Step 1: Design the Server Class

The server class may be a new class especially designed for the Automation server, or you can provide some elements of an existing class or a whole new class. You should design it in the first instance without consideration of having it operated remotely.

Step 2: Declare the Class to Be Automatic

Note: It is recommended that the class be derived from `TAutoClass`, which merely ensures that OLE is notified of the class' destruction if the class instance is deleted when still in use by OLE. This is not essential.

Within the class declaration, a series of macros are used to declare the services to be exposed. For example, this code snippet

```
DECLARE_AUTOCLASS(DataServer)
  AUTOPROPRO(Value, GetValue, int,)
  AUTOPROPRO(Text, GetText, TAutoString,)
  AUTOFUNC0(Throw,Throw,int,)
```

exposes two read-only properties and a function with no parameters that returns an `int`. There is a set of macros that includes the following:

Declaration Macro	*Member*
`AUTODATA`	Data
`AUTODATARO`	Data, read-only
`AUTOFLAG`	A bit flag
`AUTOFUNCn`	Function returning a value with *n* parameters
`AUTOFUNCnV`	Function returning void with *n* parameters
`AUTOITERATOR`	Iterator object
`AUTOPROP`	Property
`AUTOPROPRO`	Property, read-only
`AUTOPROXY`	Property containing an automated object
`AUTOSTAT`	Static member function or global function
`AUTOTHIS`	`*this`

Warning: These macros look similar but are organized differently from response tables. In particular, note that there is no comma at the end of the line and that there is an optional last parameter, where you must specify the comma that precedes it even if you do not give the final parameter.

For example, `AUTOFUNC1(OleFunction,CalledFuction,int,bool,)` calls the class member function `int CalledFunction(bool)`. The first parameter of the macro represents the OLE name for the object and is used by the controlling application. The only rule on types is that if the type is a character array, declare it as a `TAutoString`, and if the object is a pointer or reference to a C++ object, wrap it up in a `TAutoObject<>` wrapper.

Note: OCF uses the `TAuto...` templates to enable it to convert types using RTTI (Run Time Type Information). RTTI gets the type information from the actual object, not from pointers and references, so it is hard to handle. The special auto classes, therefore, create an actual object of a known type that contains a pointer or reference of a type known by template generation.

These macros allow an option to be their last parameter to enable you to hook the command—that is, execute some action when OLE accesses the exposed member. These are quite complicated except for `AUTOVALIDATE`. This enables you to place a boolean expression, which is called whenever the function or data is accessed. *`Val`* is used to represent the value when a member is accessed, *`Arg1`*, *`Arg2`*, and so forth are used to represent function parameters. For example, if the value of one pair of dice is exposed, this snippet

```
AUTODATA(DiceValue,value,int,
                  AUTOVALIDATE(Val>0 && Val <= 6))
```

ensures that a value between 1 and 6 is set; otherwise, an OLE error occurs in the controlling application.

Step 3: Define the Automatic Methods and Properties

Having exposed the members, it is necessary to describe the members to OLE.

```
DEFINE_AUTOCLASS(DataServer)
  EXPOSE_METHOD(Throw,TAutoShort,"Throw","Throw the dice",)
  EXPOSE_PROPRO(Value,TAutoShort,"Value","Last throw",)
  EXPOSE_PROPRO(Text,TAutoString,"Text","Last throw as text",)
  EXPOSE_APPLICATION(DataServer,"Dice","Dice application",)
  EXPOSE_QUIT("Quit","Quit",)
END_AUTOCLASS(DataServer,"Dice","Dice throwing class",0)
```

Note: Exposing methods enables multilingual support. This is beyond the scope of this book.

The `END_AUTOCLASS(cls, name, desc, help)` defines that the C++ class `cls` is given to OLE as `name`, described as `desc`, with a help index of `help`.

Note: You can provide a help interface by registering a help file. The identifier on the macro enables the controlling application to request context-sensitive help from WinHelp.

The macros implement methods for a class nested within your automated class, which OCF uses to communicate with the class.

Macro	*Member Declaration*
`EXPOSE_APPLICATION`	Automated application name—just for interest
`EXPOSE_METHOD`	Method
`EXPOSE_PROPRO`	Read-only property
`EXPOSE_PROPRW`	Read-write property
`EXPOSE_PROPWO`	Write-only property
`EXPOSE_QUIT`	Shutdown method (provided by `TAutoBase`)

In addition, functions with parameters need to be followed with `REQUIRED_ARG` and `OPTIONAL_ARG` macros. Remember that required arguments cannot follow optional arguments. The datatypes in the table must be special `TAuto...` data types. Refer to your *ObjectWindows Programmers' Guide*, Chapter 4, to understand the conversion table.

Step 4: Build the Application Engine

Having built the table, all that remains is to build the server application. Because this does not require object linking and embedding, the registration is much simpler. The key item is registering the application with the command-line flag of `-Automation`. The application also can use a simple hidden window so the OWL bit is trivial.

OWL doesn't provide a `ComponentFactory` macro that works with a plain `TApplication` object. Take an opportunity to write one. A `ComponentFactory` is a callback that is called three times in an executing server: to register, run, and shut down the application. However, it also may have to cope with a standard execution. The example that follows shows a simple callback. It uses a static member to store the data server object between callbacks and uses the application to run the message loop. Note that the registrar is a `TRegistrar` and that the includes required are simple, too. You also must include a `TOleAllocator(0)` object in your `OwlMain` procedure. Your target needs to include the OCF libraries.

Step 5: Build a Type Library and C++ Class

It is almost time to move on to building the controller, but first you build and run the controller with a parameter of `-TypeLib`. This does two things. It registers the automatic objects with OLE, and it builds a type library in the directory of the executable. Then, by running AutoGen (provided with Turbo C++ 4.5) and picking up the type library (selecting the Automation option), you can generate a C++ class, which can be used by the Automation controller. These are given in a C++ source and header that you can include directly in your project.

Step 6: Use the C++ Class

The AutoGen application produces a C++ class with names taken from the exposed functions. You normally can use this class without amendment merely by including the generated code in your application. AutoGen does an excellent job of generating function names, because it can take the name that you declared for each member and use that as a proxy class member. The salient points are that the class is derived from `TAutoProxy`. The function calls and class members are declared as normal C++ members. OCF then provides some simple `AUTO...` macros that combine to translate the calling function into a call to OCF. For example, here is the other end of the `DataServer` class—note that the class declaration is simple.

```
class Dice : public TAutoProxy {
  public:
    Dice() : TAutoProxy(0x409) {}
    // Throw the dice
    short Throw(); // [id(1), method]
    // Last throw of the dice
    short GetValue(); // [id(2), propget]
    // Last throw of dice in text
    TAutoString GetText(); // [id(3), propget]
    // Dice-throwing application
    void GetDice(Dice&); // [id(4), propget]
    // Quit
    void Quit(); // [id(5), method]
};
short Dice::Throw()
{
  AUTONAMES0("Throw")
  AUTOARGS0()
  AUTOCALL_METHOD_RET
}

short Dice::GetValue()
{
  AUTONAMES0("Value")
  AUTOARGS0()
  AUTOCALL_PROP_GET
}

TAutoString Dice::GetText()
{
```

20

```
    AUTONAMES0("Text")
    AUTOARGS0()
    AUTOCALL_PROP_GET
  }
```

NEW TERM A class used by an Automation controller that is supplied by an Automation server is called a *proxy class.*

Don't worry about the `TAutoString`; it converts quite nicely to a `char *`. The types aren't quite identical at the other end of the OLE conversation, but they are compatible.

To use a proxy class, you merely declare it; call the `TAutoProxy::Bind` member with the name of the application—which AutoGen even supplies at the top of the include file if you've forgotten it. Having included the CXX file in your application, use the class as a normal class. The only change required to the rest of the application is to declare a `TOleAllocator(0)` in `OwlMain`. You also need to include the OCF libraries.

Here are the applications; one will be very familiar. The first one, Listing 20.13, is DICESVR.EXE.

Listing 20.13. Source code for the DICESVR.CPP program file.

```
#include <owl\applicat.h>
#include <ocf/appdesc.h>
#include <ocf/automacr.h>
#include <ocf/ocreg.h>
#include <owl\framewin.h>

TPointer<TRegistrar> Registrar;

REGISTRATION_FORMAT_BUFFER(100)
BEGIN_REGISTRATION(AppReg)
  REGDATA(clsid,"{82F153C0-DCB6-101B-A585-040224007802}")
  REGDATA(progid,"Dice.Server")
  REGDATA(description,"Dice Thrower")
  REGDATA(cmdline, "-Automation")
END_REGISTRATION

class OleServerApp;

class DataServer: public TAutoBase
   {
    public:
    DataServer();
    ~DataServer();
    int GetValue() {return value;}
    const char* GetText();
    int Throw();
    private:
      int value;
    DECLARE_AUTOCLASS(DataServer)
      AUTOPROPRO(Value, GetValue, int,)
      AUTOPROPRO(Text, GetText, TAutoString,)
      AUTOFUNC0(Throw,Throw,int,)
```

```
    };
 DEFINE_AUTOCLASS(DataServer)
    EXPOSE_METHOD(Throw,TAutoShort,"Throw","Throw the dice",)
    EXPOSE_PROPRO(Value,TAutoShort,"Value","Last throw of the dice",)
    EXPOSE_PROPRO(Text,TAutoString,"Text","Last throw of dice in text",)
    EXPOSE_APPLICATION(DataServer,"Dice","Dice throwing application",)
    EXPOSE_QUIT("Quit","Quit",)
 END_AUTOCLASS(DataServer,"Dice","Dice throwing class",0)

 DataServer::DataServer():TAutoBase()
    {
      value = 0;
      randomize();
    }
 DataServer::~DataServer()
    {
      ::GetAppDescriptor()->InvalidateObject(this);
    }
 const char* DataServer::GetText()
    {
      const char * throwText[] = {"","One","Two","Three","Four","Five","Six"};
      return throwText[value];
    }
int DataServer::Throw()
   {
    value = rand() % 6 + 1;
    return value;
   }


class OleServerApp:public TApplication
   {
     public:
       void InitMainWindow()
         {
           SetMainWindow(new TFrameWindow(0,"Dice Throw"));
           if (Registrar->IsOptionSet(amAutomation))
             nCmdShow = SW_HIDE;
         }
   };
IUnknown* ComponentFactory(IUnknown* outer, uint32 options, uint32 /*id*/ = 0)
{
   static DataServer* dataServer = 0;     // used to hold EXE object until OLE
factory call
   IUnknown* ifc = 0;
   if (options & amShutdown)
       return (options & amServedApp) ? 0 : outer;
   //
   // Must be first time through - make server App
   // or we are going through once and running
   //
   if (!dataServer)
     dataServer = new DataServer();

   //
   // If not Automation (so is going to drop through to run)
   // or callback, is request to register use
```

continues

Listing 20.13. continued

```
  //

  if (!(options & amAutomation) ¦¦(options & amServedApp))
  //
  // Do OLE stuff
  //
    ifc = *::Registrar->CreateAutoApp
          (TAutoObjectDelete<DataServer>(dataServer),
          options, outer); // does an AddRef
  //
  // If this is a call to just run the app
  //
  if (options & amRun)
      OleServerApp().Run();
  return ifc;
}
int OwlMain(int,char*[])
  {
    TOleAllocator oleAllocator(0);
    try
      {
       Registrar = new TRegistrar(AppReg, ComponentFactory,
                                  TApplication::GetCmdLine());
       if (!Registrar->IsOptionSet(amAnyRegOption))
         Registrar->Run();
       Registrar = 0;
      }
    catch(...)
      {
      }
    return 0;
  }
```

Finally, here are Listings 20.14 through 20.19, DICECLIE.EXE, which is a client that uses an OLE-served dice throw.

Type

Listing 20.14. Source code for the DICE.H header file.

```
#ifndef _DICE_H
#define _DICE_H
#include <owl\owlall.h>
// stdio for sprintf
#include <stdio.h>
#include "dice.rh"
#include "dicedlg.h"

#endif
```

Type

Listing 20.15. Source code for the DICE.CPP program file.

```
#include "dice.h"
//
//  The usual TApplication derivative, this time
```

```
//  putting in the dice client
//
class DiceApp:public TApplication
  {
   public:
   void InitMainWindow()
         {
           TDialog* dice = new DiceDialog();
           //
           // The proper way to handle MainWindow...
           //
           SetMainWindow(new TFrameWindow(0,"Dice",dice,TRUE));
           GetMainWindow()->SetIcon(this,IDI_DICE);
           GetMainWindow()->Attr.Style
               &= ~WS_THICKFRAME & ~WS_MAXIMIZEBOX;

         }
  };
int OwlMain(int,char*[])
  {
   TOleAllocator oleAlloc(0); // NEW!
   DiceApp diceApp;
   try
     {
        return diceApp.Run(); // Standard TApplication::Run
      }
   catch (TXBase be)
     {
       MessageBox(0,be.why().c_str(),0,MB_OK);
     }
   return 0;
  }
```

Type

Listing 20.16. Source code for the DICEDLG.H header file.

```
#ifndef _DICEDIAL_H
#define _DICEDIAL_H
// Forward declaration for Dice pointer
class Dice;
class DiceDialog:public TDialog
  {
   public:
   DiceDialog();
   // new destructor
   ~DiceDialog();
   protected:
   Dice* diceThrow; // Pointer to proxy class
   TStatic* dice1;
   TStatic* dice2;
   TStatic* diceText1;
   TStatic* diceText2;
   TEdit* sum;
   TButton* pushButton;
    void SetupWindow();
   void PushButton();
   void EvTimer(uint timerId);
```

continues

Listing 20.16. continued

```
    void EvPaint();
    void Paint(TDC&,bool,TRect&);

    private:
    bool roll;
    int sumValue;
    int diceValue1;
    int diceValue2;
    TRect rectDice1;
    TRect rectDice2;
    TDib* dice;
    DECLARE_RESPONSE_TABLE(DiceDialog);
  };

#endif
```

Listing 20.17. Source code for the DICEDLG.CPP program file.

```
#include "dice.h"
// Include dicesvr source code
#include "dicesvr.cxx"
DEFINE_RESPONSE_TABLE1(DiceDialog,TDialog)
  EV_WM_TIMER,
  EV_WM_PAINT,
  EV_BN_CLICKED(IDC_PUSHBUTTON1,PushButton),
END_RESPONSE_TABLE;
DiceDialog::DiceDialog()
  :TDialog(0,DICE)
  {
     diceThrow = new Dice();          // Create proxy class
//
// Declare the controls - add some text this time
//
   dice1 = new TStatic(this,IDC_DICE1);
   diceText1 = new TStatic(this,IDC_DICETEXT1);
   dice2 = new TStatic(this,IDC_DICE2);
   diceText2 = new TStatic(this,IDC_DICETEXT2);
   sum = new TEdit(this,IDC_EDIT3);

   pushButton = new TButton(this,IDC_PUSHBUTTON1);
//
// Initialize the dice
//
   roll = FALSE;
   sumValue = 0;
   dice = new TDib(TBitmap(GetModule()->GetInstance(),
          IDB_DICE));
   diceValue1 = 0;
   diceValue2 = 0;
  };
//
```

```
// Destructor - called when instance deleted
//
DiceDialog::~DiceDialog()
  {
//
// Delete some brushes
//
   delete dice;
   diceThrow->Quit(); // Force the closure of the proxy
                      // object
   delete diceThrow;
  }
void DiceDialog::SetupWindow()
  {
   TDialog::SetupWindow();
   rectDice1 = dice1->GetWindowRect();
   rectDice2 = dice2->GetWindowRect();
   dice1->Destroy();
   dice2->Destroy();
   ScreenToClient(rectDice1.TopLeft());
   ScreenToClient(rectDice2.TopLeft());
   ScreenToClient(rectDice1.BottomRight());
   ScreenToClient(rectDice2.BottomRight());
   diceThrow->Bind("Dice.Server"); // bind to server
                                   // throws an exception
                                   // if fails
}

void DiceDialog::PushButton()
  {
   if (roll)
    {
      char diceString[5];
      KillTimer(1);
      roll = FALSE;
      pushButton->SetCaption("&Spin");
      sprintf(diceString,"%i",sumValue);
      sum->SetText(diceString);
    }
   else
    {
      roll = TRUE;
      pushButton->SetCaption("&Stop");
      sum->SetText("");
      SetTimer(1,100);
      EvTimer(1);
    }

  }
void DiceDialog::EvTimer(uint /*timerId*/)
  {
   TClientDC dc(*this);
   //
   // Four calls to the proxy class - that's
   // all that is new, replacing the call to
   // the local random number generator.
   //
```

continues

Listing 20.17. continued

```
    diceValue1 = diceThrow->Throw();
    diceText1->SetText(diceThrow->GetText());
    diceValue2 = diceThrow->Throw();
    diceText2->SetText(diceThrow->GetText());
    sumValue = diceValue1 + diceValue2;
    Paint(dc,TRUE,TRect(0,0,0,0));
  };
void DiceDialog::EvPaint()
  {
    TPaintDC dc(*this);
    TRect&   rect = *(TRect*)&dc.Ps.rcPaint;
    Paint(dc, dc.Ps.fErase, rect);
  }
void DiceDialog::Paint(TDC& dc,bool,TRect&)
  {
     TRect source1(0,0,dice->Height(),dice->Height());
     source1.Offset(dice->Height()*diceValue1,0);
     dc.StretchDIBits(rectDice1,source1,*dice);
     TRect source2(0,0,dice->Height(),dice->Height());
     source2.Offset(dice->Height()*diceValue2,0);
     dc.StretchDIBits(rectDice2,source2,*dice);
  }
```

Type **Listing 20.18. Source code for the DICE.RH resource header file.**

```
#define IDI_DICE  1
#define IDB_DICE  1
#define DICE  1
#define IDC_EDIT3  103
#define IDC_PUSHBUTTON1  104
#define IDC_DICE1  120
#define IDC_DICE2  121
#define IDC_DICETEXT1  131
#define IDC_DICETEXT2  132
```

Type **Listing 20.19. Script for the DICE.RC resource file.**

```
#include "dice.rh"
DICE DIALOG 7, 15, 85, 58
STYLE WS_CHILD | WS_VISIBLE | WS_BORDER
FONT 8, "MS Sans Serif"
{
 EDITTEXT IDC_EDIT3, 60, 6, 16, 12, ES_READONLY |
          NOT WS_TABSTOP | WS_BORDER
 LTEXT "+", -1, 25, 8, 6, 8
 LTEXT "=", -1, 52, 9, 7, 8
 DEFPUSHBUTTON "&Spin", IDC_PUSHBUTTON1, 17, 39, 50, 14
 CONTROL "", IDC_DICE1, "static", SS_BLACKFRAME | WS_CHILD
        | WS_VISIBLE, 6, 6, 16, 17
 CONTROL "", IDC_DICE2, "static", SS_BLACKFRAME | WS_CHILD
        | WS_VISIBLE, 35, 6, 16, 17
```

```
 CTEXT "", IDC_DICETEXT1, 2, 25, 25, 8
 CTEXT "", IDC_DICETEXT2, 30, 26, 25, 8
}

IDB_DICE BITMAP
{
  '42 4D F6 03 00 00 00 00 00 00 76 00 00 00 28 00'
  '00 00 70 00 00 00 10 00 00 00 01 00 04 00 00 00'
  '00 00 80 03 00 00 00 00 00 00 00 00 00 00 00 00'
  '00 00 10 00 00 00 00 00 00 00 00 00 BF 00 00 BF'
  '00 00 00 BF BF 00 BF 00 00 00 BF 00 BF 00 BF BF'
  '00 00 C0 C0 C0 00 80 80 80 00 00 00 FF 00 00 FF'
  '00 00 00 FF FF 00 FF 00 00 00 FF 00 FF 00 FF FF'
  '00 00 FF FF FF 00 91 11 11 11 11 11 11 11 91 11'
  '11 11 11 11 11 11 91 11 11 11 11 11 11 11 91 11'
  '11 11 11 11 11 11 91 11 11 11 11 11 11 11 91 11'
  '11 11 11 11 11 11 91 11 11 11 11 11 11 11 79 99'
  '99 99 99 99 99 91 79 99 99 99 99 99 99 91 79 99'
  '99 99 99 99 99 91 79 99 99 99 99 99 99 91 79 99'
  '99 99 99 99 99 91 79 99 99 99 99 99 99 91 79 99'
  '99 99 99 99 99 91 79 99 99 99 99 99 99 91 79 99'
  '99 99 99 99 99 91 79 99 99 99 99 9B BB 91 79 99'
  '99 99 99 9B BB 91 79 BB B9 99 99 9B BB 91 79 BB'
  'B9 99 99 9B BB 91 79 BB B9 99 99 9B BB 91 79 99'
  '99 99 99 99 99 91 79 99 99 99 99 99 99 91 79 99'
  '99 99 99 9B BB 91 79 99 99 99 99 9B BB 91 79 BB'
  'B9 99 99 9B BB 91 79 BB B9 99 99 9B BB 91 79 BB'
  'B9 99 99 9B BB 91 79 99 99 99 99 99 99 91 79 99'
  '99 99 99 99 99 91 79 99 99 99 99 9B BB 91 79 99'
  '99 99 99 9B BB 91 79 BB B9 99 99 9B BB 91 79 BB'
  'B9 99 99 9B BB 91 79 BB B9 99 99 9B BB 91 79 99'
  '99 99 99 99 99 91 79 99 99 99 99 99 99 91 79 99'
  '99 99 99 99 99 91 79 99 99 99 99 99 99 91 79 99'
  '99 99 99 99 99 91 79 99 99 99 99 99 99 91 79 99'
  '99 99 99 99 99 91 79 99 99 99 99 99 99 91 79 99'
  '99 99 99 99 99 91 79 99 99 99 99 99 99 91 79 99'
  '99 99 99 99 99 91 79 99 99 99 99 99 99 91 79 99'
  '99 99 99 99 99 91 79 99 99 99 99 99 99 91 79 99'
  '99 99 99 99 99 91 79 99 99 9B BB 99 99 91 79 99'
  '99 99 99 99 99 91 79 99 99 9B BB 99 99 91 79 99'
  '99 99 99 99 99 91 79 99 99 9B BB 99 99 91 79 BB'
  'B9 99 99 9B BB 91 79 99 99 99 99 99 99 91 79 99'
  '99 9B BB 99 99 91 79 99 99 99 99 99 99 91 79 99'
  '99 9B BB 99 99 91 79 99 99 99 99 99 99 91 79 99'
  '99 9B BB 99 99 91 79 BB B9 99 99 9B BB 91 79 99'
  '99 99 99 99 99 91 79 99 99 9B BB 99 99 91 79 99'
  '99 99 99 99 99 91 79 99 99 9B BB 99 99 91 79 99'
  '99 99 99 99 99 91 79 99 99 9B BB 99 99 91 79 BB'
  'B9 99 99 9B BB 91 79 99 99 99 99 99 99 91 79 99'
  '99 99 99 99 99 91 79 99 99 99 99 99 99 91 79 99'
  '99 99 99 99 99 91 79 99 99 99 99 99 99 91 79 99'
  '99 99 99 99 99 91 79 99 99 99 99 99 99 91 79 99'
  '99 99 99 99 99 91 79 99 99 99 99 99 99 91 79 99'
  '99 99 99 99 99 91 79 99 99 99 99 99 99 91 79 99'
  '99 99 99 99 99 91 79 99 99 99 99 99 99 91 79 99'
  '99 99 99 99 99 91 79 99 99 99 99 99 99 91 79 99'
  '99 99 99 99 99 91 79 BB B9 99 99 99 99 91 79 BB'
  'B9 99 99 99 99 91 79 BB B9 99 99 9B BB 91 79 BB'
```

continues

Listing 20.19. continued

```
  'B9 99 99 9B BB 91 79 BB B9 99 99 9B BB 91 79 99'
  '99 99 99 99 99 91 79 99 99 99 99 99 99 91 79 BB'
  'B9 99 99 99 99 91 79 BB B9 99 99 99 99 91 79 BB'
  'B9 99 99 9B BB 91 79 BB B9 99 99 9B BB 91 79 BB'
  'B9 99 99 9B BB 91 79 99 99 99 99 99 99 91 79 99'
  '99 99 99 99 99 91 79 BB B9 99 99 99 99 91 79 BB'
  'B9 99 99 99 99 91 79 BB B9 99 99 9B BB 91 79 BB'
  'B9 99 99 9B BB 91 79 BB B9 99 99 9B BB 91 77 77'
  '77 77 77 77 77 79 77 77 77 77 77 77 77 79 77 77'
  '77 77 77 77 77 79 77 77 77 77 77 77 77 79 77 77'
  '77 77 77 77 77 79 77 77 77 77 77 77 77 79 77 77'
  '77 77 77 77 77 79'
}


IDI_DICE ICON
{
  '00 00 01 00 01 00 20 20 10 00 00 00 00 00 E8 02'
  '00 00 16 00 00 00 28 00 00 00 20 00 00 00 40 00'
  '00 00 01 00 04 00 00 00 00 00 80 02 00 00 00 00'
  '00 00 00 00 00 00 00 00 00 00 00 00 00 00 00 00'
  '00 00 00 00 BF 00 00 BF 00 00 00 BF BF 00 BF 00'
  '00 00 BF 00 BF 00 BF BF 00 00 C0 C0 C0 00 80 80'
  '80 00 00 00 FF 00 00 FF 00 00 00 FF FF 00 FF 00'
  '00 00 FF 00 FF 00 FF FF 00 00 FF FF FF 00 00 00'
  '00 00 00 00 00 00 00 00 00 00 00 00 00 00 00 00'
  '00 00 00 00 00 00 00 00 00 00 00 00 00 00 00 00'
  '00 00 00 00 00 00 00 00 00 00 00 00 00 00 00 00'
  '00 00 00 00 00 00 00 00 00 00 00 00 00 00 00 00'
  '00 00 01 11 11 11 11 11 11 11 33 31 00 00 00 00'
  '00 01 11 11 11 11 33 31 11 11 11 11 10 00 00 00'
  '00 11 33 31 11 11 11 11 11 11 11 11 10 00 00 00'
  '00 19 99 99 99 99 99 99 99 99 91 11 10 00 00 00'
  '0D 99 99 99 99 99 99 99 99 99 99 11 10 00 00 00'
  '0D 99 99 99 99 99 99 99 9B B9 99 11 10 00 00 00'
  '0D 99 99 99 99 99 99 99 BB BB 99 11 10 00 00 00'
  '0D 99 99 99 99 99 99 99 BB BB 99 11 10 00 00 00'
  '0D 99 99 99 99 99 99 99 9B B9 99 11 10 00 00 00'
  '0D 99 99 99 99 99 99 99 99 99 99 11 10 00 00 00'
  '0D 99 99 99 99 99 99 99 99 99 99 13 10 00 00 00'
  '0D 99 99 99 99 99 99 99 99 99 99 13 10 00 00 00'
  '0D 99 99 99 99 99 99 99 99 99 99 13 10 00 00 00'
  '0D 99 99 99 99 99 99 99 99 99 99 11 10 00 00 00'
  '0D 99 99 99 99 99 99 99 99 99 99 11 10 00 00 00'
  '0D 99 99 99 99 99 99 99 99 99 99 11 10 00 00 00'
  '0D 99 99 99 99 99 99 99 99 99 99 11 10 00 00 00'
  '0D 99 99 99 99 99 99 99 99 99 99 11 10 00 00 00'
  '0D 99 BB 99 99 99 99 99 99 99 99 11 10 00 00 00'
  '0D 9B BB B9 99 99 99 99 99 99 99 11 10 00 00 00'
  '0D 9B BB B9 99 99 99 99 99 99 99 11 00 00 00 00'
  '0D 99 BB 99 99 99 99 99 99 99 99 11 00 00 00 00'
  '0D D9 99 99 99 99 99 99 99 99 99 10 00 00 00 00'
  '00 DD DD DD DD DD DD DD DD DD D0 00 00 00 00 00'
  '00 00 00 00 00 00 00 00 00 00 00 00 00 00 00 00'
  '00 00 00 00 00 00 00 00 00 00 00 00 00 00 00 00'
```

```
    '00 00 00 00 00 00 00 00 00 00 00 00 00 00 00 00'
    '00 00 00 00 00 00 00 00 00 00 00 00 00 00 FF FF'
    'FF FF FF FF FF FF FF FF FF FF FF FF FF FF FF 80'
    '00 0F FE 00 00 07 FC 00 00 07 FC 00 00 07 F8 00'
    '00 07 F8 00 00 07 F8 00 00 07 F8 00 00 07 F8 00'
    '00 07 F8 00 00 07 F8 00 00 07 F8 00 00 07 F8 00'
    '00 07 F8 00 00 07 F8 00 00 07 F8 00 00 07 F8 00'
    '00 07 F8 00 00 07 F8 00 00 07 F8 00 00 07 F8 00'
    '00 0F F8 00 00 0F F8 00 00 1F FC 00 00 7F FF FF'
    'FF FF FF FF FF FF FF FF FF FF FF FF FF FF'
}
```

The application appears in Figure 20.5.

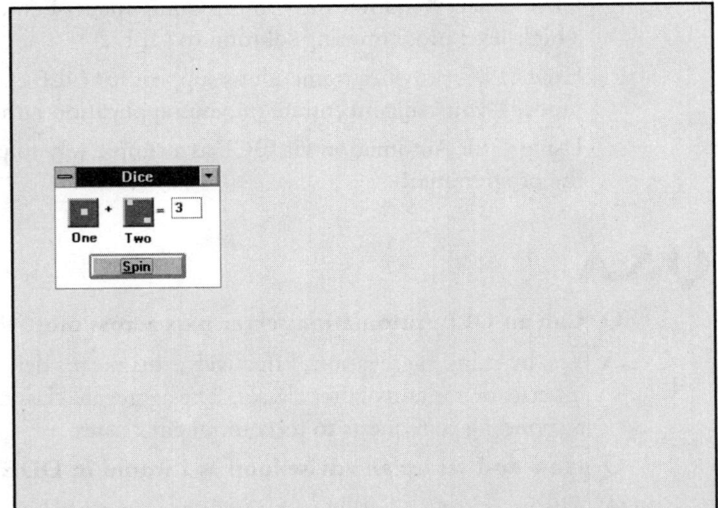

Figure 20.5.
The automatic dice.

Analysis I am sure you are surprised at how easy it is to use a proxy class with the help of OCF. Assuming that OLE can find the server, you should have no difficulty using the class. The `Bind` statement makes the connection through OLE. The destructor of the object should disconnect, but it is safest to call the `Quit` method to ensure that OLE disconnects the server. The function calls themselves are almost transparent.

For the server, the hard work is not in defining the class, but in matching up the OCF macros to the server class. This is a tedious rather than difficult task.

Whither Automation?

This was a simple example. Obviously, data exchange using Automation through OCF is simplicity itself compared to DDEML. However, at the time of writing, there isn't a proper way to send notifications back to the proxy object. Automation objects are the core of OCX, the replacement for VBX controls for 32-bit Windows. OLE defines quite a number of other features for Automation, including help file support and international translation via resources. OLE embedding servers can also provide automation.

Summary

Today, you got a taste of OLE 2. Specifically, you explored the following topics:

- OLE 2 as a method for communicating between programs and for linking and embedding views and data
- How ObjectWindows and Object Components Framework work together to provide a high-level programming solution to OLE 2
- How OWL provides tremendous support for OLE embedding via its OLE `Doc/View` model—you can concentrate on your application rather than OLE
- Using OLE Automation via OCF as a simple way to pass data between programs (for the programmer!)

Q&A

Q Can an OLE Automation server pass across more than one class?

A Yes, by using aggregation. Effectively, this means defining a controlling class that inherits or contains other classes. The aggregate class can then delegate the task of responding to requests to its component classes.

Q How do I set up an advise loop as I would in DDEML?

A The interface for notifying events is not supported yet. Eventually, this will be part of the emerging capabilities of the specification of OCX. In the meantime, one can use a more limited version of advise loops with the server informing the client when data has changed and the latter then retrieving that information via the `IDataObject` and `IAdviseSink` interfaces.

Q How do I find out more about OLE?

A If possible, work through the examples in the Borland manuals on OCF that do not use the OWL classes. These highlight some of the mechanics of OLE. I recommend that you avoid books on pure OLE as these will not explain the OCF interface. There is a full tutorial included with the Borland package; it is well worth working through it. The OWL manuals and online help are full of information about OLE and OCF.

Workshop

The Workshop provides quiz questions to help you consolidate your understanding of the material covered, and exercises to provide you with experience in using what you've learned. Try to understand the quiz and exercise answers before continuing on to the next day's lesson. Answers are provided in the Appendix A.

Quiz

1. What method of joining documents should a user use to place a document in several other documents?
2. What OWL class is responsible for managing the display of embedded objects?
3. What must you do before you can access an OLE 2 server from a container?

Exercise

Generate a copy of the SPOT application with AppExpert with all the decorations.

WEEK 3

Debugging

No matter how well you may try to write a program, and no matter how good at writing programs you ever become, you will always make mistakes and cause bugs to appear in your program. The easiest bugs to locate and fix are those caught by the compiler as it shows you your syntax and other related errors. However, it is quite possible to have a program compile flawlessly, even without any warnings, and still fail in some miserable ways. When a program fails, a debugger can be the best tool for figuring out what went wrong. In today's lesson, you learn about the following:

- The integrated debugger commands
- How to debug a simple program
- Other debugging tools

The Integrated Debugger

Built into the Integrated Development Environment (IDE) are several debugging functions. You can use these to stop a running program in the middle of its execution, to view the values of variables and member data, and to watch how programming constructs are executed on a line-by-line basis.

In the IDE's top-level menu are two submenus that can be used in debugging. The first is the Debug menu. This menu provides a number of commands that control the execution of programs and enable you to view individual variables and structures. The second menu is the View menu. Inside this menu are, among other items, commands to open various debugging windows.

The Debug Menu

The principal commands for debugging are located in the Debug menu. These are the commands that enable you to execute your program on a line-by-line basis, to set breakpoints, and evaluate individual expressions.

NEW TERM A *breakpoint* is a point in a program at which execution will stop or break. Once a breakpoint is set, you can go ahead and let the program run. When the line of code where the breakpoint is set is reached, the program will pause, and the debugger will come up with the specified line highlighted. At this point, you can evaluate expressions and execute the code one line at a time.

- The `Run` command starts a program's execution. If the source code has changed and the program isn't already in a suspended state of execution, the IDE goes through the rebuild process, compiling and linking as necessary.
- The `Step over` command is used to *single-step* through the program code on a line-by-line basis. Each time you select `Step over`, the highlighted line is executed. If that line

contains a function call, the function is called, and when it returns, the debugger will stop again on the next line.

- If you want to actually go into the function instead of skipping over it, you can use the `Trace into` command. This is the same as stepping over lines of code, except that this will follow into function calls, enabling you to step through them. If there is no function call, the trace acts exactly like a step. Note, however, that some function calls aren't as visible as others. For example, when an object is created, its constructor function will be called, even if there doesn't appear to be any direct call to that function.
- The `Toggle breakpoint` command sets or clears a breakpoint on the line of code with the cursor. If the program is executing freely when it reaches this line of code (you aren't stepping or tracing through the code), then the program will pause and the debugger will come up with the cursor on this line of code.
- If your program is paused and you move the cursor around, or perhaps you look at some other files, you might lose track of the line of code at which the program was paused. In this case, you can use the `Find execution point` command to place the cursor on the current line of executing code.
- Sometimes, you might have started a program running, and then later decided that you need to pause the program, but you didn't set any breakpoints. You can use the `Pause program` command to pause the program at its current execution point. At this point, you will be able to evaluate expressions and look at various global variables. Unfortunately, you will not always be able to locate the current execution point in the code. Also, you may not always be able to use the `Pause program` command to stop the program if, say, it's in an infinite loop. In these cases, you can sometimes use the Ctrl+Alt+SysRq key sequence to pause the program and return to the debugger.
- The `Terminate program` command stops the program's execution and then resets it to the beginning. This means that the next time you might try to run or step into the program, it will be at the beginning.
- There is a window in the debugger called the Watch window. When you use the `Add watch...` command, you are given a dialog box, shown in Figure 21.1, that enables you to add an expression. This expression will be placed in the Watch window and will be updated as the program continues execution. The watch expressions are excellent ways to see how certain variables change over the course of the program.
- Figure 21.2 shows the dialog box that is brought up when you select the `Add breakpoint...` command. This sets a breakpoint on the current line in the same way as `Toggle breakpoint`, except that you are allowed to add some parameters to the breakpoint. For example, you can have the debugger break out only when a certain condition is true (for example, a variable being equal to a certain value).

Figure 21.1.
The dialog box from which a watch expression may be added.

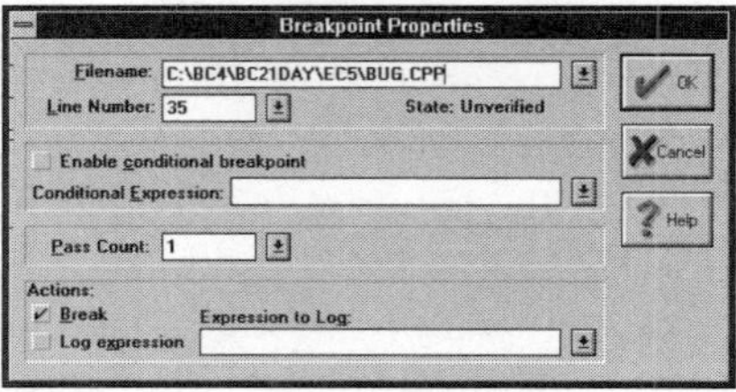

Figure 21.2.
The dialog box on which breakpoint properties may be modified.

- ☐ The `Evaluate/Modify...` command opens a dialog box that enables you to enter expressions and see what they evaluate to. It also enables you to change the value of certain variables by first evaluating them and then changing their contents.
- ☐ The `Inspect...` command yields a window for each item you inspect. This window is customized to the type of variable being inspected. If you're looking at a variable, for example, you get simple information showing the name of the variable, its location in memory, and its value. Classes, on the other hand, display all the same data in addition to their member data, their values, and the locations and names of their member functions. Figure 21.3 shows a sample inspection window.

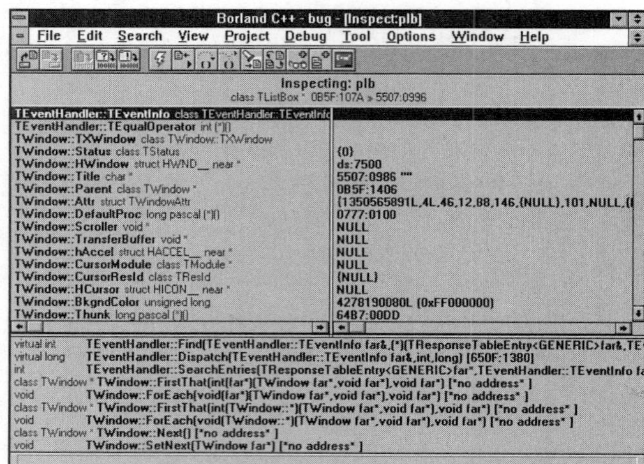

Figure 21.3.
A sample session in the IDE's debugger with an inspection window.

- Finally, the `Load symbol table...` command enables you to load a symbol table when you try to debug something like a DLL. In this case, the symbol table for the application you debug will be loaded automatically, but you will have to load the DLL's symbols by hand.

The View Menu

The View menu contains commands that display different windows. One section of that menu enables you to display windows associated with debugging. These are the Watch, Breakpoint, Call Stack, Register, and Event Log windows.

- The Watch window shows a list of expressions you've entered and their evaluation. As the program runs and the variables mentioned in the expressions change, so will the evaluations.
- The Breakpoint window shows a list of all the breakpoints set in the program. Also, when you double-click a breakpoint entry in this window, you are allowed to bring up the breakpoint properties window, enabling you to modify the breakpoint's settings.
- When you've stopped in the middle of a program, it's often helpful to see where you've come from. For example, if you find yourself in a function that could be called by any of a number of other locations, it would be useful to know which particular function called the current function and, in turn, who called that. This progression of calls is in the Call Stack window, along with the parameters of the functions for which debugging information is available.
- Although you are using C++ here, the machine itself actually deals on a much lower level, with machine code and assembly language. Basic to this lower level are registers that act like a limited set of variables for assembly language. Occasionally, it is useful to be able to view the contents of those registers during the execution of a program, and these are displayed in the Registers window. Note, however, that this usually is not very useful unless you know how your program works on the lower-level translated assembly language.
- The Event Log window displays a list of such things as when breakpoints were reached, or debugging information is displayed by the program (with the Windows `OutputDebugString` function).

21

In addition to all these menu commands, there is also the `Locate function...` command found under the Search menu. This brings up a dialog box that prompts you to enter a function name. The IDE's debugger will then attempt to find the requested function and place the cursor at that point. In order for the debugger to find the function, it must be listed in the loaded debugging information.

Debugging a Program

When debugging a program, you first must make sure that debugging information is included when the program is compiled and built. With that done, you'll be able to step through the program a line at a time, view the contents of variables as you go, set breakpoints, and so on.

Unfortunately, the standard libraries (the runtime library, the class library, and the Object Windows Library) don't come with debugging information included in them by default. Because of this, you won't be able to step or trace into its code, just as you won't be able to step or trace into the internal Windows code. You can, however, rebuild the Borland libraries to include debugging information if you have the source code. The class library and OWL source code is included with the Turbo C++ for Windows package, but the runtime library source code is available only on the CD version or at an extra cost.

The best way to learn how to debug a program is to sit down and do it. To start, type in and compile the program in Listings 21.1 and 21.2. You'll notice that it compiles with no warnings or errors, but if you try to run it and select the Dialog menu item, you'll get either a GP fault or, barring that, an hourglass that doesn't go away. In any case, the program certainly isn't doing what you would want it to do.

Type **Listing 21.1. Script for the BUG.RC resource file.**

```
#include <windows.h>
#include <owl\window.rh>

TheDialog DIALOG 6, 15, 207, 111
STYLE DS_MODALFRAME | WS_POPUP | WS_VISIBLE | WS_CAPTION |
      WS_SYSMENU
CAPTION "Dialog of the Century"
FONT 8, "MS Sans Serif"
BEGIN
   LISTBOX 101, 27, 8, 49, 88, LBS_STANDARD | WS_TABSTOP
   DEFPUSHBUTTON "OK", IDOK, 148, 6, 50, 14
   PUSHBUTTON "Cancel", IDCANCEL, 148, 24, 50, 14
END

MainMenu MENU LOADONCALL MOVEABLE PURE DISCARDABLE
BEGIN
   MENUITEM "E&xit", CM_EXIT
   MENUITEM "&Dialog", 100
END
```

Listing 21.2. Source code for the BUG.CPP program file.

```
#include <stdio.h>
#include <windows.h>
#include <owl\applicat.h>
#include <owl\dialog.h>
#include <owl\framewin.h>
```

```
#include <owl\listbox.h>
#include <owl\window.h>
#include <owl\window.rh>

class TMyDialog : public TDialog
{
public:
   TMyDialog(TWindow* parent, TModule* module = 0);

   void SetupWindow();

private:
   TListBox* numbers;
};

TMyDialog::TMyDialog(TWindow* parent, TModule* module)
   : TDialog(parent, "TheDialog", module)
{
}

void fill_lb(TListBox* plb, int count)
{
   for (int ix = 0; ix < count; ++count)
      {
      char str[25];
      sprintf(str, "%d", ix + 1);
      plb->AddString(str);
      }
}

void TMyDialog::SetupWindow()
{
   fill_lb(numbers, 20);
}

class TMyWindow : public TWindow
{
public:
   TMyWindow(TWindow* parent = 0);

protected:
   void CmExit();
   void CmDialog();

private:
   DECLARE_RESPONSE_TABLE(TMyWindow);
};
DEFINE_RESPONSE_TABLE1(TMyWindow, TWindow)
   EV_COMMAND(CM_EXIT, CmExit),
   EV_COMMAND(100, CmDialog),
END_RESPONSE_TABLE;

TMyWindow::TMyWindow(TWindow* parent)
   : TWindow(parent)
{
}

```


continues

Listing 21.2. continued

```
63: void TMyWindow::CmExit()
64: {
65:    SendMessage(WM_CLOSE);
66: }
67:
68: void TMyWindow::CmDialog()
69: {
70:    TMyDialog(this).Execute();
71: }
72:
73: class TDialogApp : public TApplication
74: {
75: public:
76:    TDialogApp() : TApplication()
77:       { nCmdShow = SW_SHOWMAXIMIZED; }
78:
79:    void InitMainWindow()
80:       {
81:       SetMainWindow(new TFrameWindow(  0,
82:                              "Dialog Testers, Inc.",
83:                              new TMyWindow ));
84:       GetMainWindow()->AssignMenu("MainMenu");
85:       }
86: };
87:
88: int OwlMain(int, char *[])
89: {
90:    return TDialogApp().Run();
91: }
```

If you run the program from the IDE, and then select the Dialog menu item, you are likely to get a dialog box that comes up entitled Unhandled Exception, with the message that a General Protection Exception occurred in BUG.CPP on line 32. By clicking OK, the IDE will come back up and place you on line 32 of the BUG.CPP file.

NEW TERM A *general protection violation* or *general protection fault* occurs when some code attempts to read or write to a part of memory that it isn't allowed. In C++, this usually means that a pointer is used that hasn't been initialized or is still pointing at memory that has been deleted and no longer exists. When running under the IDE, a general protection fault, which is Windows terminology, is reported as a general protection *exception* in keeping with C++ terminology.

Line 32 of BUG.CPP contains the following code:

```
plb->AddString(str);
```

So, remembering that a general protection exception usually has something to do with accessing memory that is off limits, you might think that the `str` variable probably is at fault, because it's a pointer. The only problem with that theory is that `str` is really a pointer to a local area of memory that's just been set up. You know that it still exists because it's still in scope.

The only other pointer here is the `plb` parameter. Considering, however, that you're just calling one of its member functions, how could it possibly be the problem? Take a look at the function it is calling, `AddString`. This function is declared in the `TListBox` class in the following manner:

```
virtual int AddString(const char far* str);
```

Note that the function is declared as virtual. This means that when the code to call it is compiled, a direct call to the member function isn't generated; rather, code to look up the location of the function is generated. The reason is that because a derived class could have written its own version of the function, the base class will need to be able to access that new function, without necessarily knowing where this function resides. So, when the pointer is used to call `AddString`, it really does use `plb` as a pointer, by looking up the function's address in the virtual table.

NEW TERM The *virtual table* is a list of pointers to virtual functions. Each class has a virtual table associated with it, in which all the virtual functions have their addresses listed. Along with each object is a *virtual table pointer*, which points to the virtual table for the appropriate class. When some code attempts to call a virtual function, the generated assembly code first looks up the virtual table, then the virtual function's address, and then actually calls the function.

The only possibility at this point is the `plb` parameter. This pointer appears to be invalid for some reason. The next step is to see who gave us this pointer. Go into the View menu and select Call Stack. A window appears that shows the current function `fill_lb` at the top. The next function down is `TMyDialog::SetupWindow`. Double-click that next line to position the cursor at the place where the `fill_lb` function was called.

You now are placed directly into the middle of the `SetupWindow` function on the following line:

```
fill_lb(numbers, 20);
```

It appears that the `numbers` member data is invalid, because that is the parameter that becomes `plb` in the `fill_lb` function. If you take a look around, you'll notice that you forgot to set `numbers` to anything. It's declared in the class, but nobody ever assigns it any value. Oops! This must be fixed before you can continue trying to run the program. Obviously, you needed to initialize `numbers` in the constructor to connect with the list box interface element in the dialog box you load from the resource. Go up to the constructor and add the following line:

```
numbers = new TListBox(this, 101, module);
```

Now if you take a look at the Debug menu, you'll notice that the Run item is grayed out. This is because you've changed the file and trying to continue running would make little sense. So use the Terminate program option to stop the program and then rebuild and run the application.

This time when you select the Dialog menu item, an hourglass that seems to hang around forever appears. After a while you may be getting the idea that something is wrong. The only way to stop the program now is to do the "three-fingered salute" and press the Ctrl+Alt+Del keys. Windows will give you a choice of going back and waiting a little longer, ending the program, or rebooting

Windows. Because waiting a little longer for the program to do something looks a little hopeless and restarting Windows seems a bit drastic, just end the program. In this case, when you get back to the IDE, the program already will have been terminated, and there will be no reason to use the Terminate program menu item.

In finding this problem, you're going to have to look at a bit of code to help narrow down where the problem might be. You know the bug occurs after you select the Dialog menu option but before the dialog box actually appears on-screen. At times like this, it's a good idea to set breakpoints on some likely areas and run through the code, one line at a time, to see what happens.

Position the cursor on the `TMyWindow::CmDialog` function and select Toggle breakpoint from the Debug menu (or press Ctrl+F8). Notice how the line changes color to reflect the state of the breakpoint. Now set breakpoints on the `TMyDialog` constructor and its `SetupWindow` function, and then run the program.

When you select the Dialog menu item now, you are returned to the IDE with the cursor on the line where you set the breakpoint, the line where `TMyWindow::CmDialog` is declared. Select the `Step over` command in the Debug menu. The screen flashes to the application and then flashes back to the source code, with the cursor on the next line, where the dialog is actually created and executed. This line looks okay, so you can step over it as well.

Now look at the `TMyDialog` constructor. Looking at the code, there doesn't seem to be anything out of the ordinary. Here you run into the nonlinearity of Windows. If you simply keep stepping, you'll end up running through the constructor and then back to the `TMyWindow::CmDialog` function. You know you have a breakpoint on the next bit of code you want to look at, so it's a good idea to just continue running from here.

When next you break into the source code, you're on the `TMyDialog::SetupWindow` function. There's only one function call in here, and it's something we wrote, so there probably is good reason to suspect that that might have inadvertently caused a problem in there. Use the `Trace` function in the Debug menu now. Your first trace takes you onto the call to `fill_lb`, and your next trace takes you right inside it.

Inside here you will see a `for` loop. It might be a good idea to walk through that one step at a time, watching the relevant variables `plb`, `count`, d, and `str`. Place the cursor on each of these variables and select the Add Watch item from the Debug menu. You are not particularly interested in any fancy displays at this point in time, so just click OK on the resultant Watch Properties dialog box. You may notice that some of the values are weird or possibly even undefined, but that's okay for right now. You are not really in the function yet, so the debugger hasn't had a chance to figure out what those values are. Also, because the `str` variable has not been declared yet, it will be listed as undefined until you get to where it is declared, at which point the Watch window will become synchronized properly.

Step over the beginning of the function. The cursor is placed on the first line of the `for` loop, and the `count` variable shows up as the number 20 in the Watch window. This is good. We specified 20 when we called this function. Step again and see that the `ix` variable is now set to `0` and the `str` variable is now recognized.

Notice how `str` is uninitialized at this point, showing random data. Stepping once more will fill `str` with what should be more reasonable data. Note, however, that the data isn't in a very readable format. It would be better if you could see it as a string. If you double-click the data item, you will bring back the Watch Properties dialog box. If you take a look in the Display As section, you will see a radio button marked String. Select this item and then click OK. When you get back to the Watch window, you'll see a string containing something a little more akin to what you expected.

Stepping again calls the `AddString` member function and brings you back to the line with the `sprintf`. Take another look at the Watch window and see how things are doing.

Wait a minute!

Why is `count` now `21`, and why is `ix` still `0`? Take a look at that `for` loop again.

```
for (int ix = 0; ix < count; ++count)
```

Oops, again! Incrementing the limit rather than the counter is a common mistake. No wonder the program seemed to have stopped. It was never leaving the loop and was trying to keep filling the list box with ever-increasing numbers. To fix that, change the line to the following:

```
for (int ix = 0; ix < count; ++ix)
```

Now terminate the application, remove the breakpoints, rebuild, and start over again. When you select the Dialog menu item now, the dialog box at least appears on-screen. Unfortunately, the list box appears to be completely empty.

The question here comes down to figuring out from where the failure is coming. You know that the pointer to the list box is valid; otherwise, you would have had another general protection exception. So the problem must be somewhere with the portion that is adding the string. Set a breakpoint on the line that reads

```
plb->AddString(str);
```

Start the program and select the Dialog menu item. When you reach the breakpoint, take a closer look at the `plb` parameter. Place the cursor over the `plb` variable and select the Inspect item from the Debug menu.

Looking at the inspection window, you can clearly see that, although you were obviously capable of creating the class object, it doesn't appear to be hooked up to the actual Windows interface item. The `TWindow::HWindow` data member is `NULL`, and the `TWindow::Attr` data member is mostly empty, except for the `101` that you passed to it earlier.

If you remember, the `SetupWindow` function is the location in which class objects become associated with their Windows counterparts. Taking a look at the `TMyDialog`'s version of the function, you can see that you forgot to call the parent's version of the `SetupWindow` function. Without that call, the actual work that connects the class with the interface element never gets done. To fix this, simply change the function to look like the following:

```
void TMyDialog::SetupWindow()
{
   TDialog::SetupWindow();
   fill_lb(numbers, 20);
}
```

Now, when you next compile and run the program, you will see a fully functional, if boring, application that enables you to display a dialog box that contains a list box of numbers 1 to 20.

Other Debugging Tools

Along with the integrated debugger included in the IDE, other tools are useful in finding and fixing problems with your applications. The first is *WinSight.* This program can display a listing of all the windows currently registered with Windows, whether those windows are visible or not. You can even see the hierarchy of the windows—which windows are children of which others. From there, you can select one or more windows and watch the messages received by them.

Of course, WinSight requires some knowledge of the lower-level Windows API that hasn't been covered in this book. OWL really does do an admirable job of hiding some of the truly messy details of the Windows API, allowing you to use an easy interface. The drawback is that, when there are problems with your code that involves the lower-level Windows API, it sometimes is difficult to track down the problem due to OWL's interface hiding.

One of the most useful programs is WinSpector. Normally, whenever you run your application from outside the IDE, general-protection (GP) faults simply will display a nasty error window and terminate your program. If you have WinSpector running when that GP fault occurs, WinSpector will record the location in your application that caused the GP fault. WinSpector also will attempt to figure out what other sections of your application had been executed immediately prior to the fault occurring, by performing a stack trace. The results of this then can be run through the DFA program to match up the memory locations with the debugging information of your program. The final results often can tell you exactly what line in your application's source code died and what functions had been called before.

Summary

Today's lesson presented a short tutorial on some of the debugging techniques provided by the IDE. You learned about the following subjects:

- The debugging commands available in the Integrated Development Environment
- Examples of some of the more common programming mistakes
- Some of the techniques used to track down and exterminate bugs

Q&A

Q Do my watches need to be limited to variables?

A No. You may supply whole expressions, such as `(count + 1) * 2`.

Q If I set a breakpoint on a line of code, do I have to stop there every single time the program comes to that line?

A No. You can set up conditions on the breakpoint so that, for example, if you are in the middle of a loop, the debugger will break in only when the iterator is equal to a certain value.

WEEK 3 IN REVIEW

15 16 17 18 19 20 21

For this review, you look at the Turbo Cribbage game supplied with the Turbo C++ 4.5 package in the TCWIN45\EXAMPLES\OWL\GAMES\CRIBBAGE directory. This implements, as the name suggests, the card game of cribbage. It includes routines for displaying cards and a pegboard, and routines for totaling scores.

How to Play

Before beginning a discussion of the program that implements the game, it probably would be useful (if not downright required) to first have a discussion about how to play the game.

The roots of cribbage extend back to the 1600s and Briton John Suckling. Cribbage is a two-person card game (actually, up to six people could play, but this version is for two players, known as the *Dealer* and the *Pone*). The rules are rather simple, but the variety and strategy still continue to make the game exciting. The numbers and point-counting make it an ideal game for children as well as adults.

Here are the stages of the game.

- The deal
- The discard
- The turn
- The play
- Counting player hands
- Counting the crib

The stages of the game are repeated until one player has acquired 121 points. As soon as 121 points are achieved, the game is over—there is no need to wait until the end of a hand.

Scoring

Different stages of the game involve different scoring possibilities, but most are used throughout the game.

15	Any combination of two or more cards whose sum is 15 (face cards count as 10). Two points are awarded.
Two, three, or four of a kind	If two, three, or four cards have the same face value, 2 points are awarded for each pair combination—the points awarded for 2, 3, and 4 of a kind are 2, 6, and 12 points, respectively.
Run	A sequential series of three or more cards. One point is awarded for each card in the run.
His Nobs	If a player holds a Jack in his or her hand (or in the crib while they're the dealer) that has the same suit as the turned extra card, one point is awarded.
His Heels	If the Starter (extra card) revealed by the Pone is a Jack, the Dealer receives two points.

31	Any combination of cards whose sum is 31 (again, face cards count as 10) scores 2 points.
Flush	Four or more cards of the same suit. One point is awarded for each card in the flush. The crib only allows a five-card flush.
Go	During the play, a player who cannot play declares "Go" and his or her opponent can receive one point if they cannot play.
Last Card	The last player to lay down a card during the play receives one point for the last card.

The Deal

The deal alternates between players every hand. In the two-player version, each player receives six cards face down.

The Discard

Each player selects two cards to discard (face down) into the *crib*. The crib is a bonus hand that awards the points to the Dealer. Because the deal alternates between players, so do the points in the crib. Throwing to the crib involves a bit of strategy because neither player can control the other's crib contribution, and the Starter, which is used as a fifth card for scoring, will not be revealed until after the throw has been made. The Pone will not want to throw obvious points to the crib, but the Dealer has the capability to throw away points to be received when they count the crib. The scoring combinations are explained in a later section ("Counting Player Hands"), but a couple of obvious bad throws would be a 5, cards which add up to 15, or a pair (all of which give points or guarantee points for the Dealer).

The Turn

After both players have thrown to the crib, the Pone cuts the remaining (undealt) cards and the top card is turned over and then is known as the *Starter*. This card is used as a fifth card for counting points in each player's hand and the crib. If a Jack (of any suit) is revealed, then the Dealer receives two points for *His Heels*.

The Play

The Play is an opportunity for both players to play the four cards they kept in their hands in a head-to-head duel. Play begins with the Pone, who plays a card face up from his or her hand and continues with each player alternating cards. Scoring occurs during *The Play* by looking at the cards played by each player as a single sequence of cards—one big hand. Scoring opportunities are available for each player in the form of sums of fifteen; two, three, or four of a kind; runs; Go, Last Card, and 31. Play continues until neither player has any cards left in his or her hand.

Each cycle of play ends when neither player can legally make a play because to do so would cause the total value of upturned cards to exceed the limit of 31 (face cards are counted as 10) or a total of 31 occurs. At the end of each playing cycle the upturned cards are turned over and a new cycle begins with the remaining cards.

As the total approaches 31, a player who cannot play declares, "Go!" and the opponent can continue playing cards (and collecting points, if possible) or collect 1 point for the Go. If a player plays a card that causes the total to become 31, then that player receives 2 points and all overturned cards are turned over for the next playing cycle.

Counting Player Hands

After the play, each player counts the points in their hand, using the Starter as a fifth, extra card. Players can earn points for 15s (commonly counted aloud as "Fifteen-two, fifteen-four", and so on); 2, 3, or 4 of a kind; a flush; runs (of 3 or more cards); or Nobs. Because the Dealer has the advantage of counting the crib's points, the Pone counts his or her hand first.

Counting the Crib

After both players have counted their hands, the Dealer picks up the crib and counts the points (again, including the Starter). The scoring opportunities available when counting the crib are the same as a regular player hand except for the Flush, which is awarded only if all five cards are the same suit.

The Cribbage Example

The base of the program starts in the CARDS.H and CARDS.CPP files where the `TCard`, `TCardGroup`, and `TDeck` classes are declared and defined. The first class models a single card and has data members to describe the card's face value (ace through king), its suit (hearts, spades, diamonds, and clubs), its back style (the card can have one of 13 styles on its back), and whether the card is faceup. All these data members are public, and the two constructors are there simply to make the object's creation simpler.

The `TCardGroup` class is used to model several cards together as a unit (such as a player's hand or a specific pile of cards). The maximum number of cards allowable in the group must be specified when instances of the class are created, and then you can insert and remove cards from the group via the `Insert` and `Remove` member functions, respectively. The `Insert` member function is overloaded to allow you to add either a single card or another group. This class also defines the array operator (`operator[]`) in order to provide easy access to the cards contained in the group.

Finally, `TDeck` is a descendant of `TCardGroup` that is used to model an entire deck of cards. Because it's derived from `TCardGroup`, it can make use of all the insertion and removal methods of its base, and `TDeck` also adds a little extra functionality. The new class has methods for shuffling the deck, cutting it, and for initializing it. This last method, `Initialize`, is called by the class constructor and simply inserts a card for each member of a standard 52-card deck. The `DealCard` member function acts to simply remove the top card from the deck.

`TDeck` also has the two methods `EncodeDeck` and `DecodeDeck`. The first function creates a 52-byte string with the contents of the current deck encoded into it. This encoding is done by placing the suit of each card into the upper four bits of a byte while filling the lower four bits with the card's face value. The encoding is done so that the contents of the deck can be saved into an INI file for future retrieval.

These classes so far only model cards and card groups in general terms. In a Windows program, we're going to want to display it. Here's where our friendly neighborhood VBX comes in. Turbo C++ 4.5 automatically installs the MHCD200.VBX file that provides routines for displaying playing cards. For each of these cards you can specify which face value and suit it's to have, and you can select from a variety of back styles. In order to use the VBX, Turbo C++ 4.5 also supplies the VBXGEN program. This reads in a VBX file and automatically creates a header file with the appropriate classes and definitions for using the VBX file. This has been done to create the MHCD200.H header file, which declares the class `TVbxMhCardDeck` as a descendant of `TVbxControl`.

The files that make use of this to actually display cards are the CARDDISP.H and CARDDISP.CPP files. These declare and define the `TCardDisplay` class as a descendant of both `TWindow` and `TCardGroup`. This particular window has its style set to that of a child in the constructor, thus making it easy to include within other windows in much the same way as child controls (pushbuttons, list boxes, and so on) can be included within windows; just create a `TCardDisplay` object in the desired location, and then use it the same way you use other controls, calling member functions to change aspects of its appearance.

The data members of the `TCardDisplay` class include a list of pointers to VBX card display objects (`cardvbx`); whether to draw a rectangle around the outside of the control (`rectangle`); the size of the border between the edge of the control and any rectangle that gets drawn (`borderSize`); a label for the control and a position for that label (`label` and `labelPos`); an array of positions for the cards in the group (`cardPos`); and an ID that can be used to distinguish this control from others (`id`).

Table R3.1 lists the member functions of the `TCardDisplay` class.

Table R3.1. `TCardDisplay` member functions.

Member Function	Usage
`TCardDisplay`	Initializes the members of the class and sets the size of the window to that specified by the parameters to the function. Also creates arrays to hold the VBX card objects and their positions.
`~TCardDisplay`	Cleans up the arrays allocated in the constructor.
`Paint`	Displays the main parts of the card display, including its border (if specified) and the label.
`SetupWindow`	Sets the background color for the window, and then hides all the VBX cards whilst setting their backs' colors to the background.
`FaceUp`	Resets the specified card to its face-up value.
`SetCardPosition`	Sets the position of the specified card.
`Show`	This is the function that actually shows a card by setting the VBX properties for the rank, suit, and back-style. The function then calls the VBX's `ShowWindow` member function.
`SetLabel`	Resets the label of the card display window.
`Insert`	Calls the base class `TCardGroup`'s `Insert` member function, and then calls the `Show` member function to display the newly inserted card.
`Remove`	Like `Insert`, this calls the base class' version of this function, and then proceeds to update the display with the new status of the cards.
`operator[]`	Accesses a card without removing it.
`VBXEventHandler`	This is the main entry from the VBX controls. In this case, the function checks to see if it was triggered by a mouse click. If so, it then passes that message along to its parent in the form of a WM_CARD_SELECTED message.

The overall effect of all these member functions, especially with the inclusion of the base classes' functionality and member functions, is that of presenting an encapsulated object that provides for all the needs of an apparent card display control. As you will see shortly, you only create this near-control in a window, and the cards will show themselves with very little prompting.

The cribbage game also includes a pegboard you use to keep track of the scoring. Like the card display, this is achieved in the program via a special child window encapsulated in a single object `TCribbageBoard` as defined in the BOARD.H and BOARD.CPP files. The data members of the `TCribbageBoard` class consist of an array to hold the players' names (`playerName`), an array to hold the players' current points (`points`), an array to hold the players' previous points (`oldpoints`), and an array that holds the locations of all the holes in the pegboard (`holes`). There also is an `enum` (`PegType`) that defines the various peg types that can be used (`ptPlayer0`, `ptPlayer1`, and `ptEmpty`). Table R3.2 describes the member functions in this `TWindow` descendant.

Table R3.2. Member functions of `TCribbageBoard`.

Member Function	Usage
`TCribbageBoard`	This constructor initializes several members and sets its window to a specific size. Most of all, though, it fills in the `holes` array with the locations of all the holes in the pegboard.
`SetupWindow`	Simply calls the base class' `SetupWindow` and then initializes the background color for the window.
`Reset`	Resets the point values to their initial values of `0` for the current points and `-1` for the previous points.
`PegHole`	This actually is what draws an individual peg hole. It does this by referring to the `holes` array and then either drawing red boxes for Player 0, drawing blue boxes for Player 1, or copying the `EMPTY_HOLE` bitmap into the specified location. Note the addition of an extra `PegHole` function that takes an `int` type for the `pegType` parameter, and then simply calls the real version of the function, casting `pegType` to the appropriate `PegType` enumeration.
`AddToScore`	Calling this member function adds a specific amount to a specific player's score. At the same time, the pegboard's peg display is updated along with the textual representation of the score. Note how the window's DC is obtained simply by declaring an instance of `TClientDC`, which then is passed to the `PegHole` and `TextOut` functions for drawing.
`SetPlayerName`	A simple function that sets a specific player's name and then makes sure it's reflected properly in the window.
`GetPlayerName`	An even simpler function that returns a specific player's name.
`Paint`	This begins by copying the `PEGBOARD` bitmap into the window, followed immediately by writing the two players' names and their scores. Finally, the member function calls `PegHole` to display the two players' scores on the pegboard.

Throughout the course of the game, a number of dialog boxes need to be displayed, the source code for which can be found in the DIALOGS.H and DIALOGS.CPP files. The dialog boxes include one that prompts the user to cut the cards (`TCutDeckDialog`); it displays the backs of 52 cards and responds to a user's click by returning to the position in the deck where the user clicked. After the user has selected a card from the deck, the `TCutResultDialog` is displayed, which shows both the card the user selected and the one selected by the computer.

The `TGoDialog` class opens a simple dialog with a single button that reads either OK or Take 1 Point depending upon whether the player can play more cards. This is used when the computer has signified that it cannot play any more cards.

The `TQuickPointsDialog` displays a number of buttons that allow the player to select the number of points he or she is entitled to. It's rather a simple dialog box, but the interesting part is where the constructor creates an array of 15 `TButton` objects to represent buttons 15 through 29. These objects will be used to hide those buttons in certain versions of the dialog, when it wouldn't be possible to select more than 14 points.

When it's time to display the total points for either the computer's hand or a hand in which the player miscounted, the `TShowPointsDialog` appears. This consists of a simple text box filled with the number of points counted and a button that enables the player to request details. If that button is pressed, the height of the dialog box is increased and the extra space at the bottom is filled with a new list box. That list box is filled with the details of the points as passed to the class constructor in the `aDetail` parameter.

Up to now I've only discussed the lower-level tools that help get the game running. The real meat is contained in the `TGameWindow` class as defined and declared in the CRIBBAGE.H and CRIBBAGE.CPP files. Just as a simple deck of cards doesn't define the game of cribbage, neither does the `TDeck` class define the cribbage game in this program; the `TGameWindow` class has all the actual functionality that defines the cribbage game itself. You should take careful note here of how the lower-level classes have been designed to model real-world objects that are then used in the main game itself. This is the kind of thing for which C++ and other object-oriented programming languages were designed.

Table R3.4 contains a brief list of the member functions contained in the `TGameWindow` class and their usage. They all act on the member data described in Table R3.3.

Table R3.3. `TGameWindow` member data.

Member Data	Meaning
`handCardPos`	An array holding the positions of all the cards that can be displayed in a player's hand
`cribCardPos`	An array holding the positions of all the cards that can be displayed in the crib

Member Data	Meaning
`pegCardPos`	An array holding the positions of all the cards that can be displayed in the playing field
`topCardPos`	An array (of one element) that holds the position of the extra card
`player`	An array holding the two `TCardDisplay` objects used as the two player hands
`crib`	The crib display
`pegCards`	The playing field cards
`topCards`	The extra card
`board`	The pegboard display
`deal`	One of the buttons used during game play
`go`	One of the buttons used during game play
`done`	One of the buttons used during game play
`take1`	One of the buttons used during game play
`take2`	One of the buttons used during game play
`instructions`	A static control that is updated throughout the game with instructions concerning the next move for the player
`state`	The current state of the game, as defined by the `TGameState` enumeration
`dealer`	A number that indicates the current dealer
`deck`	The main deck of cards being played
`currentCribPos`	Indicates the current owner of the crib
`cardBackStyle`	Holds the current style of the card backs
`pegCardOwner`	Keeps track of the owner of each card played. This is used after the game play is over to move the played cards back to their original players for point scoring.
`greenBrush`	Because green is such a heavily used color in this game (ever played at a real gambling table without green felt?), it's saved here to keep it from being recreated all the time.
`detail`	As points are tallied by the computer, their details are recorded here for the player to examine upon request.
`detailCount`	Holds the current number of lines in the `detail` list

Table R3.4. `TGameWindow` member functions.

Member Function	Usage
`TGameWindow`	The constructor initializes the window to its set size and inserts all the player controls, buttons, static text areas, and so on.
`~TGameWindow`	Deallocates the objects created in the constructor
`SetupWindow`	Sets the background color of the window to green and initializes the game state to that of waiting for a new game
`FaceValue`	Returns the face value of a card (1 through 10 for Ace through 10 and 10 for all the face cards)
`RunSize`	Checks to see if a sequence of cards form a run (a sequential list of cards)
`ComputeHandPoints`	Adds up the points in a given hand and lists the breakdown of those points in a details buffer. This looks for all combinations that total 15, series that form runs, pairs of cards, flushes, and Nobs (a Jack that matches the extra card's suit).
`ComputePegPoints`	Computes any points that might have been generated by the last card played on the playing field
`ResetPegCardDisplay`	Clears out the arrays used to keep track of the playing field and the cards' original owners
`ReclaimPegCards`	Redistributes the cards from the playing field back into their original decks
`PegCard`	Adds a card from a player to the playing field
`ScoreComputerPegPoints`	Adds points to the computer's peg score, displaying a message box to let the user know the amount of points
`ComputerPlayPegCard`	Plays a card onto the playing field for the computer
`TurnOverPegCards`	Turns over the cards on the playing field to hide their faces
`PlayableCards`	Searches a group of cards for all that can be played on the playing field without going over the maximum total of 31. It returns an index to the first one playable, and optionally fills in an array with the indices of all those that are playable.
`SetState`	Changes the game state, showing the appropriate buttons and filling the instruction box with appropriate text

Member Function	Usage
`Deal`	Shuffles the deck and deals the top card out as the extra card. Then, if it's the computer's turn to deal, `Deal` actually deals the cards to the two players. If it's the player's turn to deal, then this just sets the game state to `gsDeal` and waits for the player to click the Deal button.
`ShowPoints`	Moves the playing field cards back into their respective decks and then counts the total points for each hand. If the player miscounts, then the computer takes the missing points.
`NewGame`	Responds to the New | Game menu item by reinitializing the playing field and deck, asking the player for his or her name, asking the player to cut the deck, and then dealing the first hand
`DealButton`	Responds to the Deal button (which is visible during the `gsDeal` game state) by dealing the hands, discarding the computer's two cards, and then waiting for the user to discard
`FixDeck`	Moves all the cards from the playing field, as well as the players' hands, the crib, and the extra card back into the deck
`SaveGame`	Saves the current game state
`Exit`	Exits the program
`SaveGameEnabler`	Enables/disables the Save | Game menu item depending upon whether or not a game is currently in progress
`AboutBox`	Displays the about box dialog box
`LoadGame`	Loads a saved game
`Paint`	Draws the `DECK` bitmap. Note that all the other painting is done automatically by the other classes created.
`EvCtlColor`	Ensures that the background looks green, especially with regards to a slight idiosyncrasy with button controls (described in the source code)
`CardSelected`	This is a handler for the `WM_CARD_SELECTED` message generated by the `TCardDisplay` class in response to a VBX message. If the player currently is discarding cards to the crib, then this moves the selected cards. If the player is playing a card to the playing field, then this moves the selected card appropriately.

continues

Table R3.4. `TGameWindow` member functions.

Member Function	Usage
`PegCardsSum`	Computes the total value of all the cards in the playing field
`CanClose`	This function, which is called whenever the program is asked to quit, checks to make sure the user doesn't want to abandon any game that might currently be in progress.
`GoButton`	Responds to the Go button and checks to see if the player is capable of playing a card. If this verifies that the player is capable at this point, then it issues a warning. Otherwise it just sends the game play over to the computer.
`DoneButton`	Responds to the Done button, which is available while the player is moving cards into the crib. This checks to make sure the player moved exactly two cards into the crib and then turns the crib cards face down, the extra card face up, and then has the computer play a card.
`Take1Button`	When the computer can't play any more cards and the player can, the player is allowed to take either one or two points (if they're below or at 31 points, respectively). The Take 1 and Take 2 buttons are visible at these points and simply add the corresponding number of points to the player's score.
`Take2Button`	*See `Take1Button`*
`ComputerDiscard`	Discards two cards from the computers hand to the crib
`ComputerPlayCard`	Has the computer play a card. This includes logic to account for the times when the player has specified that he or she can't play any more cards to the playing field.
`CountPoints`	Counts the points in the playing field after the player has just played a card. This then displays a dialog box that enables the player to select the number of points gained in the last turn, and it checks to make sure the player counted properly.

There are many interrelationships within the `TGameWindow` class. Many of the functions are there simply for the use of other functions, which is evidenced by the fact that there are so

few listed in the response table. The most important lesson to learn here is how all the other classes are brought together in the main window and used to represent the various parts of the game to the user. It also is an interesting game to learn to play.

Variations and Expanding the Game

A number of variations in the game exist, including the number of players and how many points to play for in a game (achieving 121 points before your opponent scores 61 or scoring 61 before they get 31 is known as a *lurch*). Tournaments are available and special awards exist for those who receive a perfect hand (containing 29 points), those who have 0-point hands, receiving a hand whose digits are those of their ZIP code, and so on. Other variations include awarding points overlooked by one player and discovered by the other in an act known as *Muggins*.

A good project for you now would be to figure out how to implement some of the above variations or, better yet, to give the computer a little more strategy when it plays its game against you. I mean, you don't want to be able to win *all* the time, do you?

Answers

Note: Because of space limitations, not every Exercise has an answer presented here.

Answers to Day 1, "Getting Started"

Quiz

1. The program generates the string `C++ in 21 Days?`.
2. The program generates no output because the `cout` statement appears inside a comment! The function `main` simply returns 0.
3. The `cout` statement is missing the semicolon.

Exercise

```
// Exercise program

#include <iostream.h>

main()
{
   cout << "I am a C++ Programmer";
   return 0;
}
```

Answers to Day 2, "C++ The Preprocessor, Variables, and Operators"

Quiz

1. The following table indicates which identifiers are valid and which are not (and why).

Identifiers	Valid?	Reason (If Invalid)
`numFiles`	Yes	
`n0Distance_02_Line`	Yes	
`0Weight`	No	Starts with a digit
`Bin Number`	No	Contains a space
`static`	No	Reserved keyword
`Static`	Yes	

2. The output is

   12
   8
   2
   3.64851
   150.5

3. The output is

   12
   8
   2

4. The output is

   12
   27

5. The output is

   TRUE
   TRUE
   TRUE
   FALSE

Exercise

1. Here is my version of the function `max`.

```
int max(int i, int j)
{

   return (i > j) ? i : j;
}
```

2. Here is my version of the function `min`.

```
int min(int i, int j)
{
   return (i < j) ? i : j;
}
```

3. Here is my version of the function `abs`.

```
int abs(int i)
{
   return (i > 0) ? i : -i;
}
```

4. Here is my version of the function `isOdd`.

```
int isOdd(int i)
{
   return (i % 2 != 0) ? 1 : 0;
}
```

Answers to Day 3, "The Decision-Making Constructs and Loops"

Quiz

1. The simpler version is

```
if (i > 0 && i < 10)
  cout << "i = " << i << endl;
```

2. The simpler version is

```
if (i > 0) {
  j = i * i;
  cout << "j = " << j << endl;
}
else if (i < 0) {
  j = 4 * i;
  cout << "j = " << j << endl;
}
else {
  j = 10 + i;
  cout << "j = " << j << endl;
}
```

3. False. When the variable `i` stores values between -10 and -1, the statements in the clauses of the two `if` statements execute. In this case, all the assignment statements are executed. By contrast, it is impossible to execute the statements in both the `if` and `else` clauses of the supposedly equivalent `if-else` statement.

4. The simplified version is

```
if (i > 0 && i < 100)
     j = i * i;
else if (i >= 100)
     j = i;
else
     j = 1;
```

   Notice that I eliminate the original first `else if` clause because the tested condition is a subset of the first tested condition. Consequently, the condition in the first `else if` never gets examined and the associated assign statement never gets executed. This is an example of what is called *dead code.*

5. The tested condition is always false. Consequently, the statements in the clause never are executed. This is another example of dead code.

6. The statements inside the loop fail to alter the value of `i`. Consequently, the tested condition is always true and the loop iterates endlessly.

7. The output of the program consists of the numbers 3, 5, and 7.

8. The output of the program is an endless sequence of lines that display the value of `3`. The reason for the indefinite looping is that the loop control variable is not incremented.

9. The nested `for` loops use the same loop control variable. This program will not run.
10. Both `for` loops declare the variable `i` as their loop control variable. The compiler generates an error for this duplication.
11. The condition of the `while` loop is always true. Therefore, the loop iterates endlessly.
12. The program lacks a statement which explicitly initializes the variable `factorial` to 1. Without this statement, the program automatically initializes the variable `factorial` to 0—the wrong value. Consequently, the `for` loop ends up assigning 0 to the variable `factorial` in every iteration. Here is the correct version of the code.

```
int n;
double factorial = 1;
cout << "Enter positive integer: ";
cin >> n;
for (int i = 1; i <= n; i++)
   factorial *= i;
cout << n << "! = " << factorial;
```

Exercises

1. Here is my version of program IF5.CPP.

```
// C++ program to solve quadratic equation

#include <iostream.h>
#include <math.h>

main()
{
  double A, B, C, discrim, root1, root2, twoA;

  cout << "Enter coefficients for equation A*X^2 + B*X + C\n";
  cout << "Enter A: ";
  cin >> A;
  cout << "Enter B: ";
  cin >> B;
  cout << "Enter C: ";
  cin >> C;

  if (A != 0) {
     twoA = 2 * A;
     discrim = B * B - 4 * A * C;
     if (discrim > 0) {
       root1 = (-B + sqrt(discrim)) / twoA;
       root2 = (-B - sqrt(discrim)) / twoA;
       cout << "root1 = " << root1 << endl;
       cout << "root2 = " << root2 << endl
     }
     else if (discrim < 0) {

       discrim = -discrim;
       cout << "root1 = (" << -B/twoA
            << ") + i (" << sqrt(discrim) / twoA <<")\n";
```

```
        cout << "root2 = (" << -B/twoA
             << ") - i (" << sqrt(discrim) / twoA << ")\n";
      }
      else {
        root1 = -B / 2 / A;
        root2 = root1;
        cout << "root1 = " << root1 << endl;
        cout << "root2 = " << root2 << endl;
      }
    }
    else
      cout << "root = " << (-C / B) << endl;


    return 0;
  }
```

2. Here is my version of program SWITCH2.CPP.

```
// C++ program which uses the switch statement to implement
// a simple four-function calculator program

#include <iostream.h>

const int TRUE = 1;
const int FALSE = 0;

main()
{
  double x, y, z;
  char op;
  int error = FALSE;

  cout << "Enter the first operand: ";
  cin >> x;
  cout << "Enter the operator: ";
  cin >> op;
  cout << "Enter the second operand: ";
  cin >> y;

  switch (op) {
    case '+':
      z = x + y;
      break;
    case '-':
      z = x - y;
      break;
    case '*':
      z = x * y;
      break;
    case '/':
      if (y != 0)
        z = x / y;
      else
        error = TRUE;
      break;
```

```
    default:
      error = TRUE;
  }

  if (!error)
    cout << x << " " << op << " " << y << " = " << z << endl;
  else
    cout << "Bad operator or division-by-zero error\n";

  return 0;
}
```

3. Here is my version of program FOR5.CPP.

```
// Program calculates a sum of odd integers in
// the range of 11 to 121

#include <iostream.h>

const int FIRST = 11;
const int LAST = 121;

main()
{
    double sum = 0;
    for (int i = FIRST; i <= LAST; i += 2)
      sum += (double)i;

    cout << "Sum of odd integers from "
         << FIRST << " to " << LAST << " = "
         << sum << endl;
    return 0;
}
```

4. Here is my version of program WHILE2.CPP.

```
// Program calculates a sum of squared odd integers in
// the range of 11 to 121

#include <iostream.h>

const int FIRST = 11;
const int LAST = 121;

main()
{
    double sum = 0;
    int i = FIRST;
    while (i <= LAST) {
      sum += double(i * i++);
    }
    cout << "Sum of squared odd integers from "
         << FIRST << " to " << LAST << " = "
         << sum << endl;
    return 0;
}
```

5. Here is my version of program DOWHILE2.CPP.

```
// Program calculates a sum of squared odd integers in
// the range of 11 to 121

#include <iostream.h>

const int FIRST = 11;
const int LAST = 121;

main()
{
    double sum = 0;
    int i = FIRST;
    do {
      sum += double(i * i++);
    } while (i <= LAST);
    cout << "Sum of squared odd integers from "
         << FIRST << " to " << LAST << " = "
         << sum << endl;
    return 0;
}
```

Answers to Day 4, "User-Defined Types and Pointers"

Quiz

1. The enumerated values on and off appear in two different enumerated types. Here is a correct version of these statements.

```
enum Boolean { false, true };
enum State { state_on, state_off };
enum YesNo { yes, no };
enum DiskDriveStatus { drive_on , drive_off };
```

2. False. The enumerated type YesNo is correctly declared.
3. The program lacks a delete statement before the return statement. Here is the correct version.

```
#include <iostream.h>
main()
{
  int *p = new int;
  cout << "Enter a number : ";
  cin >> *p;
  cout << "The square of " << *p << " = " << (*p * *p);
  delete p;
  return 0;
}
```

Exercises

1. Here is my version of PTR6.CPP.

```
/* C++ program that demonstrates pointers to structured types */

#include <iostream.h>
#include <stdio.h>
#include <math.h>

const MAX_RECT = 4;
const TRUE = 1;
const FALSE = -1;

struct point {
  double x;
  double y;
};

struct rect {
  point ulc; // upper left corner
  point lrc; // lower right corner
  double area;
  int id;
};

typedef rect rectArr[MAX_RECT];

main()
{
  rectArr r;
  rect temp;
  rect* pr = r;
  rect* pr2;
  double length, width;
  int offset;
  int inOrder;

  for (int i = 0; i < MAX_RECT; i++, pr++) {
    cout << "Enter (X,Y) coord. for ULC of rect. # "
         << i << " : ";
    cin >> pr->ulc.x >> pr->ulc.y;
    cout << "Enter (X,Y) coord. for LRC of rect. # "
         << i << " : ";
    cin >> pr->lrc.x >> pr->lrc.y;
    pr->id = i;
    length = fabs(pr->ulc.x - pr->lrc.x);
    width = fabs(pr->ulc.y - pr->lrc.y);
    pr->area = length * width;
  }

  // sort the rectangles by areas
  offset = MAX_RECT;
  do {
    offset = (8 * offset) / 11;
    offset = (offset == 0) ? 1 : offset;
    inOrder = TRUE;
```

```
      pr = r;
      pr2 = r + offset;
      for (int i = 0;
           i < MAX_RECT - offset;
           i++, pr++, pr2++)
        if (pr->area > pr2->area) {
          inOrder = FALSE;
          temp = *pr;
          *pr = *pr2;
          *pr2 = temp;
        }
    } while (!(offset == 1 && inOrder));

    pr = r; // reset pointer
    // display rectangles sorted by area
    for (i = 0; i < MAX_RECT; i++, pr++)
      printf("Rect # %d has area %5.4lf\n", pr->id, pr->area);
    return 0;
  }
```

2. Here is my version of structure `intArrStruct`.

```
struct intArrStruct {
  int* dataPtr;
  unsigned size;
};
```

3. Here is my version of structure `matStruct`.

```
struct matStruct {
  double* dataPtr;
  unsigned rows;
  unsigned columns;
};
```

Answers to Day 5, "Functions"

Quiz

1. The output of the program is

```
a = 10 and b = 3
```

The function `swap` fails to swap the arguments `a` and `b` because it only swaps a copy of their values.

2. The output of the program is

```
a = 3 and b = 10
```

The function `swap` succeeds in swapping the arguments `a` and `b` because it uses reference parameters. Consequently, the changes in the values of parameters `i` and `j` go beyond the scope of the function itself.

3. The second version of function `inc` has a default argument, which, when used, hinders the compiler from determining which version of `inc` to call. The compiler flags a compile-time error for such functions.

4. Because the second parameter has a default argument, the third one must also have a default argument. Here is one version of the correct definition of function `volume`.

   ```
   double volume(double length, double width = 1, double height = 1)
   {
      return length * width * height;
   }
   ```

5. The parameter `i` is a lowercase letter. However, the function uses the uppercase `I` in the assignment statement. The compiler complains that the identifier `I` is not defined.
6. The function main requires a prototype of function `sqr`. The correct version of the program is

   ```
   #include <iostream.h>

   // declare prototype of function sqr
   double sqr(double);

   main()
   {
      double x = 5.2;

      cout << x << "^2 = " << sqr(x);
      return 0;
   }

   double sqr(double x)
   { return x * x; }
   ```

7. The function is

   ```
   double factorial(int i)
   { return (i > 1) ? double(i) * factorial(i-1) : 1; }
   ```

Exercises

Here is my version of program OVERLOD2.CPP.

```
// C++ program illustrates function overloading
// and default arguments

#include <iostream.h>

// inc version for int types
void inc(int& i, int diff = 1)
{
   i = i + diff;
}

// inc version for double types
void inc(double& x, double diff = 1)
{
   x = x + diff;
}
```

```
// inc version for char types
void inc(char& c, int diff = 1)
   c = c + diff;
}

main()
{
   char c = 'A';
   int i = 10;
   double x = 10.2;

   // discplay initial valus
   cout << "c = " << c << endl
        << "i = " << i << endl
        << "x = " << x << endl;

   // invoke the inc functions using default arguments
   inc(c);
   inc(i);
   inc(x);

   // display updatecd values
   cout << "After using the overloaded inc function" << endl
        << "c = " << c << endl
        << "i = " << i << endl
        << "x = " << x << endl;
   return 0;
}
```

Answers to Day 6, "Arrays"

Quiz

1. The program displays the factorials for the numbers 0 to 4.

```
x[0] = 1
x[1] = 1
x[2] = 2
x[3] = 6
x[4] = 24
```

2. The program displays the square roots for the numbers 0 to 4.

```
x[0] = 0
x[1] = 1
x[2] = 1.41421
x[3] = 1.73205
x[4] = 2
```

3. The first `for` loop should iterate between `1` and `MAX-1` and not between `0` and `MAX-1`. The first loop iteration uses an out-of-range index.

Exercise

Here is my version of program ARRAY7.CPP.

```
// C++ program that sorts arrays using the Comb sort method
#include <iostream.h>

const int MAX = 10;
const int TRUE = 1;
const int FALSE = 0;

int obtainNumData()
{
   int m;
   do { // obtain number of data points
      cout << "Enter number of data points [2 to "
           << MAX << "] : ";
      cin >> m;
      cout << endl;
   } while (m < 2 || m > MAX);
   return m;
}

void inputArray(int intArr[], int n)
{
   // prompt user for data
   for (int i = 0; i < n; i++) {
      cout << "arr[" << i << "] : ";
      cin >> intArr[i];
   }
}

void showArray(int intArr[], int n)
{
   for (int i = 0; i < n; i++) {
      cout.width(5);
      cout << intArr[i] << " ";
   }
   cout << endl;
}

void sortArray(int intArr[], int n)
{
   int offset, temp, inOrder;

   offset = n;
   while (offset > 1) {
      offset /= 2;
      do {
         inOrder = TRUE;
         for (int i = 0, j = offset; i < (n - offset); i++, j++) {
            if (intArr[i] > intArr[j]) {
               inOrder = FALSE;
               temp = intArr[i];
               intArr[i] = intArr[j];
               intArr[j] = temp;
            }
         }
```

```
        } while (!inOrder);
    }
}

main()
{
    int arr[MAX];
    int n;

    n = obtainNumData();
    inputArray(arr, n);
    cout << "Unordered array is:\n";
    showArray(arr, n);
    sortArray(arr, n);
    cout << "\nSorted array is:\n";
    showArray(arr, n);
    return 0;
}
```

Answers to Day 7, "Strings and Managing I/O"

Quiz

1. The output statement cannot contain the inserter operator >>. The statement can be corrected as follows:

   ```
   cout << "Enter a number ";
   cin >> x;
   ```

2. Because the variable x appears in the first and last items, the last number overwrites the first number.
3. The string s1 is smaller than string s2. Consequently, the call to function strcpy causes a program bug.
4. Using the function strncpy to include the constant MAX as the third argument ensures that string s1 receives MAX characters (excluding the null terminator) from string s1:

   ```
   #include <iostream.h>
   #include <string.h>
   const in MAX = 10;
   main()
   {
     char s1[MAX+1];
     char s2[] = "123456789012345678901234567890";
     strncpy(s1, s2, MAX);
     cout << "String 1 is " << s1
          << "\nString 2 is " << s2;
   ```

```
  return 0;
}
```

5. Because the string in variable `s1` is less than that in variable `s2`, the statement assigns a negative number (`-13` to be exact) in variable `i`.
6. The call to function `strcmp` compares the substrings `"C++"` with `"Pascal"` because the arguments include an offset value. Because `"C++"` is less than `"Pascal"`, the statement assigns a negative number (`-13` again) in variable `i`.
7. False! Although the basic idea for the function is sound, dimensioning the local variable requires a constant. One solution is to use the same constant, call it `MAX_STRING_SIZE`, to size up the arguments of parameter `s`.

```
int hasNoLowerCase(const char* s)
{
  char s2[MAX_STRING_SIZE+1];
  strcpy(s2, s);
  strupr(s2);
  return (strcmp(s, s2) == 0) ? 1 : 0);
}
```

The other solution uses dynamic allocation to create a dynamic local string that stores a copy of the argument of parameter `s`. This solution works with all arguments of parameter `s`:

```
int hasNoLowerCase(const char* s)
{
  char *s2 = new char[strlen(s)+1];
  int i;
  strcpy(s2, s);
  strupr(s2);
  // store result in variable i
  i = (strcmp(s, s2) == 0) ? 1 : 0);
  delete [] s2; // first delete local dynamic string
  return i; // then return the result of the function
}
```

Exercises

1. Here is my version of program OUT3.CPP.

```
// C++ program uses the printf function for formatted output

 #include <stdio.h>
 #include <math.h>

 main()
```

```
{
  double x;

  // display table heading
  printf("      X          Sqrt(X)\n");
  printf("-----------\n");
  x = 2;
  printf("    %3.0lf              %3.4lf\n", x, sqrt(x));
  x++;
  printf("    %3.0lf              %3.4lf\n", x, sqrt(x));
  x++;
  printf("    %3.0lf              %3.4lf\n", x, sqrt(x));
  x++;
  printf("    %3.0lf              %3.4lf\n", x, sqrt(x));
  x++;
  printf("    %3.0lf              %3.4lf\n", x, sqrt(x));
  x++;
  printf("    %3.0lf              %3.4lf\n", x, sqrt(x));
  x++;
  printf("    %3.0lf              %3.4lf\n", x, sqrt(x));
  x++;
  printf("    %3.0lf              %3.4lf\n", x, sqrt(x));
  x++;
  printf("    %3.0lf              %3.4lf\n", x, sqrt(x));
  return 0;
}
```

2. Here is my version of program OUT4.CPP.

```
// C++ program which displays octal and hexadecimal integers

#include <iostream.h>
#include <stdio.h>

main()
{
  long i;
  cout << "Enter an integer : ";
  cin >> i;

  printf("%ld = %lX (hex) = %lo (octal)\n", i, i, i);
  return 0;
}
```

3. Here is my version of function strlen.

```
int strlen(const char* s)
{
  int i = 0;
  while (s[i] != '\0')
    i++;
  return i;
}
```

4. Here is the other version of function strlen.

```
int strlen(const char* s)
{
  char *p = s;
  while (p++ != '\0')
    /* do nothing */;
  return p - s;
}
```

5. Here is my version of program STRING5.CPP.

```
#include <stdio.h>
#include <string.h>

main()
{
   char str[] = "2*(X+Y)/(X+Z) - (X+10)/(Y-5)";
   char strCopy[41];
   char* tkn[3] = { "+-*/ ()", "( )", "+-*/ " };
   char* ptr;

   strcpy(strCopy, str); // copy str into strCopy
   printf("%s\n", str);
   printf("Using token string %s\n", tkn[0]);
   // the first call
   ptr = strtok(str, tkn[0]);
   printf("String is broken into: ");
   while (ptr) {
     printf(", %s", ptr);
     // must make first argument a NULL character
     ptr = strtok(NULL, tkn[0]);
   }
```

```
    strcpy(str, strCopy); // restore str
    printf("\nUsing token string %s\n", tkn[1]);
    // the first call
    ptr = strtok(str, tkn[1]);
    printf("String is broken into: ");
    while (ptr) {
      printf(", %s", ptr);
      // must make first argument a NULL character
      ptr = strtok(NULL, tkn[1]);
    }

    strcpy(str, strCopy); // restore str
    printf("\nUsing token string %s\n", tkn[2]);
    // the first call
    ptr = strtok(str, tkn[2]);
    printf("String is broken into: ");
    while (ptr) {
      printf(", %s", ptr);
      // must make first argument a NULL character
      ptr = strtok(NULL, tkn[2]);
    }
    printf("\n\n");
    return 0;
}
```

Answers to Day 8, "Object-Oriented Programming and C++ Classes"

Quiz

1. By default, the members of a class are protected. Therefore, the class declaration has no public member and cannot be used to create instances.
2. The fourth constructor has a default argument, which makes it redundant with respect to the fifth constructor. The C++ compiler detects such an error.
3. True. `String("Hello Turbo C++")` creates a temporary instance of class `String` and then assigns it to the instance `s`.
4. Yes. The new statements are valid.

Exercise

Here is the implementation of function `main` in my version of program CLASS7.CPP.

```
main()
{
   Complex c[5];
   c[1].assign(3, 5);
   c[2].assign(7, 5);
   c[4].assign(2, 3);

   c[3] = c[1] + c[2];
   cout << c[1] << " + " << c[2] << " = " << c[3] << endl;
   cout << c[3] << " + " << c[4] << " = ";
   c[3] += c[4];
   cout << c[3] << endl;
   return 0;
}
```

Answers to Day 9, "Basic Stream File I/O"

Quiz

1. False. The `read` and `write` functions cannot store and recall the dynamic data, which is accessed by a pointer member of a structure or a class.
2. True.
3. True.
4. False.

Exercise

Here is the code for member function `binSearch` and the updated function `main` in program IO4.CPP. (The output also shows the new global constant `NOT_FOUND` and the updated class declaration.)

```
const unsigned NOT_FOUND = 0xffff;

class VmArray
{
protected:
   fstream f;
   unsigned size;
   double badIndex;

public:
   VmArray(unsigned Size, const char* filename);
   ~VmArray()
      { f.close(); }
   unsigned getSize() const
      { return size; }
```

```
   boolean writeElem(const char* str, unsigned index);
   boolean readElem(char* str, unsigned index);
   void Combsort();
   unsigned binSearch(const char* search);
};

unsigned VmArray::binSearch(const char* search)
{
   unsigned low = 0;
   unsigned high = size - 1;
   unsigned median;
   char str[STR_SIZE+1];
   int result;

   do {
      median = (low + high) / 2;
      readElem(str, median);
      result = strcmp(search, str);
      if (result > 0)
         low = median + 1;
      else
         high = median - 1;
   } while (result != 0 && low <= high);
   return (result == 0) ? median : NOT_FOUND;
}

main()
{
   const unsigned NUM_ELEMS = 10;
   char* data[] = { "Michigan", "California", "Virginia", "Main",
                    "New York", "Florida", "Nevada", "Alaska",
                    "Ohio", "Maryland" };
   VmArray arr(NUM_ELEMS, "arr.dat");
   char str[STR_SIZE+1];
   char c;
   unsigned index;

   // assign values to array arr
   for (unsigned i = 0; i < arr.getSize(); i++) {
      strcpy(str, data[i]);
      arr.writeElem(str, i);
   }
   // display unordered array
   cout << "Unsorted arrays is:\n";
   for (i = 0; i < arr.getSize(); i++) {
      arr.readElem(str, i);
      cout << str << endl;
   }
   // pause
   cout << "\nPress any key and then Return to sort the array...";
   cin >> c;
   // sort the array
   arr.Combsort();
   // display sorted array
   cout << "Sorted arrays is:\n";
   for (i = 0; i < arr.getSize(); i++) {
```

```
        arr.readElem(str, i);
        cout << str << endl
    }
    // pause
    cout << "\nPress any key and then Return to search the array...";
    cin >> c;
    // search for array elements using the pointer data
    for (i = 0; i < NUM_ELEMS; i++) {
        index = arr.binSearch(data[i]);
        if (index != NOT_FOUND)
            cout << "Found " << data[i]
                 << " at index " << index << endl;
        else
            cout << "No match for " << data[i] << endl;
    }
    return 0;
}
```

Answers to Day 10, "The C++ *string* Class, Templates, and the Class Library"

Quiz

1. CSTRING.H must be included to use the C++ string class.
2. A string class variable can be declared either with or without an initial value, such as the following:

   string s1;
   string s2("Initial Value");
3. The string class includes functions for comparing it to a C-style string.

   Operators ==, >, <, >=, <= and d have versions that compare string class variables to C-style strings.

   Another way is to compare the C-style element of the string class variable to the C-string, as in the following:

   result = strcmp(CStyleStr, stringClassVar.c_str());
4. The task performed by the `replace` member function finds text and substitutes for it in one call.
5. The second character in a string class variable is at index 1. Addressing is the same as with any array, with index 0 being the first item.
6. This can be done with the following declaration:

   ```
   string myString("12");
   ```

7. Given string `s1` = "11"; string `s2` = "2112";
   a. The result of `s1 + s2` is "112112"
   b. `s2.contains(s1);` returns 1 because "11" is found in "2112"
   c. `s1 > s2` is false
   d. `s2.find(s1, 0);` returns 1 because "11" is located beginning at index 1 in "2112"
8. False. Templates aren't magic; the compiler still has to be able to figure out how to execute each statement in a template exactly as if it weren't a template. For example, the < comparisons in the `Low()` template function don't make sense for classes.

```
template <class T> const T& Low(const T& a, const T& b, const T& c)
{
   if (a < b)
      {
      if (a < c)
         return a;
      }
   else if (b < c)
      return b;
   return c;
}
```

   What does the < operator mean for a class? There are two solutions.

   - Write versions of the template that know how to deal with specific classes (which almost defeats the purpose of using templates).
   - Write operators for those classes. (For example, if you wanted to use `Low()` with a class of your own, you'd need to provide an operator < function that would figure out what makes one class less than another.)

Exercises

```
1. C-style string of value "12"
   char myCStyleString[] = "12";

   C++ string class item of value "12";

   either one of the following:

   string myString("12");
   string myString = "12";
```

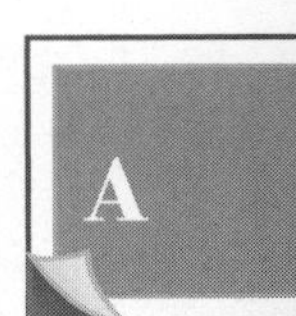

2. The following is a function that accepts a C++ string as a calling argument and that writes its value to the computer screen:

```
void ShowString(string& myString)
{
   cout << myString;
}
```

3. The following function writes out each character of the passed string individually and then returns the size of the string:

```
size_t ShowString(string& myString)
{
   size_t index;
   size_t len = myString.length();

   // write each char from the string to the screen
   // one for each pass through the loop

   for (index = 0; index < len; ++index)
      cout << myString[index];

   return len; // return the length of the string
}
```

4. The following shows a way to reverse the characters in a C++ string using the `strrev` function:

```
strrev(myString.c_str());
```

Answers to Day 11, "Programming Windows with OWL 2.5"

Quiz

1. False. The type's already changed between Windows 3.1 and Windows NT, for example. (WORD, for example, changed from an unsigned `int` to an unsigned `short`.) The idea, however, is that if you use the Windows types, you won't have to make any changes to your own code.
2. True. Even though OWL uses C++ classes, OWL itself is still written using the same functions that a C program would. Using OWL, you get to let the Borland programmers do the work for you.

Answers to Day 12, "Basic Windows"

Quiz

1. True.
2. True.
3. False.

Answers to Day 13, "OWL Controls"

Quiz

1. False. Only the text for controls with `SS_SIMPLE` style are unchangeable.
2. True.
3. True.
4. True.
5. True, because every control is a window.
6. True, but the OWL-prescribed method is to use the `EV_BN_CLICKED` macro.

Answers to Day 14, "Dialog Boxes"

Quiz

1. False. You don't need the .RES file until after linking the object modules and libraries.
2. False. There does, however, need to be a method by which the user can signal the dialog box to close itself. This is often done with buttons that, though labeled differently, return `IDOK` and `IDCANCEL`.
3. True.
4. False. The best examples of nested dialogs are those related to setting up the printer.
5. False. Dialog boxes can be stand-alone windows.

Answers to Day 15, "Grouped Controls"

Quiz

1. False. The check box can replace the two radio buttons only if these buttons offer opposite alternatives.

2. True.
3. True. Each check box can be independently toggled.
4. False.

Answers to Day 16, "List Box Controls"

Quiz

1. True.
2. True.
3. False. `LBN_SELCHANGE` indicates that a new item is selected.
4. False. `LBN_DBLCLICK` indicates that a list item is selected with a double mouse click.
5. False. `LBS_STANDARD` includes the `LBS_SORT` style and therefore creates sorted list boxes.

Answers to Day 17, "Scroll Bars, Combo Boxes, and VBX Controls"

Quiz

1. True.
2. False. You need to respond to the `CBN_EDITUPDATE` message.
3. False. The items are sorted, but not unique. You can insert multiple copies of the same string.
4. True. In order to maintain a chronological order, you must prevent automatic sorting.
5. False.
6. True.
7. False.

Answers to Day 18, "MDI Windows"

Quiz

1. False. MDI child windows cannot have their own menus.
2. False. MDI child windows are confined to the frame area of their parent window.
3. False. You cannot nest MDI child windows.

Answers to Day 20, "OLE 2"

Quiz

1. Linking. This ensures that there is one source document only.
2. `TOleWindow`. `TOleView` is derived from `TOleWindow`.
3. The server must be registered.

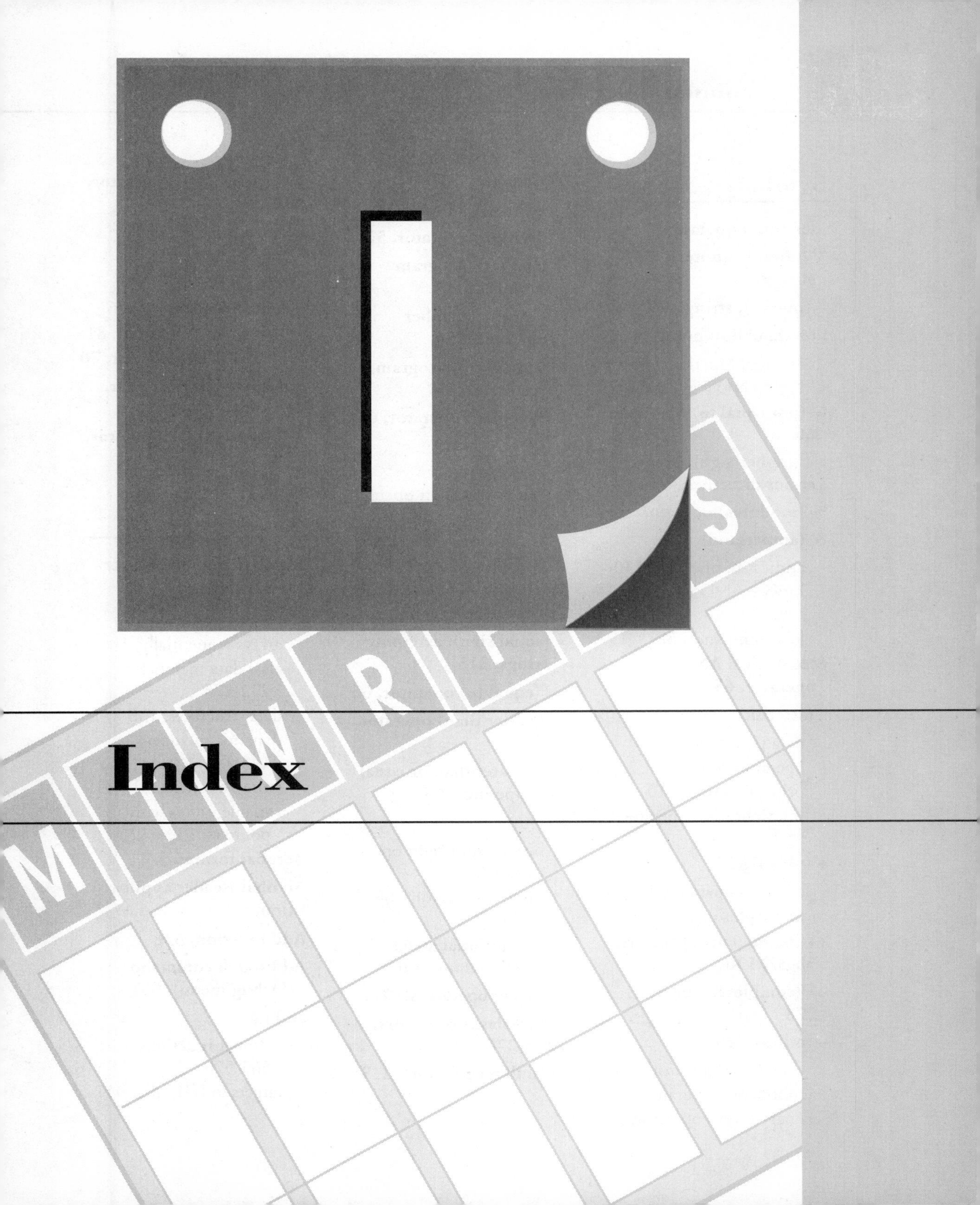

Index

Symbols

, (comma) operator, 72

“” (double quotes), strings, 37

‘’ (quotes), strings, 37

! (exclamation point)
- factorial functions, 164
- logical NOT operator, 65

!= (not equal to) operator, 66

 # (number sign), preprocessor directives, 45

% (modulus) operator, 52

& (ampersand)
- address-of operator, 130
- bitwise AND operator, 70
- key commands, 381

&& (logical AND) operator, 65

*** (asterisk)**
- data types, 131
- operator, 131
- printf function, 210
- multiplication operator, 52

+ (plus sign)
- addition operator, 52
- unary plus operator, 52

++ (increment) operators, 55-57, 136

+= (complex& operator), 278

– (minus sign)
- decrement operators, 56
- subtraction operator, 52
- unary minus operator, 52

-> operator, 138

... (ellipsis), blocks, 92

/ (division) operator, 52

// (slashes), program comments, 37

:: (colons), member functions, 254

; (semicolon), program terminators, 37

< (less than) operator, 65, 176

<<
- bitwise shift left operator, 70
- extractor operator, 286
- friend operator, 278

<= (less than or equal to) operator, 65, 176

= (equal sign), assigning strings, 315

== (equal to) operator, 66

> (greater than) operator, 65

>= (greater than or equal to) operator, 65

>>
- bitwise shift right operator, 70
- inserter operator, 208, 286

? : (conditional assignment) operator, 66

[ ] (array operators), 311

\ (backslash) operators, 275-276

\0 (null terminator), 215

^ (bitwise XOR) operator, 70

{ } (braces)
- blocks, 37
- C++ functions, 151
- initializing arrays, 176
- statement definitions, 81

| (bitwise OR) operator, 70

|| (logical OR) operator, 65

~ (bitwise NOT) operator, 70

A

About dialog box object class, 558

accessing
- arrays sequentially, 136
- class data members, 272-275
- data structures, 138
- dynamic memory, 143-144
- strings as arrays, 317-319
- variable values with pointers, 130-132

Acrobat format, 5-7

Acrobat Reader application, 5

Add function, 336

Add watch command (Debug menu), 651

adding
- member functions, 565-576
- targets to IDE files, 34

addition (+) operator, 52
address-of (&) operator, 130
addresses (variables), 129-130
addressing string characters, 311
AddString member function, 448
Admin Options subtopic (Application topic, AppExpert utility), 532
ADVFUN6.CPP program (Listing 5.5), 165-166
aliases
- data types, 118
- variables, 127

allocating memory
- to application variables, 141
- to dynamic arrays, 142

Alt+D key command, 415
Alt+F4 key command, 345
Alt+F4 key command, 36
Alt+F5 key command, 26
Alt+F7 key command, 15
Alt+F8 key command, 15
Alt+F9 key command, 22
Alt+O key command, 415
Alt+X key command, 409
altering edit control text, 388
ampersand (&), key commands, 381
ANSI (American National Standards Institute), 306
appending string characters, 325
AppExpert command (IDE Project menu), 22
AppExpert utility, 528-539
- Application topic, 529-532
- creating OLE applications, 596-631
- customizing, 563
- output, 539-540
- project files, 540

applications
- Acrobat Reader, 5
- countdown timer, 477-481
- decision-making constructs, 80
- EasyWin, 33-34
- linking, 633-646
- MDI, 502-503
- Mr. Calculator, 391-402
- OLE 2, 591-596
- Son of Mr. Calculator, 486-493
- variables, allocating memory, 141
- *see also* programs

arguments (functions)
- const type modifier, 163
- defaults, 160-162
- passing by reference, 162-163
- VBX types, 496

arithmetic
- assignment operators, 58
- expressions, 54-55
- operators, 52-54

array operators ([ ]), 311
ARRAY1.CPP program (Listing 6.1), 174-175
ARRAY2.CPP program (Listing 6.2), 177-178
ARRAY3.CPP program (Listing 6.3), 178-179
ARRAY4.CPP program (Listing 6.4), 180-181
ARRAY5.CPP program (Listing 6.5), 183-185
ARRAY6.CPP program (Listing 6.6), 188-191
arrays
- accessing sequentially, 136
- binary files, 296
- binary search method, 187
- data types, 119
- dynamic memory, 142
- elements, 176-178
- fixed-array parameters, 180
- function parameters, 179-182
- indexes, 133
- input streams, 295
- linear search method, 187
- matrices, 193-195
- multidimensional, 192-196
  - fixed-array parameter, 198
  - initializing, 196-197
  - open-array parameter, 198
  - parameters, 197-200

open-array parameters, 180
pointers, 134-136
searching, 187-192
single-dimensional, 133-134, 174-179
six-dimensional, 193
sizing automatically, 178
sizing equation, 135
smallest/largest values, 180-181
sorted-array search method, 187
sorting, 183-186
strings, passing as objects, 326
three-dimensional, 192-193
two-dimensional, 192
unordered-array search method, 187
unordered/sorted element displays, 183-185
virtual arrays, 298
writing
to binary files, 296
to output streams, 295

arrays.h header file, 332

ASCIIZ strings, 215

assigning strings, 217-219, 315-316

assignment operators, 57-60, 70

assoc.h header file, 332

asterisk (*)
data types, 131
operator, 131
printf function, 210

automating array sizing, 178

Automation (OLE), 580, 633-646

B

bags.h header file, 332

base classes, declaring, 252-256

Basic Options subtopic
Applications topic, AppExpert utiltity, 530
Main Window topic, AppExpert utility, 534
MDI Child/View topic, AppExpert utility, 539

Bell Labs, 4

binary files (arrays), 296

binary search method (arrays), 187

binarySearch function, 192

binimp.h header file, 332

bit-manipulating operators, 70-72

BITS1.CPP program (Listing 2.10), 71

bitwise operators, 70

blocks, (exception handlers), 92-93

Boolean
data types, 43
expressions, 67-69

Borland
OLE 2 implementation, 583-584
Turbo C++ documentation, 5

braces ({ })
blocks, 37
C++ functions, 151
initializing arrays, 176
statement definitions, 81

Breakpoint command (View menu), 20-21, 653

breakpoints (programs), 88, 97, 106, 650

Browse Symbol command (IDE Search menu), 17

BS_3STATE style (check box controls), 431

BS_AUTO3STATE style (check box controls), 431

BS_AUTOCHECKBOX style (check box controls), 431

BS_AUTORADIOBUTTON style (radio button controls), 432

BS_CHECKBOX style (check box controls), 431

BS_LEFTTEXT style
check box controls, 431
radio button controls, 432

BS_RADIOBUTTON style (radio button controls), 432

Buffer List command (IDE Edit menu), 14-15

buffers
data types, 414-415
Listing, 14

BUG.CPP program (Listing 21.2), 654-656

BUG.RC resource file, 654

Build All command (IDE Project menu), 25

BuildStr member function, 441

buttons (pushbutton controls), 390

BYTE macro, 343

C

C++ object class, creating for OLE Automation, 636-637

CALCJR.CPP program (Listing 17.6), 488-492

CALCJR.H header file, 487

CALCJR.RC resource file, 487-488

calculations

- rectangles, with PTR4.CPP program, 138
- square roots, 100

calculator, 486-493

- *see also* Mr. Calculator; Son of Mr. Calculator

Call Stack command (IDE View menu), 21, 653

calling functions, 152

CanClose member function, 408, 412

CanUndo member function, 385

case-sensitivity

- identifiers, 44
- string comparisons, 322-323

catch blocks (exception handlers), 92-93

CbAdd member function, 461

CbDel member function, 461

CbGetStr member function, 462

CbSetSelStr member function, 461-462

CD-ROMs (Borland Turbo C++ documentation), 5-7

char-type variables, 65

characters (strings)

- addressing, 311
- appending, 325
- converting, 313
- deleting, 326
- inserting, 310
- locating, 231-233
- removing, 310-339
- replacing, 324-325

check box controls, 430-432

child windows (MDI), 507-508, 516-525

CLASS1.CPP program (Listing 8.1), 254-255

CLASS2.CPP program (Listing 8.2), 260-261

CLASS3.CPP program (Listing 8.3), 264-265

CLASS4.CPP program (Listing 8.4), 268-269

CLASS5.CPP program (Listing 8.5), 273-274

CLASS6.CPP program (Listing 8.6), 276-278

classes (objects), 250-251

- About dialog box, 558
- base classes, 252-256
- C++, creating for OLE Automation, 636-637
- constructors, 256-258
- creating, 256-258
- data members, 272-275
- DataServer, 637
- declaring, 254
- derived classes, 262
- destructors, 258-262
- hierarchies, 262-266
- inheritance, 251
- library containers, 332-336
- OCF, 584
- OLE servers, 633-634
- OWL, 344-345
- polymorphism, 251-252, 266-272
- private sections, 253
- protected sections, 253
- proxy, 638
- public sections, 253
- removing, 258-262
- SDIDecFrame, 563
- strings, 306-315
- TAppMDIClient, 514
- TAutoClass, 634
- TButton, 389
- TCalcWindow, 399

TComboBox, 482-484
TControl, 378-379
TDialog, 406-407
TEdit, 351, 382-384
templates, 328
TListBox, 444-462
TMDIChild, 507-508
TMDIClient, 505-507
TMDIFrame, 503-504
TOleDocument, 585-586
TOleView, 586-588
TPointer, 592
TReference, 308
TResId, 406
TScrollBar, 472-475
TScroller, 366
TStatic, 379
TStringRef, 308
TSubString, 308
TVbxControl, 497-499
VBX mixin, 494
viewing, 19
VmArray, 301

Classes command (IDE View menu), 19

ClassExpert command (IDE View menu), 18

ClassExpert utility, 564-565

Clear command (IDE Edit menu), 14

Clear member function, 382, 385

client area (IDE), 9

client windows (MDI), 505-507

Clipboard editing functions, 384-385

close I/O stream function, 286

Close Project command (IDE Project menu), 24

CloseChildren member function, 514

CmCalc member function, 401, 493

CmExit member function, 402

CmStore member function, 401

code compilers, *see* compilers

Code Gen Control subtopic (Application topic, AppExpert utility), 531-532

colons (::), member functions, 254

Comb method (array sorting), 183

combo box controls, 482-486

Combsort function, 301

comma (,) operator, 72

commands
Debug menu, 25-26, 650-653
Edit menu, 13-15
File menu, 10-13
Help menu, 32-33
Options menu, 26-31
Project menu, 22-25
Search menu, 15-18
Tool menu, 26
View menu, 18-22, 653
Window menu, 31-32

comments (programs), 37

comparing strings, 223-227, 309-310, 316-318

Compile command (IDE Project menu), 24

compilers
class library containers, 332-333
#define directive, 46-49, 156-157
directives, 37
#include directive, 45
preprocessors, 44-46
templates, 327-331

complex& operator (+=), 278

ComponentFactory macro, 636

compound documents, 580
editing, 587
notifications
responses, 587
updating, 585-586

concatenating strings, 219-223, 310

conditional assignment (? :) operator, 66

conditional expressions, 66
conditional loops, 99-103
connecting OWL objects with Windows controls, 413
const type modifier (arguments), 163
CONST1.CPP program (Listing 2.2), 49-50
CONST2.CPP program (Listing 2.3), 51
constants
formal, 51-52
global, 69
macros, 49-50
programs, 48-52
constructors, 253, 256-258
controls, 413
string object class, 308-309
TAppMDIChild object class, 515, 523
TButton object class, 389
TCalcWindow object class, 400
TCheckBox object class, 413
TComboBox object class, 413, 482
TControl object class, 378
TDialog object class, 406-407
TEdit object class, 383-384
TGroupBox object class, 413
TListBox object class, 413, 445
TMDIChild object class, 508
TMDIFrame object class, 504
TRadioButton object class, 413
TScrollBar object class, 413, 473-474
TStatic object class, 379-380
TVbxControl object class, 497
constructs, *see* decision-making constructs
containers (OLE objects), 331-336, 581
controlling string spaces (characters), 324
controls
Acrobat Reader application, 6
check boxes, 430-432
combo boxes, 482-486
constructors, 413
countdown timer, 477-481
dialog boxes
initializing, 408
transferring data, 414-415
edit, 382-388
group boxes, 433
list boxes, 444, 454-455
modal dialog boxes, 415-419
modeless dialog boxes, 420
Mr. Calculator application, 391-402
pushbuttons, 389-390
radio buttons, 432
scroll bars, 472-477
static text, 379-382
VBX, 494-499
Windows, connecting OWL objects, 413
converting
string characters, 313
strings, 228
Copy command (IDE Edit menu), 14
Copy member function, 385
copying strings, 312
from sources to targets, 217
num characters, 218
returning duplicate string pointers, 218
COUNTDN.CPP program (Listing 17.3), 478-480
COUNTDN.H header file, 477
COUNTDN.RC resource file, 478
countdown timer application, 477-481
CPU (Central Processing Unit), Listing values, 21

cracking Windows messages, 348

creating

- C++ object classes for OLE Automation, 636-637
- child windows (MDI), 508
- client windows (MDI), 505-507
- dialog boxes, 407-412
- dynamic memory, 143-144
- dynamic scalar variables, 141
- EasyWin applications, 33-38
- MDI applications, 503
- object classes, 256-258
- OLE 2 applications, 591-596
- project source code files, 528-540
- read-only text windows, 360-365
- string objects, 309
- window scroll bars, 365

CSTRING.H header file, 308-315

CSTRING1.CPP program (Listing 10.1), 317-339

CSTRING2.CPP program (Listing 10.2), 319-321

CTEXT keyword (dialog boxes), 412

CTLLST.CPP program (Listing 16.3), 456-460

CTLLST.H header file, 455

CTLLST.RC resource file, 455-456

Ctrl+Alt+Del key command, 657

Ctrl+Alt+SysRq key command, 651

Ctrl+C key command, 13

Ctrl+Delete key command, 13

Ctrl+F2 key command, 25

Ctrl+F5 key command, 26

Ctrl+F8 key command, 658

Ctrl+F9 key command, 25

Ctrl+K key command, 10

Ctrl+Q A key command, 15

Ctrl+Q F key command, 15

Ctrl+S key command, 10

Ctrl+V key command, 13

Ctrl+Z key command, 13

CUA (Common User Access) standard, 502

customizing

- AppExpert utility, 563
- IDE, 28
- MDI child windows, 516

Cut command (IDE Edit menu), 14

Cut member function, 385

D

data members (object classes), accessing, 272-275

data structures

- accessing, 138
- arrays, 174
- declaring, 123-124
- dot operator, 124
- initializing, 124
- locking with const argument modifier, 163
- pointers, 138-141
- storing, 126-127
- unions, 126-127
- untagged, 123
- variables, 123

data types

- aliases, 118
- arrays, 119
- boolean, 43
- buffers, 414-415
- byte size status, 60-62
- enumerated, 119-122
- inserting into streams, 208-209
- modifiers, 42-43
- names, defining, 118-119
- printf function, 212-213
- typecasting, 62-65
- variables
  - declaring, 46-48, 64
  - Hungarian notation, 343-344
  - Windows substitutions, 342-343

DataServer object class, 637

DC (device context), 351, 361

Debug menu, 25-26, 650-653

debugging programs, 650-661

decision-making constructs

- dual-alternative if-else statement, 82-84
- exception handlers, 92-94
- if-else statements, nesting, 85-87
- multiple-alternative if-else statement, 85-87
- nesting, 91-92
- single-alternative if statement, 80-82
- switch statement, 87-90

declaring

- base classes, 252-256
- classes (objects), 254
- constants, 48-52
- data structures, 123-124
- derived classes, 262
- enumerated data types, 119-120
- fixed-array parameters, 180
- friend operators, 275-276
- functions, 150-152
- hierarchies (object classes), 262-266
- inline functions, 158
- loop control variables, 94
- multiple functions, 166-169
- open-array parameters, 180
- proxy object class, 638
- reference parameters (functions), 151
- reference variables, 127
- single-dimensional arrays, 133
- strings, 314-315
- templates as object classes, 328
- TMDIChild object class, 507-508
- TMDIClient object class, 505-506
- TMDIFrame object class, 503-504
- untagged data structures, 123
- variables, 46-48, 64
- virtual functions, 267, 270-272
- VmArray object class, 301

decrement (-) operators, 56

DEFARGS1.CPP program (Listing 5.4), 161

default arguments (functions), 160-162

#define directive (compilers), 46-49, 156-157

#define macros, 348

defining

- data type names, 118-119
- dialog boxes, 407
- functions as templates, 327
- macros, 46
- storage (OLE objects), 585
- TOleView object class, 586-588
- VBX response tables, 495-497

definition files

- EXPRTAPP.DEF, 541
- MDI1.DEF, 509
- MDI2.DEF, 516-517
- SPOTAPP.DEF, 630-638

DEFPUSHBUTTON keyword (dialog boxes), 412

delete operator, 141

DeleteString member function, 448

deleting

- modeless dialog box objects, 408
- string characters, 326

deques.h header file, 332

derived classes, declaring, 262

descendant classes, 262

Destroy member function, 408

destructors (object classes), 253, 258-262

determining string lengths, 312

device context (DC), 351, 361

dialog boxes, 406

- Add breakpoint (Debug menu), 651
- Add watch (Debug menu), 651
- AppExpert utility, 532-533, 539
- controls
  - initializing, 408
  - transferring data, 414-415
- creating, 407-412
- defining with resources, 407
- Environment Options, 28-29
- Find Text, 15
- Information, 21
- modal, 406
- modeless, 406
- New Project, 22-23
- Open a File, 10
- Print Options, 12
- Project Options, 27-28
- Save File As, 11
- Style Sheet, 31
- toggles, 409
- Tools, 29
- VBX response tables, 495-497

Dialog Client subtopic (Main Window topic, AppExpert utility), 537

DIALOG1.CPP program (Listing 14.2), 410-411

DIALOG1.RC resource file, 409

DIALOG2.CPP program (Listing 14.5), 416-418

DIALOG2.H header file, 416

DIALOG2.RC resource file, 416

DICE.CPP program (Listing 20.15), 641-642

DICE.H header file, 641-642

DICE.RC resource file, 644-645

DICE.RH resource header file, 643-645

DICEDLG.CPP program (Listing 20.17), 642-645

DICEDLG.H header file, 642

DICESVR.CPP program (Listing 20.13), 638-639

dict.h header file, 332

directives (compilers), 37

DirectoryList member function, 452-453

disabling buttons (pushbutton controls), 390

displaying

- arrays
  - elements, 177-178
  - smallest/largest values, 180-181
- variable contents, 47-48

division (/) operator, 52

dlistimp.h header file, 332

do-while loops, 99-102

dot operator (data structures), 124

double quotes (" "), strings, 37

double-linked lists (string storage), 334-335

DOWHILE1.CPP program (Listing 3.9), 100-101

drop-down combo boxes, 482

dual-alternative if-else statement (decision-making constructs), 82-84

DWORD macro, 343

dynamic memory

- accessing/creating, 143-144
- arrays, 142
- pointers, 141-145
- variables, 142

dynamic scalar variables, 141

E

EasyWin applications, 33-38

edit controls

- styles, 383-384
- text
  - altering, 388
  - retrieving, 385-387

Edit menu (IDE), 13-15

editing

Clipboard functions, 384-385

compound documents, 587

files with reference help manuals, 8

ellipsis (...), blocks, 92

embedded objects, 580, 587-588

embedding

objects, 582

see also OLE 2

empty strings, 37

EnableWindow member function, 390

enabling buttons (pushbutton controls), 390

End key command, 367

ENUM1.CPP program, 121-122

enumerated data types, 119-122

Environment command (IDE Options menu), 28-29

Environment Options dialog box, 28-29

equal to (==) operator, 66

equal sign (=), assigning strings, 315

equations (sizing arrays), 135

error message labels, 399

errors

dual-alternative if statement, 84

exception handlers (decision-making constructs), 92

runtime, 93

strings, 307-308

Evaluate/Modify command (Debug menu), 652

event handlers (OWL), 348

Event Log command (IDE View menu), 21, 653

events (VBX), 495-496

EvHandler member function, 495

EvHScroll member function, 476

EvLButtonDown member function, 400

EvTimerBar member function, 480

EvVScroll member function, 476

exception handlers (decision-making constructs), 92-94

exceptions

functions, throwing, 152-153

types, 93

see also runtime errors

exclamation point (!), factorial functions, 164

Execute member function, 408

Exit command (IDE File menu), 13

exit function, 98

exiting

functions prematurely, 160

IDE, 38

loops, 97-98, 106

Expert prototype project, 540-563

expressions

arithmetic, 54-55

Boolean, 67-69

conditional, 66

data type conversions, 62

integer-compatibility, 87

EXPRTAPP.CPP program (Listing 19.7), 558-561

EXPRTAPP.CPP program (Listing 19.8), 566-572

EXPRTAPP.DEF definition file, 541

EXPRTAPP.H header file, 545-546

EXPRTAPP.RC resource file, 548-554

EXPRTAPP.RH resource header file, 541-545

extracting substrings, 311

extractor operator (<<), 286

F

F1 key command, 8, 32
F3 key command, 15
F5 key command, 25
F7 key command, 25
F8 key command, 25
factorial functions, 164-166
fail( ) function, 286
FALSE macro, 342
__far keyword, 145
far pointers, 145
File menu (IDE), 10-13
files
- attributes , Listing, 453
- editing with reference help manuals, 8
- header, 45
- I/O, 287-289

Find command (IDE Search menu), 15-16
Find execution point command (Debug menu), 651
Find Text dialog box, 15
FindExactString member function, 448-449
finding
- string characters, 231-233
- substrings, 234-238, 326

FindString member function, 448
FIRST.CPP program (Listing 11.1), 346
fixed-array parameter
- declaring, 180
- multidimensional arrays, 198

fonts, 373
for loops, 94-99, 176
FOR1.CPP program (Listing 3.6), 95
FOR2.CPP program (Listing 3.7), 96-97
FOR3.CPP program (Listing 3.8), 98-99
FOR4.CPP program (Listing 3.11), 104-105
formal constants, 49-52
formats
- Acrobat, 5-7
- printf function, 212-214

friend functions, 272-275
friend operator (<<), 275-278
FSTREAM.H header file, 284
functions
- Add, 336
- arguments
  - const type modifier, 163
  - defaults, 160-162
  - passing by reference, 162-163
  - VBX types, 496
- arrays, 179-182
- binarySearch, 192
- BuildStr member, 441
- calling, 152
- Clipboard, 384-385
- Combsort, 301
- declaring, 150-152
- defining as templates, 327
- exceptions, throwing, 152-153
- exit, 98
- exiting prematurely, 160
- factorial, 164-166
- fail( ), 286
- friend functions, 272-275
- GetCheck( ), 431
- getInputFilename, 289
- getline, 216
- getOutputFilename, 290
- globally declared functions (strings), 313
- good( ), 286
- inline, 157-159
- inputArray, 185
- inputMatrix, 200
- Invalidate( ), 356
- linearSearch, 191
- local variables, 153-154
- main( ), OWL, 346
- member functions
  - adding, 565-576
  - AddString, 448
  - CanClose, 408, 412
  - CbAdd, 461
  - CbDel, 461
  - CbGetStr, 462
  - CbSetSelStr, 461-462
  - check box controls, 431
  - class library container iterators, 334
  - Clear, 382

close, 286
CloseChildren, 514
CmCalc, 401, 493
CmExit, 402
CmStore, 401
DeleteString, 448
Destroy, 408
DirectoryList, 452-453
EnableWindow, 390
EvHandler, 495
EvHScroll, 476
EvLButtonDown, 400
EvTimerBar, 480
EvVScroll, 476
Execute, 408
FindExactString, 448-449
FindString, 448
GetDroppedControlRect, 484
GetLine, 387
getline, 286-290
GetLineFromPos, 386
GetLineIndex, 386
GetLineLength, 387
GetNumLines, 385-386
GetRange, 475
GetSel member, 449
GetSelection, 387
GetSelIndexes, 449
GetString, 450
GetStringLen, 450
GetText, 381-382, 484-485
GetTextLen, 381
HScroll, 366
InitChild, 514
InitMainWindow, 504, 562-563
Insert, 388
InsertString, 450-451
MoveSels, 467
open, 285
Paint, 361
PreProcessMsg, 508
read, 291
SetPosition, 475
SetRange, 475
SetSel, 452
SetSelection, 388
SetSelIndex, 451
SetSelItemRange, 451
SetSelString, 451
SetText, 382, 388
SetTopIndex, 452
SetupWindow, 373-374, 408
ShowWindow, 390
string object class, 312-314, 325-327
TAppMDIClient object class, 514
TEdit object class, 385
text query (edit control), 385
TMDIClient object class, 506
TMDIFrame object class, 504
VScroll, 366
write, 291
multiple declarations, 166-169
naming, 351
non-void, 160
overloading, 166-169
Paint( ), 356
precision (streams), 207
printf, 210-215
processLines, 290
prototyping, 150-153
put_var, 401
readArray, 296
readElem, 295
recursive, 164-166
reference parameters, 151
Run( ), 347
searchInSortedArray, 192
searchInUnorderedArray, 192
SelectionChanged, 433
SetCheck ( ), 431
showArray, 186
showColumnAverage, 200
sortArray, 186
sprintf, 213
static variables, 155-156
stream I/O
close, 286
getline, 286-287
open, 285
read, 291
seekg, 297
write, 291
strings, 313
strcat, 220
strchr, 231-232
strcmp, 223-224
strcopy, 217
strcspn, 233

strdup, 218
stricmp, 224
strlen, 219
strlwr, 228
strncat, 220
strncmp, 224-225
strncpy, 218-219
strnicmp, 225
strpbrk, 233
strrchr, 232
strrev, 229-231
strspn, 232-233
strstr, 234
strtok, 234-235
_strupr, 228
TextOut, 360
TListBox object class, 446-447
trimStr, 289
VBX control property manipulation, 498
virtual functions, 266-272
declaring, 270-272
pointers, 657
void, 160
volumes, calling, 152
vs. macros, 156-157
width (streams), 207
writeArray, 296
writeElem, 295

G

General Protection Fault (GPF), programs, 131
GetCheck ( ) function, 431
GetDroppedControlRect member function, 484
getInputFilename function, 289
getline I/O stream function, 216, 286-287
GetLine member function, 387
GetLineFromPos member function, 386
GetLineIndex member function, 386
GetLineLength member function, 387
GetNumLines member function, 385-386
getOutputFilename function, 290
GetRange member function, 475
GetSel member function, 449
GetSelection member function, 387
GetSelIndexes member function, 449
GetString member function, 450
GetStringLen member function, 450
GetText member function, 381-382, 484-485
GetTextLen member function, 381
global
constants, 69
variables, 47
Globals command (IDE View menu), 19-20
good( ) function, 286
GPF (General Protection Fault), programs, 131
greater than (>) operator, 65
greater than or equal to (>=) operator, 65
group box controls, 433
GUID (Globally Unique Identifier), 593

H

handles (VBX strings), 497
handling button messages, 390
hashimp.h header file, 332
header files, 37, 45
ARRAYS.H, 332
ASSOC.H, 332
BAGS.H, 332
BINIMP.H, 332
CALCJR.H, 487
COUNTDN.H, 477
CSTRING.H, 308-315
CTLLST.H, 455
DEQUES.H, 332
DIALOG2.H, 416
DICE.H, 641-642
DICEDLG.H, 642

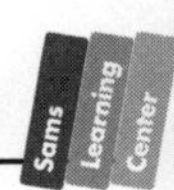

DICT.H, 332
DLISTIMP.H, 332
EXPRTAPP.H, 545-546
FSTREAM.H, 284
HASHIMP.H, 332
IOSTREAM.H, 50, 284
LISTIMP.H, 333
MDI1.H, 510
MDI2.H, 517
MRCALC.H, 392
QUEUES.H, 332
REAL.RH, 352
SETS.H, 332
SPOTAB.H, 612
SPOTAPP.H, 597
SPOTDOC.H, 601-602
SPOTVIEW.H, 605-606
STACKS.H, 333
STRING.H, 216-217
variables, 45
VECTIMP.H, 333
WIDGETS.H, 434
XFERLIST.H, 464
XPRTABTD.H, 546-547

hierarchies (operators), 72-74

HELLO.CPP program (Listing 1.1), 36-40

Help menu (IDE), 32-33

hexadecimal numbers, 43

hiding
buttons (pushbutton controls), 390
function prototypes, 152

history list boxes (combo box controls), 486

Home key command, 367

hot keys, *see* key commands

HScroll member function, 366

Hungarian notation (data type variables), 343-344

I

I/O (input/output)
files, 287-289
printf function, 210-215
streams, 206-210
string object class, 324

IDE (Integrated Development Environment), 4
components, 8-33
customizing, 28
Debug menu, 25-26
Edit menu, 13-15
exiting, 38
File menu, 10-13
files, adding targets, 34
Help menu, 32-33
loading, 8
Options menu, 26-31
Project menu, 22-25
Search menu, 15-18
Tool menu, 26
View menu, 18-22
Window menu, 31-32

identifiers, naming, 44

if-else statements, nesting, 85-87

IF1.CPP program (Listing 3.1), 81-82

IF2.CPP program (Listing 3.2), 83-84

IF3.CPP program (Listing 3.3), 86

IF4.CPP program (Listing 3.5), 91

implementing OLE 2 object classes, 593-595

IN1.CPP program (Listing 7.2), 209

#include directive (compilers), 45

increment (++) operators, 55-57

increment/decrement method (array pointers), 136-138

indexes (arrays), 133

Information command (IDE View menu), 21-22

Information dialog box, 21

inheritance (object classes), 251

InitChild member function, 514

initializing
data structures, 124
dialog box controls, 408
multidimensional arrays, 196-197
pointers (variables), 131
single-dimensional arrays, 176-179
strings, 217
VBX subsytems, 494
windows, 373-374

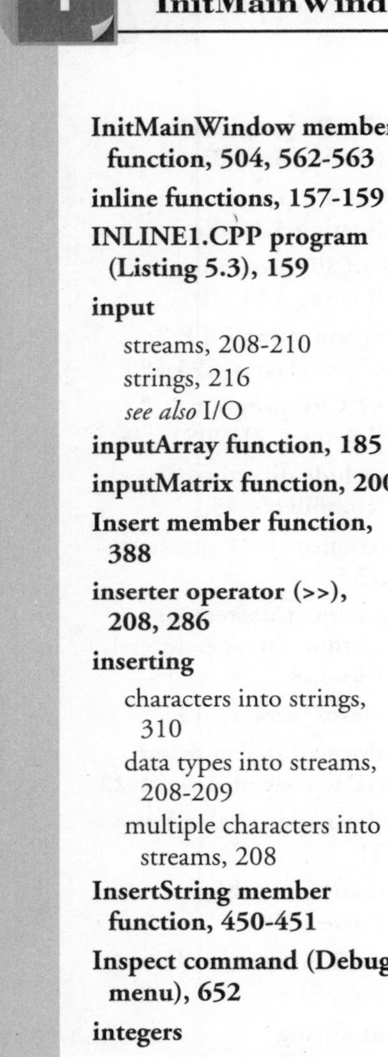

InitMainWindow member function, 504, 562-563

inline functions, 157-159

INLINE1.CPP program (Listing 5.3), 159

input
- streams, 208-210
- strings, 216
- *see also* I/O

inputArray function, 185

inputMatrix function, 200

Insert member function, 388

inserter operator (>>), 208, 286

inserting
- characters into strings, 310
- data types into streams, 208-209
- multiple characters into streams, 208

InsertString member function, 450-451

Inspect command (Debug menu), 652

integers
- arrays, sorting, 187-191
- combinations/permutations, 164-166
- compatible expressions (values), 87
- enumerated data type values, 119
- prompts, 58

Integrated Development Environment, *see* IDE

interfaces
- MDI, 502
- VBX, 472, 494-499

Invalidate( ) function, 356

IO1.CPP program (Listing 9.1), 287-289

IO2.CPP program (Listing 9.2), 292-295

IO3.CPP program (Listing 9.3), 298-301

iostream library, 284

IOSTREAM.H header file, 50, 284

ISO (International Standards Organization), 306

iterators
- class library containers, 334
- loops
  - skipping, 104-106
  - testing, 99-102

K

key commands
- Alt+D, 415
- Alt+F4, 36, 345
- Alt+F5, 26
- Alt+F7, 15
- Alt+F8, 15
- Alt+F9, 22
- Alt+O, 415
- Alt+X, 409
- Ctrl+Alt+Del, 657
- Ctrl+Alt+SysRq, 651
- Ctrl+C, 13
- Ctrl+Delete, 13
- Ctrl+F2, 25
- Ctrl+F5, 26
- Ctrl+F8, 658
- Ctrl+F9, 25
- Ctrl+K, 10
- Ctrl+Q A, 15
- Ctrl+Q F, 15
- Ctrl+S, 10
- Ctrl+V, 13
- Ctrl+Z, 13
- End, 367
- F1, 8, 32
- F3, 15
- F5, 25
- F7, 25
- F8, 25
- Home, 367
- PgDn, 367
- PgUp, 367
- Shift+Ctrl+Z, 13
- Shift+F4, 32
- Shift+F5, 31

keys (OLE 2 Registry), 589-590

keywords
- CTEXT (dialog boxes), 412
- DEFPUSHBUTTON (dialog boxes), 412
- __far, 145
- throw, 93-94
- typedef, 118-119

L

labels (error messages), 399

lengths (strings)

characters, 323

determining, 219, 312

less than (<) operator, 65, 176

less than or equal to (<=) operator, 65, 176

linear search method (arrays), 187

linearSearch function, 191

linked objects, 580

linking

applications, 633-646

objects, 581

see also OLE 2

list box controls, 444

messages, 453-454

multiple-selection, 462-467

styles, 445-446

listimp.h header file, 333

Listing

buffers, 14

CPU values, 21

file attributes, 453

Listings

1.1 HELLO.CPP program, 36-40

2.1 VAR1.CPP program, 48

2.2 CONST1.CPP program, 49-50

2.3 CONST2.CPP program, 51

2.4 OPER1.CPP program, 53-54

2.5 OPER2.CPP program, 56-57

2.6 OPER3.CPP program, 58-59

2.7 SIZEOF1.CPP program, 61

2.8 TYPCAST1.CPP program, 63-64

2.9 RELOP1.CPP program, 67-69

2.10 BITS1.CPP program, 71

3.1 IF1.CPP program, 81-82

3.2 IF2.CPP program, 83

3.3 IF3.CPP program, 86

3.4 SWITCH1.CPP program, 89-90

3.5 IF4.CPP program, 91

3.6 FOR1.CPP program, 95

3.7 FOR2.CPP program, 96-97

3.8 FOR3.CPP program, 98-99

3.9 DOWHILE1.CPP program, 100-101

3.10 WHILE1.CPP program, 103

3.11 FOR4.CPP program, 104-105

3.12 NESTFOR1.CPP program, 107

4.1 ENUM1.CPP program, 121-122

4.2 STRUCT1.CPP program, 124-125

4.3 REFVAR1.CPP program, 128

4.4 PTR1.CPP program, 132

4.5 PTR2.CPP program, 135

4.6 PTR3.CPP program, 136-137

4.7 PTR4.CPP program, 139-140

4.8 PTR5.CPP program, 143-144

5.1 VAR2.CPP program, 154

5.2 STATIC1.CPP program, 155

5.3 INLINE1.CPP program, 159

5.4 DEFARGS1.CPP program, 161

5.5 ADVFUN6.CPP program, 165

5.6 OVERLOAD.CPP program, 167-168

6.1 ARRAY1.CPP program, 174-175

6.2 ARRAY2.CPP program, 177

6.3 ARRAY3.CPP program, 178-179

6.4 ARRAY4.CPP program, 180-181

6.5 ARRAY5.CPP program, 183-185

6.6 ARRAY6.CPP program, 188-191
6.7 MAT1.CPP program, 194
6.8 MAT2.CPP program, 196-197
6.9 MAT3.CPP program, 198-199
7.1 OUT1.CPP program, 207
7.2 IN1.CPP program, 209
7.3 OUT2.CPP program, 213-214
7.4 STRING1.CPP program, 221-222
7.5 STRING2.CPP program, 225-227
7.6 STRING3.CPP program, 229-230
7.7 STRING4.CPP program, 236
8.1 CLASS1.CPP program, 254-255
8.2 CLASS2.CPP program, 260-261
8.3 CLASS3.CPP program, 264-265
8.4 CLASS4.CPP program, 268-269
8.5 CLASS5.CPP program, 273-274
8.6 CLASS6.CPP program, 276-278
9.1 IO1.CPP program, 287-289
9.2 IO2.CPP program, 292-295
9.3 IO3.CPP program, 298-300
10.1 CSTRING1.CPP program, 317-339
10.2 CSTRING2.CPP program, 319-321
10.3 templates program, 329-330
10.4 double-linked lists (string storage), 334-335
11.1 FIRST.CPP program, 346
11.2 REAL.RC files, 350
11.3 REAL.RH header file, 352
11.4 REAL.CPP program, 352-358
12.1 WINDOW1.RC program, 362
12.2 WINDOW1.CPP program, 362-364
12.3 WINDOW2.H program, 368
12.4 WINDOW2.RC program, 368
12.5 WINDOW2.CPP program, 368-372
13.1 MRCALC.H header file, 392
13.2 MRCALC.RC resource file, 393
13.3 MRCALC.CPP program, 393-399
14.1 DIALOG1.RC resource file, 409
14.2 DIALOG1.CPP program, 410-411
14.3 DIALOG2.H header file, 416
14.4 DIALOG2.RC resource file, 416
14.5 DIALOG2.CPP program, 416-418
15.1 WIDGETS.H header file, 434
15.2 WIDGETS.RC resource files, 434-435
15.3 WIDGETS.CPP program, 435-439
16.1 CTLLST.H header file, 455
16.2 CTLLST.RC resource file, 455-456
16.3 CTLLST.CPP program, 456-460
16.4 XFERLIST.H header file, 464
16.5 XFERLIST.RC resource file, 464
16.6 XFERLIST.CPP program, 464-466
17.1 COUNTDN.H header file, 477
17.2 COUNTDN.RC resource file, 478
17.3 COUNTDN.CPP program, 478-480
17.4 CALCJR.H header file, 487
17.5 CALCJR.RC resource file, 487-488
17.6 CALCJR.CPP program, 488-492
18.1 MDI1.DEF definition file, 509
18.2 MDI1.H header file, 510

18.3 MDI1.RC resource file, 510
18.4 MDI1.CPP program, 510-513
18.5 MDI2.DEF definition file, 516-517
18.6 MDI2.H header file, 517
18.7 MDI2.RC resource file, 517
18.8 MDI2.CPP program, 517
19.1 EXPRTAPP.DEF definition file, 541
19.2 EXPRTAPP.RH resource header file, 541-544
19.3 EXPRTAPP.H header file, 545-546
19.4 XPRTABTD.H header file, 546-547
19.5 EXPRTAPP.RC resource file, 548-554
19.6 XPRTABTD.CPP program, 554-557
19.7 EXPRTAPP.CPP program, 558-561
19.8 EXPRTAPP.CPP program, 566-572
20.1 SPOTAPP.H header file, 597
20.2 SPOTAPP.CPP program, 597-601
20.3 SPOTDOC.H header file, 601-602
20.4 SPOTDOC.CPP program, 602-605
20.5 SPOTVIEW.H header file, 605-606
20.6 SPOTVIEW.CPP program, 606-612
20.7 SPOTAB.H header file, 612
20.8 SPOTAB.CPP program, 613-615
20.9 SPOTAPP.RH resource header file, 615-619
20.10 SPOTAPP.RC resource file, 619-627
20.11 SPOTAPP.DEF definition file, 627
20.12 SPOT.IDE project file, 627-628
20.13 DICESVR.CPP program, 636-638
20.14 DICE.H header file, 638
20.15 DICE.CPP program, 638-639
20.16 DICEDLG.H header file, 639-640
20.17 DICEDLG.CPP program, 640-642
20.18 DICE.RH resource header file, 642
20.19 DICE.RC resource file, 642-645
21.1 BUG.RC resource file, 654
21.2 BUG.CPP program, 654-656

Load symbol tape command (Debug menu), 653

loading IDE, 8

local variables, 153-155

Locate Function command (IDE Search menu), 17

locating
- string characters, 231-233
- substrings, 234-238

locking data structures, 163

logical AND (&&) operator, 65

logical expressions, *see* Boolean expressions

logical operators, 65-66

LONG macro, 343

loops (programs), 72
- break statement, 106
- control variables, 94
- do-while, 99-102
- exiting, 97-98, 106
- for, 94-99, 176
- iterations
  - skipping, 104-106
  - testing, 99-102
- nesting, 106-108
- open, 97-99
- while, 102-103

LPCSTR macro, 343

LPSTR macro, 343

M

macros, 156-157
- ComponentFactory, 636
- constants, 49-50
- #define, 348
- defining, 46

methods (OLE Automation), 635
min, 158
Registry, 589
TAutoClass object class, 634
Windows, 342-343

Main Window topic (AppExpert utility), 533-537

main( ) function, OWL, 346

Make All command (IDE Project menu), 24-25

manipulating

buttons (pushbutton controls), 390
windows, 31

MAT1.CPP program (Listing 6.7), 194-195

MAT2.CPP program (Listing 6.8), 196-197

MAT3.CPP program (Listing 6.9), 198-200

matrices (arrays), manipulating, 193-195

MDI (Multiple Document Interface) application

child windows, 507-508
client windows, 505-507
components, 502-503
creating, 503
messages, 508-509
text viewers, 509-516
windows, 504-505, 516-525

MDI Child/View topic (AppExpert utility), 538-577

MDI Client subtopic (Main Window topic, AppExpert utility), 536

MDI1.CPP program (Listing 18.4), 510-513

MDI1.DEF definition file, 509

MDI1.H header file, 510

MDI1.RC resource file, 510

MDI2.CPP program (Listing 18.8), 517

MDI2.DEF definition file, 516-517

MDI2.H header file, 517

MDI2.RC resource file, 517

member functions, 251

adding, 565-576
AddString, 448
CanClose, 408, 412
CbAdd, 461
CbDel, 461
CbGetStr, 462
CbSetSelStr, 461-462
check box controls, 431
class library container iterators, 334
Clear, 382
close, 286
CloseChildren, 514
CmCalc, 401, 493
CmExit, 402
CmStore, 401
DeleteString, 448
Destroy, 408
DirectoryList, 452-453
EnableWindow, 390
EvHandler, 495
EvHScroll, 476
EvLButtonDown, 400
EvTimerBar, 480
EvVScroll, 476
Execute, 408
FindExactString, 448-449
FindString, 448
GetDroppedControlRect, 484
GetLine, 387
getline, 286-290
GetLineFromPos, 386
GetLineIndex, 386
GetLineLength, 387
GetNumLines, 385-386
GetRange, 475
GetSel member function, 449
GetSelection, 387
GetSelIndexes, 449
GetString, 450
GetStringLen, 450
GetText, 381-382, 484-485
GetTextLen, 381
HScroll, 366
InitChild, 514
InitMainWindow, 504, 562-563
Insert, 388

InsertString, 450-451
MoveSels, 467
open, 285
Paint, 361
PreProcessMsg, 508
read, 291
SetPosition, 475
SetRange, 475
SetSel, 452
SetSelection, 388
SetSelIndex, 451
SetSelItemRange, 451
SetSelString, 451
SetText, 382, 388
SetTopIndex, 452
SetupWindow, 373-374, 408
ShowWindow, 390
stream I/O, 284-286
string object class, 312-314, 325-327
TAppMDIClient object class, 514
TComboBox object class, 483-485
TEdit object class, 385
text query (edit control), 385
TMDIClient object class, 506
TMDIFrame object class, 504
TScrollBar object class, 474-475
VScroll, 366
write, 291
see also methods

memory
- allocating
  - to application variables, 141
  - to dynamic arrays, 142
- dynamic, 141-145
- segmented, 145

menus
- Debug, 650-653
- OWL, 349

Message command (IDE View menu), 19

messages
- buttons (pushbutton controls), handling, 390
- combo box controls, responding to, 485
- list box controls, 453-454
- MDI, 508-509
- objects, 251
- scroll bars, responding to, 475-477
- Windows, 347-349

methods, 251
- Automation (OLE), 635-645
- objects, 251
- *see also* member functions

min macro, 158

modal dialog boxes, 406
- controls, transferring data, 415-419
- creating, 407-412

modeless dialog boxes, 406
- controls, transferring data, 420
- creating, 407-412
- deleting objects, 408

modifiers (data types), 42-43

modulus (%) operator, 52

MoveSels member function, 467

Mr. Calculator application, 391-402

MRCALC.CPP program (Listing 13.3), 393-399

MRCALC.H header file, 392

MRCALC.RC resource file, 393

multidimensional arrays, 192-196
- fixed-array parameter, 198
- initializing, 196-197
- open-array parameter, 198
- parameters, 197-200

multiple-alternative if-else statement (decision-making constructs), 85-87

multiple-selection list box controls, 462-467

multiplication (*) operator, 52

N

naming
- functions, 351
- identifiers, 44
- Windows messages, 348

navigating
reference help files, 7-8
text, 365-367
near pointers, 145
NESTFOR1.CPP program (Listing 3.12), 107
nesting
decision-making constructs, 91-92
if-else statements, 85-87
loops, 106-108
New command (IDE File menu), 10
new operator, 141
New Project command (IDE Project menu), 22-23
New Project dialog box, 22-23
New Target command (IDE Project menu), 24
Next Message command (IDE Search menu), 18
nodes, 34-35
non-void functions, 160
not equal to (!=) operator, 66
notification messages (list boxes), 453-454
NULL macro, 342
null terminator (\0), 215
number sign (#), preprocessor directives, 45
numbers (hexadecimal), 43

O

ObjectComponents Framework (OCF), 8, 583-584
Object Linking and Embedding (OLE 2), 4, 250-252
object-oriented programming, *see* OOP
objects
classes, 250-251
About dialog box, 558
accessing data members, 272-275
base classes, 252-256
C++, 636, 637
constructors, 256-258
creating, 256-258
DataServer, 637
declaring, 254
destructors, 258-262
hierarchies, declaring, 262-266
inheritance, 251
library containers, 332-336
OCF, 584
OLE servers, 633-634
OWL, 344-345
polymorphism, 251-252, 266-272
private sections, 253
protected sections, 253
proxy, 638
public sections, 253
removing, 258-262
SDIDecFrame, 563
string, 306-308
strings, 308-315
TAppMDIClient, 514
TAutoClass, 634
TButton, 389
TCalcWindow, 399
TComboBox, 482-484
TControl, 378-379
TDialog, 406-407
TEdit, 351, 382-384
templates, 328
TListBox, 444-462
TMDIChild, 507-508
TMDIClient, 505-507
TMDIFrame, 503-504
TOleDocument, 585-586
TOleView, 586-588
TPointer, 592
TReference, 308
TResId, 406
TScrollBar, 472-475
TScroller, 366
TStatic, 379
TStringRef, 308
TSubString, 308
TVbxControl, 497-499
VBX mixin, 494
viewing, 19
VmArray, 301

containers, 581
embedded objects, 580, 587-588
embedding, 582
linked objects, 580
linking, 581
messages, 251
methods, 251
modeless dialog boxes, deleting, 408
OWL, connecting with Windows controls, 413
strings, 309

ObjectWindows library (TCheckBox class), 430

OCF (ObjectComponents Framework), 8, 583-584

OLE 2 (Object Linking and Embedding), 580-583
applications, creating, 591-596
Automation, 633-646
Borland implementation, 583-584
Registry, 588-590
TOleDocument implementation, 585-586

OLE 2 options (Applications topic, AppExpert utility), 531

OOP (object-oriented programming), 4, 250-252

Open a File dialog box, 10

Open command (IDE File menu), 10

open I/O stream function, 285

open loops, 97-99

Open Project command (IDE Project menu), 24

open-array parameters
declaring, 180
multidimensional arrays, 198

OPER1.CPP program (Listing 2.4), 53-54

OPER2.CPP program (Listing 2.5), 56-57

OPER3.CPP program (Listing 2.6), 58-59

operators
& (address-of), 130
* (asterisk), 131
++ (plus-plus), 136
+= (complex& operator), 278
– (decrement), 56
–>, 138
< (less than), 176
<< (friend operator), 278
<= (less than or equal to), 176
>> (inserter), 208
[ ] (arrays), 311
arithmetic, 52-54
assignment, 57-60
bit-manipulating, 70-72
comma, 72
declaring, 275-276
delete, 141
dot (data structures), 124
enumerated data types, 120
friend, 275-276
increment, 55-57
logical, 65-66
new, 141
precedence, 72-74
reference, 130
relational, 65-66
sizeof, 60-62

Options menu (IDE), 26-31

OUT1.CPP program (Listing 7.1), 207

OUT2.CPP program (Listing 7.3), 213-214

output
AppExpert utility, 539-540
device context, 361
streams, 206-208
see also I/O

OVERLOAD.CPP program (Listing 5.6), 167-168

overloading functions, 166-169

OWL (ObjectWindows Library), 7, 342-343
applications
TGroupBox class, 433
TRadioButton class, 432
event handlers, 348

main( ) function, 346
menus, 349
objects
classes, 344-345
connecting with Windows controls, 413
program, 352-358
resources, 349
TVbxControl object class, 497-499
windows, 345
Windows messages, 347-349

P

Paint( ) function, 356
passing
function arguments by reference, 162-163
string arrays as objects, 326
Paste command (IDE Edit menu), 14
Paste member function, 385
Pause program command (Debug menu), 651
PgDn key command, 367
PgUp key command, 367
plus-plus (++) operator, 136
pointers
arrays, 134-138
data structures, 138-141
dynamic memory, 141-145
far, 145
near, 145
segmented memory, 145
strings, 315
variables, 129-132
virtual functions, 657
polymorphism (object classes), 251-252, 266-272
pop-up menus, 350
precision function (streams), 207
PreProcessMsg member function, 508
preprocessors, 44-46
Previous Message command (IDE Search menu), 17
Print command (IDE File menu), 12
Print Options dialog box, 12
Print Setup command (IDE File menu), 12
printf function, 210-215
private sections (object classes), 253
processing array elements, 176
processLines function, 290
programs
ADVFUN6.CPP (Listing 5.5), 165-166
arithmetic expressions, 55
ARRAY1.CPP (Listing 6.1), 174-175
ARRAY2.CPP (Listing 6.2), 177-178
ARRAY3.CPP (Listing 6.3), 178-179
ARRAY4.CPP (Listing 6.4), 180-181
ARRAY5.CPP (Listing 6.5), 183-185
ARRAY6.CPP (Listing 6.6), 188-191
BITS1.CPP (Listing 2.10), 71
breakpoints, 88, 97, 106, 650
BUG.CPP (Listing 21.2), 654-656
CALCJR.CPP (Listing 17.6), 488-492
CLASS1.CPP (Listing 8.1), 254-255
CLASS2.CPP (Listing 8.2), 260-261
CLASS3.CPP (Listing 8.3), 264-265
CLASS4.CPP (Listing 8.4), 268-269
CLASS5.CPP (Listing 8.5), 273-274
CLASS6.CPP (Listing 8.6), 276-278
comments, 37
CONST1.CPP (Listing 2.2), 49-50
CONST2.CPP (Listing 2.3), 51
constants, 48-52

COUNTDN.CPP
(Listing 17.3), 478-480
CSTRING1.CPP
(Listing 10.1), 317-339
CSTRING2.CPP
(Listing 10.2), 319-321
CTLLST.CPP (Listing
16.3), 456-460
debugging, 650-661
DEFARGS1.CPP
(Listing 5.4), 161
DIALOG1.CPP
(Listing 14.2), 410-411
DIALOG2.CPP
(Listing 14.5), 416-418
DICE.CPP
(Listing 20.15),
641-642
DICEDLG.CPP
(Listing 20.17),
642-645
DICESVR.CPP
(Listing 20.13),
638-639
DOWHILE1.CPP
(Listing 3.9), 100-101
ENUM1.CPP
(Listing 4.1), 121-122
EXPRTAPP.CPP
(Listing 19.7), 558-561
EXPRTAPP.CPP
(Listing 19.8), 566-572
FIRST.CPP
(Listing 11.1), 346
FOR1.CPP (Listing 3.6),
95
FOR2.CPP (Listing 3.7),
96-97
FOR3.CPP (Listing 3.8),
98-99
FOR4.CPP
(Listing 3.11), 104-105
GPFs, 131
HELLO.CPP
(Listing 1.1), 36-40
IF1.CPP (Listing 3.1),
81-82
IF2.CPP (Listing 3.2),
83-84
IF3.CPP (Listing 3.3), 86
IF4.CPP (Listing 3.5), 91
IN1.CPP (Listing 7.2),
209
INLINE1.CPP
(Listing 5.3), 159
IO1.CPP (Listing 9.1),
287-289
IO2.CPP (Listing 9.2),
292-295
IO3.CPP (Listing 9.3),
298-301
loops
break statement, 106
control variables, 94
do-while, 99-102
exiting, 97-98, 106
for, 94-99, 176
iterations, 99-106
nesting, 106-108
open, 97-99
while, 102-103
MAT1.CPP
(Listing 6.7), 194-195
MAT2.CPP
(Listing 6.8), 196-197
MAT3.CPP
(Listing 6.9), 198-200
MDI1.CPP
(Listing 18.4), 510-513
MDI2.CPP
(Listing 18.8), 517
MRCALC.CPP
(Listing 13.3), 393-399
NESTFOR1.CPP
(Listing 3.12), 107
OPER1.CPP
(Listing 2.4), 53-54
OPER2.CPP
(Listing 2.5), 56-57
OPER3.CPP
(Listing 2.6), 58-59
OUT1.CPP
(Listing 7.1), 207
OUT2.CPP
(Listing 7.3), 213-214
OVERLOAD.CPP
(Listing 5.6), 167-168
OWL, 346, 352-358
PTR1.CPP (Listing 4.4),
132
PTR2.CPP (Listing 4.5),
135
PTR3.CPP (Listing 4.6),
136-140
PTR4.CPP (Listing 4.7),
139-140
PTR5.CPP (Listing 4.8),
143-144
REAL.CPP
(Listing 11.4), 352-358
REFVAR1.CPP
(Listing 4.3), 128
RELOP1.CPP
(Listing 2.9), 67-69
SIZEOF1.CPP
(Listing 2.7), 61-62

SPOTAB.CPP (Listing 20.8), 613-615
SPOTAPP.CPP (Listing 20.2), 597-601
SPOTDOC.CPP (Listing 20.4), 602-605
SPOTVIEW.CPP (Listing 20.6), 606-612
STATIC1.CPP (Listing 5.2), 155-156
stopping, 657
STRING1.CPP (Listing 7.4), 221-222
STRING2.CPP (Listing 7.5), 225-227
STRING3.CPP (Listing 7.6), 229-230
STRING4.CPP (Listing 7.7), 236-237
STRUCT1.CPP (Listing 4.2), 124-125
SWITCH1.CPP (Listing 3.4), 89-90
templates (Listing 10.3), 329-330
transparent operations, 4
TYPCAST1.CPP (Listing 2.8), 63-64
VAR1.CPP (Listing 2.1), 47-48
VAR2.CPP (Listing 5.1), 154
variables, 134
WHILE1.CPP (Listing 3.10), 103
WIDGETS.CPP (Listing 15.3), 435-439
WINDOW1.CPP (Listing 12.2), 362-368
WINDOW1.RC (Listing 12.1), 362
WINDOW2.CPP (Listing 12.5), 368-375
WINDOW2.H (Listing 12.3), 368
WINDOW2.RC (Listing 12.4), 368
WinSight debugger tool, 660
WinSpector debugging tool, 660
XFERLIST.CPP (Listing 16.6), 464-466
XFERLIST.EXE, 463
XPRTABTD.CPP (Listing 19.6), 554-557
see also applications

Project command
Options menu, 27
View menu, 19

Project menu (IDE), 22-25

Project Options dialog box, 27-28

projects, 34-35
Expert prototype, 540-563
source code files, 528-540

prompts (integers), 58

properties (VBX controls), 498-499

protected sections (object classes), 253

prototyping functions, 150-153

proxy object class, declaring, 638

PTR1.CPP program (Listing 4.4), 132

PTR2.CPP program (Listing 4.5), 135

PTR3.CPP program (Listing 4.6), 136-140

PTR4.CPP program (Listing 4.7), 139-140

PTR5.CPP program (Listing 4.8), 143-144

public sections (object classes), 253

pushbutton control, 389-390

put_var function, 401

Q–R

querying
multiple-selection list box controls, 463-467
strings, 454-462

QUEUES.H header file, 332

QuickSort method (array sorting), 183

quotes (''), strings, 37

radio button controls, 432

random access file I/O stream functions, 297-302

read I/O stream function, 291

read-only text windows, 360-365
readArray function, 296
readElem function, 295
reading
- arrays
  - binary files, 296
  - input streams, 295
- strings, 312-318

REAL.CPP program (Listing 11.4), 352-358
REAL.RC files, 350
REAL.RH header file, 352
rectangle calculations (PTR4.CPP program), 138
recursive functions, 164-166
Redo command (IDE Edit menu), 13
reference
- guides (Turbo C++), 5
- help files (Turbo C++), navigating, 7-8
- operators, 130
- parameters, declaring, 151
- variables, 127-128

references (strings), 315
REFVAR1.CPP program (Listing 4.3), 128
Register command (IDE View menu), 21
registering OLE 2 applications, 592-593
Registers command (View menu), 653
Registry (OLE 2), 588-590
relational operators, 65-66
RELOP1.CPP program (Listing 2.9), 67-69
removing
- characters from strings, 310
- classes (objects), 258-262
- *see also* deleting

Replace command (IDE Search menu), 16
replacing string characters, 324-325
resource files
- BUG.RC, 654
- CALCJR.RC, 487-488
- COUNTDN.RC, 478
- CTLLST.RC, 455-456
- DIALOG1.RC, 409
- DIALOG2.RC, 416
- DICE.RC, 644-645
- EXPRTAPP.RC, 548-554
- MDI1.RC, 510
- MDI2.RC, 517
- SPOTAPP.RC, 621
- WIDGETS.RC, 434-435
- XFERLIST.RC, 464

resource header files
- DICE.RH, 643-645
- EXPRTAPP.RH, 541-545
- SPOTAPP.RH, 615-619

Resource Workshop utility, 407, 565-576
resources
- defining dialog boxes, 407
- MRCALC.RC file, 393
- OWL, 349

responding
- to combo box control messages, 485
- to scroll bar messages, 475-477

response tables (VBX dialog boxes), 495-497
retrieving edit control text, 385-387
reversing strings, 229-231
RTTI (Run Time Type Information), 634
Run command (Debug menu), 650
Run( ) function, 347
runtime errors, 93

S

Save All command (IDE File menu), 12
Save As command (IDE File menu), 11
Save command (IDE File menu), 10
Save command (IDE Options menu), 31
Save File As dialog box, 11
scroll bars, 365
- controls, 472-477
- countdown timer, 477-481
- manipulating, 477
- notification messages, 475-477
- styles, 473-474

scrolling
- text, 365-367
- vertical requests, 367
- windows, 367-373

SDI Client subtopic (Main Window topic, AppExpert utility), 535

SDIDecFrame object class, 563

Search Again command (IDE Search menu), 17

Search menu (IDE), 15-18

searching
- arrays, 187-192
- strings, 234-235, 312, 323
- substrings, 326
- *see also* finding

searchInSortedArray function, 192

searchInUnorderedArray function, 192

seekg I/O stream function, 297

segmented memory pointers, 145

Select All command (IDE Edit menu), 14

SelectionChanged function, 433

semicolon (;), program terminators, 37

sequential binary file stream I/O functions, 290-297

sequential text stream I/O functions, 286-290

servers (OLE objects), 581-582, 636

SetCheck ( ) function, 431

SetPosition member function, 475

SetRange member function, 475

SETS.H header file, 332

SetSel member function, 452

SetSelection member function, 388

SetSelIndex member function, 451

SetSelItemRange member function, 451

SetSelString member function, 451

SetText member function, 382, 388

setting string parameters, 313-314

SetTopIndex member func-tion, 452

SetupWindow member function, 373-374, 408

Shell-Metzner method (array sorting), 183

Shift+Ctrl+Z key command, 13

Shift+F4 key command, 32

Shift+F5 key command, 31

shortcut keys, *see* key commands

showArray function, 186

showColumnAverage function, 200

showing buttons (pushbutton controls), 390

ShowWindow member function, 390

single-alternative if statement (decision-making constructs), 80-82

single-dimensional arrays, 174-176
- declaring, 133-134
- initializing, 176-179

single-letter variables, 392

six-dimensional arrays, 193

sizeof operator, 60-62

SIZEOF1.CPP program (Listing 2.7), 61-62

sizing arrays automatically, 178

slashes (//), program comments, 37

Son of Mr. Calculator application, 486-493

sortArray function, 186

sorted-array search method, 187

sorting
- arrays, 183-186
- integer arrays, 187-191

source code files (projects), creating, 528-540

spaces (strings), controlling, 324

speed bar (IDE), 8

SPOT.IDE project file, 630

SPOTAB.CPP program (Listing 20.8), 613-615

SPOTAB.H header file, 612

SPOTAPP.CPP program (Listing 20.2), 597-601

SPOTAPP.DEF definition file, 630

SPOTAPP.H header file, 597

SPOTAPP.RC resource file, 619

SPOTAPP.RH resource header file, 615-619

SPOTDOC.CPP program (Listing 20.4), 602-605

SPOTDOC.H header file, 601-602

SPOTVIEW.CPP program (Listing 20.6), 606-612

SPOTVIEW.H header file, 605-606

sprintf function, 213

square roots, calculating values, 100

stacks.h header file, 333

statements
- break, 88
- dual-alternative if-else, 82-84
- multiple-alternative if-else, 85-87
- single-alternative if, 80-82
- switch, 87-90
- *see also* decision-making constructs

static text, 379-382

static variables, 155-156

STATIC1.CPP program (Listing 5.2), 155-156

status line (IDE), 9

Step over command (Debug menu), 650

storing
- data structures, 126-127
- multidimensional arrays, 193
- OLE objects, 581, 585

strcat string function, 220

strchr string function, 231-232

strcmp string function, 223-224

strcopy string function, 217

strcspn string function, 233

strdup string function, 218

streams, 37
- I/O functions
  - close, 286
  - getline, 216, 286-287
  - open, 285
  - read, 291
  - printf , 210-215
  - random access file, 297-302
  - seekg, 297
  - sequential binary file, 290-297
  - sequential text, 286-290
  - write, 291
- input, 208-210
- inserting
  - data types, 208-209
  - multiple characters, 208
- output, 206-208

stricmp string function, 224

STRING.H header file, 216-217

STRING1.CPP program (Listing 7.4), 221-222

STRING2.CPP program (Listing 7.5), 225-227

STRING3.CPP program (Listing 7.6), 229-230

STRING4.CPP program (Listing 7.7), 236-237

strings, 215
- arrays
  - accessing as, 317-319
  - passing as objects, 326
- assigning, 217-219, 315-316
- characters
  - addressing, 311
  - appending, 325
  - converting, 313
  - deleting, 326
  - inserting, 310
  - locating, 231-233
  - removing, 310
  - replacing, 324-325

comparing, 223-227, 316-318
concatenating, 219-223
converting, 228
copying, 312
  from sources to targets, 217
  num characters, 218
  returning duplicate string pointers, 218
declaring, 314-315
determining lengths, 219
double-linked list storage (Listing 10.4), 334-335
empty strings, 37
functions
  globally declared, 313
  I/O, 313
  strcat, 220
  strchr, 231-232
  strcmp, 223-224
  strcopy, 217
  strcspn, 233
  strdup, 218
  stricmp, 224
  strlen, 219
  strlwr, 228
  strncat, 220
  strncmp, 224-225
  strncpy, 218-219
  strnicmp, 225
  strpbrk, 233
  strrchr, 232
  strrev, 229-231
  strspn, 232-233
  strstr, 234
  strtok, 234-235
  strupr, 228
initializing, 217
input, 216
lengths
  determining, 312
  in characters, 323
object class
  comparing, 309-310
  concatenating, 310
  constructors, 308-309
  I/O, 324
  member functions, 312-314, 325-327
  reading/setting parameters, 313-314
objects, creating, 309
parameters, reading/setting, 312
printf function format, 212
querying, 454-462
reading, 316-318
references, 315
reversing, 229-231
searching, 312, 323
spaces, controlling, 324
substituting, 319-325
substrings
  extracting, 311
  finding, 326
  locating, 234-238
tokens, searching, 234-235
troubleshooting, 307
VBX, 497
writing, 316-317

strlen string function, 219
strlwr string function, 228
strncat string function, 220
strncmp string function, 224-225
strncpy string function, 218-219
strnicmp string function, 225
strpbrk string function, 233
strrchr string function, 232
strrev string function, 229-231
strspn string function, 232-233
strstr string function, 234
strtok string function, 234-235
STRUCT1.CPP program (Listing 4.2), 124-125
strupr string function, 228
Style Sheet dialog box, 31
Style Sheets command (IDE Options menu), 31
styles
  combo box controls, 483
  edit control, 383-384
  list box controls, 445-446
  static text, 380-381
  scroll bars, 473-474
substituting strings, 319-325

substrings
extracting, 311
finding, 326
locating, 234-238
subsytems (VBX), initializing, 494
subtraction (–) operator, 52
switch statements (decision-making constructs), 87-90
SWITCH1.CPP program (Listing 3.4), 89-90
system menu (IDE), 8

T

tags (variables), 129
TApplication object class (OWL), 345
TAppMDIClient object class, 514
Target command (IDE Options menu), 28
TAutoClass object class, 634
TButton object class, 389
TCalcWindow object class, 399
TCheckBox class (check box controls), 430
TComboBox object class, 482-485
TControl object class, 378-379
TDialog object class, 406-407
TEdit object class, 351, 382-384
member functions, 385
text query member functions, 385-387
templates, 327
declaring as object classes, 328
program (Listing 10.3), 329-330
Terminate program command (Debug menu), 651
testing multiple-selection list box controls, 463-467
TEventHandler object class (OWL), 344
text
compiling, 45
edit controls
altering, 388
retrieving, 385-387
MDI viewers, 509-516
query member functions, 385
replacing macro-based constants, 46
scrolling, 365-367
static controls, 379-382
windows (read-only), 360-365
TextOut function, 360-361
TGroupBox class (group box controls), 433
three-dimensional arrays, 192-193
throw keyword, 93-94
TListBox object class, 444-462
TMDIChild object class, 507-508
TMDIClient object class, 505-507
TMDIFrame object class, 503-504
TModule object class (OWL), 345
Toggle breakpoint command (Debug menu), 651
toggles
check box controls, 430
dialog boxes, 409
tokens (strings), searching, 234-235
TOleDocument object class, 585-586
TOleView object class, 586-588
Tool menu (IDE), 26
tools (debugging) 660-661
Tools command (IDE Options menu), 29-30
Tools dialog box, 29
TPointer object class, 592
Trace into command (Debug menu), 651
TRadioButton class (radio button controls), 432
transferring dialog box control data , 414-420
transparent operations (programs), 4

TReference object class, 308

TResId object class, 406

trimStr function, 289

troubleshooting
- strings, 307
- *see also* debugging

TRUE macro, 342

try blocks (exception handlers), 92-93

TScrollBar object class, 472-475

TScroller object class, 366

TStatic object class, 379

TStreamableBase object class (OWL), 345

TStringRef object class, 308

TSubString object class, 308

Turbo C++
- Borland documentation, 5
- reference guides, 5
- reference help files, navigating, 7-8

TVbxControl object class, 497-499

TWindow object class (OWL), 345

two-dimensional arrays, 192

TYPCAST1.CPP program (Listing 2.8), 63-64

typecasting data types, 62-65

typedef keyword, 118-119

typeface, 373

U

UINT macro, 343

unary operators, 52

Undo command (IDE Edit menu), 13

Undo member function, 385

unions (data structures), 126-127

unordered-array search method, 187

untagged data structures, 123

updating compound document notifications, 585-586

utilities
- AppExpert, 22, 528-539
  - customizng, 563
  - output, 539-540
  - project files, 540
- ClassExpert, 564-565
- Resource Workshop, 407, 565-576

V

VAR1.CPP program (Listing 2.1), 47-48

VAR2.CPP program (Listing 5.1), 154

variables
- accessing values with pointers, 130-132
- addresses, 129-130
- applications, allocating memory, 141
- arrays, 133-134
- byte size status, 60
- char-type, 65
- contents, displaying, 47-48
- data structures, 123
- data types, Hungarian notation, 343-344
- declaring, 46-48, 64
- dynamic, 142
- global, 47
- header files, 45
- local (functions), 153-154
- loops, 72
- pointers, 129-130
- programs, 134
- reference variables, 127-128
- single-letter, 392
- static (functions), 155-156
- tags, 129

VBX (Visual Basic eXchange)
- arguments (functions), 496
- controls, 494-499
- dialog box response tables, 495-497
- events, 495-496
- mixin object class, 494

strings, 497
subsytems, initializing, 494
vectimp.h header file, 333
View menu (IDE), 18-22, 653
viewing object classes, 19
viewports (windows), 365
views (windows), 653-661
virtual arrays, 298
virtual functions, 266-272, 657
VmArray object class, 301
void functions, 160
VOID macro, 343
volumes (functions), calling, 152
VScroll member function, 366

W

Watch command (IDE View menu), 20, 653
while loops, 102-103
WHILE1.CPP program (Listing 3.10), 103
WIDGETS.CPP program (Listing 15.3), 435-439
WIDGETS.H header file, 434
WIDGETS.RC resource file, 434-435
width function (streams), 207
Window menu (IDE), 31-32
WINDOW1.CPP program (Listing 12.2), 362-368
WINDOW1.RC program (Listing 12.1), 362
WINDOW2.CPP program (Listing 12.5), 368-375
WINDOW2.H program (Listing 12.3), 368
WINDOW2.RC program (Listing 12.4), 368
Windows
controls, connecting OWL objects, 413
data type substitutions, 342-343
macros, 342-343
menus, 349
messages, 347-349
windows
breakpoints, 20
child windows (MDI), 507-508
initializing, 373-374
manipulating, 31
MDI, 502-505, 516-525
OWL, 345
scroll bars, creating, 365
scrolling, 367-373
text (read-only), 360-365
viewports, 365
views, 653-661
WinSight program debugger tool, 660
WinSpector program debugging tool, 660
WORD macro, 343
write I/O stream function, 291
writeArray function, 296
writeElem function, 295
writing
arrays
to binary files, 296
to output streams, 295
strings, 316-317
WYSIWYG (What You See is What You Get), 581

X–Y–Z

XFERLIST.CPP program (Listing 16.6), 464-466
XFERLIST.EXE program, 463
XFERLIST.H header file, 464
XFERLIST.RC resource file, 464
XPRTABTD.CPP program (Listing 19.6), 554-557
XPRTABTD.H header file, 546-547

Book ISBN 0-672-30727-8